ALGORITHM DESIGN WITH HASKELL

This book is devoted to five main principles of algorithm design: divide and conquer, greedy algorithms, thinning, dynamic programming, and exhaustive search. These principles are presented using Haskell, a purely functional language, leading to simpler explanations and shorter programs than would be obtained with imperative languages. Carefully selected examples, both new and standard, reveal the commonalities and highlight the differences between algorithms. The algorithm developments use equational reasoning where applicable, clarifying the applicability conditions and correctness arguments. Every chapter concludes with exercises (nearly 300 in total), each with complete answers, allowing the reader to consolidate their understanding and apply the techniques to a range of problems. The book serves students (both undergraduate and postgraduate), researchers, teachers, and professionals who want to know more about what goes into a good algorithm and how such algorithms can be expressed in purely functional terms.

ALGORITHM DESIGN WITH HASKELL

RICHARD BIRD
University of Oxford

JEREMY GIBBONS
University of Oxford

CAMBRIDGE
UNIVERSITY PRESS

University Printing House, Cambridge CB2 8BS, United Kingdom

One Liberty Plaza, 20th Floor, New York, NY 10006, USA

477 Williamstown Road, Port Melbourne, VIC 3207, Australia

314-321, 3rd Floor, Plot 3, Splendor Forum, Jasola District Centre, New Delhi - 110025, India

79 Anson Road, #06-04/06, Singapore 079906

Cambridge University Press is part of the University of Cambridge.

It furthers the University's mission by disseminating knowledge in the pursuit of education, learning and research at the highest international levels of excellence.

www.cambridge.org
Information on this title: www.cambridge.org/9781108491617
DOI: 10.1017/9781108869041

First published 2020

A catalogue record for this publication is available from the British Library

ISBN 978-1-108-49161-7 Hardback

For Stephen Gill (RB) and Sue Gibbons (JG).

Contents

Preface

Our aim in this book is to provide an introduction to the principles of algorithm design using a purely functional approach. Our language of choice is Haskell and all the algorithms we design will be expressed as Haskell functions. Haskell has many features for structuring function definitions, but we will use only a small subset of them.

Using functions, rather than loops and assignment statements, to express algorithms changes everything. First of all, an algorithm expressed as a function is composed of other, more basic functions that can be studied separately and reused in other algorithms. For instance, a sorting algorithm may be specified in terms of building a tree of some kind and then flattening it in some way. Functions that build trees can be studied separately from functions that consume trees. Furthermore, the properties of each of these basic functions and their relationship to others can be captured with simple equational properties. As a result, one can talk and reason about the 'deep' structure of an algorithm in a way that is not easily possible with imperative code. To be sure, one can reason formally about imperative programs by formulating their specifications in the predicate calculus, and using loop invariants to prove they are correct. But, and this is the nub, one cannot easily reason about the properties of an imperative program directly in terms of the language of its code. Consequently, books on formal program design have a quite different tone from those on algorithm design: they demand fluency in both the predicate calculus and the necessary imperative dictions. In contrast, many texts on algorithm design traditionally present algorithms with a step-by-step commentary, and use informally stated loop invariants to help one understand why the algorithm is correct.

With a functional approach there are no longer two separate languages to think about, and one can happily calculate better versions of algorithms, or parts of algorithms, by the straightforward process of equational reasoning. That, perhaps, is the main contribution of this book. Although it contains a fair amount of equational reasoning, we have tried to maintain a light touch. The plain fact of the matter is that calculation is fun to do but boring to read – well, too much of it is. Although it does not matter very much whether imperative algorithms are expressed in C or Java or pseudo-code, the situation changes completely when algorithms are expressed functionally.

Many of the problems considered in this book, especially in the later parts, begin with a specification of the task in hand, expressed as a composition of standard functions such as maps, filters, and folds, as well as other functions such as *perms* for computing all the permutations of a list, *parts* for computing all the partitions, and *mktrees* for building all the trees of a particular kind. These component functions are then combined, or *fused*, in various ways to construct a final algorithm with the required time complexity. A final sorting algorithm may not refer to the underlying tree, but the tree is still there in the structure of the algorithm. The notion of fusion dominates the technical and mathematical aspects of the design process and is really the driving force of the book.

The disadvantage for any author of taking a functional approach is that, because functional languages such as Haskell are not so well known as mainstream procedural languages, one has to spend some time explaining them. That would add substantially to the length of the book. The simple solution to this problem is just to assume the necessary knowledge. There is a growing range of textbooks on languages like Haskell, including our own *Thinking Functionally with Haskell* (Cambridge University Press, 2014), and we will just assume the reader is familiar with the necessary material. Indeed, the present book was designed as a companion volume to the earlier book. A brief summary of what we do assume, and an even briefer reprise of some essential ideas, is given in the first chapter, but you will probably not be able to learn enough about Haskell there to understand the rest of the book. Even if you do know something about functional programming, but not about how equational reasoning enters the picture (some books on functional programming simply don't mention equational reasoning), you will probably still have to refer to our earlier book. In any case, the mathematics involved in equational reasoning is neither new nor difficult.

Books on algorithm design traditionally cover three broad areas: a collection of design principles, a study of useful data structures, and a number of interesting and intriguing algorithms that have been discovered over the centuries. Sometimes the books are arranged by principles, sometimes by topic (such as graph algorithms, or text algorithms), and sometimes by a mixture of both. This book mostly takes the first approach. It is devoted to five main design strategies underlying many effective algorithms: divide and conquer, greedy algorithms, thinning algorithms, dynamic programming, and exhaustive search. These are the design strategies that every serious programmer should know. The middle strategy, on thinning algorithms, is new, and serves in many problems as an alternative to dynamic programming.

Each design strategy is allocated a part to itself, and the chapters on each strategy cover a variety of algorithms from the well-known to the new. There is only a little material on data structures – only as much as we need. In the first part of the book we do discuss some basic data structures, but we will also rely on some of Haskell's libraries of other useful ways of structuring data. One reason for doing so is that we wanted the book not to be too voluminous; another reason is that there does exist one text, Chris Okasaki's *Purely Functional Data Structures* (Cambridge University Press, 1998), that covers a lot of the material. Other books on functional data structures have been published since we began writing this book, and more are beginning to appear.

Another feature of this book is that, as well as some firm favourites, it describes a number of algorithms that do not usually appear in books on algorithm design. Some of these algorithms have been adapted, elaborated, and simplified from yet another book published by Cambridge University Press: *Pearls of Functional Algorithm Design* (2010). The reason for this novelty is simply to make the book entertaining as well as instructive. Books on algorithm design are read, broadly speaking, by three kinds of people: academics who need reference material, undergraduate or graduate students on a course, and professional programmers simply for interest and enjoyment. Most professional programmers do not design algorithms but just take them from a library. Yet they too are a target audience for this book, because sometimes professional programmers want to know more about what goes into a good algorithm and how to think about them.

Algorithms in real life are a good deal more intricate than the ones presented in this book. The shortest-path algorithm in a satellite navigation system is a good deal more complicated than a shortest-path algorithm as presented in a textbook on algorithm design. Real-life algorithms have to cope with the problems of scale, with the effective use of a computer's hardware, with user interfaces, and with many other things that go into a well-designed and useful product. None of these aspects is covered in the present book, nor indeed in most books devoted solely to the principles of algorithm design.

There is another feature of this book that deserves mention: all exercises are answered, if sometimes somewhat briefly. The exercises form an integral part of the text, and the questions and answers should be read even if the exercises are not attempted. Rather than have a complete bibliography at the end of the book, each chapter ends with references to (some of) the books and articles pertinent to the chapter.

Most of the major programs in this book are available on the web site

www.cs.ox.ac.uk/publications/books/adwh

You can also use this site to see a list of all known errors, as well as report new ones. We also welcome suggestions for improvement, including ideas for new exercises.

Acknowledgements

Preparation of this book has benefited enormously from careful reading by Sue Gibbons, Hsiang-Shang Ko, and Nicolas Wu. The manuscript was prepared using the lhs2TEX system of Ralf Hinze and Andres Löh, which pretty-prints the Haskell code and also allows it to be extracted and type-checked. The extracted code was then tested using the wonderful QuickCheck tool developed by Koen Claessen and John Hughes. Type-checking and QuickChecking the code has saved us from many infelicities; any errors that remain are, of course, our own responsibility.

We also thank David Tranah and the team at Cambridge University Press for their advice and hard work in the generation of the final version of the text.

Richard Bird
Jeremy Gibbons

PART ONE

BASICS

What makes a good algorithm? There are as many answers to this question as there are to the question of what makes a good cookbook recipe. Is the recipe clear and easy to follow? Does the recipe use standard and well-understood techniques? Does it use widely available ingredients? Is the preparation time reasonably short? Does it involve many pots and pans and a lot of kitchen space? And so on and so on. Some people when asked this question say that what is most important about a recipe is whether the dish is attractive or not, a point we will try to bear in mind when expressing our functional algorithms.

In the first three chapters we review the ingredients we need for designing good recipes for attractive algorithms in a functional kitchen, and describe the tools we need for analysing their efficiency. Our functional language of choice is Haskell, and the ingredients are Haskell functions. These ingredients and the techniques for combining them are reviewed in the first chapter. Be aware that the chapter is *not* an introduction to Haskell; its main purpose is to outline what should be familiar territory to the reader, or at least territory that the reader should feel comfortable travelling in.

The second chapter concerns efficiency, specifically the running time of algorithms. We will ignore completely the question of space efficiency, for the plain fact of the matter is that executing a functional program can take up quite a lot of kitchen space. There are methods for controlling the space used in evaluating a functional expression, but we refer the reader to other books for their elaboration. That chapter reviews asymptotic notation for stating running times, and explores how recurrence relations, which are essentially recursive functions for determining the running times of recursive functions, can be solved to give asymptotic estimates. The chapter also introduces, albeit fairly briefly, the notion of amortised running times because it will be needed later in the book.

The final chapter in this part introduces a small number of basic data structures that will be needed at one or two places in the rest of the book. These are symmetric lists, random-access lists, and purely functional arrays. Mostly we postpone discussion of any data structure required to make an algorithm efficient until the algorithm itself is introduced, but these three form a coherent group that can be discussed without having specific applications in mind.

Chapter 1

Functional programming

Haskell is a large and powerful language, brimming with clever ideas about how to structure programs and possessing many bells and whistles. But in this book we will use only a small subset of the host of available features. So, no Monads, no Applicatives, no Foldables, and no Traversables. In this chapter we will spell out what we do need to construct effective algorithms. Some of the material will be revisited when particular problems are put under the microscope, so you should regard the chapter primarily as a way to check your understanding of the basic ideas of Haskell.

1.1 Basic types and functions

We will use only simple types, such as Booleans, characters, strings, numbers of various kinds, and lists. Most of the functions we use can be found in Haskell's Standard Prelude (the *Prelude* library), or in the library *Data.List*. Be warned that the definitions we give of some of these functions may not be exactly the definitions given in these libraries: the library definitions are tuned for optimal performance and ours for clarity. We will use type synonyms to improve readability, and **data** declarations of new types, especially trees of various kinds. When necessary we make use of simple type classes such as *Eq*, *Ord*, and *Num*, but we will not introduce new ones. Haskell provides many kinds of number, including two kinds of integer, *Int* and *Integer*, and two kinds of floating-point number, *Float* and *Double*. Elements of *Int* are restricted in range, usually $[-2^{63}, 2^{63})$ on 64-bit computers, though Haskell compilers are only required to cover the range $[-2^{29}, 2^{29})$. Elements of *Integer* are unrestricted. We will rarely use the floating-point numbers provided by *Float* and *Double*. In one or two places we will use *Rational* arithmetic, where a *Rational* number is the ratio of two *Integer* values. Haskell does not have a type of natural numbers,[1] though the library *Numeric.Natural* does provide arbitrary-precision ones. Instead, we will sometimes use the type synonym

   type *Nat* = *Int*

Haskell cannot enforce the constraint that elements of *Nat* be natural numbers, and we use the synonym purely to document intention. For example, we can assert that *length* :: [*a*] → *Nat* because the length of a list, as defined in the Prelude, is a nonnegative element of *Int*. Haskell also provides unsigned numbers in the *Data.Word* library. Elements of *Word* are unsigned numbers and can represent natural numbers *n* in the range $0 \leqslant n < 2^{64}$ on 64-bit machines. However, defining **type** *Nat* = *Word* would be inconvenient simply because we could not then assert that *length* :: [*a*] → *Nat*.

   Most important for our purposes are the basic functions that manipulate lists. Of these the most useful are *map*, *filter*, and folds of various kinds. Here is the definition of *map*:

   $$map :: (a \rightarrow b) \rightarrow [a] \rightarrow [b]$$
   $$map\, f\, [] \quad = []$$
   $$map\, f\, (x:xs) = f\, x : map\, f\, xs$$

The function *map* applies its first argument, a function, to every element of its second argument, a list. The function *filter* is defined as follows:

   $$filter :: (a \rightarrow Bool) \rightarrow [a] \rightarrow [a]$$
   $$filter\, p\, [] \quad = []$$
   $$filter\, p\, (x:xs) = \textbf{if}\; p\, x\; \textbf{then}\; x : filter\, p\, xs\; \textbf{else}\; filter\, p\, xs$$

The function *filter* filters a list, retaining only those elements that satisfy the given test. There are various fold functions on lists, most of which will be explained in due course. Two of the important ones are *foldr* and *foldl*. The former is defined as follows:

   $$foldr :: (a \rightarrow b \rightarrow b) \rightarrow b \rightarrow [a] \rightarrow b$$
   $$foldr\, f\, e\, [] \quad = e$$
   $$foldr\, f\, e\, (x:xs) = f\, x\, (foldr\, f\, e\, xs)$$

The function *foldr* folds a list from right to left, starting with a value *e* and using a binary operator ⊕ to reduce the list to a single value. For example,

   $$foldr\, (\oplus)\, e\, [x, y, z] = x \oplus (y \oplus (z \oplus e))$$

In particular, *foldr* (:) [] *xs* = *xs* for *all* lists *xs*, including infinite lists. However, we will not make much use of infinite lists in what follows, except for idioms such as

---

[1] In the documentation for the GHC libraries, there is the statement "It would be very natural to add a type *Natural* providing an unbounded size unsigned integer, just as *Prelude.Integer* provides unbounded size signed integers. We do not do that yet since there is no demand for it." Maybe this book will create such a demand.

$$label :: [a] \rightarrow [(Nat, a)]$$
$$label\ xs = zip\ [0..]\ xs$$

As another example, we can write

$$length :: [a] \rightarrow Nat$$
$$length = foldr\ succ\ 0\ \textbf{where}\ succ\ x\ n = n + 1$$

The second main function, *foldl*, folds a list from left to right:

$$foldl :: (b \rightarrow a \rightarrow b) \rightarrow b \rightarrow [a] \rightarrow b$$
$$foldl\ f\ e\ []\quad = e$$
$$foldl\ f\ e\ (x:xs) = foldl\ f\ (f\ e\ x)\ xs$$

Thus

$$foldl\ (\oplus)\ e\ [x,y,z] = ((e \oplus x) \oplus y) \oplus z$$

For example, we could also write

$$length :: [a] \rightarrow Nat$$
$$length = foldl\ succ\ 0\ \textbf{where}\ succ\ n\ x = n + 1$$

Note that *foldl* returns a well-defined value only on finite lists; evaluation of *foldl* on an infinite list will never terminate. There is an alternative definition of *foldl*, namely

$$foldl\ f\ e = foldr\ (flip\ f)\ e \cdot reverse$$

where *flip* is a useful prelude function defined by

$$flip :: (a \rightarrow b \rightarrow c) \rightarrow b \rightarrow a \rightarrow c$$
$$flip\ f\ x\ y = f\ y\ x$$

Since one can reverse a list in linear time, this definition is asymptotically as fast as the former. However, it involves two traversals of the input, one to reverse it and the second to fold it.

1.2 Processing lists

The difference between *foldr* and *foldl* prompts a general observation. When a programmer brought up in the imperative programming tradition meets functional programming for the first time, they are likely to feel that many computations seem to be carried out in the wrong order. Recursion has been described as the curious process of reaching one's goal by walking backwards towards it. Specifically, lists often seem to be processed from right to left when the natural way surely appears to be from left to right. Appeals to naturalness are often suspicious, and appearances can be deceptive. We normally read an English sentence from left to right, but when we encounter a phrase such as "a lovely little old French silver butter knife" the adjectives have to be applied from right to left. If the knife was made of French silver, but not necessarily made in France, we have to write "a lovely little old French-silver butter knife" to avoid ambiguity. Mathematical expressions too are usually understood from right to left, certainly those involving a chain of functional compositions. As to deceptiveness, the definition

$$head = foldr \ (\ll) \perp \ \textbf{where} \ x \ll y = x$$

though a little strange is certainly correct and takes constant time. The evaluation of *foldr* $(\ll)$, conceptually from right to left, is abandoned after the first element is encountered. Thus

$$
\begin{aligned}
head \ (x:xs) &= foldr \ (\ll) \perp (x:xs) \\
&= x \ll foldr \ (\ll) \perp xs \\
&= x
\end{aligned}
$$

The last step follows from the fact that Haskell is a *lazy* language in which evaluations are performed only when needed, so evaluation of $\ll$ does not require evaluation of its second argument.

Sometimes the direction of travel *is* important. For example, consider the following two definitions of *concat*:

$$
\begin{aligned}
concat_1, concat_2 &:: [[a]] \to [a] \\
concat_1 &= foldr \ (+\!\!+) \ [] \\
concat_2 &= foldl \ (+\!\!+) \ []
\end{aligned}
$$

We have $concat_1 \ xss = concat_2 \ xss$ for all finite lists xss (see Exercise 1.10), but which definition is better? We will look at the precise running times of the two functions in the following chapter, but here is one way to view the problem. Imagine a long table on which there are a number of piles of documents. You have to assemble these documents into one big pile ensuring that the correct order is maintained, so the second pile (numbering from left to right) has to go under the first pile, the third pile under the second pile, and so on. You could start from left to right, picking up the first pile, putting it on top of the second pile, picking the combined pile up and putting it on top of the third pile, and so on. Or you could start at the other end, placing the penultimate pile on the last pile, the antepenultimate pile on top of that, and so on (even English words are direction-biased: the words 'first', 'second', and 'third' are simple, but 'penultimate' and 'antepenultimate' are not). The left to right solution involves some heavy lifting, particularly at the last step when a big pile of documents has to be lifted up and placed on the last pile, but the right to left solution involves picking up only one pile at each step. So $concat_1$ is potentially a much more efficient way to concatenate a list of lists than $concat_2$.

Here is another example. Consider the problem of breaking a list of words into a list of lines, ensuring that the width of each line is at most some given bound. This problem is known as the *paragraph problem*, and there is a section devoted to it in Chapter 12. It seems natural to process the input from left to right, adding successive words to the end of the current line until no more words will fit, in which case a new line is started. This particular algorithm is a greedy one. There are also non-greedy algorithms for the paragraph problem that process words from right to left. Part Three of the book is devoted to the study of greedy algorithms. Nevertheless, these two examples apart, the direction of travel is often unimportant.

The direction of travel is also related to another concept in algorithm design, the notion of an *online* algorithm. An online algorithm is one that processes a list without having the entire list available from the start. Instead, the list is regarded as a potentially infinite *stream* of values. Consequently, any online algorithm for solving a problem for a given stream also has to solve the problem for every prefix of the stream. And that means the stream has to be processed from left to right. In contrast, an *offline* algorithm is one that is given the complete list to start with, and can process the list in any order it wants. Online algorithms can usually be defined in terms of another basic Haskell function *scanl*, whose definition is as follows:

$$scanl :: (b \rightarrow a \rightarrow b) \rightarrow b \rightarrow [a] \rightarrow [b]$$
$$scanl\, f\, e\, [] \quad\quad = [e]$$
$$scanl\, f\, e\, (x:xs) = e : scanl\, f\, (f\, e\, x)\, xs$$

For example,

$$scanl\, (\oplus)\, e\, [x,y,z,...] = [e, e \oplus x, (e \oplus x) \oplus y, ((e \oplus x) \oplus y) \oplus z, ...]$$

In particular, *scanl* can be applied to an infinite list, producing an infinite list as result.

1.3 Inductive and recursive definitions

While most functions make use of recursion, the nature of the recursion is different in different functions. The functions *map*, *filter*, and *foldr* all make use of *structural recursion*. That is, the recursion follows the structure of lists built from the empty list [] and the cons constructor (:). There is one clause for the empty list and another, recursive clause for $x:xs$ in terms of the value of the function for xs. We will call such definitions *inductive* definitions. Most inductive definitions can be expressed as instances of *foldr*. For example, both *map* and *filter* can be so expressed (see the exercises).

Here is another example, an inductive definition of the function *perms* that returns a list of all the permutations of a list (we call it $perms_1$ because later on we will meet another definition, $perms_2$):

$$perms_1\, [] \quad\quad = [[]]$$
$$perms_1\, (x:xs) = [zs \mid ys \leftarrow perms_1\, xs, zs \leftarrow inserts\, x\, ys]$$

The permutations of a nonempty list are obtained by taking each permutation of the tail of the list and returning all the ways the first element can be inserted. The function *inserts* is defined by

$$inserts :: a \rightarrow [a] \rightarrow [[a]]$$
$$inserts \; x \; [] \qquad = [[x]]$$
$$inserts \; x \; (y : ys) = (x : y : ys) : map \; (y:) \; (inserts \; x \; ys)$$

For example,

$$inserts \; 1 \; [2,3] = [[1,2,3],[2,1,3],[2,3,1]]$$

The definition of $perms_1$ uses explicit recursion and a list comprehension, but another way is to use a *foldr*:

$$perms_1 = foldr \; step \; [[]] \quad \textbf{where} \; step \; x \; xss = concatMap \; (inserts \; x) \; xss$$

The useful function *concatMap* is defined by

$$concatMap :: (a \rightarrow [b]) \rightarrow [a] \rightarrow [b]$$
$$concatMap \; f = concat \cdot map \; f$$

Observe that since

$$step \; x \; xss = (concatMap \cdot inserts) \; x \; xss$$

the definition of $perms_1$ can be expressed even more briefly as

$$perms_1 = foldr \; (concatMap \cdot inserts) \; [[]]$$

The idiom *foldr* (*concatMap* · *steps*) *e* will be used frequently in later chapters for various definitions of *steps* and *e*, so keep the abbreviation in mind.

Here is another way of generating permutations, one that is recursive rather than inductive:

$$perms_2 \; [] = [[]]$$
$$perms_2 \; xs = [x : zs \mid (x,ys) \leftarrow picks \; xs, zs \leftarrow perms_2 \; ys]$$
$$picks :: [a] \rightarrow [(a,[a])]$$
$$picks \; [] \qquad = []$$
$$picks \; (x : xs) = (x,xs) : [(y,x:ys) \mid (y,ys) \leftarrow picks \; xs]$$

The function *picks* picks an arbitrary element from a list in all possible ways, returning both the element and what remains. The function $perms_2$ computes a permutation by picking an arbitrary element of a nonempty list as a first element, and following it with a permutation of the rest of the list.

The function $perms_2$ uses a list comprehension, but an equivalent way is to write

$$perms_2 \; [] = [[]]$$
$$perms_2 \; xs = concatMap \; subperms \; (picks \; xs)$$
$$\textbf{where} \; subperms \; (x,ys) = map \; (x:) \; (perms_2 \; ys)$$

Expressing $perms_2$ in this way rather than by a list comprehension helps with equational reasoning, and also with the analysis of its running time. We will return to both $perms_1$ and $perms_2$ in the following chapter.

The different styles, recursive or inductive, of the definitions of basic combinatorial functions, such as permutations, partitions, or subsequences, lead to different kinds of final algorithm. For example, divide-and-conquer algorithms are usually recursive, while greedy and thinning algorithms are usually inductive. To appreciate that there may be different algorithms for one and the same problem, one has to go back to the definitions of the basic functions used in the specification of the problem and see if they can be defined differently. For example, the inductive definition of $perms_1$ leads to Insertion sort, while the recursive definition of $perms_2$ leads to Selection sort. These two sorting algorithms will be introduced in the context of greedy algorithms in Part Three. The general point is a key one for functional algorithm design: different solutions for problems arise simply because there are different but equally clear definitions of one or more of the basic functions describing the solution.

While functional programming relies solely on recursion to define arbitrarily long computations, imperative programming can also make use of loops of various kinds, including *while* and *until* loops. We can define and use loops in Haskell too. For example,

$$until :: (a \rightarrow Bool) \rightarrow (a \rightarrow a) \rightarrow a \rightarrow a$$
$$until\ p\ f\ x = \textbf{if}\ p\ x\ \textbf{then}\ x\ \textbf{else}\ until\ p\ f\ (f\ x)$$

is a recursive definition of the function *until* that repeatedly applies a function to a value until the result satisfies some condition. We will encounter *until* again later in the book. Given *until* we can define *while* by

$$while\ p = until\ (not \cdot p)$$

We can also define a functional version of simple for-loops in which a function is applied to an argument a specified number of times (see the exercises).

1.4 Fusion

The most powerful technique for constructing efficient algorithms lies in our ability to *fuse* two computations together into one computation. Here are three simple examples:

$$
\begin{aligned}
map\ f \cdot map\ g &= map\ (f \cdot g) \\
concatMap\ f \cdot map\ g &= concatMap\ (f \cdot g) \\
foldr\ f\ e \cdot map\ g &= foldr\ (f \cdot g)\ e
\end{aligned}
$$

The first equation says that the two-step process of applying one function to every element of a list, and then applying a second function to every element of the result, can be replaced by a one-step traversal in which the composition of the two functions is applied to each element. The second equation is an instance of the first one, and the third is yet another example of when two traversals can be replaced by a single traversal.

Here is an another example of a fusion law, one for you to solve:

$$foldr\ f\ e \cdot concat = ????$$

Pause for a minute or so to try and complete the right-hand side. It is a good test of your understanding of the material so far. But do not be discouraged if you cannot find the answer, because it is not too obvious and many experienced functional programmers would fail to spot it. In a moment we will show how this particular fusion rule follows from one single master rule. Indeed, that is how we ourselves know the right-hand side, not by memorising it but by reconstructing it from the master rule.

You probably paused for a short time, gave up and then read on. But you don't get away that easily. Try this simpler version first:

$$foldr\ f\ e\ (xs + ys) = ????$$

Having answered this question, can you now answer the first one?

The answers to both questions will be given shortly. The master fusion rule is the fusion law of *foldr*. This law states that

$$h\ (foldr\ f\ e\ xs) = foldr\ g\ (h\ e)\ xs$$

for all finite lists *xs* provided

$$h\ (f\ x\ y) = g\ x\ (h\ y)$$

for all *x* and *y*. The proviso is called the *fusion condition*. Without one extra proviso, the restriction to finite lists is necessary (see the exercises). The proof of the fusion rule is by induction on the structure of a list. There are two cases, a base case and an induction step. The base case is

$$\begin{aligned}
&h\ (foldr\ f\ e\ [])\\
=\quad &\{\ \text{definition of } foldr\ \}\\
&h\ e\\
=\quad &\{\ \text{definition of } foldr\ \}\\
&foldr\ g\ (h\ e)\ []
\end{aligned}$$

The induction step is

$$h \ (foldr \ f \ e \ (x:xs))$$
$$= \quad \{ \text{ definition of } foldr \ \}$$
$$h \ (f \ x \ (foldr \ f \ e \ xs))$$
$$= \quad \{ \text{ fusion condition } \}$$
$$g \ x \ (h \ (foldr \ f \ e \ xs))$$
$$= \quad \{ \text{ induction } \}$$
$$g \ x \ (foldr \ g \ (h \ e) \ xs)$$
$$= \quad \{ \text{ definition of } foldr \ \}$$
$$foldr \ g \ (h \ e) \ (x:xs)$$

This completes the induction and the proof of the fusion law of *foldr*.

Returning to our two problems, the answer to the easier one is

$$foldr \ f \ e \ (xs + \!\!\!+ \ ys) = foldr \ f \ (foldr \ f \ e \ ys) \ xs$$

For the more difficult one we have $concat = foldr \ (+\!\!\!+) \ [\,]$, and the fusion law says that

$$h \ (foldr \ (+\!\!\!+) \ [\,] \ xss) = foldr \ g \ (h \ [\,]) \ xss$$

provided g satisfies

$$h \ (xs + \!\!\!+ \ ys) = g \ xs \ (h \ ys)$$

But $h = foldr \ f \ e$, and the solution to the easier problem says we can satisfy the fusion condition by taking $g = flip \ (foldr \ f)$. Thus

$$foldr \ f \ e \cdot concat = foldr \ (flip \ (foldr \ f)) \ e$$

over finite lists. Well done if you got it.

Before ending the section, let us make a remark about styles of reasoning. The proof of the fusion rule for *foldr* was carried out at the *point-level*, meaning that all functions were fully applied to their arguments. It is also called *point-wise* reasoning. Contrast this with the following proof:

$$map \ f \cdot filter \ p \cdot concat$$
$$= \quad \{ \text{ distributing } filter \text{ over } concat \ \}$$
$$map \ f \cdot concat \cdot map \ (filter \ p)$$
$$= \quad \{ \text{ distributing } map \text{ over } concat \ \}$$
$$concat \cdot map \ (map \ f) \cdot map \ (filter \ p)$$
$$= \quad \{ \text{ property of } map \ \}$$
$$concat \cdot map \ (map \ f \cdot filter \ p)$$
$$= \quad \{ \text{ definition of } concatMap \ \}$$
$$concatMap \ (map \ f \cdot filter \ p)$$

This calculation is carried out at the function level using functional composition as the basic combining form. It is also called *point-free* reasoning (and sometimes

pointless reasoning by wags). When applicable, point-free reasoning is more attractive than point-wise reasoning, if only because there are fewer parentheses to write.
For this reason we often write things like

$$h \cdot foldr\, f\; e = foldr\, g\; (h\; e)$$

without mentioning the list to which both sides are applied. However, as we said
above, without an additional proviso the fusion law is true only for finite lists. For
that reason we often state point-free equations with a rider "for all finite lists" or
"over finite lists". We did exactly this at the end of the previous section, though it so
happens that the equation

$$foldr\, f\; e \cdot concat = foldr\, (flip\, (foldr\, f))\; e$$

is true for *all* lists, infinite as well as finite.

1.5 Accumulating and tupling

Sometimes a clean and simple definition has to be tweaked to make it efficient. Here
is one rather artificial example. Given a list *xss* of lists of integers, consider the
problem of concatenating the shortest prefix of *xss* whose total sum is positive. If
no sum is positive, then the whole list is concatenated. Let *collapse* be the function
that carries out this process, so for example

$$
\begin{aligned}
collapse\; [[1],[-3],[2,4]] \quad &= [1] \\
collapse\; [[-2,1],[-3],[2,4]] &= [-2,1,-3,2,4] \\
collapse\; [[-2,1],[3],[2,4]] \quad &= [-2,1,3]
\end{aligned}
$$

The simplest way to define *collapse* is in terms of a helper function which *accumu-
lates* the required prefix in its first argument:

$$
\begin{aligned}
collapse &:: [[Int]] \to [Int] \\
collapse\; xss &= help\; [\,]\; xss \\
help\; xs\; xss &= \textbf{if}\; sum\; xs > 0 \lor null\; xss\; \textbf{then}\; xs \\
&\qquad \textbf{else}\; help\; (xs \mathbin{+\!\!+} head\; xss)\; (tail\; xss)
\end{aligned}
$$

Ignore completely what this particular function might be useful for and concentrate
only on the fact that *collapse* appears to be doing a lot of work in recomputing sums.
As each list is constructed in the first argument (the *accumulating parameter*) of
help, its sum is recomputed from scratch. We can do better by *tupling* each list with
its sum. Replace the definition of *collapse* with the following one:

$$
\begin{aligned}
collapse\; xss \quad &= help\; (0,[\,])\; (labelsum\; xss) \\
labelsum\; xss \quad &= zip\; (map\; sum\; xss)\; xss \\
help\; (s,xs)\; xss &= \textbf{if}\; s > 0 \lor null\; xss\; \textbf{then}\; xs \\
&\qquad \textbf{else}\; help\; (cat\; (s,xs)\; (head\; xss))\; (tail\; xss) \\
cat\; (s,xs)\; (t,ys) &= (s+t, xs \mathbin{+\!\!+} ys)
\end{aligned}
$$

Each list is paired with its sum and this pairing is threaded through the computation. There are no *sum* computations in the revised definition of *help* but only in the function *labelsum*. There is, however, a single + operation in the definition of *cat*. In the worst case, the cost of computing these sums is now linear in the total length of the input, whereas with the previous definition it was quadratic.

The remaining problem with *collapse* is the ++ operation in *cat*. The concatenations are performed from left to right. For example,

$$collapse\ [[-5,3],[-2],[-4],[-4,1]] = $$
$$((([\,] + [-5,3]) + [-2]) + [-4]) + [-4,1]$$

As we have seen, this is an inefficient way to concatenate lists. One way to solve the problem is to replace the accumulating list in the definition of *help* with an accumulating *function*:

$$collapse\ xss\ = (help\ (0, id)\ (labelsum\ xss))\ [\,]$$
$$help\ (s, f)\ xss = \textbf{if } s > 0 \lor null\ xss \textbf{ then } f \textbf{ else } help\ (s + t, f \cdot (xs+\!\!+))\ (tail\ xss)$$
$$\textbf{where } (t, xs) = head\ xss$$

At the end of the computation the accumulating function is applied to the empty list. For example, we now have

$$collapse\ [[-5,3],[-2],[-4],[-4,1]]$$
$$= (([-5,3]+\!\!+) \cdot ([-2]+\!\!+) \cdot ([-4]+\!\!+) \cdot ([-4,1]+\!\!+))\ [\,]$$
$$= [-5,3] + ([-2] + ([-4] + ([-4,1] + [\,])))$$

The concatenation is now from right to left and is more efficient. This trick of using an accumulating function to achieve efficient concatenation will appear again at various places in the book.

The general point we want to make with this example is the idea of *tupling*, whereby a computation can be made more efficient by tupling values of interest together and threading them through the computation. In that way such values do not have to be recomputed from scratch each time. Tupling is, in fact, a simple version of the idea of *memoising* the values of a function to save computing them more than once. Memoisation will be treated more fully in Part Five on dynamic programming algorithms. Generally, though not always, we will leave such tupling optimisations to the last stage in the design of an efficient algorithm because they add little by way of understanding and can clutter and obscure the code. Premature optimisation is the root of all evil in programming. We mention the tupling optimisation now because it is used a number of times in the final versions of some algorithms.

The twin techniques of accumulating parameters and tupling are useful devices for improving the running time of algorithms, but the mother of all such devices is fusion. Practically every algorithm in this book benefits from fusion of some kind, so if you take away anything from this chapter, make sure to include the two central principles of good algorithm design: (i) formulate the problem in terms of basic, well-understood ingredients; and (ii) fuse the components into a dish that is finally ready to leave the kitchen.

1.6 Chapter notes

The particular version of Haskell used in this book is Haskell 8.0, released in May 2016. The website www.haskell.org shows you how to download the Haskell Platform, a bundled system with lots of useful libraries. In addition to a compiler, the platform also provides an interpreter GHCi that we will use to illustrate some computations. The website also contains a wealth of material about Haskell, including a complete list of books on Haskell programming and a number of on-line tutorials about various aspects and features of the language. The wikibook en.wikibooks.org/wiki/Haskell also contains much useful information. Our own book on functional programming in Haskell [1] gives some help on how the use of a special function *seq* can be deployed to control the amount of space it takes to evaluate (some) functional expressions.

The quote about premature optimisation being the root of all evil in programming is due to Don Knuth [4], though it may have appeared earlier. The phrase "a lovely little old rectangular green French silver whittling knife" was used by Mark Forsyth [2] to show that adjectives in English absolutely have to be in the following order: opinion, size, age, shape, colour, origin, material, purpose. Any deviation from this order just sounds wrong. However, the linguistic device known as *hyperbaton* changes the word order for rhetorical effect.

The technique of using an accumulating function to change the order in which concatenations are performed was first written up in [3], though it was used earlier by a number of programmers.

References

[1]   Richard Bird. *Thinking Functionally with Haskell*. Cambridge University Press, Cambridge, 2014.
[2]   Mark Forsyth. *The Elements of Eloquence*. Icon Books, London, 2013.
[3]   John Hughes. A novel representation of lists and its application to the function "reverse". *Information Processing Letters*, 22(3):141–144, 1986.
[4]   Donald E. Knuth. Structured programming with go to statements. *ACM Computing Surveys*, 6(4):261–301, 1974.

Exercises

Exercise 1.1 Here are some other basic list-processing functions we will need:

> *maximum*, *take*, *takeWhile*, *inits*, *splitAt*, *null*, *elem*, *zipWith*,
> *minimum*, *drop*, *dropWhile*, *tails*, *span*, *all*, (!!)

To check your understanding, just give appropriate types.

Exercise 1.2 Trawling through *Data.List* we discovered the function

$$uncons :: [a] \rightarrow Maybe\,(a, [a])$$

of whose existence we were quite unconscious. Guess the definition of *uncons*.

Exercise 1.3 The library *Data.List* does not provide functions

$$wrap \quad :: a \rightarrow [a]$$
$$unwrap :: [a] \rightarrow a$$
$$single \quad :: [a] \rightarrow Bool$$

for wrapping a value into a singleton list, unwrapping a singleton list into its sole occupant, and testing a list for being a singleton. This is a pity, for the three functions can be very useful on occasions and will appear a number of times in the rest of this book. Give appropriate definitions.

Exercise 1.4 Write down a definition of *reverse* that takes linear time. One possibility is to use a *foldl*.

Exercise 1.5 Express both *map* and *filter* as an instance of *foldr*.

Exercise 1.6 Express *foldr f e · filter p* as an instance of *foldr*.

Exercise 1.7 The function *takeWhile* returns the longest initial segment of a list all of whose elements satisfy a given test. Moreover, its running time is proportional to the length of the result, not the length of the input. Express *takeWhile* as an instance of *foldr*, thereby demonstrating once again that a *foldr* need not process the whole of its argument before terminating.

Exercise 1.8 The *Data.List* library contains a function *dropWhileEnd* which drops the longest suffix of a list all of whose elements satisfy a given Boolean test. For example

$$dropWhileEnd\ even\ [1, 4, 3, 6, 2, 4] = [1, 4, 3]$$

Define *dropWhileEnd* as an instance of *foldr*.

Exercise 1.9 An alternative definition of *foldr* is

$$foldr\ f\ e\ xs = \textbf{if}\ null\ xs\ \textbf{then}\ e\ \textbf{else}\ f\ (head\ xs)\ (foldr\ f\ e\ (tail\ xs))$$

Dually, an alternative definition of *foldl* is

$$foldl\ f\ e\ xs = \textbf{if}\ null\ xs\ \textbf{then}\ e\ \textbf{else}\ f\ (foldl\ f\ e\ (init\ xs))\ (last\ xs)$$

where *last* and *init* are dual to *head* and *tail*. What is the problem with this definition of *foldl*?

Exercise 1.10 Bearing the examples

$$foldr\ (\oplus)\ e\ [x,y,z] = x \oplus (y \oplus (z \oplus e))$$
$$foldl\ (\oplus)\ e\ [x,y,z] = ((e \oplus x) \oplus y) \oplus z$$

in mind, under what simple conditions on $\oplus$ and e do we have

$$foldr\ (\oplus)\ e\ xs = foldl\ (\oplus)\ e\ xs$$

for all finite lists xs?

Exercise 1.11 Given a list of digits representing a natural number, construct a function *integer* which converts the digits into that number. For example,

$$integer\ [1,4,8,4,9,3] = 148493$$

Next, given a list of digits representing a real number r in the range $0 \leqslant r < 1$, construct a function *fraction* which converts the digits into the corresponding fraction. For example,

$$fraction\ [1,4,8,4,9,3] = 0.148493$$

Exercise 1.12 Complete the right-hand sides of

$$map\ (foldl\ f\ e) \cdot inits\ = ????$$
$$map\ (foldr\ f\ e) \cdot tails\ = ????$$

Exercise 1.13 Define the function

$$apply :: Nat \rightarrow (a \rightarrow a) \rightarrow a \rightarrow a$$

that applies a function a specified number of times to a value.

Exercise 1.14 Can the function *inserts* associated with the inductive definition of $perms_1$ be expressed as an instance of *foldr*?

Exercise 1.15 Give a definition of *remove* for which

$$perms_3\ [] = [[]]$$
$$perms_3\ xs = [x:ys \mid x \leftarrow xs, ys \leftarrow perms_3\ (remove\ x\ xs)]$$

computes the permutations of a list. Is the first clause necessary? What is the type of $perms_3$, and can one generate the permutations of a list of functions with this definition?

Exercise 1.16 What extra condition is needed for the fusion law of *foldr* to be valid over all lists, finite and infinite?

Exercise 1.17 As stated, the fusion law for *foldr* requires the proviso

$$h\ (f\ x\ y) = g\ x\ (h\ y)$$

for all x and y. The proviso is actually too general. Can you spot what the necessary and sufficient fusion condition is? To help you, here is an example, admittedly a rather artificial one, where a more restricted version of the fusion condition is necessary. Define the function *replace* by

$$replace\ x = \textbf{if } even\ x \textbf{ then } x \textbf{ else } 0$$

We claim that $replace \cdot foldr\ f\ 0 = foldr\ f\ 0$ on finite lists, where

$$f :: Int \rightarrow Int \rightarrow Int$$
$$f\ x\ y = 2 \times x + y$$

Prove this fact by using the more restricted proviso.

Exercise 1.18 We referred to the fusion rule of *foldr* as *the* master fusion rule, but there is another master rule, the fusion rule for *foldl*. What is this rule?

Exercise 1.19 Is the following statement true or false? "The original definition of *collapse* is more efficient than the optimised versions in the best case, when the first prefix has positive sum, because the sums of the remaining lists are not required. In the optimised version the sums of all the component lists are required."

Exercise 1.20 Find a definition of *op* so that

$$concat\ xss = foldl\ op\ id\ xss\ [\ ]$$

Exercise 1.21 A list of numbers is said to be *steep* if each number is greater than the sum of the elements following it. Give a simple definition of the Boolean function *steep* for determining whether a sequence of numbers is steep. What is the running time and how can you improve it by tupling?

Answers

Answer 1.1 We have

$$
\begin{array}{ll}
maximum, minimum & :: Ord\ a \Rightarrow [a] \rightarrow a \\
take, drop & :: Nat \rightarrow \qquad\ \ [a] \rightarrow [a] \\
takeWhile, dropWhile & :: (a \rightarrow Bool) \rightarrow [a] \rightarrow [a] \\
inits, tails & :: [a] \rightarrow [[a]] \\
splitAt & :: Nat \rightarrow \qquad\ \ [a] \rightarrow ([a],[a]) \\
span & :: (a \rightarrow Bool) \rightarrow [a] \rightarrow ([a],[a]) \\
null & :: \qquad\qquad\qquad [a] \rightarrow Bool \\
all & :: (a \rightarrow Bool) \rightarrow [a] \rightarrow Bool \\
elem & :: Eq\ a \Rightarrow a \rightarrow\ \ [a] \rightarrow Bool \\
(!!) & :: [a] \rightarrow Nat \rightarrow a \\
zipWith & :: (a \rightarrow b \rightarrow c) \rightarrow [a] \rightarrow [b] \rightarrow [c]
\end{array}
$$

In Haskell 8.0 some of these functions have more general types. For example,

$$maximum, minimum :: (Foldable\ t, Ord\ a) \Rightarrow t\ a \rightarrow a$$

The type class *Foldable* describes data structures that can be folded. For instance *Foldable t* contains a method *foldr* of type

$$foldr :: (a \to b \to b) \to b \to t\, a \to b$$

Lists are foldable and we will use *foldr* only on lists.

Answer 1.2 The function *uncons* is defined by

$$uncons\ [] \qquad = Nothing$$
$$uncons\ (x:xs) = Just\ (x,xs)$$

Answer 1.3 The simple definitions are

$$wrap\ x \qquad = [x]$$
$$unwrap\ [x] = x$$
$$single\ [x] \quad = True$$
$$single\ \_ \quad = False$$

Note that *head* and *unwrap* are different functions.

Answer 1.4 The definition is

$$reverse :: [a] \to [a]$$
$$reverse = foldl\ (flip\ (:))\ []$$

Answer 1.5 We have

$$map\ f \quad = foldr\ op\ [] \quad \textbf{where}\ op\ x\ xs = f\ x:xs$$
$$filter\ p = foldr\ op\ [] \quad \textbf{where}\ op\ x\ xs = \textbf{if}\ p\ x\ \textbf{then}\ x:xs\ \textbf{else}\ xs$$

Answer 1.6 We have *foldr f e · filter p = foldr op e*, where

$$op\ x\ y = \textbf{if}\ p\ x\ \textbf{then}\ f\ x\ y\ \textbf{else}\ y$$

Answer 1.7 We have

$$takeWhile :: (a \to Bool) \to [a] \to [a]$$
$$takeWhile\ p = foldr\ op\ [] \quad \textbf{where}\ op\ x\ xs = \textbf{if}\ p\ x\ \textbf{then}\ x:xs\ \textbf{else}\ []$$

For example,

$$takeWhile\ even\ [2,3,4,5]$$
$$= op\ 2\ (takeWhile\ even\ [3,4,5])$$
$$= 2: takeWhile\ even\ [3,4,5]$$
$$= 2: op\ 3\ (takeWhile\ even\ [4,5])$$
$$= 2: []$$

Answer 1.8 We have

$$dropWhileEnd :: (a \rightarrow Bool) \rightarrow [a] \rightarrow [a]$$
$$dropWhileEnd\ p = foldr\ op\ [\,]$$
$$\textbf{where}\ op\ x\ xs = \textbf{if}\ p\ x \wedge null\ xs\ \textbf{then}\ [\,]\ \textbf{else}\ x : xs$$

Answer 1.9 While

$$head :: [a] \rightarrow a$$
$$head\ (x : xs) = x$$
$$tail :: [a] \rightarrow [a]$$
$$tail\ (x : xs)\ \ = xs$$

both take constant time, the dual functions

$$last :: [a] \rightarrow a$$
$$last\ [x]\ \ \ \ \ = x$$
$$last\ (x : xs) = last\ xs$$

$$init :: [a] \rightarrow [a]$$
$$init\ [x]\ \ \ \ \ = [\,]$$
$$init\ (x : xs) = x : init\ xs$$

both take linear time because the whole list has to be traversed. That makes the alternative definition of *foldl* very inefficient.

Answer 1.10 One simple condition is that $\oplus$ is associative operation with identity element e. For example, addition is an associative operation with identity element 0, so *foldr* $(+)$ $0\ xs = foldl$ $(+)$ $0\ xs$ for all finite lists xs.

Answer 1.11 For the function that converts a decimal to an integer, a definition by *foldl* is appropriate:

$$integer = foldl\ shiftl\ 0\ \ \textbf{where}\ shiftl\ n\ d = 10 \times n + d$$

For the function that converts a decimal to a fraction, a definition by *foldr* is appropriate:

$$fraction = foldr\ shiftr\ 0\ \ \textbf{where}\ shiftr\ d\ x = (fromIntegral\ d + x)/10$$

The use of *fromIntegral* is necessary to convert a digit (an integer) to a floating-point number since division is not defined on integers.

Answer 1.12 We have

$$map\ (foldl\ f\ e) \cdot inits = scanl\ f\ e$$
$$map\ (foldr\ f\ e) \cdot tails = scanr\ f\ e$$

where *scanr* is a prelude function, dual to *scanl*. These results are known collectively as the *Scan Lemma* and can be very useful in text-processing algorithms such as those in Chapter 11.

Answer 1.13 There are two possible definitions:

$$apply\ 0\ f = id$$
$$apply\ n\ f = f \cdot apply\ (n-1)\ f$$

$$apply\ 0\ f = id$$
$$apply\ n\ f = apply\ (n-1)\ f \cdot f$$

Functional composition is an associative operation, so the definitions are equivalent.

Answer 1.14 Yes it can, although the definition is not immediately obvious:

$$inserts\ x = foldr\ step\ [[x]]$$
$$\textbf{where}\ step\ y\ yss = (x:y:ys):map\ (y:)\ yss$$
$$\textbf{where}\ ys = tail\ (head\ yss)$$

This definition relies on the fact that $head\ (inserts\ x\ ys) = x:ys$.

Answer 1.15 The function *remove* removes the first occurrence of a given element in a given list:

$$remove :: Eq\ a \Rightarrow a \rightarrow [a] \rightarrow [a]$$
$$remove\ x\ [] \quad = []$$
$$remove\ x\ (y:ys) = \textbf{if}\ x == y\ \textbf{then}\ ys\ \textbf{else}\ y:remove\ x\ ys$$

The first clause of $perms_3$ is indeed necessary; without it we have $perms_3\ [] = []$. From this one can show that $perms_3$ returns the empty list for all arguments. The type of $perms_3$ is $perms_3 :: Eq\ a \Rightarrow [a] \rightarrow [[a]]$, so, no, one cannot generate the permutations of a list of functions using this definition since functions cannot be tested for equality.

Answer 1.16 We would have to show the validity of fusion when the input is the undefined list $\perp$. Since $foldr\ f\ e\ \perp = \perp$ we require that h has to be a *strict* function, returning the undefined value if the argument is undefined.

Answer 1.17 Taking the example first, the original fusion condition requires that

$$replace\ (2 \times x + y) = 2 \times x + replace\ y$$

which is not true if y is odd. But we do have

$$replace\ (f\ x\ (foldr\ f\ 0\ xs)) = f\ x\ (replace\ (foldr\ f\ 0\ xs))$$

because $foldr\ f\ 0\ xs$ is always an even number. The more general fusion law, which we will call *context-sensitive* fusion, is that

$$h\ (foldr\ f\ e\ xs) = foldr\ g\ (h\ e)\ xs$$

for all finite lists xs provided that

$$h\ (f\ x\ (foldr\ f\ e\ xs)) = g\ x\ (h\ (foldr\ f\ e\ xs))$$

for all x and finite lists xs. Context-sensitive fusion will be needed in order to show that some problems can be solved by greedy algorithms.

Answer 1.18 We have

$$h \, (foldl \, f \, e \, xs) = foldl \, g \, (h \, e) \, xs$$

for all finite lists xs provided that

$$h \, (f \, y \, x) = g \, (h \, y) \, x$$

for all y and x. The proof that this proviso is sufficient is by induction, but we have to be careful and first generalise the induction hypothesis by replacing e by an arbitrary value y:

$$h \, (foldl \, f \, y \, xs) = foldl \, g \, (h \, y) \, xs$$

Then we have

$$
\begin{aligned}
& h \, (foldl \, f \, y \, (x:xs)) \\
=\ & \{ \text{ definition of } foldl \, \} \\
& h \, (foldl \, f \, (f \, y \, x) \, xs) \\
=\ & \{ \text{ induction } \} \\
& foldl \, g \, (h \, (f \, y \, x)) \, xs \\
=\ & \{ \text{ proviso } \} \\
& foldl \, g \, (g \, (h \, y) \, x) \, xs \\
=\ & \{ \text{ definition of } foldl \, \} \\
& foldl \, g \, (h \, y) \, (x:xs)
\end{aligned}
$$

The induction step would not be valid without the generalisation.

Answer 1.19 No, it is false. Haskell is a lazy language in which only those values which contribute to the answer are computed. In the best case of *collapse* the remaining sums are discarded so they are never computed.

Answer 1.20 We can take $op \, f \, xs \, ys = f \, (xs \mathbin{+\!\!+} ys)$, though of course we cannot concatenate an infinite list of lists this way.

Answer 1.21 A simple definition:

$$
\begin{aligned}
steep \, [] \quad &= True \\
steep \, (x:xs) &= x > sum \, xs \land steep \, xs
\end{aligned}
$$

This definition computes *sum* on every tail of the list. Since computation of *sum'* takes linear time, computation of *steep* takes quadratic time. To obtain a linear-time algorithm we can tuple *sum* and *steep*, leading to the definition

$$
\begin{aligned}
steep &= snd \cdot faststeep \\
faststeep \, [] \quad &= (0, True) \\
faststeep \, (x:xs) &= (x + s, x > s \land b) \ \textbf{where} \ (s, b) = faststeep \, xs
\end{aligned}
$$

Chapter 2

Timing

The secret of a successful algorithm, like the secret of successful comedy, is all about timing. In this chapter we review the tools needed for analysing the running times of functional algorithms and illustrate their use on one or two examples. The criteria for success should include space as well as time, but analysing the space requirements of a functional algorithm can be a complicated process, so we will ignore it almost entirely. The three tools we need are: asymptotic notation for describing the growth of functions; recurrence relations for estimating running times; and the notion of amortised running times.

2.1 Asymptotic notation

Asymptotic notation is used to compare the order of growth of functions without worrying about the constants involved. There are three kinds of asymptotic notation: Θ, O, and Ω ('big theta', 'big omicron', and 'big omega').

Let f and g be two functions taking natural numbers as arguments and returning nonnegative results, not necessarily integers. We say that f is of *order* g, and write $f = \Theta(g)$, if there are positive constants C and D and a number n_0 such that

$$Cg(n) \leqslant f(n) \leqslant Dg(n)$$

for all $n > n_0$. For example[1]

$$
\begin{aligned}
n(n+1)/2 &= \Theta(n^2) \\
n^3 + n^2 + n \log n &= \Theta(n^3) \\
n(1 + 1/2 + 1/3 + \cdots) &= \Theta(n \log n)
\end{aligned}
$$

The notation is abused to the extent that we write $f(n) = \Theta(g(n))$ rather than the more correct $f = \Theta(g)$. In particular, $\Theta(1)$ stands for an anonymous function whose values lie between two positive constants. For instance, we can be confident that

---

[1] In this book, except where otherwise stated, logarithms are taken in base two, so $\log n$ means $\log_2 n$.

taking the head of a list is a constant-time operation. Exactly what this constant is does not really matter – well, as long as it is small. Instead we say that *head* takes $\Theta(1)$ steps.

If we want only to put an upper bound on the values of a function, then we can use O notation. We say that f is of order *at most* g, and write $f = O(g)$, if there is a positive constant C and a natural number n_0 such that

$$f(n) \leqslant Cg(n)$$

for all $n > n_0$. In particular, $O(1)$ stands for an anonymous function whose values are bounded above by some positive constant. For example, the running time of *takeWhile* on a list of length n is $O(n)$ steps, assuming the test takes constant time. In the worst case the running time is $\Theta(n)$ steps but in the best case, when the first element does not pass the test, the running time is $\Theta(1)$ steps.

A running time of $O(n^2)$ does not imply that the running time is not also $O(n)$; so to claim, for example, that a sorting algorithm is inefficient because its running time is $O(n^2)$ is mathematically illiterate. Instead we can use Ω notation. We say that f is of order *at least* g, and write $f = \Omega(g)$, if there is a positive constant C and a natural number n_0 such that

$$f(n) \geqslant Cg(n)$$

for all $n \geqslant n_0$. It follows that $f = \Theta(g)$ if and only if $f = O(g)$ and $f = \Omega(g)$. Use of Ω notation is therefore for putting lower bounds on the values of a function. It is legitimate to assert that a sorting algorithm is inefficient if its running time is $\Omega(n^2)$ in the worst case. As we will see in due course, this statement is correct as well as legitimate, because there are sorting algorithms with superior running times.

Of the three kinds of asymptotic estimate, Θ notation and O notation are the ones we will use the most. For example, we can estimate sums such as $\sum_{k=1}^{n} k = \Theta(n^2)$ and $\sum_{k=1}^{n} k^2 = \Theta(n^3)$ without bothering about the exact constants involved.

There are two dangerous bends one has to navigate with asymptotic notation. Firstly, the equality sign in $f = \Theta(g)$ is not true equality with all the attendant properties that equality entails. For instance, $n^2 = \Theta(n^2)$ and $n^2 + n = \Theta(n^2)$ does not imply $n^2 = n^2 + n$. With Θ notation the equality goes one way, from the sharper to the looser estimate. Another way to define Θ notation is to say that $\Theta(g)$ denotes the *set* of all functions f with the stated property, and to write "$f \in \Theta(g)$" instead of "$f = \Theta(g)$". However, use of one-way equality rather than inclusion is traditional and there is no compelling reason to break from it. Consequently, we will never write $\Theta(g) = f$. We can, however, write

$$n^2 + \Theta(n) = \Theta(n^2)$$

for this assertion does make perfect mathematical sense.

The second danger concerns reasoning about asymptotic notation. We cannot reasonably assert, for example, that

$$\Theta(1) + \Theta(2) + \cdots + \Theta(n) = \Theta(n^2)$$

because the left-hand side does not have a clear meaning. But we can write

$$\sum_{i=1}^{n} \Theta(i) = \Theta(n^2)$$

because there is only one occurrence of Θ on the left and we assume that it stands for a single anonymous function of i.

We say that the running time of an algorithm is linear if it takes $\Theta(n)$ steps for an input of size n, quadratic if it takes $\Theta(n^2)$ steps, and so on. However, to claim that an algorithm is linear should, strictly speaking, mean that it takes this time in all cases. That is true for a function like *reverse*, but often the time taken differs in different cases. Use of Θ notation is therefore usually confined to one particular case. For instance, we might say that an algorithm takes $\Theta(n^2)$ steps in the worst case, but only $\Theta(n)$ steps in the best case. Best- and worst-case times are rarely the same. Most often we concentrate on the worst-case running time of an algorithm, only occasionally mentioning the best case.

There are two other measures of an algorithm's performance: the time it takes in the average case, and a measure of how common the average case can be expected to be. For any average-case analysis we have to assume some probability distribution of the input values. For example, we could analyse the average case of a sorting algorithm by assuming that the input is a permutation of 1 to n and that all such permutations are equally likely. That may or may not be a sensible assumption to make. Average-case analysis is a fascinating subject and can involve some sophisticated mathematics, but in what follows we will almost always ignore this measure of running time.

2.2 Estimating running times

So far we have used but not defined the phrase "the running time of a function". It is, of course, a function of the input size that measures the number of basic steps executed before the result is determined. The difficulty is that we simply do not know what the notion of a basic step means, at least not without looking closely at the details of a particular Haskell compiler and the architecture of the machine on which the algorithm is executed. The simplest alternative, and the one we will use, is to count *reduction* steps. Haskell evaluates an expression by reducing it to normal form and printing the result. At each step some reducible expression, or *redex*, is selected and simplified, by applying definitions supplied by the programmer or built-in operations like +. However, not all reduction steps take exactly the same time, nor does counting them take into account the time required to find the next redex in a large and possibly complicated expression, and so the number of reduction steps is not a completely faithful measure of time. Alternatively, we could look at the elapsed time between the start and finish points, but again such a measure depends on the particular computer on which the function is evaluated. GHCi, a Haskell interpreter that comes bundled with the Haskell Platform, does provide statistics of performance if requested, including a measure of the elapsed time. Hugs, an earlier interpreter for Haskell, counted reduction steps.

The second difficulty with estimating running times is that Haskell is a lazy language and evaluates expressions only as far as necessary to obtain the required value. For instance, in the evaluation of f (g x) it may or may not be the case that g x is evaluated fully in order to determine the value computed by f. We will see an example or two of this phenomenon in the following section. However, in most of the algorithms in this book every subexpression will be fully evaluated at some point in the computation, so the laziness of Haskell is not critical for timing purposes. Instead we will assume *eager* evaluation for the purposes of timing. In particular, if $T_g(n)$ is an estimate of the number of reduction steps required to compute g on an input of size n, for some appropriate definition of size, and g on such an input returns a value of size m, and $T_f(m)$ is similarly the number of steps required to compute f on an input of size m, then the running time $T(n)$ of the computation of $f \cdot g$ on an input of size n is given by

$$T(n) = T_g(n) + T_f(m)$$

Since lazy evaluation never requires more reduction steps than eager evaluation, any upper bound of the running time of a function under eager evaluation will also be an upper bound under lazy evaluation.

In order to count, or at least estimate, the number of reduction steps in the evaluation of a recursive function, we need the idea of a *recurrence relation*. Associated with every recursively defined function is another recursively defined function for estimating the first function's running time. The definition of the second function is usually referred to as a recurrence relation. Sometimes the relation is an equality (=), sometimes an inequality ($\leqslant$ or $\geqslant$), depending on whether we are seeking exact, upper, or lower bounds on the running time. To *solve* a recurrence relation means to find some way of expressing the function involved in a closed form.

For example, here is a simple recurrence relation for the running time T of some algorithm as a function of the input size n:

$$T(n) = T(n-1) + \Theta(n)$$

There is no real need to state the base case $T(0) = \Theta(1)$. The solution is given by

$$T(n) = \sum_{k=0}^{n} \Theta(k) = \Theta(n^2)$$

The solution is not quite so obvious with the recurrence

$$T(n) = 2T(n-1) + \Theta(n) \tag{2.1}$$

One way to solve (2.1) is to *unfold* it to see if a general pattern appears. Replacing $\Theta(n)$ by cn to avoid tripping up over multiple Θs, we have

$$
\begin{aligned}
T(n) &= cn + 2T(n-1) \\
&= cn + 2(c(n-1) + 2T(n-2)) \\
&= cn + 2c(n-1) + 4c(n-2) + \cdots + 2^{n-1}c + 2^n cT(0)
\end{aligned}
$$

and so

$$
\begin{aligned}
T(n) &= c\sum_{k=0}^{n-1} 2^k(n-k) + 2^n cT(0) \\
&= c\sum_{k=1}^{n} k2^{n-k} + 2^n cT(0) \\
&= c2^n \sum_{k=1}^{n} \frac{k}{2^k} + 2^n cT(0) \\
&= \Theta(2^n)
\end{aligned}
$$

since $\sum_{k=1}^{n} k/2^k < 2$. Strictly speaking, the above calculation solves only the recurrence

$$T(n) = 2T(n-1) + cn$$

However, (2.1) can be replaced by two recurrence relations:

$$
\begin{aligned}
T(n) &\leqslant 2T(n-1) + c_2 n \\
T(n) &\geqslant 2T(n-1) + c_1 n
\end{aligned}
$$

and the reasoning above can be repeated with inequalities instead of equalities, showing that $T(n) = \Omega(n)$ and $T(n) = O(n)$, and thus $T(n) = \Theta(n)$. There is no real harm in replacing $\Theta(f(n))$ by $c \times f(n)$, and we shall continue to do so.

Next, consider the recurrence

$$T(n) = nT(n-1) + \Theta(n)$$

This time we have

$$
\begin{aligned}
T(n) &= cn + nT(n-1) \\
&= cn + n(c(n-1) + (n-1)T(n-2)) \\
&= cn + cn(n-1) + cn(n-1)(n-2) + \cdots
\end{aligned}
$$

Hence

$$T(n) = c\sum_{k=1}^{n} \frac{n!}{(n-k)!} = \Theta(n!)$$

Later on, when we discuss divide-and-conquer algorithms, we will encounter other recurrence relations and show how to solve them.

Let us now look at some specific examples of how to time a Haskell function. Consider again the following two definitions of the function *concat*:

$$concat_1 \; xss = foldr \; (+\!\!+) \; [\,] \; xss$$
$$concat_2 \; xss = foldl \; (+\!\!+) \; [\,] \; xss$$

Since $+\!\!+$ is an associative operation with the empty list as identity element, these two definitions are equivalent provided *xss* is a finite list. Let $T_1(m,n)$ and $T_2(m,n)$ denote asymptotic estimates of the running times of the definitions when *xss* is a list of length *m* consisting of lists each of length *n*. The total length of *xss* is therefore mn. Under this assumption, the worst-case and the best-case running times coincide, so we can give asymptotic estimates without focusing on different cases.

To estimate T_1, it is best first to rewrite the definition of *concat*$_1$ in explicitly recursive terms:

$$concat_1 \; [\,] \qquad = [\,]$$
$$concat_1 \; (xs:xss) = xs +\!\!+ concat_1 \; xss$$

The recursive definition of *concat*$_1$ leads to the following definition of T_1:

$$T_1(0,n) \qquad = \Theta(1)$$
$$T_1(m+1,n) = T_1(m,n) + C(n,mn)$$

where $C(m,n)$ is the time taken to concatenate a list of length *m* with a list of length *n*. Here the base case is necessary. The cost of $+\!\!+$ is proportional to the length of the first argument, so $C(m,n) = \Theta(m)$. That means we can replace the second equation in the definition of T_1 by

$$T_1(m+1,n) = T_1(m,n) + \Theta(n)$$

Now we have

$$T_1(m,n) = \sum_{k=0}^{m} \Theta(n) = \Theta(mn)$$

The running time of *concat*$_1$ is therefore linear in the total length of the input, the best we can expect. Turning to *concat*$_2$, we again first rewrite the definition as an explicitly recursive function:

$$concat_2 \; xss \qquad = step \; [\,] \; xss$$
$$step \; ws \; [\,] \qquad = ws$$
$$step \; ws \; (xs:xss) = step \; (ws +\!\!+ xs) \; xss$$

Here *step* is an abbreviation for *foldl* $(+\!\!+)$. That leads to the recurrence

$$T_2(m,n) \qquad = S(0,m,n)$$
$$S(k,0,n) \qquad = \Theta(1)$$
$$S(k,m+1,n) = S(k+n,m,n) + \Theta(k)$$

where $S(k,m,n)$ is the cost of evaluating *step ws xss* when *ws* has length *k*, and $\Theta(k)$ accounts for the $+\!\!+$ operation in the recursive definition of *step*. We have

$$S(k,m,n) = \sum_{j=0}^{m-1} \Theta(k+jn) = \Theta(km+m^2n)$$

and so $T_2(m,n) = \Theta(m^2 n)$. The running time of $concat_2$ is therefore not linear in the total length of the input. Experiments with GHCi confirm the difference in running times:

```
> sum $ concat2 (replicate 2000 (replicate 100 1))
200000
(2.84 secs, 14,502,482,208 bytes)
> sum $ concat1 (replicate 2000 (replicate 100 1))
200000
(0.03 secs, 29,292,184 bytes)
```

By the way, experiments such as these are useful guides for guessing the running time of a function. Try running the function on inputs of sizes n, $2n$, $4n$, and so on. If the elapsed time doubles at each run, then the function takes linear time; if the elapsed time is greater by a factor of four at each step, then the function probably takes quadratic time; and if the time is greater by a factor of eight, then the function takes cubic time. And so on.

Here is another example. Consider again the two permutation-generating functions of the previous chapter:

$perms_1 = foldr \ (concatMap \cdot inserts) \ [[]]$
$inserts \ x \ [] \quad = [[x]]$
$inserts \ x \ (y:ys) = (x:y:ys) : map \ (y:) \ (inserts \ x \ ys)$

$perms_2 \ [] = [[]]$
$perms_2 \ xs = concatMap \ subperms \ (picks \ xs)$
$\qquad\qquad$ **where** $subperms \ (x,ys) = map \ (x:) \ (perms_2 \ ys)$
$picks \ [] \quad = []$
$picks \ (x:xs) = (x,xs) : [(y,x:ys) \mid (y,ys) \leftarrow picks \ xs]$

Let $T_1(n)$ and $T_2(n)$ be the running times of $perms_1$ and $perms_2$ on a list of length n. The recurrence relation for T_1 satisfies

$$T_1(n+1) = T_1(n) + n! \, (I(n) + \Theta(n^2))$$

The function $I(n)$ is the time to compute the list of insertions of a new element in a permutation of length n. There are $n+1$ results, each of which is a list of length $n+1$, and it takes $\Theta(n^2)$ to concatenate them. Finally, there are $n!$ permutations of a list of length n, so the insertions are computed $n!$ times. Now

$$I(n+1) = I(n) + \Theta(n)$$

There are $n+1$ ways to add a new element to a list of length n, so it takes $\Theta(n)$ steps to perform the map operations. That gives $I(n) = \Theta(n^2)$, and $I(n)\,n! = \Theta((n+2)!)$, so we have

$$T_1(n+1) = T_1(n) + \Theta((n+2)!)$$

Hence

$$T_1(n) = \sum_{k=0}^{n-1} \Theta((k+2)!) = \sum_{k=2}^{n+1} \Theta(k!)$$

But

$$\sum_{k=0}^{n} k! = n! \left(1 + \frac{1}{n} + \frac{1}{n(n-1)} + \cdots + \frac{1}{n!}\right) = \Theta(n!)$$

Therefore $T_1(n) = \Theta((n+1)!)$ and so the running time of $perms_1$ is proportional to the total length of the output, namely $n \times n!$.

Turning to $T_2(n)$, we have the recurrence relation

$$T_2(n) = P(n) + n\left(T_2(n-1) + \Theta(n!)\right) + \Theta((n+1)!)$$

where $P(n)$ is the time taken to compute *picks*. The second term accounts for the total time spent computing n evaluations of *subperms*, and the final term is the cost of the *concat* operation, which takes linear time in the length of the output. The function $P(n)$ satisfies

$$P(n) = P(n-1) + \Theta(n)$$

where the $\Theta(n)$ term accounts for the map operations implicit in the list comprehension. Thus

$$T_2(n) = n\,T_2(n-1) + \Theta((n+1)!)$$

To solve this recurrence we can guess that $T_2(n)$ takes the form

$$T_2(n) = f(n)\,n!$$

for some function f. Then we have

$$f(n)\,n! = nf(n-1)\,(n-1)! + \Theta((n+1)!)$$

which on division by $n!$ gives $f(n) = f(n-1) + \Theta(n)$. Hence $f(n) = \Theta(n^2)$ and $T_2(n) = \Theta((n+2)!)$. Thus the running time of $perms_2$ is a factor of n greater than the running time of $perms_1$.

2.3 Running times in context

As we said above, Haskell is a lazy language that evaluates expressions only as far as necessary to obtain the answer. In this section we take a brief look at some of the consequences of lazy evaluation. The material is not necessary for understanding the rest of the book, so it can be skipped, especially at a first reading.

The major point at issue is that we have to be careful about what running time we actually assign to a given function when it occurs in a particular context. For instance we have seen that evaluation of $concat_1$ on a list of length m of lists all of length n takes $\Theta(mn)$ steps. However, evaluating $head \cdot concat_1$ does not take this time. In fact, evaluation of $head \cdot concat_1$ on a nonempty list of nonempty lists proceeds essentially as follows:

$$head \; (concat_1 \; ((x:xs):xss))$$
$$= head \; ((x:xs) + concat_1 \; xss)$$
$$= head \; (x:(xs + concat_1 \; xss))$$
$$= x$$

There are only $\Theta(1)$ reduction steps. The running time of $head \cdot concat_2$ is, however, $\Theta(m)$ steps because it takes this time to reduce

$$(([] + xs_1) + xs_2) + \cdots + xs_m$$

to $xs_1 + \cdots$ before the head of xs_1 can be extracted.

Here is another instructive example. Consider the functions $inits$ and $tails$:

$$inits, tails :: [a] \to [[a]]$$
$$inits \; [] \quad = [[]]$$
$$inits \; (x:xs) = []:map \; (x:) \; (inits \; xs)$$
$$tails \; [] \quad = [[]]$$
$$tails \; (x:xs) = (x:xs):tails \; xs$$

For instance

$$inits \; \texttt{"abcd"} = [\texttt{""}, \texttt{"a"}, \texttt{"ab"}, \texttt{"abc"}, \texttt{"abcd"}]$$
$$tails \; \texttt{"abcd"} = [\texttt{"abcd"}, \texttt{"bcd"}, \texttt{"cd"}, \texttt{"d"}, \texttt{""}]$$

The running times $I(n)$ and $T(n)$ of $inits$ and $tails$ satisfy

$$I(n+1) = I(n) + \Theta(n)$$
$$T(n+1) = T(n) + \Theta(1)$$

with solutions $I(n) = \Theta(n^2)$ and $T(n) = \Theta(n)$. However, for both functions there are $\Theta(n^2)$ symbols in the output for a list of length n, so it takes this time to print the result. The difference between the running times of $inits$ and $tails$ emerges when we want to produce some function of the final list rather than the final list itself. For instance one can *count* the number of suffixes in linear time, but it requires quadratic time to count the prefixes:

```
length $ tails [1..10000]
10001
(0.00 secs, 2,407,104 bytes)
length $ inits [1..10000]
10001
(1.39 secs, 5,901,977,160 bytes)
```

To compute the length of a list one only has to know the number of elements, not the values of the elements themselves. The much greater space required in the second evaluation is due to the fact that evaluation of *inits* builds up a long chain of maps:

$$[[],$$
$$map\ (1:)\ [[]],$$
$$map\ (1:)\ (map\ (2:)\ [[]]),$$
$$...$$
$$map\ (1:)\ (map\ (2:)\ ...\ map\ (10000:)\ [[]])]$$

The values of these elements are not needed for computing the length of the result, but nevertheless the unevaluated expressions have to be stored, which is why the total amount of space required is about the square of the space needed for counting the number of suffixes. We will return to *inits* and *tails* in the following chapter.

Here is one more example. Consider the cost of computing $length \cdot perms_1$, where $perms_1$ was defined in the previous section. Since only the number of permutations has to be found, no expression denoting an individual permutation has to be evaluated and the running time, $L(n)$ say, satisfies the recurrence relation

$$L(n+1) = L(n) + n!\,I(n)$$

where $I(n) = \Theta(n^2)$, the same as before. The recurrence has the same asymptotic solution as before, so it takes $\Theta((n+1)!)$ steps to compute the number of permutations. This time can be brought down to $\Theta(n!)$ steps by redefining *inserts*. The trick is to use an accumulating function:

$$inserts\ x \qquad = help\ id\ x$$
$$help\ f\ x\ [] \qquad = [f\ [x]]$$
$$help\ f\ x\ (y:ys) = f\ (x:y:ys) : help\ (f \cdot (y:))\ x\ ys$$

For example,

$$help\ id\ 1\ [2,3]$$
$$= id\ [1,2,3] : help\ (2:)\ 1\ [3]$$
$$= id\ [1,2,3] : (2:)\ [1,3] : help\ ((2:) \cdot (3:))\ 1\ []$$
$$= id\ [1,2,3] : (2:)\ [1,3] : (2:)\ ((3:)\ [1]) : []$$

It now takes only $\Theta(n)$ steps to count the number of insertions, so

$$L(n+1) = L(n) + \Theta((n+1)!)$$

with the solution $L(n) = \Theta(n!)$. However, the total running time $T_1(n)$ of $perms_1$ is not affected by this change.

2.4 Amortised running times

Sometimes the total cost of a sequence of n operations is $O(n)$ steps even though the cost of an individual operation is not $O(1)$. Consider the function

$$build :: (a \rightarrow a \rightarrow Bool) \rightarrow [a] \rightarrow [a]$$
$$build\ p = foldr\ insert\ [] \textbf{ where } insert\ x\ xs = x : dropWhile\ (p\ x)\ xs$$

For example, $build\ (==)$ removes adjacent duplicates from a list:

$$build\ (==)\ [4,4,2,1,1,1,2,5] = [4,2,1,2,5]$$

The running time $I(n)$ of *insert* on a list of length n is $O(n)$ steps, assuming evaluation of p takes constant time. Hence the running time $B(n)$ of *build* on a list of length n satisfies

$$B(n+1) = B(n) + O(n)$$

with solution $B(n) = O(n^2)$. The running time of *insert* is certainly not constant because *dropWhile* can take $\Omega(n)$ steps when applied to a list of length n. It therefore appears that the assertion $B(n) = O(n^2)$ is the best we can say about the running time of *build p*.

In fact the running time of *build p* is $O(n)$ steps, not just $O(n^2)$ steps. To see why, observe that each element added to the list can be dropped at most once. Thus the total number of elements that can be dropped is at most the total number of elements that can be added, namely n. That gives a total running time of $O(n)$ steps. The *amortised* cost of a single operation is obtained by dividing the total cost of the operations by the number of such operations, namely n. The amortised cost of *insert* in the computation of *build* is therefore $O(1)$ steps. Note that no assumption about probability distributions is involved in this analysis.

As another example, consider the following function which increments a binary integer a given number of times:

$$bits :: Int \rightarrow [[Bit]]$$
$$bits\ n = take\ n\ (iterate\ inc\ [])$$
$$\textbf{where } inc\ []\ \ \ \ \ = [1]$$
$$inc\ (0:bs) = 1:bs$$
$$inc\ (1:bs) = 0:inc\ bs$$

The Standard Prelude function *iterate* generates an infinite list:

$$iterate :: (a \rightarrow a) \rightarrow a \rightarrow [a]$$
$$iterate\ f\ x = x : iterate\ f\ (f\ x)$$

The function *inc* increments a binary integer, written in reverse order with the least significant bit first: for example, $inc\ 101 = 011$ and $inc\ 111 = 0001$. How long does it take to compute *bits n*? Since the running time of *inc* on a list of length k is $\Omega(k)$ in the worst case (when all the bits are 1), it seems that the best we can say about the total cost of n increments is that it takes $O(n^2)$ steps. Certainly it takes this time both to compute and print the result, but we are concerned only with the computation time. In fact the cost is $O(n)$ steps. To see why, observe that in half of the cases only the first bit is changed; in a quarter of the cases only the first two bits are changed; in an eighth of the cases only the first three bits are changed; and so on. Taking the cost of changing a bit to be 1 step, the total cost is

$$\frac{n}{2}+\frac{2n}{4}+\frac{3n}{8}+\cdots = O(n)$$

The amortised cost of each increment is therefore $O(1)$ steps.

The most important use of amortised costs occurs when building data structures of various kinds. We will see examples in the following chapter. Typical operations on data structures include inserting an element into the structure, deleting an element, and perhaps merging two structures in some way. When each individual operation is considered in isolation, upper and lower bounds can be given for the cost of the operation. However, when some computation involves a sequence of n such operations, whether they are grouped together or distributed throughout the computation, the total cost as a function of n may be lower than the sum of the individual estimates of the costs of each operation in the sequence.

The amortised costs of *build p* and a sequence of *inc* operations were obtained using different insights, but there is a more uniform way of computing amortised costs, not restricted to costs that are $O(1)$. We will need this method in the following chapter. To do so we first change the cost model to one that counts the costs of operations in terms of definite integers rather than asymptotic notation. For example with *build p* we can charge a cost of 1 for each evaluation of p (remember p is assumed to be a constant-time operation) and 1 for each cons operation. The actual running times are proportional to these costs. Similarly, when a bit sequence begins with exactly t bits set to 1, the cost of *inc* is defined to be $t+1$.

Now suppose n successive applications of some function f applied to x_0 produces a sequence of values $x_0, x_1, ..., x_n$. Let $C(x_i)$ be the cost of computing f on input x_i and $A(x_i)$ the amortised cost. The aim is to show

$$\sum_{i=0}^{n-1} C(x_i) \leqslant \sum_{i=0}^{n-1} A(x_i) \tag{2.2}$$

In particular, if $A(x_i) = O(1)$, then the total cost of n operations is $O(n)$.

To establish (2.2) we construct a function S, a 'size' function that returns nonnegative integers, and show for some appropriate definition of A that

$$C(x_i) \leqslant S(x_i) - S(x_{i+1}) + A(x_i) \tag{2.3}$$

for $0 \leqslant i < n$. In words, the cost of f on an input is bounded above by the difference in sizes between the input and output, plus the amortised cost. The inequality (2.2) can be summed, giving

$$\sum_{i=0}^{n-1} C(x_i) \leqslant S(x_0) - S(x_n) + \sum_{i=0}^{n-1} A(x_i)$$

so (2.2) is certainly satisfied if $S(x_0) = 0$.

Here are our two examples again. In the case of *build p* we take $S(xs) = length\ xs$. Let $C(xs_i)$ be the cost of computing xs_{i+1}, counting a cost of 1 for each p or cons operation. We have

$$C(xs_i) = length\ xs_i - length\ xs_{i+1} + 2$$

The cost is positive because if the output is longer than the input, it can only be so by one element. Hence we can take $A(xs) = 2$.

In the case of *inc* we can define $S(bs)$ to be the number of bits in bs that are set to 1. If there are b_1 bits set to 1 before an *inc* operation, including t initial bits, and b_2 bits set after the operation, then $b_2 = b_1 - t + 1$, equivalently $t + 1 = b_1 - b_2 + 2$. Hence

$$C(bs_i) = S(bs_i) - S(bs_{i+1}) + 2$$

and so $A(bs) = 2$.

Here is one more example. Consider the function

$$prune :: ([a] \rightarrow Bool) \rightarrow [a] \rightarrow [a]$$
$$prune\ p = foldr\ cut\ [\ ]\ \textbf{where}\ cut\ x\ xs = until\ done\ init\ (x:xs)$$
$$done\ xs = null\ xs \lor p\ xs$$

The value of *cut x xs* is the result of repeatedly dropping the last element of $x:xs$ until a list satisfying p is obtained. For example, if *ordered* is the test for whether a sequence is in ascending order, we have

$$prune\ ordered\ [3,7,8,2,3] = [3,7,8]$$

This is obviously a very silly way to find the longest ordered prefix of a list, but never mind – only the running time is of interest. If evaluation of p on a list of length k takes $O(k)$ steps, then evaluation of *cut* on a list of length k takes $O(k^2)$ steps. So it seems that the best we can say is that *prune* applied to a list of length n takes $O(n^3)$ steps. In fact, *prune* takes $O(n^2)$ steps, which means that the amortised running time of *cut* is $O(n)$ steps.

To see why, suppose the result of *cut* on a list of length k_1 is a list of length k_2, where $0 \leqslant k_2 \leqslant k_1 + 1$. Suppose we charge evaluation of each of *done* and *init* on a list of length k as k units. Then *init* is performed $k_1 + 1 - k_2$ times with a total cost of

$$(k_1 + 1) + k_1 + (k_1 - 1) + \cdots + (k_2 + 1) = \frac{(k_1 + 1)(k_1 + 2)}{2} - \frac{k_2(k_2 + 1)}{2}$$

Since *done* is performed one more time than *init*, for a cost of k_2, its total cost is

$$\frac{(k_1 + 1)(k_1 + 2)}{2} - \frac{k_2(k_2 - 1)}{2}$$

Summing these two quantities and adding in 1 unit for the cons operation, we have that the total cost of *cut* on a list of length k_1 is

$$(k_1 + 1)(k_1 + 2) - k_2^2 + 1 = k_1^2 - k_2^2 + 3(k_1 + 1)$$

We can therefore take

$$S(xs_i) = (length\ xs_i)^2$$
$$A(xs_i) = 3 \times (length\ xs_i + 1)$$

to satisfy (2.3). But no list can have length greater than n, so $A(xs_i) = O(n)$ and the total cost of *prune* on a list of length n is $O(n^2)$ steps.

2.5 Chapter notes

As will be appreciated, a fair amount of combinatorial mathematics is involved in the analysis of running times. We have mentioned sums and factorials, but later on we will also need floors and ceilings, modulus operations, and binomial coefficients. The best source book for these concepts is [1]. The history of asymptotic notation is discussed in [2] and also appears in [3]. To complete a quartet of books authored by Donald Knuth, the inventor of the name 'Analysis of Algorithms', we also recommend [4].

There are a number of algorithms for generating permutations, and a comprehensive review can be found in Section 7.2.1.2 of [5], yet another book by Knuth. The method of choice used in *Data.List* is one that achieves maximal laziness. For a fascinating discussion of this rather complicated definition, see http://stackoverflow.com/questions/24484348/.

References

[1] Ronald L. Graham, Donald E. Knuth, and Oren Patashnik. *Concrete Mathematics*. Addison-Wesley, Reading, MA, second edition, 1994.
[2] Donald E. Knuth. Big omicron and big omega and big theta. *ACM SIGACT News*, 8(2):18–23, 1976.
[3] Donald E. Knuth. *The Art of Computer Programming*, volume 1: Fundamental Algorithms. Addison-Wesley, Reading, MA, third edition, 1997.
[4] Donald E. Knuth. *Selected Papers on Analysis of Algorithms*. Center for the Study of Language and Information, Stanford University, CA, 2000.
[5] Donald E. Knuth. *The Art of Computer Programming*, volume 4A: Combinatorial Algorithms. Addison-Wesley, Reading, MA, 2011.

Exercises

Exercise 2.1 Is the assertion $f(n) = O(1)$ the same as the assertion $f(n) = \Theta(1)$?

Exercise 2.2 Are the following two assertions true?

$$O(f(n) \times g(n)) = f(n) \times O(g(n))$$
$$O(f(n) + g(n)) = f(n) + O(g(n))$$

Exercise 2.3 Prove formally that $(n+1)^2 = \Theta(n^2)$ by exhibiting the necessary constants.

Exercise 2.4 What are the exact values of the sums $\sum_{k=1}^{n} k$ and $\sum_{k=1}^{n} k^2$?

Exercise 2.5 Some of the following are correct and some are wrong. Which are which?

$$2n^2 + 3n = \Theta(n^2)$$
$$2n^2 + 3n = O(n^3)$$
$$n \log n = O(n\sqrt{n})$$
$$n + \sqrt{n} = O(\sqrt{n} \log n)$$
$$\sum_{k=1}^{n} 1/k = \Theta(\log n)$$
$$2^{\log n} = O(n)$$
$$\log(n!) = \Theta(n \log n)$$

Exercise 2.6 Sums of the form $\sum_{k=0}^{n} k x^k$ for various x come up surprisingly often in the analysis of running times. One way of finding the solution is to start with the simpler geometric series

$$\sum_{k=0}^{n} x^k = \frac{1 - x^{n+1}}{1 - x}$$

which is valid provided $x \neq 1$, and to differentiate both sides with respect to x. Using the fact that the derivative of a sum is the sum of its derivatives, carry out this differentiation and hence estimate the sums $\sum_{k=0}^{n} k 2^k$ and $\sum_{k=0}^{n} k/2^k$.

Exercise 2.7 Using Θ notation, estimate the sum $\sum_{k=1}^{n} k \log k$.

Exercise 2.8 Solve the recurrence relation

$$T(0,n) = \Theta(n^2)$$
$$T(m,n) = T(m-1,n) + \Theta(m)$$

Exercise 2.9 Use the fusion law of *foldr* to simplify *head · concat*$_1$. Can the fusion law of *foldl* be used to simplify *head · concat*$_2$?

Exercise 2.10 Analyse the running time of *perms*$_3$, where

perms$_3$ [] = [[]]
perms$_3$ *xs* = *concatMap subperms xs*
          where *subperms x* = *map* (*x*:) (*perms*$_3$ (*remove x xs*))

Exercise 2.11 Do *perms*$_1$, *perms*$_2$, and *perms*$_3$ all return the same first list? If so, what is it?

Exercise 2.12 Can the trick of using an accumulating function work with *inits*?

Exercise 2.13 Suppose you are given a list of n digits and you want to find the position, reading from left to right, of the first digit d for which $d \geqslant 5$. If no such digit occurs, then the result is some negative position, say -1. In the best case the algorithm examines one digit and in the worst case all n digits. Assuming that every sequence of n digits is equally likely, what is the average number of digits that have to be examined?

Exercise 2.14 Using the function *iterate*, give a one-line definition of the function *tails1* that returns the nonempty suffixes of a list.

Exercise 2.15 Consider the problem of maintaining a *dynamic array*. Apart from inspecting and updating the elements, suppose that new elements can be added to the array but only at the front. At some point the array, which is of a fixed given size, can become full. To solve this problem, a new array of double the size of the old one can be allocated and all the existing elements copied into the upper half of the new array, leaving space for further additions in the bottom half. Then we can carry on until the new array becomes full, in which case the process is repeated. Show that, in a sequence of add operations, each addition has an amortised cost of $O(1)$.

Answers

Answer 2.1 Strictly speaking, no. We have $f(n) = O(1)$ if there is a positive constant C and an integer n_0 such that $f(n) \leqslant C$ for all $n > n_0$, while $f(n) = \Theta(n)$ if there are positive constants C and D and an integer n_0 such that $D \leqslant f(n) \leqslant C$ for all $n > n_0$. Hence the function *const* 0 is $O(1)$ but not $\Theta(1)$.

Answer 2.2 No, the first one is true, but the second one is false. For example, take $f(n) = n^2$ and $g(n) = 1$. Then $h(n) = O(n^2 + 1)$ holds if there exists a C and n_0 such that $h(n) \leqslant C(n^2 + 1)$ for all $n > n_0$, but it does not follow that that there exists a C and n_0 such that $h(n) \leqslant n^2 + C$ for all $n > n_0$.

Answer 2.3 We have $n^2 \leqslant (n+1)^2 \leqslant 4n^2$ for all $n > 0$. The second inequality follows from the fact that $3n^2 - 2n - 1 = (3n+1)(n-1)$, which is nonnegative if $n \geqslant 1$.

Answer 2.4 We have
$$\sum_{k=1}^{n} k = \frac{n(n+1)}{2}$$
$$\sum_{k=1}^{n} k^2 = \frac{n(n+1)(2n+1)}{6}$$

Answer 2.5 They are all true except for $n + \sqrt{n} = O(\sqrt{n} \log n)$. The last one, $\log(n!) = \Theta(n \log n)$, is a crude form of Stirling's approximation, which states that

$$n! = \sqrt{2\pi n} \left(\frac{n}{e}\right)^n (1 + O(1/n))$$

Answer 2.6 Differentiating, we obtain

$$\sum_{k=0}^{n} kx^{k-1} = \frac{1 - (n+1)x^n + nx^{n+1}}{(1-x)^2}$$

so

$$\sum_{k=0}^{n} kx^{k} = \frac{x(1 - (n+1)x^n + nx^{n+1})}{(1-x)^2}$$

Taking $x = 2$, we find that the right-hand side is $\Theta(n2^n)$, and taking $x = 1/2$ and letting n tend to infinity, the right-hand side tends to the value 2.

Answer 2.7 We have

$$\sum_{k=1}^{n} k \log k \leqslant \log n \sum_{k=1}^{n} k = O(n^2 \log n)$$

We also have

$$\sum_{k=1}^{n} k \log k \geqslant \sum_{k=n/2}^{n} k \log k \geqslant \log(n/2) \sum_{k=n/2}^{n} k = \Omega(n^2 \log n)$$

Hence the sum is $\Theta(n^2 \log n)$.

Answer 2.8 We have $T(m,n) = \Theta(mn + n^2)$.

Answer 2.9 To simplify $head \cdot foldr \,(+\!\!+)\, []$ we have to find a function op_1 so that

$$head\,(xs +\!\!+ ys) = op_1\,xs\,(head\,ys)$$

It is easy to see what the definition should be:

$$op_1\,xs\,y = \textbf{if } null\,xs \textbf{ then } y \textbf{ else } head\,xs$$

That gives

$$head \cdot concat_1 = foldr\,op_1 \perp$$

since $head\,[] = \perp$.

To simplify $head \cdot foldl \,(+\!\!+)\, []$ using the fusion law of $foldl$ we have to find a function op_2 so that

$$head\,(xs +\!\!+ ys) = op_2\,(head\,xs)\,ys$$

But, unless xs is known to be nonempty, no such op_2 exists because we would have to have $op_2 \perp ys = head\,ys$ and $op_2\,x\,ys = x$.

Answer 2.10 We have

$$T(0) = \Theta(1)$$
$$T(n) = n\,(R(n) + T(n-1) + \Theta((n-1)!)) + \Theta((n+1)!)$$

where $R(n)$ is the time needed for removing an element from a list of length n.

The first term is the time needed to compute all evaluations of *subperms*. For each evaluation we remove an element, costing $R(n)$ steps, compute the permutations of the resulting list, and then cons the element on the $(n-1)!$ results. The final term accounts for the concatenations. Since $nR(n) = O((n+1)!)$ we have

$$T(n) = nT(n-1) + \Theta((n+1)!)$$

and, as we have seen, this leads to $T(n) = \Theta((n+2)!)$, a factor of n worse than the total length of the output.

Answer 2.11 Yes. Applied to *xs*, all three methods return *xs* as the first permutation (in the case of *perms*$_3$ it is required that the elements of *xs* can be compared with equality).

Answer 2.12 Yes. Here is the definition:

$$inits = help\ id$$
$$\textbf{where}\ help\ f\ [] \qquad = f\ []:[]$$
$$help\ f\ (x:xs) = f\ []:help\ (f \cdot (x:))\ xs$$

It now takes linear time to compute *length · inits*.

Answer 2.13 Since exactly half the digits are greater than or equal to 5, the algorithm inspects just one digit half of the time, two digits a quarter of the time, and so on. Therefore in the average case $\sum_{k=0}^{n} k/2^k$ digits are inspected, which is 2 as we saw in Exercise 2.6. The average case is therefore only twice as bad as the best case.

Answer 2.14 The definition is

$$tails1 = takeWhile\ (not \cdot null) \cdot iterate\ tail$$

Answer 2.15 If the array has size 1 to begin with, the add operations take, in order, times proportional to $1, 2, 1, 4, 1, 1, 1, 8, \ldots$ The total cost of n add operations is therefore

$$n + \sum_{k=1}^{p} 2^k - 1 \leqslant n + 2^{p+1}$$

where $2^p \leqslant n < 2^{p+1}$. Hence the amortised cost of an add operation is $O(1)$ steps. A similar situation occurs in Haskell. Periodically memory becomes full, and computation is suspended while a garbage collection takes place. Thus a cons operation is not actually guaranteed to take $O(1)$ steps in all cases.

Chapter 3

Useful data structures

Most of the algorithms in this book can be implemented with acceptable efficiency using just common-or-garden lists. One or two others require more specialised data structures, such as binary search trees, heaps, and queues of various kinds. The general philosophy of this book is not to consider data structures in isolation from the algorithms that depend on them, so we postpone discussion of such structures to the appropriate time and place. However, there is a small group of interrelated data structures that we will introduce now. They are symmetric lists, random-access lists, and arrays. Each is designed in its own way to overcome an obvious deficiency in the running times of some of the basic operations on standard lists.

3.1 Symmetric lists

As we have seen, some operations on lists are lopsided with regard to efficiency: while adding an element to the front of a list takes constant time, adding it to the rear takes linear time. In what follows these two functions will be called *cons* and *snoc*; the former is defined by *cons x xs = x:xs*, and the latter by *snoc x xs = xs ++ [x]*. Similarly, while *head* and *tail* take constant time, *last* and *init* take linear time. The data type known as *symmetric lists* overcomes this one-sidedness, guaranteeing amortised constant time for all six operations. The basic idea is quite simple: break the list into two and reverse the second half. In that way, a *snoc* can be implemented as a *cons* on the second half, *last* as a *head*, and so on. The problem occurs with *init* and *tail* when one attempts to remove an element; in some cases the list has first to be reorganised into two new halves.

Here are the details. A symmetric list is introduced as a pair of lists

type *SymList a* = ([a], [a])

with the understanding that the symmetric list (*xs, ys*) represents the standard list

$xs + reverse\ ys$. That means we can convert back from symmetric lists to standard lists by

$$fromSL :: SymList\ a \rightarrow [a]$$
$$fromSL\ (xs, ys) = xs + reverse\ ys$$

A function such as *fromSL* which converts a representation back into the structure it is designed to represent is called an *abstraction* function. Using an abstraction function we can capture the required relationship between the implementation of an operation on the representing type and its 'abstract' definition with a simple equation.

There is another aspect to the representation, the clever part that makes everything fit together. The two invariants

$$null\ xs \implies null\ ys \lor single\ ys$$
$$null\ ys \implies null\ xs \lor single\ xs$$

are maintained on symmetric lists (xs, ys). Here, *single* is the test for a singleton list. In words, if one or other component is the empty list, then the other component has to be either the empty list or a singleton list. The operations on symmetric lists both exploit this *representation invariant* as well as maintain it.

Apart from *fromSL* there are six other operations we are going to implement on symmetric lists; we will call them

$$consSL,\ snocSL,\ headSL,\ lastSL,\ tailSL,\ initSL$$

The implementations are designed to satisfy the six equations

$$cons\ x \cdot fromSL = fromSL \cdot consSL\ x$$
$$snoc\ x \cdot fromSL = fromSL \cdot snocSL\ x$$
$$tail \cdot fromSL \quad = fromSL \cdot tailSL$$
$$init \cdot fromSL \quad = fromSL \cdot initSL$$
$$head \cdot fromSL \ = headSL$$
$$last \cdot fromSL \ = lastSL$$

Here are the definitions of *snocSL* and *lastSL*:

$$snocSL :: a \rightarrow SymList\ a \rightarrow SymList\ a$$
$$snocSL\ x\ (xs, ys) = \textbf{if}\ null\ xs\ \textbf{then}\ (ys, [x])\ \textbf{else}\ (xs, x : ys)$$

$$lastSL :: SymList\ a \rightarrow a$$
$$lastSL\ (xs, ys) \quad = \textbf{if}\ null\ ys\ \textbf{then}\ head\ xs\ \textbf{else}\ head\ ys$$

Both of these definitions make use of, and maintain, the representation invariant. In the case of *snocSL* we cannot just add x to the front of ys, because that would break the invariant if xs happens to be the empty list and ys a singleton. But when xs is empty we can return $(ys, [x])$, because ys is either empty or a singleton, and

$$[] +\!\!+ reverse\ [] +\!\!+ [x] = [] +\!\!+ reverse\ [x]$$
$$[] +\!\!+ reverse\ [y] +\!\!+ [x] = [y] +\!\!+ reverse\ [x]$$

In the case of *lastSL*, if *ys* is the empty list, then *xs* is either empty or a singleton and, in the second case, the last element is the sole member of *xs*. We should really have defined *lastSL* to read

> *lastSL* (*xs*, *ys*) = **if** *null ys*
> > **then if** *null xs*
> > > **then** *error* "lastSL of empty list"
> > > **else** *head xs*
> > **else** *head ys*

Otherwise we would get a confusing "head of empty list" error message when trying to obtain the last element of an empty symmetric list. However, we will keep the code simple by omitting error messages, using a simple $\perp$ instead. Once the definitions of these two functions are understood, there should be no difficulty with implementing the entirely dual functions *consSL* and *headSL*, so we will leave them as exercises.

Two functions remain, and here things get interesting. The definition of *tailSL* is as follows:

> *tailSL* :: *SymList a* $\rightarrow$ *SymList a*
> *tailSL* (*xs*, *ys*)
> > | *null xs*   = **if** *null ys* **then** $\perp$ **else** *nilSL*
> > | *single xs* = (*reverse vs*, *us*)
> > | *otherwise* = (*tail xs*, *ys*)
> > **where** (*us*, *vs*) = *splitAt* (*length ys* **div** 2) *ys*

Let us look at the three cases. In the first case, when *xs* is an empty list, the representation invariant guarantees that *ys* is either the empty list or a singleton list. If the former, then *tailSL* should really give a suitable error message rather than simply returning $\perp$. If *ys* is a singleton, then *tailSL* correctly returns the empty symmetric list. The next easy case is the third one, in which *xs* is a list of length at least two. Then we can simply drop the first element of *xs* without destroying the invariant. The most interesting case is the second one, when *xs* is a singleton list, so *ys* can be a list of any length whatsoever. Here we split *ys* into two equal halves *us* and *vs*, and then return the value (*reverse vs*, *us*). That's correct because

$$[] +\!\!+ reverse\ (us +\!\!+ vs) = reverse\ vs +\!\!+ reverse\ us$$

The implementation of *initSL* is entirely dual to that of *tailSL* and we will leave it as another exercise. The definition of *nilSL* is also left as an exercise.

Each of the operations apart from *tailSL* and *initSL* takes constant time. Although *tailSL* and *initSL* can take linear time in the worst case, they both take amortised constant time. For the proof we employ the size method of the previous chapter. Consider a sequence of n symmetric list operations producing a sequence $x_0, x_1, ..., x_n$ of symmetric lists, where we suppose x_0 is the empty symmetric list $([\,],[\,])$. Recall that we have to construct a cost function C, a size function S, and an amortised function A to satisfy

$$C(x_i) \leqslant S(x_i) - S(x_{i+1}) + A(x_i) \qquad (3.1)$$

For the size function S, we choose

$$S(x_i) = abs \, (length \; xs_i - length \; ys_i)$$

where $x_i = (xs_i, ys_i)$ and abs is the function that returns the absolute value of a number:

$$abs \; n = \textbf{if} \; n \geqslant 0 \; \textbf{then} \; n \; \textbf{else} - n$$

For the amortised time we choose $A(x_i) = 2$. As to the costs of the individual operations, we can charge a cost of 1 for each of the constant-time operations, *headSL*, *lastSL*, *consSL*, and *snocSL*. Neither of the first two change the symmetric list, so (3.1) is satisfied for *headSL* and *lastSL*. Next consider *snocSL*, which, applied to a symmetric list with component lengths (m, n), produces a symmetric list with component lengths $(n, 1)$ if $m = 0$ and $(m, n+1)$ if $m \neq 0$. That means S increases or decreases by 1 and so (3.1) is again satisfied. The same argument holds for *consSL*. Finally, except in one case, both *tailSL* and *initSL* also increase or decrease S by at most 1. The exceptional case is when one of xs or ys is a singleton and the other has length k. In this case S has the value $k - 1$ before the operation and at most 1 afterwards. Since $k \leqslant k - 1 - 1 + 2$ we can therefore charge k units for the cost of the operation in this case, again satisfying (3.1).

For a fully serviceable library of symmetric list operations, we should of course provide additional operations, such as *nullSL* and *singleSL* for testing whether a symmetric list is empty or a singleton, and *lengthSL* for computing the length of a symmetric list. These are left as exercises.

We will illustrate the use of symmetric lists on just one example. Consider again the function *inits* from Chapter 2:

$$inits :: [a] \rightarrow [[a]]$$
$$inits \, [\,] \qquad = [[\,]]$$
$$inits \, (x : xs) = [\,] : map \, (x :) \, (inits \; xs)$$

As we have seen, computing $length \cdot inits$ takes quadratic time. Can we find some other way of defining *inits* so that this time is reduced to linear time? The definition

$$inits = map \; reverse \cdot reverse \cdot tails \cdot reverse$$

achieves this aim but is unsatisfactory for another reason: what we really want is an *online* algorithm for *inits*, so that given an infinite list, *inits* returns an infinite list of its finite prefixes. The above definition is not online because one cannot reverse an infinite list. A better definition, and the one given in *Data.List* in all essential details, is to write

$$inits = map\ fromSL \cdot scanl\ (flip\ snocSL)\ nilSL$$

It still takes quadratic time to print all the prefixes, but only linear time to compute *length* · *inits* (assuming of course that the input list is finite). There is another definition of *inits* for which *length* · *inits* takes linear time, one that does not use symmetric lists; we will leave that as an exercise.

Before leaving the subject of symmetric lists, we should mention that Haskell provides an alternative method for providing efficient list operations in the library *Data.Sequence*. This library supports a number of operations on lists, including those above. Instead of using the idea of representing a list as two component lists, the library is based on 2-3 finger trees, a data structure that we will not discuss.

3.2 Random-access lists

Some algorithms, though not too many, rely on being able to retrieve the kth element of a list for various k. Haskell provides a list-indexing operator (!!) for this purpose, though we will rename it as *fetch*:

$$fetch :: Nat \rightarrow [a] \rightarrow a$$
$$fetch\ k\ xs = \textbf{if}\ k == 0\ \textbf{then}\ head\ xs\ \textbf{else}\ fetch\ (k-1)\ (tail\ xs)$$

Fetching the kth element of a list takes $\Theta(k)$ steps. In this section, and also in the following one, we discuss two methods for making *fetch* more efficient. In the present section we describe a data structure known as a *random-access list*. With random-access lists each of the operations *cons*, *head*, *tail*, and *fetch* takes logarithmic time in the length of the list, that is, $O(\log n)$ steps for a list of length n. While the performance of the first three operations deteriorates, the last one is made more efficient. You pays your money and you makes your choice, as the saying goes. Another important consequence of the representation is that, also in logarithmic time, we can update an element at a specified position with a new element, an operation that would take linear time with standard lists.

A random-access list is constructed out of two other data structures, the first of which is a binary tree:

data *Tree a* = *Leaf a* | *Node* (*Tree a*) (*Tree a*)

A tree is either a leaf containing a value, or a node consisting of two subtrees. The size of a tree is the number of leaves in the tree:

$$size\ (Leaf\ x)\quad = 1$$
$$size\ (Node\ t_1\ t_2) = size\ t_1 + size\ t_2$$

Some operations on trees depend on knowing the size of a tree. Since we do not want to recompute *size* from scratch each time, we can install its value in the tree, redefining *Tree* to read:

data *Tree a = Leaf a | Node Nat (Tree a) (Tree a)*

Provided size information is correctly installed each time we build a tree, we can now define *size* as a selector function:

$size :: Tree\ a \rightarrow Nat$
$size\ (Leaf\ x) \qquad = 1$
$size\ (Node\ n\ \_\ \_) = n$

The function *node*, known as a *smart constructor*, constructs a *Node* ensuring that size information is correctly installed:

$node :: Tree\ a \rightarrow Tree\ a \rightarrow Tree\ a$
$node\ t_1\ t_2 = Node\ (size\ t_1 + size\ t_2)\ t_1\ t_2$

A binary tree can have many shapes and arbitrary sizes, but we are only going to construct *perfect* binary trees in which all leaves have the same depth. For example,

$t = Node\ 4\ (Node\ 2\ (Leaf\ 'a')\ (Leaf\ 'b'))\ (Node\ 2\ (Leaf\ 'c')\ (Leaf\ 'd'))$

is a perfect tree of size 4. All perfect trees have sizes of the form 2^p for some $p \geqslant 0$. We will see in due course how this perfection is guaranteed.

The second data structure is a sequence of perfect trees. But what we need is not just an arbitrary list of trees, but a sequence of a special kind. The sequence is designed to reflect the binary numerical representation described in the previous chapter. Consider, for example, the number 6, which in (reversed) binary notation is 011 with the least significant bit first. The idea is to represent a six-element list, say "abcdef", by a sequence

$[Zero,$
$\quad One\ (Node\ 2\ (Leaf\ 'a')\ (Leaf\ 'b')),$
$\quad One\ (Node\ 4\ (Node\ 2\ (Leaf\ 'c')\ (Leaf\ 'd'))$
$\qquad\qquad (Node\ 2\ (Leaf\ 'e')\ (Leaf\ 'f')))]$

Similarly, 5 is 101 in binary, and a five-element list, say "abcde", is represented by

$[One\ (Leaf\ 'a'),$
$\quad Zero,$
$\quad One\ (Node\ 4\ (Node\ 2\ (Leaf\ 'b')\ (Leaf\ 'c'))$
$\qquad\qquad (Node\ 2\ (Leaf\ 'd')\ (Leaf\ 'e')))]$

An empty list can be represented by []. We will not allow trailing zeros in random-access lists, so the representations are unique.

Here, finally, is the definition of a random-access list:

data *Digit a* = *Zero* | *One* (*Tree a*)
type *RAList a* = [*Digit a*]

The abstraction function *fromRA* converts random-access lists into standard lists:

fromRA :: *RAList a* → [*a*]
fromRA = *concatMap from*
                where *from Zero*   = []
                       from (*One t*) = *fromT t*

fromT :: *Tree a* → [*a*]
fromT (*Leaf x*)   = [*x*]
fromT (*Node* _ t_1 t_2) = *fromT* t_1 ++ *fromT* t_2

It is possible to make *fromT* more efficient, but we leave that to the exercises.

The point of a random-access list is that we can skip over chunks of the list when looking up an element at a specified location:

fetchRA :: *Nat* → *RAList a* → *a*
fetchRA k (*Zero* : *xs*) = *fetchRA k xs*
fetchRA k (*One t* : *xs*) = **if** *k* < *size t*
                             then *fetchT k t* **else** *fetchRA* (*k* − *size t*) *xs*

fetchT :: *Nat* → *Tree a* → *a*
fetchT 0 (*Leaf x*) =   *x*
fetchT k (*Node n* t_1 t_2) = **if** *k* < *m*
                           then *fetchT k* t_1 **else** *fetchT* (*k* − *m*) t_2
                           where *m* = *n* div 2

The function *fetchRA* skips over trees whose elements have positions that are too small, taking into account the number of elements it has skipped over. When a tree is found that does contain a value at the desired position, the function *fetchT* is invoked. Using the size information stored in a tree the required element can be found either by searching the left subtree or the right subtree at each step. Provided *k* is in the range $0 \leqslant k < n$ when looking up the *k*th element in a list containing *n* elements, we have

fetch k · *fromRA* = *fetchRA k*

Furthermore, *fetchRA* takes $O(\log k)$ steps. To see this, suppose $2^p \leqslant k < 2^{p+1}$. The computation of *fetchRA* skips over *p* elements in $O(p)$ steps, and then searches a perfect binary tree of size 2^p in a further $O(p)$ steps. A better definition of *fetchRA* would produce an "index too large" error message if $n \leqslant k$, but we will leave that definition as an exercise.

In addition to *fetchRA* and *fromRA*, five other basic operations are supported by random-access lists:

$$nullRA \quad :: RAList \ a \to Bool$$
$$nilRA \quad :: RAList \ a$$
$$consRA \quad :: a \to RAList \ a \to RAList \ a$$
$$unconsRA :: RAList \ a \to (a, RAList \ a)$$
$$updateRA :: Nat \to a \to RAList \ a \to RAList \ a$$

The function *nullRA* tests whether a list is empty, *nilRA* returns an empty list, and *updateRA* updates a random-access list at a specified location with a new value. Its definition is similar to that of *fetchRA* and we will leave it as an exercise. The definition of *consRA* stems directly from that of the *inc* operation of the previous chapter:

$$inc \ [] \quad = [1]$$
$$inc \ (0:bs) = 1:bs$$
$$inc \ (1:bs) = 0:inc \ bs$$

Here is the definition of *consRA*:

$$consRA \ x \ xs = consT \ (Leaf \ x) \ xs$$
$$consT \ t_1 \ [] \quad\quad\quad = [One \ t_1]$$
$$consT \ t_1 \ (Zero:xs) \quad = One \ t_1 : xs$$
$$consT \ t_1 \ (One \ t_2 :xs) = Zero : consT \ (node \ t_1 \ t_2) \ xs$$

The definition of *unconsRA* follows that of the *dec* operation, which decrements a binary counter:

$$dec \ [1] \quad = []$$
$$dec \ (1:ds) = 0:ds$$
$$dec \ (0:ds) = 1:dec \ ds$$

Here is the definition of *unconsRA*:

$$unconsRA \ xs = (x, ys) \ \textbf{where} \ (Leaf \ x, ys) = unconsT \ xs$$
$$unconsT :: RAList \ a \to (Tree \ a, RAList \ a)$$
$$unconsT \ (One \ t:xs) = \textbf{if} \ null \ xs \ \textbf{then} \ (t, []) \ \textbf{else} \ (t, Zero:xs)$$
$$unconsT \ (Zero:xs) \ = (t_1, One \ t_2 : ys) \ \textbf{where} \ (Node \ \_ \ t_1 \ t_2, ys) = unconsT \ xs$$

The code is a little subtle. To illustrate the fact that *unconsT xs* always returns a leaf as first component when *xs* is a well-formed random-access list, it is instructive to play through the example

$$[Zero, Zero, One \ t]$$

where *t* is the perfect tree of size 4 that flattens to "abcd" from page 48. According to the second clause of *unconsT*, the result is

$$(t_1, One \ t_2 : ys) \ \textbf{where} \ (Node \ \_ \ t_1 \ t_2, ys) = unconsT \ [Zero, One \ (tree \ "abcd")]$$

Again according to the second clause, the right-hand side returns

$(t_3, One\ t_4 : zs)$ **where** $(Node \_\ t_3\ t_4, zs) = unconsT\ [One\ (tree\ "abcd")]$

Finally, according to the first clause of $unconsT$, we have

$unconsT\ [One\ (tree\ "abcd")] = (tree\ "abcd", [])$

That gives $t_3 = tree\ "ab"$, $t_4 = tree\ "cd"$ and $zs = []$. Hence we have $t_1 = Leaf\ 'a'$, $t_2 = Leaf\ 'b'$, and $ys = []$, and so

$$unconsT\ [Zero, Zero, One\ (tree\ "abcd")]$$
$$= (Leaf\ 'a', [One\ (Leaf\ 'b'), One\ (tree\ "cd")])$$

as required.

Given $unconsRA$, we can define $headRA$ and $tailRA$ quite simply (see the exercises). As we have seen in the previous chapter, a sequence of n cons operations, or n uncons operations, on an initially empty list takes $O(n)$ steps, so considered separately they take amortised constant time. But when they are mixed, the best we can say is that they each take $O(\log n)$ steps. The lookup and update operations also take this time. In the following section we look at a data structure in which a lookup operation takes constant time, though an update operation goes from logarithmic time to linear time.

3.3 Arrays

One of the main differences between functional and procedural algorithms is that the former rely on lists as the basic carrier of information while the latter rely on arrays. In functional algorithms input usually consists of a list of values, whereas in procedural algorithms input values are usually assumed to be presented as the elements of an array. For a procedural programmer array updates are *destructive*: once an array is updated by changing the value at a particular index, the old array is lost. In functional programming, data structures are *persistent* because any named structure may be referred to at some other point in the computation and therefore has to continue to exist. Consequently, any update operation, even at a single index, has to be implemented by making a new copy of the whole array. Because they cannot be changed but only copied, purely functional arrays are known as *immutable* arrays. It is possible to get round this problem and allow mutable structures by encapsulating the operations in a suitable monad, but we will not introduce monads in this book.

Wholesale or *monolithic* updates, on the other hand, are fine. Changing all or some of the entries at one go involves copying the array only once. Haskell provides a number of such wholesale operations in the library *Data.Array*. The purpose of this section is simply to describe the main functions in this library.

The type *Array i e* consists of arrays with indices of type i and elements of type e. The basic operation for constructing arrays is a function

$$array :: Ix\ i \Rightarrow (i,i) \rightarrow [(i,e)] \rightarrow Array\ i\ e$$

The type class *Ix* restricts what can be an index; usually this is an integer or a character, types that can be converted into a contiguous range of values. The first argument to *array* is a pair of bounds, the lowest and highest indices in the array. The second argument is an *association* list of index–value pairs. Building an array through *array* takes linear time in the length of the association list and the size of the array.

A simple variant of *array* is *listArray*, which takes just a list of elements:

$$listArray :: Ix\ i \Rightarrow (i,i) \rightarrow [e] \rightarrow Array\ i\ e$$
$$listArray\ (l,r)\ xs = array\ (l,r)\ (zip\ [l..r]\ xs)$$

Finally, there is another way of building arrays, called *accumArray*, whose type seems rather complicated:

$$accumArray :: Ix\ i \Rightarrow (e \rightarrow v \rightarrow e) \rightarrow e \rightarrow (i,i) \rightarrow [(i,v)] \rightarrow Array\ i\ e$$

The arguments are: an 'accumulating' function for transforming array entries *e* and new values *v* into new entries; an initial entry for each index; a pair of bounds for the array; and an association list of index–value pairs. The result of *accumArray f e* (l,r) *ivs* is an array with bounds (l,r) and initial entries *e* everywhere, built by processing the association list *ivs* from left to right, combining old entries and values into new entries using the accumulating function *f*. The process takes linear time in the length of the association list, assuming that the accumulating function take constant time. In symbols we have

$$accumArray\ f\ e\ (l,r)\ ivs =$$
$$array\ (l,r)\ [(j, foldl\ f\ e\ [v \mid (i,v) \leftarrow ivs, i == j]) \mid j \leftarrow [l..r]]$$

Well, nearly. In the *Data.Array* definition there is an added restriction on *ivs*, namely that every index in *ivs* should lie in the specified range (l,r). If this condition is not met, then the left-hand side returns an error while the right-hand side does not.

For example, we have

$$accumArray\ (+)\ 0\ (1,3)\ [(1,20),(2,30),(1,40),(2,50)]$$
$$= array\ (1,3)\ [(1,60),(2,80),(3,0)]$$
$$accumArray\ (flip\ (:))\ [\,]\ (\texttt{'A'},\texttt{'C'})\ [(\texttt{'A'},\texttt{"Apple"}),(\texttt{'A'},\texttt{"Apricot"})]$$
$$= array\ (\texttt{'A'},\texttt{'C'})\ [(\texttt{'A'},[\texttt{"Apricot"},\texttt{"Apple"}]),(\texttt{'B'},[\,]),(\texttt{'C'},[\,])]$$

As just one useful application of *accumArray*, suppose we are given a list of *n* natural numbers, all in the range $(0,m)$ for some *m*. We can sort this list in $\Theta(m+n)$ steps in the following way:

$$sort :: Nat \rightarrow [Nat] \rightarrow [Nat]$$
$$sort\ m\ xs = concatMap\ copy\ (assocs\ a)$$
$$\textbf{where}\ a = accumArray\ (+)\ 0\ (0,m)\ (zip\ xs\ (repeat\ 1))$$
$$copy\ (x,k) = replicate\ k\ x$$

The function $assocs :: Array\ i\ e \rightarrow [(i,e)]$ returns the list of index–value pairs in index order. The function $elems$, which can be defined by

$$elems :: Ix\ i \Rightarrow Array\ i\ e \rightarrow [e]$$
$$elems = map\ snd \cdot assocs$$

converts an array to a list of its elements in index order. Thus $elems$ is the abstraction function for converting arrays back into standard lists.

The good news is that with arrays the lookup function, (!), takes constant time. For instance,

$$assocs\ xa = [(i, xa\,!\,i)\ |\ i \leftarrow range\ (bounds\ xa)]$$

takes time proportional to the size of the array. The *Data.Array* function $bounds$ returns the bounds of an array, and $range$ enumerates the values between the lower and upper bound.

The bad news, as we have said, is that array updates take linear time in the size of the array. The update function is $//$, with type

$$(//) :: Ix\ i \Rightarrow Array\ i\ e \rightarrow [(i,e)] \rightarrow Array\ i\ e$$

Thus the operation $xa\ //\ ies$ updates the array xa with the associations in ies. For example,

$$foldl\ update\ (array\ (1,n)\ [])\ (zip\ [1..n]\ xs)$$
$$\textbf{where}\ update\ xa\ (i,x) = xa\ //\ [(i,x)]$$

builds an array but takes $\Theta(n^2)$ steps to do it, while the equivalent expression

$$array\ (1,n)\ (zip\ [1..n]\ xs)$$

takes $\Theta(n)$ steps.

In summary, indexing and wholesale operations are efficient for arrays, while individual updates are not. "We can remember it for you wholesale", as Philip K. Dick entitled one of his short stories (see [1]).

3.4 Chapter notes

The idea of modelling a symmetric list, also known as a double-ended queue or *deque*, by a pair of lists has been thought of many times. It appears in Okasaki's book [5] on functional data structures, where the idea is attributed to Gries [2] and Hood and Melville [3]. See also [4], which introduces the representation invariant used above. Random-access lists, also known as *one-sided flexible arrays*, are discussed in Chapter 9 of [5]. That chapter also presents some alternative number representations, including binary numbers constructed from 1s and 2s rather than 0s and 1s. Using such a representation, one can implement *headRA* to run in $O(1)$ worst-case time. The monolithic array operations of *Data.Array* were proposed by

Philip Wadler in [6], although others had earlier suggested similar operations. The Haskell Platform provides a number of other libraries for handling arrays, including unboxed, mutable, and storable arrays.

References

[1]   Philip K. Dick. We can remember it for you wholesale. In *The Collected Short Stories of Philip K. Dick*, Volume 2. Citadel Twilight, New York, 1990.
[2]   David Gries. *The Science of Programming*. Springer, New York, 1981.
[3]   Robert Hood and Robert Melville. Real-time queue operations in pure Lisp. *Information Processing Letters*, 13(2):50–53, 1981.
[4]   Rob R. Hoogerwoord. A symmetric set of efficient list operations. *Journal of Functional Programming*, 2(4):294–303, 1992.
[5]   Chris Okasaki. *Purely Functional Data Structures*. Cambridge University Press, Cambridge, 1998.
[6]   Philip L. Wadler. A new array operation. In J. F. Fasel and R. M. Keller, editors, *Graph Reduction*, volume 279 of *Lecture Notes in Computer Science*, pages 328–333. Springer-Verlag, Berlin, 1986.

Exercises

Exercise 3.1 Write down all the ways `"abcd"` can be represented as a symmetric list. Give examples to show how each of these representations can be generated.

Exercise 3.2 Define the value *nilSL* that returns an empty symmetric list, and the two functions *nullSL* and *singleSL* for testing whether a symmetric list is empty or a singleton. Also, define *lengthSL*.

Exercise 3.3 Define the functions *consSL* and *headSL*.

Exercise 3.4 Define the function *initSL*.

Exercise 3.5 Implement *dropWhileSL* so that

$$dropWhile \cdot fromSL = fromSL \cdot dropWhileSL$$

Exercise 3.6 Define *initsSL* with the type

$$initsSL :: SymList\ a \rightarrow SymList\ (SymList\ a)$$

Write down the equation that expresses the relationship between *fromSL*, *initsSL*, and *inits*.

Exercise 3.7 Give an online definition of *inits* that does not use symmetric lists for which *length* · *inits* takes linear time.

Exercise 3.8 Estimate the running time of *fromT* when applied to a perfect tree of size 2^p, where *fromT* was defined by

$$fromT :: Tree\ a \rightarrow [a]$$
$$fromT\ (Leaf\ x) \qquad = [x]$$
$$fromT\ (Node\ \_\ t_1\ t_2) = fromT\ t_1 +\!\!+ fromT\ t_2$$

One way to reduce the running time is to introduce a function

$$fromTs :: [Tree\ a] \rightarrow [a]$$

and define $fromT\ t = fromTs\ [t]$. Give an efficient definition of $fromTs$. Variations of this particular optimisation for *flattening* a tree will be used a number of times in the rest of the book.

Exercise 3.9 What change to the definition of *fetchRA* is needed to produce a suitable error message when the index is too large?

Exercise 3.10 Give a definition of the function $toRA :: [a] \rightarrow RAList\ a$ that converts a list into a random-access list.

Exercise 3.11 Give a definition of *updateRA*.

Exercise 3.12 Following on from the previous exercise, give a one-line definition of a function

$$(//) :: RAList\ a \rightarrow [(Nat, a)] \rightarrow RAList\ a$$

so that $xs\ //\ kxs$ is the result of carrying out a sequence of updates kxs on a random-access list xs. The updates should be applied from left to right. Hint: both *flip* and the standard Haskell function

$$uncurry :: (a \rightarrow b \rightarrow c) \rightarrow (a, b) \rightarrow c$$
$$uncurry f\ (x, y) = f\ x\ y$$

will be useful.

Exercise 3.13 Define *headRA* and *tailRA*.

Exercise 3.14 Suppose you want to define an array *fa* with bounds $(0, n)$ whose kth entry is $k!$, the factorial of k. Complete the definition

$$fa = listArray\ (0, n)\ ????$$

in two different ways, one using *scanl* and one not. (Hint: for the second definition use the fact that $fa\ !\ i = i \times fa\ !\ (i - 1)$.)

Exercise 3.15 There is another function *accum* in *Data.Array* with the type

$$accum :: Ix\ i \Rightarrow (e \rightarrow v \rightarrow e) \rightarrow Array\ i\ e \rightarrow [(i, v)] \rightarrow Array\ i\ e$$

This function takes an accumulating function, an array, and an association list. It computes new array entries by combining elements from the association list with the accumulating function. More precisely,

$$(accum\ f\ a\ ivs)\ !\ j = foldl\ f\ (a\ !\ j)\ [v \mid (i, v) \leftarrow ivs, i == j]$$

Define *accumArray* in terms of *accum*.

Answers

Answer 3.1 There are three ways:

$$("a","dcb"),("ab","dc"),("abc","d")$$

We have, for example,

$("a","dcb") = foldl\ (flip\ snocSL)\ nilSL\ "abcd"$
$("abc","d") = foldr\ consSL\ nilSL\ "abcd"$
$("ab","dc") = consSL\ 'a'\ (snocSL\ 'd'\ (foldr\ consSL\ nilSL\ "bc"))$

Answer 3.2 We have

$nilSL :: SymList\ a$
$nilSL = ([],[])$

$nullSL :: SymList\ a \rightarrow Bool$
$nullSL\ (xs,ys) = null\ xs \wedge null\ ys$

$singleSL :: SymList\ a \rightarrow Bool$
$singleSL\ (xs,ys) = (null\ xs \wedge single\ ys) \vee (null\ ys \wedge single\ xs)$

$lengthSL :: SymList\ a \rightarrow Nat$
$lengthSL\ (xs,ys) = length\ xs + length\ ys$

Answer 3.3 We have

$consSL :: a \rightarrow SymList\ a \rightarrow SymList\ a$
$consSL\ x\ (xs,ys) = \textbf{if}\ null\ ys\ \textbf{then}\ ([x],xs)\ \textbf{else}\ (x:xs,ys)$

$headSL :: SymList\ a \rightarrow a$
$headSL\ (xs,ys)\ \ = \textbf{if}\ null\ xs\ \textbf{then}\ head\ ys\ \textbf{else}\ head\ xs$

Answer 3.4 We have

$initSL :: SymList\ a \rightarrow SymList\ a$
$initSL\ (xs,ys)$
$\quad |\ null\ ys\ \ \ \ = \textbf{if}\ null\ xs\ \textbf{then}\ \bot\ \textbf{else}\ nilSL$
$\quad |\ single\ ys\ = (us, reverse\ vs)$
$\quad |\ otherwise = (xs, tail\ ys)$
$\quad \textbf{where}\ (us,vs) = splitAt\ (length\ xs\ \text{div}\ 2)\ xs$

Answer 3.5 We have

$dropWhileSL\ p\ xs$
$\quad |\ nullSL\ xs\ \ \ \ \ \ \ = nilSL$
$\quad |\ p\ (headSL\ xs) = dropWhileSL\ p\ (tailSL\ xs)$
$\quad |\ otherwise\ \ \ \ \ \ = xs$

Answer 3.6 We can define

> $initsSL\ xs = $ **if** $nullSL\ xs$
> > **then** $snocSL\ xs\ nilSL$
> > **else** $snocSL\ xs\ (initsSL\ (initSL\ xs))$

The relationship is

> $inits \cdot fromSL = map\ fromSL \cdot fromSL \cdot initsSL$

Answer 3.7 We have

> $inits = map\ reverse \cdot scanl\ (flip\ (:))\ [\,]$

Answer 3.8 We have

$$T(p) = 2\,T(p-1) + \Theta(2^{p-1})$$

where the $\Theta(2^{p-1})$ term accounts for the concatenation. That gives $T(p) = \Theta(p\,2^p)$. The new definition is

> $fromT\ t = fromTs\ [t]$
> $fromTs\ [\,] \qquad\qquad\ = [\,]$
> $fromTs\ (Leaf\ x:ts) \qquad = x:fromTs\ ts$
> $fromTs\ (Node\ \_\ t_1\ t_2:ts) = fromTs\ (t_1:t_2:ts)$

This definition has a running time of $\Theta(2^p)$ steps. Another method is to use an accumulating function.

Answer 3.9 Add a clause

> $fetchRA\ k\ [\,] = error$ `"index too large"`

Answer 3.10 We have

> $toRA :: [a] \rightarrow RAList\ a$
> $toRA = foldr\ consRA\ nilRA$

Answer 3.11 We have

> $updateRA\ k\ x\ (Zero:xs)\ = Zero:updateRA\ k\ x\ xs$
> $updateRA\ k\ x\ (One\ t:xs) = $ **if** $k < size\ t$
> > **then** $One\ (updateT\ k\ x\ t):xs$
> > **else** $One\ t:updateRA\ (k - size\ t)\ x\ xs$

> $updateT :: Nat \rightarrow a \rightarrow Tree\ a \rightarrow Tree\ a$
> $updateT\ 0\ x\ (Leaf\ y) \qquad\ = Leaf\ x$
> $updateT\ k\ x\ (Node\ n\ t_1\ t_2) \ = $ **if** $k < m$
> > **then** $Node\ n\ (updateT\ k\ x\ t_1)\ t_2$
> > **else** $Node\ n\ t_1\ (updateT\ (k - m)\ x\ t_2)$
> > **where** $m = n$ **div** 2

Answer 3.12 We have

$$(//) :: RAList\ a \rightarrow [(Nat, a)] \rightarrow RAList\ a$$
$$(//) = foldl\ (flip\ (uncurry\ updateRA))$$

For example,

$$fromRA\ (toRA\ [0..3]\ //\ [(1,7),(2,3),(3,4),(2,8)]) = [0,7,8,4]$$

The intermediate updates are

$$[0,1,2,3],\ \ [0,7,2,3],\ \ [0,7,3,3],\ \ [0,7,3,4],\ \ [0,7,8,4]$$

If there are m updates on a random-access list of length n, the running time of $//$ is $\Theta(m \log n)$ steps.

Answer 3.13 The definitions are

$$headRA\ xs = fst\ (unconsRA\ xs)$$
$$tailRA\ xs\ = snd\ (unconsRA\ xs)$$

Answer 3.14 We have

$$fa = listArray\ (0,n)\ (scanl\ (\times)\ 1\ [1..n])$$
$$fa = listArray\ (0,n)\ (1 : [i \times fa\ !\ (i-1)\ |\ i \leftarrow [1..10]])$$

The $listArray$ construction is not strict in the array elements, so recursive definitions such as the one above are legitimate.

Answer 3.15 We have

$$accumArray\ f\ e\ bnds\ ivs = accum\ f\ (array\ bnds\ [(i,e)\ |\ i \leftarrow range\ bnds])\ ivs$$

PART TWO

DIVIDE AND CONQUER

Divide and conquer (from the Latin *divide et impera*, and more accurately translated as divide and rule) is the first algorithm design technique we will study in depth. Given a problem to solve, either solve it directly if its size is sufficiently small and it is easy to do so, or else divide it into one or more subproblems, solve each of these subproblems, and then combine the solutions to give a solution to the original problem. Such a strategy covers pretty much everything about problem solving in computer science, or mathematics, or life for that matter, but the feature that makes it into a simple and effective computational tool is that each subproblem is simply the original problem on an input of smaller size. Hence each subproblem is solved by the same strategy. A divide-and-conquer algorithm is therefore essentially recursive in nature.

Phrased this way, every functional algorithm that depends on explicit recursion can be thought of as a divide-and-conquer algorithm. After all, one possible decomposition of a problem of size $n > 0$ is to divide it into a problem of size $n - 1$ and a problem of size 1. For instance, an algorithm expressed as a *foldr* has essentially this decomposition. But in a truly divide-and-conquer algorithm there are two other important aspects. One is that each subproblem should have a size that is some fraction of the input size, a fraction like $n/2$ or $n/4$. In many cases the subproblems will have equal size, or as close to equal size as possible. A problem of size n might therefore be divided into two subproblems each of size $n/2$, a very common form of decomposition that we will meet later on. There are also examples of divide-and-conquer algorithms in which the subproblems have different sizes, for example one of size $n/5$ and the other of size $7 \times n/10$. We will encounter such an example in Chapter 6. The second important aspect is that the subproblems should be independent of each other, so the work done in solving them is not duplicated. Problems in which the subproblems overlap and have many sub-subproblems in common can be tackled by the dynamic programming strategy, a topic we will take up in Part Five.

Finally, because the subproblems are independent and can be solved concurrently as well as sequentially, divide-and-conquer algorithms are highly suited to exploiting parallelism. We will not pursue parallel programming in this book, but see Simon Marlow's book *Parallel and Concurrent Programming in Haskell* (O'Reilly, 2013), for an excellent coverage of the topic.

Chapter 4

Binary search

Binary search is probably the simplest example of divide and conquer. A search problem is solved by dividing it into two subproblems, each of size approximately half the original. The distinguishing feature of binary search is that one of these subproblems is trivial. In this chapter we introduce binary search by looking at two examples that can profitably use it, and then go on to encapsulate binary search as a data structure, a binary search tree.

4.1 A one-dimensional search problem

In the first problem we are given a strictly increasing function f from natural numbers to natural numbers (so $x < y \Rightarrow f\,x < f\,y$ for all x and y) together with a target number t. The object is to find x, if it exists, such that $t = f(x)$. Since f is strictly increasing, there is at most one solution. Furthermore, $x < f(x+1)$ if f is strictly increasing, so the search can be confined to the interval $0 \leqslant x \leqslant t$ (inclusive). Recalling that Nat is a Haskell type synonym for Int, we have

$$search :: (Nat \rightarrow Nat) \rightarrow Nat \rightarrow [Nat]$$
$$search\,f\,t = [x \mid x \leftarrow [0..t], t == f\,x]$$

The result of $search$ is either an empty list or a singleton list. The only assumption we have really used about f is that $t = f(x) \Rightarrow 0 \leqslant x \leqslant t$ for all x and t. This method, which searches for a value incrementally in steps of one, is called *linear search*.

There are better methods than linear search for solving our problem, and we are going to give two. In both methods the first step is to make the search interval explicit:

$$search\,f\,t = seek\,(0,t) \quad \textbf{where } seek\,(a,b) = [x \mid x \leftarrow [a..b], t == f\,x]$$

The next step is to find a better version of $seek$. If $a > b$, then $seek\,(a,b) = [\,]$. Otherwise, let m be any number in the range $a \leqslant m \leqslant b$. We then have

$$seek\ (a,b) = [x \mid x \leftarrow [a..m-1], t == f\ x] +\!\!+$$
$$[m \mid t == f\ m] +\!\!+$$
$$[x \mid x \leftarrow [m+1..b], t == f\ x]$$

The key observation is that if $t < f(m)$, then the last two lists are empty; if $t = f(m)$, then we are done; and if $t > f(m)$, then the first two lists are empty. Here we do use the fact that f is increasing. Hence we can define

$$search :: (Nat \to Nat) \to Nat \to [Nat]$$
$$search\ f\ t = seek\ (0,t)$$
$$\textbf{where}\ seek\ (a,b) \mid a > b \quad\ = []$$
$$\mid t < f\ m \ = seek\ (a, m-1)$$
$$\mid t == f\ m = [m]$$
$$\mid otherwise = seek\ (m+1, b)$$
$$\textbf{where}\ m = choose\ (a,b)$$

It remains to choose m. The obvious choice to balance the two subproblems is to take $m = \lfloor (a+b)/2 \rfloor$, the middle of the interval. In other words,

$$choose\ (a,b) = (a+b)\ \text{div}\ 2$$

This is binary search. A search problem is divided into a single subproblem of about half the size. It is easy to appreciate that binary search takes logarithmic time in the size of the interval being searched, because the interval halves at each step. Thus $search\ f\ t$ takes $O(\log t)$ steps. To be more precise we have to formulate and solve the associated recurrence relation, but we will leave that discussion until after we have dealt with the second method for solving our problem.

There are a number of aspects of the above definition of *search* that make another solution worth exploration, not the least of which is the fact that the definition is incorrect! For example, suppose $f(n) = 2^n$. Then evaluation of *search f* 1024 returns [] instead of the correct answer [10]. Pause for a moment to see if you can spot the bug.

What has gone wrong is not the definition of *search* but its type. The first step requires evaluation of the test $1024 < 2^{512}$, and 2^{512} is a huge number, well beyond the capabilities of limited-precision arithmetic. In fact, as an element of *Nat*, evaluation of 2^{512} returns 0, causing the test to incorrectly return *False*. The situation can be remedied by changing *Nat* to *Integer*, but the numbers are still huge and the calculations can be very time-consuming.

The second, minor problem with *search* is that f is evaluated twice at each step. That is easily solved with a suitable local definition, but the fact still remains that in the worst case there are three comparison tests at each step. Can we do better?

Yes, and here is the idea: we first find integers a and b such that $f(a) < i \leqslant f(b)$

and then search only the interval $[a+1..b]$. If $t \leqslant f(0)$, then we can invent a fictitious value $f(-1) = -\infty$ and set $(a,b) = (-1,0)$; otherwise we can find a and b by looking at the values of f for the numbers $1,2,4,8,\ldots$ until a value p is found for which $f(2^{p-1}) < t \leqslant f(2^p)$. Such a value is guaranteed to exist, because f is strictly increasing. The function *bound* computes such an interval:

$$bound :: (Nat \to Nat) \to Nat \to (Int, Nat)$$
$$bound\ f\ t = \textbf{if}\ t \leqslant f\ 0\ \textbf{then}\ (-1,0)\ \textbf{else}\ (b\ \text{div}\ 2, b)$$
$$\textbf{where}\ b = until\ done\ (\times 2)\ 1$$
$$done\ b = t \leqslant f\ b$$

It takes $p+1$ evaluations to compute *bound* $f\ t$ when $f(2^{p-1}) < t \leqslant f(2^p)$. In the worst case, when $f = id$, that gives $O(\log n)$ evaluations, but when $f(n) = 2^n$, only $O(\log(\log n))$ evaluations are required.

Now, to search the interval $[a+1..b]$ we need only to find the smallest x such that $t \leqslant f(x)$. Such a value is guaranteed to exist because $t \leqslant f(b)$. That gives

$$search\ f\ t = \textbf{if}\ f\ x == t\ \textbf{then}\ [x]\ \textbf{else}\ []$$
$$\textbf{where}\ x = smallest\ (bound\ f\ t)$$
$$smallest\ (a,b) = head\ [x \mid x \leftarrow [a+1..b], t \leqslant f\ x]$$

The definition of *smallest* uses linear search, but, as we have seen above, a better method is to split the interval: if $a+1 < b$ then for any m in the range $a < m < b$ we have

$$smallest\ (a,b) = head\ ([x \mid x \leftarrow [a+1..m], t \leqslant f\ x] \mathbin{+\!\!+}$$
$$[x \mid x \leftarrow [m+1..b], t \leqslant f\ x])$$

This time, if $t \leqslant f(m)$, then the first list is not empty; otherwise it is. Hence we can write

$$search :: (Nat \to Nat) \to Nat \to [Nat]$$
$$search\ f\ t = \textbf{if}\ f\ x == t\ \textbf{then}\ [x]\ \textbf{else}\ []\ \textbf{where}$$
$$x = smallest\ (bound\ f\ t)\ f\ t$$

where

$$smallest\ (a,b)\ f\ t \mid a+1 == b = b$$
$$\mid t \leqslant f\ m \quad = smallest\ (a,m)\ f\ t$$
$$\mid otherwise \quad = smallest\ (m,b)\ f\ t$$
$$\textbf{where}\ m = (a+b)\ \text{div}\ 2$$

This is our second version of binary search. We have made *smallest* a separate top-level function because we will need it in the following section. Note that *smallest* $(a,b)\ f\ t$ is well defined even if there is no x in the range $a < x \leqslant b$ such that $t \leqslant f\ x$; in this case the value returned is b. In this version of binary search there is only one comparison involving f at each step, as compared with two in the worst case of the previous version. Moreover, *search* works with limited-precision arithmetic. Note, finally, that $f(a)$ is never evaluated during the algorithm, so the fictitious value $f(-1) = -\infty$ is never required.

To time this version, let $T(n)$ denote the number of evaluations of f in the computation of *smallest* $(a,b) f t$ when interval (a,b) contains n numbers, so that $n = b - a + 1$. The fast and loose way to define $T(n)$ is to write

$$T(2) = 0$$
$$T(n) = T(n/2) + 1$$

To solve this recurrence, we can unfold it to give

$$T(n) = 1 + T(n/2) = 2 + T(n/4) = 3 + T(n/8) = \cdots = k + T(n/2^k)$$

It follows that $T(n) = k$ if $n = 2^{k+1}$. If n is not a power of two, so $2^k < n < 2^{k+1}$, then we can appeal to the assumption that $T(n)$ is an increasing function of n to arrive at the estimate $T(n) \leqslant \lceil \log n \rceil$. If f takes constant time, then binary search takes $\Theta(\log t)$ steps.

Here is where we are playing fast and loose. For one thing, the subproblems do not both have size $n/2$. If n is odd, then both subproblems have size $\lceil (n+1)/2 \rceil$, while if n is even, then just one of the subproblems has this size. For another thing, the sizes of intervals are natural numbers and $T(n)$ is defined only when n is a natural number, so $T(n/2)$ is not well-defined. Finally, the assumption that when the problem size increases the complexity cannot decrease is not always valid – it depends on the algorithm. Neither of the first two issues usually matters, especially when we are after only asymptotic bounds, such as $T(n) = \Theta(\log n)$. But sometimes they do. This is certainly the case when we are after an exact number. For instance, the exact number of evaluations of f in the worst case of *smallest* on an interval of size n is given by the recurrence $T(n) = T\lceil (n+1)/2 \rceil + 1$ and $T(2) = 0$. The exact solution turns out to be $T(n) = \lceil \log (n-1) \rceil$ for $2 \leqslant n$ (see Exercise 4.3). However, in the main we will ignore floors and ceilings in recurrences, and carry on with fast and loose reasoning.

Here is another recurrence relation that we will mention now, one that will crop up frequently in the following chapter: $T(n) = 2T(n/2) + \Theta(n)$. To solve this recurrence we unfold it, replacing $\Theta(n)$ by cn to avoid tripping up on multiple Θs. Then we obtain

$$T(n) = cn + 2T(n/2)$$
$$= cn + 2(cn/2 + 2T(n/4))$$
$$= 2cn + 4T(n/4)$$
$$= \cdots$$
$$= kcn + 2^k T(n/2^k)$$

Supposing $2^{k-1} < n \leqslant 2^k$, so $k = \lceil \log n \rceil$, we obtain

521	693	768	799	821	829	841	869	923	947	985	999
519	621	752	797	801	827	833	865	917	924	945	998
507	615	673	676	679	782	785	819	891	894	897	913
475	597	627	630	633	717	739	742	845	848	851	894
472	523	583	586	589	612	695	698	701	704	767	810
403	411	441	444	547	583	653	656	679	691	765	768
397	407	432	434	444	510	613	626	627	673	715	765
312	313	363	366	411	472	523	601	612	647	698	704
289	312	327	330	333	336	439	472	527	585	612	691
272	245	283	296	299	302	313	441	523	529	587	589
217	237	245	264	267	296	303	376	471	482	537	588
116	128	131	134	237	240	267	346	469	481	515	523
103	107	113	126	189	237	264	318	458	480	497	498
100	101	112	124	176	212	257	316	452	472	487	497

Figure 4.1 An example grid

$$T(n) = cn \lceil \log n \rceil + \Theta(2^{\lceil \log n \rceil})$$

and so $T(n) = \Theta(n \log n)$. Such a running time is sometimes called *linearithmic*, a portmanteau word that combines *linear* and *logarithmic*. We will meet other more difficult recurrence relations in the following section.

4.2 A two-dimensional search problem

The second problem is much more interesting. This time we are given a function f from *pairs* of natural numbers to natural numbers with the property that f is strictly increasing in each argument. Given t, we have to find all pairs (x,y) such that $f(x,y) = t$. Unlike the one-dimensional case, there can be many solutions. To get a feel for the problem, take a look at the grid in Figure 4.1. Positions on the grid are given by Cartesian coordinates (x,y), where x is the column number and y is the row number. The bottom-left element is at position $(0,0)$ and the top-right element is at position $(11,13)$. What systematic procedure would you use to find all the positions that contain the number 472? Pause for a moment to answer this question.

Did you try to use binary search? After all, that is what the chapter is about. The difficulty is that it is not easy to see exactly how to program the search in this two-dimensional case. So we will start slowly and begin with the obvious generalisation of one-dimensional search to a two-dimensional $(t+1) \times (t+1)$ grid:

$$search\, f\, t = [(x,y) \mid x \leftarrow [0..t], y \leftarrow [0..t], t == f(x,y)]$$

This method, which takes $\Theta(t^2)$ steps, searches the grid upwards column by column, starting at the leftmost column. Also it takes no account of the fact that searching a column can be abandoned as soon as an (x,y) is found for which $t \leqslant f(x,y)$. There has to be a better way; we shall describe no fewer than four, including three versions that employ binary search.

The first improvement is to start at the top-left rather than the bottom-left corner:

$$search\, f\; t = [(x,y) \mid x \leftarrow [0..t], y \leftarrow [t, t-1..0], t == f(x,y)]$$

As in binary search, a more general version is obtained by making the search interval explicit:

$$searchIn\, (a,b)\, f\; t = [(x,y) \mid x \leftarrow [a..t], y \leftarrow [b, b-1..0], t == f(x,y)]$$

Thus $search = searchIn\,(0,t)$. Next, we examine the various cases that can arise. First, it follows at once from the definition of $searchIn$ that

$$searchIn\, (a,b)\, f\; t \quad \mid a > t \lor b < 0 = [\,]$$

Now suppose the search interval is not empty and $f(a,b) < t$. In this case column a can be eliminated from further consideration since $f(a,b') \leqslant f(a,b)$ for $b' \leqslant b$. That means

$$searchIn\, (a,b)\, f\; t \quad \mid f(a,b) < t = searchIn\, (a+1,b)\, f\; t$$

In the dual case, $f(a,b) > t$, row b can be eliminated since $f(a',b) \geqslant f(a,b)$ for $a' \geqslant a$. That means

$$searchIn\, (a,b)\, f\; t \quad \mid f(a,b) > t = searchIn\, (a,b-1)\, f\; t$$

Finally, if $f(a,b) = t$, then both column a and row b can be eliminated since $f(a,b') < f(a,b)$ if $b' < b$ and $f(a',b) > f(a,b)$ if $a' > a$. It is only in this last case that we use the fact that f is strictly increasing, rather than just weakly increasing, in both arguments.

Putting the four cases together, and renaming (a,b) as (x,y), we arrive at

$$search\, f\; t = searchIn\, (0,t)$$
$$\textbf{where}\ searchIn\, (x,y) \mid x > t \lor y < 0 = [\,]$$
$$\qquad\qquad\qquad \mid z < t \qquad = searchIn\, (x+1,y)$$
$$\qquad\qquad\qquad \mid z == t \qquad = (x,y) : searchIn\, (x+1,y-1)$$
$$\qquad\qquad\qquad \mid z > t \qquad = searchIn\, (x,y-1)$$
$$\qquad\qquad\qquad \textbf{where}\ z = f(x,y)$$

This method is known as *saddleback search*. It is fairly easy to see it requires only $\Theta(t)$ evaluations of f. More precisely, suppose there is a $p \times q$ rectangle to search. In the best case, when the search proceeds along the diagonal of the rectangle, finding occurrences of t at each step, there are $(p \min q)$ evaluations of f. In the worst case, when the search proceeds along the edges of the rectangle, there are $p + q - 1$ evaluations of f. As just one example, with $f(x,y) = x^2 + 3^y$ and $t = 20259$, it takes 20402 evaluations of f to obtain the answer $[(24,9)]$. That is quite close to the best case.

Saddleback search can be improved because starting with the corners $(0,t)$ and

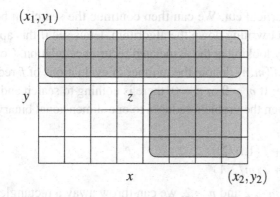

Figure 4.2 A divide-and-conquer decomposition

$(t,0)$ can be an overly pessimistic estimate of where the required values lie. Instead we can use binary search to obtain better starting intervals. Recall from the previous section that, provided $t \leqslant f\ b$, the value of *smallest* $(a,b)\ f\ t$ is the smallest x in the range $a < x \leqslant b$ such that $t \leqslant f\ x$. Hence, if we define

$$p = smallest\ (-1,t)\ (\lambda y.f(0,y))\ t$$
$$q = smallest\ (-1,t)\ (\lambda x.f(x,0))\ t$$

then we can start saddleback search with the corners $(0,p)$ and $(q,0)$. This version of saddleback search takes $\Theta(\log t) + \Theta(p+q)$ steps. Since p and q may be substantially less than t, we can end up with a search that takes $\Theta(\log t)$ steps. For example, again with $f(x,y) = x^2 + 3^y$ and $t = 20259$, we have $p = 10$ and $q = 143$. It now takes a total of only 181 evaluations of f (including those evaluations in the two binary searches) to compute the answer, a substantial saving over the previous version.

A third way to search a grid is to head for a proper divide-and-conquer solution, looking at the middle element of the grid first. After all, that would be the obvious two-dimensional analogue of binary search. Suppose we have confined the search to a rectangle with top-left corner (x_1,y_1) and bottom-right corner (x_2,y_2). What if we first inspected the value $f(x,y)$ where $x = \lfloor (x_1 + x_2)/2 \rfloor$ and $y = \lfloor (y_1 + y_2)/2 \rfloor$? If $f(x,y) < t$, we can throw away all elements of the lower-left rectangle. A picture of this situation is given in Figure 4.2, in which $f(x,y) = z < t$ and the shaded rectangles are those we need to keep. Similarly, if $f(x,y) > t$ the upper-right rectangle can be discarded. And finally if $f(x,y) = t$, then both can be discarded.

This strategy will not, of course, maintain the property that the search space is always a rectangle; instead we will have either two rectangles or an L-shape. We can split an L-shape into two rectangles by making either a horizontal cut (as in the figure) or a vertical cut. We can then continue the search in both the smaller rectangles. Without writing down the algorithm, let us see if this approach yields a faster algorithm by looking at the associated recurrence relation. Consider an $m \times n$ rectangle, and let $T(m,n)$ denote the number of evaluations of f required to search it in the worst case. If $m = 0$ or $n = 0$, there is nothing to search and $T(m,n) = 0$. If $m = 1$ or $n = 1$, then the problem reduces to one-dimensional binary search and we have

$$T(1,n) = 1 + T(1,n/2)$$
$$T(m,1) = 1 + T(m/2,1)$$

Otherwise, when $m \geqslant 2$ and $n \geqslant 2$, we can throw away a rectangle of size at least $m/2 \times n/2$. If we make a horizontal cut, then we are left with two rectangles, one of size $m/2 \times n/2$ and the other of size $m/2 \times n$. Hence

$$T(m,n) = 1 + T(m/2,n/2) + T(m/2,n)$$

If we make a vertical cut, then we have

$$T(m,n) = 1 + T(m/2,n/2) + T(m,n/2)$$

In order to reach a base case quickly, it is better to make a horizontal cut if $m \leqslant n$, and a vertical cut if $m > n$.

To solve these recurrences assume m and n are powers of two and define U by $U(i,j) = T(2^i, 2^j)$. Supposing $i \leqslant j$ and making a horizontal cut, we therefore have

$$U(0,j) \qquad = j$$
$$U(i+1,j+1) = 1 + U(i,j) + U(i,j+1)$$

It is not easy to solve this recurrence, but we can make an educated guess and assume that the solution is exponential in i. If we set $U(i,j) = 2^i f(i,j) - 1$ for some function f, then we obtain

$$f(0,j) \qquad = j+1$$
$$2f(i+1,j+1) = f(i,j) + f(i,j+1)$$

The second equation suggests another educated guess, namely that f is a linear function of i and j. Setting $f(i,j) = ai + bj + c$, we obtain

$$bj + c \qquad\qquad = j+1$$
$$2(a(i+1) + b(j+1) + c) = ai + bj + c + ai + b(j+1) + c$$

These equations are satisfied by taking $a = -1/2$, $b = 1$ and $c = 1$. Putting the pieces together, we arrive at the solution

$$U(i,j) = 2^i(j - i/2 + 1) - 1$$

Setting $i = \log m$ and $j = \log n$, we therefore have

$$T(m,n) = 2^{\log m}(\log n - (\log m)/2 + 1) - 1 \leqslant m \log(2n/\sqrt{m})$$

If $m \geqslant n$ we should make a vertical cut rather than a horizontal one; then we get an

(x_1, y_1)

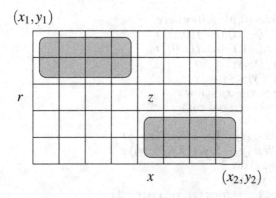

r z

x (x_2, y_2)

Figure 4.3 A two-dimensional divide-and-conquer decomposition

algorithm with at most $n \log (2m/\sqrt{n})$ evaluations of f. In either case, if one of m or n is much smaller than the other we get a better algorithm than saddleback search. For example, again with $f(x,y) = x^2 + 3^y$ and $t = 20259$, this method needs only 96 evaluations of f to compute the answer, about half the number of the previous version.

But we can do better still. As before, suppose we have confined the search to a rectangle with top-left corner (x_1, y_1) and bottom-right corner (x_2, y_2). Assume that $y_1 - y_2 \leqslant x_2 - x_1$, so there are at least as many columns as rows. Suppose we carry out a binary search

$$x = smallest \ (x_1 - 1, x_2) \ (\lambda x. f(x,r)) \ t$$

along the middle row, $r = \lfloor (y_1 + y_2)/2 \rfloor$. Recall that x is the smallest x in the range $x_1 \leqslant x \leqslant x_2$, if it exists, such that $t \leqslant f(x,r)$; otherwise $x = x_2$. If $t < f(x,r)$, then we need continue the search only on the two rectangles $((x_1, y_1), (x-1, r+1))$ and $((x, r-1), (x_2, y_2))$. Figure 4.3 shows a picture of this case, where $z = f(x,r)$. If $f(x,r) = t$, then we can cut out column x and continue the search on the two rectangles $((x_1, y_1), (x-1, r+1))$ and $((x+1, r-1), (x_2, y_2))$. Finally, if $f(x,r) > t$, so every entry in the row r is greater that t, then we can continue the search on the single rectangle $((x_1, r-1), (x_2, y_2))$. The reasoning is dual if there are more rows than columns. As a result, we can eliminate about half the elements of the array with a logarithmic number of probes. The algorithm incorporating this method is given in Figure 4.4.

As to the analysis, again let $T(m,n)$ denote the number of evaluations of f required to search an $m \times n$ rectangle. Suppose $m \leqslant n$. In the best case, when each binary search on a row returns the leftmost or rightmost element, we have

$$T(m,n) = \log n + T(m/2, n)$$

$$search\, f\, t = from\ (0,p)\ (q,0)\ \textbf{where}$$

$$\quad p = smallest\ (-1,t)\ (\lambda y.f(0,y))\ t$$
$$\quad q = smallest\ (-1,t)\ (\lambda x.f(x,0))\ t$$
$$\quad from\ (x_1,y_1)\ (x_2,y_2)$$
$$\qquad |\ x_2 < x_1 \lor y_1 < y_2\ = [\,]$$
$$\qquad |\ y_1 - y_2 \leqslant x_2 - x_1 = row\ x$$
$$\qquad |\ otherwise\qquad\quad = col\ y$$

$$\quad\textbf{where}$$
$$\quad x = smallest\ (x_1 - 1, x_2)\ (\lambda x.f(x,r))\ t$$
$$\quad y = smallest\ (y_2 - 1, y_1)\ (\lambda y.f(c,y))\ t$$
$$\quad c = (x_1 + x_2)\ \text{div}\ 2$$
$$\quad r = (y_1 + y_2)\ \text{div}\ 2$$
$$\quad row\ x\ |\ z < t\quad = from\ (x_1,y_1)\ (x_2, r+1)$$
$$\qquad\quad |\ z == t = (x,r) : from\ (x_1,y_1)\ (x-1, r+1)\ +\!\!+ from\ (x+1, r-1)\ (x_2,y_2)$$
$$\qquad\quad |\ z > t\quad = from\ (x_1,y_1)\ (x-1, r+1)\ +\!\!+ from\ (x, r-1)\ (x_2,y_2)$$
$$\qquad\quad\textbf{where}\ z = f\ (x,r)$$
$$\quad col\ y\ |\ z < t\quad = from\ (c+1, y_1)\ (x_2,y_2)$$
$$\qquad\quad |\ z == t = (c,y) : from\ (x_1,y_1)\ (c-1, y+1)\ +\!\!+ from\ (c+1, y-1)\ (x_2,y_2)$$
$$\qquad\quad |\ z > t\quad = from\ (x_1,y_1)\ (c-1, y)\ +\!\!+ from\ (c+1, y-1)\ (x_2,y_2)$$
$$\qquad\quad\textbf{where}\ z = f\ (c,y)$$

Figure 4.4 The final program

---

with solution $T(m,n) = \Theta(\log m \times \log n)$. In the worst case, when each binary search returns the middle element, we have

$$T(m,n) = \log n + 2\, T(m/2, n/2)$$

To solve this recurrence relation, again set $U(i,j) = T(2^i, 2^j)$. Then we have

$$U(i,j) = \sum_{k=0}^{i-1} 2^k\, (j-k) = \Theta(2^i\,(j-i+1))$$

Hence $T(m,n) = \Theta(m \log(1 + n/m))$. Dually, if $n < m$, we obtain a running time of $T(m,n) = \Theta(n \log(1 + m/n))$. For our example function $f(x,y) = x^2 + 3^y$ and $t = 20259$, the final program of Figure 4.4 needs only 72 evaluations of f to compute the answer, about three-quarters of the previous best time.

These bounds are asymptotically optimal. Any algorithm for searching an $m \times n$ rectangle has to perform at least

$$\Omega(m \log(1 + n/m) + n \log(1 + m/n))$$

evaluations of f. This lower bound shows that when $m = n$ we cannot do better than $\Omega(m + n)$ comparisons. So saddleback search is the best possible method on a square grid. But if $m < n$, then $m \leqslant n \log(1 + m/n)$ since $x \leqslant \log(1 + x)$ if $0 \leqslant x \leqslant 1$. Thus when $m \leqslant n$ we have the lower bound $\Omega\ (m \log(n/m))$, and when $m > n$ we have the lower bound $\Omega\ (n \log(m/n))$.

The proof of the lower bound depends on the *decision tree* associated with the problem. The role of decision trees in putting a lower bound on the running time of a problem will be explained at the end of the next section in the context of sorting. So, it is perhaps better to read that section first and then come back to what follows. But here is the idea. Suppose there are $A(m,n)$ different possible answers to the problem. For example, $A(1,1) = 2$ because there are two possible outcomes, either an empty list or a singleton list; and $A(2,2) = 6$ because the possible outcomes are one empty list, four possible singleton lists, and one possible doubleton list. Each test of $f(x,y)$ has three possible outcomes, $f(x,y) < t, f(x,y) = t$, and $f(x,y) > t$, so the height h of the ternary decision tree has to satisfy $h \geqslant \log_3 A(m,n)$. Provided we can estimate $A(m,n)$, this gives us a lower bound on the number of tests that have to be performed.

To estimate $A(m,n)$, observe that each list of pairs (x,y) in the range $0 \leqslant x < n$ and $0 \leqslant y < m$ with $f(x,y) = z$ is in a one-to-one correspondence with a step-shaped path from the top-left corner of the $m \times n$ rectangle to the bottom-right corner, in which the value z appears at the inner corners of the steps. This step shape is not necessarily the one traced by the function *search*. The path from the top-left to bottom-right corner contains m down-moves and n right-moves in some order, so the number of such paths is $\binom{m+n}{n}$ (which is the same as $\binom{m+n}{m}$), so that is the value of $A(m,n)$.

Another way to calculate $A(m,n)$ is to suppose there are k solutions. The required value can appear in k rows in exactly $\binom{m}{k}$ ways, and for each way there are $\binom{n}{k}$ possible choices for the columns. Hence

$$A(m,n) = \sum_{k=0}^{m} \binom{m}{k}\binom{n}{k} = \binom{m+n}{n}$$

since the summation is an instance of Vandermonde's convolution, see [7]. Taking logarithms, we obtain the lower bound

$$\log A(m,n) = \Omega(m \log (1+n/m) + n \log (1+m/n))$$

which is the result given above.

4.3 Binary search trees

Binary search trees capture the essence of binary search as a data structure. The trees are based on the following type:

data *Tree a = Null | Node (Tree a) a (Tree a)*

A tree either is the null tree or consists of a node, which has a left subtree, a node value (also called its label), and a right subtree. This kind of tree is different from the one used in the construction of random-access lists in the previous chapter, in that values are stored at nodes rather than leaves. In general, trees can be classified according to the precise form of the branching structure, the location of information in the tree, the presence or otherwise of subsidiary information, and the relationship between the information stored in different parts of the tree. We will encounter other kinds of tree in subsequent chapters.

The size of a tree is the number of labels it contains:

size :: *Tree a* → *Nat*
size Null   = 0
size (*Node l x r*) = 1 + *size l* + *size r*

The values in a tree can be turned into a list by the function *flatten*:

flatten :: *Tree a* → [*a*]
flatten Null   = []
flatten (*Node l x r*) = *flatten l* ++ [*x*] ++ *flatten r*

The running time of this definition of *flatten* is not linear in the size of the tree, an issue we have encountered before in Exercise 3.8. The solution is to use an accumulating parameter (see the exercises).

By definition, a tree is a *binary search tree* if flattening it returns a list of values in strictly increasing order. Thus the label of a binary search tree is greater than any label in its left subtree and smaller than any label in its right subtree.

The definition of a binary search tree can be modified in various ways. For example, one can allow duplicate node labels, so that flattening the tree produces a list only in nondecreasing order. More useful in practice is to allow labels to be records of some kind, with each record containing a key field unique to that record. The tree is ordered by key, so flattening it produces a list of records in increasing order of key. Such trees can be used to search *dictionaries*, in which the keys are 'words' of some kind, and the records contain information associated with a given word.

Here is the counterpart of binary search in terms of records and key fields:

search :: *Ord k* ⇒ (*a* → *k*) → *k* → *Tree a* → *Maybe a*
search key k Null = *Nothing*
search key k (*Node l x r*)
    | *key x* < *k*   = *search key k r*
    | *key x* == *k* = *Just x*
    | *key x* > *k*   = *search key k l*

The search returns *Nothing* if there is no record with the given key; otherwise it returns *Just x*, the (unique) record with the given key. The tree is searched by following either the left or the right subtree of a node depending on whether the key at the node is greater than or less than the given key. In the worst case, the search takes time proportional to the height of the tree, where

$height :: Tree\ a \to Nat$

$height\ Null \qquad = 0$

$height\ (Node\ l\ x\ r) = 1 + max\ (height\ l)\ (height\ r)$

Thus the search is guaranteed to take $O(\log n)$ steps for a tree of size n only if its height is $O(\log n)$. Later on we will see how to ensure that the height of a tree is logarithmic in its size.

Although two trees of the same size need not have the same height, the two measures are not independent. The height h and size n of a tree satisfy the relationship $h \leqslant n < 2^h$. In particular, $h \geqslant \lceil \log(n+1) \rceil$. The proof of this fundamental relationship is by structural induction, a proof we leave as an exercise. By definition a tree is *balanced* if the heights of the left and right subtrees of each node differ by at most one. There are other definitions of what it means for a tree to be balanced, but we will stick to this one. Although a balanced tree of size n need not have the minimum possible height $\lceil \log(n+1) \rceil$, its height is always reasonably small. More precisely, if t is a balanced tree of size n and height h, then we have

$$h \leqslant 1.4404 \log(n+1) + \Theta(1)$$

The proof of this result uses induction in rather an indirect way. Suppose $H(n)$ is the maximum possible height of a balanced tree of size n. Our objective is to put an upper bound on $H(n)$. We will do this by turning the problem around. Suppose $S(h)$ is the minimum possible size of a balanced tree of height h. Taking a tree of size n and height $H(n)$, we therefore have $S(H(n)) \leqslant n$. Hence we can put an upper bound on $H(n)$ by putting a lower bound on $S(n)$: if $S(n) \geqslant f(n)$, then $n \geqslant f(H(n))$ and so $f^{-1}(n) \geqslant H(n)$.

Since *Null* is the only tree with height 0, it is clear that $S(0) = 0$. Similarly, there is only one kind of tree with height 1, so $S(1) = 1$. The smallest possible balanced tree with height $h+2$ has two balanced subtrees, one with height $h+1$ and the other with height h. Hence

$$S(h+2) = S(h+1) + S(h) + 1$$

It is at this point that induction comes in. A simple induction argument shows that $S(h) = fib(h+2) - 1$, where *fib* is the Fibonacci function. To complete the proof we will need the following fact about the Fibonacci function, which can also be proved by induction. Let φ and ψ be the two roots of the equation $x^2 - x - 1 = 0$, that is, $\varphi = (1 + \sqrt{5})/2$ and $\psi = (1 - \sqrt{5})/2$. Then $fib(n) = (\varphi^n - \psi^n)/\sqrt{5}$. Furthermore, since $\psi^n < 1$, we obtain that $fib(n) > (\varphi^n - 1)/\sqrt{5}$. Hence

$$(\varphi^{H(n)+2} - 1)/\sqrt{5} - 1 < fib(H(n)+2) - 1 = S(H(n)) \leqslant n$$

Taking logarithms, we obtain

$$(H(n) + 2) \log \varphi < \log(n+1) + \Theta(1)$$

Since $\log \varphi > 1/1.4404$, the result now follows.

We now turn to the task of building a balanced binary search tree from a list of distinct values. One way to build a tree, though the result is not necessarily balanced, is to partition the list into two lists, one containing those elements smaller than some fixed element, and those elements which are not. That leads to

$mktree :: Ord \ a \Rightarrow [a] \rightarrow Tree \ a$
$mktree \ [] \quad = Null$
$mktree \ (x:xs) = Node \ (mktree \ ys) \ x \ (mktree \ zs)$
$\quad\quad\quad\quad\quad\quad$ **where** $(ys, zs) = partition \ (<x) \ xs$
$partition \ p \ xs = (filter \ p \ xs, filter \ (not \cdot p) \ xs)$

In the best case, when partitioning splits a list of length n into two lists of lengths $n/2$, the running time $T(n)$ satisfies $T(n+1) = 2T(n/2) + \Theta(n)$. This recurrence, a slight variant of one we have seen before, also has the solution $T(n) = \Theta(n \log n)$. In the worst case, when partitioning splits a list of length n into a list of length 0 and a list of length n, the recurrence relation is $T(n+1) = T(n) + \Theta(n)$ with solution $T(n) = \Theta(n^2)$.

In order to construct an efficient version of *mktree* that guarantees a balanced tree, we need to maintain information about the heights of the subtrees of a node. The way to do that is to modify the type *Tree* to read

data $Tree \ a = Null \mid Node \ Nat \ (Tree \ a) \ a \ (Tree \ a)$

The extra label in a node is the height of the tree. Thus, we have

$height \ Null \quad\quad\quad\quad = 0$
$height \ (Node \ h \ \_ \ \_ \ \_) = h$

We can build these augmented trees with the help of a smart constructor *node*, defined by

$node :: Tree \ a \rightarrow a \rightarrow Tree \ a \rightarrow Tree \ a$
$node \ l \ x \ r = Node \ h \ l \ x \ r \ \textbf{where} \ h = 1 + max \ (height \ l) \ (height \ r)$

We will meet another smart constructor in a moment, and yet a third later on.

A balanced tree can be constructed by inserting values one by one into an initially empty tree:

$mktree :: Ord \ a \Rightarrow [a] \rightarrow Tree \ a$
$mktree = foldr \ insert \ Null$

The definition of *insert* starts off easily enough:

$insert \ x \ Null = node \ Null \ x \ Null$
$insert \ x \ (Node \ h \ l \ y \ r)$
$\quad \mid x < y \quad = balance \ (insert \ x \ l) \ y \ r$
$\quad \mid x == y = Node \ h \ l \ y \ r$
$\quad \mid y < x \quad = balance \ l \ y \ (insert \ x \ r)$

The value x is discarded if it is already present in the tree; otherwise x is inserted into either the left subtree or the right subtree. But we cannot simply apply *node* to the result since the result may not be a balanced tree. That is where *balance* comes in. It is a second smart constructor, smarter than *node* in that it restores balance as well as installing height information.

To implement *balance* we have to consider three cases. First of all, observe that a single insertion can increase the height of a tree by at most one. That means it is sufficient to implement *balance* under the assumption that both subtrees are balanced and that they differ in height by at most two. The easy case is when the two subtrees differ in height by at most one. Then we can implement *balance* by *node*. The other two cases are entirely symmetrical, so we shall consider just the case when the left subtree has height two more than the right subtree, that is,

$$height\ l = height\ r + 2$$

We have to inspect the subtrees of the left subtree, so let l have left subtree ll and right subtree rl. In the first case, suppose $height\ rl \leqslant height\ ll$. Because l is assumed to be balanced, all of the following four relationships hold:

$$height\ r = height\ l - 2 = height\ ll - 1 \leqslant height\ rl \leqslant height\ ll$$

In this case we can implement *balance* with a *right rotation*:

$$balance\ l\ x\ r = rotr\ (node\ l\ x\ r)$$
$$rotr\ (Node\ \_\ (Node\ \_\ ll\ y\ rl)\ x\ r) = node\ ll\ y\ (node\ rl\ x\ r)$$

Here is a picture of a right rotation:

To check this leads to a balanced tree, we reason as follows:

$$abs\ (height\ ll - height\ (node\ rl\ x\ r))$$
$$=\quad \{\ \text{definition of } height\ \}$$
$$abs\ (height\ ll - 1 - height\ rl\ \text{max}\ height\ r)$$
$$=\quad \{\ \text{since } height\ r \leqslant height\ rl\ \text{(see above)}\ \}$$
$$abs\ (height\ ll - 1 - height\ rl)$$
$$\leqslant\quad \{\ \text{since } height\ ll - 1 \leqslant height\ rl \leqslant height\ ll\ \text{(see above)}\ \}$$
$$1$$

Thus the tree on the right of the picture is indeed balanced.

In the second case we have *height ll* < *height rl*. But again *l* is assumed to be balanced, so

    height ll + 1 = *height rl*

In this case we have to inspect the subtrees of *rl*, so let *lrl* and *rrl* be the left and right subtrees of *rl*. In this case all of the following relationships hold:

    height r = height l − 2 = *height rl* − 1 = *height ll* = *height lrl* max *height rrl*

In this case we can implement *balance* with a left rotation followed by a right rotation:

    balance l x r = rotr (*node* (*rotl l*) *x r*)
    rotl (*Node _ ll y* (*Node _ lrl z rrl*)) = *node* (*node ll y lrl*) *z rrl*

Here is the picture:

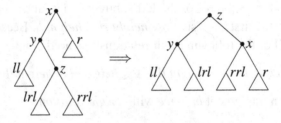

To check this leads to a balanced tree, note that

    balance l x r = rotr (*node* (*node* (*node ll y lrl*) *z rrl*) *x r*)
           = *node* (*node ll y lrl*) *z* (*node rrl x r*)

We can then argue as follows:

       abs (*height* (*node ll y lrl*) − *height* (*node rrl x r*))
  =   { definition of *height* }
       abs (*height ll* max *height lrl* − *height rrl* max *height r*)
  =   { since *height rrl* ⩽ *height r* (see above) }
       abs (*height ll* max *height lrl* − *height r*)
  =   { since *height lrl* ⩽ *height ll* (see above) }
       abs (*height ll* − *height r*)
  =   { since *height ll* = *height r* (see above) }
       0

The remaining case *height r = height l* + 2 is treated in an entirely dual manner. To give the complete definition of *balance* we will need a function *bias*, defined by

    bias :: *Tree a* → *Int*
    bias (*Node _ l x r*) = *height l* − *height r*

Then the full definition of *balance* is given by

$$balance :: Tree\ a \rightarrow a \rightarrow Tree\ a \rightarrow Tree\ a$$
$$balance\ t_1\ x\ t_2$$
$$\quad |\ abs\ (h_1 - h_2) \leqslant 1 = node \quad t_1\ x\ t_2$$
$$\quad |\ h_1 == h_2 + 2 \qquad = rotateR\ t_1\ x\ t_2$$
$$\quad |\ h_2 == h_1 + 2 \qquad = rotateL\ t_1\ x\ t_2$$
$$\quad \textbf{where}\ h_1 = height\ t_1;\ \ h_2 = height\ t_2$$
$$rotateR\ t_1\ x\ t_2 = \textbf{if}\ 0 \leqslant bias\ t_1\ \textbf{then}\ rotr\ (node\ t_1\ x\ t_2)$$
$$\textbf{else}\quad rotr\ (node\ (rotl\ t_1)\ x\ t_2)$$
$$rotateL\ t_1\ x\ t_2 = \textbf{if}\ bias\ t_2 \leqslant 0\ \textbf{then}\ rotl\ (node\ t_1\ x\ t_2)$$
$$\textbf{else}\quad rotl\ (node\ t_1\ x\ (rotr\ t_2))$$

The definition returns an error when applied to two trees whose heights differ by more than two, but it is easy enough to define a balancing function that works for two trees of any height. This function, which we will call *gbalance*, will be needed in the following section. To compute *gbalance* $t_1\ x\ t_2$, suppose first that $h_1 > h_2 + 2$. In this case the subtrees $r_1, r_2, \ldots$ along the right spine of t_1 can be traversed to find a subtree $r = r_k$ satisfying

$$0 \leqslant height\ r - height\ t_2 \leqslant 1$$

Such a tree is guaranteed to exist because the subtrees $r_1, r_2, \ldots$ decrease in height by at least one and at most two at each step. Furthermore, if l is the left-sibling of r, then

$$abs\ (height\ l - height\ (node\ r\ x\ t_2)) \leqslant 2$$

because t_1 is a balanced tree and $abs\ (height\ l - height\ r) \leqslant 1$. That means l and *node* $r\ x\ t_2$ can be combined with *balance*. Rebalancing can increase the height of a tree by at most one, so further rebalancing up the tree maintains the precondition on *balance*. The traversal is captured by *balanceR*, defined by

$$balanceR :: Set\ a \rightarrow a \rightarrow Set\ a \rightarrow Set\ a$$
$$balanceR\ (Node\ \_\ l\ y\ r)\ x\ t_2 = \textbf{if}\ height\ r \geqslant height\ t_2 + 2$$
$$\textbf{then}\ balance\ l\ y\ (balanceR\ r\ x\ t_2)$$
$$\textbf{else}\ balance\ l\ y\ (node\ r\ x\ t_2)$$

The situation is dual when $h_2 > h_1 + 2$ and is expressed by a function *balanceL*, whose definition is left as an exercise. It is clear that *balanceR* $t_1\ x\ t_2$ takes $O(h_1 - h_2)$ steps, where h_1 and h_2 are the heights of t_1 and t_2. Dually, *balanceL* $t_1\ x\ t_2$ takes $O(h_2 - h_1)$ steps.

With that, the complete definition of *gbalance* is as follows:

$gbalance :: Set\ a \rightarrow a \rightarrow Set\ a \rightarrow Set\ a$
$gbalance\ t_1\ x\ t_2$
$\quad |\ abs\ (h_1 - h_2) \leqslant 2 = balance\quad t_1\ x\ t_2$
$\quad |\ h_1 > h_2 + 2\qquad = balanceR\ t_1\ x\ t_2$
$\quad |\ h_1 + 2 < h_2\qquad = balanceL\ t_1\ x\ t_2$
$\quad \textbf{where}\ h_1 = height\ t_1;\ \ h_2 = height\ t_2$

Evaluation of *balance* certainly takes constant time, even though *gbalance* does not. That means each insertion takes logarithmic time in the size of the tree, and building the tree takes $\Theta(n \log n)$ steps.

Can we build a binary search tree from a list of elements over an arbitrary ordered type in better than $\Theta(n \log n)$ steps? To answer this question, observe first that any information we can discover about the elements of the underlying type arises solely as a result of comparison tests of the form $x \leqslant y$ or $x == y$ between the elements. That means it is sufficient to put a lower bound to the number of such comparisons required in the construction of the tree. If we can show that, say, $\Omega(f(n))$ comparison tests are needed in the worst case, then that is a lower bound on the total time to build the tree. The argument is not valid when we are building a tree of integers or words, since there may be cunning methods that avoid comparison tests altogether. Now suppose the computation of *mktree* on a list of length n can be achieved with $B(n)$ comparison tests of the form $x \leqslant y$. Then, since we can sort a list of elements over an arbitrary ordered type by

$sort :: (Ord\ a) \Rightarrow [a] \rightarrow [a]$
$sort = flatten \cdot mktree$

and since *flatten* involves no comparisons whatsoever, it follows that sorting a list of elements can be achieved with $B(n)$ comparisons.

We now put a lower bound to $B(n)$. Every algorithm based on binary comparisons can be associated with a certain tree, called a *decision tree*. The decision tree is a binary tree whose labels are binary comparisons of the form $x \leqslant y$. The left subtree is a decision tree for the case $x \leqslant y$ and the right subtree is a decision tree for the case $x > y$. The execution of any sorting algorithm based on binary comparisons traces a path from the root of the decision tree to a leaf, each leaf being associated with a unique permutation that sorts the list. Each permutation of the input determines a sorted list, so there have to be at least $n!$ leaves for an input of length n because there are $n!$ possible permutations that can sort the list. Since a binary tree of height h has no more than 2^h leaves, the decision tree has to have some height h such that $n! \leqslant 2^h$. Taking logarithms, that means $h \geqslant \log(n!)$. To estimate the right-hand side, we can use Stirling's approximation (see Answer 2.5) to arrive at $h = \Omega(n \log n)$. But h estimates the total number of comparisons that may be needed to sort the list in the worst case, so we have our lower bound $B(n) = \Omega(n \log n)$. So, the answer to the original question is: No, we cannot build a binary search tree in better than $\Theta(n \log n)$ steps.

4.4 Dynamic sets

Sets that can grow or shrink over time are called *dynamic sets*. Operations on such sets include a membership test, adding a value to a set, and deleting an element from a set. One may also want to take the union of two sets, or to split a set into two sets, one containing those elements at most some given value, and the other those elements greater than the value. As a special case of set union, one may also want to *combine* two sets when it is known that the elements of the first are all less than any element of the second. Thus, splitting a set and then combining the results gives back the original set.

In this section we will show how to implement these operations when sets are represented by balanced binary search trees:

type *Set a = Tree a*

The membership test is a simple variant of the function *search* of the previous section:

$$member :: Ord\ a \Rightarrow a \rightarrow Set\ a \rightarrow Bool$$
$$member\ x\ Null \qquad\qquad\qquad = False$$
$$member\ x\ (Node\ \_\ l\ y\ r)\ |\ x<y\ \ = member\ x\ l$$
$$\qquad\qquad\qquad\qquad |\ x == y = True$$
$$\qquad\qquad\qquad\qquad |\ x>y\ \ = member\ x\ r$$

Insertion is implemented by the function *insert* of the previous section. The function *delete* is more interesting:

$$delete :: Ord\ a \Rightarrow a \rightarrow Set\ a \rightarrow Set\ a$$
$$delete\ x\ Null \qquad\qquad\qquad = Null$$
$$delete\ x\ (Node\ \_\ l\ y\ r)\ |\ x<y\ \ = balance\ (delete\ x\ l)\ y\ r$$
$$\qquad\qquad\qquad\qquad |\ x == y = combine\ l\ r$$
$$\qquad\qquad\qquad\qquad |\ x>y\ \ = balance\ l\ y\ (delete\ x\ r)$$

Deleting a single value from a tree can reduce its height by at most one, so the smart constructor *balance* can be used to restore balance. Recall that *balance* t_1 x t_2 was defined only for the case that the heights of t_1 and t_2 differed by at most two. That leaves *combine*, which in effect has to concatenate two trees.

We will give two definitions of *combine*, the second of which generalises the first. In the first definition, *combine* is defined only for two balanced trees that differ in height by at most one. This is certainly sufficient for its use in *delete*. The easy case is when one of the trees is null; in such a case we can simply return the other tree.

When neither tree is null we have to find an appropriate label for the combined tree, and there are two sensible options: either take the leftmost label of the second tree, or the rightmost label of the first tree. We choose the former, defining *deleteMin* by

$$deleteMin :: Ord\ a \Rightarrow Set\ a \rightarrow (a, Set\ a)$$
$$deleteMin\ (Node\ \_\ Null\ x\ r) = (x, r)$$
$$deleteMin\ (Node\ \_\ l\ x\ r)\quad = (y, balance\ t\ x\ r)\ \textbf{where}\ (y, t) = deleteMin\ l$$

The function *deleteMin* returns the minimum element of a nonempty set, together with the set that remains after deleting the minimum element. The function *balance* can then be invoked to ensure that this set is balanced (see Exercise 4.15). Now we can define *combine* by

$$combine :: Ord\ a \Rightarrow Set\ a \rightarrow Set\ a \rightarrow Set\ a$$
$$combine\ l\ Null = l$$
$$combine\ Null\ r = r$$
$$combine\ l\ r\quad = balance\ l\ x\ t\ \textbf{where}\ (x, t) = deleteMin\ r$$

The second definition of *combine* is exactly the same, except that *balance* is replaced by the more general function *gbalance* of the previous section. Therefore *combine* can be used to combine any two sets as long as all the elements of the first set are less than any element of the second set. Combining two sets of sizes m and n takes $O\ (\log n + \log m)$ steps.

The final function we will implement is a function *split* with type

$$split :: Ord\ a \Rightarrow a \rightarrow Set\ a \rightarrow (Set\ a, Set\ a)$$

The value of *split x t* is a pair of sets, the first containing those elements of t which are at most x, and the second those elements that are greater than x. Thus, combining the two sets gives back the original set. In symbols,

$$split\ x\ xs = (ys, zs)\quad \Rightarrow\quad combine\ ys\ zs = xs$$

Even more briefly, *uncurry combine · split x = id*. For example, consider the 1973 two-volume edition of the Shorter Oxford English Dictionary. If *soed* is the set of all the words in the dictionary, then the contents of each volume is given by *split* "Markworthy" *soed*.

To define *split* we have to split a tree into pieces and then sew the pieces together to make the final pair of sets:

$$split\ x\ t = sew\ (pieces\ x\ t)$$

A piece consists of a tree minus one of its subtrees, so it consists of a label and either a left or a right subtree:

data *Piece a = LP (Set a) a | RP a (Set a)*

A left piece *LP l x* is missing its right subtree, and a right piece *RP x r* is missing its left subtree. The function *pieces* is defined by

$pieces :: Ord\ a \Rightarrow a \to Set\ a \to [Piece\ a]$
$pieces\ x\ t = addPiece\ t\ []\ \textbf{where}$
$\quad addPiece\ Null\ ps \qquad\qquad = ps$
$\quad addPiece\ (Node\ \_\ l\ y\ r)\ ps\ |\ x < y\ = addPiece\ l\ (RP\ y\ r : ps)$
$\qquad\qquad\qquad\qquad\quad\ \ |\ x \geqslant y\ = addPiece\ r\ (LP\ l\ y : ps)$

For example, $pieces\ 9\ t$, where t is the tree

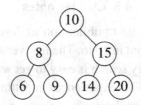

produces the list of three pieces

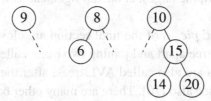

in which the missing tree is indicated by a dashed line. We can sew a list of pieces together by

$sew :: [Piece\ a] \to (Set\ a, Set\ a)$
$sew = foldl\ step\ (Null, Null)$
$\quad \textbf{where}\ step\ (t_1, t_2)\ (LP\ t\ x) = (gbalance\ t\ x\ t_1, t_2)$
$\qquad\qquad\ step\ (t_1, t_2)\ (RP\ x\ t) = (t_1, gbalance\ t_2\ x\ t)$

For example, sewing the three pieces above produces the two trees

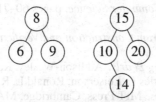

We claim that $split\ x\ t$ takes $O(h)$ steps, where $h = height\ t$. Certainly, $pieces\ x\ t$ takes this time, so we have to show that sew does too. If we define the height of a piece to be the height of the tree associated with the piece, then $pieces\ x\ t$ produces a list of pieces whose heights $h_1, h_2, ..., h_k$ are strictly increasing and bounded above by h. For example, the pieces pictured above have heights $0, 1, 2$. The total cost of sew is proportional to

$$(h_1 - 0) + (h_2 - h_1) + \ldots + (h_k - h_{k-1}) \leqslant h$$

because each call of *gbalance* t_1 x t_2 takes time proportional to the difference between the heights of t_1 and t_2. Thus both *piece* and *sew* take logarithmic time in the size of the sets, so *split* does too. We will need *combine* and a variant of *split* in Chapter 14.

4.5 Chapter notes

According to Knuth [10], the first publication to describe binary search (for the special case $n = 2^k - 1$) appeared in 1946. The first version that worked for all n was not published until 1960. Binary search is easy to get wrong; see Bentley's book [4] for an interesting discussion of his experiences in getting professional programmers to implement binary search. Saddleback search was so named by David Gries, see [3, 6, 8], probably because the shape of the three-dimensional grid, with the smallest element at the bottom left, the largest at the top right, and two wings, is a bit like an equestrian saddle.

The functions *sew* and *pieces* of the final section are closely related to a more general way of taking a tree apart and joining two trees, called the *Zipper*; see [9].

Balanced binary trees are also called AVL trees, after their inventors Adelson-Velskiĭ and Landis [1]; see also [10]. There are many other balanced tree schemes; for example [5] describes red–black trees, and [2] describes a simple scheme based on two operations, skew and split.

References

[1]   Georgy M. Adelson-Velskiĭ and Evgenii M. Landis. An algorithm for the organisation of information. *Soviet Mathematics – Doklady*, 3(5):1259–1263, 1962. English translation in *Doklady Akademia Nauk SSSR*, 146(2): 263–266.

[2]   Arne Andersson. Binary trees made simple. In F. Dehne, J. R. Sack, N. Santoro, and S. Whitesides, editors, *Workshop on Algorithm Design and Data Structures*, volume 709 of *Lecture Notes in Computer Science*, pages 60–71, Springer-Verlag, Berlin, 1993.

[3]   Roland Backhouse. *Program Construction and Verification*. Prentice-Hall, Hemel Hempstead, 1986.

[4]   Jon Bentley. *Programming Pearls*. Addison-Wesley, Reading, MA, 1986.

[5]   Thomas H. Cormen, Charles E. Leiserson, Ronald L. Rivest, and Clifford Stein. *Introduction to Algorithms*. MIT Press, Cambridge, MA, third edition, 2009.

[6]   Edsger W. Dijkstra. The saddleback search. EWD-934, http://www.cs.utexas.edu/users/EWD/index09xx.html, 1985.

[7]   Ronald L. Graham, Donald E. Knuth, and Oren Patashnik. *Concrete Mathematics*. Addison-Wesley, Reading, MA, second edition, 1994.

[8]   David Gries. *The Science of Programming*. Springer, New York, 1981.

[9]   Gérard Huet. The Zipper. *Journal of Functional Programming*, 7(5):549–554, 1997.

[10] Donald E. Knuth. *The Art of Computer Programming*, volume 3: Sorting and Searching. Addison-Wesley, Reading, MA, second edition, 1998.

Exercises

Exercise 4.1 The *rule of floors* states that for integers n and real numbers r we have $n \leqslant \lfloor r \rfloor \Leftrightarrow n \leqslant r$. This useful rule will appear in a number of problems. Using just the rule of floors (no case analysis) prove that for integers a and b we have $a < (a+b) \text{ div } 2 < b$ if and only if $a+1 < b$.

The dual *rule of ceilings* states that for integers n and real numbers r we have $\lceil r \rceil \leqslant n \Leftrightarrow r \leqslant n$. Using this rule prove that if h is an integer such that $n < 2^h$, then $\lceil \log (n+1) \rceil \leqslant h$. This result was stated in Section 4.3.

Exercise 4.2 Look again at the expression

$$head ([x \mid x \leftarrow [a+1..m], t \leqslant f \, x] \mathbin{+\!\!+} [x \mid x \leftarrow [m+1..b], t \leqslant f \, x])$$

where $a < m < b$ and $f(a) < t \leqslant f(b)$. If nothing else is assumed about f, then we cannot assert that the first list is empty if $f(m) < t$. Nevertheless, the definition of *smallest* (a,b) returns some value. What is it?

Exercise 4.3 Recall that the exact number $T(n)$ of evaluations of f required in the worst case of evaluating *smallest* $(a,b) f \, t$, where $n = b - a + 1$ is the number of integers in the interval, satisfies $T(2) = 0$ and

$$T(n) = T(\lceil (n+1)/2 \rceil) + 1$$

for $n > 2$. Use the rule of ceilings to show that $T(n) = \lceil \log (n-1) \rceil$.

Exercise 4.4 Following on from the previous question, given that $f(a) < t \leqslant f(b)$, show that any algorithm for computing *smallest* $(a,b) f \, t$ requires $\lceil \log (n-1) \rceil$ comparison tests of the form $t \leqslant f(x)$.

Exercise 4.5 What are the positions of 472 in the grid of Figure 4.1?

Exercise 4.6 With $f(x,y) = x^3 + y^3$, what is the result of saddleback search for $t = 1729$? Does the final algorithm return the same result?

Exercise 4.7 To obtain a linear-time definition of *flatten* we can use an accumulating parameter. There is more than one way of doing so, but a simple method is to introduce *flatcat* defined by

> *flatcat* :: *Tree a* → $[a]$ → $[a]$
> *flatcat t xs* = *flatten t* $\mathbin{+\!\!+}$ *xs*

We have *flatten t* = *flatcat t* $[\,]$, so it remains to produce a recursive definition of *flatcat* that does not use *flatten* or any $\mathbin{+\!\!+}$ operations. Give details of the synthesis.

Exercise 4.8 Prove by structural induction that

$$height\ t \leqslant size\ t < 2^{height\ t}$$

for all binary trees t.

Exercise 4.9 The definition

$$partition\ p\ xs = (filter\ p\ xs, filter\ (not \cdot p)\ xs)$$

involves two traversals of its second argument. Give a definition of *partition* that makes only one traversal of the input.

Exercise 4.10 Another way to build a binary tree for a list containing duplicates is to build a tree of type *Tree* $[a]$ in which node labels are lists of equal values. Show how to build such a tree.

Exercise 4.11 Consider the recurrences

$$B(n+1) = 2B(n/2) + \Theta(n)$$
$$W(n+1) = W(n) + \Theta(n)$$

for the best and worst cases for building a binary search tree by partitioning the input. Prove that $B(n) = \Theta(n \log n)$ and $W(n) = \Theta(n^2)$.

Exercise 4.12 Show that $\log(n!) = \Omega(n \log n)$ without using Stirling's approximation.

Exercise 4.13 For the (second) definition of *combine* we have

$$flatten\ (combine\ t_1\ t_2) = flatten\ t_1 + flatten\ t_2$$

Anticipating the following chapter, give a definition of *merge* for which

$$flatten\ (union\ t_1\ t_2) = merge\ (flatten\ t_1)\ (flatten\ t_2)$$

Exercise 4.14 One method of defining *union* is to flatten one of the trees and then insert the elements one by one into the other tree:

$$union :: Ord\ a \Rightarrow Set\ a \to Set\ a \to Set\ a$$
$$union\ t_1\ t_2 = foldr\ insert\ t_1\ (flatten\ t_2)$$

Supposing the first tree has size m and the second tree has size n, how long does *union* take?

Another method is to flatten both trees, merge the results to obtain a sorted list, and then to build a tree from the sorted list:

$$union\ t_1\ t_2 = build\ (merge\ (flatten\ t_1)\ (flatten\ t_2))$$

We can build a tree from a sorted list in linear time if we bring in arrays. Here is the first line of the definition:

$$build\ xs = from\ (0, n)\ (listArray\ (0, n-1)\ xs)\ \textbf{where}\ n = length\ xs$$

(recall from Chapter 3 that the expression *listArray* $(0, length\ xs - 1)$ *xs* converts a list of length n into an array whose indices run from 0 to $n - 1$). Construct a definition of *from*. How long does this method of defining *union* take?

Exercise 4.15 Why is the use of *balance* justified in the definitions of *deleteMin* and *combine*?

Exercise 4.16 Give the definition of *balanceL*.

Exercise 4.17 Suppose *pair* $f\ (x, y) = (f\ x, f\ y)$. Using *pair* give a one-line, linear-time definition of *split x*.

Answers

Answer 4.1 Here is the proof:

$$a < (a+b)\ div\ 2 < b$$
$$\Leftrightarrow\quad \{\ \text{definition of } div\ \}$$
$$a < \lfloor (a+b)/2 \rfloor < b$$
$$\Leftrightarrow\quad \{\ \text{arithmetic}\ \}$$
$$a+1 \leqslant \lfloor (a+b)/2 \rfloor < b$$
$$\Leftrightarrow\quad \{\ \text{rule of floors (twice)}\ \}$$
$$a+1 \leqslant (a+b)/2 < b$$
$$\Leftrightarrow\quad \{\ \text{arithmetic}\ \}$$
$$a+1 < b$$

The rule of floors is used twice in the above proof, the second appeal being the equivalent form: $\lfloor r \rfloor < x \Leftrightarrow r < x$.

For the second part we have $n < 2^h \Leftrightarrow n+1 \leqslant 2^h \Leftrightarrow \log(n+1) \leqslant h$, and the result follows by appeal to the rule of ceilings.

Answer 4.2 We have *smallest* $(a, b) = x \Rightarrow f(x) < t \leqslant f(x+1)$.

Answer 4.3 The proof is by induction and for the induction step we have to show

$$\lceil \log(n-1) \rceil = \lceil \log(\lceil (n+1)/2 \rceil - 1) \rceil + 1$$

To do so, we can reason by *indirect equality*, showing that $a = b$ by showing $a \leqslant k$ if and only if $b \leqslant k$ for all k. Using the rule of ceilings on the left-hand side gives $\lceil \log(n-1) \rceil \leqslant k \Leftrightarrow n-1 \leqslant 2^k$. On the right-hand side we have

$$\lceil \log(\lceil (n+1)/2 \rceil - 1) \rceil + 1 \leqslant k$$
$\Leftrightarrow$ { arithmetic }
$$\lceil \log(\lceil (n+1)/2 \rceil - 1) \rceil \leqslant k - 1$$
$\Leftrightarrow$ { rule of ceilings }
$$\log(\lceil (n+1)/2 \rceil - 1) \leqslant k - 1$$
$\Leftrightarrow$ { arithmetic }
$$\lceil (n+1)/2 \rceil - 1 \leqslant 2^{k-1}$$
$\Leftrightarrow$ { arithmetic }
$$\lceil (n+1)/2 \rceil \leqslant 2^{k-1} + 1$$
$\Leftrightarrow$ { rule of ceilings }
$$(n+1)/2 \leqslant 2^{k-1} + 1$$
$\Leftrightarrow$ { arithmetic }
$$n - 1 \leqslant 2^k$$

establishing the result.

Answer 4.4 From the answer to Exercise 4.2, we have that *smallest* $(a,b) f\, t$ can return any one of $b - a$ answers, namely those of the form $f(x) < t \leqslant f(x+1)$ for some x in the range $a \leqslant x < b$. A decision tree with internal nodes labelled with tests of the form $t \leqslant f(x)$ therefore has to have a height h satisfying $2^h \geqslant b - a$. Since $b - a = n - 1$ we have the lower bound $h \geqslant \lceil \log(n-1) \rceil$.

Answer 4.5 The positions are $(0,9)$, $(5,6)$, $(7,5)$, and $(9,0)$.

Answer 4.6 The four answers are $(9,10)$, $(10,9)$, $(1,12)$, and $(12,1)$. The only issue is the order in which these four values are produced. With saddleback search the answers are found in the order $(12,1), (10,9), (9,10), (1,12)$, but they are listed in reverse order. With the final algorithm it depends on the order in which the subrectangles are searched. It turns out that the final algorithm produces the list $[(9,10), (1,12), (10,9), (12,1)]$.

Answer 4.7 Here is the recursive case:

$flatcat\ (Node\ l\ x\ r)\ xs$
$=$ { specification of *flatcat* }
$flatten\ (Node\ l\ x\ r) \mathbin{+\!\!+} xs$
$=$ { definition of *flatten* }
$flatten\ l \mathbin{+\!\!+} [x] \mathbin{+\!\!+} flatten\ r \mathbin{+\!\!+} xs$
$=$ { specification of *flatcat* }
$flatten\ l \mathbin{+\!\!+} [x] \mathbin{+\!\!+} flatcat\ r\ xs$
$=$ { specification of *flatcat* }
$flatcat\ l\ (x : flatcat\ r\ xs)$

Answer 4.8 There are two cases, depending on whether the tree is *Null* or a *Node*. The former case is easy. For the latter, we will prove only the second inequality, which can be written in the form *size t* $\leqslant 2^{height\ t} - 1$ since both size and height are integers. We reason as follows:

$$
\begin{aligned}
& size\ (node\ l\ x\ y) \\
= \quad & \{\ \text{definition of } size\ \} \\
& size\ l + 1 + size\ r \\
\leqslant \quad & \{\ \text{induction hypothesis}\ \} \\
& 2^{height\ l} - 1 + 1 + 2^{height\ r} - 1 \\
\leqslant \quad & \{\ \text{arithmetic}\ \} \\
& 2^{1 + max\ (height\ l)\ (height\ r)} - 1 \\
\leqslant \quad & \{\ \text{definition of } height\ \} \\
& 2^{height\ t} - 1
\end{aligned}
$$

Answer 4.9 We have *partition p* $[\,] = ([\,],[\,])$. Setting $(ys,zs) = filter\ p\ xs$ gives

$$
\begin{aligned}
& partition\ p\ (x : xs) \\
= \quad & \{\ \text{definition of } partition\ \} \\
& (filter\ p\ (x : xs), filter\ (not \cdot p)\ (x : xs)) \\
= \quad & \{\ \text{definition of } filter\ \} \\
& \mathbf{if}\ p\ x\ \mathbf{then}\ (x : ys, zs)\ \mathbf{else}\ (ys, x : zs)
\end{aligned}
$$

from which we obtain

$$
partition\ p\ xs = foldr\ op\ ([\,],[\,])\ xs
$$
$$
\mathbf{where}\ op\ x\ (ys,zs) = \mathbf{if}\ p\ x\ \mathbf{then}\ (x : ys, zs)\ \mathbf{else}\ (ys, x : zs)
$$

Answer 4.10 The best way of computing *mktree* is to partition the input into three lists: those elements less than some given element, those elements equal to it, and those elements greater than it:

$$
partition3 :: Ord\ a \Rightarrow a \rightarrow [a] \rightarrow ([a],[a],[a])
$$
$$
partition3\ y = foldr\ op\ ([\,],[\,],[\,])
$$
$$
\mathbf{where}\ op\ x\ (us, vs, ws) \mid x < y \quad = (x : us, vs, ws)
$$
$$
\mid x == y = (us, x : vs, ws)
$$
$$
\mid x > y \quad = (us, vs, x : ws)
$$

Now we can define

$$
mktree :: Ord\ a \Rightarrow [a] \rightarrow Tree\ [a]
$$
$$
mktree\ [\,] = Null
$$
$$
mktree\ xs = Node\ (mktree\ us)\ vs\ (mktree\ ws)
$$
$$
\mathbf{where}\ (us, vs, ws) = partition3\ (head\ xs)\ xs
$$

This definition of *partition3* will be needed in Chapter 6.

Answer 4.11 By unfolding the recurrence for B we obtain

$$
\begin{aligned}
B(n+1) &= cn + 2B(n/2) \\
&= 2cn + 4B((n/2-1)/2) \\
&\leqslant 2cn + 4B(n/4) \\
&\leqslant \cdots \\
&\leqslant kcn + 2^k B(n/2^k)
\end{aligned}
$$

giving $B(n) = O(n \log n)$. We also have $B(n) = \Omega(n \log n)$. Similarly,

$$
\begin{aligned}
W(n+1) &= cn + W(n) \\
&= cn + c\,(n-1) + W(n-1) \\
&= cn + c\,(n-1) + \cdots + c \\
&= cn\,(n+1)/2
\end{aligned}
$$

giving $W(n) = \Theta(n^2)$.

Answer 4.12 For even n we have

$$
n! \geqslant n\,(n-1)\,(n-2)\cdots(n/2) \geqslant (n/2)^{n/2}
$$

so $\log(n!) \geqslant (n/2) \log(n/2) \geqslant (n/4) \log n$ for $n \geqslant 4$. The case for odd n is similar.

Answer 4.13 The definition is

$$
\begin{aligned}
&merge :: Ord\ a \Rightarrow [a] \rightarrow [a] \rightarrow [a] \\
&merge\ [\,]\ ys &&= ys \\
&merge\ xs\ [\,] &&= xs \\
&merge\ (x:xs)\ (y:ys)\ |\ x < y &&= x:merge\ xs\ (y:ys) \\
&\qquad\qquad\qquad\quad\ |\ x == y &&= x:merge\ xs\ ys \\
&\qquad\qquad\qquad\quad\ |\ x > y &&= y:merge\ (x:xs)\ ys
\end{aligned}
$$

The function *merge* merges two sorted lists, removing duplicates. Merging two lists of lengths m and n takes $\Theta(m+n)$ steps. We will return to merging in the following chapter.

Answer 4.14 Inserting a new element into a balanced tree of size m takes $\Theta(\log m)$ steps and produces a tree of size $m + 1$. Hence, if we do it for n elements, then the number of steps is

$$
\log m + \log(m+1) + \cdots + \log(m+n-1)
$$

which is $\Theta\left((m+n)\log(m+n)\right)$ steps.

The definition of *from* is

$$
\begin{aligned}
&from\ (l,r)\ xa = \\
&\quad \textbf{if}\ l == r\ \textbf{then}\ Null\ \textbf{else}\ node\ (from\ (l,m)\ xa)\ (xa\,!\,m)\ (from\ (m+1,r)\ xa) \\
&\quad \textbf{where}\ m = (l+r)\ \text{div}\ 2
\end{aligned}
$$

This method of defining *union* takes $\Theta(m+n)$ steps.

Answer 4.15 In the case of *deleteMin*, if *l* and *r* are two trees whose height difference is at most one and *t* is a tree whose height differs from that of *l* by at most one, then the height difference of *t* and *r* is at most two, meeting the precondition on *balance*. The argument for *combine* is similar.

Answer 4.16 We have

$$balanceL :: Set\ a \to a \to Set\ a \to Set\ a$$
$$balanceL\ t_1\ x\ (Node\ \_\ l\ y\ r) = \textbf{if}\ height\ l \geqslant height\ t_1 + 2$$
$$\textbf{then}\ balance\ (balanceL\ t_1\ x\ l)\ y\ r$$
$$\textbf{else}\ \ balance\ (node\ t_1\ x\ l)\ y\ r$$

Answer 4.17 We have $split\ x = pair\ mktree \cdot partition\ (\leqslant x) \cdot flatten$.

Chapter 5

Sorting

If binary search is the simplest example of the divide-and-conquer strategy, then sorting is arguably the most representative. By sorting we mean putting the elements of a given list into nondecreasing order. In this chapter we consider two basic divide-and-conquer algorithms for sorting. Nothing is assumed about the elements of the input except that they can be compared under $\leqslant$, so the type of *sort* is *sort* :: *Ord a* $\Rightarrow$ $[a]$ $\rightarrow$ $[a]$. In both algorithms the problem is divided into two subproblems, each of about half the size of the original, which are then combined to give the final result. Together, the dividing and combining phases involve $\Theta(n)$ comparisons on an input of length n, so the associated recurrence relation takes the form

$$T(n) = 2T(n/2) + \Theta(n)$$

which we have seen has the solution $T(n) = \Theta(n \log n)$. As we have also seen at the end of the previous chapter, this is asymptotically the best bound for a sorting algorithm based on comparisons.

We will also consider one other comparison-based algorithm, and two more that assume additional properties of the elements. All five algorithms have a common theme, which is that sorting can be viewed as a two-stage process in which one first builds a tree of some kind and then flattens it. In symbols,

sort = *flatten* · *mktree*

It seems a bit wasteful of space to erect a potentially large data structure and then demolish it, but under lazy evaluation the tree only exists in very small pieces at any one moment. In any case, it is usually easy to synthesise another definition of *sort* in which the tree no longer appears. Building a tree encapsulates the division stage of a divide-and-conquer algorithm, while flattening it captures the combining phase.

There are many different ways of sorting and it is not straightforward to say which is best. When expressed functionally, some famous sorting algorithms have different characteristics from when expressed as imperative code. What is a good algorithm in one setting may not be so good in the other. Naturally, we will concentrate only on good functional sorting algorithms.

A good sorting algorithm should aim for four qualities, whose combination is not always easy to achieve. First, it should be *fast*. Ideally, not only should it be asymptotically optimal in the number of comparisons it makes, but the constants involved in other operations should also be small. What would you prefer for sorting a list of small size n, an algorithm that takes $2n^2$ steps or one that takes $1000n \log n$ steps? An algorithm with a blindingly fast performance on average, but a quadratic-time performance in the worst case, might be acceptable. But then again it might not. Second, the algorithm should be *smooth*, meaning that the more sorted the input is, the faster the algorithm performs. In real life, large amounts of data are unlikely to be in truly random order and a good algorithm should take advantage of this fact. Third, the algorithm should be *stable*. When sorting records by key values, records with equal keys should appear in the same order in the output as in the input. One can always convert an unstable sorting algorithm into a stable one by first recording the position of each element in the list, then sorting the input by key, keeping elements with equal keys in separate 'buckets'. Then each bucket is sorted by the positions of the elements in the original list. Finally, the positions are discarded. Bucket sort is one of the algorithms we will describe later in the chapter. Finally, a sorting algorithm should be *compact*, meaning that it should be economical in its use of space as well as running time. This is much more difficult to achieve in a purely functional setting, especially a lazy one, and we will quietly ignore the problem of compactness in what follows. In summary, sorting algorithms, like cars, should be fast, smooth, stable, and compact.

5.1 Quicksort

Following on from the previous chapter, our first sorting algorithm arises as a result of flattening a binary search tree. Here is the relevant data type again:

data *Tree a* = *Null* | *Node* (*Tree a*) *a* (*Tree a*)

The function *mktree* builds a tree:

$$
\begin{aligned}
&mktree :: Ord\ a \Rightarrow [a] \to Tree\ a \\
&mktree\ [] \qquad = Null \\
&mktree\ (x : xs) = Node\ (mktree\ ys)\ x\ (mktree\ zs) \\
&\qquad\qquad\qquad \textbf{where}\ (ys, zs) = partition\ (<x)\ xs
\end{aligned}
$$

The function *partition* ($<x$) splits a list into two lists, comprising those elements less than x and those not less than x:

$$partition :: (a \rightarrow Bool) \rightarrow [a] \rightarrow ([a],[a])$$
$$partition\ p\ xs = foldr\ op\ ([],[])\ xs$$
$$\textbf{where}\ op\ x\ (ys,zs) = \textbf{if}\ p\ x\ \textbf{then}\ (x:ys,zs)\ \textbf{else}\ (ys,x:zs)$$

The function *flatten* flattens a tree:

$$flatten :: Tree\ a \rightarrow [a]$$
$$flatten\ Null \qquad = []$$
$$flatten\ (Node\ l\ x\ r) = flatten\ l \mathbin{+\mkern-10mu+} [x] \mathbin{+\mkern-10mu+} flatten\ r$$

Now define

$$qsort = flatten \cdot mktree$$

It is easy to eliminate the tree (see Exercise 5.2) and the result is one version of the famous algorithm known as Quicksort:

$$qsort :: Ord\ a \Rightarrow [a] \rightarrow [a]$$
$$qsort\ [] \qquad = []$$
$$qsort\ (x:xs) = qsort\ ys \mathbin{+\mkern-10mu+} [x] \mathbin{+\mkern-10mu+} qsort\ zs$$
$$\textbf{where}\ (ys,zs) = partition\ (<x)\ xs$$

However, this version of *qsort* is not fast, not smooth, and not compact. But it is stable. Stability is a result of the fact that *partition* does not change the order of the elements in the input. It is not fast because in the worst case *qsort* requires $\Theta(n^2)$ comparisons to sort a list of length n. One worst case arises when the input is already sorted, so *qsort* certainly isn't smooth. The problem lies in the choice of the partitioning element (or *pivot*) x, a choice that determines how equal in size the two sublists produced by *partition* will be. Choosing the first element of the input as pivot can lead to two very unbalanced subproblems. Better is to choose a random element of the input; better still is to choose the median element. But finding the median takes time. We will consider two median-finding algorithms in the following chapter. It is the case that *qsort* is fast on average, requiring only $\Theta(n \log n)$ steps with a small constant of proportionality. Finally, *qsort* as defined above can be very inefficient in its use of space, requiring $\Theta(n^2)$ units in the worst case. Space efficiency can be improved by tweaking the definition of *qsort* but we won't go into details.

Nevertheless, Quicksort is a decent sorting algorithm when implemented in an imperative setting. In such a setting, Quicksort can be formulated in terms of mutable arrays rather than lists, and the partitioning phase can be carried out *in place*, meaning that the input array can be used as working space for partitioning. No other space, apart from the stack needed to implement the recursion, is required. But the space-efficient version sacrifices stability. We will not dwell further on the merits and demerits of Quicksort, partly because the topic has been addressed in

[1], and partly because there are better functional algorithms for sorting. Additional aspects of Quicksort are taken up in the exercises.

5.2 Mergesort

Quicksort is a divide-and-conquer algorithm in which the hard work is done in the dividing phase – the combining phase is just concatenation. By contrast, the next sorting algorithm, Mergesort, performs more work in the combining phase and less in the partition phase.

Again we begin with a tree. This time the tree is a slightly different species:

data *Tree a* = *Null* | *Leaf a* | *Node* (*Tree a*) (*Tree a*)

There are no constraints on the order of the elements in a tree and one can build a tree for lists of arbitrary type. The ordering on the elements comes into play when we flatten a tree:

$$
\begin{aligned}
&flatten :: Ord\ a \Rightarrow Tree\ a \to [a] \\
&flatten\ Null && = [] \\
&flatten\ (Leaf\ x) && = [x] \\
&flatten\ (Node\ t_1\ t_2) = merge\ (flatten\ t_1)\ (flatten\ t_2)
\end{aligned}
$$

The function *merge* merges two sorted lists into one:

$$
\begin{aligned}
&merge :: Ord\ a \Rightarrow [a] \to [a] \to [a] \\
&merge\ []\quad\ ys && = ys \\
&merge\ xs\quad [] && = xs \\
&merge\ (x:xs)\ (y:ys)\ |\ x \leqslant y && = x:merge\ xs\ (y:ys) \\
&\qquad\qquad\qquad\qquad |\ otherwise = y:merge\ (x:xs)\ ys
\end{aligned}
$$

Merging two lists of lengths m and n by *merge* requires at most $m+n$ comparisons (see the exercises). The cost of flattening a tree depends on the number of leaves in each subtree. If a tree of size n has two subtrees each of size $n/2$, then the number of comparisons $T(n)$ required satisfies

$$T(n) = 2T(n/2) + n$$

with solution $T(n) = \Theta(n \log n)$. It follows that if we can build a tree for a list of length n in this time, and the tree has the *size-balanced* property that each node has two subtrees that differ in size by at most 1, then sorting a list of length n can be done with $\Theta(n \log n)$ comparisons.

Here is a divide-and-conquer algorithm to build a size-balanced tree:

$$
\begin{aligned}
&mktree :: [a] \to Tree\ a \\
&mktree\ []\quad = Null \\
&mktree\ [x]\ = Leaf\ x \\
&mktree\ xs\ = Node\ (mktree\ ys)\ (mktree\ zs)\ \textbf{where}\ (ys, zs) = halve\ xs
\end{aligned}
$$

The function *halve* splits a list into two equal halves:

$$halve\ xs = (take\ m\ xs, drop\ m\ xs)\ \textbf{where}\ m = length\ xs\ \text{div}\ 2$$

This definition involves three traversals of the list, one to compute its length, and two more to perform the splitting. No human would split up a list this way. Instead, they would simply deal out the elements alternately into two piles:

$$halve = foldr\ op\ ([],[])\ \textbf{where}\ op\ x\ (ys,zs) = (zs,x:ys)$$

This version of *halve* produces a different result, but the two sublists have the same sizes as before and each is a subsequence of the input. For example,

$$halve\ [1..9] = ([2,4,6,8],[1,3,5,7,9])$$

Since the order of the elements in the tree is immaterial, this definition of *halve* is perfectly adequate.

The running time of *mktree* satisfies essentially the same recurrence as *flatten* so it takes $\Theta(n\log n)$ steps to build a tree. Clearly the tree has the size-balanced property. Now if we define

$$msort = flatten \cdot mktree$$

then we obtain another famous algorithm called Mergesort. It is easy to eliminate the tree, and the result is

$$\begin{aligned}
msort\ [] &= []\\
msort\ [x] &= [x]\\
msort\ xs &= merge\ (msort\ ys)\ (msort\ zs)\\
&\quad\textbf{where}\ (ys,zs) = halve\ xs
\end{aligned}$$

Unlike Quicksort, Mergesort has a $\Theta(n\log n)$ running time, so it is fast. It is stable with the first definition of *halve*, but not with the second definition. However, Mergesort is not smooth, taking $\Theta(n\log n)$ steps even when the input is already sorted.

Returning to *mktree*, it is possible to build a size-balanced tree in linear time. The method was covered in [1] as an example of the tupling technique, so we will just sketch the idea and state the result. The idea is to avoid repeated halving, by defining *mkpair n xs* = (*mktree* (*take n xs*), *drop n xs*). A direct recursive definition of *mkpair* can then be derived, leading to

$$\begin{aligned}
mktree\ xs &= fst\ (mkpair\ (length\ xs)\ xs)\\
mkpair\ 0\ xs &= (Null,xs)\\
mkpair\ 1\ xs &= (Leaf\ (head\ xs), tail\ xs)\\
mkpair\ n\ xs &= (Node\ t_1\ t_2, zs)\\
&\quad\textbf{where}\ (t_1, ys) = mkpair\ m\ xs\\
&\qquad\quad (t_2, zs) = mkpair\ (n-m)\ ys\\
&\qquad\quad m\quad\ \ = n\ \text{div}\ 2
\end{aligned}$$

The running time $T(n)$ of *mkpair n* satisfies $T(n) = 2T(n/2) + \Theta(1)$, with solution $T(n) = \Theta(n)$.

There is another way of building a tree in linear time. Although the result will not be a size-balanced tree, it will be good enough to ensure that the corresponding version of Mergesort still has optimal asymptotic time complexity. The idea is to switch from a divide-and-conquer scheme to a *bottom-up* scheme. First, the list of elements is converted into a list of leaves. Provided this list is not empty or a singleton list, it is then halved in size by combining adjacent pairs of trees into larger trees. The halving process is repeated until only one tree is left:

> *mktree* [] = *Null*
> *mktree xs* = *unwrap* (*until single* (*pairWith Node*) (*map Leaf xs*))

> *pairWith f* []   = []
> *pairWith f* [x]   = [x]
> *pairWith f* (x : y : xs) = f x y : pairWith f xs

The functions *unwrap* and *single* (and *wrap*, used below) were defined in Exercise 1.3. The running time $T(n)$ of this version of *mktree* satisfies

$$T(n) = T(n/2) + \Theta(n)$$

Thus $T(n) = \Theta(n)$, the same as before. If we use this bottom-up version of *mktree* in the definition of *msort*, then we can synthesise another definition:

> *msort* [] = []
> *msort xs* = *unwrap* (*until single* (*pairWith merge*) (*map wrap xs*))

This synthesis is more interesting than the previous one, and the details are provided in the exercises. This version of Mergesort, called *Bottom-up* Mergesort (and sometimes *Straight* Mergesort), converts the input into a list of singleton lists and then repeatedly merges those lists in pairs until a single list is left. To time this version of *msort* assume that the length n of the input is a power of two. The first pass involves repeatedly merging two singleton lists, taking at most $2 \times n/2 = n$ comparisons. The second pass involves repeatedly merging two lists of length two, taking at most $4 \times n/4 = n$ comparisons, and so on. That gives a total of at most kn comparisons, where $n = 2^k$. For general n we have that Bottom-up Mergesort takes $\Theta(n \log n)$ comparisons.

Looking deeper into Bottom-up Mergesort, we can see that it is not essential to start with a list of singleton lists. Instead, we could split the input into nondecreasing runs and begin the merging process with that:

> *msort* [] = []
> *msort xs* = *unwrap* (*until single* (*pairWith merge*) (*runs xs*))

The function *runs* splits a list into runs of nondecreasing values:

$$runs :: Ord\ a \Rightarrow [a] \to [[a]]$$
$$runs = foldr\ op\ []$$

$$\textbf{where}\ op\ x\ [] \qquad\qquad\qquad = [[x]]$$
$$op\ x\ ((y:xs):xss)\ |\ x \leqslant y \quad = (x:y:xs):xss$$
$$|\ otherwise = [x]:(y:xs):xss$$

The function *runs* processes the input from right to left. The next element is added
to the front of the current run if possible; otherwise it begins a new run. This version
of *msort*, called *Smooth* Mergesort (and sometimes *Natural* Mergesort), is smooth;
in particular, if the input is already sorted, it needs only $\Theta(n)$ comparisons to return
the input untouched. The Haskell *Data.List* function *sort* is similar, except that it
is more cunning and splits the input into both ascending runs and descending runs,
taking care to reverse the descending runs. Here is the definition:

$$runs\ [x] \qquad = [[x]]$$
$$runs\ (x:y:xs)$$
$$\quad |\ x \leqslant y \qquad = upruns\ y\ (x:)\ xs$$
$$\quad |\ otherwise = dnruns\ y\ [x]\ xs$$

$$upruns\ x\ f\ [] \ = [f\ [x]]$$
$$upruns\ x\ f\ (y:ys)$$
$$\quad |\ x \leqslant y \qquad = upruns\ y\ (f \cdot (x:))\ ys$$
$$\quad |\ otherwise = f\ [x]:runs\ (y:ys)$$

$$dnruns\ x\ xs\ [] \ = [x:xs]$$
$$dnruns\ x\ xs\ (y:ys)$$
$$\quad |\ x > y \qquad = dnruns\ y\ (x:xs)\ ys$$
$$\quad |\ otherwise = (x:xs):runs\ (y:ys)$$

This time, *runs* processes the input from left to right. The second argument of both
upruns and *dnruns* is an accumulating parameter, a list in the case of *dnruns* and a
function in the case of *upruns*. The first argument of *dnruns* is the minimum value
encountered so far, while the first argument of *upruns* is the maximum. In the case
of *dnruns*, if the next value in the input is strictly smaller than the minimum, then
the minimum is added to the front of the run, and the new value becomes the current
minimum. Thus, the runs produced by *dnruns* are in strictly increasing order. In
the case of *upruns*, if the next value is no smaller than the maximum, then the
maximum is added, in effect, to the back of the run, and the next value becomes the
new maximum. Thus, the runs produced by *upruns* are in weakly increasing order.
The asymmetry between *dnruns* and *upruns*, the first producing strictly increasing
runs and the second only weakly increasing runs, has as a consequence that the
resulting sorting algorithm is stable. We omit a formal proof, but simply give an
example. Using *a*, *b*, and *c* to indicate relative order in the original list, we have

$$runs \ [6,4,3_a,2_a,2_b,1_a,1_b,2_c,1_c,3_b]$$
$$= [[2_a,3_a,4,6],[1_a,2_b],[1_b,2_c],[1_c,3_b]]$$

Merging these lists in pairs, and then merging the results, produces the sorted list

which is the required order for a stable sort.

Four versions of Mergesort have been covered in this section, all of which have relatively short definitions. The final one is probably the best, being fast, smooth, and stable. As we said above, it is this definition of Mergesort that is provided in the Haskell library *Data.List*. Well, not quite. The Haskell definition is more general in that the comparison test is provided as an extra argument. To motivate the definition, consider how you would sort a list into descending rather than ascending order. All the algorithms above have tacitly assumed that sorting means sorting into ascending order. One can of course define *sortDown = reverse · sort*, but this definition involves another traversal and that adds overhead. There are other kinds of comparison between elements that one can think of. For instance, we might conceivably want to sort a list of numbers so that all the even ones come first. To achieve this generality, *Data.List* provides two more functions

$$sortBy :: (a \rightarrow a \rightarrow Ordering) \rightarrow [a] \rightarrow [a]$$
$$sortOn :: Ord \ b \Rightarrow (a \rightarrow b) \rightarrow [a] \rightarrow [a]$$

The type *Ordering* is defined in the Standard Prelude:

data *Ordering* $= LT \mid EQ \mid GT$

The function *compare* is a method in the type class *Ord* and has the type

$$compare :: Ord \ a \Rightarrow a \rightarrow a \rightarrow Ordering$$

For example, *compare* $3 \ 4 = LT$. As two examples,

$$sortBy \ compare \ [3,1,4] \qquad = [1,3,4]$$
$$sortBy \ (flip \ compare) \ [3,1,4] = [4,3,1]$$

The function *sortBy cmp* sorts according to the weird even–odd ordering described above, where *cmp* is defined by

$$cmp \ x \ y = compare \ (odd \ x, x) \ (odd \ y, y)$$

This definition exploits the fact that *False* < *True* in Haskell. For example

$$sortBy \ cmp \ [1 .. 10] = [2,4,6,8,10,1,3,5,7,9]$$

The variant *sortOn* sorts according to the values of a given function. For example, *sortOn fst* sorts a list of pairs in order of first components. Exercise 5.12 asks you to define this variant. We will need *sortBy* and *sortOn* later on in the book, but for the while we continue with the assumption that sorting means sorting into ascending order.

5.3 Heapsort

Our next sorting algorithm, Heapsort, involves a different kind of tree from that in the previous section, one that is identical to the type of binary search trees except that node labels are placed before the two subtrees:

data *Tree a* = *Null* | *Node a* (*Tree a*) (*Tree a*)

We can flatten such a tree by

$$flatten :: Ord\ a \Rightarrow Tree\ a \rightarrow [a]$$
$$flatten\ Null \qquad = []$$
$$flatten\ (Node\ x\ u\ v) = x : merge\ (flatten\ u)\ (flatten\ v)$$

By definition a tree is a *heap* if flattening it produces a list in nondecreasing order. Thus a heap is a tree in which the value at a node is no larger than the values in either of its subtrees. If the tree is size-balanced, then flattening it takes $\Theta\ (n \log n)$ steps for a tree of size n.

It is easy enough to build a size-balanced heap in linearithmic time (i.e. $O(n \log n)$ steps for a list of length n) – see Exercise 5.13. However, as we will now show, it is possible to build such a heap in linear time. The idea is to compute *mkheap* as the composition of two other functions: *mktree*, which builds a size-balanced tree, and *heapify*, which reorganises the labels to ensure the heap condition. We will leave the linear-time implementation of *mktree* as another exercise and concentrate on *heapify*. The definition starts out easily enough:

$$heapify :: Ord\ a \Rightarrow Tree\ a \rightarrow Tree\ a$$
$$heapify\ Null \qquad = Null$$
$$heapify\ (Node\ x\ u\ v) = siftDown\ x\ (heapify\ u)\ (heapify\ v)$$

It remains to define *siftDown*. This function is another smart constructor, taking a value and two heaps and building a heap by sifting the value downwards until the heap property is restored:

$$siftDown :: Ord\ a \Rightarrow a \rightarrow Tree\ a \rightarrow Tree\ a \rightarrow Tree\ a$$
$$siftDown\ x\ Null\ Null = Node\ x\ Null\ Null$$
$$siftDown\ x\ (Node\ y\ u\ v)\ Null$$
$$\quad | x \leqslant y \qquad = Node\ x\ (Node\ y\ u\ v)\ Null$$
$$\quad | otherwise \quad = Node\ y\ (siftDown\ x\ u\ v)\ Null$$
$$siftDown\ x\ Null\ (Node\ y\ u\ v)$$
$$\quad | x \leqslant y \qquad = Node\ x\ Null\ (Node\ y\ u\ v)$$
$$\quad | otherwise \quad = Node\ y\ Null\ (siftDown\ x\ u\ v)$$
$$siftDown\ x\ (Node\ y\ ul\ ur)\ (Node\ z\ vl\ vr)$$
$$\quad | x \leqslant min\ y\ z = Node\ x\ (Node\ y\ ul\ ur)\ (Node\ z\ vl\ vr)$$
$$\quad | y \leqslant min\ x\ z = Node\ y\ (siftDown\ x\ ul\ ur)\ (Node\ z\ vl\ vr)$$
$$\quad | z \leqslant min\ x\ y = Node\ z\ (Node\ y\ ul\ ur)\ (siftDown\ x\ vl\ vr)$$

Note that *heapify* does not change the structure of a heap, so *heapify* returns a size-balanced tree if given one. To show that *heapify* takes $\Theta(n)$ steps when applied to a size-balanced tree t of size n, observe that *siftDown* is applied to every subtree of t, including t itself, and in the worst case can take time proportional to the height of the subtree. Suppose t has height h. Then t has one subtree of height h, at most two subtrees of height $h-1$, at most four subtrees of height $h-2$, and so on. Hence the total running time of *heapify* is proportional to at most

$$h + 2(h-1) + 4(h-2) + \cdots + 2^{h-1} = \sum_{k=1}^{h} 2^{h-k} k = 2^h \sum_{k=1}^{h} k/2^k < 2^{h+1}$$

Finally, a size-balanced tree of size n has height $\Theta(\log n)$ (in fact it has the minimum possible height $\lceil \log(n+1) \rceil$ – see the exercises) and so $T(n) = \Theta(n)$.

Here, finally, is the definition of Heapsort:

> *hsort* :: *Ord a* $\Rightarrow$ $[a] \to [a]$
> *hsort* = *flatten* · *heapify* · *mktree*

A tree is built in $\Theta(n)$ steps, heapified in $\Theta(n)$ steps, and flattened in $\Theta(n \log n)$ steps. Thus *hsort* takes $\Theta(n \log n)$ steps. Unlike Quicksort or Mergesort, the tree cannot be eliminated by fusing the component functions, so Heapsort necessarily involves building a tree. In an imperative setting, when the input is given in an array, the tree can be stored in the array by juggling with array indices, so Heapsort can be made in-place. Heapsort is fast, but not smooth, stable, or compact. On random data it turns out to be somewhat slower than the best version of Mergesort, so we still have a champion. On the other hand, heaps are useful for other purposes, including the implementation of priority queues, a topic we will take up in Chapter 8.

5.4 Bucketsort and Radixsort

We turn now to two completely different kinds of sorting algorithm. Neither is based on comparisons between elements of some arbitrary type, so sorting no longer has the type *sort* :: *Ord a* $\Rightarrow$ $[a] \to [a]$. Instead these two algorithms exploit the structure of the elements to be sorted. To set the scene, consider sorting a list of words, where a word is a list of alphabetic characters. That means sorting the words into lexical order. We can use Mergesort for this purpose:

> **type** *Word* = $[Char]$
> *sortWords* :: $[Word] \to [Word]$
> *sortWords* = *msort*

As we have seen, sorting a list of n words this way involves $O(n \log n)$ comparisons between words. However, comparing two words does not take constant time. If there are at most k letters in each word, then comparing them will take $\Theta(k)$ character comparisons in the worst case. That means the true cost of computing *sortWords* is $O(kn \log n)$ steps. The two algorithms in this section reduce the cost to $O(kn)$ steps.

The way we will view the problem is to think of a word as containing *fields* of information, the fields being the first character of the word, the second character, and so on. Similarly, an integer can be defined in terms of the fields of its decimal digits. These fields can be extracted by providing a list of total functions, which we will call *discriminators*, each of which extracts one possible field. For instance with decimals of length k, there will be k discriminators, one for each decimal digit. Given a list of discriminators, two elements x and y are lexically ordered if the following test returns *True*:

> *ordered* :: *Ord b* $\Rightarrow$ $[a \to b] \to a \to a \to Bool$
> *ordered* $[\,]$ $x\,y$ $= True$
> *ordered* $(d:ds)\,x\,y = (d\,x < d\,y) \lor ((d\,x == d\,y) \land ordered\,ds\,x\,y)$

In this formulation of the problem, the fields themselves have to be elements from some ordered type.

The obvious way to sort a list of words is to divide them into piles, or *buckets*, according to their first letter. Each bucket is then sorted in the same way, but on the second letter, and so on. At the end of this process there will be lots of little buckets, each containing a single word. These buckets then have to be combined in the right order to give the final sorted list. The simplest way to implement this idea is in terms of a tree, and the kind of tree we will need is as follows:

> **data** *Tree a = Leaf a | Node [Tree a]*

This kind of tree is sometimes called a *rose tree*. A rose tree therefore is either a leaf containing a value, or a node that can have an arbitrary list of subtrees. We can build a rose tree by

> *mktree* :: *(Bounded b, Enum b, Ord b)* $\Rightarrow$ $[a \to b] \to [a] \to Tree\,[a]$
> *mktree* $[\,]$ xs $= Leaf\,xs$
> *mktree* $(d:ds)\,xs = Node\,(map\,(mktree\,ds)\,(ptn\,d\,xs))$

A rose tree is built by partitioning the list into buckets according to the first field. Each bucket is then converted into a tree by applying the algorithm recursively to the remaining fields. Later on we will modify this definition in the interests of efficiency. The reason for the type-class constraints on *mktree* will become apparent in a moment.

The function *ptn* partitions a list into buckets according to the field extracted by the discriminator:

$$ptn :: (Bounded\ b, Enum\ b, Ord\ b) \Rightarrow (a \rightarrow b) \rightarrow [a] \rightarrow [[a]]$$
$$ptn\ d\ xs = [filter\ (\lambda x.d\ x == m)\ xs \mid m \leftarrow rng]$$
$$\mathbf{where}\ rng = [minBound .. maxBound]$$

The definition of rng explains why the result type of a discriminator has to be both bounded and enumerable. The definition of ptn is very inefficient, and for two quite separate reasons. Firstly, rng may be a very long list. For example, since Haskell's *Char* type represents all Unicode characters, the length of $rng :: [Char]$ is over a million. Secondly, the result of ptn is computed by repeatedly traversing the input. If rng has length r and the input has length n, then ptn requires $r \times n$ evaluations of the discriminator. We will address this problem of efficiency later on.

Having built a tree, we can now flatten it:

$$flatten :: Tree\ [a] \rightarrow [a]$$
$$flatten\ (Leaf\ xs) = xs$$
$$flatten\ (Node\ ts) = concatMap\ flatten\ ts$$

The resulting sorting algorithm is known as Bucketsort:

$$bsort\ ds\ xs = flatten\ (mktree\ ds\ xs)$$

Well, not quite. In Bucketsort as traditionally presented there are no trees. We should be familiar with this situation by now, and the next step is to eliminate the intermediate tree. The base case $bsort\ [\ ]\ xs = xs$ is easy. For the induction step we reason

$$\begin{array}{ll}
& bsort\ (d:ds)\ xs \\
= & \{\ \text{definition of } bsort\ \} \\
& flatten\ (mktree\ (d:ds)\ xs) \\
= & \{\ \text{definition of } mktree\ \} \\
& flatten\ (Node\ (map\ (mktree\ ds)\ (ptn\ d\ xs))) \\
= & \{\ \text{definition of } flatten\ \} \\
& concatMap\ (flatten \cdot mktree\ ds)\ (ptn\ d\ xs) \\
= & \{\ \text{definition of } bsort\ \} \\
& concatMap\ (bsort\ ds)\ (ptn\ d\ xs)
\end{array}$$

Hence we have shown

$$bsort\ [\ ]\ xs \qquad = xs$$
$$bsort\ (d:ds)\ xs = concatMap\ (bsort\ ds)\ (ptn\ d\ xs)$$

So far, so good. But we can push the calculation one more step if we exploit a simple but important fact, namely that

$$map\ (bsort\ ds)\ (ptn\ d\ xs) = ptn\ d\ (bsort\ ds\ xs)$$

Informally, this identity asserts that ptn is stable: partitioning a sorted sequence yields a collection of sorted buckets. A detailed proof is given in the exercises. Assuming it holds, we can continue:

$$concatMap\ (bsort\ ds)\ (ptn\ d\ xs)$$
$$=\quad \{\ above\ stability\ property\ \}$$
$$concat\ (ptn\ d\ (bsort\ ds\ xs))$$

And that gives us Radixsort:

$$rsort :: (Bounded\ b, Enum\ b, Ord\ b) \Rightarrow [a \rightarrow b] \rightarrow [a] \rightarrow [a]$$
$$rsort\ [\ ]\ xs\quad\ \ = xs$$
$$rsort\ (d:ds)\ xs = concat\ (ptn\ d\ (rsort\ ds\ xs))$$

Whereas *bsort* sorts on the most significant field first, *rsort* sorts on the most significant field last. The difference is that in *bsort* the buckets have to be kept separate; sorting each bucket means dividing each bucket into further buckets, and so on. At the end there will be a long array of singleton buckets, which are only then reassembled into the final list. In *rsort* the buckets can be combined after each pass. Indeed, Radixsort was used in the early days of sorting punched cards with a mechanical sorter. The sorter was used to divide the cards into buckets on the least significant column of a card. The buckets were then carefully reassembled by a human sorter into a single deck of cards without changing the order of any of the cards in a single bucket or the order of the buckets themselves. The entire deck was then replaced in the sorter and sorted again on the next least significant digit, and so on. A much simpler process for a human to carry out.

Let us now return to the problem of computing *ptn* efficiently. To avoid a potentially huge range of values, most of which will probably not occur in a given field, it is best to make the range (l, u) of values in a field explicit. We will assume for simplicity that all fields have the same range. Second, we suppose that field elements are of a type that can be array indices, which is to say they are elements of the type class *Ix*. Then we can avoid multiple traversals of the input by accumulating the elements into an array:

$$ptn :: Ix\ b \Rightarrow (b, b) \rightarrow (a \rightarrow b) \rightarrow [a] \rightarrow [[a]]$$
$$ptn\ (l, u)\ d\ xs = elems\ xa$$
$$\textbf{where}\ xa = accumArray\ snoc\ [\ ]\ (l, u)\ (zip\ (map\ d\ xs)\ xs)$$
$$snoc\ xs\ x = xs \mathbin{+\mkern-8mu+} [x]$$

It is important for the stability property above that *ptn* should ensure that the order in each bucket is the same as in the input, which explains why array entries are computed by adding a new value to the end of a list via *snoc*. But *snoc* is not a constant-time operation, so building the array can take $\Theta(n^2)$ steps in the worst case, when all the elements go into the same slot. One solution is to use symmetric lists; another is to insert elements in reverse order, and then to reverse each list when extracting the array elements:

$$ptn\ (l,u)\ d\ xs = map\ reverse\ (elems\ xa)$$
$$\textbf{where}\ xa = accumArray\ (flip\ (:))\ [\,]\ (l,u)\ (zip\ (map\ d\ xs)\ xs)$$

This version of ptn takes $\Theta(n)$ steps for an input of length n. Here is the revised definition of $rsort$ that uses the new ptn:

$$rsort :: Ix\ b \Rightarrow (b,b) \to [a \to b] \to [a] \to [a]$$
$$rsort\ bb\ [\,]\ xs\qquad = xs$$
$$rsort\ bb\ (d:ds)\ xs = concat\ (ptn\ bb\ d\ (rsort\ bb\ ds\ xs))$$

If there are k discriminators, then $rsort$ takes $\Theta(kn)$ steps because there are k calls of ptn, each of which takes $\Theta(n)$ steps, and one application of $concat$, which also takes linear time.

Finally, let us specialise $rsort$ to the case where the input is a nonempty list of natural numbers. Each number is converted into a list of digits by applying $show$, and then padded with leading zeros to ensure that each decimal has the same length. We can define the discriminator functions by

$$discs :: [Nat] \to [Nat \to Char]$$
$$discs\ xs\ = [\lambda x.pad\ k\ (show\ x)\ !!\ i\ |\ i \leftarrow [0..k-1]]$$
$$\qquad\qquad\textbf{where}\ k = maximum\ (map\ (length \cdot show)\ xs)$$
$$pad\ k\ xs = replicate\ (k - length\ xs)\ \text{'0'} + xs$$

And now we have

$$irsort :: [Nat] \to [Nat]$$
$$irsort\ xs = rsort\ (\text{'0'}, \text{'9'})\ (discs\ xs)\ xs$$

How does $irsort$ compare with the current champion, Smooth Mergesort? As one experiment, we sorted a list of a million randomly generated integers, all in the range $(0, 10000)$ – so there are five discriminators. Radixsort took 65% of the time of Smooth Mergesort. In fact, Smooth Mergesort only begins to pull ahead when there are eight or more discriminators.

5.5 Sorting sums

We end the chapter by taking a look at a famous unsolved problem connected with sorting. Suppose A is some ordered type and $+$ is some monotonic binary operation on A, so

$$x \leqslant x' \wedge y \leqslant y' \;\Rightarrow\; x+y \leqslant x'+y'$$

In concrete code we take A to be a synonym for *Integer* and $+$ to be numerical addition. Consider the problem of computing *sortsums*, where

$$sortsums :: [A] \to [A] \to [A]$$
$$sortsums\ xs\ ys = sort\ [x+y\ |\ x \leftarrow xs, y \leftarrow ys]$$

Supposing both lists have length n, what is asymptotically the best possible running time of any algorithm for computing *sortsums*? There are n^2 sums, so sorting involves $\Omega(n^2 \log n)$ comparisons on elements of A in the worst case. The bound $\Omega(n^2 \log n)$ does not depend on $+$ being monotonic but, even if it is, the bound is the same. We will prove this fact below.

But now suppose we assume more about $+$ and A, specifically that $(A, +)$ is an *Abelian group*. Thus $+$ is associative and commutative, with an identity element we will write as 0, and an operation *negate* such that $x + negate\ x = 0$. For example, the integers form an Abelian group under addition. What is the best bound in this case? The answer is that nobody knows. It cannot be better than $O(n^2)$ because it takes n^2 steps to produce the answer, but there is still a gap between $O(n^2)$ and $O(n^2 \log n)$.

What if additional properties of A were assumed? After all, integers have more structure than just being an Abelian group under addition. Integers can be multiplied as well as added – they form an algebraic *ring*. Does that help? Again, nobody knows. It remains an open problem, some 40 years after it was first posed in [6], as to whether the total cost of computing *sortsums* can be reduced to $O(n^2)$ steps.

However, some progress has been made. In particular, Jean-Luc Lambert [9] proved that, if $(A, +)$ is an Abelian group, then *sortsums* can be computed with $O(n^2)$ comparisons between elements of A. His algorithm is another nifty example of divide and conquer, and we describe it below. However, Lambert's algorithm does require $Cn^2 \log n$ additional operations, including other 'housekeeping' comparisons; moreover C is quite large. Thus the total running time does not beat the $O(n^2 \log n)$ bound.

Here is a proof that $\Omega(n^2 \log n)$ is a lower bound on *sortsums* when the only assumption made is that $+$ is monotonic. Suppose xs and ys are both sorted into increasing order and consider the $n \times n$ matrix $[[x + y \mid y \leftarrow ys] \mid x \leftarrow xs]$. Each row and column of the matrix is therefore in increasing order. The grid is of the same kind that we saw in two-dimensional search in the previous chapter. The matrix is an example of what is known as a standard Young tableau, and it follows from Theorem H of Section 5.1.4 of [8] that there are precisely

$$E(n) = (n^2)! \left/ \left(\frac{(2n-1)!}{(n-1)!} \frac{(2n-2)!}{(n-2)!} \cdots \frac{n!}{0!} \right) \right.$$

ways of assigning the values 1 to n^2 to the elements of the matrix. Each such assignment determines a potential permutation that can sort the input, so in the associated decision tree there have to be at least $E(n)$ leaves. Using the fact that $\log E(n) = \Omega(n^2 \log n)$, we conclude that at least this number of comparisons between elements of A is required.

Now for the meat of the exercise. Lambert's algorithm depends on two simple facts. Define the subtraction operation $(-)$ by $x - y = x + negate\ y$. Then we have

$$x + y = x - negate\ y \tag{5.1}$$

and

$$x - y \leqslant x' - y' \iff x - x' \leqslant y - y' \tag{5.2}$$

Verification of (5.1) is easy, but (5.2), which we leave as an exercise, requires all the properties of an Abelian group. Here in outline is how (5.1) and (5.2) are used. First, we use fact (5.1) to sort subtractions rather than sums:

> $sortsums\ xs\ ys = sortsubs\ xs\ (map\ negate\ ys)$
> $sortsubs\ xs\ ys\ =\ sort\ [x - y \mid x \leftarrow xs, y \leftarrow ys]$

Second, we use fact (5.2) to compute $sortsubs\ xs\ ys$ by computing instead the two lists $xxs = sortsubs\ xs\ xs$ and $yys = sortsubs\ ys\ ys$. By using a divide-and-conquer scheme, Lambert showed how the two lists xxs and yys can be computed with only $O(n^2)$ comparisons between elements of A. The two lists can be merged to give $sortsubs\ xs\ ys$ – but crucially, *without any further comparisons* on elements of A. Since $x - y \leqslant x' - y'$ precisely in the case that $x - x'$ precedes $y - y'$ in the merged list, the merged list can be computed using *precedence comparisons* only, comparisons between suitable integer labels, not elements of A.

Let us deal first with the merging step. We label values of type A with natural numbers and change the definition of $sortsubs$ to read

> $sortsubs\ xs\ ys = map\ fst\ (sortWith\ abs\ xis\ yis)$
> $\quad$ **where** $xis\ =\ zip\ xs\ [0..n-1]$
> $\qquad\qquad yis\ =\ zip\ ys\ [n..]$
> $\qquad\qquad n\quad =\ length\ xs$
> $\qquad\qquad abs = merge\ (sortsubs_1\ xis)\ (sortsubs_1\ yis)$

The elements of the two lists xs and ys are given distinct labels, from 0 upwards. With *Label* a type synonym for natural numbers, and *Pair* a synonym for pairs of labels, the two component sorting functions in the new definition of $sortsubs$ have types

> $sortsubs_1 :: [(A, Label)] \rightarrow [(A, Pair)]$
> $sortWith :: [(A, Pair)] \rightarrow [(A, Label)] \rightarrow [(A, Label)] \rightarrow [(A, Pair)]$

The first function, $sortsubs_1$, is defined in the first instance by

> $sortsubs_1\ xis = sort\ (subs\ xis\ xis)$
> $subs\ xis\ yis = [(x - y, (i,j)) \mid (x,i) \leftarrow xis, (y,j) \leftarrow yis]$

Thus $sortsubs_1$ sorts subtractions over a single labelled list, retaining label information to show the origin of the subtraction. For example, the element $(6, (11, 3))$ records that 6 is the result of subtracting the element in position 3 in xis from the element in position 11. As defined, $sortsubs_1$ takes $O(n^2 \log n)$ steps. Below we show how this can be reduced to $O(n^2)$ steps.

We deal with *sortWith* next. The definition, which uses both the Haskell function *sortBy* and an array, is as follows:

$sortWith\ abs\ xis\ yis = sortBy\ cmp\ (subs\ xis\ yis)$
    where $cmp\ (\_,(i,k))\ (\_,(j,l)) = compare\ (a\,!\,(i,j))\ (a\,!\,(k,l))$
       $a = array\ bs\ (zip\ labelPairs\ [0..])$
       $labelPairs = map\ snd\ abs$
       $bs = (minimum\ labelPairs, maximum\ labelPairs)$

Now consider

$abs = merge\ (sortsubs_1\ xis)\ (sortsubs_1\ yis)$

Here *map fst abs* is a list of A-values in nondecreasing order, and *map snd abs* is a list of corresponding pairs of labels. This second list is just what we need to determine the result of a comparison test, for $x_i - y_k \leqslant x_j - y_l$ if and only if (i,j) precedes (k,l) in the list *labelPairs*. We compute precedence information quickly by creating an array indexed by pairs of labels whose entries are positive integers. Although *sortWith* depends on comparisons, the comparisons are between pairs of labels, not elements of A.

It remains to compute a better version of $sortsubs_1$, and it is here that divide and conquer enters the picture. We make use of the identity

$sortsubs_1\ (xis \mathbin{+\!\!+} yis)\ (xis \mathbin{+\!\!+} yis) =$
   $merge\ (merge\ (sortsubs_1\ xis\ xis)\ (sortsubs_1\ xis\ yis))$
       $(merge\ (sortsubs_1\ yis\ xis)\ (sortsubs_1\ yis\ yis))$

Two of the subterms, $sortsubs_1\ xis\ xis$ and $sortsubs_1\ yis\ yis$, are computed recursively, and the results are merged to give *abs*. Next, $sortsubs_1\ xis\ yis$ is computed via

$sortsubs_1\ xis\ yis = sortWith\ abs\ (subs\ xis\ yis)$

Finally, $sortsubs_1\ yis\ xis$ can be computed quickly from $sortsubs\ xis\ yis$ by negating values, swapping labels, and reversing the list. The complete program is summarised in Figure 5.1. Counting comparisons between elements of A only, the number $C(n)$ of comparisons to compute $sortsubs_1$ on a list of length n satisfies $C(n) = 2C(n/2) + \Theta(n^2)$ with solution $C(n) = \Theta(n^2)$. However, the total time $T(n)$ taken to carry out the complete sorting is given by $T(n) = 2T(n/2) + \Theta(n^2 \log n)$, with solution $T(n) = \Theta(n^2 \log n)$. The logarithmic factor can be removed from $T(n)$ if *sortBy cmp* in the definition of *sortWith* can be computed in quadratic time, but this result remains elusive. In any case, the additional complexity arising from replacing comparisons between elements of A by comparisons between integers makes the algorithm very inefficient in practice.

$$sortsums\ xs\ ys = sortsubs\ xs\ (map\ negate\ ys)$$
$$sortsubs\ xs\ ys = map\ fst\ (sortWith\ abs\ xis\ yis)$$
$$\textbf{where}\ xis\ = zip\ xs\ [0..n-1]$$
$$yis\ = zip\ ys\ [n..]$$
$$n\ \ \ = length\ xs$$
$$abs = merge\ (sortsubs_1\ xis)\ (sortsubs_1\ yis)$$

$$sortWith\ abs\ xis\ yis = sortBy\ cmp\ (subs\ xis\ yis)$$
$$\textbf{where}\ cmp\ (\_,(i,k))\ (\_,(j,l)) = compare\ (a\,!\,(i,j))\ (a\,!\,(k,l))$$
$$a = array\ bs\ (zip\ labelPairs\ [0..])$$
$$labelPairs = map\ snd\ abs$$
$$bs = (minimum\ labelPairs, maximum\ labelPairs)$$

$$subs\ xis\ yis = [\,(x-y,(i,j))\mid (x,i)\leftarrow xis,(y,j)\leftarrow yis\,]$$
$$sortsubs_1\ [\,]\ \ \ \ \ = [\,]$$
$$sortsubs_1\ [(x,i)] = [(0,(i,i))]$$
$$sortsubs_1\ xis\ \ \ \ = merge\ abs\ (merge\ cs\ ds)$$
$$\textbf{where}\ abs = merge\ (sortsubs_1\ xis_1)\ (sortsubs_1\ xis_2)$$
$$cs\ \ = sortWith\ abs\ xis_1\ xis_2$$
$$ds\ \ = reverse\ (map\ switch\ cs)$$
$$(xis_1,xis_2) = splitAt\ (length\ xis\ \text{div}\ 2)\ xis$$

$$switch\ (x,(i,j)) = (negate\ x,(j,i))$$

Figure 5.1 The complete program

5.6 Chapter notes

The ultimate source of information about sorting is Knuth's comprehensive treatment in [8]. Quicksort was invented by Tony Hoare, see [7]. Mergesort is even older and goes back to John von Neumann, who first suggested the method in 1945. The Haskell implementation of Mergesort is attributed to Lennart Augustsson and Thomas Nordin. Heapsort was discovered by J. W. J. Williams [10], although an earlier version, simply called Treesort, was due to Robert W. Floyd. The derivation of Radixsort is due to Jeremy Gibbons [5].

The problem of sorting sums is Problem 41 in the Open Problems Project [2], a web resource devoted to recording open problems of interest to researchers in computational geometry and related fields. The earliest known reference to the problem is by Michael Fredman [4], who attributed the problem to Elwyn Berlekamp. All these references consider the problem in terms of numbers rather than Abelian groups, but the idea is the same.

References

[1] Richard Bird. *Thinking Functionally with Haskell*. Cambridge University Press, Cambridge, 2014.

[2]   Erik D. Demaine, Joseph S. B. Mitchell, and Joseph O'Rourke. The open problems project. http://cs.smith.edu/~jorourke/TOPP/, 2009.

[4]   Michael L. Fredman. How good is the information theory lower bound in sorting? *Theoretical Computer Science*, 1(4):355–361, 1976.

[5]   Jeremy Gibbons. A pointless derivation of radix sort. *Journal of Functional Programming*, 9(3):339–346, 1999.

[6]   Lawrence H. Harper, Thomas H. Payne, John E. Savage, and Ernst G. Straus. Sorting $x + y$. *Communications of the ACM*, 18(6):347–349, 1975.

[7]   Charles A. R. Hoare. Quicksort. *Computer Journal*, 5(1):10–16, 1962.

[8]   Donald E. Knuth. *The Art of Computer Programming*, volume 3: Sorting and Searching. Addison-Wesley, Reading, MA, second edition, 1998.

[9]   Jean-Luc Lambert. Sorting the sums $(x_i + y_j)$ in $O(n^2)$ comparisons. *Theoretical Computer Science*, 103(1):137–141, 1992.

[10] John W. J. Williams. Algorithm 232 – Heapsort. *Communications of the ACM*, 7(6):347–348, 1964.

Exercises

Exercise 5.1 Four species of tree have been described in this chapter. Name the sorting algorithms associated with the following five tree structures, identifying the odd one out:

> **data** *Tree a = Null | Leaf a | Node (Tree a) (Tree a)*
> **data** *Tree a = Null | Node a (Tree a) (Tree a)*
> **data** *Tree a = Null | Node a [Tree a]*
> **data** *Tree a = Null | Node (Tree a) a (Tree a)*
> **data** *Tree a = Leaf a | Node [Tree a]*

Exercise 5.2 Starting with *qsort = flatten · mktree*, where *flatten* is as defined in the text, construct the definition of *qsort (x : xs)*.

Exercise 5.3 Recall from the previous chapter the following definition of *flatten* in which the concatenation operations have been eliminated:

> *flatten t = flatcat t* []
> *flatcat Null xs   = xs*
> *flatcat (Node l x r) xs = flatcat l (x : flatcat r xs)*

Starting with *qsort = flatten · mktree*, synthesise a version of Quicksort for this version of *flatten*.

Exercise 5.4 Would it be sensible to choose as pivot the middle element of the list, that is, the one whose position is the middle position? How about the mean value, or the median?

Exercise 5.5 Define *minimum = head · qsort*. How long does it take to compute the minimum of a nonempty list this way?

More generally, define *select k xs* = (*qsort xs*) !! *k*. Synthesise a more efficient definition. (This exercise will be answered in the following chapter.)

Exercise 5.6 Synthesise a space-efficient version of *qsort* by introducing two accumulating parameters:

$$qsort\ (x\!:\!xs) = help\ x\ xs\ [\,]\ [\,]$$
$$\textbf{where}\ help\ x\ xs\ us\ vs = qsort\ (us + ys) + [x] + qsort\ (vs + zs)$$
$$\textbf{where}\ (ys, zs) = partition\ (<x)\ xs$$

Your task is simply to obtain a recursive definition of *help*.

Exercise 5.7 The number of comparisons $T(m,n)$ required by *merge* to merge two lists of lengths m and n in the worst case satisfies

$$T(0,n) = 0$$
$$T(m,0) = 0$$
$$T(m,n) = 1 + T(m-1,n)\ \text{max}\ T(m,n-1)$$

Prove that $T(m,n) \leqslant m+n$.

Exercise 5.8 In the recursive definition of *msort*, are the two base cases both necessary?

Exercise 5.9 Synthesise the bottom-up version of Mergesort. You will need the following fusion law of *until*:

$$f \cdot until\ p\ g = until\ q\ h \cdot f$$

provided that $f \cdot g = h \cdot f$ and $p\ x \Leftrightarrow q\ (f\ x)$ for all x.

Exercise 5.10 What common functions do the following two expressions represent?

$$flip\ (foldl\ (\lambda f\ x.\,(x\!:)\cdot f)\ id)\ [\,]$$
$$flip\ (foldr\ (\lambda x f.f \cdot (x\!:))\ id)\ [\,]$$

Exercise 5.11 A playing card can be represented by two characters, the first being one of the letters of SHDC (Spades, Hearts, Diamonds, Clubs) and the second one of the letters of AKQJT98765432 (Ace, King, Queen, Jack, Ten, etc.). Bridge players sort their 13 cards from left to right in the order given by these lists. For example,

$$[SA, SQ, S9, S8, S2, HK, H5, H3, H2, CA, CT, C7, C2]$$

Bridge players would describe this hand as "Five spades to the Ace-Queen, four hearts to the King, void diamonds and four clubs to the Ace-Ten". Be that as it may, use *sortBy* to sort a Bridge hand into order.

Exercise 5.12 Using the Haskell *Data.Ord* function

$$comparing :: Ord\ b \Rightarrow (a \to b) \to a \to a \to Ordering$$
$$comparing\ f\ x\ y = compare\ (f\ x)\ (f\ y)$$

give a simple definition of *sortOn*. Explain why this definition can be inefficient, and use tupling to give a better version.

Exercise 5.13 Give a divide-and-conquer algorithm for building a size-balanced heap in linearithmic time.

Exercise 5.14 Given that we can build a heap in linearithmic time, it seems that another way to define Heapsort is simply to define

$$hsort = flatten \cdot mkheap$$

In other words, build a heap and then flatten it. Show the result of eliminating the intermediate heap from this definition. Why did we not include this version of *hsort* in the text?

Exercise 5.15 Show how to build a size-balanced tree, of the kind described in Heapsort, in linear time. Start with

$$mktree\ [] \quad = Null$$
$$mktree\ (x : xs) = Node\ x\ (mktree\ (take\ m\ xs))\ (mktree\ (drop\ m\ xs))$$
$$\textbf{where } m = length\ xs\ \text{div}\ 2$$

Exercise 5.16 Prove that a size-balanced tree, of the kind described in Heapsort, has minimum possible height $\lceil \log (n + 1) \rceil$, where n is the size of the tree.

Exercise 5.17 Suppose you are given a list of n integers, all of which lie in some given range $(0, m)$. Show how to sort the list in $\Theta(m + n)$ steps.

Exercise 5.18 Here is the stability property of Bucketsort again:

$$map\ (bsort\ ds)\ (ptn\ d\ xs) = ptn\ d\ (bsort\ ds\ xs) \tag{5.3}$$

The aim of this exercise is to prove (5.3) using the original definition of *bsort* as a function that flattens a tree. First, define the function

$$tmap :: (a \to b) \to Tree\ a \to Tree\ b$$

for mapping a function over a tree. This function will be needed below.

Next, use the following subsidiary claims to prove (5.3):

$$mktree\ ds \cdot filter\ p \quad = tmap\ (filter\ p) \cdot mktree\ ds \tag{5.4}$$
$$flatten \cdot tmap\ (filter\ p) = filter\ p \cdot flatten \tag{5.5}$$

Next, use the following claim to prove (5.4): provided p is a total predicate, we have

$$ptn\ d \cdot filter\ p = map\ (filter\ p) \cdot ptn\ d \tag{5.6}$$

Now prove (5.6). You can assume that filters of total predicates commute, so

$$filter\ p \cdot filter\ q = filter\ q \cdot filter\ p$$

Finally, prove (5.5). That's a lot of work for one exercise, but it does demonstrate that the pages of explanation found in some textbooks as to why Radixsort works can be reduced to simple calculation.

Exercise 5.19 Specialise Radixsort to the problem of sorting a list of words, where a word is made up of lower-case letters only.

Exercise 5.20 Prove that, if $(A, +)$ is an Abelian group, then

$$x - y \leqslant x' - y' \iff x - x' \leqslant y - y'$$

Answers

Answer 5.1 Mergesort, Heapsort, odd one out, QuickSort, and Bucketsort.

Answer 5.2 We have

$$\begin{aligned}
& qsort\ (x : xs) \\
= \quad & \{ \text{definition} \} \\
& flatten\ (mktree\ (x : xs)) \\
= \quad & \{ \text{definition of } mktree \text{ with } (ys, zs) = partition\ (<x)\ xs \} \\
& flatten\ (Node\ (mktree\ ys)\ x\ (mktree\ zs)) \\
= \quad & \{ \text{definition of } flatten \} \\
& flatten\ (mktree\ ys) +\!\!+ [x] +\!\!+ flatten\ (mktree\ zs) \\
= \quad & \{ \text{definition of } qsort \} \\
& qsort\ ys +\!\!+ [x] +\!\!+ qsort\ zs
\end{aligned}$$

Answer 5.3 Let $qcat\ xs\ ys = flatcat\ (mktree\ xs)\ ys$. Then we obtain

$$\begin{aligned}
qsort\ xs &= qcat\ xs\ [\,] \\
qcat\ [\,]\ ys\ \ &= ys \\
qcat\ (x : xs)\ ys &= qcat\ us\ (x : qcat\ vs\ ys) \\
&\quad \textbf{where}\ (us, vs) = partition\ (<x)\ xs
\end{aligned}$$

Answer 5.4 No, choosing the middle element is as likely to produce two unbalanced lists as choosing the first element. The only advantage of such a choice is that if the input is already sorted into strictly increasing order, then $qsort$ will take $\Theta(n \log n)$ steps rather than $\Theta(n^2)$ steps. Choosing the mean value as pivot is better, but of course the notion of a mean value depends on the input being a list of numbers, so this method is not available for an arbitrary ordered type. Choosing the median value as pivot would guarantee the list is evenly split, but of course such a choice depends on there being an efficient method for computing the median, a problem that is addressed in the following chapter.

Answer 5.5 It could take quadratic time, for example when the input is in decreasing order.

Answer 5.6 The base case

$$help \; x \; [\,] \; us \; vs = qsort \; us \; +\!\!+ \; [x] \; +\!\!+ \; qsort \; vs$$

is easy. For the recursive case assume $y < x$. We argue as follows:

$$help \; x \; (y : xs) \; us \; vs$$
$$= \quad \{ \text{ with } (ys, zs) \text{ as above } \}$$
$$qsort \; (us +\!\!+ y : ys) +\!\!+ [x] +\!\!+ qsort \; (vs +\!\!+ zs)$$
$$= \quad \{ \text{ claim (see below) } \}$$
$$qsort \; (y : us +\!\!+ ys) +\!\!+ [x] +\!\!+ qsort \; (vs +\!\!+ zs)$$
$$= \quad \{ \text{ definition of } help \}$$
$$help \; x \; (y : us) \; vs$$

The claim is that $qsort$ is unchanged when the input is permuted. A dual calculation in the remaining case yields

$$qsort \; [\,] \quad = [\,]$$
$$qsort \; (x : xs) = help \; xs \; [\,] \; [\,]$$
$$\quad \textbf{where} \; help \; [\,] \; us \; vs \qquad\qquad = qsort \; us +\!\!+ [x] +\!\!+ qsort \; vs$$
$$\qquad\qquad help \; (y : xs) \; us \; vs \mid x \leqslant y \qquad = help \; xs \; us \; (y : vs)$$
$$\qquad\qquad\qquad\qquad\qquad\quad \mid otherwise = help \; xs \; (y : us) \; vs$$

Answer 5.7 The base cases $T(0, n) = 0 \leqslant n$ and $T(m, 0) = 0 \leqslant m$ are immediate and the induction step is

$$1 + T(m - 1, n) \; \max \; T(m, n - 1) \leqslant 1 + (m - 1 + n) \; \max \; (m + n - 1) = m + n$$

In fact one can prove rather more: for $m > 0$ and $n > 0$ we have $T(m, n) = m + n - 1$.

Answer 5.8 Oh yes. Since $halve \; [x] = ([\,], [x])$ the recursion would not terminate if either clause were missing. It is an easy mistake to make. The first two clauses of $sortsubs_1$ in Figure 5.1 are necessary for the same reason.

Answer 5.9 Arguing at the function level for a nonempty list, we have

$$flatten \cdot unwrap \cdot until \; single \; (pairWith \; Node) \cdot map \; Leaf$$
$$= \quad \{ \text{ since } flatten \cdot unwrap = unwrap \cdot map \; flatten \}$$
$$unwrap \cdot map \; flatten \cdot until \; single \; (pairWith \; Node) \cdot map \; Leaf$$
$$= \quad \{ \text{ fusion law of } until \text{ (see below) } \}$$
$$unwrap \cdot until \; single \; (pairWith \; merge) \cdot map \; (flatten \cdot Leaf)$$
$$= \quad \{ \text{ since } flatten \cdot Leaf = wrap \}$$
$$unwrap \cdot until \; single \; (pairWith \; merge) \cdot map \; wrap$$

The two fusion conditions are

$$single \cdot map \; flatten = single$$
$$map \; flatten \cdot pairWith \; Node = pairWith \; merge \cdot map \; flatten$$

Verification of the conditions is omitted.

Answer 5.10 In both cases the function is *reverse*. Of course, a shorter definition is *foldl* (*flip* (:)) [].

Answer 5.11 We have to define a comparison function *cmp* for playing cards. With *suit* as a synonym for *head*, and *rank* a synonym for *head* · *tail*, and noting that "SHDC" is in reverse alphabetical order, we can define

$$cmp\ c_1\ c_2 = \textbf{if}\ suit\ c_1 == suit\ c_2$$
$$\textbf{then}\ compare\ (posn\ (rank\ c_1))\ (posn\ (rank\ c_2))$$
$$\textbf{else}\ \ compare\ (suit\ c_2)\ (suit\ c_1)$$
$$posn\ r = head\ [i \mid (c,i) \leftarrow zip\ ranks\ [0..], c == r]$$
$$ranks = \texttt{"AKQJT98765432"}$$

Answer 5.12 We can define

$$sortOn\ f = sortBy\ (comparing\ f)$$

However, the value of f on one and the same argument may be computed many times under this definition. A better method is to define

$$sortOn\ f\ xs = map\ snd\ (sortBy\ (comparing\ fst)\ (zip\ (map\ f\ xs)\ xs))$$

Even this definition is not as good as it might be because the list xs is traversed twice in the final term. A better definition still is

$$sortOn\ f = map\ snd \cdot sortBy\ (comparing\ fst) \cdot map\ (\lambda x.(f\ x, x))$$

This is essentially the definition given in *Data.List*.

Answer 5.13 The function *mkheap* is defined by

$$mkheap :: Ord\ a \Rightarrow [a] \rightarrow Tree\ a$$
$$mkheap\ [] \quad\quad = Null$$
$$mkheap\ (x:xs) = Node\ y\ (mkheap\ ys)\ (mkheap\ zs)$$
$$\textbf{where}\ (y, ys, zs) = split\ (x:xs)$$
$$split :: Ord\ a \Rightarrow [a] \rightarrow (a, [a], [a])$$
$$split\ (x:xs) = foldr\ op\ (x, [], [])\ xs$$
$$\textbf{where}\ op\ x\ (y, ys, zs) \mid x \leqslant y \quad\ = (x, y:zs, ys)$$
$$\mid otherwise = (y, x:zs, ys)$$

The function *split* returns three components. The first component is the smallest element in the input, while the other two are lists, of as equal a size as possible.

Answer 5.14 Eliminating the tree gives

$$hsort\ [] = []$$
$$hsort\ xs = y:merge\ (hsort\ ys)\ (hsort\ zs)$$
$$\textbf{where}\ (y, ys, zs) = split\ xs$$

But this is just another version of Mergesort.

Answer 5.15 The method is similar to the one used in Mergesort. Define

$mkpair :: Nat \rightarrow [a] \rightarrow (Tree\ a, [a])$
$mkpair\ n\ xs = (mktree\ (take\ n\ xs), drop\ n\ xs)$
$mktree\ xs\quad = fst\ (mkpair\ (length\ xs)\ xs)$

This time we obtain

$mkpair\ 0\ xs\quad\ = (Null, xs)$
$mkpair\ n\ (x : xs) = (Node\ x\ l\ r, zs)$
   where $(l, ys) = mkpair\ m\ xs$
       $(r, zs) = mkpair\ (n - 1 - m)\ ys$
       $m = (n - 1)$ div 2

Answer 5.16 A size-balanced tree of size n has height $H(n)$, where $H(0) = 0$ and $H(n+1) = 1 + H(\lceil n/2 \rceil)$. The solution to this recurrence is $H(n) = \lceil \log(n+1) \rceil$. The induction step follows from $\lceil \log(n+2) \rceil = 1 + \lceil \log(\lceil n/2 \rceil + 1) \rceil$, whose proof is another application of the rule of ceilings.

Answer 5.17 The answer is simply to count the number of times each element occurs. An array can be used to store the count of each element, and the final sorted output can then be read off from the array:

$csort :: Nat \rightarrow [Int] \rightarrow [Int]$
$csort\ m\ xs = concat\ [replicate\ k\ x \mid (x, k) \leftarrow assocs\ a]$
       where $a = accumArray\ (+)\ 0\ (0, m)\ [(x, 1) \mid x \leftarrow xs]$

This is Countsort, and takes $\Theta(m + n)$ steps. It was also presented in Section 3.3.

Answer 5.18 We have

$tmap\ f\ (Leaf\ x)\ = Leaf\ (f\ x)$
$tmap\ f\ (Node\ ts) = Node\ (map\ (tmap\ f)\ ts)$

Here is the proof of (5.3):

$\quad map\ (bsort\ ds)\ (ptn\ d\ xs)$
$=\quad$ { definition of ptn }
$\quad [bsort\ ds\ (filter\ ((== m) \cdot d)\ xs) \mid m \leftarrow rng]$
$=\quad$ { definition of $bsort$ }
$\quad [(flatten \cdot mktree\ ds \cdot filter\ ((== m) \cdot d))\ xs \mid m \leftarrow rng]$
$=\quad$ { assumptions (5.4) and (5.5) }
$\quad [(filter\ ((== m) \cdot d) \cdot flatten \cdot mktree\ ds)\ xs \mid m \leftarrow rng]$
$=\quad$ { definition of $bsort$ }
$\quad [filter\ ((== m) \cdot d)\ (bsort\ ds\ xs) \mid m \leftarrow rng]$
$=\quad$ { definition of ptn }
$\quad ptn\ d\ (bsort\ ds\ xs)$

The proof of (5.4) is by induction over the discriminators. Unlike the proof above, it is carried out in a point-free style. It is easy to show

$$mktree\;[\,]\cdot filter\;p = tmap\;(filter\;p)\cdot mktree\;[\,]$$

and that establishes the base case. For the induction step we reason

$$
\begin{array}{rl}
& mktree\;(d:ds)\cdot filter\;p \\
= & \{\text{ definition of } mktree\ \} \\
& Node\cdot map\;(mktree\;ds)\cdot ptn\;d\cdot filter\;p \\
= & \{\text{ assumption (5.6) }\} \\
& Node\cdot map\;(mktree\;ds\cdot filter\;p)\cdot ptn\;d \\
= & \{\text{ induction }\} \\
& Node\cdot map\;(tmap\;(filter\;p)\cdot mktree\;ds)\cdot ptn\;d \\
= & \{\text{ definition of } tmap\ \} \\
& tmap\;(filter\;p)\cdot Node\cdot map\;(mktree\;ds)\cdot ptn\;d \\
= & \{\text{ definition of } mktree\ \} \\
& tmap\;(filter\;p)\cdot mktree\;(d:ds)
\end{array}
$$

For the proof of (5.6) we reason

$$
\begin{array}{rl}
& map\;(filter\;p)\;(ptn\;d\;xs) \\
= & \{\text{ definition of } ptn\ \} \\
& [filter\;p\;(filter\;((==m)\cdot d)\;xs)\mid m \leftarrow rng] \\
= & \{\text{ filters of total predicates commute }\} \\
& [filter\;((==m)\cdot d)\;(filter\;p\;xs)\mid m \leftarrow rng] \\
= & \{\text{ definition of } ptn\ \} \\
& ptn\;(filter\;p\;xs)
\end{array}
$$

Finally, we prove (5.5) by induction over the tree. The induction step is

$$
\begin{array}{rl}
& flatten\;(tmap\;(filter\;p)\;(Node\;ts)) \\
= & \{\text{ definition of } tmap\ \} \\
& flatten\;(Node\;(map\;(tmap\;(filter\;p))\;ts)) \\
= & \{\text{ definition of } flatten\ \} \\
& concat\;(map\;(flatten\cdot tmap\;(filter\;p))\;ts) \\
= & \{\text{ induction }\} \\
& concat\;(map\;(filter\;p\cdot flatten)\;ts) \\
= & \{\text{ claim; see below }\} \\
& filter\;p\;(concat\;(map\;flatten\;ts)) \\
= & \{\text{ definition of } flatten\ \} \\
& filter\;p\;(flatten\;(Node\;ts))
\end{array}
$$

The claim is that

$$concat\cdot map\;(filter\;p) = filter\;p\cdot concat$$

But enough is enough, and we omit the proof.

Answer 5.19 One way:

$$wsort :: [Word] \rightarrow [Word]$$
$$wsort\ [] = []$$
$$wsort\ xss = rsort\ (\text{'a'},\text{'z'})\ ds\ xss$$
$$\mathbf{where}\ ds = [\lambda xs.(xs + \!\!+ repeat\ \text{'a'})\ !!\ i\ |\ i \leftarrow [0..k-1]]$$
$$k\ = maximum\ [length\ xs\ |\ xs \leftarrow xss]$$

Answer 5.20 The proof is as follows:

$$(x-y) \leqslant (x'-y')$$
$$\Leftrightarrow\ \{\ \text{adding } y \text{ to both sides }\}$$
$$(x-y)+y \leqslant (x'-y')+y$$
$$\Leftrightarrow\ \{\ \text{associativity and commutativity }\}$$
$$x+(y-y) \leqslant (y-y')+x'$$
$$\Leftrightarrow\ \{\ \text{since } y-y=0 \text{ and } x+0=x\ \}$$
$$x \leqslant (y-y')+x'$$
$$\Leftrightarrow\ \{\ \text{subtracting } x' \text{ from both sides }\}$$
$$(x-x') \leqslant (y-y')$$

Chapter 6

Selection

This chapter describes four related problems in which a divide-and-conquer strategy can be employed to good effect. All involve selection of some kind, whether from one set, two sets, or the complement of a set. The primary example is the problem of selecting the kth smallest element in a set, where k can be anything from 1 to n, the size of the set. Finding the minimum element (the 1st smallest) or the maximum element (the nth smallest) are special cases, as is the problem of finding the median element (roughly, the $\lfloor n/2 \rfloor$th smallest, but see below). We shall also consider the problem of selecting the kth smallest in the union of two given sets, and finding the smallest number not in a given set of natural numbers. Efficient solutions to these problems depend on how the set is represented, whether by a list, with or without duplicates, by an array, or by a tree of some kind.

6.1 Minimum and maximum

By way of a warm-up, let us start with the problem of computing the minimum and maximum elements of a finite nonempty list. The standard definitions are

$$minimum, maximum :: Ord\ a \Rightarrow [a] \rightarrow a$$
$$minimum = foldr1\ min$$
$$maximum = foldr1\ max$$

The prelude function *foldr1*, and its companion *foldl1*, are fold functions for nonempty lists:

$$foldr1, foldl1 :: (a \rightarrow a \rightarrow a) \rightarrow [a] \rightarrow a$$
$$foldr1\ f\ [x] \quad = x$$
$$foldr1\ f\ (x:xs) = f\ x\ (foldr1\ f\ xs)$$
$$foldl1\ f\ (x:xs) = foldl\ f\ x\ xs$$

For example,

$$foldr1 \ (\oplus) \ [w,x,y,z] = w \oplus (x \oplus (y \oplus z))$$
$$foldl1 \ (\oplus) \ [w,x,y,z] = ((w \oplus x) \oplus y) \oplus z$$

The definition of *minimum* and *maximum* uses a *foldr1*, which processes the list from right to left; we can also use a *foldl1* and process from left to right because *min* and *max* are associative operations. In either direction there are $n-1$ evaluations of *min* or *max* for a list of length n. Each evaluation involves a single comparison, so there are $n-1$ comparisons in total. This is the best one can achieve. Think of an algorithm for determining the maximum as a tennis tournament between n players, in which the outcome of a single match corresponds to the outcome of a single comparison. Every player apart from the eventual winner must lose a match, so there must be $n-1$ matches.

If we want both the minimum and maximum elements, then $2n-2$ comparisons are certainly sufficient. The obvious method involves two passes over the input, but it can be reduced to one pass by making use of the tupling law

$$(foldr \ f_1 \ e_1 \ xs, foldr \ f_2 \ e_2 \ xs) = foldr \ f \ (e_1, e_2) \ xs$$
$$\textbf{where} \ f \ x \ (y,z) = (f_1 \ x \ y, f_2 \ x \ z)$$

Although it is not true in general that

$$foldr1 \ f \ (x : xs) = foldr \ f \ x \ xs$$

we do have

$$minimum \ (x : xs) = foldr \ min \ x \ xs$$
$$maximum \ (x : xs) = foldr \ max \ x \ xs$$

because both *min* and *max* are commutative as well as associative. It follows that

$$minmax :: Ord \ a \Rightarrow [a] \rightarrow (a,a)$$
$$minmax \ (x : xs) = foldr \ op \ (x,x) \ xs$$
$$\textbf{where} \ op \ x \ (y,z) = (min \ x \ y, max \ x \ z)$$

The number of comparisons can be reduced by rewriting *op*, using the fact that the current minimum is never greater than the current maximum:

$$minmax :: Ord \ a \Rightarrow [a] \rightarrow (a,a)$$
$$minmax \ (x : xs) = foldr \ op \ (x,x) \ xs$$
$$\textbf{where} \ op \ x \ (y,z) \ | \ x < y \qquad = (x,z)$$
$$| \ z < x \qquad = (y,x)$$
$$| \ otherwise = (y,z)$$

At each step the current minimum and maximum are updated according to whether the new element is smaller than the current minimum, larger than the current maximum, or in between. In the worst case there are two comparisons at each step, giving $2n-2$ comparisons in total, the same number as before. However, in the best case there are only $n - 1$ comparisons. Examples of best-case and worst-case inputs are set as exercises.

Here is a divide-and-conquer algorithm for the same problem:

$$minmax\ [x]\quad = (x,x)$$
$$minmax\ [x,y] = \textbf{if } x \leqslant y \textbf{ then } (x,y) \textbf{ else } (y,x)$$
$$minmax\ xs\quad = (min\ a_1\ a_2, max\ b_1\ b_2)$$
$$\textbf{where } (a_1,b_1) = minmax\ ys$$
$$(a_2,b_2) = minmax\ zs$$
$$(ys,zs) = halve\ xs$$

The function *halve* was defined in Section 5.2. The minimum and maximum element in a singleton list coincide, so the answer can be computed with zero comparisons. Otherwise, the input is divided into two equal halves, the results for both halves are computed recursively, and the final answer is obtained by comparing the two minimums and the two maximums. The case of a doubleton list is treated separately simply because the total number of comparisons can be reduced from two to one in this case.

The total running time of this version of *minmax* goes up to $\Theta(n \log n)$ steps, which hardly seems to make it worthwhile. But, counting comparisons only, the number $C(n)$ of comparisons satisfies the recurrence relation

$$C(1) = 0$$
$$C(2) = 1$$
$$C(n) = C(\lfloor n/2 \rfloor) + C(\lceil n/2 \rceil) + 2$$

This recurrence is difficult to solve exactly, though it is easy enough to show that $C(n) = 3n/2 - 2$ when n is a positive power of two. Thus the divide-and-conquer algorithm can save a quarter of the comparisons.

In fact, the divide-and-conquer algorithm is not the best possible. For example, $C(12) = 18$ but the minimum and maximum of 12 elements can be computed with only 16 comparisons. To see why, here is an algorithm for *minmax* obtained by switching to a bottom-up scheme:

$$minmax = unwrap \cdot until\ single\ (pairWith\ op) \cdot mkPairs$$
$$\textbf{where } op\ (a_1,b_1)\ (a_2,b_2) = (min\ a_1\ a_2, max\ b_1\ b_2)$$

$$pairWith\ f\ []\quad\quad = []$$
$$pairWith\ f\ [x]\quad\quad = [x]$$
$$pairWith\ f\ (x:y:xs) = f\ x\ y : pairWith\ f\ xs$$

$$mkPairs\ []\quad\quad = []$$
$$mkPairs\ [x]\quad\quad = [(x,x)]$$
$$mkPairs\ (x:y:xs) = \textbf{if } x \leqslant y \textbf{ then } (x,y) : mkPairs\ xs \textbf{ else } (y,x) : mkPairs\ xs$$

With $C(n)$ as the comparison count, we have

$$C(1) = 0$$
$$C(1) = 1$$
$$C(n) = \lfloor n/2 \rfloor + D(\lceil n/2 \rceil)$$

where $\lfloor n/2 \rfloor$ accounts for the number of comparisons to compute *mkPairs* and

$$D(1) = 0$$
$$D(n) = 2 \lfloor n/2 \rfloor + D(\lceil n/2 \rceil)$$

It is easy enough to show that $D(n) = 2(n-1)$, so $C(n) = n + \lceil n/2 \rceil - 2$. In particular $C(12) = 16$. In fact, $C(n)$ is also a lower bound on the number of comparisons needed to compute the minimum and maximum of n elements in the worst case (see Answer 6.7). Moreover, the total running time of *minmax* is $\Theta(n)$ steps. However, the bottom-up algorithm is not recommended as a method for computing *minmax* because the other constants involved are larger than with the naive version.

6.2 Selection from one set

By definition, the kth smallest element of a set (or a list without duplicates – see Exercise 6.1) with n elements has exactly $k - 1$ elements smaller than it, so the 1st smallest is the smallest, and the nth smallest is the largest. The median m of a set with an odd size n is an element of the set for which there are exactly $\lfloor n/2 \rfloor$ elements smaller than m and $\lfloor n/2 \rfloor$ elements greater than m. When n is even there is a choice of definition, and we pick the one that has $\lfloor n/2 \rfloor - 1$ smaller elements and $\lfloor n/2 \rfloor$ larger elements. This defines what is sometimes called the *lower median*. Combining the two cases, we have that the median of a set of size n has $\lfloor (n+1)/2 \rfloor - 1$ smaller elements and $\lceil (n+1)/2 \rceil - 1$ greater elements.

When a set is represented by a list with no duplicates, the kth smallest appears at position $k - 1$ in a sorted list. Hence we can define

$$select :: Ord\ a \Rightarrow Nat \rightarrow [a] \rightarrow a$$
$$select\ k\ xs = (sort\ xs)\ !!\ (k-1)$$

In particular,

$$median\ xs = select\ k\ xs\ \textbf{where}\ k = (length\ xs + 1)\ \text{div}\ 2$$

The definitions of *select* and *median* make sense when xs contains duplicates, and in what follows we will not assume that the elements of xs are all different. Since sorting a list takes $O(n \log n)$ steps, the running time of *select* is $O(n \log n)$ steps. This is an upper bound rather than an exact bound because, under lazy evaluation, the whole list may not have to be sorted in order to retrieve the kth element – it depends on the sorting algorithm. On the other hand, the running time is $\Omega(n)$ steps because it takes this time just to inspect every element of the input. Can these lower and upper bounds be made to coincide, that is, can *select* be computed in linear time? The answer is yes, and the algorithm is yet another clever example of divide and conquer.

First, though, let us replace the function *sort* in the definition of *select* by a modified version of *qsort*, the Quicksort algorithm described in the previous chapter:

$$qsort\ [] = []$$
$$qsort\ xs = qsort\ us \mathbin{+\!\!+} vs \mathbin{+\!\!+} qsort\ ws$$
$$\textbf{where}\ (us, vs, ws) = partition3\ (pivot\ xs)\ xs$$

Here *pivot* chooses some element of a list as the pivot and *partition3*, whose definition was given in Answer 4.10, splits a list into three lists: those elements less than, equal to, or greater than the pivot. Splitting a list into three sublists rather than two is better whenever duplicate elements may be present.

We can synthesise a faster version of *select* by exploiting the following divide-and-conquer property of the list-indexing operation:

$$(xs \mathbin{+\!\!+} ys)\ !!\ k = \textbf{if}\ k < n\ \textbf{then}\ xs\ !!\ k\ \textbf{else}\ ys\ !!\ (k-n)\ \textbf{where}\ n = length\ xs$$

Now we can reason for nonempty *xs*:

$$select\ k\ xs$$
$$=\quad \{\ \text{definition}\ \}$$
$$qsort\ xs\ !!\ (k-1)$$
$$=\quad \{\ \text{with}\ (us, vs, ws) = partition3\ (pivot\ xs)\ xs\ \}$$
$$(qsort\ us \mathbin{+\!\!+} vs \mathbin{+\!\!+} qsort\ ws)\ !!\ (k-1)$$
$$=\quad \{\ \text{assuming}\ k-1 < length\ us\ \}$$
$$qsort\ us\ !!\ (k-1)$$
$$=\quad \{\ \text{definition of}\ select\ \}$$
$$select\ k\ us$$

The other cases can be dealt with in a similar fashion, and we end up with the following definition of *select*:

$$select :: Ord\ a \Rightarrow Nat \rightarrow [a] \rightarrow a$$
$$select\ k\ xs$$
$$\mid k \leqslant m \qquad = select\ k\ us$$
$$\mid k \leqslant m+n = vs\ !!\ (k-m-1)$$
$$\mid k > m+n = select\ (k-m-n)\ ws$$
$$\textbf{where}\ (us, vs, ws) = partition3\ (pivot\ xs)\ xs$$
$$\qquad\quad (m, n) \qquad = (length\ us, length\ vs)$$

The middle list *vs* is not empty because it contains at least one copy of the pivot. Let $T(n)$ be the running time of this version of *select* on an input of length n. Assuming *partition3* splits the list into three lists, the first and third having length at most $(n-1)/2$, we have

$$T(n) \leqslant T((n-1)/2) + \Theta(n)$$

with solution $T(n) = O(n)$. On the other hand, *partition3* may return a very unequal split, so the running time in the worst case satisfies

$$T(n) = T(n-1) + \Theta(n)$$

with solution $T(n) = \Theta(n^2)$. If the partitioning uses the median of the list as pivot, then there will be an equal split and the result will be a linear-time algorithm for *select*. But that involves finding the median in linear time, which is essentially what we are trying to achieve in the first place. The idea therefore seems circular and without obvious merit.

However, it can be made to work. The wiggle room is that we do not have to choose the actual median as the pivot: any value will do as long as the result of partitioning is three lists, the sum of the lengths of the first and third lists being some proper fraction of the input. We shall see why later on. The method for choosing *pivot* is a very cunning divide-and-conquer scheme. First, divide the input into groups of five by applying *group* 5, where

$$group :: Nat \rightarrow [a] \rightarrow [[a]]$$
$$group\ n\ [] = []$$
$$group\ n\ xs = ys : group\ n\ zs\ \textbf{where}\ (ys, zs) = splitAt\ n\ xs$$

If the length of the input is not an exact multiple of five, there will be a trailing group of shorter length. For example,

$$group\ 5\ [1..12] = [[1..5], [6..10], [11,12]]$$

There are therefore $\lceil n/5 \rceil$ groups. Computing *group* takes linear time.

Next, find the median of each group by sorting each group and taking the middle element of the result. That is, compute

$$medians = map\ (middle \cdot sort) \cdot group\ 5$$
$$\textbf{where}\ middle\ xs = xs\ !!\ ((length\ xs + 1)\ \text{div}\ 2 - 1)$$

For example, *medians* $[1..12] = [3,8,11]$. Computing *medians* also takes linear time: sorting each group of five elements takes constant time, as does evaluation of *middle*, and there are $\lceil n/5 \rceil$ groups.

Finally, define *pivot* to select the median of these medians by applying the algorithm for *select* recursively. That gives

$$pivot :: Ord\ a \Rightarrow [a] \rightarrow a$$
$$pivot\ [x] = x$$
$$pivot\ xs\ = median\ (medians\ xs)$$
$$\textbf{where}\ median\ xs = select\ ((length\ xs + 1)\ \text{div}\ 2)\ xs$$

The clause *pivot* $[x] = x$ has to be included as a special case: without it we would have *pivot* $[x] = select\ 1\ [x]$, and computing the right-hand side would involve computing *pivot* [x] again, so the whole program would spin off into an infinite loop.

To estimate the running time $T(n)$ of *select* in the worst case, observe that finding the median of the medians takes $T(\lceil n/5 \rceil) + \Theta(n)$ steps because *pivot* calls *select* recursively on a list of length $\lceil n/5 \rceil$. The partitioning step takes $\Theta(n)$ steps on a list of length n. To these times we have also to add in the running time to select from either the first or third list returned by *partition3*. We claim that each of these lists has length at most $7n/10$ for an input of length n. To appreciate why, here is a picture for a particular input of length 28:

$$
\begin{array}{cccccc}
42 & 37 & 99 & 70 & 95 & \\
17 & 36 & 43 & 69 & 79 & 88 \\
11 & 23 & \mathbf{29} & 61 & 73 & 87 \\
06 & 13 & 28 & 52 & 30 & 32 \\
01 & 09 & 21 & 38 & 18 &
\end{array}
$$

The columns are the groups of length 5, except for the last column. Each of these groups has been sorted, and the columns have been arranged in increasing order of their median. The median $m = 29$ of the medians has been highlighted. The algorithm does not arrange the columns in this way; the picture is there just to explain what we can say about how m partitions the list.

The key property of m is as follows. The bottom-left rectangle with upper-right corner at m contains only elements less than or equal to m. The number of elements in this rectangle, apart from m, is

$$3 \lfloor (\lceil n/5 \rceil + 1)/2 \rfloor - 1 \geqslant 3n/10$$

(see Exercise 6.10). That means the number of elements greater than m is at most $7n/10$. By reasoning similarly about the top-right rectangle with bottom-left corner at m we have that the number of elements less than m is at most $7n/10$. That means that in the worst case *select* is called recursively on a list of size at most $7n/10$. Ignoring floors and ceilings, the total running time therefore satisfies

$$T(n) \leqslant T(n/5) + T(7n/10) + cn$$

for some c. It is easy to show by induction that $T(n) \leqslant bn$ for some appropriately chosen b. For the induction step, we have to show

$$bn/5 + 7bn/10 + cn \leqslant bn$$

This inequality is immediate on taking $b = 10c$. In summary, *select* can be computed in linear time.

6.3 Selection from two sets

Continuing the theme of selection, consider the problem of computing *select*, where this time we define

$$select :: Ord\ a \Rightarrow Nat \rightarrow [a] \rightarrow [a] \rightarrow a$$
$$select\ k\ as\ bs = (merge\ as\ bs)\ !!\ k$$

Thus *select* takes a number k and two sorted lists, and returns the element at position k in the merged list. In particular, *select 0 as bs* returns the smallest element in *merge as bs*.

How long does the computation of *select* take? Clearly, if both lists have length n, then *select* takes $O(n)$ steps because two lists can be merged in this time. However, if they are given as two sorted arrays, or two balanced binary search trees, then the time can be reduced to $O(\log n)$ steps. The result is a little surprising because two arrays or two binary search trees certainly cannot be merged in less than linear time. The faster algorithm is yet another example of divide and conquer, and the proof that it works hinges on a subtle relationship between merging and selection.

Here is the relationship: provided the arguments of *merge* are two sorted lists, we have

$$merge\ (xs + [a] + ys)\ (us + [b] + vs)\ !!\ k$$
$$\mid a \leqslant b \wedge k \leqslant p+q = merge\ (xs + [a] + ys)\ us\ !!\ k$$
$$\mid a \leqslant b \wedge k > p+q = merge\ ys\ (us + [b] + vs)\ !!\ (k-p-1)$$
$$\mid b \leqslant a \wedge k \leqslant p+q = merge\ xs\ (us + [b] + vs)\ !!\ k$$
$$\mid b \leqslant a \wedge k > p+q = merge\ (xs + [a] + ys)\ vs\ !!\ (k-q-1)$$
$$\textbf{where } p = length\ xs; q = length\ us$$

The proof is given later on. Using the relationship, it is possible to derive the following definition of *select*:

$$select\ k\ [\ ]\ bs = bs\ !!\ k$$
$$select\ k\ as\ [\ ] = as\ !!\ k$$
$$select\ k\ as\ bs \mid\ \ a \leqslant b \wedge k \leqslant p+q = select\ k\ as\ us \qquad\qquad \text{-- line 3}$$
$$\mid\ \ a \leqslant b \wedge k > p+q = select\ (k-p-1)\ ys\ bs \qquad \text{-- line 4}$$
$$\mid\ \ b \leqslant a \wedge k \leqslant p+q = select\ k\ xs\ bs \qquad\qquad \text{-- line 5}$$
$$\mid\ \ b \leqslant a \wedge k > p+q = select\ (k-q-1)\ as\ vs \qquad \text{-- line 6}$$
$$\textbf{where } p = (length\ as)\ div\ 2$$
$$q = (length\ bs)\ div\ 2$$
$$(xs,a:ys) = splitAt\ p\ as$$
$$(us,b:vs) = splitAt\ q\ bs$$

The derivation is similar to the one involving *qsort* in the previous section and we won't go into details. Instead, here is the trace of an example of *select* in which $k = 6$:

p q k	as	bs	
3 3 6	$[1,4,4,\underline{7},8,11,15]$	$[2,5,9,\underline{11},15,16,20]$	-- line 3
3 1 6	$[1,4,4,\underline{7},8,11,15]$	$[2,\underline{5},9]$	-- line 6
3 0 4	$[1,4,4,\underline{7},8,11,15]$	$[\underline{9}]$	-- line 4
1 0 0	$[8,\underline{11},15]$	$[\underline{9}]$	-- line 5
0 0 0	$[\underline{8}]$	$[\underline{9}]$	-- line 3
0 0 0	$[\underline{8}]$	$[]$	

The values of a and b have been underlined. The last column gives the line number of the recursive call of *select* used for the next step. The final value of *select* on the two lists is 8.

Since *select* chooses the values of a and b to be the middle elements of the two lists, half of one of the lists is discarded at each step. Ignoring completely the cost of evaluating the local definitions, the running time of *select* therefore satisfies

$$T(m,n) = T(m,n/2) \text{ max } T(m/2,n) + \Theta(1)$$

with solution $T(m,n) = \Theta(\log m + \log n)$. Of course, evaluations of the local definitions take linear rather than constant time, so the true timing estimate is

$$T(m,n) = T(m,n/2) \text{ max } T(m/2,n) + \Theta(m+n)$$

with solution $T(m,n) = \Theta(m+n)$. The divide-and-conquer-algorithm is therefore no faster than the naive version we started out with. The pay-off comes when the two lists are given as two arrays or two binary search trees. Then we can arrange that the cost of the local evaluations is indeed constant.

We will spell out the details for binary search trees, leaving arrays to the exercises. Recall from Chapter 4 that a binary search tree is a tree of type

data *Tree a = Null | Node Nat (Tree a) a (Tree a)*

with the property that, provided the tree labels are values of an ordered type, flattening a tree produces a list in ascending order. Recall also that the *Nat* component of a *Node* contains the height of the tree. However, this time we need to assume that the integer is not the height, but the *size* of the tree. Thus

size Null $= 0$
size (Node s l x r) $= s$

Of course, installing such information takes time, but we will ignore the cost of doing so. With that assumption, the task is to compute

select :: *Ord a* $\Rightarrow$ *Nat* $\to$ *Tree a* $\to$ *Tree a* $\to$ *a*
select k t₁ t₂ = merge (flatten t₁) (flatten t₂) !! k

The faster algorithm is given by

$$select\ k\ t_1\ Null = index\ t_1\ k$$
$$select\ k\ Null\ t_2 = index\ t_2\ k$$
$$select\ k\ (Node\ h_1\ l_1\ a\ r_1)\ (Node\ h_2\ l_2\ b\ r_2)$$
$$\qquad |\ a \leqslant b \wedge k \leqslant p+q = select\ k\ (Node\ h_1\ l_1\ a\ r_1)\ l_2$$
$$\qquad |\ a \leqslant b \wedge k > p+q = select\ (k-p-1)\ r_1\ (Node\ h_2\ l_2\ b\ r_2)$$
$$\qquad |\ b \leqslant a \wedge k \leqslant p+q = select\ k\ l_1\ (Node\ h_2\ l_2\ b\ r_2)$$
$$\qquad |\ b \leqslant a \wedge k > p+q = select\ (k-q-1)\ (Node\ h_1\ l_1\ a\ r_1)\ r_2$$
$$\qquad \mathbf{where}\ p = size\ l_1;\ q = size\ l_2$$

The function *index* is specified by

$$index\ t\ k = flatten\ t\ !!\ k$$

It is easy to derive

$$index\ (Node\ \_\ l\ x\ r)\ k$$
$$\quad |\ k < p\quad = index\ l\ k$$
$$\quad |\ k == p = x$$
$$\quad |\ k > p\quad = index\ r\ (k-p-1)$$
$$\quad \mathbf{where}\ p = size\ l$$

and we leave details as an exercise.

Now for the tricky part, the proof of the relationship between merging and selection. Recall that we have to simplify

$$merge\ (xs \mathbin{+\!\!+} [a] \mathbin{+\!\!+} ys)\ (us \mathbin{+\!\!+} [b] \mathbin{+\!\!+} vs)\ !!\ k$$

We will assume that $a \leqslant b$; the case $a \geqslant b$ is entirely dual. Furthermore, let p be the length of xs and q the length of us in what follows.

We will need to make use of two decomposition rules, one for list-indexing and one for merging. The decomposition rule for indexing has been used before:

$$(xs \mathbin{+\!\!+} ys)\ !!\ k = \mathbf{if}\ k < n\ \mathbf{then}\ xs\ !!\ k\ \mathbf{else}\ ys\ !!\ (k-n)\ \mathbf{where}\ n = length\ xs$$

To state the decomposition rule for *merge*, first define $\lll$ by

$$(\lll) :: Ord\ a \Rightarrow [a] \to [a] \to Bool$$
$$xs \lll ys = and\ [x \leqslant y \mid x \leftarrow xs, y \leftarrow ys]$$

Thus $xs \lll ys$ holds if no element of xs is larger than any element of ys. The decomposition rule for *merge* now states that

$$merge\ (xs \mathbin{+\!\!+} ys)\ (us \mathbin{+\!\!+} vs) = merge\ xs\ us \mathbin{+\!\!+} merge\ ys\ vs$$

provided $xs \lll vs$ and $us \lll ys$. For the proof observe that $xs \lll ys$ because the list $xs \mathbin{+\!\!+} ys$ is sorted. If $xs \lll vs$ holds as well, then

$$xs \lll merge\ ys\ vs$$

Similarly, $us \lll merge\ ys\ vs$ if $us \lll ys$. Hence, if both hold, then

$$merge\ xs\ us \lll merge\ ys\ vs$$

from which the decomposition rule for *merge* follows.

As well as the two decomposition rules, we will need two other observations. First, suppose $ys = ys_1 \mathbin{+\!\!+} ys_2$, where ys_1 is the longest prefix of ys such that

$$xs \mathbin{+\!\!+} [a] \mathbin{+\!\!+} ys_1 \lll [b] \mathbin{+\!\!+} vs$$

Then we claim $us \lll ys_2$. Either ys_2 is empty, in which case the result is immediate, or its first element is greater than b, which means it is greater than any element in us. As a consequence, we have

$$\begin{aligned}
&merge\ (xs \mathbin{+\!\!+} [a] \mathbin{+\!\!+} ys_1 \mathbin{+\!\!+} ys_2)\ (us \mathbin{+\!\!+} [b] \mathbin{+\!\!+} vs) \\
&= merge\ (xs \mathbin{+\!\!+} [a] \mathbin{+\!\!+} ys_1)\ us \mathbin{+\!\!+} merge\ ys_2\ ([b] \mathbin{+\!\!+} vs)
\end{aligned}$$

by the decomposition rule for *merge*.

The second observation is dual. Suppose $us = us_1 \mathbin{+\!\!+} us_2$, where us_2 is the longest suffix of us such that

$$xs \mathbin{+\!\!+} [a] \lll us_2 \mathbin{+\!\!+} [b] \mathbin{+\!\!+} vs$$

then $us_1 \lll ys$. That means

$$\begin{aligned}
&merge\ (xs \mathbin{+\!\!+} [a] \mathbin{+\!\!+} ys)\ (us_1 \mathbin{+\!\!+} us_2 \mathbin{+\!\!+} [b] \mathbin{+\!\!+} vs) \\
&= merge\ (xs \mathbin{+\!\!+} [a])\ us_1 \mathbin{+\!\!+} merge\ ys\ (us_2 \mathbin{+\!\!+} [b] \mathbin{+\!\!+} vs)
\end{aligned}$$

We are now ready for the main calculation. Assume first that $k \leqslant p + q$. We reason

$$\begin{aligned}
&\quad merge\ (xs \mathbin{+\!\!+} [a] \mathbin{+\!\!+} ys)\ (us \mathbin{+\!\!+} [b] \mathbin{+\!\!+} vs)\ !!\ k \\
&= \quad \{\ \text{choose } ys_1 \text{ and } ys_2 \text{ as above}\ \} \\
&\quad merge\ (xs \mathbin{+\!\!+} [a] \mathbin{+\!\!+} ys_1 \mathbin{+\!\!+} ys_2)\ (us \mathbin{+\!\!+} [b] \mathbin{+\!\!+} vs)\ !!\ k \\
&= \quad \{\ \text{decomposition rule of } merge; \text{ see above}\ \} \\
&\quad (merge\ (xs \mathbin{+\!\!+} [a] \mathbin{+\!\!+} ys_1)\ us \mathbin{+\!\!+} merge\ ys_2\ ([b] \mathbin{+\!\!+} vs))\ !!\ k \\
&= \quad \{\ \text{assumption } k \leqslant p + q \text{ and decomposition rule of } (!!)\ \} \\
&\quad merge\ (xs \mathbin{+\!\!+} [a] \mathbin{+\!\!+} ys_1)\ us\ !!\ k \\
&= \quad \{\ \text{decomposition rule of } (!!) \text{ again}\ \} \\
&\quad (merge\ (xs \mathbin{+\!\!+} [a] \mathbin{+\!\!+} ys_1)\ us \mathbin{+\!\!+} merge\ ys_2\ [])\ !!\ k \\
&= \quad \{\ \text{decomposition rule of } merge \text{ again}\ \} \\
&\quad merge\ (xs \mathbin{+\!\!+} [a] \mathbin{+\!\!+} ys)\ us\ !!\ k
\end{aligned}$$

The second case is when $k > p + q$. Let q_1 be the length of us_1, where us_1 is as defined above. Then we have

$$p + 1 + q_1 \leqslant p + 1 + q \leqslant k$$

This time we reason

$$merge\ (xs \mathbin{+\!\!+} [a] \mathbin{+\!\!+} ys)\ (us \mathbin{+\!\!+} [b] \mathbin{+\!\!+} vs)\ !!\ k$$
$=$ { choose us_1 and us_2 as above }
$$merge\ (xs \mathbin{+\!\!+} [a] \mathbin{+\!\!+} ys)\ (us_1 \mathbin{+\!\!+} us_2 \mathbin{+\!\!+} [b] \mathbin{+\!\!+} vs)\ !!\ k$$
$=$ { decomposition property of $merge$; see above }
$$(merge\ (xs \mathbin{+\!\!+} [a])\ us_1 \mathbin{+\!\!+} merge\ ys\ (us_2 \mathbin{+\!\!+} [b] \mathbin{+\!\!+} vs))\ !!\ k$$
$=$ { assumption on $k > p + q$ and decomposition rule of $(!!)$ }
$$merge\ ys\ (us_2 \mathbin{+\!\!+} [b] \mathbin{+\!\!+} vs)\ !!\ (k - p - 1 - q_1)$$
$=$ { decomposition properties of $(!!)$ and $merge$ again }
$$merge\ ys\ (us \mathbin{+\!\!+} [b] \mathbin{+\!\!+} vs)\ !!\ (k - p - 1)$$

The proof is complete.

6.4 Selection from the complement of a set

Sometimes we want to select from the complement of a set. For example, given a set of five-letter words, we might want the (lexically) smallest five-letter word not in the set. Or we might want the smallest natural number not in a given finite set of natural numbers. The problem is a simplification of a common programming task in which the set represents objects currently in use and one wants to select some object not in use, say the one with the smallest name. In this section we tackle the natural number version of the problem, supposing the set is given as a list without duplicates in no particular order. For example,

$$[08, 23, 09, 00, 12, 11, 01, 10, 13, 07, 41, 04, 14, 21, 05, 17, 03, 19, 02, 06]$$

How would you go about finding the smallest natural number not in this list?
Here is the specification of the problem:

$$select :: [Nat] \rightarrow Nat$$
$$select\ xs = head\ ([0..] \mathbin{\backslash\backslash} xs)$$

$$(\mathbin{\backslash\backslash}) :: Eq\ a \Rightarrow [a] \rightarrow [a] \rightarrow [a]$$
$$xs \mathbin{\backslash\backslash} ys = filter\ (\notin ys)\ xs$$

The value $xs \mathbin{\backslash\backslash} ys$ (pronounced 'xs minus ys') is what remains when every element of ys is removed from xs. Evaluation of $select$ on a list of length n takes $\Omega(n^2)$ steps. For example, evaluation of $select\ [0..n-1]$ requires $n+1$ membership tests, the total cost of which is $n(n+1)/2$ equality tests.

One idea that quickly springs to mind for improving the running time of $select$ is to sort the input. Since the order of the elements in the input is not material, we have

$$select\ xs = head\ ([0..] \mathbin{\backslash\backslash} sort\ xs)$$

Now that the right-hand argument to \\ is ordered, we can simply look for the first gap:

$$select\ xs \qquad\qquad = searchFrom\ 0\ (sort\ xs)$$
$$searchFrom\ k\ [\,] \qquad = k$$
$$searchFrom\ k\ (x:xs) = \textbf{if}\ k == x\ \textbf{then}\ searchFrom\ (k+1)\ xs\ \textbf{else}\ k$$

This improves the running time of *select* to $O(n \log n)$ steps, assuming an asymptotically optimal sorting algorithm is used. However, we can do better still and reduce the time to $\Theta(n)$ steps. The key observation is that it is not necessary to sort all of the input: only those elements that are at most n, the size of the set, need be sorted. The reason is that not every number in $\{0, 1, ..., n\}$ can be in the set: there are $n+1$ numbers in the former and only n in the latter. That means we can define

$$select\ xs = searchFrom\ 0\ (sort\ (filter\ (\leqslant n)\ xs))\ \textbf{where}\ n = length\ xs$$

Unlike general sorting, we can sort a list of n natural numbers, all of which are in the range $(0, n)$, in $\Theta(n)$ steps. For example, we can use Countsort (see Answer 5.17):

$$select\ xs \ = searchFrom\ 0\ (csort\ n\ (filter\ (\leqslant n)\ xs))$$
$$\qquad \textbf{where}\ n = length\ xs$$
$$csort\ n\ xs = concat\ [replicate\ k\ x\ |\ (x,k) \leftarrow assocs\ a]$$
$$\qquad \textbf{where}\ a = accumArray\ (+)\ 0\ (0,n)\ [(x,1)\ |\ x \leftarrow xs]$$

In fact there is no need to produce the sorted list: we can simply look for the first index with count 0:

$$select\ xs = length\ (takeWhile\ (\neq 0)\ (elems\ a))$$
$$\qquad \textbf{where}\ a = accumArray\ (+)\ 0\ (0,n)\ [(x,1)\ |\ x \leftarrow xs, x \leqslant n]$$
$$\qquad n = length\ xs$$

This algorithm does not depend on the input being a list without duplicates.

It is also possible to devise a linear-time divide-and-conquer solution that does not make use of arrays. The idea is to decompose the lists into two equal-size sublists and then compute the solution recursively by continuing with just one of the sublists, the same strategy that was used with binary search. Assuming the decomposition takes $\Theta(n)$ steps, we then obtain the recurrence relation

$$T(n) = T(n/2) + \Theta(n)$$

for the running time $T(n)$, with solution $T(n) = \Theta(n)$.

We can split *xs* by partitioning *xs* on a suitably chosen natural number b (the choice will be made later on), using the function *partition* of Quicksort. With $(ys, zs) = partition\ (<b)\ xs$ we have

$$[0..]\,\backslash\backslash\,xs = ([0..b-1]\,\backslash\backslash\,ys) +\!\!+ ([b..]\,\backslash\backslash\,zs)$$

Here is the proof:

$$[0..] \setminus\setminus xs$$
$$= \quad \{ \text{ since } [0..] = [0..b-1] + [b..] \}$$
$$([0..b-1] + [b..]) \setminus\setminus xs$$
$$= \quad \{ \text{ since } (as + bs) \setminus\setminus xs = (as \setminus\setminus xs) + (bs \setminus\setminus xs) \}$$
$$([0..b-1] \setminus\setminus xs) + ([b..] \setminus\setminus xs)$$
$$= \quad \{ \text{ since } as \setminus\setminus xs = (as \setminus\setminus ys) \setminus\setminus zs = (as \setminus\setminus zs) \setminus\setminus ys \}$$
$$((([0..b-1] \setminus\setminus zs) \setminus\setminus ys) + (([b..] \setminus\setminus ys) \setminus\setminus zs))$$
$$= \quad \{ \text{ since } [0..b-1] \setminus\setminus zs = [0..b-1] \text{ and } [b..] \setminus\setminus ys = [b..] \}$$
$$([0..b-1] \setminus\setminus ys) + ([b..] \setminus\setminus zs)$$

Next, since

$$head\ (as + bs) = \textbf{if } null\ as \textbf{ then } head\ bs \textbf{ else } head\ as$$

we obtain

$$select\ xs = \textbf{if } null\ ([0..b-1] \setminus\setminus ys)$$
$$\textbf{then } head\ ([b..] \setminus\setminus zs)$$
$$\textbf{else } \ head\ ([0..b-1] \setminus\setminus ys)$$
$$\textbf{where } (ys, zs) = partition\ (<b)\ xs$$

Now comes a second key observation. Since ys does not contain duplicates and every element of ys is less than b, we have

$$null\ ([0..b-1] \setminus\setminus ys) = (length\ ys == b)$$

Inspection of the code for $select$ suggests that we should generalise $select$ to a function, $selectFrom$ say, defined by

$$selectFrom :: Nat \to [Nat] \to Nat$$
$$selectFrom\ a\ xs = head\ ([a..] \setminus\setminus xs)$$

under the invariant that no element of xs is smaller than a. Then, provided b is chosen so that the lengths of both partitioned lists are at most half the length of the original, the following recursive definition of $select$ is well-founded:

$$select\ xs = selectFrom\ 0\ xs$$
$$selectFrom\ a\ xs \mid null\ xs \qquad\qquad = a$$
$$\mid length\ ys == b - a = selectFrom\ b\ zs$$
$$\mid otherwise \qquad\quad = selectFrom\ a\ ys$$
$$\textbf{where } (ys, zs) = partition\ (<b)\ xs$$

It remains to choose b. Clearly we want $b > a$, but we would also like to ensure the lengths p and q of the two lists ys and zs are as equal as possible. The appropriate choice to satisfy these requirements is $b = a + 1 + \lfloor n/2 \rfloor$, where n is the length of xs. If $n \neq 0$ and $p < b - a$, then $p \leqslant b - a - 1 = \lfloor n/2 \rfloor$, while if $p = b - a$, then $q = n - (b - a) = n - \lfloor n/2 \rfloor - 1 \leqslant \lfloor n/2 \rfloor$. As a final optimisation we can avoid repeatedly computing $length$ by tupling each list with its length. All of that leads to

$$select\ xs = selectFrom\ 0\ (length\ xs, xs)$$

$$selectFrom\ a\ (n, xs)\ |\ n == 0\quad = a$$
$$|\ l == b - a = selectFrom\ b\ (n - l, zs)$$
$$|\ otherwise\ = selectFrom\ a\ (l, ys)$$
$$\mathbf{where}\ (ys, zs) = partition\ (<b)\ xs$$
$$b\qquad = a + 1 + n\ \mathrm{div}\ 2$$
$$l\qquad = length\ ys$$

This solution also takes linear time.

6.5 Chapter notes

The lower bound on the number of comparisons required to compute *minmax* (see Answer 6.7) is from Pohl [5]. The linear-time selection algorithm was first described by Blum *et al.* [2]. The selection algorithm derived from Quicksort is due to Hoare [3]. It is still not known exactly how many comparisons are required to find the median; see Paterson [4]. The problems of selecting from the union of two sets and from the complement of a set were treated in [1].

References

[1]   Richard Bird. *Pearls of Functional Algorithm Design*. Cambridge University Press, Cambridge, 2010.

[2]   Manuel Blum, Robert W. Floyd, Vaughan Pratt, Ronald L. Rivest, and Robert E. Tarjan. Time bounds for selection. *Journal of Computer and System Sciences*, 7(4):448–461, 1973.

[3]   Charles A. R. Hoare. Algorithm 63 (PARTITION) and Algorithm 65 (FIND). *Communications of the ACM*, 4(7):321–322, 1961.

[4]   Michael S. Paterson. Progress in selection. In R. Karlsson and A. Lingas, editors, *Scandinavian Workshop on Algorithm Theory*, volume 1097 of *Lecture Notes in Computer Science*, pages 368–379. Springer-Verlag, Berlin, 1996.

[5]   Ira Pohl. A sorting problem and its complexity. *Communications of the ACM*, 15(6):462–464, 1972.

Exercises

Exercise 6.1 Does it make sense to define the *k*th smallest element of an arbitrary list as an element with exactly $k - 1$ elements smaller than it?

Exercise 6.2 Define combinators *cross* and *pair* so that

$$pair\ (foldr\ f_1\ e_1, foldr\ f_2\ e_2) = foldr\ (cross \cdot pair\ (f_1, f_2))\ (e_1, e_2)$$

Exercise 6.3 Describe two lists of length n for which the second definition of *minmax* uses $n - 1$ and $2n - 2$ comparisons, respectively.

Exercise 6.4 Show that in the divide-and-conquer algorithm for *minmax* the comparison count $C(n)$ satisfies $C(n) = 3n/2 - 2$ when n is a positive power of two.

Exercise 6.5 Show that $D(n) = 2(n-1)$ in the bottom-up algorithm for *minmax*.

Exercise 6.6 Suppose a set is given by a balanced binary search tree. Asymptotically, how long does it take to find the minimum and maximum elements?

Exercise 6.7 Consider a particularly brutal tennis tournament with the twist that the tournament has to determine both the best and the worst player. Initially all n players are potential champions or potential losers, and the overlap between the two groups is n. The best we can do is to play a match between two players in the overlap, placing the winner in a potential champion category, and the loser in a potential loser category. Assuming n is even, it follows that after $n/2$ matches the overlap is reduced to zero. How would you complete the tournament and how many matches are there?

Exercise 6.8 Show that $n + \lceil \log n \rceil - 2$ matches are sufficient to determine the best and second-best players in a tennis tournament involving n players.

Exercise 6.9 Are there any other ways apart from setting *pivot* $[x] = x$ to ensure the definition of the linear-time algorithm for *select* is well-founded?

Exercise 6.10 Use the rules of floors and ceilings to show that

$$3 \lfloor (\lceil n/5 \rceil + 1)/2 \rfloor - 1 \geqslant 3n/10$$

No case analysis is allowed.

Exercise 6.11 Instead of grouping elements into blocks of 5, suppose we group into blocks of 3. Does this lead to a linear-time algorithm for *select*? How about grouping into blocks of 7?

Exercise 6.12 Counting only comparisons between list elements, how many comparisons are required to compute *select* $4 [1..7]$ when *pivot* chooses the first element of a list, and when *pivot* is as defined in the linear-time version of *select*? For the second question you can assume that sorting n elements for $3 \leqslant n \leqslant 5$ requires 3 comparisons for $n = 3$, 5 comparisons for $n = 4$, and 7 comparisons for $n = 5$.

Exercise 6.13 Is $\lll$ a transitive relation, that is, does $xs \lll ys$ and $ys \lll zs$ imply $xs \lll zs$?

Exercise 6.14 Suppose $xs \mathbin{+\mkern-10mu+} ys$ and $us \mathbin{+\mkern-10mu+} vs$ are both sorted. Prove that $xs \lll vs$ or $us \lll ys$.

Exercise 6.15 Assuming arrays are indexed from 0, write down a definition of

$$select :: Ord\ a \Rightarrow Nat \rightarrow Array\ Nat\ a \rightarrow Array\ Nat\ a \rightarrow a$$

Answers

Answer 6.1 No. Consider the third smallest element of the list $[1,2,2,3]$. There is no element with exactly two smaller elements.

Answer 6.2 We can define

$$pair :: (a \rightarrow b, a \rightarrow c) \rightarrow a \rightarrow (b,c)$$
$$pair\ (f,g)\ x = (f\ x, g\ x)$$
$$cross :: (a \rightarrow c, b \rightarrow d) \rightarrow (a,b) \rightarrow (c,d)$$
$$cross\ (f,g)\ (x,y) = (f\ x, g\ y)$$

Then we have

$$(cross \cdot pair\ (f,g))\ x\ (y,z) = cross\ (pair\ (f,g)\ x)\ (y,z)$$
$$= cross\ (f\ x, g\ x)\ (y,z)$$
$$= (f\ x\ y, g\ x\ z)$$

Answer 6.3 One worst case is when the input is in ascending order. One best case is when the input is in ascending order but with the first and last elements swapped.

Answer 6.4 When n is a power of two we have $C(n) = 2C(n/2) + 2$ and a simple induction yields the answer.

Answer 6.5 The induction step is $D(n) = 2\lfloor n/2 \rfloor + 2(\lceil n/2 \rceil - 1) = 2(n-1)$.

Answer 6.6 We have to find the leftmost and rightmost elements in the tree, each of which takes $\Theta(\log n)$ steps.

Answer 6.7 After reducing the overlap to zero, the best one can do thereafter is to play $n/2 - 1$ matches among the potential losers to determine the worst player, and $n/2 - 1$ matches among the potential winners to determine the champion. That comes to a total of $3n/2 - 2$ matches. A similar argument holds for odd n and shows that $\lceil 3n/2 \rceil - 2$ matches are sufficient, which is the same bound as for the bottom-up algorithm for *minmax*.

The tennis tournament analogy can be used to show that $\lceil 3n/2 \rceil - 2$ matches are necessary in the worst case to determine both the champion and the worst player. We cannot, of course, construct a worst case, because that would depend on the particular algorithm being executed. Instead we can use an *adversarial argument*. In this scenario, the adversary chooses the answers to each comparison test asked for by a particular algorithm as it runs in order to force a worst case. The only restriction on the adversary is that the answers must be consistent with all previous answers. Now, at any stage of the tournament there are four possible groups of players: those that haven't played any matches so far (group A), those that have played some matches and never lost (group B); those that have played some matches and never won (group C); and those that have both won and lost a match (group

D). Let the quadruple (a, b, c, d) denote the number of players in each of these categories at some stage of the tournament. Any algorithm starts with $(n, 0, 0, 0)$ and ends with $(0, 1, 1, n-2)$. The adversary can always arrange that the answer to each comparison test either leaves (a, b, c, d) unchanged or else produces one of the following quadruples (as long as all values are nonnegative):

$$(a-2, b+1, c+1, d) \quad (a-1, b, c+1, d) \quad (a-1, b+1, c, d)$$
$$(a, b-1, c, d+1) \quad (a, b, c-1, d+1)$$

In the first case, a match between two group A players – an AA match – will always produce one extra member of group B and one extra member of group C. In the second case, the adversary can arrange that an AB match produces only one extra member of group C (by having the player in group B win). And so on, for each of the ten cases AA, AB, AC, AD, BB, BC, BD, CC, CD, and DD. The final step is to consider the value $k = 3a + 2b + 2c$. At the start of the tournament $k = 3n$ and at the conclusion $k = 4$. But the value of k can decrease by at most two at each step, so it takes at least $\lceil (3n-4)/2 \rceil = \lceil 3n/2 \rceil - 2$ matches to determine the outcome.

Answer 6.8 It requires $n-1$ matches to determine the best player. Any player who lost to the eventual winner of the tournament may be the second-best player. Since there are $\lceil \log n \rceil$ players who lost to the eventual winner, a second tournament of $\lceil \log n \rceil - 1$ matches can be played to determine the second-best player. That gives a total of $n + \lceil \log n \rceil - 2$ matches. Using another adversarial argument, it can also be shown that this number of matches is necessary.

Answer 6.9 Yes, either set *select* $1 [x] = x$ or set *median* $[x] = x$.

Answer 6.10 The proof goes as follows:

$$3k - 1 \leqslant 3 \lfloor (\lceil n/5 \rceil + 1)/2 \rfloor - 1$$
$$\Leftrightarrow \quad \{ \text{ arithmetic of integers } \}$$
$$k \leqslant \lfloor (\lceil n/5 \rceil + 1)/2 \rfloor$$
$$\Leftrightarrow \quad \{ \text{ rule of floors } \}$$
$$2k - 1 \leqslant \lceil n/5 \rceil$$
$$\Leftrightarrow \quad \{ \text{ arithmetic of integers } \}$$
$$2k - 2 < \lceil n/5 \rceil$$
$$\Leftrightarrow \quad \{ \text{ (contrapositive) rule of ceilings } \}$$
$$10k - 10 < n$$
$$\Leftrightarrow \quad \{ \text{ arithmetic } \}$$
$$k \leqslant (n+9)/10$$

Hence

$$3n/10 \leqslant 3(n+9)/10 - 1 \leqslant 3 \lfloor (\lceil n/5 \rceil + 1)/2 \rfloor - 1$$

Answer 6.11 No, dividing into blocks of 3 will not give a linear-time algorithm. We have

$$2\lfloor(\lceil n/3\rceil+1)/2\rfloor - 1 \geqslant n/3$$

so the associated recurrence relation is

$$T(n) = T(n/3) + T(2n/3) + \Theta(n)$$

whose solution is $\Theta(n \log n)$. However, dividing into blocks of 7 is okay because the associated recurrence relation is

$$T(n) = T(n/7) + T(5n/7) + \Theta(n)$$

whose solution is $T(n) = \Theta(n)$.

Answer 6.12 When the pivot is chosen to be the first element of the list, the value of *select* 4 $[1..7]$ is obtained by computing *partition3 p* $[p..7]$ for $p = 1,2,3,4$. Partitioning a list of n elements requires n comparisons, so $7+6+5+4 = 22$ comparisons are required.

To answer the second question, the calling structure with associated comparison counts is given by

> *select* 4 $[1..7]$
>> *pivot* $[1..7]$
>>> *sort* $[1..5]$ (7 comparisons)
>>> *sort* $[6,7]$ (1 comparisons)
>>> *select* 1 $[3,6]$ (4 comparisons)
>> *partition3* 3 $[1..7]$ (7 comparisons)
>> *select* 1 $[4..7]$ (11 comparisons)

The counts, 4 and 11, for the recursive calls *select* 1 $[3,6]$ and *select* 1 $[4..7]$ of *select* are given by

> *select* 1 $[3,6]$
>> *pivot* $[3,6]$
>>> *sort* $[3,6]$ (1 comparisons)
>>> *select* 1 $[3]$ (1 comparisons)
>> *partition3* 3 $[3,6]$ (2 comparisons)

for a total count of 4 and

> *select* 1 $[4..7]$
>> *pivot* $[4..7]$
>>> *sort* $[4..7]$ (5 comparisons)
>>> *select* 1 $[5]$ (1 comparisons)
>> *partition3* 5 $[4..7]$ (4 comparisons)
>> *select* 1 $[4]$ (1 comparisons)

for a total count of 11. Calls of the form *select* 1 [*x*] each take one comparison. That gives a grand total of 30 comparisons.

Answer 6.13 No, not if *ys* is empty. Transitivity holds only for nonempty lists.

Answer 6.14 The result is immediate if any of the four lists is empty. Otherwise either *last xs* $\leqslant$ *head vs* or *last us* $\leqslant$ *head ys* because if both are false, then

$$head\ vs < last\ xs \leqslant head\ ys < last\ us$$

contradicting the assumption that *us* ++ *vs* is sorted.

Answer 6.15 To help understand the program below, suppose *xa* $[0..n-1]$ denotes an array of *n* elements. Then *bounds xa* $= (0, n-1)$. The segment *xa* $[lx..rx]$ of *xa* has length $rx - lx + 1$, and so is empty if $lx = rx + 1$. The midpoint of the segment is *xa*!*p*, where $p = (lx + rx)$ div 2. The element at position *k*, counting from 0, is at position $lx + rx$ in the segment, and at position $k + lx + ly$ in the result of merging *xs* $[lx..rx]$ with *ya* $[ly..ry]$. With that understood, the function

$$select :: Ord\ a \Rightarrow Nat \rightarrow Array\ Nat\ a \rightarrow Array\ Nat\ a \rightarrow a$$

is defined by

$$
\begin{aligned}
&select\ k\ xa\ ya = search\ k\ (bounds\ xa)\ (bounds\ ya)\ \textbf{where}\\
&\quad search\ k\ (lx, rx)\ (ly, ry)\\
&\quad\ |\ lx == rx + 1 && = ya\ !\ (ly + k)\\
&\quad\ |\ ly == ry + 1 && = xa\ !\ (lx + k)\\
&\quad\ |\ a \leqslant b \wedge k + lx + ly \leqslant p + q = search\ k\ (lx, rx)\ (ly, q - 1)\\
&\quad\ |\ a \leqslant b \wedge k + lx + ly > p + q = search\ (k + lx - p - 1)\ (p + 1, rx)\ (ly, ry)\\
&\quad\ |\ b \leqslant a \wedge k + lx + ly \leqslant p + q = search\ k\ (lx, p - 1)\ (ly, ry)\\
&\quad\ |\ b \leqslant a \wedge k + lx + ly > p + q = search\ (k + ly - q - 1)\ (lx, rx)\ (q + 1, ry)\\
&\quad\ \textbf{where}\ p = (lx + rx)\ \text{div}\ 2\\
&\qquad\qquad\ q = (ly + ry)\ \text{div}\ 2\\
&\qquad\qquad\ a = xa\ !\ p\\
&\qquad\qquad\ b = ya\ !\ q
\end{aligned}
$$

PART THREE

GREEDY ALGORITHMS

Many computational problems involve selecting some best candidate from a set of possible candidates. Candidates can be lists, trees, layouts of a document, routes in a network of roads, and so on. The best candidate may be the shortest list, the least wasteful paragraph, or the quickest route. Even sorting can be regarded as an optimisation problem; after all, the aim of a sorting algorithm is to find some permutation of the input that minimises the number of out-of-order elements. Greedy sorting algorithms will be our first topic in Chapter 7. In general there may be more than one best candidate and the task is to find just one of them.

The input to such problems is normally not the set of candidates but a list of components out of which the candidates can be built. For example, the raw materials may be a list of words that constitute the paragraph, a list of numbers that form the fringe of a tree, or a list of towns and roads in a shortest-path algorithm. A *greedy* algorithm solves such a problem in a *step-by-step* fashion by constructing a single best *partial* candidate at each step. A partial candidate may be a fully formed candidate for the components used so far in its construction, but it may be something more general. The idea of a step-by-step algorithm is easy to grasp intuitively but not so easy to formalise, especially in a purely functional language. For example, a divide-and-conquer algorithm for sorting will minimise the number of out-of-order elements but it is not, conceptually at least, a step-by-step algorithm. Finally, in most of our examples a best candidate is one that minimises some notion of cost, so the word 'greedy' may seem a little inappropriate. Perhaps 'frugal' or 'parsimonious' would be better adjectives. However, the name 'greedy' has become the standard way of referring to these algorithms.

The idea of maintaining a single best candidate at each step will not always lead to a best final candidate. Suppose you are out walking on a hillside and wish to climb to the highest point. If you are in a mist and cannot see where to go, you may decide on the strategy of choosing to walk along a path of steepest ascent at each step. That may work, but it may also lead to the top of a little hillock when there is a much bigger hill in the background. The same is true of greedy algorithms (which have also been called hillclimbing algorithms): you may get to a locally optimal solution that is not globally optimal. We will say that a greedy algorithm *works* if it does lead to a globally optimal solution.

Greedy algorithms can be tricky things. The trickiness is not in the algorithm itself, which is usually quite short and easy to understand, but in the proof that it does produce a best solution. With a greedy algorithm the correctness of the program is less obvious than with, say, a sorting algorithm; after all we did not spend any time in previous chapters on proving that the various sorting algorithms actually did sort. The main difficulty with proving that a greedy algorithm works is that for many problems equational reasoning is simply not up to the task and has to be replaced by reasoning about *refinement*. We will see what this entails in due course.

In the following chapters we consider a number of greedy algorithms. Rather than just giving the algorithm and proving it works, we will take a more structured approach, one that will pay dividends when we come to discuss dynamic programming and exhaustive search algorithms. First we show how to define a function *candidates* that generates the set of *all* possible candidates. This function may be defined recursively or by using a suitable higher-order function such as *foldr*, *until*, or *apply* (a function that applies another function a given number of times). Sometimes more than one style is available, each leading to an equally clear definition, so it is a free choice as to which one to employ. Next we define the selection criterion explicitly. This can also sometimes be done in various ways because a given greedy algorithm may work for more than one cost function. The choice of how the candidates are generated and how the cost function is defined can have a significant effect on the ease with which the correctness of the algorithm is proved. Finally, the generation and selection functions are combined, or *fused*, into one function. When *candidates* is defined as an instance of a standard higher-order function such as *foldr* we can appeal to standard fusion conditions to carry out the fusion step. We have already seen this two-stage process with sorting, when algorithms were described in terms of building a tree and then flattening it. The deep structure of an algorithm is revealed by expressing it in terms of more basic components and then combining them.

Chapter 7

Greedy algorithms on lists

This chapter deals with three problems in which the candidates are lists. The problems are drawn from three different areas of computing, and appear to have nothing in common. Nevertheless, they can all be solved by an appropriate greedy algorithm and the method for obtaining the greedy algorithm is the same in all three cases. The problems will repay careful study, so we will try to take things slowly. To set the scene, we begin with an abstract formulation of the essential ingredients behind a successful greedy algorithm.

7.1 A generic greedy algorithm

The following function *mcc* selects a candidate with minimum cost:

$$mcc :: [Component] \to Candidate$$
$$mcc = minWith\ cost \cdot candidates$$

This function is defined as the composition of a function *candidates* that builds a finite list of candidates out of a list of components, and a function *minWith cost* that selects a candidate with minimum cost. The function *minWith* can be defined in the following way (alternatives are discussed in the exercises):

$$minWith :: Ord\ b \Rightarrow (a \to b) \to [a] \to a$$
$$minWith\ f = foldr1\ (smaller\ f)$$
$$\textbf{where}\ smaller\ f\ x\ y = \textbf{if}\ f\ x \leqslant f\ y\ \textbf{then}\ x\ \textbf{else}\ y$$

The function *foldr1* was introduced in the previous chapter. Since *foldr1* returns the undefined value when applied to an empty list, so does *minWith*. Thus *minWith* returns a well-defined value only when applied to finite nonempty lists. If there is more than one candidate with minimum cost, then the above definition selects the first such candidate on the list. Changing *smaller* to read

$$smaller\ f\ x\ y = \textbf{if}\ f\ x < f\ y\ \textbf{then}\ x\ \textbf{else}\ y$$

would mean that the last candidate with minimum cost is selected. Consequently, the result returned by *minWith* depends on the precise order in which candidates are generated. As will be appreciated by the end of the chapter, this fact will seriously restrict our ability to reason equationally about greedy algorithms. The function *candidates* takes a finite list of components, whatever they may be, and returns a finite nonempty list of candidates. Candidate construction can be achieved in a number of ways, but for the moment we will focus on one that uses *foldr*:

$$candidates :: [Component] \rightarrow [Candidate]$$
$$candidates\ xs = foldr\ step\ [c_0]\ xs$$
$$\textbf{where}\ step\ x\ cs = concatMap\ (extend\ x)\ cs$$

Here c_0 is some default partial candidate for an empty list of components. We could have written

$$candidates = foldr\ (concatMap \cdot extend)\ [c_0]$$

but *step* is certainly a shorter name. The type of *extend* is

$$extend :: Component \rightarrow Candidate \rightarrow [Candidate]$$

This function takes a component and a candidate and returns a finite list of extended candidates. The fully formed candidates are those constructed when all the components have been processed. If the candidates were, say, the permutations of a list, then c_0 would be the empty list and *extend x* would be a list of all the ways x can be inserted into a given permutation. For example,

$$extend\ 1\ [2,4,3] = [[1,2,4,3],[2,1,4,3],[2,4,1,3],[2,4,3,1]]$$

It is assumed in what follows that *extend x* returns a *nonempty* finite list of candidates for all x.

A greedy algorithm for computing *mcc* arises as the result of successfully fusing *minWith cost* with *candidates*. Operationally speaking, instead of building the complete list of candidates and then selecting a best one, we construct a single best candidate at each step. We met the fusion rule for *foldr* in Chapter 1, but here it is again: we have

$$h\ (foldr\ f\ e\ xs) = foldr\ g\ e'\ xs$$

for all finite lists xs, provided $e' = h\ e$ and the fusion condition

$$h\ (f\ x\ y) = g\ x\ (h\ y)$$

holds for all x and y. For our problem, $h = minWith\ cost$ and $f = step$, but g is unknown. The fusion condition reads

$$minWith\ cost\ (step\ x\ cs) = gstep\ x\ (minWith\ cost\ cs)$$

for some function *gstep* (a 'greedy step'). To see if it holds, and to discover *gstep* in the process, we can reason as follows:

$$minWith\ cost\ (step\ x\ cs)$$

$= \quad \{\ \text{definition of } step\ \}$

$$minWith\ cost\ (concatMap\ (extend\ x)\ cs)$$

$= \quad \{\ \text{distributive law (see below)}\ \}$

$$minWith\ cost\ (map\ (minWith\ cost \cdot extend\ x)\ cs)$$

$= \quad \{\ \text{define } gstep\ x = minWith\ cost \cdot extend\ x\ \}$

$$minWith\ cost\ (map\ (gstep\ x)\ cs)$$

$= \quad \{\ \text{greedy condition (see below)}\ \}$

$$gstep\ x\ (minWith\ cost\ cs)$$

The distributive law used in the second step is the fact that

$$minWith\ f\ (concat\ xss) = minWith\ f\ (map\ (minWith\ f)\ xss)$$

provided xss is a finite list of finite nonempty lists. Equivalently,

$$minWith\ f\ (concatMap\ g\ xs) = minWith\ f\ (map\ (minWith\ f \cdot g)\ xs)$$

provided xs is a finite list and g returns finite nonempty lists. The proof of the distributivity law is left as Exercise 7.3.

Summarising this short calculation, we have shown that

$$mcc = foldr\ gstep\ c_0\ \textbf{where}\ gstep\ x = minWith\ cost \cdot extend\ x$$

provided the following *greedy condition* holds:

$$minWith\ cost\ (map\ (gstep\ x)\ cs) = gstep\ x\ (minWith\ cost\ cs)$$

That all seems simple enough, so let's look at some concrete examples.

7.2 Greedy sorting algorithms

Here is one specification of the function *sort* that sorts a list into ascending order:

$$sort :: Ord\ a \Rightarrow [a] \to [a]$$
$$sort = minWith\ ic \cdot perms$$

The function $ic :: Ord\ a \Rightarrow [a] \to Int$, short for 'inversion count', counts the number of *inversions* in a list. The notion of an inversion is one of the first concepts that arise in the study of the combinatorial properties of permutations. An inversion is a pair of elements that are out of place, so (x,y) is an inversion if x appears before y in the list but $x > y$. For example, $ic\ [7,1,2,3] = 3$ and $ic\ [3,2,1,7] = 3$. We can define ic by

$$ic :: Ord\ a \Rightarrow [a] \to Int$$
$$ic\ xs = length\ [(x,y)\ |\ (x,y) \leftarrow pairs\ xs, x > y]$$
$$pairs :: [a] \to [(a,a)]$$
$$pairs\ xs = [(x,y)\ |\ x : ys \leftarrow tails\ xs, y : zs \leftarrow tails\ ys]$$

The function *pairs* returns a list of all pairs of elements in a list in the order they appear in the list, and *ic* counts the number of pairs for which the first component is greater than the second. A list with minimum inversion count has count 0 and is a list in ascending order. Two distinct permutations cannot both be in ascending order, so there is only one permutation of a list that minimises *ic*, namely the sorted permutation.

The function *perms* can be defined in various ways, including by a divide-and-conquer algorithm – see the exercises. Here is the first method used in Chapter 1:

$$perms :: [a] \to [[a]]$$
$$perms = foldr\ (concatMap \cdot extend)\ [[\,]]$$

$$extend :: a \to [a] \to [[a]]$$
$$extend\ x\ [\,] \qquad = [[x]]$$
$$extend\ x\ (y:xs) = (x:y:xs) : map\ (y:)\ (extend\ x\ xs)$$

The function *extend* inserts a new element into a list in all possible positions. In particular, the function *gstep*, where

$$gstep\ x = minWith\ ic \cdot extend\ x$$

inserts a new element into a list so as to minimise the inversion count of the result. For example,

$$gstep\ 6\ [7,1,2,3] = [7,1,2,3,6]$$
$$gstep\ 6\ [3,2,1,7] = [3,2,1,6,7]$$

The first list has inversion count 4, while the second has inversion count 3. The greedy condition for *sort* is the assertion

$$minWith\ ic\ (map\ (gstep\ x)\ xss) = gstep\ x\ (minWith\ ic\ xss)$$

for all x and xss. However, this assertion is false. Take $xss = [[7,1,2,3],[3,2,1,7]]$. We have

$$minWith\ ic\ xss = [7,1,2,3]$$

because both lists have inversion count 3 and *minWith* returns the first list with the smallest inversion count. Hence

$$gstep\ 6\ (minWith\ ic\ xss) = [7,1,2,3,6]$$

with inversion count 4, while

$$minWith\ ic\ (map\ (gstep\ 6)\ xss) = [3,2,1,6,7]$$

with inversion count 3. The greedy condition therefore fails. Of course, the greedy condition does hold if we swap the order of the two lists in *xss*, but what if *xss* were a longer list of permutations? It is not clear that we can always reorder a list of candidates to ensure that the greedy condition holds. In any case, such a step is the wrong route to take, because candidate generation should be an independent activity from finding one with minimum cost. We therefore appear to be well and truly stuck.

There are three possible solvents to free us from this sticky situation. Two of them will be described now, but the third and most important one will be left to the end of the chapter.

The first way of freeing ourselves is to use context-sensitive fusion. We discussed this in Exercise 1.17, but here is the essential point again. Although the fusion condition

$$h (f\, x\, y) = g\, x\, (h\, y)$$

for all x and y is sufficient to establish the fusion rule for *foldr*, it is not a necessary one. All that does have to be shown is that the fusion condition holds for all x and all y of the form $y = foldr\, f\, e\, xs$. This version of the fusion condition is called *context-sensitive* fusion. That means, in the case of sorting, that all we have in fact to show is the context-sensitive fusion condition

$$minWith\ ic\ (map\ (gstep\ x)\ (perms\ xs)) = gstep\ x\ (minWith\ ic\ (perms\ xs))$$

for all x and xs. Luckily, this condition does hold. The proof follows from the fact that there is a *unique* permutation that minimises *ic*, namely the ordered permutation with inversion count 0, and that

$$ic\ xs = 0 \ \Rightarrow\ ic\ (gstep\ x\ xs) = 0$$

Sometimes context-sensitive fusion is not enough to establish the greedy condition. This happens when there is no unique candidate with minimum cost. The second way of becoming unstuck is to *change the cost function*. Suppose you are climbing some hills and want to reach a highest point, of which there maybe more than one. At each step you can take the steepest ascending path, a strategy that may or may not work. Nevertheless, it may also be the case that there is a unique point in the climb with the best view, and that point is also a highest one. An alternative strategy at each step is to take the path that best improves the view. The proof that this strategy works may go through when the first one does not. We will see many examples of this trick in the following chapters.

In the case of sorting there is a simple alternative to *ic*, in fact an alternative that can be accomplished at a stroke! It is to replace *ic* with *id*, the identity function. We did not claim that the cost function had to return a single numerical value. We have $minWith\ id = minimum$, so $sort = minimum \cdot perms$. In words, the sorted permutation is the lexically least permutation. The context-sensitive greedy condition in this case reads

$$minimum\ (map\ (gstep\ x)\ (perms\ xs)) = gstep\ x\ (minimum\ (perms\ xs))$$

where $gstep\ x\ xs = minimum\ (extend\ x\ xs)$. As before, the greedy condition holds because the sorted permutation is the unique permutation that minimises *id*, and

$$sorted \; xs \; \Rightarrow \; sorted \; (gstep \; x \; xs)$$

When xs is a sorted list we can define $gstep \; x \; xs$ by

$$gstep \; x \; [] \qquad = [x]$$
$$gstep \; x \; (y:xs) = \textbf{if } x \leqslant y \textbf{ then } x:y:xs \textbf{ else } y:gstep \; x \; xs$$

The result, namely $sort = foldr \; gstep \; []$, is a simple sorting algorithm usually known as Insertion sort.

Insertion sort is not the only greedy sorting algorithm. Here is the other definition of $perms$ from Chapter 1:

$$perms \; [] = [[]]$$
$$perms \; xs = concatMap \; subperms \; (picks \; xs)$$
$$\qquad\qquad \textbf{where } subperms \; (x, ys) = map \; (x:) \; (perms \; ys)$$

$$picks \; [] \qquad = []$$
$$picks \; (x:xs) = (x, xs):[(y, x:ys) \mid (y, ys) \leftarrow picks \; xs]$$

The function $picks$ picks an arbitrary element from a list in all possible ways, returning both the element and what remains. This version of $perms$ is defined recursively rather than through the use of $foldr$. Nevertheless, it is straightforward to fuse $minimum$ and $perms$. Firstly, we have

$$minimum \; (perms \; []) = minimum \; [[]] = []$$

Secondly, for nonempty xs we reason as follows:

$$
\begin{aligned}
& minimum \; (perms \; xs) \\
= \; & \{ \text{ above definition of } perms \} \\
& minimum \; (concatMap \; subperms \; (picks \; xs)) \\
= \; & \{ \text{ distributive law } \} \\
& minimum \; (map \; (minimum \cdot subperms) \; (picks \; xs)) \\
= \; & \{ \text{ claim: see below } \} \\
& minimum \; (subperms \; (minimum \; (picks \; xs))) \\
= \; & \{ \text{ suppose } (x, ys) = minimum \; (picks \; xs) \} \\
& minimum \; (subperms \; (x, ys)) \\
= \; & \{ \text{ definition of } subperms \} \\
& minimum \; (map \; (x:) \; (perms \; ys)) \\
= \; & \{ \text{ since } minimum \cdot map \; (x:) = (x:) \cdot minimum \text{ on nonemtpy lists } \} \\
& x:minimum \; (perms \; ys)
\end{aligned}
$$

The claim takes the form

$$minimum \cdot map \; f = f \cdot minimum$$

where $f = minimum \cdot subperms$. It is left as an exercise to show that the claim holds if f is a *monotonic* function, that is, $x \leqslant y \Rightarrow f \; x \leqslant f \; y$. To verify the claim for *minimum · subperms*, suppose (x_1, ys_1) and (x_2, ys_2) are two picks of the same list. It is easy to check that

$$(x_1, ys_1) \leqslant (x_2, ys_2) \;\Rightarrow\; x_1 : sort\ ys_1 \leqslant x_2 : sort\ ys_2$$

But, as we have seen, *minimum* (*subperms* (x, ys)) $= x : sort\ ys$ so the claim follows. We have therefore shown

$$sort\ [] = []$$
$$sort\ xs = x : sort\ ys \;\textbf{where}\; (x, ys) = pick\ xs$$

where *pick xs* = *minimum* (*picks xs*). The function *pick* takes quadratic time, but it can be implemented to take linear time, see Exercise 7.10. The result is another well-known algorithm for sorting called Selection sort. Both Insertion sort and Selection sort take quadratic time in the worst case, so they are not fast. But they are simple.

7.3 Coin-changing

Our second problem is about giving change in coins. Suppose you were a cashier in a supermarket and had to give 2.56 in change to a customer. How would you do it? Pause for a moment to answer this question.

We cannot answer this question for you because we do not know your nationality and the currency of your country (though we have assumed in the statement of the question that it is a decimal currency). The denominations of the available coins have to be known. In the United States the denominations are a penny (1c), a nickel (5c), a dime (10c), a quarter (25c), a half-dollar (50c), and a dollar ($1). In the UK they are 1p, 2p, 5p, 10p, 20p, 50p, £1, and £2. (Even 50 years after decimalisation, there are no nicknames for UK coins.) Pre-decimalisation, the UK coinage system was a very odd one, consisting of a halfpenny (0.5d), a penny (1d), a threepence (3d), a sixpence (6d), a shilling (12d), a florin (24d), and a half-crown (30d). The British coped with this system somehow, but fortunately it is now consigned to history. Note that, whatever the system, there has to be a coin that allows change of one unit of currency, be it a penny, a halfpenny, or a cent.[1]

We also cannot answer the question until you say what criterion you are adopting for giving the change. Are you trying to minimise the number of coins in the change or maybe the total weight? Although some people delight in carrying around lots of loose change, the coins can weigh a lot in the pocket or handbag, so maybe minimum weight should be the criterion to go for. The weights in grams of the UK and US coins are given in the following table:

---

[1] That is not strictly true. For example the smallest coin in Australia is 5c but one can buy items for, say, $9.99. When paying by cash with a $10 note, the cashier rounds the amount down to $9.95 and gives 5c change.

	1	2	5	10	20	25	50	100	200
UK	3.56	7.12	3.25	6.5	5.0	–	8.0	9.5	12.0
US	2.5	–	5.0	2.27	–	5.67	11.54	8.1	–

Inspection shows that for UK currency each coin of a given denomination weighs no more than the value of the coin in smaller denominations. But that is not quite enough to prove that minimising the number of coins also minimises the total weight. In US currency two quarters weigh 11.34 grams, which is less than the weight of a half-dollar (11.54 grams). And a quarter and a nickel together weigh 10.67 grams, while three dimes weigh only 6.81 grams. Certainly in the United States minimising the number of coins does not minimise their total weight. The statement *is* true for UK currency, as one can check by exhaustive search (see the exercises).

There is an obvious greedy algorithm for minimising the number of coins: at each step give the customer a coin of largest value as long as it is no larger than the remaining amount. Cashiers regularly adopt such a strategy the world over. For $2.56 that would mean five coins:

$$2 \times \$1 + 1 \times 50c + 1 \times 5c + 1 \times 1c$$

For £2.56 that would mean four coins:

$$1 \times £2 + 1 \times 50p + 1 \times 5p + 1 \times 1p$$

Does the greedy algorithm work? The answer is no, not necessarily: it depends on the coinage system. Before 1971 when decimalisation occurred in the UK, a greedy algorithm for giving change of 48d would use three coins, a half-crown, a shilling and a sixpence, whereas two florins would suffice. Another reason to be grateful for decimalisation. As a simpler example, with denominations $[4, 3, 1]$ the greedy algorithm would give three coins for a change of 6 units, while two coins of denomination 3 would suffice.

To specify the problem, suppose we are given a list of denominations in decreasing order, ending with a denomination of 1. For example,

type *Denom* = *Nat*
type *Tuple* = *[Nat]*

usds, ukds :: *[Denom]*
usds = $[100, 50, 25, 10, 5, 1]$
ukds = $[200, 100, 50, 20, 10, 5, 2, 1]$

By definition, a *tuple* is a list of natural numbers, of the same length as the list of denominations, representing the given change (we prefer 'tuple' to 'change' simply because 'tuples' reads better than 'changes'). For example, $[2, 1, 0, 0, 1, 1]$ represents $2.56 in US currency. The amount a tuple represents is given by

amount :: *[Denom]* → *Tuple* → *Nat*
amount ds cs = *sum* (*zipWith* (×) *ds cs*)

The number of coins in a tuple, its count, is defined by $count = sum$. We can now define

$mkchange :: [Denom] \rightarrow Nat \rightarrow Tuple$

$mkchange\ ds = minWith\ count \cdot mktuples\ ds$

The function $mktuples$ gives all possible ways of making change for a given amount with the given denominations. One simple definition is

$mktuples :: [Denom] \rightarrow Nat \rightarrow [Tuple]$

$mktuples\ [1]\ n = [[n]]$

$mktuples\ (d : ds)\ n = [c : cs \mid c \leftarrow [0 .. n \text{ div } d], cs \leftarrow mktuples\ ds\ (n - c \times d)]$

By assumption the last coin has denomination 1, so to make up change of n using just this coin we have to use n coins. Otherwise, for the next denomination d any number c in the range $0 \leqslant c \leqslant \lfloor n/d \rfloor$ can be chosen. The rest of the computation is a recursive call with the remaining denominations and the remaining amount $n - cd$. Another reasonable definition of $mktuples$ based on $foldr$ is given as Exercise 7.14.

The function $mktuples$ can return a long list of candidate tuples. For example,

$length\ (mktuples\ usds\ 256) = 6620$

$length\ (mktuples\ ukds\ 256) = 223195$

Hence computation with the above definition of $mkchange$ is quite slow.

There is another important feature of $mkchange$ to take into account: unlike the case of sorting there may be more than one tuple with minimum count. For example, take the denominations $[7, 3, 1]$. Then both $[6, 4, 0]$ and $[7, 1, 2]$ are tuples for 54 units of change with minimum count 10. The definition of $minWith$ given in the previous section chooses the first tuple with minimum count in the list of candidates. That means the above definition of $mkchange$ returns $[6, 4, 0]$ (why?) but the greedy algorithm, as outlined in the preamble, chooses the second tuple $[7, 1, 2]$. These results are different and again we seem to be stuck. One can resolve this difficulty by modifying the definition of $mktuples$ to produce the tuples in a different order. But two wrongs do not make a right and this is not the path to take. One alternative, as we have seen, is to change the cost function.

This time we replace $minWith\ count$ by $maxWith\ id$. Thus we define

$mkchange\ ds = maximum \cdot mktuples\ ds$

since $maxWith\ id = maximum$. Instead of choosing a tuple with minimum count, $mkchange$ chooses the lexically largest tuple. Whether or not the largest tuple is also one with minimum count depends on the denominations of the coins. We return to this essential point in a short while. Note that, while there may be more than one tuple with minimum count, there is always a unique largest tuple.

So, let us calculate it. The base case

$mkchange\ [1]\ n = [n]$

is immediate. For the induction step we first rewrite the definition of *mktuples* to avoid an explicit list comprehension:

> $mktuples\ [1]\ n = [[n]]$
> $mktuples\ (d:ds)\ n = concatMap\ (extend\ ds)\ [0..n\ \text{div}\ d]$
> > **where** $extend\ ds\ c = map\ (c:)\ (mktuples\ ds\ (n - c \times d))$

The translation is straightforward and details are omitted. The advantage of higher-order functions such as *concatMap* over list comprehensions is that the rules of the game can be stated more simply. In particular,

> $maximum\ (concatMap\ f\ xs) = maximum\ (map\ (maximum \cdot f)\ xs)$
> $maximum\ (map\ (x:)\ xs) \quad = x : maximum\ xs$

for all finite nonempty lists. The first law is an instance of the distributive law of the previous section; as before it is valid only if f returns a finite nonempty list. That is not a problem here because *extend* does return such a list. The second is not valid if xs is the empty list (why?), but that is also not a problem here because *mktuples* returns a nonempty list.

We now reason as follows:

> $\quad mkchange\ (d:ds)\ n$
> $=\quad \{\text{ definition }\}$
> $\quad maximum\ (mktuples\ (d:ds)\ n)$
> $=\quad \{\text{ definition of } mktuples \text{ with } m = n\ \text{div}\ d\ \}$
> $\quad maximum\ (concatMap\ (extend\ ds)\ [0..m])$
> $=\quad \{\text{ first law above }\}$
> $\quad maximum\ (map\ (maximum \cdot extend\ ds)\ [0..m])$

We continue with the inner term:

> $\quad maximum\ (extend\ ds\ c)$
> $=\quad \{\text{ definition of } extend\ \}$
> $\quad maximum\ (map\ (c:)\ (mktuples\ ds\ (n - c \times d)))$
> $=\quad \{\text{ second law above }\}$
> $\quad c : maximum\ (mktuples\ ds\ (n - c \times d))$
> $=\quad \{\text{ definition of } mkchange\ \}$
> $\quad c : mkchange\ ds\ (n - c \times d)$

Hence

> $\quad maximum\ (map\ (maximum \cdot extend\ ds)\ [0..m])$
> $=\quad \{\text{ above }\}$
> $\quad maximum\ [c : mkchange\ ds\ (n - c \times d)\ |\ c \leftarrow [0..m]]$
> $=\quad \{\text{ definition of lexicographic maximum }\}$
> $\quad m : mkchange\ ds\ (n - m \times d)$

That gives the greedy algorithm:

$$mkchange :: [Denom] \rightarrow Nat \rightarrow Tuple$$
$$mkchange\,[1]\,n \quad = [n]$$
$$mkchange\,(d:ds)\,n = c:mkchange\,ds\,(n-c\times d)\ \textbf{where}\ c = n\ \text{div}\ d$$

At each step the maximum number of coins of the next denomination is chosen. For example,

$$mkchange\ ukds\ 256 \ = [1,0,1,0,0,1,0,1]$$
$$mkchange\ usds\ 256 \ = [2,1,0,0,1,1]$$
$$mkchange\,[7,3,1]\,54 = [7,1,2]$$

All of the calculation above is valid for the earlier definition of *mkchange* in terms of minimising *count*, except for the very last step.

Finally, but crucially, we revisit the question of when *mkchange* does produce a tuple with minimum count. Equivalently, when is the lexically largest tuple also the one with minimum count?

Let us prove this is the case for UK currency (the case of US currency is slightly simpler and left as an exercise). Let $[c_8, c_7, ..., c_1]$ be a tuple with minimum count and $[g_8, g_7, ..., g_1]$ be the tuple returned by the greedy algorithm, namely the lexically largest tuple. The aim is to show that $c_j = g_j$ for $1 \leqslant j \leqslant 8$, so the largest tuple for UK currency is the unique tuple with minimum count. This is not necessarily true for other currencies for which the greedy algorithm works. The amount A in the change satisfies

$$A = 200\,c_8 + 100\,c_7 + 50\,c_6 + 20\,c_5 + 10\,c_4 + 5\,c_3 + 2\,c_2 + c_1$$
$$A = 200\,g_8 + 100\,g_7 + 50\,g_6 + 20\,g_5 + 10\,g_4 + 5\,g_3 + 2\,g_2 + g_1$$

We first show that $c_1 = g_1$ and $c_2 = g_2$. First of all, $0 \leqslant g_1 < 2$ for otherwise we could increase g_2 to obtain a lexically larger tuple. Also $0 \leqslant c_1 < 2$ for otherwise we could increase c_2 to obtain a larger tuple with a smaller count. The next step is to prove that $0 \leqslant 2c_2 + c_1 < 5$ and $0 \leqslant 2g_2 + g_1 < 5$. This is done by showing that, if $2c_2 + c_1 \geqslant 5$, then there is a larger tuple for the same amount with the same or a smaller count. Details are given in Exercise 7.15. The proof of the second inequality is the same. As a result we have

$$A \bmod 5 = 2c_2 + c_1 = 2g_2 + g_1$$

and so $2(c_2 - g_2) = g_1 - c_1 < 2$. Hence $c_1 = g_1$ and $c_2 = g_2$. Next, setting

$$B = (A - (2c_2 + c_1))/5$$

we have

$$B = 40\,c_8 + 20\,c_7 + 10\,c_6 + 4\,c_5 + 2\,c_4 + c_3$$
$$B = 40\,g_8 + 20\,g_7 + 10\,g_6 + 4\,g_5 + 2\,g_4 + g_3$$

Now $0 \leqslant g_3 < 2$, for otherwise we could increase g_4 to obtain a larger tuple. And $0 \leqslant c_3 < 2$, for otherwise there would be a tuple with smaller count. Hence

$$B \bmod 2 = c_3 = g_3$$

For the next step, set $C = (B - c_3)/2$. Then

$$C = 20\,c_8 + 10\,c_7 + 5\,c_6 + 2\,c_5 + c_4$$
$$C = 20\,g_8 + 10\,g_7 + 5\,g_6 + 2\,g_5 + g_4$$

The same reasoning as in the first step shows that $c_4 = g_4$ and $c_5 = g_5$. For the next step, set $D = (C - (2\,c_5 + c_4))/5$, so

$$D = 4\,c_8 + 2\,c_7 + c_6$$
$$D = 4\,g_8 + 2\,g_7 + g_6$$

The same argument as in the second step shows $c_6 = g_6$. Setting $E = (D - c_6)/2$ we have

$$E = 2\,c_8 + c_7$$
$$E = 2\,g_8 + g_7$$

and now we can repeat the argument in the first step once again to show that $c_7 = g_7$ and $c_8 = g_8$.

There is no shortcut to this rather lengthy reasoning about currency; each denomination has to be dealt with separately. After all, the argument might break down only with larger denominations. Essentially the same argument works for US currency. It also works for denominations that are successive powers of some base or, more generally, when each denomination is a multiple of the next lower denomination. But there appears to be no simple characterisation of when it works in general.

7.4 Decimal fractions in TEX

Our third problem involving lists of numbers has to do with Knuth's typesetting system TEX, the system used to typeset this book. The source language of TEX is decimal. For instance, one can use \hspace{0.2134156in} to get a space of that width: | |. But internally TEX uses integer arithmetic with all fractions expressed as an integer multiple of $1/2^{16} = 1/65536$. For example, 0.2134156 is represented by the integer 13986, as is the shorter fraction 0.21341. There is therefore the problem of converting a decimal fraction to its closest internal representation and, conversely, converting an internal representation to its shortest decimal fraction. In either direction only limited-precision integer arithmetic is allowed, the arithmetic of *Int*. The first direction is easy but the other one involves a greedy algorithm.

Let us consider the external-to-internal problem first. With *Digit* as a synonym for *Int* restricted to digits d in the range $0 \leqslant d < 10$, a decimal fraction representing a real number r in the range $0 \leqslant r < 1$ can be converted into a floating-point number (see Exercise 1.11) by

> $fraction :: [Digit] \rightarrow Double$
> $fraction = foldr\ shiftr\ 0$
>
> $shiftr :: Digit \rightarrow Double \rightarrow Double$
> $shiftr\ d\ r = (fromIntegral\ d + r)/10$

For example, $0.d_1 d_2 d_3$ is converted into the real number

$$(d_1 + (d_2 + (d_3 + 0)/10)/10)/10 = \frac{d_1}{10} + \frac{d_2}{100} + \frac{d_3}{1000}$$

The conversion function $fromIntegral$ is needed in Haskell to convert an integer (here a digit) into a floating-point number before it can be added to another floating-point number. Such conversion functions obscure the arithmetic and from now on we will silently ignore them in arithmetic reasoning.

The function $scale$ converts the result r into the nearest multiple of 2^{-16}, namely

$$\lfloor 2^{16} r + 1/2 \rfloor = \left\lfloor \frac{2^{17} r + 1}{2} \right\rfloor$$

Hence, since $2^{17} = 131072$, we can define

> $scale :: Double \rightarrow Int$
> $scale\ r = \lfloor (131072 \times r + 1)/2 \rfloor$

The external-to-internal TEX problem is now specified by

> $intern :: [Digit] \rightarrow Int$
> $intern = scale \cdot fraction$

Well and good, but $intern$ uses fractional arithmetic to compute the result and the requirement was to use only limited-precision integer arithmetic. So there is still a problem to overcome.

The solution is to try to fuse $scale$ and $fraction$ into one function using the fusion law of $foldr$. But this turns out not to be possible (see Exercise 7.19). The best we can do is to decompose $scale$ into two functions and fuse just one of them with $fraction$. We have for all integers a and b, with $b > 0$, and real x that

$$\left\lfloor \frac{x+a}{b} \right\rfloor = \left\lfloor \frac{\lfloor x \rfloor + a}{b} \right\rfloor \tag{7.1}$$

The proof, which uses the rule of floors (see Exercise 4.1), is left as another exercise. In particular, taking $x = 131072\,r$, $a = 1$, and $b = 2$, it follows that

> $scale = halve \cdot convert$

where

> $halve\ n = (n+1)\ \text{div}\ 2$
> $convert\ r = \lfloor 131072 \times r \rfloor$

It *is* possible to fuse *convert* and *fraction*. We have

$$convert \cdot foldr\ shiftr\ 0 = foldr\ shiftn\ 0$$

provided we can find a function *shiftn* to satisfy the fusion condition

$$convert\ (shiftr\ d\ r) = shiftn\ d\ (convert\ r)$$

To discover *shiftn* we reason

$$
\begin{aligned}
&convert\ (shiftr\ d\ r) \\
= \quad &\{\ \text{definitions}\ \} \\
&\lfloor 131072 \times (d+r)/10 \rfloor \\
= \quad &\{\ (7.1)\ \} \\
&(131072 \times d + \lfloor 131072 \times r \rfloor)\ \text{div}\ 10 \\
= \quad &\{\ \text{definition of}\ convert\ \} \\
&(131072 \times d + convert\ r)\ \text{div}\ 10
\end{aligned}
$$

Hence we can define

$$shiftn\ d\ n = (131072 \times d + n)\ \text{div}\ 10$$

We have shown that

$$intern :: [Digit] \rightarrow Int$$
$$intern = halve \cdot foldr\ shiftn\ 0$$

That solves the external-to-internal problem. The largest integer that can arise during this computation is at most 1310720, so *Int* arithmetic is sufficient. Notice that we have nowhere exploited any property of 131072 except that it was a positive integer. But for 2^{17} the algorithm can be optimised: except for the first 17 digits, all the other digits of the fraction can be discarded because they cannot affect the answer. The proof is left as Exercise 7.20.

The other direction is to find for a given n in the range $0 \leqslant n < 2^{16}$ some shortest decimal fraction whose internal representation is n. Again, only limited-precision integer arithmetic is allowed. We know by now how to set up the problem:

$$extern :: Int \rightarrow [Digit]$$
$$extern\ n = minWith\ length\ (externs\ n)$$

where n is restricted to the range $0 \leqslant n < 2^{16}$. Ideally, the function *externs n* should return a list of all finite decimals whose internal value is n. The problem is that this is an infinite list, so any execution of *extern* would fail to terminate. For example, the 17-digit fraction 0.01525115966796875 and the 5-digit fraction 0.01526 both have internal value 1000, and so does any fraction between these bounds. Sometimes, as here, the set of candidates is infinite, and selecting a best one, though expressible mathematically, cannot be formulated as an executable expression.

One solution, as we have seen above, is to generate only decimals of length at most 17. In fact, it is sufficient to generate decimals of length at most 5 (see

Exercise 7.22). Indeed, in the first implementation of T_EX a decimal of exactly length five was always chosen. But this choice proved unsatisfactory (a user who asked for a 0.4-point rule was told that T_EX had actually typeset a 0.39999-point rule), so Knuth implemented a greedy algorithm.

Instead we will look at another way to generate a finite list of possible decimals, one guaranteed to include all the shortest decimals. This method will lead to the greedy algorithm. To determine the list, observe that a decimal ds is an element of *externs n* if and only if *scale* (*fraction ds*) $= n$. Abbreviating 131072 to w in what follows, we have

$$scale \, r = n \iff 2n - 1 \leqslant wr < 2n + 1$$

since *scale* $r = \lfloor (wr + 1)/2 \rfloor$. That suggests generalising *externs* to a function, *decimals* say, that takes an interval as argument:

$$externs \, n = decimals \, (2n - 1, 2n + 1)$$

where, provided $a < b$ and $b > 0$, the value of *decimals* (a, b) is any list of decimals ds satisfying

$$a \leqslant w \times fraction \, ds < b$$

as long as it includes all the shortest decimals satisfying the constraint. To arrive at a definition of *decimals*, observe first that

$$a \leqslant w \times fraction \, [\,] < b \iff a \leqslant 0 < b$$

so we can set *decimals* $(a, b) = [[\,]]$ if $a \leqslant 0$. Secondly, we have

$$a \leqslant w \times fraction \, (d : ds) < b$$
$\iff$ { definition of *fraction* }
$$a \leqslant w \times shiftr \, d \, (fraction \, ds) < b$$
$\iff$ { definition of *shiftr*, writing $r = fraction \, ds$ }
$$a \leqslant w(d + r)/10 < b$$
$\iff$ { arithmetic }
$$10a - wd \leqslant wr < 10b - wd$$
$\iff$ { since $0 \leqslant r < 1$ (and $P \iff P \wedge Q$ if $P \Rightarrow Q$) }
$$(10a/w - 1 < d < 10b/w) \wedge (10a - wd \leqslant wr < 10b - wd)$$
$\iff$ { since d is an integer }
$$(\lfloor 10a/w \rfloor \leqslant d \leqslant \lfloor 10b/w \rfloor) \wedge (10a - wd \leqslant wr < 10b - wd)$$
$\iff$ { since d is a digit }
$$(max \, 0 \, \lfloor 10a/w \rfloor \leqslant d \leqslant min \, 9 \, \lfloor 10b/w \rfloor \wedge$$
$$(10a - wd \leqslant wr < 10b - wd)$$

Hence

$$a \leqslant w \times fraction \, (d : ds) < b$$
$$\iff \quad l \leqslant d \leqslant u \wedge 10a - wd \leqslant fraction \, ds < 10b - wd$$

where $l = max\ 0\ \lfloor 10a/w \rfloor$ and $u = min\ 9\ \lfloor 10b/w \rfloor$. That suggests the following definition of *decimals*:

> $decimals :: (Int, Int) \rightarrow [[Digit]]$
> $decimals\ (a,b) =$
>   **if** $a \leqslant 0$ **then** $[[\ ]]$
>   **else** $[d : ds \mid d \leftarrow [l..u], ds \leftarrow decimals\ (10 \times a - w \times d, 10 \times b - w \times d)]$
>   **where** $w = 131072$
> $l\ = 0\ max\ ((10 \times a)\ \text{div}\ w)$
> $u = 9\ min\ ((10 \times b)\ \text{div}\ w)$

Given this definition, we claim that *externs n* returns a list of all decimals *ds* such that *intern ds = n* but *intern ds′ < n* for any proper prefix *ds′* of *ds*. For the proof, observe that the successive intervals generated by *decimals* (a,b) have lower bounds

$$a,\ 10a - wd_1,\ 10(10a - wd_1) - wd_2, \dots$$

The *k*th term of this sequence is

$$10^k a - w(10^{k-1} d_1 + \cdots + 10^0 d_k) = 10^k (a - w \times fraction\ ds)$$

Hence *decimals* (a,b) produces a list of the shortest *ds* such that $a \leqslant wr$, where $r = fraction\ ds$. Furthermore, $2n - 1 \leqslant wr$ if and only if $n \leqslant scale\ r$, so *externs n* produces decimals *ds* that scale to *n* but no prefix of *ds* does.

However, the above definition of *decimals* contains a bug that we have encountered before in the definition of binary search. The problem is that the numbers can get quite large and the arithmetic of *Int* is not up to the job. Instead we have to move over to *Integer* arithmetic and define *decimals* as a function with type

$$decimals :: (Integer, Integer) \rightarrow [[Digit]]$$

The reason for the bug and the necessary revisions of *decimals* and *externs* are left as an exercise.

Now that we have ensured that *externs* returns a finite list, we can return to consideration of *extern*. As in the coin-changing problem, there may be more than one shortest fraction with the same internal representation. For example, both 0.05273 and 0.05274 are shortest fractions whose internal representation is 3456. The above definition of *extern* returns the first fraction while, as we will see, the greedy algorithm returns the second. Once again the solution is to change the cost function.

The revised definition of *extern* should cause no surprise:

$$extern = maximum \cdot externs$$

As with coin-changing, we switch to selecting the lexically largest decimal fraction. The proof that the largest fraction returned by *externs* is a shortest fraction is given later on.

We will omit the calculation that gives the following greedy algorithm:

$extern :: Int \rightarrow [Digit]$

$extern \; n = decimal \; (2 \times n - 1, 2 \times n + 1)$

where

$decimal :: (Int, Int) \rightarrow [Digit]$

$decimal \; (a, b) = \textbf{if } a \leqslant 0 \textbf{ then } [\,]$

$\qquad\qquad\qquad\quad \textbf{else } d : decimal \; (10 \times a - w \times d, 10 \times b - w \times d)$

$\qquad\qquad\qquad\quad \textbf{where } d = (10 \times b) \; \text{div} \; w$

$\qquad\qquad\qquad\qquad\qquad\; w = 131072$

Note first that *Integer* arithmetic has been replaced by *Int* arithmetic again. We claim that $b < w$ for all calls of *decimal* (a, b). With $n < 2^{16}$ we have

$$2n + 1 \leqslant 2(2^{16} - 1) + 1 = 2^{17} - 1 < 2^{17} = w$$

so the claim holds for the initial call. Furthermore

$$10b - w \lfloor 10b/w \rfloor = 10b \bmod w < w$$

so the claim holds for recursive calls. With $b < w$ we have $0 \leqslant \lfloor 10b/w \rfloor < 10$, so d is always a valid digit.

It remains to show that the largest decimal fraction is also a shortest one. We do this by showing that if ds_1 and ds_2 are two different decimals in *decimals* (a, b), then $ds_1 < ds_2 \Rightarrow length \; ds_2 \leqslant length \; ds_1$. We saw above that, if *decimals* (a, b) produces a decimal ds, then it cannot also produce a proper prefix of ds. Hence ds_1 cannot be a prefix of ds_2. Now, by definition of lexical order, we have $ds_1 = us \mathbin{+\!\!+} d_1 : vs_1$ and $ds_2 = us \mathbin{+\!\!+} d_2 : vs_2$, where $d_1 < d_2$. Let k be the length of us and n be the decimal integer formed from the digits in us. It is easy to show that both $d_1 : vs_1$ and $d_2 : vs_2$ are in

$decimals \; (10^k \times a - 131072 \times n, 10^k \times b - 131072 \times n)$

But $d_1 < d_2$, and that means $[d_2]$ is also in this list. And since $[d_2]$ and $d_2 : vs_2$ cannot both be in the list unless vs_2 is the empty list, we conclude that $ds_2 = us \mathbin{+\!\!+} [d_2]$, which is no longer than ds_1.

7.5 Nondeterministic functions and refinement

All three problems in this chapter have been successfully dealt with by changing the cost function into another one that guarantees a linear order, so minimum and maximum elements are unique. However, this device is not always possible. In general, in order to establish a (context-sensitive) greedy condition of the form

$gstep \; x \; (minWith \; cost \; (candidates \; xs))$

$\quad = minWith \; cost \; (map \; (gstep \; x) \; (candidates \; x))$

when there may be more than one candidate with minimum cost, we have to prove the very strong property

$$cost\ c \leqslant cost\ c' \iff cost\ (gstep\ x\ c) \leqslant cost\ (gstep\ x\ c') \qquad (7.2)$$

for all candidates c and c'. To see why, observe that, if c is the first candidate returned by *candidates* with minimum cost, then *gstep x c* has to be the first candidate with minimum cost in the list of extended candidates. This follows from our definition of *minWith*, which selects the first element with minimum cost in a list of candidates. To ensure that the extension of a candidate c' earlier in the list has a larger cost, we have to show that

$$cost\ c' > cost\ c \implies cost\ (gstep\ x\ c') > cost\ (gstep\ x\ c) \qquad (7.3)$$

for all candidates c and c'. To ensure that the extension of a candidate c' later in the list does not have a smaller cost, we have to show that

$$cost\ c \leqslant cost\ c' \implies cost\ (gstep\ x\ c) \leqslant cost\ (gstep\ x\ c') \qquad (7.4)$$

for all c and c'. The conjunction of (7.3) and (7.4) is (7.2).

The problem is that (7.2) is so strong that it rarely holds in practice. A similar condition is needed if, say, *minWith* returned the last element in a list with minimum cost. What we really need is a form of reasoning that allows us to establish the necessary fusion condition from the simple monotonicity condition (7.4) alone, and the plain fact of the matter is that equational reasoning with any definition of *minWith* is simply not adequate to provide it.

It follows that we have to abandon equational reasoning, at least for a function like *minWith*. One general approach is to replace our functional framework with a *relational* one, and to reason instead about the inclusion of one relation in another. But for our purposes this solution is way too drastic, more akin to a heart transplant than a tube of solvent for occasional use. The alternative, if it can be made to work smoothly, is to introduce a *nondeterministic* variant of *minWith* and to reason about the refinement of one expression by another instead of the equality of two expressions.

Suppose we introduce *MinWith cost* as a nondeterministic function, specified by the assertion that x is a possible value of *MinWith cost xs* precisely when xs is a finite nonempty list of well-defined values, x is an element of xs, and $cost\ x \leqslant cost\ y$ for all elements y of xs. Note the initial capital letter: *MinWith* is not part of Haskell. It is not our intention to extend Haskell with nondeterministic functions. Instead, *MinWith* is simply there to extend our powers of specification and will not appear in any final algorithm.

We will write $x \leftarrow MinWith\ cost\ xs$ to mean that x is one possible element of xs with minimum cost. The symbol $\leftarrow$ is read as "is a refinement of". Think of *MinWith cost xs* as the *set* of elements of xs with minimum cost and interpret $\leftarrow$

as set membership. The situation is analogous to order notation, in which $O(g(n))$ is interpreted as a set of functions and the equality sign in $f(n) = O(g(n))$ as set membership. For example, $1 \leftarrow \textit{MinWith cost} \, [1,2]$ is a true assertion provided $\textit{cost} \, 1 \leqslant \textit{cost} \, 2$. On the other hand, neither $\textit{MinWith cost} \, [\,]$ nor $\textit{MinWith cost} \, [1, \bot, 2]$ is well-defined.

More generally, if E_1 and E_2 are possibly nondeterministic expressions of the same type T, then we will write $E_1 \leftarrow E_2$ to mean that

$$v \leftarrow E_1 \;\Rightarrow\; v \leftarrow E_2$$

for all values v of type T. Thus the symbol $\leftarrow$ in $E_1 \leftarrow E_2$ should be thought of as *set inclusion*. The situation is analogous to an assertion such as $2n^2 + O(n^2) = O(n^2)$ in which the $=$ sign really means set inclusion.

Next, suppose E and E_1 are possibly nondeterministic expressions. Then we interpret $x \leftarrow E(E_1)$ to mean that there exists a y such that $y \leftarrow E_1$ and $x \leftarrow E(y)$. Consequently, we have

$$E_1 \leftarrow E_2 \;\Rightarrow\; E(E_1) \leftarrow E(E_2)$$

Thus all expressions are monotonic under refinement.

As an example, consider the greedy condition

$\textit{gstep} \, x \, (\textit{MinWith cost} \, (\textit{candidates xs}))$
$\qquad \leftarrow \textit{MinWith cost} \, (\textit{map} \, (\textit{gstep} \, x) \, (\textit{candidates xs}))$

First of all, this assertion is meaningful only if $\textit{candidates xs}$ is a finite nonempty list of well-defined values and $\textit{gstep} \, x$ returns well-defined results on well-defined arguments. In such a case, the assertion

$c \leftarrow \textit{gstep} \, x \, (\textit{MinWith cost} \, (\textit{candidates xs}))$

holds if $c = \textit{gstep} \, x \, c'$ for some c' such that $c' \leftarrow \textit{MinWith cost} \, (\textit{candidates xs})$. The greedy condition asserts that, for some candidate c' in the list $cs = \textit{candidates xs}$ with minimum cost, $\textit{gstep} \, x \, c'$ is a candidate with minimum cost in $\textit{map} \, (\textit{gstep} \, x) \, cs$. Unlike the previous version of the greedy condition, this assertion does follow from the simple monotonicity condition (7.4). To spell out the details, suppose c' is a candidate in cs with minimum cost. We have only to show that

$$\textit{cost} \, (\textit{gstep} \, x \, c') \leqslant \textit{cost} \, (\textit{gstep} \, x \, c'')$$

for all candidates c'' in cs. But this follows at once from (7.4) and the assumption $\textit{cost} \, c' \leqslant \textit{cost} \, c''$.

Next, we define two nondeterministic expressions of the same type to be equal if they both have the same set of refinements. Thus

$$E_1 = E_2 \;\Leftrightarrow\; E_1 \leftarrow E_2 \wedge E_2 \leftarrow E_1$$

For example, consider the distributive law

$$\textit{MinWith cost} \, (\textit{concat xss}) = \textit{MinWith cost} \, (\textit{map} \, (\textit{MinWith cost}) \, \textit{xss})$$

where xss is a finite nonempty list of finite nonempty lists. This is a law we definitely want to hold. The equality sign here means that there is no refinement of one side that is not also a refinement of the other side. We interpret the assertion

$$xs \leftarrow map\ (MinWith\ cost)\ xss$$

to mean that, if $xss = [xs_1, xs_2, ..., xs_n]$ is a list of finite nonempty lists of well-defined values, then $xs = [x_1, x_2, ..., x_n]$, where $x_j \leftarrow MinWith\ cost\ xs_j$. The proof that the distributive law holds is left as Exercise 7.23.

What else do we want? Well, we certainly want a refinement version of the fusion law for $foldr$, namely that

$$foldr\ gstep\ c_0\ xs \leftarrow MinWith\ cost\ (foldr\ fstep\ [c_0]\ xs)$$

for all finite lists xs provided

$$gstep\ x\ (MinWith\ cost\ ys) \leftarrow MinWith\ cost\ (fstep\ x\ ys)$$

for all x and all ys of the form $ys = foldr\ fstep\ [c_0]\ xs$. Here is the proof of the fusion law. The base case is immediate and the induction step is as follows:

$$
\begin{aligned}
& foldr\ gstep\ c_0\ (x:xs) \\
=\quad & \{\ \text{definition of } foldr\ \} \\
& gstep\ x\ (foldr\ gstep\ c_0\ xs) \\
\leftarrow\quad & \{\ \text{induction and monotonicity of refinement}\ \} \\
& gstep\ x\ (MinWith\ cost\ (foldr\ fstep\ [c_0]\ xs)) \\
\leftarrow\quad & \{\ \text{fusion condition}\ \} \\
& MinWith\ cost\ (fstep\ x\ (foldr\ fstep\ [c_0]\ xs)) \\
=\quad & \{\ \text{definition of } foldr\ \} \\
& MinWith\ (foldr\ fstep\ [c_0]\ (x:xs))
\end{aligned}
$$

Let us see what else we might need by redoing the calculation of the greedy algorithm for mcc. This time we start with the specification

$$mcc\ xs \leftarrow MinWith\ cost\ (candidates\ xs)$$

For the fusion condition we reason, with $cs = candidates\ xs$,

$$
\begin{aligned}
& MinWith\ cost\ (fstep\ x\ cs) \\
=\quad & \{\ \text{with } fstep = concatMap \cdot extend\ \} \\
& MinWith\ cost\ (concatMap\ (extend\ x)\ cs) \\
=\quad & \{\ \text{distributive law}\ \} \\
& MinWith\ cost\ (map\ (MinWith\ cost \cdot extend\ x)\ cs) \\
\rightarrow\quad & \{\ \text{suppose } gstep\ x\ xs \leftarrow MinWith\ cost\ (extend\ x\ xs)\ \} \\
& MinWith\ cost\ (map\ (gstep\ x)\ cs) \\
\rightarrow\quad & \{\ \text{greedy condition}\ \} \\
& gstep\ x\ (MinWith\ cost\ (candidates\ xs))
\end{aligned}
$$

We write $E_1 \rightarrow E_2$ as an alternative to $E_2 \leftarrow E_1$. The second step makes use of the distributive law, and the third step makes use of the monotonicity of refinement. As we saw above, the greedy condition follows from (7.4).

We have introduced a single nondeterministic function *MinWith cost*, which will be sufficient for the following two chapters. In Part Four of the book, on thinning algorithms, we will need another nondeterministic function, *ThinBy*, and that function will be dealt with in the same way as *MinWith*, namely by simply stating the valid rules of reasoning about refinement.

7.6 Summary

Let us summarise the general points that emerge from this chapter:

1. A greedy algorithm arises from the successful fusion of a function that selects a best candidate with a function that generates all candidates, or at least all candidates that may turn out to be best ones.
2. The best candidate can sometimes be defined in different ways. In hillwalking terms, the highest point may also be the one with the best view and one can choose to maximise the height or to maximise the view. In either case the result is the same.
3. Sometimes the simple statement of the greedy condition is too strong because it does not take context into account.
4. While it may be possible to prove that a context-sensitive fusion condition holds in special cases, usually by changing the cost function, in general one may have to replace reasoning with equality by reasoning with refinement in order to prove that a greedy algorithm works.

7.7 Chapter notes

Both Insertion sort and Selection sort are well-known sorting algorithms, though they are not usually described as being greedy algorithms. Knuth starts his comprehensive text [6] with a study of inversions, and many interesting properties of inversions can be found there.

The coin-changing problem has a long history. Recent references include [1, 5]. The TeX problem was first discussed in [7], under the title "A simple program whose proof isn't", and considered further in [3]. It is remarkable that both of these problems succumbed to exactly the same calculation.

For further information about how to reason about nondeterminism in a functional setting, see [4]. There are many articles about nondeterministic functions and refinement, and many ways of formalising these ideas. One way is to regard a nondeterministic function as a relation, and refinement as the inclusion of one relation in another. The relational approach to programming, in a categorical setting, is described in [2]; this book also contains the TEX problem as an example. Another approach, which we have more or less followed above with minor syntactic changes, is given in [8] and the earlier [9]. These two articles record the pitfalls one can tumble into if sufficient care is not taken.

References

[1] Michal Adamaszek and Anna Niewiarowska. Combinatorics of the change-making problem. *European Journal of Combinatorics*, 31(1):47–63, 2010.

[2] Richard S. Bird and Oege de Moor. *The Algebra of Programming*. Prentice-Hall, Hemel Hempstead, 1997.

[3] Richard S. Bird. Two greedy algorithms. *Journal of Functional Programming*, 2(2):237–244, 1992.

[4] Richard Bird and Florian Rabe. How to calculate with nondeterministic functions. In G. Hutton, editor, *Mathematics of Program Construction*, volume 11825 of *Lecture Notes in Computer Science*. Springer-Verlag, Cham, pages 138–154, 2019.

[5] Xuan Cai. Canonical coin systems for change-making problems. In *Hybrid Intelligent Systems*, IEEE, pages 499–504, 2009.

[6] Donald E. Knuth. *The Art of Computer Programming*, volume 3: Sorting and Searching. Addison-Wesley, Reading, MA, second edition, 1998.

[7] Donald E. Knuth. A simple program whose proof isn't. In W. H. J. Feijen, A. J. M. van Gasteren, D. Gries, and J. Misra, editors, *Beauty is Our Business: A Birthday Salute to Edsger W. Dijkstra*. Springer-Verlag, Berlin, 1990.

[8] Joseph M. Morris and Malcolm Tyrrell. Dually nondeterministic functions. *ACM Transactions on Programming Languages and Systems*, 30(6):34, 2008.

[9] Joseph M. Morris and Alexander Bunkenburg. Specificational functions. *ACM Transactions on Programming Languages and Systems*, 21(3):677–701, 1999.

Exercises

Exercise 7.1 The *Data.List* library provides a function

$$minimumBy :: (a \rightarrow a \rightarrow Ordering) \rightarrow [a] \rightarrow a$$

Define *minWith* using *minimumBy*.

Exercise 7.2 Write down a definition of a function *minsWith f* that returns *all* the elements of a finite nonempty list that minimise f. In particular the statement $x \leftarrow MinWith f\ xs$ can be read as $x \in minsWith f\ xs$.

Exercise 7.3 Prove that, if f is associative, then

$$foldr1\ f\ (xs +\!\!+ ys) = f\ (foldr1\ f\ xs)\ (foldr1\ f\ ys)$$

for all nonempty lists *xs* and *ys*. Hence show that

$$foldr1\ f\ (concat\ xss) = foldr1\ f\ (map\ (foldr1\ f)\ xss)$$

provided *xss* contains only nonempty lists. Finally, show that

$$minWith f\ (concat\ xss) = minWith f\ (map\ (minWith f)\ xss)$$

provided *xss* contains only nonempty lists.

Exercise 7.4 Write down a divide-and-conquer definition of *perms*.

Exercise 7.5 Why is the law

$$minimum \cdot map\ (x:) = (x:) \cdot minimum$$

not valid on empty lists?

Exercise 7.6 Show that $minimum \cdot map\ f = f \cdot minimum$ on nonempty lists if f is monotonic. Is the monotonicity condition necessary?

Exercise 7.7 Given that $gstep\ x = minimum \cdot extend\ x$, derive a recursive definition of *gstep*.

Exercise 7.8 With *gstep* as defined in the previous question, show that

$$minimum\ (map\ (gstep\ x)\ xss) = gstep\ x\ (minimum\ xss)$$

provided all lists in *xss* have the same length. Give an example to show the condition fails if *xss* can contain lists of different length.

Exercise 7.9 Suppose (x_1, ys_1) and (x_2, ys_2) are two picks of the same list. Show that

$$(x_1, ys_1) \leqslant (x_2, ys_2) \implies x_1 : sort\ ys_1 \leqslant x_2 : sort\ ys_2$$

Exercise 7.10 Write down a linear-time algorithm for computing *pick*.

Exercise 7.11 Consider evaluation of Insertion sort on the list $[3,4,2,5,1]$. Keeping in mind that Haskell is a lazy language, continue the following sequence of evaluation steps until the first element of the result is obtained:

$$gstep\ 3\ (gstep\ 4\ (gstep\ 2\ (gstep\ 5\ (gstep\ 1\ []))))$$
$$gstep\ 3\ (gstep\ 4\ (gstep\ 2\ (gstep\ 5\ (1:[]))))$$
$$gstep\ 3\ (gstep\ 4\ (gstep\ 2\ (1: gstep\ 5\ [])))$$

Now answer the following questions. How long does it take to compute $head \cdot isort$ on a nonempty list? What is the precise sequence of comparisons made for sorting $[3,4,2,5,1]$? Does Insertion sort actually work by inserting a new element into a sorted list at each step?

Exercise 7.12 Explain why $mkchange\ [7,3,1]\ 54 = [6,4,0]$, where

$$mkchange\ ds = minWith\ count \cdot mktuples\ ds$$

What change to the definition of *mktuples* would produce $[7,1,2]$?

Exercise 7.13 Here is the weight-based version of coin-changing:

type *Weights* = [*Int*]

weight :: *Weights* → *Tuple* → *Int*
weight ws cs = *sum* (*zipWith* (×) *ws cs*)

mkchangew :: *Weights* → [*Denom*] → *Nat* → *Tuple*
mkchangew ws ds = *minWith* (*weight ws*) · *mktuples ds*

In the UK it is the case that minimising count also minimises weight. We could prove this by simply carrying out an exhaustive test:

ukws = [1200, 950, 800, 500, 650, 325, 712, 356]
test = [*n* | *n* ← [1..200], *mkchange ukds n* ≠ *mkchangew ukws ukds n*]

We only need to check amounts up to £2. But *test* returns a nonempty list beginning with 2 because

mkchange ukds 2   = [0, 0, 0, 0, 0, 0, 1, 0]
mkchangew ukws ukds 2 = [0, 0, 0, 0, 0, 0, 0, 2]

One 2p coin weighs the same as two 1p coins. What has gone wrong, and how can the test be corrected?

Exercise 7.14 Express the function *mktuples* as an instance of *foldr*. (Hint: maintain a list of pairs, where a pair consists of a tuple and a residual amount, and then at the end select the first component of a pair with a zero residue.) Write down the associated greedy algorithm. We will use such a definition when we come to discuss a thinning algorithm for the same problem.

Exercise 7.15 Consider the denominations [5, 2, 1] and a largest tuple [c_3, c_2, c_1] with minimum count. Show that, if $2 c_2 + c_1 \geqslant 5$, then there is a larger tuple for the same amount but with a smaller count. If the denominations were [4, 3, 1], do we necessarily have $3 c_2 + c_1 < 4$?

Exercise 7.16 Consider the UR (United Region) currency whose denominations are [100, 50, 20, 15, 5, 2, 1]. Explain carefully where the argument as to why the greedy algorithm works for UK currency breaks down with UR currency. Does the greedy algorithm work for UR currency?

Exercise 7.17 Prove that, if each denomination is a multiple of the next lower denomination, then the greedy algorithm works.

Exercise 7.18 Prove (7.1) using the rule of floors.

Exercise 7.19 We calculated that

intern = *halve* · *foldr shiftn* 0

Suppose $halve \cdot foldr\ shiftn\ 0 = foldr\ op\ 0$ for some function op. The associated fusion condition is

$$halve\ (shiftn\ d\ n) = op\ d\ (halve\ n)$$

for all n of the form $n = foldr\ shiftn\ 0\ ds$. Using the rule of floors, we have

$$halve\ (shiftn\ d\ n) = (2^{17} \times d + n + 10)\ \text{div}\ 20$$

Now, since $halve\ (2 \times n) = halve\ (2 \times n - 1)$, the fusion condition requires that

$$(2^{17} \times d + 2 \times n + 10)\ \text{div}\ 20 = (2^{17} \times d + 2 \times n + 9)\ \text{div}\ 20$$

Your task is to find a two-digit decimal ds with $n = foldr\ shiftn\ 0\ ds$ such that the above statement is false for $d = 0$.

Exercise 7.20 Why can all but the first 17 digits of the input be ignored?

Exercise 7.21 Why does the first definition of *decimals* contain a bug? Hint: as we said in the very first chapter, Haskell does not guarantee that the type *Int* covers a greater range than $[-2^{29}, 2^{29})$. Would the bug still occur if a Haskell compiler allowed the range $[-2^{63}, 2^{63})$ for *Int*? Give the necessary revisions of *decimals* and *externs* that solve the problem.

Exercise 7.22 For $n < 2^{16}$ the integer D, where

$$D = \left\lfloor 10^5 \frac{n}{2^{16}} + \frac{1}{2} \right\rfloor$$

satisfies $D < 10^5$ and so has at most 5 digits. Using this fact, show that *extern n* has at most 5 digits.

Exercise 7.23 To verify the distributive law for *MinWith cost*, we have to show that, if $x \leftarrow MinWith\ (concat\ xss)$, then there exists a list xs such that

$$xs \leftarrow map\ (MinWith\ cost)\ xss\ \wedge\ x \leftarrow MinWith\ cost\ xs$$

Conversely, we also have to show

$$xs \leftarrow map\ (MinWith\ cost)\ xss\ \wedge\ x \leftarrow MinWith\ cost\ xs$$
$$\Rightarrow\ x \leftarrow MinWith\ cost\ (concat\ xss)$$

Prove these two claims.

Exercise 7.24 Suppose $MCC\ xs = MinWith\ cost\ (candidates\ xs)$. Show that

$$foldr\ gstep\ e\ xs \leftarrow MCC\ xs$$

provided $e \leftarrow MCC\ []$ and

$$c \leftarrow MCC\ xs\ \Rightarrow\ gstep\ x\ c \leftarrow MCC\ (x:xs)$$

for all candidates c, components x, and lists of components xs.

Exercise 7.25 Define $Flip :: Bool \to Bool$ by

$Flip\ x = MinWith\ (const\ 0)\ [x, not\ x]$

Which of the following assertions are true?

$id \leftarrow Flip \qquad\qquad not \leftarrow Flip \qquad\qquad not \cdot not = not \qquad\qquad Flip \cdot Flip = Flip$

Answers

Answer 7.1 One simple definition:

$minWith\ f = minimumBy\ cmp$
$\qquad\qquad$**where** $cmp\ x\ y = compare\ (f\ x)\ (f\ y)$

A more efficient definition:

$minWith\ f = snd \cdot minimumBy\ cmp \cdot map\ tuple$
$\qquad\qquad$**where** $tuple\ x = (f\ x, x)$
$\qquad\qquad\qquad\qquad cmp\ (x, \_)\ (y, \_) = compare\ x\ y$

Answer 7.2 One simple definition:

$minsWith\ f\ xs = [x \mid x \leftarrow xs, and\ [f\ x \leqslant f\ y \mid y \leftarrow xs]]$

A more efficient definition:

$minsWith\ f = map\ snd \cdot foldr\ step\ [] \cdot map\ tuple$
$\qquad$**where** $tuple\ x = (f\ x, x)$
$\qquad\qquad step\ x\ [] \qquad\qquad\qquad = [x]$
$\qquad\qquad step\ x\ (y:xs) \mid a < b \quad = [x]$
$\qquad\qquad\qquad\qquad\qquad \mid a == b = x:y:xs$
$\qquad\qquad\qquad\qquad\qquad \mid a > b \quad = y:xs$
$\qquad\qquad\qquad\qquad$**where** $a = fst\ x; b = fst\ y$

Answer 7.3 We can prove

$foldr1\ f\ (xs \mathbin{+\!\!+} ys) = f\ (foldr1\ f\ xs)\ (foldr1\ f\ ys)$

by induction on xs. The induction step is

$\qquad foldr1\ f\ (x:xs \mathbin{+\!\!+} ys)$
$= \quad \{$ definition of $foldr1$ $\}$
$\qquad f\ x\ (foldr1\ f\ (xs \mathbin{+\!\!+} ys))$
$= \quad \{$ induction $\}$
$\qquad f\ x\ (f\ (foldr1\ f\ xs)\ (foldr1\ f\ ys))$
$= \quad \{$ associativity of f $\}$
$\qquad f\ (f\ x\ (foldr1\ f\ xs))\ (foldr1\ f\ ys)$
$= \quad \{$ definition of $foldr1$ $\}$
$\qquad f\ (foldr1\ f\ (x:xs))\ (foldr1\ f\ ys)$

The proof of

$$foldr1\ f\ (concat\ xss) = foldr1\ f\ (map\ (foldr1\ f)\ xss)$$

is also by induction. The induction step is

$$foldr1\ f\ (concat\ (xs:xss))$$
$$= \quad \{\ \text{definition of } concat\ \}$$
$$foldr1\ f\ (xs \mathbin{+\mkern-8mu+} concat\ xss)$$
$$= \quad \{\ \text{above}\ \}$$
$$f\ (foldr1\ f\ xs)\ (foldr1\ f\ (concat\ xss))$$
$$= \quad \{\ \text{induction}\ \}$$
$$f\ (foldr1\ f\ xs)\ (foldr1\ f\ (map\ (foldr1\ f)\ xss))$$
$$= \quad \{\ \text{definition of } foldr1\ \}$$
$$foldr1\ f\ (foldr1\ f\ xs:map\ (foldr1\ f)\ xss)$$
$$= \quad \{\ \text{definition of } map\ \}$$
$$foldr1\ (map\ (foldr1\ f)\ (xs:xss))$$

The final claim holds because *smaller f* is associative.

Answer 7.4 One definition is

$$perms :: [a] \rightarrow [[a]]$$
$$perms\ []\ = [[]]$$
$$perms\ [x] = [[x]]$$
$$perms\ xs\ = concatMap\ interleave\ (cp\ yss\ zss)$$
$$\quad \textbf{where } yss = perms\ ys$$
$$\quad\quad\quad\quad zss = perms\ zs$$
$$\quad\quad\quad\quad (ys,zs) = splitAt\ (length\ xs\ \text{div}\ 2)\ xs$$

$$cp :: [a] \rightarrow [b] \rightarrow [(a,b)]$$
$$cp\ xs\ ys = [(x,y) \mid x \leftarrow xs, y \leftarrow ys]$$

$$interleave :: ([a],[a]) \rightarrow [[a]]$$
$$interleave\ (xs,[]) \quad = [xs]$$
$$interleave\ ([],ys) \quad = [ys]$$
$$interleave\ (x:xs,y:ys) = map\ (x:)\ (interleave\ (xs,y:ys)) \mathbin{+\mkern-8mu+}$$
$$\quad\quad\quad\quad\quad\quad\quad\quad map\ (y:)\ (interleave\ (x:xs,ys))$$

Answer 7.5 We have

$$minimum\ (map\ (x:)\ []) = \perp$$
$$x:minimum\ [] \quad\quad\quad = x:\perp$$

This is a consequence of the fact that the (:) operation is not strict in Haskell.

Answer 7.6 The result clearly holds for a singleton list. For the induction step we argue as follows:

$minimum\ (map\ f\ (x:xs))$

$=$ { definition of map }

$minimum\ (f\ x:map\ f\ xs)$

$=$ { definition of $minimum$ }

$min\ (f\ x)\ (minimum\ (map\ f\ xs))$

$=$ { induction }

$min\ (f\ x)\ (f\ (minimum\ xs))$

$=$ { claim: $min\ (f\ x)\ (f\ y) = f\ (min\ x\ y)$ }

$f\ (min\ x\ (minimum\ xs))$

$=$ { definition of $minimum$ }

$f\ (minimum\ (x:xs))$

The claim is equivalent to the condition that f is monotonic.

For the second question, suppose that $a<b<c, f\ a<min\ (f\ b)\ (f\ c)$, and $f\ c<f\ b$. Then f is not monotonic but, nevertheless,

$$minimum\ [f\ a, f\ b, f\ c] = f\ (minimum\ [a,b,c])$$

Answer 7.7 It is easy to show $gstep\ x\ [] = [x]$. For the induction step we argue

$gstep\ x\ (y:xs)$

$=$ { definition of $gstep$ }

$minimum\ (extend\ x\ (y:xs))$

$=$ { definition of $extend$ }

$minimum\ ((x:y:xs):map\ (y:)\ (extend\ x\ xs))$

$=$ { definition of $minimum$ }

$min\ (x:y:xs)\ (minimum\ (map\ (y:)\ (extend\ x\ xs)))$

$=$ { since $minimum \cdot map\ (y:) = (y:) \cdot minimum$ on nonempty lists }

$min\ (x:y:xs)\ (y:minimum\ (extend\ x\ xs))$

$=$ { definition of $gstep$ }

$min\ (x:y:xs)\ (y:gstep\ x\ xs)$

Hence we have the definition

$gstep\ x\ [] \qquad = [x]$

$gstep\ x\ (y:xs) = min\ (x:y:xs)\ (y:gstep\ x\ xs)$

Answer 7.8 We show that $gstep\ x$ is monotonic, that is,

$$as \leqslant bs \implies gstep\ x\ as \leqslant gstep\ x\ bs \qquad (7.5)$$

whenever as and bs have the same length. The proof is by induction. The claim is immediate if both as and bs are the empty list. For the induction step, suppose $a:as$ and $b:bs$ are two lists of the same length with $a:as \leqslant b:bs$, so either $a<b$, or $a=b$ and $as \leqslant bs$. If $a<b$, then

$$x:a:as < x:b:bs \quad \wedge \quad a:gstep\ x\ as < b:gstep\ x\ bs$$

so $gstep\ x\ (a:as) < gstep\ x\ (b:bs)$. In the case $a = b$ and $as \leqslant bs$ we have

$$x:a:as \leqslant x:a:bs \quad \wedge \quad a:gstep\ x\ as \leqslant a:gstep\ x\ bs$$

because, by induction, $gstep\ x\ as \leqslant gstep\ x\ bs$.

For the second question, we have $[] < [1]$, but

$$gstep\ 2\ [] = [2] > [1,2] = gstep\ 2\ [1]$$

Answer 7.9 Either $x_1 < x_2$, in which case the implication is immediate, or $x_1 = x_2$, in which case ys_1 and ys_2 contain exactly the same elements and sorting these lists produces the same result.

Answer 7.10 The definition is

$$pick\ [x] \quad = (x, [])$$
$$pick\ (x:xs) = \textbf{if } x \leqslant y \textbf{ then } (x, xs) \textbf{ else } (y, x:ys) \textbf{ where } (y, ys) = pick\ xs$$

Answer 7.11 The evaluation sequence is as follows:

$$gstep\ 3\ (gstep\ 4\ (gstep\ 2\ (gstep\ 5\ (gstep\ 1\ []))))$$
$$gstep\ 3\ (gstep\ 4\ (gstep\ 2\ (gstep\ 5\ (1:[]))))$$
$$gstep\ 3\ (gstep\ 4\ (gstep\ 2\ (1:gstep\ 5\ [])))$$
$$gstep\ 3\ (gstep\ 4\ (1:gstep\ 2\ (gstep\ 5\ [])))$$
$$gstep\ 3\ (1:gstep\ 4\ (gstep\ 2\ (gstep\ 5\ [])))$$
$$1:gstep\ 3\ (gstep\ 4\ (gstep\ 2\ (gstep\ 5\ [])))$$

In answer to the first question, it takes $\Theta(n)$ steps to compute the head of Insertion sort on a list of length n. In answer to the second question, the precise sequence of comparisons is

$$(5,1)\ (2,1)\ (4,1)\ (3,1)\ (2,5)\ (4,2)\ (3,2)\ (4,5)\ (3,4)\ (4,5)$$

In answer to the third question, Insertion sort is not really sorting by insertion, at least when evaluated lazily. It is more akin to a sorting algorithm known as Bubble sort, though not exactly the same sequence of comparisons is performed. The lesson here is that under lazy evaluation you don't always get what you think you are getting.

Answer 7.12 Because *mktuples* produces tuples in increasing lexical order. If we change the definition to read

$$mktuples :: [Denom] \rightarrow Nat \rightarrow [Tuple]$$
$$mktuples\ [1]\ n \quad = [[n]]$$
$$mktuples\ (d:ds)\ n = [c:cs \mid c \leftarrow [m, m-1..0], cs \leftarrow mktuples\ ds\ (n - c \times d)]$$
$$\textbf{where } m = n \textbf{ div } d$$

then *mktuples* would produce tuples in decreasing lexical order and we would have $mkchange\ [7,3,1]\ 54 = [7,1,2]$.

Answer 7.13 The culprits, once again, are the definitions of *minWith cost* and *mktuples*. Since one 2p coin weighs exactly the same as two 1p coins, there is no unique minimum-weight tuple. The test can be corrected by redefining *mktuples* as in the previous exercise to generate tuples in decreasing lexical order. Then *test* does return the empty list.

Answer 7.14 Expressing *mktuples* in terms of *foldr* means processing the list of denominations from right to left. It follows that, in order to process denominations in decreasing order of value, we have to reverse given lists of currencies like *ukds*. Thus we define

$$mktuples\ ds\ n = finish\ (foldr\ (concatMap \cdot extend)\ [([],n)]\ (reverse\ ds))$$
$$\textbf{where}\ finish = map\ fst \cdot filter\ (\lambda(cs,r).r == 0)$$
$$extend\ d\ (cs,r) = [(cs + [c], r - c \times d) \mid c \leftarrow [0..r\ \text{div}\ d]]$$

That leads to the greedy algorithm

$$mkchange\ ds\ n = fst\ (foldr\ gstep\ ([],n)\ (reverse\ ds))$$
$$\textbf{where}\ gstep\ d\ (cs,r) = (cs + [c], r - c \times d)\ \textbf{where}\ c = r\ \text{div}\ d$$

The greedy algorithm can be calculated by fusing *maximum* with *mktuples*.

Answer 7.15 We have $2\,c_2 + c_1 \geqslant 5$ if $c_2 \geqslant 3$ or if $(c_2,c_1) = (2,1)$. In the first case we can increase c_3 by one and replace (c_2,c_1) either by $(c_2 - 3, 1)$, if $c_1 = 0$, or by $(c_2 - 2, 0)$, if $c_1 = 1$. In the second case we can increase c_3 by one and set both c_1 and c_2 to zero. In each case this gives a larger tuple with a smaller count.

The answer to the second question is no, because the tuple $[c_3, 2, 0]$ has a smaller count than $[c_3 + 1, 0, 2]$.

Answer 7.16 Let $[c_7, c_6, ..., c_1]$ be the optimal solution and let $[g_7, g_6, ..., g_1]$ be the greedy one, so

$$A = 100\,c_7 + 50\,c_6 + 20\,c_5 + 15\,c_4 + 5\,c_3 + 2\,c_2 + c_1$$
$$A = 100\,g_7 + 50\,g_6 + 20\,g_5 + 15\,g_4 + 5\,g_3 + 2\,g_2 + g_1$$

The same argument as in the text shows that $c_1 = g_1$ and $c_2 = g_2$. Next, with $B = (A - (2\,c_2 + c_1))/5$ we have

$$B = 20\,c_7 + 10\,c_6 + 4\,c_5 + 3\,c_4 + c_3$$
$$B = 20\,g_7 + 10\,g_6 + 4\,g_5 + 3\,g_4 + g_3$$

But now the argument breaks down since we cannot show that $c_3 = g_3$. In UR currency we have $1 \times 20 + 2 \times 5$ as the greedy choice for 30 units, while 2×15 is the same amount with one coin fewer.

Answer 7.17 Suppose, as in the previous solution, we have

$$A = d_k\,c_k + \cdots + d_2\,c_2 + c_1$$
$$A = d_k\,g_k + \cdots + d_2\,g_2 + g_1$$

Since d_2 divides into each other denomination, we have $A \bmod d_2 = c_1 = g_1$. Next, with $B = (A - c_1)/d_2$ we have $B \bmod d_3 = c_2 = g_2$. And so on.

Answer 7.18 We can reason as follows:

$$k \leqslant \lfloor (x+a)/b \rfloor$$
$$\Leftrightarrow \quad \{ \text{rule of floors} \}$$
$$kb \leqslant x+a$$
$$\Leftrightarrow \quad \{ \text{rule of floors} \}$$
$$kb - a \leqslant \lfloor x \rfloor$$
$$\Leftrightarrow \quad \{ \text{rule of floors} \}$$
$$k \leqslant \lfloor (\lfloor x \rfloor + a)/b \rfloor$$

Hence $\lfloor (x+a)/b \rfloor = \lfloor (\lfloor x \rfloor + a)/b \rfloor$.

Answer 7.19 Take $ds = [0,7]$. We have $n = foldr\ shiftn\ 0\ [0,7] = 9175$ and

$$(2^{17} \times 0 + 2 \times 9175 + 10)\ \mathrm{div}\ 20 = 918$$
$$(2^{17} \times 0 + 2 \times 9175 + 9)\ \mathrm{div}\ 20\ = 917$$

Answer 7.20 Let $r = fraction\ ds$ and $r' = fraction\ (take\ 17\ ds)$. Then $\lfloor 10^{17} r \rfloor = \lfloor 10^{17} r' \rfloor$. Furthermore,

$$\left\lfloor \frac{2^{17} r + 1}{2} \right\rfloor = \left\lfloor \frac{10^{17} r + 5^{17}}{2 \times 5^{17}} \right\rfloor$$

so $scale\ r = scale\ r'$ by (7.1). So, only 17 digits matter. The smallest internal value is 0, which occurs only if the input decimal is strictly less than the decimal 0.00000762939453125, the value of 2^{-17}. The largest internal value is $2^{16} = 65536$, which occurs only if the input is greater than the decimal representation of $1 - 2^{17}$, namely 0.99999237060546875. Hence 17 digits are sometimes necessary.

Answer 7.21 The reason for the bug is that, since $10b - w \lfloor 10a/w \rfloor \geqslant 10(b-a)$, the size of the interval argument to *decimals* can grow from 2 to 2×10^{17}. Since $2 \times 10^{17} \geqslant 2^{29}$, the upper bound of an interval can exceed the range of *Int*. However, $2 \times 10^{17} < 2^{63}$, so the problem does not arise with 64-bit computers. The revised definition of *externs* is

$$externs :: Int \rightarrow [[Digit]]$$
$$externs\ n = decimals\ (2 \times n' - 1, 2 \times n' + 1)$$
$$\textbf{where}\ n' = fromIntegral\ n$$

The definition of $decimals :: (Integer, Integer) \rightarrow [[Digit]]$ is as before except that the term $d : ds$ has to be replaced with $fromInteger\ d : ds$ because digits are elements of *Int*, not *Integer*.

Answer 7.22 The fraction $D/10^5$ produces the internal number n', where

$$\left| \frac{D}{10^5} - \frac{n'}{2^{16}} \right| \leqslant 2^{-17}$$

We also have

$$\left| D - 10^5 \frac{n}{2^{16}} \right| \leqslant \frac{1}{2}$$

by definition of D. Now

$$|n - n'| \leqslant \left| n - 2^{16} D/10^5 \right| + \left| n' - 2^{16} D/10^5 \right| \leqslant 2^{15}/10^5 + 1/2 < 1$$

so $n = n'$.

Answer 7.23 Suppose $xss = [xs_1, ..., xs_n]$ is a finite nonempty list of finite nonempty lists. If $x \leftarrow MinWith\ cost\ (concat\ xss)$, then x is an element of some list xs_i with a cost that is no greater than any other element of $concat\ xss$. Suppose $x_j \leftarrow MinWith\ cost\ xs_j$ for each $j \neq i$. Then the list $xs = [x_1, .., x_{i-1}, x, x_{i+1}, ..x_n]$ is such that

$$xs \leftarrow map\ (MinWith\ cost)\ xss \quad \wedge \quad x \leftarrow MinWith\ cost\ xs$$

Conversely, suppose $xs = [x_1, ..., x_n]$ satisfies

$$xs \leftarrow map\ (MinWith\ cost)\ xss$$

so $x_j \leftarrow MinWith\ cost\ xs_j$ for each $1 \leqslant j \leqslant n$. Now take $x = x_i$ for some i such that $x_i \leftarrow MinWith\ cost\ xs$. Then $x \leftarrow MinWith\ cost\ (concat\ xss)$. The proof really only relies on the fact that, if $cost\ x \leqslant cost\ y$ and $cost\ y \leqslant cost\ z$, then $cost\ x \leqslant cost\ z$.

Answer 7.24 The proof is by induction on xs. The base step is immediate, and for the induction step we can argue

$$\begin{aligned}
& foldr\ gstep\ e\ (x:xs) \\
=\ & \{ \text{definition of } foldr \} \\
& gstep\ x\ (foldr\ gstep\ e\ xs) \\
\leftarrow\ & \{ \text{induction} \} \\
& gstep\ x\ (MCC\ xs) \\
\leftarrow\ & \{ \text{greedy condition} \} \\
& MCC\ (x:xs)
\end{aligned}$$

This reasoning is valid for any definition of *candidates*. However, unlike the greedy algorithm based on fusion, it gives no hint about how *gstep* may be defined.

Answer 7.25 The assertion $not \cdot not = not$ is, of course, false. The others are true, including the last one because there is no refinement of $Flip \cdot Flip$ that is not also a refinement of $Flip$ and vice versa.

Chapter 8

Greedy algorithms on trees

The next two problems are about trees, so the greedy algorithms take place in a wood rather than on a hillside. The problems concern the task of building a tree with minimum cost, for two different definitions of cost. The first problem is closely related to the tree-building algorithms we have seen before in binary search and sorting. The second problem, Huffman coding trees, is of practical importance in compressing data effectively. Unlike the problems in the previous chapter, the two greedy tree-building algorithms require us to reason about the nondeterministic function *MinWith* in order to prove that they work.

8.1 Minimum-height trees

Throughout the chapter we fix attention on one type of tree, called a *leaf-labelled* tree:

data *Tree a = Leaf a | Node (Tree a) (Tree a)*

A leaf-labelled tree is therefore a binary tree with information stored only at the leaves. Essentially this species of tree, though with an additional constructor *Null*, was described in Section 5.2 on Mergesort.

The size of a leaf-labelled tree is the number of its leaves:

size :: *Tree a → Nat*
size (Leaf x) = 1
size (Node u v) = *size u + size v*

The height of a tree is defined by

height (Leaf x) = 0
height (Node u v) = 1 + *height u* max *height v*

With a leaf-labelled tree of size n and height h we have the relationship $h < n \leqslant 2^h$, so $h \geqslant \lceil \log n \rceil$.

The *fringe* of a tree is the list of leaf labels in left-to-right order:

$$fringe :: Tree\ a \rightarrow [a]$$
$$fringe\ (Leaf\ x)\ \ \ = [x]$$
$$fringe\ (Node\ u\ v) = fringe\ u \mathbin{+\!\!+} fringe\ v$$

Thus *fringe* is essentially the same function that we have previously called *flatten*. Note that the fringe of a tree is always a nonempty list.

Consider the problem of building a tree of minimum height with a given list as fringe. We have already encountered two ways of solving this problem, both of which can be implemented to take linear time. The first solution is the divide-and-conquer, or top-down, method of Section 5.2:

$$mktree :: [a] \rightarrow Tree\ a$$
$$mktree\ [x] = Leaf\ x$$
$$mktree\ xs\ \ = Node\ (mktree\ ys)\ (mktree\ zs)$$
$$\textbf{where}\ (ys, zs) = splitAt\ (length\ xs\ \text{div}\ 2)\ xs$$

This definition does not take linear time, but it is easy to convert it into one that does. The trick, as we have seen in the treatment of Mergesort in Section 5.2, is to avoid repeated halving by tupling. Second, we have the bottom-up method, also described in Section 5.2:

$$mktree = unwrap \cdot until\ single\ (pairWith\ Node) \cdot map\ Leaf$$

These two ways of building a tree lead to different trees but both have minimum height. To show that this property holds for the first definition of *mktree*, let $H(n)$ denote the height of *mktree* for an input of length n. Then H satisfies the recurrence $H(1) = 0$ and $H(n) = 1 + H(\lceil n/2 \rceil)$ with solution $H(n) = \lceil \log n \rceil$ (see Exercise 8.1), the minimum height possible. The reason why the bottom-up method also produces a minimum-height tree is left as another exercise.

Let us now change the problem slightly: given a nonempty list of natural numbers, can we find a linear-time algorithm for building a tree with minimum cost and the given list as fringe, where

$$cost :: Tree\ Nat \rightarrow Nat$$
$$cost\ (Leaf\ x)\ \ \ = x$$
$$cost\ (Node\ u\ v) = 1 + cost\ u\ \text{max}\ cost\ v$$

The function *cost* has the same definition as *height* except that the 'height' of a leaf is the label value rather than 0. In fact, if each leaf is replaced by a tree whose height is given by the label value, the problem is really of the following form: given a list of trees together with their heights, can we find a linear-time algorithm to combine them into a single tree of minimum height without changing the shape or order of the component trees? To appreciate the problem consider the two trees with the same fringe

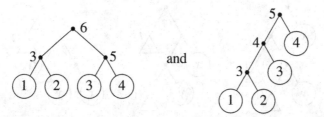

in which each node is labelled with its cost. The tree on the left has cost 6, but the tree on the right has minimum cost 5. It is not obvious how to construct a tree with minimum cost, at least not efficiently, and that is where a greedy algorithm enters the stage. We start off with a specification and then calculate the algorithm.

The specification is phrased as one of refinement:

$$mct :: [Nat] \rightarrow Tree\ Nat$$
$$mct\ xs \leftarrow MinWith\ cost\ (mktrees\ xs)$$

for finite nonempty lists xs, where $mktrees\ xs$ is a list of all possible trees with fringe xs. In words, $mct\ xs$ is some element of $mktrees\ xs$ with minimum cost.

The function $mktrees$ can be defined in a number of ways. We are going to give two inductive definitions; other possibilities are discussed in the exercises. The first method is to define

$$mktrees :: [a] \rightarrow [Tree\ a]$$
$$mktrees\ [x] \quad = [Leaf\ x]$$
$$mktrees\ (x : xs) = concatMap\ (extend\ x)\ (mktrees\ xs)$$

The function $extend$ returns a list of all the ways in which a new element can be added as a leftmost leaf in a tree:

$$extend :: a \rightarrow Tree\ a \rightarrow [Tree\ a]$$
$$extend\ x\ (Leaf\ y) \quad = [Node\ (Leaf\ x)\ (Leaf\ y)]$$
$$extend\ x\ (Node\ u\ v) = [Node\ (Leaf\ x)\ (Node\ u\ v)] \mathbin{+\!\!+}$$
$$\qquad\qquad\qquad\quad [Node\ u'\ v \mid u' \leftarrow extend\ x\ u]$$

For example, applying $extend\ x$ to the tree

produces the three trees

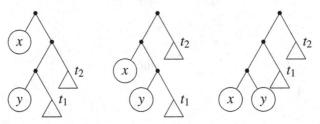

We might have taken *mktrees* $[] = []$ and so defined *mktrees* as an instance of *foldr*. But *MinWith* is not defined on an empty list and we have to restrict the input to nonempty lists. The Haskell standard library does not provide a sufficiently general fold function for nonempty lists (the function *foldr1* is not quite general enough), but if we define *foldrn* by

$$foldrn :: (a \rightarrow b \rightarrow b) \rightarrow (a \rightarrow b) \rightarrow [a] \rightarrow b$$
$$foldrn\, f\, g\, [x] \quad = g\, x$$
$$foldrn\, f\, g\, (x:xs) = f\, x\, (foldrn\, f\, g\, xs)$$

then the definition of *mktrees* above can be recast in the form

$$mktrees = foldrn\, (concatMap \cdot extend)\, (wrap \cdot Leaf)$$

where *wrap* converts a value into a singleton list.

The second inductive way of building a tree is to first build a forest, a list of trees:

type *Forest a* $= [Tree\ a]$

A forest can be 'rolled up' into a tree using

$$rollup :: [Tree\ a] \rightarrow Tree\ a$$
$$rollup = foldl1\ Node$$

The function *foldl1* is the Haskell prelude function for folding a nonempty list from left to right. For example,

$$rollup\ [t_1, t_2, t_3, t_4] = Node\ (Node\ (Node\ t_1\ t_2)\ t_3)\ t_4$$

The converse to *rollup* is the function *spine*, defined by

$$spine :: Tree\ a \rightarrow [Tree\ a]$$
$$spine\ (Leaf\ x) \quad = [Leaf\ x]$$
$$spine\ (Node\ u\ v) = spine\ u \mathbin{+\!\!+} [v]$$

This function returns the leftmost leaf of a tree, followed by a list of the right subtrees along the path from the leftmost leaf of the tree to the root. Provided the first tree in a forest *ts* is a leaf, we have

$$spine\ (rollup\ ts) = ts$$

We can now define

$$mktrees :: [a] \rightarrow [Tree\ a]$$
$$mktrees = map\ rollup \cdot mkforests$$

where *mkforests* builds the forests:

$mkforests :: [a] \to [Forest\ a]$

$mkforests = foldrn\ (concatMap \cdot extend)\ (wrap \cdot wrap \cdot Leaf)$

$extend :: a \to Forest\ a \to [Forest\ a]$

$extend\ x\ ts = [Leaf\ x : rollup\ (take\ k\ ts) : drop\ k\ ts \mid k \leftarrow [1 .. length\ ts]]$

The new version of *extend* is arguably simpler than the previous one. It works by rolling up some initial segment of the forest into a tree and adding a new leaf as the first tree in the new forest. For example,

$$extend\ x\ [t_1, t_2, t_3] = [[Leaf\ x, t_1, t_2, t_3],$$
$$[Leaf\ x, Node\ t_1\ t_2, t_3],$$
$$[Leaf\ x, Node\ (Node\ t_1\ t_2)\ t_3]]$$

The two versions of *mktrees* are not the same function simply because they produce the trees in a different order. We will come back to *spine* and *rollup* later on.

Let us now return to the first definition of *mktrees*, the one expressed directly as an instance of *foldrn*. To fuse the two component functions in the definition of *mct* we can appeal to the fusion law of *foldrn*. The context-sensitive version of this law states that

$$foldrn\ f_2\ g_2\ xs \leftarrow M\ (foldrn\ f_1\ g_1\ xs)$$

for all finite, nonempty lists *xs*, provided $g_2\ x \leftarrow M\ (g_1\ x)$ and

$$f_2\ x\ (M\ (foldrn\ f_1\ g_1\ xs)) \leftarrow M\ (f_1\ x\ (foldrn\ f_1\ g_1\ xs))$$

For our problem, $M = MinWith\ cost$, $f_1 = concatMap \cdot extend$, and $g_1 = wrap \cdot leaf$. Since $Leaf\ x = MinWith\ cost\ [Leaf\ x]$, we can take $g_2 = Leaf$. For the second fusion condition we have to find a function, *gstep* say, so that

$$gstep\ x\ (MinWith\ cost\ (mktrees\ xs))$$
$$\leftarrow MinWith\ cost\ (concatMap\ (extend\ x)\ (mktrees\ xs))$$

As we saw at the end of the previous chapter, this condition is satisfied if the monotonicity condition

$$cost\ t \leqslant cost\ t' \quad \Rightarrow \quad cost\ (gstep\ x\ t) \leqslant cost\ (gstep\ x\ t')$$

holds for all trees *t* and *t'* in *mktrees xs*. However, no such function *gstep* exists to satisfy the monotonicity condition. Consider the two trees t_1 and t_2:

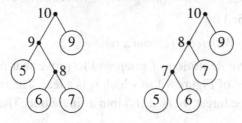

which, along with the three trees

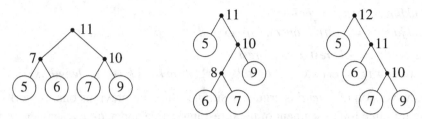

are the five trees that can be built with fringe $[5,6,7,9]$. The subtrees of each tree have been labelled with their costs, so both t_1 and t_2 have the minimum possible cost 10. However, the monotonicity condition

$$cost\ t_1 \leqslant cost\ t_2 \implies cost\ (gstep\ x\ t_1) \leqslant cost\ (gstep\ x\ t_2)$$

fails for any definition of *gstep*. Take, for example, $x = 8$. Adding 8 to t_1 in the best possible way gives a tree with minimum cost 11, while adding 8 to t_2 in the best possible way gives a tree with cost 10. So there is no way we can define a function *gstep* for which the fusion condition holds. Once again we appear to be stuck, even with a refinement version of fusion.

The only way out of the wood is to change the cost function, and once again lexical ordering comes to the rescue. Notice that the list of costs $[10,8,7,5]$ reading downwards along the left spine of t_2 is lexically less than the costs $[10,9,5]$ along the left spine of t_1. The lexical cost, *lcost* say, is defined by

lcost :: *Tree Nat* → $[Nat]$
lcost = *reverse* · *scanl1 op* · *map cost* · *spine*
    where *op x y* = $1 + (x\ max\ y)$

The costs of the trees along the left spine are accumulated from left to right by *scanl1 op* and then reversed. For example, *spine* t_2 has tree costs $[5,6,7,9]$ and accumulation gives the list $[5,7,8,10]$, which, when reversed, gives the lexical cost of t_2. Minimising *lcost* also minimises *cost* (why?), so we can revise the second fusion condition to read

    gstep x (*MinWith lcost* (*mktrees xs*))
       ← *MinWith lcost* (*concatMap* (*extend x*) (*mktrees xs*))

This time we can show

    lcost t_1 ⩽ *lcost* t_2 ⟹ *lcost* (*gstep x* t_1) ⩽ *lcost* (*gstep x* t_2)

where *gstep* is specified by

    gstep x ts ← *MinWith lcost* (*extend x ts*)

To give a constructive definition of *gstep* and to prove that monotonicity holds, consider the two trees of Figure 8.1 in which t_i is a leaf. The tree on the left is the result of rolling up the forest $[t_1, t_2, ..., t_n]$ into a single tree. The tree on the right is

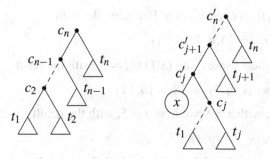

Figure 8.1 Inserting x into a tree

obtained by adding x as a new leaf after rolling up the first j elements of the forest. The trees are labelled with cost information, so

$$c_1 = cost\ t_1$$
$$c_k = 1 + (c_{k-1} \max cost\ t_k)$$

for $2 \leqslant k \leqslant n$. In particular, $[c_1, c_2, ..., c_n]$ is strictly increasing. A similar definition holds for the costs on the right:

$$c'_j = 1 + (x \max c_j)$$
$$c'_k = 1 + (c'_{k-1} \max cost\ t_k)$$

for $j + 1 \leqslant k \leqslant n$. In particular, since adding a new leaf cannot reduce costs, we have $c_k \leqslant c'_k$ for $j \leqslant k \leqslant n$.

The aim is to define *gstep* by choosing j to minimise $[c'_n, c'_{n-1}, ..., c'_j, x]$. For example, consider the five trees $[t_1, t_2, ..., t_5]$ with costs $[5, 2, 4, 9, 6]$. Then

$$[c_1, c_2, ..., c_5] = [5, 6, 7, 10, 11]$$

Take $x = 8$. There are five possible ways of adding x to the forest, namely by rolling up j trees for $1 \leqslant j \leqslant 5$. Here they are, with costs on the left and accumulated costs on the right:

$$[8, 5, 2, 4, 9, 6] \longrightarrow [8, 9, 10, 11, 12, 13]$$
$$[8, 6, 4, 9, 6] \longrightarrow [8, 9, 10, 11, 12]$$
$$[8, 7, 9, 6] \longrightarrow [8, 9, 10, 11]$$
$$[8, 10, 6] \longrightarrow [8, 11, 12]$$
$$[8, 11] \longrightarrow [8, 12]$$

The forest which minimises *lcost* is the third one, whose lexical cost is the reverse of $[8, 9, 10, 11]$.

We claim that the best choice of j is the smallest value in the range $1 \leqslant j < n$, if it exists, such that

$$1 + (x \max c_j) < c_{j+1} \tag{8.1}$$

If no such j exists, then choose $j = n$. For example, with

$$[c_1, c_2, c_3, c_4, c_5] = [5, 6, 7, 10, 11]$$

and $x = 8$, the smallest j satisfying (8.1) is $j = 3$, with the result

$$[x, 1 + (x \max c_3), c_4, c_5] = [8, 9, 10, 11]$$

On the other hand, with $x = 9$ we have $j = 5$, with the result

$$[x, 1 + (x \max c_5)] = [9, 12]$$

To prove (8.1), suppose the claim holds for both j and k, where $1 \leqslant j < k < n$. Then, setting $c'_j = 1 + (x \max c_j)$ and $c'_k = 1 + (x \max c_k)$, the two sequences

$$\begin{aligned} as &= [x, c'_j, c_{j+1}, ..., c_{k-1}, c_k, c_{k+1}, ..., c_n] \\ bs &= \qquad\qquad [x, \quad c'_k, c_{k+1}, ..., c_n] \end{aligned}$$

are such that *reverse as* < *reverse bs* because $c_k < c'_k$. Hence, the smaller the value of j, the lower is the cost.

To show that *gstep x* is monotonic with respect to *lcost*, suppose

$$\begin{aligned} lcost\ t_1 &= [c_n, c_{n-1}, ..., c_1] \\ lcost\ t_2 &= [d_m, d_{m-1}, ..., d_1] \end{aligned}$$

where *lcost* $t_1 \leqslant$ *lcost* t_2. If these costs are equal, then so are the costs of adding a new leaf to either tree. Otherwise, if *lcost* $t_1 <$ *lcost* t_2 and we remove the common prefix, say one of length k, then we are left with two trees t'_1 and t'_2 with

$$\begin{aligned} lcost\ t'_1 &= [c_p, ..., c_1] \\ lcost\ t'_2 &= [d_q, ..., d_1] \end{aligned}$$

where $p = n - k$, $q = m - k$ and $c_p < d_q$. It is sufficient to show that

$$lcost\ (gstep\ x\ t'_1) \leqslant lcost\ (gstep\ x\ t'_2)$$

Firstly, suppose (8.1) holds for t'_1 and $j < p$. Then

$$lcost\ (gstep\ x\ t'_1) = [c_p, ..., c_{j+1}, 1 + (x \max c_j), x]$$

But $c_p < d_q$, and since *gstep x* t'_2 can only increase the cost of t'_2, we have in this case that

$$lcost\ (gstep\ x\ t'_1) < lcost\ t'_2 \leqslant lcost\ (gstep\ x\ t'_2)$$

In the second case, suppose (8.1) does not hold for t'_1. In this case

$$lcost\ (gstep\ x\ t'_1) = [1 + (x \max c_p), x]$$

Now, either $1 + (x \max c_p) < d_q$, in which case

$$lcost\ (gstep\ x\ t'_1) < lcost\ t'_2 \leqslant lcost\ (gstep\ x\ t'_2)$$

or $1 + (x \max c_p) \geqslant d_q$, in which case $x \geqslant d_q - 1$ and $1 + (x \max d_{q-1}) \geqslant d_q$. That means that (8.1) does not hold for t'_2 either, and so we have

$$lcost\ (gstep\ x\ t'_1) = [1 + (x\ max\ c_p), x]$$
$$\leqslant [1 + (x\ max\ d_q), x] = lcost\ (gstep\ x\ t'_2)$$

That completes the proof of monotonicity.

The next task is to implement *gtep*. We can rewrite (8.1) by arguing

$$1 + (x\ max\ c_j) < c_{j+1}$$
$$\Leftrightarrow 1 + (x\ max\ c_j) < 1 + (c_j\ max\ cost\ t_{j+1})$$
$$\Leftrightarrow (x\ max\ c_j) < cost\ t_{j+1}$$

Hence *mct* = *foldrn gstep Leaf*, where

$$gstep :: Nat \to Tree\ Nat \to Tree\ Nat$$
$$gstep\ x = rollup \cdot add\ x \cdot spine$$

where *add* is defined by

$$add\ x\ ts = Leaf\ x : join\ x\ ts$$
$$join\ x\ [u] \qquad = [u]$$
$$join\ x\ (u : v : ts) = \textbf{if}\ x\ max\ cost\ u < cost\ v$$
$$\textbf{then}\ u : v : ts\ \textbf{else}\ join\ x\ (Node\ u\ v : ts)$$

However, instead of computing spines at each step and then rolling up the spine again, we can roll up the forest at the end of the computation. What is wanted for this step are functions *hstep* and *g* for which

$$foldrn\ gstep\ Leaf = rollup \cdot foldrn\ hstep\ g$$

We can discover *hstep* and *g* by appealing to the fusion law for *foldrn*. Notice that here we are applying the fusion law for *foldrn* in the anti-fusion, or *fission* direction, splitting a fold into two parts.

Firstly, we require *rollup · g* = *Leaf*. Since *rollup* [*Leaf x*] = *Leaf x*, we can define *g* by *g* = *wrap · Leaf*. Secondly, we want

$$rollup\ (hstep\ x\ ts) = gstep\ x\ (rollup\ ts)$$

for all *x* and all *ts* of the form *ts* = *foldrn hstep g xs*. Now,

$$gstep\ x\ (rollup\ ts)$$
$$= \quad \{ \text{ definition of } gstep \}$$
$$rollup\ (add\ x\ (spine\ (rollup\ ts)))$$
$$= \quad \{ \text{ provided the first element of } ts \text{ is a leaf} \}$$
$$rollup\ (add\ x\ ts)$$

Hence we can take *hstep* = *add*, provided the first element of *ts* is a leaf. But *ts* = *foldrn add* (*wrap · Leaf*) *xs* for some *xs* and it is immediate from the definition of *add* that the first element of *ts* is indeed a leaf.

We now have *mct* = *rollup · foldrn add* (*wrap · Leaf*). As a final step, repeated evaluations of *cost* can be eliminated by pairing each tree in the forest with its cost. That leads to the final algorithm

type *Pair* = (*Tree Nat*, *Nat*)

mct :: [*Nat*] → *Tree Nat*
mct = *rollup* · *map fst* · *foldrn hstep* (*wrap* · *leaf*)

hstep :: *Nat* → [*Pair*] → [*Pair*]
hstep x ts = *leaf x* : *join x ts*

join :: *Nat* → [*Pair*] → [*Pair*]
join x [*u*]   = [*u*]
join x (*u* : *v* : *ts*) = **if** *x* max *snd u* < *snd v*
                    then *u* : *v* : *ts* **else** *join x* (*node u v* : *ts*)

The functions *leaf* and *node* are the smart constructors

leaf :: *Nat* → *Pair*
leaf x = (*Leaf x*, *x*)

node :: *Pair* → *Pair* → *Pair*
node (*u*, *c*) (*v*, *d*) = (*Node u v*, 1 + *c* max *d*)

For example, the greedy algorithm applied to the list $[5, 3, 1, 4, 2]$ produces the forests

[*Leaf* 2]
[*Leaf* 4, *Leaf* 2]
[*Leaf* 1, *Node* (*Leaf* 4) (*Leaf* 2)]
[*Leaf* 3, *Leaf* 1, *Node* (*Leaf* 4) (*Leaf* 2)]
[*Leaf* 5, *Node* (*Node* (*Leaf* 3) (*Leaf* 1)) (*Node* (*Leaf* 4) (*Leaf* 2))]

The final forest is then rolled up into the final tree

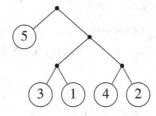

with cost 7.

It remains to estimate the running time of *mct*. The critical measure is the number of calls to *join*. We can prove by induction that any sequence of *hstep* operations applied to a list of length n and returning a forest of length m involves at most $2n - m$ calls to *join*. The base case, $n = 1$ and $m = 1$, is obvious. For the induction step, note that *join* applied to a list of length m' and returning a list of length m is called $m' - m$ times. Thus, using the induction step that *hstep* applied to a list of length $n - 1$ and returning a forest of length m' involves at most $2(n - 1) - m'$ calls of *join*, we have *hstep* applied to a list of length n, and returning a forest of length m involves at most

$$(2(n-1) - m') + 1 + (m' - m) \leqslant 2n - m$$

calls of *join*, establishing the induction. Hence the algorithm takes linear time.

Before leaving the problem of building a minimum-cost tree, we make one final remark. Observe that, when the input is a list consisting entirely of zeros, building a minimum-cost tree means building a minimum-height tree. It follows that the greedy algorithm, with minor changes, also works when the cost is the height of the tree. The changes are left as an exercise.

8.2 Huffman coding trees

Our second example is Huffman coding trees. As older computer users know only too well, it is often necessary to store files of information as compactly as possible. Suppose the information to be stored is a text consisting of a sequence of characters. Haskell uses Unicode internally for its *Char* data type, but the standard text I/O functions assume that texts are sequences of 8-bit characters, so a text of n characters contains $8n$ bits of information. Each character is represented by a fixed-length code, so the characters of a text can be recovered by decoding each successive group of eight bits.

One idea for reducing the total number of bits required to code a text is to abandon the notion of fixed-length codes, and seek instead a coding scheme based on the relative frequency of occurrence of the characters in the text. The basic idea is to take a sample piece of text, estimate the number of times each character appears, and choose short codes for the more frequent characters and longer codes for the rarer ones. For example, if we take the codes

$$\text{'t'} \longrightarrow 0$$
$$\text{'e'} \longrightarrow 10$$
$$\text{'x'} \longrightarrow 11$$

then "text" can be coded as the bit sequence 010110 of length 6. However, it is important that codes are chosen in such a way as to ensure that the coded text can be deciphered uniquely. To illustrate, suppose the codes had been

$$\text{'t'} \longrightarrow 0$$
$$\text{'e'} \longrightarrow 10$$
$$\text{'x'} \longrightarrow 1$$

Under this scheme, "text" would be coded as the sequence 01010 of length 5. However, the string "tee" would also be coded by 01010. Obviously this is not what is wanted. The simplest way to prevent the problem arising is to choose codes so that no code is a proper prefix of any other – a *prefix-free code*.

As well as requiring unique decipherability, we also want the coding to be optimal. An optimal coding scheme is one that minimises the expected length of the coded text. More precisely, if characters c_j, for $1 \leqslant j \leqslant n$, have frequencies of occurrence p_j, then we want to choose codes with lengths ℓ_j such that

$$\sum_{j=1}^{n} p_j \ell_j$$

is as small as possible.

One method for constructing an optimal code satisfying the prefix property is called Huffman coding. Each character is stored in a leaf of a binary tree, the structure of which is determined by the computed frequencies. The code for a character c is the sequence of binary values describing the path in the tree to the leaf containing c. For instance, with the tree

Node (*Node* (*Leaf* 'b') (*Leaf* 'e')) (*Leaf* 't')

the character 'b' is coded by 00, the character 'e' by 01, and the character 't' by 1. Clearly, such a scheme yields a prefix-free code.

There are four aspects to the problem of implementing Huffman coding: (i) collecting information from a sample; (ii) building a binary tree; (iii) coding a text; and (iv) decoding a bit sequence. We deal only with the problem of building a tree.

So, having analysed the sample, suppose we are given a list of pairs:

$$[(c_1, w_1), (c_2, w_2), ..., (c_n, w_n)]$$

where for $1 \leqslant j \leqslant n$ the c_j are the characters and the w_j are positive integers, called *weights*, indicating the frequencies of the characters in the text. The relative frequency of character c_j occurring is therefore w_j/W, where $W = \sum w_j$. We will suppose $w_1 \leqslant w_2 \leqslant \cdots \leqslant w_n$, so that the weights are given in ascending order.

In terms of trees, the cost function we want to minimise can be defined in the following way. By definition, the *depth* of a leaf is the length of the path from the root of the tree to the leaf. We can define the list of depths of the leaves in a tree by

> *depths* :: *Tree a* → [*Nat*]
> *depths* = *from* 0
> > **where** *from n* (*Leaf x*)   = [n]
> > *from n* (*Node u v*) = *from* (n + 1) u ++ *from* (n + 1) v

Now introduce the types

> **type** *Weight* = *Nat*
> **type** *Elem*   = (*Char*, *Weight*)
> **type** *Cost*   = *Nat*

and define *cost* by

$$cost :: Tree\ Elem \rightarrow Cost$$
$$cost\ t = sum\ [w \times d \mid ((\_, w), d) \leftarrow zip\ (fringe\ t)\ (depths\ t)]$$

It is left as an exercise to derive the following alternative definition of *cost*:

$$cost\ (Leaf\ e)\quad = 0$$
$$cost\ (Node\ u\ v) = cost\ u + cost\ v + weight\ u + weight\ v$$

$$weight :: Tree\ Elem \rightarrow Nat$$
$$weight\ (Leaf\ (c, w)) = w$$
$$weight\ (Node\ u\ v)\quad = weight\ u + weight\ v$$

We might now follow the previous section and specify

$$huffman :: [Elem] \rightarrow Tree\ Elem$$
$$huffman \leftarrow MinWith\ cost \cdot mktrees$$

where *mktrees* builds all the trees with a given list as fringe. But this specification is too strong: it is not required that the input list be the fringe, only that some permutation of it is. (However, in Chapter 14 we will consider a version of the problem in which the input *is* required to be the fringe.) One way of correcting the definition is to replace *mktrees* by *concatMap mktrees · perms*. Another way, and the one we will pursue, is to design a new version of *mktrees*. This version will construct all *unordered* binary trees. In an unordered binary tree the two children of a node are regarded as a set of two trees rather than an ordered pair. Thus *Node u v* is regarded as the same tree as *Node v u*. For example, there are 12 ordered binary trees whose fringe is a permutation of $[1, 2, 3]$, two trees for each of the six permutations, but only three essentially different unordered trees:

$$Node\ (Node\ (Leaf\ 1)\ (Leaf\ 2))\ (Leaf\ 3)$$
$$Node\ (Node\ (Leaf\ 1)\ (Leaf\ 3))\ (Leaf\ 2)$$
$$Node\ (Node\ (Leaf\ 2)\ (Leaf\ 3))\ (Leaf\ 1)$$

Each tree can be flipped in three ways (flipping the children of the top tree, the children of the left subtree, or both) to give the 12 different ordered binary trees. For Huffman coding it is sufficient to consider unordered trees because two sibling characters have the same codes except for the last bit and it does not matter which sibling is on the left. To compute all the unordered Huffman trees we can start with a list of leaves in weight order, and then repeatedly combine pairs of trees until a single tree remains. The pairs are chosen in all possible ways and a combined pair can be placed back in the list so as to maintain weight order. Thus, in an unordered tree *Node u v* we can assume $cost\ u \leqslant cost\ v$ without loss of generality.

Here is an example to see the idea at work. Showing only the weights, consider the following list of four trees in weight order:

$[Leaf\ 3, Leaf\ 5, Leaf\ 8, Leaf\ 9]$

As a first step we can choose to combine the first and third trees (among six possible choices) to give

$[Leaf\ 5, Leaf\ 9, Node\ (Leaf\ 3)\ (Leaf\ 8)]$

The new tree, with weight 11, is placed last in the list to maintain weight order. As the next step we can choose to combine the first two trees (among three possible choices), giving

$[Node\ (Leaf\ 3)\ (Leaf\ 8), Node\ (Leaf\ 5)\ (Leaf\ 9)]$

The next step is forced as there are only two trees left, and we end up with a singleton tree

$[Node\ (Node\ (Leaf\ 3)\ (Leaf\ 8))\ (Node\ (Leaf\ 5)\ (Leaf\ 9))]$

whose fringe is $[3, 8, 5, 9]$. This bottom-up method for building trees will generate $6 \times 3 = 18$ trees in total, more than the total number of unordered trees on four elements, because some trees, such as the one above, are generated twice (see the exercises). However, the list of trees includes all that are needed.

Now for the details. We define

$mktrees :: [Elem] \rightarrow [Tree\ Elem]$
$mktrees = map\ unwrap \cdot mkforests \cdot map\ Leaf$

where *mkforests* builds the list of forests, each forest consisting of a singleton tree. On way to define this function uses *until*:

$mkforests :: [Tree\ Elem] \rightarrow [Forest\ Elem]$
$mkforests = until\ (all\ single)\ (concatMap\ combine) \cdot wrap$

The function *mkforests* takes a list of trees, turns them into a singleton list of forests by applying *wrap*, and then repeatedly combines two trees in every possible way until every forest is reduced to a single tree. Each singleton forest is then unwrapped to give the final list of trees. The function *combine* is defined by

$combine :: Forest\ Elem \rightarrow [Forest\ Elem]$
$combine\ ts = [insert\ (Node\ t_1\ t_2)\ us\ |\ ((t_1, t_2), us) \leftarrow pairs\ ts]$

$pairs :: [a] \rightarrow [((a, a), [a])]$
$pairs\ xs = [((x, y), zs)\ |\ (x, ys) \leftarrow picks\ xs, (y, zs) \leftarrow picks\ ys]$

The function *picks* was defined in Chapter 1. The function *insert*, whose definition is left as an exercise, inserts a tree into a list of trees so as to maintain weight order. Hence *combine* selects, in all possible ways, a pair of trees from a forest, combines them into a new tree, and inserts the new tree into the remaining trees.

Another way to define *mkforests* uses the function *apply*. Recall the answer to Question 1.13, which gives the following definition of *apply*:

$$apply :: Nat \rightarrow (a \rightarrow a) \rightarrow a \rightarrow a$$
$$apply\ n\ f = \textbf{if}\ n == 0\ \textbf{then}\ id\ \textbf{else}\ f \cdot apply\ (n-1)\ f$$

Thus *apply n* applies a function *n* times to a given value. The alternative definition of *mkforests* is to write

$$mkforests :: [Tree\ Elem] \rightarrow [Forest\ Elem]$$
$$mkforests\ ts = apply\ (length\ ts - 1)\ (concatMap\ combine)\ [ts]$$

The two definitions give the same result because at each step the number of trees in each forest is reduced by one, so it takes exactly $n-1$ steps to reduce an initial forest of n trees to a list of singleton forests.

Our problem now takes the form

$$huffman :: [Elem] \rightarrow Tree\ Elem$$
$$huffman \leftarrow MinWith\ cost \cdot mktrees$$

Since *mktrees* is defined in terms of *until*, we will aim for a constructive definition of *huffman* of the same form. The task is to find a function *gstep* so that

$$unwrap\ (until\ single\ gstep\ (map\ Leaf\ xs)) \leftarrow MinWith\ cost\ (mktrees\ xs)$$

for all finite nonempty lists *xs* of type [*Elem*]. More generally, we will seek a function *gstep* such that

$$unwrap\ (until\ single\ gstep\ ts) \leftarrow MinWith\ cost\ (map\ unwrap\ (mkforests\ ts))$$

for all finite nonempty lists of trees *ts*. Problems of this form will arise in the following chapter too, so let us pause for a little more theory on greedy algorithms.

Another generic greedy algorithm

Suppose in this section that the list of candidates is given by a function

$$candidates :: State \rightarrow [Candidate]$$

for some type *State*. For Huffman coding, states are lists of trees and candidates are trees:

$$candidates\ ts = map\ unwrap\ (mkforests\ ts)$$

For the problems in the following chapter, states are combinations of values.

The aim of this section is to give conditions for which the refinement

$$extract\ (until\ final\ gstep\ sx) \leftarrow MinWith\ cost\ (candidates\ sx) \qquad (8.2)$$

holds for all states *sx*. The functions on the left have the following types:

$$gstep\ :: State \rightarrow State$$
$$final\ :: State \rightarrow Bool$$
$$extract :: State \rightarrow Candidate$$

In words, (8.2) states that repeatedly applying a greedy step to any initial state *sx* will result in a final state from which a candidate x can be extracted with the property that x is a candidate in *candidates sx* with minimum cost. In order for the refinement to be meaningful, it is assumed that the left-hand side returns a well-defined value for any initial state. Unlike the formulation of a generic greedy algorithm in Section 7.1, nothing is known about how the candidates are constructed.

For brevity in what follows, define

$$MCC\ sx\ \ = MinWith\ cost\ (candidates\ sx)$$
$$mincost\ sx = minimum\ (map\ cost\ (candidates\ sx))$$

In particular, for all x in *candidates sx* we have

$$x \leftarrow MCC\ sx\ \ \Leftrightarrow\ \ cost\ x = mincost\ sx$$

There are two conditions that ensure (8.2). The first is

$$final\ sx\ \Rightarrow\ extract\ sx \leftarrow MCC\ sx \qquad (8.3)$$

This condition holds for Huffman coding, when *final* = *single* and *extract* = *unwrap*, since *map unwrap* (*mkforests* $[t]$) = $[t]$ and *MinWith cost* $[t]$ = t.

The second condition is the greedy condition. We can state it in two ways. The first way is

$$not\ (final\ sx)\ \Rightarrow\ (\exists x : x \leftarrow MCC\ (gstep\ sx) \land x \leftarrow MCC\ sx) \qquad (8.4)$$

In hillclimbing terms, the greedy condition asserts that, from any starting point not already on top of the hill, there is some path to a highest point that starts out with a greedy step.

The second way of stating the greedy condition appears to be stronger:

$$not\ (final\ sx)\ \Rightarrow\ MCC\ (gstep\ sx) \leftarrow MCC\ sx \qquad (8.5)$$

However, with one extra proviso, (8.4) implies (8.5). The proviso is that applying *gstep* to a state may reduce the number of final candidates but will never introduce new ones. In symbols,

$$candidates\ (gstep\ sx) \subseteq candidates\ sx \qquad (8.6)$$

Suppose $x \leftarrow MCC\ (gstep\ sx)$ and $x \leftarrow MCC\ sx$. Then, by definition of *MCC* and *mincost*, we have

$$mincost\ (gstep\ sx) = cost\ x = mincost\ sx$$

Now suppose $y \leftarrow MCC\ (gstep\ sx)$, so $y \in candidates\ sx$ by (8.6). Then

$$cost\ y = mincost\ (gstep\ sx) = mincost\ sx$$

and so $y \leftarrow MCC\ sx$. Although, in general, $E_1 \leftarrow E_2$ is a stronger statement than one that merely asserts there exists some value v such that $v \leftarrow E_1 \land v \leftarrow E_2$, that is not the case here.

To prove (8.2), suppose that k is the smallest integer – assumed to exist – for which *apply k gstep sx* is a final state. That means *until final gstep sx = apply k gstep sx*

It follows that *apply j gstep sx* is not a final state for $0 \leqslant j < k$, so, by the stronger greedy condition, we have

$MCC\ (apply\ (j+1)\ gstep\ sx) \leftarrow MCC\ (apply\ j\ gstep\ sx)$

for $0 \leqslant j < k$. Hence $MCC\ (apply\ k\ gstep\ sx) \leftarrow MCC\ sx$. Furthermore, by (8.3) we have

$extract\ (apply\ k\ gstep\ sx) \leftarrow MCC\ (apply\ k\ gstep\ sx)$

establishing (8.2).

This style of reasoning about greedy algorithms is very general. However, unlike greedy algorithms derived by fusion, it gives no hint as to what form *gstep* might take.

Huffman coding continued

Returning to Huffman coding, in which candidates are trees, it remains to define *gstep* and to show that the greedy condition holds. For Huffman coding we have

$MCC\ ts = MinWith\ cost\ (map\ unwrap\ (mkforests\ ts))$

We take *gstep* to be the function that combines the two trees in the forest with smallest weights. Since trees are kept in weight order, that means

$gstep\ (t_1 : t_2 : ts) = insert\ (Node\ t_1\ t_2)\ ts$

For the greedy condition, let $ts = [t_1, t_2, ..., t_n]$ be a list of trees in weight order, with weights $[w_1, w_2, ..., w_n]$. The task is to construct a tree t for which

$t \leftarrow MCC\ (gstep\ ts) \quad \wedge \quad t \leftarrow MCC\ ts$

Suppose $t' \leftarrow MCC\ ts$. We construct t by applying tree surgery to t'. Every tree in *ts* appears somewhere as a subtree of t', so imagine that t_i appears at depth d_i in t' for $1 \leqslant i \leqslant n$. Now, among the subtrees of t', there will be a pair of sibling trees at greatest depth. There may be more than one such pair, but there will be at least one. Suppose two such trees are t_i and t_j and let $d = d_i = d_j$. Then $d_1 \leqslant d$ and $d_2 \leqslant d$. Furthermore, t_i and t_j could have been chosen as the first step in the construction of t'. Without loss of generality, suppose $w_1 \leqslant w_i$ and $w_2 \leqslant w_j$. Construct t by swapping t_i with t_1 and t_j with t_2. Then t can be constructed by taking a greedy first step. Furthermore

$$cost\ t' - cost\ t = d_1 w_1 + d_2 w_2 + d\,(w_i + w_j) - (d_1 w_i + d_2 w_j + d\,(w_1 + w_2))$$
$$= (d - d_1)\,(w_i - w_1) + (d - d_2)\,(w_j - w_2)$$
$$\geqslant 0$$

But $cost\ t'$ is as small as possible, so $cost\ t' = cost\ t$. Hence $t \leftarrow MCC\ ts$ and $t \leftarrow MCC\ (gstep\ ts)$.

The same tree surgery can be used to show that the stronger greedy condition holds by a direct argument. Suppose $t \leftarrow MCC \ (gstep \ ts)$ but t is not a value in $MCC \ ts$. That means there exists a tree $t' \leftarrow MCC \ ts$ with $cost \ t' < cost \ t$. We now get a contradiction by applying the surgical procedure to t' to produce another tree $t'' \leftarrow MCC \ (gstep \ ts)$ with $cost \ t = cost \ t'' \leqslant cost \ t'$.

Here is the greedy algorithm we have derived:

$$huffman \ es = unwrap \ (until \ single \ gstep \ (map \ Leaf \ es))$$
$$\textbf{where} \ gstep \ (t_1 : t_2 : ts) = insert \ (Node \ t_1 \ t_2) \ ts$$

However, simple as it is, the algorithm is not quite ready to leave the kitchen. There are two sources of inefficiency. Firstly, the function *insert* recomputes weights at each step, an inefficiency that can easily be brushed aside by tupling. The more serious issue is that, while finding two trees of smallest weights is a constant-time operation, inserting the combined tree back into the forest can take linear time in the worst case. That means the greedy algorithm takes quadratic time in the worst case. The final step is to show how this can be reduced to linear time.

The key observation behind the linear-time algorithm is the fact that, in any call of *gstep*, the argument to *insert* has a weight at least as large as any previous argument. Suppose we combine two trees with weights w_1 and w_2 and, later on, two trees with weights w_3 and w_4. We have $w_1 \leqslant w_2 \leqslant w_3 \leqslant w_4$, and it follows that $w_1 + w_2 \leqslant w_3 + w_4$. This suggests maintaining the non-leaf trees as a simple queue, whereby elements are added to the rear of the queue and removed only from the front. Instead of maintaining a single list we therefore maintain two lists, the first being a list of leaves and the second a queue of node trees. Since elements are never added to the first list, but only removed from the front, the first list could also be a queue. But a simple list suffices. We will call the first list a *stack* simply to distinguish it from the second one. At each step, *gstep* selects two lightest trees from either the stack or the queue, combines them, and adds the result to the end of the queue. At the end of the algorithm the queue will contain a single tree, the greedy solution. Figure 8.2, which shows the weights only, gives an example of how the method works out. The method is viable only if the various queue operations take constant time. But we have already met symmetric lists in Chapter 3, which satisfy the requirements exactly.

Here are the details. First we set up the type *SQ* of Stack-Queues:

$$\textbf{type} \ SQ \ a \quad = (Stack \ a, Queue \ a)$$
$$\textbf{type} \ Stack \ a \ = [a]$$
$$\textbf{type} \ Queue \ a = SymList \ a$$

Now we can define

$$huffman :: [Elem] \ \text{>} \ Tree \ Elem$$
$$huffman = extractSQ \cdot until \ singleSQ \ gstep \cdot makeSQ \cdot map \ leaf$$

Stack of weights	Queue of combined weights
1, 2, 4, 4, 6, 9	
4, 4, 6, 9	$1+2$
4, 6, 9	$4+(1+2)$
9	$4+(1+2), 4+6$
	$4+6, 9+(4+(1+2))$
	$(4+6)+(9+(4+(1+2)))$

Figure 8.2 Example of the stack and queue operations

The component functions on the right-hand side are defined in terms of the type

   type $Pair = (Tree\ Elem, Weight)$

of pairs of trees and weights. First of all, the functions *leaf* and *node* (needed in the definition of *gstep*) are smart constructors that install weight information correctly:

   $leaf :: Elem \to Pair$
   $leaf\ (c, w) = (Leaf\ (c, w), w)$

   $node :: Pair \to Pair \to Pair$
   $node\ (t_1, w_1)\ (t_2, w_2) = (Node\ t_1\ t_2, w_1 + w_2)$

Next, the function *makeSQ* initialises a Stack-Queue:

   $makeSQ :: [Pair] \to SQ\ Pair$
   $makeSQ\ xs = (xs, nilSL)$

Recall that the function *nilSL* returns an empty symmetric list.

   Next, the function *singleSQ* determines whether a Stack-Queue is a singleton, and *extractSQ* extracts the tree:

   $singleSQ :: SQ\ a \to Bool$
   $singleSQ\ (xs, ys) = null\ xs \wedge singleSL\ ys$

   $extractSQ :: SQ\ Pair \to Tree\ Elem$
   $extractSQ\ (xs, ys) = fst\ (headSL\ ys)$

The function *singleSL*, whose definition is left as an exercise, tests for whether a symmetric list is a singleton.

   Finally, we define

   $gstep :: SQ\ Pair \to SQ\ Pair$
   $gstep\ ps = add\ (node\ p_1\ p_2)\ rs$
      where $(p_1, qs) = extractMin\ ps$
         $(p_2, rs) = extractMin\ qs$

   $add :: Pair \to SQ\ Pair \to SQ\ Pair$
   $add\ y\ (xs, ys) = (xs, snocSL\ y\ ys)$

It remains to define *extractMin* for extracting a tree with minimum weight from a
Stack-Queue:

$$extractMin :: SQ\ Pair \rightarrow (Pair, SQ\ Pair)$$
$$extractMin\ (xs, ys)$$
$$\quad |\ nullSL\ ys \quad = (head\ xs, (tail\ xs, ys))$$
$$\quad |\ null\ xs \quad\quad = (headSL\ ys, (xs, tailSL\ ys))$$
$$\quad |\ snd\ x \leqslant snd\ y = (x, (tail\ xs, ys))$$
$$\quad |\ otherwise \quad = (y, (xs, tailSL\ ys))$$
$$\quad \textbf{where}\ x = head\ xs;\quad y = headSL\ ys$$

If both the stack and the queue are nonempty, then the tree with the smallest weight
from either list is selected. If one of the stack and the queue is empty, the selection
is made from the other component.

The linear-time algorithm for Huffman coding depends on the assumption that
the input is sorted into ascending order of weight. If this were not the case, then
$O(n \log n)$ steps have to be spent sorting. Strictly speaking, that means Huffman
coding actually takes $O(n \log n)$ steps. There is an alternative implementation of the
algorithm with this running time, and that is to use a *priority queue*. Priority queues
will be needed again, particularly in Part Six, so we will consider them now.

8.3 Priority queues

A *priority queue* is a data structure *PQ* for maintaining a list of values so that the
following two operations take at most logarithmic time in the length of the list:

$$insertQ :: Ord\ p \Rightarrow a \rightarrow p \rightarrow PQ\ a\ p \rightarrow PQ\ a\ p$$
$$deleteQ :: Ord\ p \Rightarrow PQ\ a\ p \rightarrow ((a, p), PQ\ a\ p)$$

The function *insertQ* takes a value and a *priority* and inserts the value into the queue
with the given priority. The function *deleteQ* takes a nonempty queue and extracts a
value whose priority is the *smallest*, returning the value and its associated priority,
together with the remaining queue. In a *max-priority queue* the function *deleteQ*
would extract a value with the *largest* priority.

As well as the two functions above, we also need some other functions on priority
queues, including

$$emptyQ \quad :: PQ\ a\ p$$
$$nullQ \quad\quad :: PQ\ a\ p \rightarrow Bool$$
$$addListQ :: Ord\ p \Rightarrow [(a, p)] \rightarrow PQ\ a\ p \rightarrow PQ\ a\ p$$
$$toListQ \quad :: Ord\ p \Rightarrow PQ\ a\ p \rightarrow [(a, p)]$$

The constant *emptyQ* represents an empty queue, and *nullQ* tests for an empty
queue. The function *addListQ* adds a list of value-priority pairs in one fell swoop,

while *toListQ* returns a list of value-priority pairs in order of priority. The function *addListQ* can be defined in terms of *insertQ* (see the exercises).

One simple implementation of priority queues is to maintain the queue as a list in ascending order of priority. But, as we have seen with Huffman's algorithm, this means that insertion is a linear-time operation. A better method is to use a heap, similar to the heaps described in Section 5.3. Using a heap guarantees logarithmic time for an insertion or deletion, as we will now see.

The relevant data type for heaps is the following:

    data $PQ\ a\ p = Null \mid Fork\ Rank\ a\ p\ (PQ\ a\ p)\ (PQ\ a\ p)$
    type $Rank\ \ \ = Nat$

A queue is therefore a binary tree. (We use *Fork* as a constructor rather than *Node* to avoid a name clash with Huffman trees, but continue to refer to 'nodes' rather than 'forks'.) The heap condition is that flattening a queue returns a list of elements in ascending order of priority:

    $toListQ :: Ord\ p \Rightarrow PQ\ a\ p \rightarrow [(a,p)]$
    $toListQ\ Null \qquad\qquad\quad = [\ ]$
    $toListQ\ (Fork\ \_\ x\ p\ t_1\ t_2) = (x,p) : mergeOn\ snd\ (toListQ\ t_1)\ (toListQ\ t_2)$

The definition of *mergeOn* is left as an exercise. Thus a queue is a heap in which the element at a node has a priority that is no larger than the priorities in each of its subtrees. Each node of the queue stores an additional piece of information, the *rank* of that node. By definition, the rank of a tree is the length of the shortest path in the tree from the root to a *Null* tree. A queue is not just a heap but a variety called a *leftist* heap. A tree is leftist if the rank of the left subtree of any node is no smaller than the rank of its right subtree. This property makes heaps taller on the left, whence its name. A simple consequence of the leftist property is that the length of the shortest path from the root of a tree to a *Null* is always along the right spine of the tree. We leave it as an exercise to show that, for a tree of size n, this length is at most $\lfloor \log(n+1) \rfloor$.

We can maintain rank information with the help of a smart constructor *fork*:

    $fork :: a \rightarrow p \rightarrow PQ\ a\ p \rightarrow PQ\ a\ p \rightarrow PQ\ a\ p$
    $fork\ x\ p\ t_1\ t_2$
       $\mid r_2 \leqslant r_1 \quad = Fork\ (r_2+1)\ x\ p\ t_1\ t_2$
       $\mid otherwise = Fork\ (r_1+1)\ x\ p\ t_2\ t_1$
       where $r_1 = rank\ t_1;\ \ r_2 = rank\ t_2$
    $rank :: PQ\ a\ p \rightarrow Rank$
    $rank\ Null \qquad\qquad = 0$
    $rank\ (Fork\ r\ \_\ \_\ \_\ \_) = r$

In order to maintain the leftist property, the two subtrees are swapped if the left subtree has lower rank than the right subtree.

Two leftist heaps can be combined into one by the function $combineQ$, where

$combineQ :: Ord\ p \Rightarrow PQ\ a\ p \rightarrow PQ\ a\ p \rightarrow PQ\ a\ p$
$combineQ\ Null\ t = t$
$combineQ\ t\ Null = t$
$combineQ\ (Fork\ k_1\ x_1\ p_1\ l_1\ r_1)\ (Fork\ k_2\ x_2\ p_2\ l_2\ r_2)$
$\quad |\ p_1 \leqslant p_2 \quad = fork\ x_1\ p_1\ l_1\ (combineQ\ r_1\ (Fork\ k_2\ x_2\ p_2\ l_2\ r_2))$
$\quad |\ otherwise = fork\ x_2\ p_2\ l_2\ (combineQ\ (Fork\ k_1\ x_1\ p_1\ l_1\ r_1)\ r_2)$

In the worst case, $combineQ$ traverses the right spines of the two trees. Hence the running time of $combineQ$ on two leftist heaps of rank at most r is $O(\log r)$ steps. Now we can define the insertion and deletion operations (the functions $emptyQ$ and $nullQ$ are left as exercises):

$insertQ :: Ord\ p \Rightarrow a \rightarrow p \rightarrow PQ\ a\ p \rightarrow PQ\ a\ p$
$insertQ\ x\ p\ t = combineQ\ (fork\ x\ p\ Null\ Null)\ t$

$deleteQ :: Ord\ p \Rightarrow PQ\ a\ p \rightarrow ((a,p), PQ\ a\ p)$
$deleteQ\ (Fork\ \_\ x\ p\ t_1\ t_2) = ((x,p), combineQ\ t_1\ t_2)$

Both operations take logarithmic time in the size of the queue. Summarising, by using a priority queue of n elements rather than an ordered list we can reduce the time for an insertion to $O(\log n)$ steps rather than $O(n)$ steps. The price paid for this reduction is that the time to find a smallest value goes up from $O(1)$ steps to $O(\log n)$ steps.

Finally, here is the implementation of Huffman's algorithm using a priority queue:

$huffman :: [Elem] \rightarrow Tree\ Elem$
$huffman = extract \cdot until\ singleQ\ gstep \cdot makeQ \cdot map\ leaf$

$extract :: PQ\ (Tree\ Elem)\ Weight \rightarrow Tree\ Elem$
$extract = fst \cdot fst \cdot deleteQ$

$gstep :: PQ\ (Tree\ Elem)\ Weight \rightarrow PQ\ (Tree\ Elem)\ Int$
$gstep\ ps = insertQ\ t\ w\ rs$
$\qquad\qquad\quad \textbf{where}\ (t,w) \quad = node\ p_1\ p_2$
$\qquad\qquad\qquad\qquad (p_1, qs) = deleteQ\ ps$
$\qquad\qquad\qquad\qquad (p_2, rs) = deleteQ\ qs$

$makeQ :: Ord\ p \Rightarrow [(a,p)] \rightarrow PQ\ a\ p$
$makeQ\ xs = addListQ\ xs\ emptyQ$

$singleQ :: Ord\ p \Rightarrow PQ\ a\ p \rightarrow Bool$
$singleQ = nullQ \cdot snd \cdot deleteQ$

This algorithm runs in $O(n \log n)$ steps without making the assumption that the input is sorted by weight.

8.4 Chapter notes

The minimum-cost tree problem was first described in [1]. Another way to build a minimum-cost tree is to use either the Hu–Tucker [2] or the Garsia–Wachs algorithm [5]. The Hu–Tucker algorithm applies because *cost* is a *regular* cost function as defined in [2]. But the best implementation of the Hu–Tucker algorithm takes $\Theta(n \log n)$ steps. The Garsia–Wachs algorithm will be discussed in Section 14.6.

Huffman's algorithm is a firm favourite in the study of greedy algorithms. It first appeared in [3]. The linear-time greedy algorithm based on queues is described in [4], which also shows how the algorithm can be generalised to deal with k-ary trees rather than just binary trees. If one insists that the fringe of the tree is exactly the given character–weight pairs in the order they are given, then the resulting tree, called an *alphabetic* tree by Hu, can be built using the Garsia–Wachs algorithm.

There are many implementations of priority queues, including leftist heaps, skew heaps, and maxiphobic heaps. All these can be found in [6, 7].

References

[1]   Richard Bird. *Pearls of Functional Algorithm Design*. Cambridge University Press, Cambridge, 2010.
[2]   Te Chiang Hu. *Combinatorial Algorithms*. Addison-Wesley, Reading, MA, 1982.
[3]   David A. Huffman. A method for the construction of minimum-redundancy codes. *Proceedings of the IRE*, 40(9):1098–1101, 1952.
[4]   Donald E. Knuth. *The Art of Computer Programming*, volume 1: Fundamental Algorithms. Addison-Wesley, Reading, MA, third edition, 1997.
[5]   Donald E. Knuth. *The Art of Computer Programming*, volume 3: Sorting and Searching. Addison-Wesley, Reading, MA, second edition, 1998.
[6]   Chris Okasaki. *Purely Functional Data Structures*. Cambridge University Press, Cambridge, 1998.
[7]   Chris Okasaki. Fun with binary heap trees. In J. Gibbons and O. de Moor, editors, *The Fun of Programming*, pages 1–16. Palgrave, Macmillan, Hampshire, 2003.

Exercises

Exercise 8.1 Consider the recurrence $H(1) = 0$ and $H(n) = 1 + H(\lceil n/2 \rceil)$. Prove by induction that $H(n) = \lceil \log n \rceil$.

Exercise 8.2 Prove that the bottom-up algorithm

$$mktree = unwrap \cdot until \ single \ (pairWith \ Node) \cdot map \ Leaf$$

of Section 8.1 produces a tree of minimum height.

Exercise 8.3 We claimed in Section 8.1 that minimising *lcost* also minimises *cost*. Why is this true?

Exercise 8.4 Why is the claim *rollup · spine = id* not true for all possible lists of trees?

Exercise 8.5 The (context-free) fusion rule for *foldrn* asserts that

$$foldrn\ f_2\ g_2\ xs \leftarrow M\ (foldrn\ f_1\ g_1\ xs)$$

for all finite lists *xs*, provided

$$g_2\ x \quad\quad \leftarrow M\ (g_1\ x)$$
$$f_2\ x\ (M\ y) \leftarrow M\ (f_1\ x\ y)$$

Prove this result.

Exercise 8.6 Specialise the final greedy algorithm of Section 8.1 as suggested to build a minimum-height tree.

Exercise 8.7 The function $splits :: [a] \rightarrow [([a],[a])]$ splits a list *xs* into all pairs of lists (ys, zs) such that $xs = ys \mathbin{+\!\!+} zs$. The function *splitsn* is similar, except that it splits a list into pairs of nonempty lists. Give recursive definitions of *splits* and *splitsn*.

Exercise 8.8 Using *splitsn*, give a recursive definition of the function *mktrees* of Section 8.1. Write down a recurrence relation for the function $T(n)$ that counts the number of trees with *n* leaves. It can be shown that

$$T(n) = \frac{1}{n}\binom{2n-2}{n-1}$$

These values are called the *Catalan numbers*.

Exercise 8.9 Here is another way of defining the function *mktrees* of Section 8.1, one similar to that used in Huffman coding:

$$mktrees :: [a] \rightarrow [Tree\ a]$$
$$mktrees = map\ unwrap \cdot until\ (all\ single)\ (concatMap\ combine) \cdot$$
$$\quad\quad wrap \cdot map\ Leaf$$
$$combine :: Forest\ a \rightarrow [Forest\ a]$$
$$combine\ xs = [ys \mathbin{+\!\!+} [Node\ x\ y] \mathbin{+\!\!+} zs \mid (ys, x:y:zs) \leftarrow splits\ xs]$$

The function *combine* combines two adjacent trees in a forest in all possible ways. The process is repeated until only singleton forests remain, forests that consist of just one tree. Finally the trees are extracted to give a list of trees. This method may generate the same tree more than once, but all possible trees are nevertheless produced. Write down the associated greedy algorithm for this version of *mktrees* (no justification is required).

Exercise 8.10 In Huffman coding, why does the second, recursive definition of *cost* follow from the first?

Exercise 8.11 Define the function *insert* used in Huffman's algorithm.

Exercise 8.12 Give the two ways that the tree

[*Node* (*Node* (*Leaf* 3) (*Leaf* 8)) (*Node* (*Leaf* 5) (*Leaf* 9))]

can be generated from [*Leaf* 3, *Leaf* 5, *Leaf* 8, *Leaf* 9].

Exercise 8.13 The number of trees generated in the specification of Huffman's algorithm is given for $n \geqslant 2$ by

$$\binom{n}{2}\binom{n-1}{2}\cdots\binom{2}{2}$$

Show that this number equals

$$\frac{n!\,(n-1)!}{2^{n-1}}$$

Exercise 8.14 Define *MCC k xs* = *MinWith cost* (*apply k fstep* [*xs*]). Show that

$$apply\ k\ gstep\ xs \leftarrow MCC\ k\ xs$$

provided *MCC k* (*gstep xs*) ← *MCC* (*k* + 1) *xs*.

Exercise 8.15 Define the function *singleSL* :: *SymList a* → *Bool* for determining whether a symmetric list is a singleton.

Exercise 8.16 Define *addListQ* in terms of *insertQ*.

Exercise 8.17 Define *mergeOn*.

Exercise 8.18 Show that, for the trees considered in Section 8.3, a tree of size n has rank at most $\lfloor \log(n+1) \rfloor$.

Exercise 8.19 Define *emptyQ* and *nullQ*.

Answers

Answer 8.1 The base case is immediate and the induction step follows from

$$\lceil \log n \rceil = 1 + \lceil \log \lceil n/2 \rceil \rceil$$

This equation can be proved by showing

$$\lceil \log n \rceil \leqslant k \;\Leftrightarrow\; 1 + \lceil \log \lceil n/2 \rceil \rceil \leqslant k$$

for any k. Both sides reduce to $n \leqslant 2^k$ by appeal to the rule of ceilings, establishing the result.

Answer 8.2 For a list of length n the bottom-up algorithm builds a tree t whose left child is a perfectly balanced binary tree with 2^k leaves, where $2^k < n \leqslant 2^{k+1}$. The height of t is therefore $k+1 = \lceil \log n \rceil$, the smallest height possible.

Answer 8.3 Because $cost = head \cdot lcost$ and

$$us \leqslant vs \;\Rightarrow\; head\ us \leqslant head\ vs$$

Answer 8.4 The function *spine* returns the undefined value on trees with an infinite spine, so the equation fails.

Answer 8.5 The base case is easy, and the induction step is

$$
\begin{aligned}
&foldrn\, f_2\, g_2\, (x\!:\!xs) \\
=\quad & \{\text{ definition of } foldrn \,\} \\
&f_2\, x\, (foldrn\, f_2\, g_2\, xs) \\
\leftarrow\quad & \{\text{ induction }\} \\
&f_2\, x\, (M\, (foldrn\, f_1\, g_1\, xs)) \\
\leftarrow\quad & \{\text{ fusion condition }\} \\
&M\, (f_1\, x\, (foldrn\, f_1\, g_1\, xs)) \\
=\quad & \{\text{ definition of } foldrn \,\} \\
&M\, (foldrn\, f_1\, g_1\, (x\!:\!xs))
\end{aligned}
$$

Answer 8.6 The algorithm is

$$greedy = rollup \cdot map\, fst \cdot foldrn\, insert\, (wrap \cdot leaf)$$

$$
\begin{aligned}
\mathbf{where}\ & insert\, x\, ts = leaf\, x : join\, ts \\
& join\, [u] \qquad = [u] \\
& join\, (u\!:\!v\!:\!ts) = \mathbf{if}\ snd\, u < snd\, v\ \mathbf{then}\ u\!:\!v\!:\!ts\ \mathbf{else}\ join\, (node\, u\, v\!:\!ts) \\
& leaf\, x = (Leaf\, x, 0)
\end{aligned}
$$

Answer 8.7 The definitions are

$$
\begin{aligned}
splits\, [] \quad &= \quad [([],[])] \\
splits\, (x\!:\!xs) &= \quad ([], x\!:\!xs) : [(x\!:\!ys, zs) \mid (ys, zs) \leftarrow splits\, xs] \\
splitsn\, [] \quad &= \quad [] \\
splitsn\, [x] \quad &= \quad [] \\
splitsn\, (x\!:\!xs) &= ([x], xs) : [(x\!:\!ys, zs) \mid (ys, zs) \leftarrow splitsn\, xs]
\end{aligned}
$$

Answer 8.8 We have

$$
\begin{aligned}
mktrees\, [x] &= [Leaf\, x] \\
mktrees\, xs\ &= [Node\, u\, v \mid (ys, zs) \leftarrow splitsn\, xs, \\
&\qquad\qquad\quad u \leftarrow mktrees\, ys, v \leftarrow mktrees\, zs]
\end{aligned}
$$

The recurrence relation is given by $T(1) = 1$ and, for $n > 1$,

$$T(n) = \sum_{k=1}^{n-1} T(k)\, T(n-k)$$

Answer 8.9 The greedy algorithm is

$mct :: [Nat] \rightarrow Tree\ Nat$
$mct = unwrap \cdot until\ single\ combine \cdot map\ Leaf$

$combine :: Forest\ Nat \rightarrow Forest\ Nat$
$combine\ ts = us \mathbin{+\!\!+} [Node\ u\ v] \mathbin{+\!\!+} vs$
$\qquad$ **where** $(us, u:v:vs) = bestjoin\ ts$

The omitted function *bestjoin* splits a forest into two sub-forests in which the first two trees of the second forest are trees whose combined cost is minimal. For example, for the input $[5,3,1,4,2,2]$ this version of *mct* produces the tree

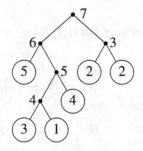

In the case of a minimum-height tree this greedy algorithm can be simplified to give the bottom-up algorithm described at the beginning of the chapter.

Answer 8.10 If the cost of tree u is $\sum w_i\, l_i$ and the cost of tree v is $\sum w'_i\, l'_i$, then the cost of *Node u v* is

$$\sum w_i\,(l_i+1) + \sum w'_i\,(l'_i+1) = cost\ u + cost\ v + weight\ u + weight\ v$$

Answer 8.11 We can implement *insert* by linear search, leading to

$insert :: Tree\ Elem \rightarrow Forest\ Elem \rightarrow Forest\ Elem$
$insert\ t_1\ [] \quad = [t_1]$
$insert\ t_1\ (t_2:ts) = \textbf{if}\ weight\ t_1 \leqslant weight\ t_2\ \textbf{then}\ t_1:t_2:ts\ \textbf{else}\ t_2 : insert\ t_1\ ts$

Answer 8.12 The same tree is generated either by combining *Leaf* 3 and *Leaf* 8 as a first step, followed by combining *Leaf* 5 and *Leaf* 9, or vice versa.

Answer 8.13 The proof is by induction. Both expressions equal 1 for $n = 2$, and the induction step is an easy calculation.

Answer 8.14 The proof is by induction. The case $k = 0$ is immediate, and for the induction step we can argue as follows:

$$apply\ (k+1)\ gstep\ xs$$
$$=\quad \{\ \text{definition of } apply\ \}$$
$$apply\ k\ gstep\ (gstep\ xs)$$
$$\leftarrow\quad \{\ \text{induction}\ \}$$
$$MCC\ k\ (gstep\ xs)$$
$$\leftarrow\quad \{\ \text{given}\ \}$$
$$MCC\ (k+1)\ xs$$

Answer 8.15 The definition is

$$singleSL :: SymList\ a \rightarrow Bool$$
$$singleSL\ (xs, ys) = (null\ xs \wedge single\ ys) \vee (null\ ys \wedge single\ xs)$$

Answer 8.16 We can define

$$addListQ\ xs\ q = foldr\ (uncurry\ insertQ)\ q\ xs$$

Answer 8.17 We have

$$mergeOn :: Ord\ b \Rightarrow (a \rightarrow b) \rightarrow [a] \rightarrow [a] \rightarrow [a]$$
$$mergeOn\ key\ xs\ [\,] = xs$$
$$mergeOn\ key\ [\,]\ ys = ys$$
$$mergeOn\ key\ (x:xs)\ (y:ys)$$
$$\quad |\ key\ x \leqslant key\ y\ = x : mergeOn\ key\ xs\ (y:ys)$$
$$\quad |\ otherwise\qquad = y : mergeOn\ key\ (x:xs)\ ys$$

Answer 8.18 Essentially we have to show that a tree of rank r and size n satisfies $2^r - 1 \leqslant n$. Such a tree has one node at depth 0, two nodes at depth 1, and so on. The tree also has 2^{r-1} nodes at depth $r - 1$. All this is because the first null node does not appear until level r. Hence the size of the tree is at least

$$1 + 2 + \cdots + 2^{r-1} = 2^r - 1$$

which establishes the claim.

Answer 8.19 We have

$$emptyQ = Null$$
$$nullQ\ Null = True$$
$$nullQ\ \_\quad = False$$

Chapter 9

Greedy algorithms on graphs

In this chapter we consider two problems for which the candidates are graphs, in fact special forms of graph called *spanning trees*. The first problem is about computing a spanning tree with minimum cost for a connected graph, while the second is about computing a spanning tree for a directed graph whose edges determine a shortest path from a given starting vertex to all other vertices. All these terms are made precise below. The shortest-paths algorithm is then used to solve another problem, called the *jogger's problem*, for computing a cyclic path with minimum total cost.

9.1 Graphs and spanning trees

We start with some terminology. There are two kinds of graph, a *directed* graph, also called a *digraph*, and an *undirected* graph, just called a *graph*. Certain definitions are slightly different for digraphs and graphs, so it is best to consider them as separate though closely related species. The minimum-cost spanning tree problem deals with graphs, while the shortest-paths problem deals with digraphs.

By definition, a *digraph D* is a pair (V, E), where V is a set of *vertices*, also called *nodes*, and E is a set of *edges*. An edge consists of a pair of vertices (u, v), where u is the *source* of the edge and v is the *target*. Such an edge is *directed* from u to v. In a digraph it is possible to have *loops* – edges of the form (u, u). Because E is a set it cannot contain an edge more than once, so there is at most one edge with the same source and target. It follows that a digraph of n vertices cannot have more that n^2 edges, or $n(n-1)$ edges if there are no loops.

A *graph G* is also given by a pair (V, E) of vertices and edges, but this time each edge is a set $\{u, v\}$ of exactly two vertices. It follows that graphs cannot have loops. For the purposes of representation we write (u, v) for this set of two vertices, but (u, v) and (v, u) are considered to be the same edge. A graph of n vertices cannot have more than $n(n-1)/2$ edges. In a *sparse* graph or digraph with n vertices and e edges we have $e = O(n)$, while in a *dense* graph or digraph we have $e = \Omega(n^2)$.

Certain algorithms are better tailored for sparse graphs, while others are better for dense graphs.

For the purposes of this chapter we will need *labelled* graphs and digraphs. By definition, a labelled graph or digraph is a graph in which each edge carries a label, usually called its *weight*. For simplicity, weights are assumed to be integers. The weight of an edge is recorded along with the edge, so both for graphs and for digraphs the relevant type declarations are:

> **type** *Graph* $= ([Vertex], [Edge])$
> **type** *Edge* $= (Vertex, Vertex, Weight)$
> **type** *Vertex* $= Int$
> **type** *Weight* $= Int$

We will also fix on the definitions

> $nodes\ (vs, es)\quad = vs$
> $edges\ (vs, es)\quad = es$
> $source\ (u, v, w) = u$
> $target\ (u, v, w) = v$
> $weight\ (u, v, w) = w$

The representation of a graph as lists of vertices and edges mirrors the mathematical definition and is acceptable for many problems. For other problems an alternative representation is superior. This is to view a graph as an *adjacency* function of type $Vertex \rightarrow [(Vertex, Weight)]$. The domain of this function is the set of vertices, and for each vertex u the value of the function applied to u is a set of pairs (v, w) such that (u, v, w) is a labelled edge. Assuming that vertices are named by integers in the range 1 to n for some n, a simple implementation of the adjacency function is by an array, so an alternative description of a graph is

> **type** *AdjArray* $= Array\ Vertex\ [(Vertex, Weight)]$

We leave it as an exercise to convert between the two descriptions. The adjacency array representation of a graph is used for some of the problems in Part Six.

A *path* in a graph or digraph is a sequence $[v_0, v_1, ..., v_k]$ of vertices such that (v_j, v_{j+1}) is an edge (directed from v_j to v_{j+1} in the case of digraphs) for $0 \leqslant j < k$. Such a path *connects* v_0 and v_k. A *cycle* in a graph or digraph is a path $[v_0, v_1, ..., v_0]$ whose edges and vertices are all distinct apart from the two endpoints. In a graph the path $[v_0, v_1, v_0]$ is not a cycle because (v_0, v_1) and (v_1, v_0) are the same edge; consequently, cycles in a graph have lengths greater than two. A graph or digraph is *acyclic* if there are no cycles; a graph is *connected* if there is a path from every vertex to every other vertex. In an acyclic graph there can be at most one path between any two vertices.

A connected acyclic graph is called a *tree*, and a set of trees is called a *forest*:

type *Tree* = *Graph*
type *Forest* = [*Tree*]

Trees are therefore not a data type in the sense used in previous chapters, but merely a synonym for a special kind of graph. Every graph can be decomposed into the set of its connected components.

A *spanning* forest of a graph $G = (V, E)$ is a disjoint set of trees

$$(V_1, E_1), (V_2, E_2), ..., (V_k, E_k)$$

with $V = \bigcup_{1 \leqslant i \leqslant k} V_i$ and whose combined edges $E' = \bigcup_{1 \leqslant i \leqslant k} E_i$ constitute a *maximal* subset of E in the sense that no further edge of G can be added to E' without creating a cycle. If G is connected, then a spanning forest consists of a single spanning tree. A spanning tree of a connected graph with n vertices has exactly $n - 1$ edges (why?). Finally, a minimum-cost spanning tree (MCST) of a connected graph G is a spanning tree T of G in which the sum of the weights of the edges in T is as small as possible. Our aim in this section is to find efficient methods for computing a MCST of a connected graph. It is left as an exercise to generalise the solutions to compute a minimum-cost spanning forest of a graph that is not connected.

To add some life to these definitions, consider a country with a given network of towns and roads. The towns are the vertices and each road is an edge connecting two towns. Each road can be travelled in either direction, so the graph is undirected. We suppose there is at most one road connecting two given towns and the weight associated with a road is its length. The network may be connected in that there is a route (a path) between every two towns, but it may not. For instance, the country may consist of several islands not connected by bridges. If all the towns are connected by road, then a MCST is a network of roads with no cyclic routes[1] and of minimum total cost connecting all the towns.

Finding a MCST does not help with planning shortest routes. The path between two towns in a MCST is not necessarily the shortest route between the two towns. We will consider the problem of planning shortest routes in Section 9.5. Finding a MCST also does not help with a superficially similar problem in which one is given a connected graph and a subset T of vertices, with the aim of finding a minimum-cost tree that includes every vertex in T. This problem, called the *Steiner tree* problem, is much more challenging and beyond the scope of this book.

Here is a specification of the MCST problem, expressed in our standard way:

mcst :: *Graph* → *Tree*
mcst ← *MinWith cost · spats*

The function *cost* returns the sum of the weights of the edges of the tree:

---

[1] Though routes for cyclists are certainly allowed.

$$cost :: Tree \rightarrow Int$$
$$cost = sum \cdot map\ weight \cdot edges$$

The function *spats* (short for 'spanning trees') generates all the spanning trees of a given connected graph. For a graph (V, E) with n vertices, that means finding all subsets of E of size $n - 1$ which are both acyclic and connected. One way to define *spats* is to add edges one by one into an initially empty set, ensuring at each step that the set of edges is acyclic, that is, a forest. Only at the final step when the last edge is added is the forest guaranteed to coalesce into a single tree (provided of course that the graph is connected). Another way is also to add edges one by one, but to ensure at each step that the set of edges is both acyclic and connected, that is, a tree. These two methods for generating spanning trees lead to two different greedy algorithms, known respectively as Kruskal's algorithm and Prim's algorithm. Let us examine each in turn.

9.2 Kruskal's algorithm

In Kruskal's algorithm, the definition of *spats* is very similar to the definition of *mktrees* in Huffman's algorithm, except that it works on a list of *states* rather than a list of trees. Each state is a pair consisting of a forest and the list of edges from which the next edge can be chosen:

type $State = (Forest, [Edge])$

$spats :: Graph \rightarrow [Tree]$
$spats = map\ extract \cdot until\ (all\ done)\ (concatMap\ steps) \cdot wrap \cdot start$

$extract :: State \rightarrow Tree$
$extract\ ([t], \_) = t$

$done :: State \rightarrow Bool$
$done = single \cdot fst$

$start :: Graph \rightarrow State$
$start\ g = ([([v], []) \mid v \leftarrow nodes\ g], edges\ g)$

The starting state consists of a forest of trees, each of which is a graph with a single vertex and no edges, and the full set of edges of the graph. A final state is a pair consisting of a singleton tree and the list of edges not used in its construction. The function *extract* takes a final state, discards the unused edges, and extracts the spanning tree.

That leaves us with the definition of $steps :: State \rightarrow [State]$, which takes a forest and a list of edges and selects every possible edge that can be added to the forest without creating a cycle. An edge can be so added if its endpoints belong to different trees. The result is a forest in which the two trees are combined into one larger tree. Hence we define

$$steps :: State \rightarrow [State]$$
$$steps\ (ts, es) = [(add\ e\ ts, es') \mid (e, es') \leftarrow picks\ es, safeEdge\ e\ ts]$$

Recall that the function $picks :: [a] \rightarrow [(a, [a])]$ picks an element of a nonempty list in all possible ways, returning both the element and the remaining list. The function *safeEdge* is defined by

$$safeEdge :: Edge \rightarrow Forest \rightarrow Bool$$
$$safeEdge\ e\ ts = find\ ts\ (source\ e) \neq find\ ts\ (target\ e)$$

$$find :: Forest \rightarrow Vertex \rightarrow Tree$$
$$find\ ts\ v = head\ [t \mid t \leftarrow ts, any\ (== v)\ (nodes\ t)]$$

The value *find ts v* is the unique tree in the forest *ts* that contains *v* as one of its vertices. Each *find* operation can take $\Theta(n)$ steps in the worst case, since every vertex of the graph may have to be inspected. A more efficient definition is given later on. Finally, the function *add* combines two trees and adds the result to the forest:

$$add :: Edge \rightarrow Forest \rightarrow Forest$$
$$add\ e\ ts = (nodes\ t_1 \mathbin{+\!\!+} nodes\ t_2, e : edges\ t_1 \mathbin{+\!\!+} edges\ t_2) : rest$$
$$\textbf{where}\ t_1\quad = find\ ts\ (source\ e)$$
$$t_2\quad = find\ ts\ (target\ e)$$
$$rest = [t \mid t \leftarrow ts, t \neq t_1 \wedge t \neq t_2]$$

It follows that each *add* operation, like *find*, takes $O(n)$ steps (ignoring tree comparisons). Again, a more efficient definition is given later on.

The greedy algorithm for computing a minimum-cost spanning tree is obtained by following the path mapped out by the theory in the previous chapter. First, define

$$MCC = MinWith\ cost \cdot map\ extract \cdot until\ (all\ done)\ (concatMap\ steps) \cdot wrap$$

Recall that we have

$$extract\ (until\ done\ gstep\ sx) \leftarrow MCC\ sx$$

for all states *sx*, provided two conditions are satisfied. The first one is

$$done\ sx \implies extract\ sx \leftarrow MCC\ sx$$

This condition follows from the definition of *MCC*, since

$$extract\ ([t], es) = t \leftarrow MCC\ ([t], es)$$

The second condition is the greedy condition: there exists a tree *t* such that

$$t \leftarrow MCC\ (gstep\ sx)\ \wedge\ t \leftarrow MCC\ sx$$

To verify the greedy condition we have to choose a definition of *gstep*. The obvious choice is to define *gstep* to select a safe edge of minimum weight. Assuming the list of edges is in ascending order of weight, we can define *gstep* by

$gstep :: State \rightarrow State$
$gstep\ (ts, e : es) = \textbf{if}\ t_1 \neq t_2\ \textbf{then}\ (ts', es)\ \textbf{else}\ gstep\ (ts, es)$
    $\textbf{where}\ t_1\ \ = find\ ts\ (source\ e)$
           $t_2\ \ = find\ ts\ (target\ e)$
           $ts'\ \ = (nodes\ t_1 \mathbin{+\!\!+} nodes\ t_2, e : edges\ t_1 \mathbin{+\!\!+} edges\ t_2) : rest$
           $rest = [t \mid t \leftarrow ts, t \neq t_1 \wedge t \neq t_2]$

The function $gstep$ selects the first edge whose endpoints are in different trees t_1 and t_2, and combines t_1 and t_2 into one tree.

Now, to verify the greedy condition, consider a state $sx = (ts, es)$ consisting of a forest ts and a list es of unused edges. Let e be an element of es of lightest weight that is a safe edge for ts. Suppose $t \leftarrow MCC\ sx$. If t contains the edge e, then t can always be constructed by choosing e as a first step. Hence $t \leftarrow MCC\ (gstep\ sx)$ and the greedy condition is satisfied. Otherwise, t does not contain e, and adding e to t would create a (unique) cycle. Remove any edge e' in the cycle and replace it with e. The result is another spanning tree t' with $cost\ t' \leqslant cost\ t$, because $weight\ e \leqslant weight\ e'$. Furthermore, since t' contains e and t' can be constructed by choosing e as a first step, we can take $t = t'$ to satisfy the greedy condition.

Hence one way to formulate Kruskal's algorithm is as follows:

$kruskal :: Graph \rightarrow Tree$
$kruskal = extract \cdot until\ done\ gstep \cdot start$
$start\ g\ \ = ([([v], []) \mid v \leftarrow nodes\ g], sortOn\ weight\ (edges\ g))$

The function $sortOn$ in the Haskell library $Data.List$ appeared in Exercise 5.12. There is another way to formulate the algorithm, which is to write

$kruskal :: Graph \rightarrow Tree$
$kruskal\ g = extract\ (apply\ (n-1)\ gstep\ (start\ g))$
   $\textbf{where}\ n = length\ (nodes\ g)$

Given a connected graph with n vertices, we know that $gstep$ will be applied exactly $n-1$ times.

It remains to time the program. Suppose the graph has n vertices and e edges. As the graph is assumed to be connected and there is at most one edge between any two vertices, we have $n - 1 \leqslant e \leqslant n(n-1)/2$. Sorting the edges takes $O(e \log e)$ steps. As we have seen, each $find$ and add operation takes $O(n)$ steps. In the worst case, all e edges may have to be considered, so there are $2e$ calls of $find$ and $n-1$ calls of add, for a total running time of $O(e \log e + en + n^2) = O(en)$ steps.

The bottleneck in this algorithm is the time complexity of $find$ and add. A faster implementation of these functions makes use of a special data structure for computing with disjoint sets. We turn to this topic next.

9.3 Disjoint sets and the union–find algorithm

The computationally expensive part of Kruskal's algorithm lies in the maintenance of a collection of disjoint sets, the vertices of the trees in the forest. Initially, each vertex is in a set by itself. Each union operation reduces the number of disjoint sets by one. The function *find* has to discover which set in the collection contains a given vertex. Rather than returning the whole set, we can define *find* to return the *name* of the set. The name of a set is some designated vertex in the set. Let *DS* be some data type for maintaining disjoint sets of vertices v in the range $1 \leqslant v \leqslant n$ for some n. What we need are the following three operations on *DS*, in which *Name* is a synonym for *Vertex*:

> *startDS* $:: Nat \rightarrow DS$
> *findDS* $:: DS \rightarrow Vertex \rightarrow Name$
> *unionDS* $:: Name \rightarrow Name \rightarrow DS \rightarrow DS$

The function *startDS* takes a positive integer n and returns a collection of n singleton sets, each containing a unique vertex v in the range $1 \leqslant v \leqslant n$. The function *findDS* takes a vertex v and returns the name of the set in the collection that contains v. The function *unionDS* takes two different names and replaces the two named sets in the collection by a single set with an appropriately chosen name, in fact the name of the larger set.

Here is the implementation of Kruskal's algorithm that uses these three functions. The disjoint sets of vertices are separated out from the trees in the forest, and all the tree edges are combined into one set. Thus we change the state to read

> **type** $State = (DS, [Edge], [Edge])$

Then we can define

> $kruskal :: Graph \rightarrow Tree$
> $kruskal\ g = extract\ (apply\ (n-1)\ gstep\ s)$
> $\qquad\qquad$ **where** $extract\ (\_, es, \_) = (nodes\ g, es)$
> $\qquad\qquad\qquad\quad n = length\ (nodes\ g)$
> $\qquad\qquad\qquad\quad s = (startDS\ n, [\,], sortOn\ weight\ (edges\ g))$

The revised definition of *gstep* is

> $gstep :: State \rightarrow State$
> $gstep\ (ds, fs, e : es) = $ **if** $n_1 \neq n_2$ **then** $(unionDS\ n_1\ n_2\ ds, e : fs, es)$
> $\qquad\qquad\qquad\qquad\qquad\qquad$ **else** $gstep\ (ds, fs, es)$
> $\qquad\qquad\qquad$ **where** $n_1 = findDS\ ds\ (source\ e)$
> $\qquad\qquad\qquad\qquad\quad n_2 = findDS\ ds\ (target\ e)$

In the simple implementation of Kruskal's algorithm described above, the three operations *startDS*, *findDS*, and *unionDS* can each be implemented to take $O(n)$

steps. But we can do better with two other implementations, which we will call implementations A and B. In implementation A, the function *findDS* takes $O(\log n)$ steps in the worst case, while *unionDS* takes $O(n)$ steps. Recalling that Kruskal's algorithm may require $2e$ calls of *findDS* and $n-1$ calls of *unionDS*, that means a total running time of $O(e \log n + n^2)$ steps, a significant improvement on $O(en)$ steps. In implementation B, the function *findDS* takes $O(\log^2 n)$ steps, but *unionDS* takes only $O(\log n)$ steps. That means a total running time of $O(e \log^2 n + n \log n)$ steps, again an improvement on $O(en)$ steps.

These timing bounds are not the best that can be achieved: one can construct implementations of *findDS* and *unionDS* so that a sequence of $O(e)$ find operations and up to $n-1$ union operations takes $O(e \log n)$ steps. However, this implementation seems impossible to achieve in a purely functional setting because it relies on mutable arrays with a constant-time update function. Although mutable data structures can be handled with monadic programming, we choose not to do so. The so-called *Union–Find* problem is a well-known example of a problem in which the complexity of the best purely functional solution seems to be inferior to that of the best imperative one.

Implementation A of *DS* also uses an array, but the array is an immutable one. Recall the following three functions from Section 3.3:

$$listArray :: Ix\ i \Rightarrow (i,i) \rightarrow [e] \rightarrow Array\ i\ e$$
$$(!) \qquad :: Ix\ i \Rightarrow Array\ i\ e \rightarrow i \rightarrow e$$
$$(//) \qquad :: Ix\ i \Rightarrow Array\ i\ e \rightarrow [(i,e)] \rightarrow Array\ i\ e$$

The first function constructs an array from a pair of bounds and a list of values in index order, the second is the array lookup function, and the third is an update function. Building an array takes linear time, a lookup takes constant time, but an update takes linear time even for an update at a single position. We will use the following tailored versions of the three operations above:

$$fromList :: [a] \rightarrow Array\ Vertex\ a$$
$$fromList\ xs = listArray\ (1, length\ xs)\ xs$$

$$index :: Array\ Vertex\ a \rightarrow Vertex \rightarrow a$$
$$index\ a\ v = a\ !\ v$$

$$update :: Vertex \rightarrow a \rightarrow Array\ Vertex\ a \rightarrow Array\ Vertex\ a$$
$$update\ v\ x\ a = a\ //\ [(v,x)]$$

Here is the definition of *DS* based on arrays:

type $Size = Nat$
data $DS = DS\ \{names :: Array\ Vertex\ Vertex, sizes :: Array\ Vertex\ Size\}$

The implementation consists of just two arrays, one for naming the sets in the collection, and one for computing their sizes. The sets themselves can be determined from the fact that two elements have the same name if and only if they are in the same set.

The definition of *startDS* is

$startDS :: Nat \rightarrow DS$
$startDS\ n = DS\ (fromList\ [1..n])\ (fromList\ (replicate\ n\ 1))$

Recall that we assume vertices are labelled from 1 to n for some n. Initially every set is a singleton set of size 1. The name of a set is the value of its sole occupant. In the general case, the name of a set is a value k such that

$index\ (names\ ds)\ k = k$

Each entry in the *names* array is either a name or a vertex whose entry is either a name or another vertex with the same property. Thus we can find the name of the set containing a specified vertex by tracing back in the *names* array until an entry is found that points to itself. That gives us the definition of *findDS*:

$findDS :: DS \rightarrow Vertex \rightarrow Name$
$findDS\ ds\ x = $ **if** $x == y$ **then** x **else** $findDS\ ds\ y$
$\qquad$ **where** $y = index\ (names\ ds)\ x$

The time complexity of this operation depends on how far away a vertex is from the name of the set containing it. We will show how this distance is kept small in a moment. Finally, *unionDS* is defined by

$unionDS :: Name \rightarrow Name \rightarrow DS \rightarrow DS$
$unionDS\ n_1\ n_2\ ds = DS\ ns\ ss$
$\quad$ **where** $(ns, ss) =$
$\qquad\qquad$ **if** $s_1 < s_2$
$\qquad\qquad$ **then** $(update\ n_1\ n_2\ (names\ ds), update\ n_2\ (s_1 + s_2)\ (sizes\ ds))$
$\qquad\qquad$ **else** $(update\ n_2\ n_1\ (names\ ds), update\ n_1\ (s_1 + s_2)\ (sizes\ ds))$
$\qquad\qquad s_1 = index\ (sizes\ ds)\ n_1$
$\qquad\qquad s_2 = index\ (sizes\ ds)\ n_2$

The first two arguments of *unionDS* are different names, *not* arbitrary vertices. The sizes of the sets corresponding to the two names are computed, and the smaller set is absorbed into the larger by renaming the smaller set with the name of the larger. Finally, the size of the larger set is increased accordingly. The sole but critical purpose of maintaining size information is to ensure that the number of *findDS* operations used in looking up the name of a set is as small as possible. If the first lookup does not yield the name of a set, it is because the set has been absorbed into a larger one. A set of size 1 is absorbed into a set of size at least 1, which in turn is absorbed into a set of size at least 2, which in turn is absorbed into a set of size 4, and so on. It follows that, if there are k lookups in a search for the name of a set S, then S has size at least 2^{k-1}. That gives us the bound $k \leqslant \lfloor \log n \rfloor + 1$.

	1	2	3	4	5	6	7
startDS 7	1	2	3	4	5	6	7
	1	1	1	1	1	1	1
unionDS 1 2	1	1	3	4	5	6	7
	2	1	1	1	1	1	1
unionDS 6 7	1	1	3	4	5	6	6
	2	1	1	1	1	2	1
unionDS 3 6	1	1	6	4	5	6	6
	2	1	1	1	1	3	1
unionDS 1 6	6	1	6	4	5	6	6
	2	1	1	1	1	5	1

Figure 9.1 An example of Union–Find with seven vertices. After each operation, the two rows show the resulting names and sizes.

An example of the use of these operations is given in Figure 9.1. Observe that the second rows show the size correctly only for the name of the set; for example, after *unionDS* 1 2 the set with name 1 has the correct size 2, but the size associated with 2 (which is no longer a name) remains 1. At the end of the four union operations we have

$$map\ (findDS\ ds)\ [1..7] = [6,6,6,4,5,6,6]$$

Thus the set of disjoint sets is reduced to three sets: $\{1,2,3,6,7\}$ with name 6 and two singleton sets $\{4\}$ and $\{5\}$ with names 4 and 5, respectively. In particular, to find the name of the set containing 2 we have to evaluate *findDS* three times:

$$findDS\ ds\ 2 = findDS\ ds\ 1 = findDS\ ds\ 6 = 6$$

But the set containing 2 is a set of size 5, and $\lfloor \log 5 \rfloor + 1 = 3$, which is just what the bound above predicts.

The second implementation, implementation B, of *DS* uses the data structure of random-access lists from Chapter 3. This time we have

data $DS = DS\ \{names :: RAList\ Vertex, sizes :: RAList\ Size\}$

The definition of *startDS* is

$startDS :: Nat \to DS$
$startDS\ n = DS\ (toRA\ [1..n])\ (toRA\ (replicate\ n\ 1))$

$toRA :: [a] \to RAList\ a$
$toRA = foldr\ consRA\ nilRA$

The definitions of *findDS* and *unionDS* remain the same, except for the changes

$$index \; xs \; x \qquad = lookupRA \; (x-1) \; xs$$
$$update \; n_1 \; n_2 \; xs = updateRA \; (n_1 - 1) \; n_2 \; xs$$

because positions in random-access lists are indexed from 0 rather than 1.

Now we can restate the various running times. The implementation of *unionDS* involves two lookups and two updates, for a total of $O(n)$ steps for implementation A, and $O(\log n)$ steps for implementation B. Implementation A of *findDS* takes $O(\log n)$ steps, whereas implementation B takes $O(\log^2 n)$ steps. With implementation A the total running time of Kruskal's algorithm is $O(n^2)$ steps on a sparse graph and $O(n^2 \log n)$ steps on a dense graph. With implementation B the times are $O(n \log^2 n)$ steps for a sparse graph and $O(n^2 \log^2 n)$ steps for a dense graph. It follows that implementation B is better for sparse graphs, while implementation A is better for dense graphs.

9.4 Prim's algorithm

The only difference between Prim's algorithm and Kruskal's algorithm is that a tree is constructed at each step rather than a forest. Here is the revised definition of states and *spats*:

type *State* = (*Tree*, [*Edge*])

spats :: *Graph* → [*Tree*]

spats g = *map fst* (*until* (*all done*) (*concatMap steps*) [*start g*])
        where *done* (*t, es*) = (*length* (*nodes t*) == *length* (*nodes g*))
start g = (([*head* (*nodes g*)], []), *edges g*)

This time the starting state is defined by arbitrarily selecting the first vertex of *g* as the initial tree. The function *steps* is virtually the same as in Kruskal's algorithm, namely

steps :: *State* → [*State*]
steps (*t, es*) = [(*add e t, es'*) | (*e, es'*) ← *picks es, safeEdge e t*]

except for different definitions of *add* and *safeEdge*. This time, *safeEdge* determines whether an edge has exactly one endpoint in the tree:

safeEdge :: *Edge* → *Tree* → *Bool*
safeEdge e t = *elem* (*source e*) (*nodes t*) ≠ *elem* (*target e*) (*nodes t*)

The function *add* adds an edge to a tree:

add :: *Edge* → *Tree* → *Tree*
add e (*vs, es*) = **if** *elem* (*source e*) *vs* **then** (*target e* : *vs, e* : *es*)
                                  else (*source e* : *vs, e* : *es*)

The greedy algorithm is derived in the same way as Kruskal's algorithm. First of all, define

$$MCC = MinWith\ cost \cdot map\ fst \cdot until\ (all\ done)\ (concatMap\ steps) \cdot wrap$$

We then have

$$extract\ (until\ done\ gstep\ sx) \leftarrow MCC\ sx$$

provided we can show that there exists a tree t for which

$$t \leftarrow MCC\ (gstep\ sx) \quad \wedge \quad t \leftarrow MCC\ sx$$

As before, we can establish the greedy condition by defining $gstep$ to select a safe edge of minimum weight. Assuming the list of edges is in ascending order of weight, that means

$$gstep\ (t, e : es) = \textbf{if}\ safeEdge\ e\ t\ \textbf{then}\ (add\ e\ t, es)\ \textbf{else}\ keep\ e\ (gstep\ (t, es))$$
$$\textbf{where}\ keep\ e\ (t, es) = (t, e : es)$$

The function $keep$ is needed because, unlike Kruskal's algorithm, an edge that cannot be added to a tree at one step could still be added at a later step when the tree has grown some more.

The proof of the greedy condition is also very similar to that for Kruskal, but it is worth spelling out the details. Consider an incomplete state $sx = (t_1, es)$, so more edges can be added to t_1, and let e be an element of es of lightest weight that is a safe edge for t_1. Without loss of generality, suppose $source\ e$ is a vertex of t_1 and $target\ e$ is not. Now let $t_2 \leftarrow MCC\ sx$. If t_2 contains the edge e, then t_2 can be constructed by choosing e as a first step. Hence $t_2 \leftarrow MCC\ (gstep\ sx)$ and we can choose $t = t_2$ to satisfy the greedy condition. Otherwise, t_2 does not contain e and adding e to t_2 would create a (unique) cycle. This time we have to be more careful in selecting an edge of t_2 that can be replaced by e. Observe that among the edges of the cycle there has to be an edge e' such that $source\ e'$ is a vertex in t_1 and $target\ e'$ is not. If this were not the case, then e would not be a safe edge for t_1. Replacing e' by e in t_2 gives another tree t_3 whose cost is no greater than $cost\ t_2$. And now we can take $t = t_3$ to satisfy the greedy condition.

The greedy algorithm can be expressed in almost the same way as the first version of Kruskal's algorithm:

$$prim :: Graph \rightarrow Tree$$
$$prim\ g = fst\ (until\ done\ gstep\ (start\ g))$$
$$\textbf{where}\ done\ (t, es) = (length\ (nodes\ t) == length\ (nodes\ g))$$

As an alternative we can write

$$prim\ g = fst\ (apply\ (n - 1)\ gstep\ (start\ g))$$
$$\textbf{where}\ n = length\ (nodes\ g)$$

with a somewhat more efficient definition of the termination condition. However, the main problem with this version of Prim's algorithm is that it is not very efficient. At step k, when the tree has k vertices and $k - 1$ edges, the number of edges that may have to be checked before finding a safe edge is $O(e-k)$. That means *gstep* takes $O(k(e-k))$ steps, because *safeEdge* takes $O(k)$ steps. Summing over all steps gives a running time of

$$\sum_{k=1}^{n-1} O(k(e-k)) = \sum_{k=1}^{n-1} O(ke) = O(en^2)$$

steps for Prim's algorithm, compared with $O(en)$ steps for the first version of Kruskal's algorithm. The bound can be improved by using an efficient implementation of sets with a membership test that takes logarithmic time. That reduces the times for *safeEdge* and *add* to $O(\log k)$ steps, and the total time to $O(en \log n)$ steps. But the result is still worse than Kruskal's algorithm.

In fact, we can reduce the running time of Prim's algorithm to $O(n^2)$ steps by reducing the number of edges that have to be considered at each step. The idea is to maintain for each vertex v off the tree at most one edge, that edge being one of least weight that connects v to some tree vertex. When the tree is updated with a new vertex, the candidate edges for the next step can be updated as well. The number of candidate edges is therefore $O(n)$ at each stage. The result will be a version of Prim's algorithm that takes $O(n^2)$ steps both for sparse and for dense graphs, which is better than the $O(e \log n + n^2)$ bound for Kruskal's algorithm.

To implement the idea we need two arrays. First we suppose that vertices are named by integers in the range 1 to n for some n, so they can be used as array indices. States are redefined to be

> **type** *State* $= (Links, [Vertex])$
> **type** *Links* $= Array\ Vertex\ (Vertex, Weight)$

The first component of a state is now an array rather than a tree. The entry for a vertex v not in the tree is a pair (u, w) for which the edge (u, v, w) is a lightest edge linking v to any vertex u on the tree. The vertex u is called the *parent* of v. We therefore define

> *parent* :: *Links* $\rightarrow$ *Vertex* $\rightarrow$ *Vertex*
> *parent ls v* $= fst\ (ls\ !\ v)$
>
> *weight* :: *Links* $\rightarrow$ *Vertex* $\rightarrow$ *Weight*
> *weight ls v* $= snd\ (ls\ !\ v)$

If there is no edge connecting v to a tree vertex, then the parent of v is v itself and the associated weight is infinitely large. Apart from the root, the parent of a vertex v in the tree is the vertex of the tree to which v was linked when it was added to the tree.

The second component of a state is a list of vertices, not edges. These are the *fresh* vertices, vertices not yet on the tree. For example, in the following state the tree vertices are $[1, 2, 3, 4, 5]$ while $[6, 7, 8]$ are fresh:

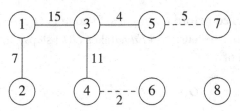

The dashed line connecting 4 and 6 indicates that the lightest edge connecting the vertex 6 to the tree is the edge $(4,6,2)$; similarly, the lightest edge connecting 7 to the tree is $(5,7,5)$. Vertex 8 has no edges connecting it to the tree. In this state the first component is the array

	1	2	3	4	5	6	7	8
parent	1	1	1	3	3	4	5	8
weight	0	7	15	11	4	2	5	∞

The second array is a fixed one and is needed simply to be able to determine the weight of an edge in constant time rather than having to search through the edges each time:

type *Weights* $= Array\ (Vertex, Vertex)\ Weight$

We will leave the definition of *weights* :: *Graph* $\to$ *Weights* as Exercise 9.9. The final version of Prim's algorithm can now be expressed as follows:

$prim :: Graph \to Tree$
$prim\ g = extract\ (apply\ (n-1)\ (gstep\ wa)\ (start\ n))$
         where $n\ \ = length\ (nodes\ g)$
                $wa = weights\ g$

In the initial state, all vertices are fresh and all except vertex 1 have infinite weights:

$start :: Nat \to State$
$start\ n = (array\ (1,n)\ ((1,(1,0)) : [(v,(v,maxInt))\ |\ v \leftarrow [2..n]]), [1..n])$

$maxInt :: Int$
$maxInt = maxBound$

The value *maxInt*, the largest possible element of *Int*, represents an infinite weight. Vertex 1 has zero weight and the default parent vertex for each entry is the vertex itself. The function *gstep* is defined by

$gstep :: Weights \to State \to State$
$gstep\ wa\ (ls,vs) = (ls',vs')$
     where $(\_,v) = minimum\ [(weight\ ls\ v,v)\ |\ v \leftarrow vs]$
            $vs'\ \ = filter\ (\neq v)\ vs$
            $ls'\ \ \ = accum\ better\ ls\ [(u,(v,wa\ !\ (u,v)))\ |\ u \leftarrow vs']$
            $better\ (v_1,w_1)\ (v_2,w_2) = \textbf{if}\ w_1 \leqslant w_2\ \textbf{then}\ (v_1,w_1)\ \textbf{else}\ (v_2,w_2)$

The function *gstep* selects a fresh vertex v closest to the tree and updates the links by replacing each parent of a fresh vertex u with v and the weight of the edge (u, v) if the replacement yields a lighter link to the tree. Finally, the function *extract* extracts the final tree from the final state:

> *extract* :: *State* → *Tree*
> *extract* $(ls, \_) = (indices\ ls, [(u, v, w) \mid (v, (u, w)) \leftarrow assocs\ ls, v \neq 1])$

Each *gstep* operation takes $O(n)$ steps, so the revised definition of *prim* therefore takes $O(n^2)$ steps. As we will see in the following section, essentially the same algorithm can be used for computing shortest paths on a directed graph.

9.5 Single-source shortest paths

We turn now to directed graphs and shortest paths. The notion of getting from one point to another involves a direction of travel, so graphs with directed edges are an appropriate basis for studying shortest routes. There is no loss in moving to digraphs because a graph can always be modelled as a digraph by representing each edge as two directed edges, each with the same weight. Typical of the problems we can solve using a shortest-paths algorithm is: given a network of streets in a city that may include one-way streets, what is the shortest route by car from one address to another?

Normally, the cost of a route is the sum of the lengths (that is, the weights) of the edges along the route, but there are examples where other aggregation functions are required. For instance, if you are a hiker and the routes are footpaths, the best route may be one with the shallowest uphill climb. Each footpath is associated with a measure of its gradient and the cost of a route is the maximum of the individual gradients along the path. In such a case, the best route for an unfit walker is one that minimises this cost. As a dual example, some roads may have height restrictions owing to bridges over the roads. Here the best route for the driver of a high-sided vehicle is one that maximises the minimum of the heights of the bridges along a route. In what follows we will focus on distances and their sums, but the algorithm we will describe, a version of Dijkstra's algorithm, is easily adapted to other situations.

Finding a shortest path P from A to B necessarily involves finding a shortest path from A to every node along P: shortest paths have shortest sub-paths. In the worst case, the route to B may be discovered only after finding the routes from A to all other nodes in the network. In other words, the algorithm may have to compute a *shortest-paths spanning tree* (SPST) rooted at A. Note that a SPST is a different animal from a MCST. In this section we will concentrate on finding a SPST for any digraph for which there is a path from the given source vertex to every other vertex.

The algorithm can be modified to terminate as soon as the shortest path to a given destination is discovered.

Until now we have assumed nothing about edge weights except that, for simplicity, they were integers. But from now on we need the assumption that no weight is negative. With negative weights there is the possibility of having cycles with negative costs, and that allows paths with infinite negative costs. Some algorithms can cope with negative weights (as long as there are no cycles with negative costs), but not the algorithm we describe. We will see why we need this assumption later on.

Another feature of the problem is that, unlike the case of a MCST, the optimality of a SPST rooted at A cannot be expressed in terms of a single numerical value. The cost of a tree depends on the path costs from A to all other vertices on the tree. The obvious way to state that one tree is no worse than another is to require that the distances to every vertex in the first tree are no greater than the corresponding distances in the second. This requirement defines a preorder on trees but not a total preorder.

A final point to bear in mind is that the algorithm we will discuss is not the one found in a car navigation system for computing real-life shortest routes. Actual road networks are based on real distances, and adjacent towns in the network are more or less closer than towns separated by long routes. That means certain heuristics can be employed for finding shortest routes quickly. The resulting algorithm, called the A* search algorithm, will be discussed in Chapter 16.

9.6 Dijkstra's algorithm

Our shortest-paths spanning tree algorithm, a version of Dijkstra's algorithm, uses essentially the same definition of states as in the final version of Prim's algorithm, except that edge weights in the links array are replaced by distances, where the distance from the source vertex 1 to vertex v is the sum of the weights of the edges along the path from 1 to v:

```
type State    = (Links, [Vertex])
type Links    = Array Vertex (Vertex, Distance)
type Distance = Int

parent :: Links → Vertex → Vertex
parent ls v = fst (ls ! v)

distance :: Links → Vertex → Distance
distance ls v = snd (ls ! v)
```

For example, the state

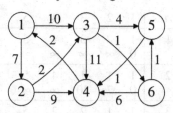

Figure 9.2 An example digraph

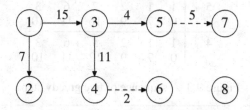

in which the fresh vertices are $[6,7,8]$ is represented by the array

	1	2	3	4	5	6	7	8
parent	1	1	1	3	3	4	5	8
distance	0	7	15	26	19	28	24	∞

In particular, the fresh vertex closest to the tree is vertex 7, with a distance from vertex 1 of $15+4+5 = 24$.

Except for one or two small changes, Dijkstra's algorithm is identical to Prim's algorithm:

> $dijkstra :: Graph \rightarrow Tree$
> $dijkstra\ g = extract\ (apply\ (n-1)\ (gstep\ wa)\ (start\ n))$
> $\qquad$ **where** $n\ \ = length\ (nodes\ g)$
> $\qquad\qquad\ wa = weights\ g$

The function *weights* has to be defined differently from how it was in Prim's algorithm because we are now dealing with a directed graph (see Exercise 9.9). The functions *start* and *extract* are exactly the same as in Prim's algorithm, and *gstep* is defined by

> $gstep :: Weights \rightarrow State \rightarrow State$
> $gstep\ wa\ (ls, vs) = (ls', vs')$
> $\quad$ **where** $(d, v) = minimum\ [(distance\ ls\ v, v) \mid v \leftarrow vs]$
> $\qquad\qquad vs'\ \ = filter\ (\neq v)\ vs$
> $\qquad\qquad ls'\ \ = accum\ better\ ls\ [(u, (v, sum\ d\ (wa\ !\ (v, u)))) \mid u \leftarrow vs']$
> $\qquad\qquad\quad$ **where** $sum\ d\ w = $ **if** $w == maxInt$ **then** $maxInt$ **else** $d + w$
> $\qquad\qquad better\ (v_1, d_1)\ (v_2, d_2) = $ **if** $d_1 \leqslant d_2$ **then** (v_1, d_1) **else** (v_2, d_2)

Greedy algorithms on graphs

vertex	1	2	3	4	5	6
1	1	2	3	4	5	6
	0	∞	∞	∞	∞	∞
2	1	1	1	4	5	6
	0	7	10	∞	∞	∞
3	1	1	2	2	5	6
	0	7	9	16	∞	∞
6	1	1	2	2	3	3
	0	7	9	16	13	10
5	1	1	2	2	6	3
	0	7	9	16	11	10
4	1	1	2	5	6	3
	0	7	9	12	11	10

Figure 9.3 A sequence of five greedy steps

Each application of *gstep* selects a fresh vertex v of minimum distance from the source vertex 1. There are $n-1$ fresh vertices, so *gstep* is applied $n-1$ times. After selecting v, the function *gstep* updates the parents and distances for each fresh vertex u whenever there is a path to u going through v that is shorter. For instance, in the example above, adding 7 as a new tree node, with distance 24, we may find an edge $(7,6,1)$, so the distance from 1 to the fresh vertex 6 can be reduced to $24+1$, which is better than the current best distance 28. Note the necessity for the function *sum* in the definition of *gstep*. The reason is that if (v,u) is not an edge, so its weight is *maxInt*, then the new distance of u from the source vertex should also be *maxInt*. That requires $d+maxInt = maxInt$ for any finite distance d, an equation that does not hold in Haskell.

The function *extract* extracts the spanning tree as a graph, but a better result is to return the actual paths from the source node to each other vertex:

type *Path* = ([*Vertex*], *Distance*)

extract :: *State* → [*Path*]
extract (*ls*, _) = [(*reverse* (*getPath ls v*), *distance ls v*) | $v \leftarrow$ *indices ls*]
getPath ls v   = **if** $u == v$ **then** [u] **else** v : *getPath ls u*
          where $u = $ *parent ls v*

Let us walk through an example to show how Dijkstra's algorithm works out in practice. Consider the digraph of Figure 9.2 in which $n=6$. There is a path from the source vertex 1 to every other vertex, so it is possible to construct a SPST rooted at vertex 1. Figure 9.3 shows the sequence of $n-1$ greedy steps. The vertex on the left is the vertex found at the beginning of each step. The final distances in Figure 9.3 are

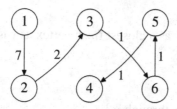

Figure 9.4 The shortest-paths spanning tree from vertex 1

the costs of the shortest paths from the source vertex 1 to all vertices. In particular, the shortest route to vertex 4 has cost 12 and is along the path $[1,2,3,6,5,4]$. The spanning tree is shown in Figure 9.4.

It remains to prove that Dijkstra's algorithm works correctly. We did not give a definition of the list of all shortest-paths spanning trees, so a proof based on the generic greedy condition of the previous chapter is not available to us. Instead, we give a direct proof. We show that, at each step, the distance recorded in the state for every vertex on the tree is indeed the shortest distance from the source. In symbols, if

$(ls, vs) = apply\ k\ (gstep\ wa)\ (start\ n)$

then for all tree vertices v (those not in vs), we have

$distance\ ls\ v = shortest\ g\ v$

where $shortest\ g\ v$ is the cost of the shortest path in the graph g from the source vertex to v. The proof of the claim is by induction on k. The base case $k = 0$ is immediate since the only tree vertex is the source vertex 1 and the shortest path is the empty path with distance 0. For the induction step, let v be the vertex selected by $gstep$ and let P be a path of shortest distance in the graph from the source vertex to v. Such a path has to contain a fresh vertex because v itself is fresh. Suppose that (x, y, w) is the first edge in P for which y is fresh. Since x is a tree vertex, and the distances to tree vertices are never changed once they are set, we have by induction that

$distance\ ls\ x = shortest\ g\ x$

After selecting x, the function $gstep$ updates the distances to each fresh vertex, including y, and, since such distances are never increased, we have

$distance\ ls\ y \leqslant distance\ ls\ x + w = shortest\ g\ x + w = shortest\ g\ y$

Hence, since computed distances are never shorter than the shortest possible distance, we have $distance\ ls\ y = shortest\ g\ y$.

We can now reason

>   *distance ls v*
> $\leqslant$ { definition of *v* as a closest fresh vertex as *y* is fresh }
>   *distance ls y*
> $=$ { above }
>   *shortest g y*
> $\leqslant$ { since *P* passes through *y* }
>   *shortest g v*

So, by the same argument as before, *distance ls v* = *shortest g v*. Note that it is in the very last step that we exploit the fact that edge weights are not negative, so the initial section of the path *P* to *y* cannot cost more than *P* itself.

We have introduced Dijkstra's algorithm as a variant of Prim's algorithm, but there is another way of formulating Dijkstra's algorithm, namely as a version of *breadth-first* search, a topic we will take up in Part Six (see Chapter 16 for details).

9.7 The jogger's problem

Finally, here is one application of Dijkstra's algorithm. Consider the plight of a reluctant jogger who, while willing to undertake exercise, wishes to suffer as little unpleasantness as possible. The jogger is confronted with a network of footpaths, each of which possesses some nonnegative measure of undesirability, say its length. Beginning at some specified point, called 'home', the jogger wishes to plan a circular route, no footpath being traversed more than once, of minimum total undesirability. We will suppose that the undesirability of a footpath is independent of the direction of travel, so we are dealing with an undirected network of footpaths. Such a route will be a cycle in the network, that is, a circular path consisting of distinct vertices (footpath junctions) as well as distinct edges (why?).

Abstractly put, the problem is to determine, given a graph $G = (V, E)$ and a specified home vertex *a*, a cycle that begins and ends at *a* and is of minimum total cost, where the cost of each individual footpath is some given positive value. Since no footpath can be travelled more than once, there must be at least three different edges in the cycle. In what follows we assume *G* is a connected graph and that such a cycle exists. For example, the graph

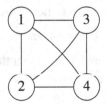

has five possible cycles from the source node 1, each of which can be travelled in either direction: $1231, 12341, 1241, 12431, 1341$.

A simple method for computing a minimum jog J in a graph G is to observe that the path P defined by J from a to the last vertex, say x, before returning to a via the edge (x, a) has to be a shortest path from a to x in a modified graph $G(x)$ in which the edge between a and x is removed. If there were a shorter path, then there would be a shorter cycle. That means Dijkstra's algorithm can be used on $G(x)$ to find P, provided that each undirected edge in G is replaced by two directed edges with the same weight. A best possible jog can then be found by running Dijkstra's algorithm on all graphs $G(x)$ for which x is incident on a. Since Dijkstra's algorithm can take $\Theta(n^2)$ steps, this method can take $\Theta(n^3)$ steps if there are $\Theta(n)$ edges incident on a. The algorithm works equally well for both graphs and digraphs. Nevertheless, there seems to be a lot of duplicated effort in the method, so it is sensible to ask whether there is a way of using Dijkstra's algorithm just once to solve the jogger's problem. The answer is yes, as we will now see.

Let T be a shortest-path spanning tree of a graph G rooted at vertex a. We are going to show that there is some minimum jog J of G with the property that all the constituent edges of J are in T except one. There has to be at least one such edge since T is acyclic. This property is called the *single-edge property*.

Let J be a minimum jog with the fewest number of non-T edges. Suppose x is the first vertex in J such that the edge from x is not in T, and let y be the last vertex such that the edge to y is not in T. The case $x = a$ is not excluded, nor is $y = a$, but x and y have to be different vertices. Since the graph is undirected, the roles of x and y are dual. Here is a picture in which solid lines are paths in T:

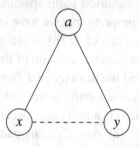

Our aim is to show that the dashed line is a single non-T edge. Using the notation $(u \cdots v)_G$ to mean a path from u to v with vertices and edges in G, we have

$$J = (a \cdots x)_T \, (x \cdots y)_J \, (y \cdots a)_T$$

Since J is a cycle in which no vertex, apart from a, is repeated, x and y have no common ancestor in T apart from a; in symbols,

$$(a \cdots x)_T \cap (y \cdots a)_T = (a)$$

We now show that the assumption that there is some intermediate vertex z on the path $(x \cdots y)_J$ leads to a contradiction. Suppose such a z exists. Here is the picture:

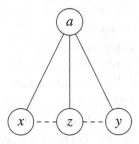

Consider the jog J', defined by

$$J' = (a \cdots x)_T (x \cdots z)_J (z \cdots a)_T$$

The jog J' has fewer non-T edges than J. Furthermore, since T is a shortest-paths spanning tree of an undirected graph, we have

$$cost \mid (z \cdots a)_T \mid \leqslant cost (z \cdots y)_J (y \cdots a)_T$$

Hence

$$\begin{aligned}
cost\, J' &= cost\, (a \cdots x)_T + cost\, (x \cdots z)_J + cost\, (z \cdots a)_T \\
&\leqslant cost\, (a \cdots x)_T + cost\, (x \cdots z)_J + cost\, (z \cdots y)_T + cost\, (y \cdots a)_T \\
&\leqslant cost\, J
\end{aligned}$$

This contradicts the assumption that J is a shortest jog with the fewest non-T edges. So no such vertex z exists.

Now we are ready to describe the algorithm. Suppose, as usual, that the home vertex is vertex 1 and let T be a shortest-paths spanning tree with source vertex 1. It follows from the single-edge property that we have to find an edge $e = (x, y)$, with $x < y$, such that: (i) e is not an edge of T; (ii) e creates a cycle containing vertex 1 when added to T; and (iii) e minimises the sum of the distance in T from vertex 1 to vertex x, the weight of e, and the distance in T from vertex y to vertex 1 (which, since the graph is undirected, is the same as the distance from 1 to y). In fact it is not necessary to insist that (x, y) is a real edge, because if it is not then its weight is infinite and cannot minimise the sum. Call any pair (x, y) satisfying the first two properties a *candidate* pair.

We can identify a candidate pair by considering two cases. In the first case $x = 1$, so y cannot be connected directly to vertex 1 in T; that is, the parent of y in T cannot be 1. In the second case, neither x nor y is vertex 1. In this case define the *subtrees* of T to be those trees that result from deleting all edges of T incident on vertex 1. In this case, (x, y) is a candidate pair if x and y belong to different subtrees. Call the root of the subtree to which x belongs the *root* of x. Then a pair of vertices is a candidate pair in the second case if they have different roots.

For example, in the spanning tree

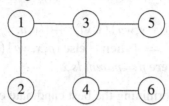

the roots of the two subtrees are 2 and 3, and the candidate pairs are $(1,4)$, $(1,5)$, $(1,6)$, $(2,3)$, $(2,4)$, $(2,5)$, and $(2,6)$. However, none of the pairs $(3,6)$, $(4,5)$, $(5,6)$ is a candidate, because these pairs have the same root, namely 3. The root of a vertex can be computed from the links array constructed by Dijkstra's algorithm:

$root :: Links \rightarrow Vertex \rightarrow Vertex$
$root\ ls\ v = \textbf{if}\ p == 1\ \textbf{then}\ v\ \textbf{else}\ root\ ls\ p$
$\qquad \textbf{where}\ p = parent\ ls\ v$

A better method, left as an exercise, is to install a third component in the links array, one that computes the root associated with each vertex, and to update this component when processing vertices. In this way we can ensure that evaluation of *root* takes constant time. Now we can define

$candidate :: Links \rightarrow (Vertex, Vertex) \rightarrow Bool$
$candidate\ ls\ (x,y) = \textbf{if}\ x == 1\ \textbf{then}\ parent\ ls\ y \neq 1\ \textbf{else}\ root\ ls\ x \neq root\ ls\ y$

The jogger's problem can now be solved by defining

$jog :: Graph \rightarrow [Edge]$
$jog\ g = getPath\ ls\ wa\ (bestEdge\ ls\ wa)$
$\qquad \textbf{where}\ ls\ = fst\ (apply\ (n-1)\ (gstep\ wa)\ (start\ n))$
$\qquad\qquad wa = weights\ g$
$\qquad\qquad n\ \ = length\ (nodes\ g)$

The functions *gstep* and *start* are the same as in Dijkstra's algorithm, while *weights* is the same as in Prim's algorithm because the graph is undirected. The function *bestEdge* is defined by

$bestEdge :: Links \rightarrow Weights \rightarrow (Vertex, Vertex)$
$bestEdge\ ls\ wa =$
$\qquad minWith\ cost\ [(x,y)\ |\ x \leftarrow [1..n], y \leftarrow [x+1..n], candidate\ ls\ (x,y)]$
$\qquad \textbf{where}\ n = snd\ (bounds\ ls)$
$\qquad\qquad cost\ (x,y) = \textbf{if}\ w == maxInt\ \textbf{then}\ maxInt$
$\qquad\qquad\qquad\qquad\qquad\ \textbf{else}\ distance\ ls\ x + w + distance\ ls\ y$
$\qquad\qquad\qquad\qquad \textbf{where}\ w = wa\ !\ (x,y)$

If (x,y) is not an edge, so its weight is *maxInt*, then *cost* (x,y) should also be *maxInt*. The function *getPath* is defined by

$getPath :: Links \rightarrow Weights \rightarrow (Vertex, Vertex) \rightarrow [Edge]$
$getPath\ ls\ wa\ (x,y) =$
  $reverse\ (path\ x) + [(x,y,wa\ !\ (x,y))] + [(v,u,w)\ |\ (u,v,w) \leftarrow path\ y]$
  $\mathbf{where}\ path\ x = \mathbf{if}\ x == 1\ \mathbf{then}\ [\,]\ \mathbf{else}\ (p,x,wa\ !\ (p,x)) : path\ p$
                $\mathbf{where}\ p = parent\ ls\ x$

Building the array and determining the best candidate edge takes $O(n^2)$ steps, so the jogger's problem can be solved in this time.

9.8 Chapter notes

For an interesting history of the minimum-cost spanning tree problem, see [4]. The four proofs of Cayley's formula (see Answer 9.3) can be found in [1]. The Steiner tree problem mentioned in the introduction is studied in [7].

A fast Union–Find algorithm is presented and analysed in [8]. Kruskal's algorithm was described in [5] and Prim's algorithm in [6]. Prim's algorithm should perhaps be called Jarník's algorithm because it was invented earlier by Vojtěch Jarník in 1930 and rediscovered by Prim in 1957, and again by Dijkstra in 1959. Alternative descriptions of these algorithms can be found in most textbooks on algorithm design. Dijkstra's shortest-paths algorithm was described in a short article in [3]. The jogger's problem is taken from [2], where a second version involving digraphs is also discussed.

References

[1] Martin Aigner and Günter M. Ziegler. *Proofs from The Book*. Springer-Verlag, Berlin, third edition, 2004.
[2] Richard S. Bird. The jogger's problem. *Information Processing Letters*, 13(2):114–117, 1981.
[3] Edsger W. Dijkstra. A note on two problems in connexion with graphs. *Numerische Mathematik*, 1(1):269–271, 1959.
[4] Ronald L. Graham and Pavol Hell. On the history of the minimum spanning tree problem. *Annals of the History of Computing*, 7(1):43–57, 1985.
[5] Joseph B. Kruskal. On the shortest spanning subtree of a graph and the traveling salesman problem. *Proceedings of the American Mathematical Society*, 7(1):48–50, 1956.
[6] Robert C. Prim. Shortest connection networks and some generalizations. *Bell Systems Technical Journal*, 36(6):1389–1401, 1957.
[7] Hans Jürgen Prömel and Angelika Steger. *The Steiner Tree Problem*. Springer-Verlag, Berlin, 2002.
[8] Robert E. Tarjan. Efficiency of a good but not linear set union algorithm. *Journal of the ACM*, 22(2):215–225, 1975.

Exercise 9.1 Some quick questions on graphs and digraphs:

1. Why can a digraph of n vertices contain up to n^2 edges, while a graph can contain no more than $n(n-1)/2$ edges?
2. Can a digraph have a cycle of length two?
3. Why is it the case that in an acyclic graph there is at most one path between any two vertices? Is this true of acyclic digraphs?
4. Can a labelled graph have more than one edge between two vertices?
5. Why is a spanning forest of a connected graph necessarily a spanning tree?
6. Why does a spanning tree of a connected graph of n vertices have exactly $n-1$ edges?
7. What is the maximum number of edges in a longest possible cycle of a graph of n vertices?

Exercise 9.2 Assuming vertices are labelled from 1 to n, define functions

$$toAdj \quad :: Graph \rightarrow AdjArray$$
$$toGraph :: AdjArray \rightarrow Graph$$

for converting a digraph into its adjacency representation and vice versa.

Exercise 9.3 Draw all the spanning trees for the following graph:

Exercise 9.4 Assign weights to the edges AB and CD in the following graph to show that the path from A to D in a MCST is not necessarily the shortest path from A to D.

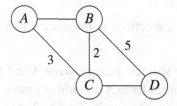

Exercise 9.5 Here is a possible divide-and-conquer algorithm for computing a MCST. Divide the vertices V of the graph into two sets V_1 and V_2 that differ in size by at most one. Let E_i be the set of edges whose endpoints are in V_i. Recursively find a MCST for $G_1 = (V_1, E_1)$ and $G_2 = (V_2, E_2)$. Finally, select a lightest edge, one of whose endpoints is in V_1 and the other in V_2, and add it to the two MCSTs to form a single MCST. Does this algorithm work?

Exercise 9.6 The function *steps* in the specification of Kruskal's algorithm does not discard an edge if it creates a cycle in a given forest, even though it will also create a cycle in any subsequent forest. Write down a version of *steps* that does discard such edges.

Exercise 9.7 What is the output of Kruskal's algorithm if the input is not a connected graph? Adapt the algorithm to find the minimum-cost spanning forest of an unconnected graph.

Exercise 9.8 Why is the test $t_1 \neq t_2$ in the specification of Kruskal's algorithm sufficient to determine whether two trees in a forest are different? After all, the trees $t_1 = ([1,2],[(1,2,3)])$ and $t_2 = ([2,1],[(1,2,3)])$ are the same tree but the test $t_1 \neq t_2$ returns *True*. As a supplementary question, can the test be made more efficient?

Exercise 9.9 Construct the function *weights* as used in Prim's algorithm when the input is an undirected graph. What is the definition when the input is a directed graph?

Exercise 9.10 Consider the problem of finding a *maximum*-cost spanning tree. Is there a greedy algorithm for this problem?

Exercise 9.11 Here is the specification of a shortest-paths spanning tree:

$$spst \leftarrow MinWith \; cost \cdot spats$$

The function *spats* returns all spanning trees of a directed graph. Give a definition of *spats*. To define *cost*, we need to compute the path from the source vertex to every other vertex in the tree. Define a function

$$pathsFrom :: Vertex \rightarrow Tree \rightarrow [Path]$$

where *Path* is a synonym for [*Edge*], such that *pathsFrom* 1 *t* returns the paths from the source vertex 1 to every other vertex in the tree. Finally, define

$$cost :: Tree \rightarrow [Distance]$$

so that $cost \; t = [d_2,...,d_n]$, where d_v is the distance from the source vertex 1 to vertex v.

Exercise 9.12 To find the shortest path between A and B, suppose we simultaneously compute shortest routes from A to various towns, and shortest routes from various towns to B, stopping when some intermediate town C has been found in both directions. Does this idea work?

Exercise 9.13 Give an example to show that Dijkstra's algorithm does not work with negative lengths even if there are no negative-length cycles.

Exercise 9.14 How would you modify Dijkstra's algorithm to stop as soon as the shortest path to a given vertex is found?

Exercise 9.15 In the jogger's problem we can install a third component in the links array to represent the root associated with each vertex:

> **type** *Links = Array Vertex (Vertex, Vertex, Distance)*
> **type** *State = (Links, [Vertex])*
>
> *parent :: Links → Vertex → Vertex*
> *parent ls v = u* **where** $(u, \_, \_) = ls\,!\,v$
>
> *root :: Links → Vertex → Vertex*
> *root ls v = r* **where** $(\_, r, \_) = ls\,!\,v$
>
> *distance :: Links → Vertex → Distance*
> *distance ls v = d* **where** $(\_, \_, d) = ls\,!\,v$

The starting state is then given by

> *start :: Nat → State*
> *start n =*
> $(array\ (1, n)\ ((1, (1, 1, 0)) : [(v, (v, v, maxInt)) \mid v \leftarrow [2 .. n]]), [1 .. n])$

Give the modified definition of *gstep :: Weights → State → State*.

Answers

Answer 9.1 Some quick answers:

1. Because in a digraph every vertex may contain an edge to every vertex, including itself, while in a graph there are no edges from a vertex to itself, and at most one edge between two vertices.

2. Yes, if the digraph contains both the edges (u, v) and (v, u).

3. Suppose there were two different paths between u and v. Let these two paths first meet at some vertex w after u, where w could be v. The two paths P and Q from u to w contain no edge in common, so the path P followed by the reverse of Q creates a cycle. In an acyclic digraph there can be many paths that connect two vertices.

4. It is certainly possible to have both (u, v, w_1) and (u, v, w_2) as labelled edges when $w_1 \neq w_2$.

5. Because if the forest consisted of two trees there would be a vertex in each tree connected by an edge (or the graph would not be connected), and so the edges in the forest would not be a maximal set.

6. Because a tree with n nodes has exactly $n - 1$ edges, a result that is easily proved by induction.

7. A maximum-length cycle will pass through every vertex once apart from the two endpoints, which gives a total number of n edges.

Answer 9.2 For a directed graph g we can define

$toAdj :: Graph \rightarrow AdjArray$

$toAdj\ g = accumArray\ (flip\ (:))\ [\ ]\ (1, n)\ [(u, (v, w)) \mid (u, v, w) \leftarrow edges\ g]$
  where $n = length\ (nodes\ g)$

$toGraph :: AdjArray \rightarrow Graph$

$toGraph\ a = (indices\ a, [(u, v, w) \mid (u, vws) \leftarrow assocs\ a, (v, w) \leftarrow vws])$

For an undirected graph the last argument to $accumArray$ has to be replaced by

$$[(u, (v, w)) \mid (u, v, w) \leftarrow edges\ g] +\!\!+ [(v, (u, w)) \mid (u, v, w) \leftarrow edges\ g]$$

Answer 9.3 There are 16 spanning trees:

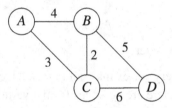

In fact, the number of possible spanning trees for n vertices is given by Cayley's formula n^{n-2}. Four proofs of this remarkable result are given in [1].

Answer 9.4 One fully labelled graph is as follows:

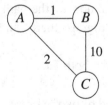

The shortest path from A to D has total length 9, while the path in the MCST has length 10.

Answer 9.5 No. Take a triangle

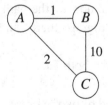

Let $V_1 = [A]$ and $V_2 = [B, C]$. The divide-and-conquer algorithm returns the edges AB and BC with cost 11, but the MCST has edges AB and AC with cost 3.

Answer 9.6 Simply change the definition of $steps$ to read

$steps :: State \rightarrow [State]$

$steps\ (ts, es) = [(add\ e\ ts, es') \mid e : es' \leftarrow tails\ es, safeEdge\ e\ ts]$

Answer 9.7 Kruskal's algorithm will return an error because it attempts to take the head of an empty list. The algorithm for finding a minimum-cost spanning forest (MCSF) is as follows:

$$mcsf :: Graph \rightarrow Forest$$
$$mcsf \ g = fst \ (until \ (null \cdot snd) \ gstep \ s)$$
$$\textbf{where} \ s = ([([v],[]) \mid v \leftarrow nodes \ g], sortOn \ weight \ (edges \ g))$$

This time the algorithm searches all the unused edges and terminates when this list is empty.

Answer 9.8 Because the test $t_1 \neq t_2$ is applied only to two identical trees or to two trees with disjoint sets of nodes. If, however, the two trees are identical, the test will take linear time in the size of the trees. A faster definition is

$$notEqual \ t_1 \ t_2 = head \ (nodes \ t_1) \neq head \ (nodes \ t_2)$$

Answer 9.9 One method is to set up an array with infinite weights and then update the array with the actual edge weights:

$$weights \ g = listArray \ ((1,1),(n,n)) \ (repeat \ maxInt)$$
$$// \ [((u,v),w) \mid (u,v,w) \leftarrow edges \ g]$$
$$// \ [((v,u),w) \mid (u,v,w) \leftarrow edges \ g]$$
$$\textbf{where} \ n = length \ (nodes \ g)$$

When the graph is directed the definition simplifies to

$$weights :: Graph \rightarrow Array \ (Vertex, Vertex) \ Weight$$
$$weights \ g = listArray \ ((1,1),(n,n)) \ (repeat \ maxInt)$$
$$// \ [((u,v),w) \mid (u,v,w) \leftarrow edges \ g]$$
$$\textbf{where} \ n = length \ (nodes \ g)$$

Answer 9.10 Yes, both Kruskal's and Prim's algorithm can be adapted by negating all the edge weights. In symbols,

$$maxWith \ cost = minWith \ newcost$$

where the new cost *newcost* is defined by

$$newcost :: Tree \rightarrow Int$$
$$newcost = sum \cdot map \ (negate \cdot weight) \cdot edges$$

With Kruskal's algorithm that means edges are listed in decreasing order of weight.

Answer 9.11 The definition of *spats* is exactly the same as in Prim's algorithm but with a modified definition of *add* and *safeEdge* to take account of the fact that edges are directed:

$spats :: Graph \rightarrow [Tree]$
$spats\ g = map\ fst\ (apply\ (n-1)\ (concatMap\ steps)\ [s])$
$\qquad\quad \textbf{where}\ n = length\ (nodes\ g)$
$\qquad\qquad\qquad s = (([head\ (nodes\ g)],[\,]),edges\ g)$

$steps :: (Tree,[Edge]) \rightarrow [(Tree,[Edge])]$
$steps\ (t,es) = [(add\ e\ t,es') \mid (e,es') \leftarrow picks\ es, safeEdge\ e\ t]$

$add :: Edge \rightarrow Tree \rightarrow Tree$
$add\ e\ (vs,es) = (target\ e : vs, e : es)$

$safeEdge :: Edge \rightarrow Tree \rightarrow Bool$
$safeEdge\ e\ t = elem\ (source\ e)\ ns \wedge not\ (elem\ (target\ e)\ ns)$
$\qquad\qquad \textbf{where}\ ns = nodes\ t$

The definition of *pathsFrom* is

$pathsFrom\ u\ t =$
$\quad [\,] : [(u,v,w) : es \mid (u',v,w) \leftarrow edges\ t, u' == u, es \leftarrow pathsFrom\ v\ t]$

Finally, *cost* is defined by

$cost = map\ (sum \cdot map\ weight) \cdot sortOn\ (target \cdot last) \cdot tail \cdot pathsFrom\ 1$

Answer 9.12 Not obviously. For example, consider the graph

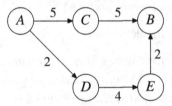

The closest vertex from A is D with cost 2. The closest vertex to B is E with cost 2. The next closest vertex from A is C with cost 5, and the next closest vertex to B is C with cost 5. That gives the answer ACB with cost 10, but the path $ADEB$ has cost 8.

Answer 9.13 A good example is the following digraph:

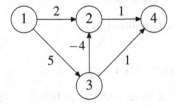

The distances from 1 to the vertices $[1,2,3,4]$ are $[0,1,5,2]$, but the greedy algorithm returns the following distances after three greedy steps (the parent array is not shown):

	1	2	3	4
start	0	∞	∞	∞
update 1	0	2	5	∞
update 2	0	2	5	3
update 4	0	2	5	3

The distances to vertices 2 and 4 are incorrectly calculated as 2 and 3.

Answer 9.14 Change the main definition to

$$dijkstra :: Graph \rightarrow Vertex \rightarrow Path$$
$$dijkstra\ g\ v = path\ (until\ done\ (gstep\ wa)\ (start\ n))$$
$$\mathbf{where}\ path\ (ls, vs) = (reverse\ (getPath\ ls\ v), distance\ ls\ v)$$
$$done\ (ls, vs) = v \notin vs$$
$$n = length\ (nodes\ g)$$
$$wa = weights\ g$$

Answer 9.15 The modified definition is

$$gstep :: Weights \rightarrow State \rightarrow State$$
$$gstep\ wa\ (ls, vs) = (ls', vs')\ \mathbf{where}$$
$$(d, v) = minimum\ [(distance\ ls\ v, v) \mid v \leftarrow vs]$$
$$vs' = filter\ (\neq v)\ vs$$
$$ls' = accum\ better\ ls\ [(u, (v, new\ u, sum\ d\ (wa\ !\ (v, u)))) \mid u \leftarrow vs']$$
$$\quad\mathbf{where}\ sum\ d\ w = \mathbf{if}\ w == maxInt\ \mathbf{then}\ maxInt\ \mathbf{else}\ d + w$$
$$better\ (v_1, r_1, d_1)\ (v_2, r_2, d_2) =$$
$$\quad\mathbf{if}\ d_1 \leqslant d_2\ \mathbf{then}\ (v_1, r_1, d_1)\ \mathbf{else}\ (v_2, r_2, d_2)$$
$$new\ u = \mathbf{if}\ v == 1\ \mathbf{then}\ u\ \mathbf{else}\ root\ ls\ v$$

PART FOUR

THINNING ALGORITHMS

We turn now to a powerful strategy for solving an optimisation problem when a greedy algorithm is not possible. The strategy is called *thinning*, and an algorithm that employs it a *thinning algorithm*.

The principle at work behind thinning is really quite simple: if maintaining a single best candidate at each step is not guaranteed to deliver a best candidate overall, then maybe one can get away with maintaining a *subset* of the candidates. Provided we can quickly identify those partial candidates that can never grow into fully fledged best candidates, we can remove them from further consideration. The key factor in the success of the enterprise is the size of the set that remains. When the set of all possible candidates is exponential in the length of the input, we want a subset that is much smaller, say one of linear or quadratic size. We have already encountered one simple instance of thinning in the computation of *externs* in the TEX problem of Chapter 7. There we thinned an infinite set of candidates into a finite one simply in order to make *externs* a computable function.

Thinning algorithms therefore sit between the extremes of greedy algorithms and exhaustive search algorithms. However, with some exceptions, thinning has not traditionally been suggested as a separate design technique in the algorithms literature. Instead, problems that are susceptible to thinning have more often been solved by a related technique, called *dynamic programming*, a topic we will pursue in Part Five. As we will see, dynamic programming can be thought of as a gener-alisation of the divide-and-conquer strategy. Although the parentage of thinning algorithms and dynamic programming algorithms is different, both techniques can often be applied to one and the same problem. What makes thinning important is that many algorithms traditionally regarded as paradigms of dynamic programming can be formulated, often more effectively, as thinning algorithms.

Chapter 10

Introduction to thinning

In this chapter we explore the basic theory of thinning and discuss three simple examples of the idea. As with most of the algorithms we have seen so far, the key step that makes thinning a viable design technique involves fusion. For fusion to work, we will need to reason about refinement and another nondeterministic function, called *ThinBy*. The first section enumerates the essential properties that we need this function to possess. The chapter ends with a general thinning algorithm that captures most of the essential points about how to introduce thinning.

10.1 Theory

The theory behind thinning algorithms is all about a nondeterministic function

$$ThinBy :: (a \rightarrow a \rightarrow Bool) \rightarrow [a] \rightarrow [a]$$

This function takes a comparison function and a list as arguments and returns a list as its result. It is specified by two properties: firstly, if *ys* is a possible output of the expression *ThinBy* $(\preccurlyeq)$ *xs*, that is, if

$$ys \leftarrow ThinBy\ (\preccurlyeq)\ xs$$

then *ys* is a subsequence of *xs*; and secondly, for every *x* in *xs* we can find an element *y* in *ys* such that $y \preccurlyeq x$. In symbols,

$$ys \sqsubseteq xs\ \wedge\ \forall x \in xs : \exists y \in ys : y \preccurlyeq x$$

where $ys \sqsubseteq xs$ means that *ys* is a subsequence of *xs*. It is assumed throughout that $\preccurlyeq$ is a *preorder*, a relation which is reflexive and transitive. But we do not assume $\preccurlyeq$ is a *total* preorder; that is, we do not assume that for all *x* and *y* either $x \preccurlyeq y$ or $y \preccurlyeq x$ holds. Any definition of the form

$$x \preccurlyeq y = (cost\ x \leqslant cost\ y)$$

for a total function $cost :: Ord\ b \Rightarrow a \rightarrow b$ would mean that $\preccurlyeq$ is a total preorder. Working with total preorders turns out to be too restrictive for the purposes of thinning, which is why we choose as our basic construct thinning *by* a comparison function rather than thinning *with* a cost function.

Here is an example. Suppose $\preceq$ is defined on pairs of numbers by

$$(a,b) \preceq (c,d) = (a \geqslant c) \wedge (b \leqslant d)$$

Then $\preceq$ is a preorder, in fact a *partial* order because it is also anti-symmetric, meaning that $x \preceq y \wedge y \preceq x \Rightarrow x = y$ for all x and y; but $\preceq$ is not a total preorder. For example, $(4,3)$ and $(5,4)$ are not comparable under $\preceq$. Now consider the expression

$$\mathit{ThinBy}\ (\preceq)\ [(1,2),(4,3),(2,3),(5,4),(3,1)]$$

This expression has four possible refinements:

$$[(4,3),(5,4),(3,1)]$$
$$[(4,3),(2,3),(5,4),(3,1)]$$
$$[(1,2),(4,3),(5,4),(3,1)]$$
$$[(1,2),(4,3),(2,3),(5,4),(3,1)]$$

The most effective implementation of *ThinBy* would be to return a subsequence of shortest length, but computing such a sequence (see the exercises) can involve a quadratic number of evaluations of $\preceq$. Instead we prefer sub-optimal implementations of *ThinBy* that take linear time. One legitimate but pointless implementation is to take $\mathit{thinBy}\ (\preceq) = id$. However, the refinement law $id \leftarrow \mathit{ThinBy}\ (\preceq)$ is useful in establishing other properties of *ThinBy*.

One sensible implementation of *ThinBy* is to define

$$\mathit{thinBy}\ (\preceq) = \mathit{foldr}\ \mathit{bump}\ []$$
$$\textbf{where}\ \mathit{bump}\ x\ []\quad = [x]$$
$$\mathit{bump}\ x\ (y\!:\!ys)$$
$$\qquad | \ x \preceq y\quad = x\!:\!ys$$
$$\qquad | \ y \preceq x\quad = y\!:\!ys$$
$$\qquad | \ \mathit{otherwise} = x\!:\!y\!:\!ys$$

This function processes a list from right to left. Each new element x can 'bump' the current first element y if $x \preceq y$, or be bumped by y if $y \preceq x$. Otherwise it is added to the list. For example,

$$\mathit{thinBy}\ (\preceq)\ [(1,2),(4,3),(2,3),(5,4),(3,1)] = [(1,2),(4,3),(5,4),(3,1)]$$

In this example, thinning is more effective if the list elements are in ascending order of first component, or ascending order of second component:

$$\mathit{thinBy}\ (\preceq)\ [(1,2),(2,3),(3,1),(4,3),(5,4)] = [(3,1),(4,3),(5,4)]$$
$$\mathit{thinBy}\ (\preceq)\ [(3,1),(1,2),(2,3),(4,3),(5,4)] = [(3,1),(4,3),(5,4)]$$

We can maintain order when building candidates in a step-by-step manner by merging sublists at each step rather than full-scale sorting. That is the primary reason why we insist that thinning a list xs should return a subsequence of xs – the relative order of the elements is not changed. There are other sensible definitions of *thinBy*, including one that processes elements from left to right; see the exercises for examples.

In addition to the identity law, there are six other basic laws about thinning, some of which are more useful in calculations than others. Proofs of the laws are relegated to the exercises so that we can concentrate here on what they say. The first law is that

$$ThinBy\ (\preccurlyeq) = ThinBy\ (\preccurlyeq) \cdot ThinBy\ (\preccurlyeq)$$

In words, thinning a list twice has the same possible outcomes as thinning it once. The law is interesting theoretically but not of much practical use.

By contrast, the next law is used as the very first step in every derivation that follows. It is called *thin introduction*, and it asserts that

$$MinWith\ cost = MinWith\ cost \cdot ThinBy\ (\preccurlyeq)$$

provided $x \preccurlyeq y \Rightarrow cost\ x \leqslant cost\ y$. Thin introduction is the law that lets us restate an optimisation problem as a problem about thinning.

The next law is called *thin elimination*:

$$wrap \cdot MinWith\ cost \leftarrow ThinBy\ (\preccurlyeq)$$

provided $cost\ x \leqslant cost\ y \Rightarrow x \preccurlyeq y$. Thin elimination is dual to thin introduction, and so is its proviso.

The next law also makes an appearance in virtually every calculation about thinning involving *concat*. It is the *distributive* law, and it states that

$$ThinBy\ (\preccurlyeq) \cdot concat = ThinBy\ (\preccurlyeq) \cdot concatMap\ (ThinBy\ (\preccurlyeq))$$

In words, one can thin the concatenation of a list of lists by thinning each list, concatenating the results, and thinning again. Without the final thinning, the law would be only a refinement. That is,

$$concatMap\ (ThinBy\ (\preccurlyeq)) \leftarrow ThinBy\ (\preccurlyeq) \cdot concat$$

This version is not strong enough to be of much practical help.

The next law is the *thin-map* law, which comes in two flavours. Firstly,

$$map\ f \cdot ThinBy\ (\preccurlyeq) \leftarrow ThinBy\ (\preccurlyeq) \cdot map\ f$$

provided $x \preccurlyeq y \Rightarrow f\ x \preccurlyeq f\ y$. Secondly,

$$ThinBy\ (\preccurlyeq) \cdot map\ f \leftarrow map\ f \cdot ThinBy\ (\preccurlyeq)$$

provided $f\ x \preccurlyeq f\ y \Rightarrow x \preccurlyeq y$. It follows that

$$map\ f \cdot ThinBy\ (\preccurlyeq) = ThinBy\ (\preccurlyeq) \cdot map\ f$$

if $x \preccurlyeq y \Leftrightarrow f\ x \preccurlyeq f\ y$. Appeal to the thin-map law often relies on context. For example,

$$map\ f \cdot ThinBy\ (\preccurlyeq) \cdot filter\ p = ThinBy\ (\preccurlyeq) \cdot map\ f \cdot filter\ p$$

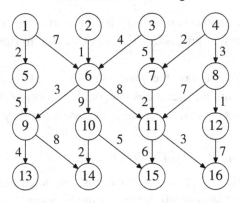

Figure 10.1 A layered network

provided $p\,x \wedge p\,y \Rightarrow (x \preccurlyeq y \Leftrightarrow f\,x \preccurlyeq f\,y)$. We will see an example of this context-sensitive version in the following section.

The final law is the *thin-filter* law:

$$ThinBy\,(\preccurlyeq) \cdot filter\,p = filter\,p \cdot ThinBy\,(\preccurlyeq)$$

provided $(x \preccurlyeq y \wedge p\,y) \Rightarrow p\,x$.

We will come back to the theory of thinning after first exploring some sample problems to see what thinning can contribute to the study of efficient functional algorithms.

10.2 Paths in a layered network

Our first problem is a shortest-paths problem. Consider the digraph in Figure 10.1. Reading from top to bottom, the graph consists of a number of *layers*, each layer consisting of a number of vertices and each edge going from one layer to the one beneath. It so happens in the example that there are the same number of vertices in each layer, but this is not a requirement. Each edge is given by a triple (u, v, w), where u is the source vertex of the edge, v is the target vertex, and w is a numerical weight, not necessarily positive. We assume that there is at least one path from some vertex in the top layer to some vertex in the bottom layer (in the example there are 27 such paths). The problem is to find one with minimum total weight. For the example the answer is the path $[(4,7,2),(7,11,2),(11,16,3)]$ of total weight 7. It is easy to see that Dijkstra's algorithm can be used to solve this problem, at least if the weights are nonnegative. Imagine another vertex U with zero-weight edges to each of the vertices in the top layer, and another vertex V with zero-weight edges from each of the vertices in the bottom layer. Then a shortest path from U to V

includes a shortest path from the top layer to the bottom layer. Dijkstra's algorithm takes $O(n^2)$ steps, where n is the total number of vertices in the network, but it is possible to reduce this time with a thinning algorithm.

To calculate the thinning algorithm, suppose the layered network is given by a list of lists of edges, each list describing the edges between two adjacent layers:

type *Net* $= [[Edge]]$
type *Path* $= [Edge]$
type *Edge* $= (Vertex, Vertex, Weight)$
type *Vertex* $= Int$
type *Weight* $= Int$

We will make use of the following selector functions:

source, *target* :: *Edge* $\rightarrow$ *Vertex*
source $(u, v, w) = u$
target $(u, v, w) = v$

weight :: *Edge* $\rightarrow$ *Weight*
weight $(u, v, w) = w$

Our problem is to compute *mcp* (a minimum-cost path), specified by

mcp :: *Net* $\rightarrow$ *Path*
mcp $\leftarrow$ *MinWith cost* · *paths*

The cost function on paths is defined by

cost :: *Path* $\rightarrow$ *Int*
cost = *sum* · *map weight*

The function *paths* can be defined in terms of the Cartesian-product function *cp*:

$cp :: [[a]] \rightarrow [[a]]$
$cp = foldr\ op\ [[\ ]]$ **where** $op\ xs\ yss = [x : ys \mid x \leftarrow xs, ys \leftarrow yss]$

For example,

$cp\ ["abc", "de", "f"] = ["adf", "aef", "bdf", "bef", "cdf", "cef"]$

We have

paths :: *Net* $\rightarrow$ [*Path*]
paths = *filter connected* · *cp*

where *connected* is the predicate

connected :: *Path* $\rightarrow$ *Bool*
connected $[\ ]$ = *True*
connected $(e : es) = linked\ e\ es \wedge connected\ es$

and *linked* is the predicate

$linked :: Edge \rightarrow Path \rightarrow Bool$
$linked\ e_1\ []\qquad = True$
$linked\ e_1\ (e_2 : es) = target\ e_1 == source\ e_2$

As a first step we can fuse *filter* and *cp* to arrive at another definition of *paths*:

$paths = foldr\ step\ [[\,]]$
$\qquad\qquad$ **where** $step\ es\ ps = [e : p \mid e \leftarrow es, p \leftarrow ps, linked\ e\ p]$

Details of the fusion step are left as an exercise. We can also rewrite *step* in the equivalent form

$step\ es\ ps = concat\ [cons\ e\ ps \mid e \leftarrow es]$
$\qquad\qquad$ **where** $cons\ e\ ps = [e : p \mid p \leftarrow ps, linked\ e\ p]$

Now we arrive at the heart of the problem. A greedy algorithm, one that maintains a single path at each step, is not possible because the source of a minimum-cost path at one level may not be among the target vertices of the edges at the next level up. So we introduce thinning. The thin-introduction law says we can rewrite the specification as

$mcp \leftarrow MinWith\ cost \cdot ThinBy\ (\preccurlyeq) \cdot paths$

provided we choose $\preccurlyeq$ so that $p_1 \preccurlyeq p_2 \Rightarrow cost\ p_1 \leqslant cost\ p_2$. An appropriate choice for $\preccurlyeq$ is the partial preorder

$(\preccurlyeq) :: Path \rightarrow Path \rightarrow Bool$
$p_1 \preccurlyeq p_2 = source\ (head\ p_1) == source\ (head\ p_2) \wedge cost\ p_1 \leqslant cost\ p_2$

In words, when building paths from bottom to top, there is no point in keeping a path if there is another path with the same source vertex and lower cost.

The aim now is to fuse *ThinBy* $(\preccurlyeq)$ and *paths*. That means finding a function *tstep* so that the fusion condition

$tstep\ es\ (ThinBy\ (\preccurlyeq)\ ps) \leftarrow ThinBy\ (\preccurlyeq)\ (step\ es\ ps)$

holds. We can establish the fusion condition by arguing as follows:

$\qquad ThinBy\ (\preccurlyeq)\ (step\ es\ ps)$
$=\quad \{\ \text{definition of } step\ \}$
$\qquad ThinBy\ (\preccurlyeq)\ (concat\ [cons\ e\ ps \mid e \leftarrow es])$
$=\quad \{\ \text{distributive law}\ \}$
$\qquad ThinBy\ (\preccurlyeq)\ (concat\ [ThinBy\ (\preccurlyeq)\ (cons\ e\ ps) \mid e \leftarrow es])$
$=\quad \{\ \text{claim: see below}\ \}$
$\qquad ThinBy\ (\preccurlyeq)\ (concat\ [cons\ e\ (ThinBy\ (\preccurlyeq)\ ps) \mid e \leftarrow es])$
$=\quad \{\ \text{definition of } step\ \}$
$\qquad ThinBy\ (\preccurlyeq)\ (step\ es\ (ThinBy\ (\preccurlyeq)\ ps))$
$\rightarrow\quad \{\ \text{defining } tstep\ es\ ps \leftarrow ThinBy\ (\preccurlyeq)\ (step\ es\ ps)\ \}$
$\qquad tstep\ es\ (ThinBy\ (\preccurlyeq)\ ps)$

We have shown that

$$foldr\ tstep\ [[\,]] \leftarrow ThinBy\ (\preccurlyeq) \cdot foldr\ step\ [[\,]]$$

where

$$tstep\ es\ ps \leftarrow ThinBy\ (\preccurlyeq)\ (step\ es\ ps)$$

The claim in the third step is the assertion

$$ThinBy\ (\preccurlyeq)\ (cons\ e\ ps) = cons\ e\ (ThinBy\ (\preccurlyeq)\ ps)$$

Here is the proof:

$$ThinBy\ (\preccurlyeq) \cdot cons\ e$$
$$=\quad \{\ \text{definition of } cons\ \}$$
$$ThinBy\ (\preccurlyeq) \cdot map\ (e{:}) \cdot filter\ (linked\ e)$$
$$=\quad \{\ \text{thin-map law; see below}\ \}$$
$$map\ (e{:}) \cdot ThinBy\ (\preccurlyeq) \cdot filter\ (linked\ e)$$
$$=\quad \{\ \text{thin-filter law; see below}\ \}$$
$$map\ (e{:}) \cdot filter\ (linked\ e) \cdot ThinBy\ (\preccurlyeq)$$
$$=\quad \{\ \text{definition of } cons\ \}$$
$$cons\ e \cdot ThinBy\ (\preccurlyeq)$$

The thin-filter law is justified because

$$p_1 \preccurlyeq p_2 \wedge linked\ e\ p_2 \ \Rightarrow\ linked\ e\ p_1$$

The thin-map law is justified because

$$e{:}p_1 \preccurlyeq e{:}p_2 \ \Leftrightarrow\ p_1 \preccurlyeq p_2$$

provided $linked\ e\ p_1$ and $linked\ e\ p_2$. The appeal to the thin-map law in the above calculation therefore relies on context.

In summary, we have the final algorithm

$$mcp = minWith\ cost \cdot foldr\ tstep\ [[\,]]$$
$$\textbf{where}\ tstep\ es\ ps = thinBy\ (\preccurlyeq)\ [e{:}p \mid e \leftarrow es, p \leftarrow ps, linked\ e\ p]$$

where $minWith$ is some implementation of $MinWith$ and $thinBy$ is some suitable implementation of $ThinBy$. As a further optimisation we can tuple paths with their costs to avoid recomputation of $cost$.

There is one further and important optimisation. Thinning will be most effective if each list of edges is sorted so that edges with the same source vertex appear together. Then thinning with the definition of $thinBy$ given in the first section will produce just one path for every source vertex. For example, in the network of Figure 10.1 the first step will produce the four singleton paths

$$[[(9,13,4)],[(10,14,2)],[(11,16,3)],[(12,16,7)]]$$

Each additional step will also produce exactly four paths because each layer has four vertices. As to the running time, observe that, because the number of paths maintained at each step is at most the number of vertices in the current layer, the cost of each step is proportional to at most the product of the number of edges between two layers and the number of vertices in the lower layer. If each layer has no more than k vertices, then the running time is $O(ek)$ steps, where e is the total number of edges. If there are d layers, then $e \leqslant (d-1)k^2$. Furthermore, the total number n of vertices is at most dk. The thinning algorithm therefore takes $O(dk^3)$ steps, while Dijkstra's algorithm takes $O(d^2 k^2)$ steps. The thinning algorithm is therefore superior when the network is deeper than it is wide. By renaming vertices so that the vertices in each layer are labelled with 1 to k, and using an array to store the best paths at each step, it is possible to shave a factor of k off this running time, giving an optimal $O(dk^2)$ algorithm. This extension is left as Exercise 10.14.

10.3 Coin-changing revisited

For the next problem we revisit the coin-changing problem of Chapter 7. Recall that the greedy algorithm is not guaranteed to produce the smallest number of coins for all possible denominations. In particular, the greedy algorithm does not work for the United Regions (UR) denominations (see Exercise 7.16). However, the UR is a rich country and can afford automated change-giving systems. Which algorithm should we design to guarantee a minimum number of coins is given for any possible set of denominations?

One answer is a thinning algorithm. To set things up for a thinning step we need to replace the recursive definition of *mktuples* given in Chapter 7 with a definition using an appropriate higher-order function such as a fold of some kind. As we will see in Part Five, working directly with recursive definitions leads to thinking about dynamic programming solutions, but thinning typically involves a fusion step with a higher-order function such as a fold. For compatibility with the other algorithms in this chapter we choose *foldr*, so denominations are considered in order from right to left. We still want to consider denominations in decreasing order of value, so we take currencies in increasing order; for example

$ukds = [1, 2, 5, 10, 20, 50, 100, 200]$
$urds = [1, 2, 5, 15, 20, 50, 100]$

Here are the relevant definitions:

type *Denom* $= Nat$
type *Coin* $= Nat$
type *Residue* $= Nat$
type *Count* $= Nat$
type *Tuple* $= ([Coin], Residue, Count)$

And here are the selector functions we will need:

$coins :: Tuple \rightarrow [Coin]$
$coins\ (cs, \_, \_) = cs$

$residue :: Tuple \rightarrow Residue$
$residue\ (\_, r, \_) = r$

$count :: Tuple \rightarrow Count$
$count\ (\_, \_, k) = k$

This time a tuple consists of three things: a list of coin counts $[c_k, c_{k-1}, ..., c_1]$ for a given list of denominations $[d_1, d_2, ..., d_k]$, the residual amount r after giving these coins in change, and a count of the number of coins used. The function $mktuples$ is redefined as follows:

$mktuples :: Nat \rightarrow [Denom] \rightarrow [Tuple]$
$mktuples\ n = foldr\ (concatMap \cdot extend)\ [([], n, 0)]$

$extend :: Denom \rightarrow Tuple \rightarrow [Tuple]$
$extend\ d\ (cs, r, k) = [(cs \mathbin{+\!\!+} [c], r - c \times d, k + c)\ |\ c \leftarrow [0 .. r\ \mathbf{div}\ d]]$

We start with no coins and a residue n, the amount of change required. At each step the next lower denomination is considered, and every possible choice for a number of coins of this denomination is considered. The new residue and count are calculated and the algorithm proceeds to the next step. Evaluation of $mktuples$ returns many more values than the one in Chapter 7 because it returns *all* the partial tuples, including those with a non-zero residue. For example,

$length\ (mktuples\ 256\ ukds) = 10640485$

The function $mkchange$ is now specified by

$mkchange :: Nat \rightarrow [Denom] \rightarrow [Coin]$
$mkchange\ n \leftarrow coins \cdot MinWith\ cost \cdot mktuples\ n$

where

$cost :: Tuple \rightarrow (Residue, Count)$
$cost\ t = (residue\ t, count\ t)$

A candidate with minimum cost is one whose residue is as small as possible and, among such candidates, one with minimum count. Since we are assuming there is a denomination with value 1, there are candidates with zero residue, so a minimum-cost candidate has zero residue and minimum count.

As in the layered network problem, we now introduce a thinning step, writing

$mkchange\ n \leftarrow coins \cdot MinWith\ cost \cdot ThinBy\ (\preceq) \cdot mktuples\ n$

where preorder $\preceq$ has to be chosen to satisfy

$t_1 \preceq t_2 \implies cost\ t_1 \leqslant cost\ t_2$

The right choice of $\preceq$ is the following one:

$(\preccurlyeq) :: Tuple \to Tuple \to Bool$

$t_1 \preccurlyeq t_2 = (residue\ t_1 == residue\ t_2) \wedge (count\ t_1 \leqslant count\ t_2)$

In words, there is no point in keeping a tuple in play if there is another tuple whose residue is the same but whose count is smaller. That sounds reasonable, but it might be thought that a stronger statement is true, namely that there is no point in keeping a tuple if there is another tuple whose residue and count are both smaller. However, this statement is false (see Exercise 10.16).

The aim now is to fuse $ThinBy\ (\preccurlyeq)$ and $mktuples$. For this to work we need to verify the fusion condition

$$tstep\ d\ (ThinBy\ (\preccurlyeq)\ ts) \leftarrow ThinBy\ (\preccurlyeq)\ (step\ d\ ts)$$

for some function $tstep$ satisfying

$$tstep\ d\ ts \leftarrow ThinBy\ (\preccurlyeq)\ (step\ d\ ts)$$

That means we have to verify the condition

$$ThinBy\ (\preccurlyeq)\ (step\ d\ (ThinBy\ (\preccurlyeq)\ ts)) \leftarrow ThinBy\ (\preccurlyeq)\ (step\ d\ ts) \tag{10.1}$$

where $step = concatMap \cdot extend$. Following exactly the same path as in the layered network problem, we reason

$$\begin{aligned}
& ThinBy\ (\preccurlyeq)\ (step\ d\ ts) \\
= \quad & \{\ \text{definition of } step\ \} \\
& ThinBy\ (\preccurlyeq)\ (concatMap\ (extend\ d)\ ts) \\
= \quad & \{\ \text{distributive law}\ \} \\
& ThinBy\ (\preccurlyeq)\ (concatMap\ (ThinBy\ (\preccurlyeq) \cdot extend\ d)\ ts)
\end{aligned}$$

However, the calculation can proceed no further because

$$ThinBy\ (\preccurlyeq) \cdot extend\ d = extend\ d$$

The reason is that the tuples in $extend\ d\ t$ have different residues and thinning can never eliminate any tuples.

Instead, we have to back up and find an alternative proof that (10.1) holds. For this we need the key fact that, if $t_1 \preccurlyeq t_2$, then

$$\forall e_2 \in extend\ d\ t_2 : \exists e_1 \in extend\ d\ t_1 : e_1 \preccurlyeq e_2 \tag{10.2}$$

To prove (10.2), let $t_1 = (cs_1, r, k_1)$ and $t_2 = (cs_2, r, k_2)$, where $t_1 \preccurlyeq t_2$ so $k_1 \leqslant k_2$. Suppose $e_2 = (cs_2 \mathbin{+\!\!+} [c], r - c \times d, k_2 + c)$. Then $e_1 = (cs_1 \mathbin{+\!\!+} [c], r - c \times d, k_1 + c)$ is in $extend\ d\ t_1$ and $e_1 \preccurlyeq e_2$, establishing the result.

Now to prove (10.1), let $us \leftarrow ThinBy\ (\preccurlyeq)\ ts$ and $vs \leftarrow ThinBy\ (\preccurlyeq)\ (step\ d\ us)$. We have to show that $vs \leftarrow ThinBy\ (\preccurlyeq)\ (step\ d\ ts)$, that is,

$$vs \sqsubseteq step\ d\ ts \quad \wedge \quad \forall w \in step\ d\ ts : (\exists v \in vs : v \preccurlyeq w)$$

Recall that $\sqsubseteq$ denotes the subsequence relation. For the first conjunct, we can reason as follows:

$$vs$$
$\sqsubseteq$ { definitions of vs and *ThinBy* }
   step d us
$\sqsubseteq$ { since $xs \sqsubseteq ys \Rightarrow step\ d\ xs \sqsubseteq step\ d\ ys$ }
   step d ts

For the second conjunct suppose $w \in extend\ d\ t$, where $t \in ts$. Since there exists $u \in us$ with $u \preccurlyeq t$, appeal to (10.2) says there exists $e \in extend\ d\ u$ with $e \preccurlyeq w$. But by definition of vs there exists a $v \in vs$ with $v \preccurlyeq e$, so (10.1) follows on appeal to the transitivity of $\preccurlyeq$.

Summarising, we have shown that

$$foldr\ tstep\ [([],n,0)] \leftarrow ThinBy\ (\preccurlyeq) \cdot mktuples\ n$$

where

$$tstep\ d \leftarrow ThinBy\ (\preccurlyeq) \cdot concatMap\ (extend\ d)$$

As with the layered network problem, the thinning step will be more effective if tuples with the same residue are brought together. This can be achieved by keeping tuples in decreasing order of residue. Since *extend* produces tuples in this order, it is sufficient to define *tstep* by

$$tstep\ d = thinBy\ (\preccurlyeq) \cdot mergeBy\ cmp \cdot map\ (extend\ d)$$
$$\textbf{where}\ cmp\ t_1\ t_2 = residue\ t_1 \geqslant residue\ t_2$$

The definition of $mergeBy :: (a \to a \to Bool) \to [[a]] \to [a]$ is left as an exercise. The complete algorithm now reads

$$mkchange :: Nat \to [Denom] \to [Coin]$$
$$mkchange\ n = coins \cdot minWith\ cost \cdot foldr\ tstep\ [([],n,0)]$$

The running time of *mkchange* is $O(n^2 k)$ steps, where n is the amount for which change is required and k is the number of denominations. At each step the number of candidates in play is at most $n+1$ because there is at most one candidate for each residual amount r and $0 \leqslant r \leqslant n$. A candidate with residue r has $O(r)$ extensions, so there can be $O(n^2)$ new candidates before thinning. Processing each denomination therefore requires $O(n^2)$ steps, and there are k steps in total.

As a final remark, the coin-changing problem can be thought of as an instance of the layered network problem. Each layer contains one vertex for each residual amount and for the denominations considered so far. The edges between the layers correspond to the choices for the number of coins for the next denomination. For example, with change 17 and denominations $[1,2,5,10]$ the first three layers of the network are illustrated in Figure 10.2. The connection between the two problems is no accident because *all* thinning algorithms involving a fold can be regarded as a shortest-path problem on a directed acyclic graph of some kind. This connection will be examined more closely later when we discuss dynamic programming.

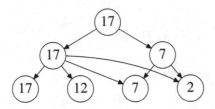

Figure 10.2 Coin-changing as a layered network

10.4 The knapsack problem

Our third and final problem in this chapter is a famous one called the *knapsack* problem. This problem is usually given as a model instance of the dynamic programming strategy, but we are going to give a thinning algorithm. The dynamic programming solution (see Chapter 13) is more restrictive in that it depends on certain quantities being integers.

Here is the setting. Suppose a thief comes to your room in the night bearing a knapsack. Surveying the room, he discovers the following items:

item	value	weight	value/weight
Laptop	30	14	2.14
Television	67	31	2.16
Jewellery	19	8	2.38
CD collection	50	24	2.08

Each item here has an integer value and weight but, in general, values and weights can be arbitrary positive real numbers. The thief would like to steal everything in the room, but his knapsack can support only a limited weight. Assuming the maximum weight the knapsack can hold is 50 units, what items should the thief steal in order to maximise the total value of his haul?

He could decide to pack items in decreasing order of value. That gives

$$swag = \text{Television} + \text{Laptop} \quad \text{(value 97, weight 45)}$$

He could decide to pack items in ascending order of weight. That gives

$$swag = \text{Jewellery} + \text{Laptop} + \text{CDs} \quad \text{(value 99, weight 46)}$$

He could decide to pack in decreasing value/weight ratio. That gives

$$swag = \text{Jewellery} + \text{Television} \quad \text{(value 86, weight 39)}$$

Each of these strategies is, of course, a greedy strategy, trying to obtain a global optimum by making a sequence of locally optimal decisions. For this example the best strategy is the second one, but it is easy to give examples to show that packing items in ascending order of weight is not always the best policy. In fact, there is no greedy algorithm for the problem.

The scenario above is known as the *0/1 knapsack problem*: either an item is chosen or it is not. In the more general *integer knapsack problem*, the scenario changes to a warehouse rather a room. The warehouse contains large numbers of each individual item and the thief can choose an arbitrary number of each item subject to the capacity of his knapsack. There is no greedy algorithm for this problem either. There is, however, one version of the knapsack problem for which a greedy algorithm does work. That is the *fractional knapsack problem* in which the items are things like gold dust in which an arbitrary *proportion* of each item can be chosen. In what follows we will concentrate on the 0/1 version of the knapsack problem, leaving the other two as exercises.

We start off by defining various types and selector functions:

type *Name* $= String$
type *Value* $= Nat$
type *Weight* $= Nat$
type *Item* $= (Name, Value, Weight)$
type *Selection* $= ([Name], Value, Weight)$

Each item has a name, a value, and a weight. A selection is a triple consisting of a list of item names, the total value of the selection, and its total weight. We will need the following three selector functions, the last two of which can be applied both to items and to selections, and hence are given a polymorphic type:

$name :: Item \rightarrow Name$
$name\ (n, \_, \_) = n$

$value :: (a, Value, Weight) \rightarrow Value$
$value\ (\_, v, \_) = v$

$weight :: (a, Value, Weight) \rightarrow Weight$
$weight\ (\_, \_, w) = w$

We can now specify *swag* ('swag' means money or goods taken by a thief) by

$swag :: Weight \rightarrow [Item] \rightarrow Selection$
$swag\ w \leftarrow MaxWith\ value \cdot filter\ (within\ w) \cdot selections$

The nondeterministic function *MaxWith cost* is dual to *MinWith cost* in that the possible refinements are those with maximum cost rather than minimum cost. The first argument to *swag* is the maximum weight the knapsack can hold. The predicate *within w* is defined by

$within :: Weight \rightarrow Selection \rightarrow Bool$
$within\ w\ sn = weight\ sn \leqslant w$

There are two reasonable ways to define *selections*. One way is to write

> *selections* :: [*Item*] → [*Selection*]
> *selections* = *foldr* (*concatMap* · *extend*) [([], 0, 0)]
>   **where** *extend i sn* = [*sn*, *add i sn*]
>
> *add* :: *Item* → *Selection* → *Selection*
> *add i* (*ns*, *v*, *w*) = (*name i* : *ns*, *value i* + *v*, *weight i* + *w*)

The other way is left as Exercise 10.21. At each step we can extend a selection either by omitting the next item or by including it. The function *selections* returns all possible subsequences of the given list of items, so there are 2^n selections for a list of n items.

As a first step, we fuse *filter* with *selections* to obtain a new function, which we will call *choices*:

> *choices* :: *Weight* → [*Item*] → [*Selection*]
> *choices w* = *foldr* (*concatMap* · *extend*) [([], 0, 0)]
>   **where** *extend i sn* = *filter* (*within w*) [*sn*, *add i sn*]

The function *choices* generates only those selections whose total weight is at most the carrying capacity of the knapsack. This step alone can significantly reduce the number of selections that have to be considered, but we can do even better with a thinning step. We rewrite the specification as

> *swag w* ← *MaxWith value* · *ThinBy* ($\preccurlyeq$) · *choices w*

where the appropriate choice here of preorder $\preccurlyeq$ is the following one:

> ($\preccurlyeq$) :: *Selection* → *Selection* → *Bool*
> $sn_1 \preccurlyeq sn_2$ = *value* $sn_1 \geqslant$ *value* $sn_2 \wedge$ *weight* $sn_1 \leqslant$ *weight* sn_2

In words, there is no point in keeping a selection from a list of items in play if there is another selection from the same list with a greater value and a smaller weight. We have $sn_1 \preccurlyeq sn_2 \Rightarrow$ *value* $sn_1 \geqslant$ *value* sn_2, the necessary proviso for the thin-introduction step in the case of *MaxWith*.

We can now fuse *ThinBy* and *choices* to arrive at the new definition

> *swag w* = *maxWith value* · *foldr tstep* [([], 0, 0)]
>   **where** *tstep i*   = *thinBy* ($\preccurlyeq$) · *concatMap* (*extend i*)
>   *extend i sn* = *filter* (*within w*) [*sn*, *add i sn*]

The details are left as Exercise 10.20. As with the other thinning algorithms in this chapter, the thinning step will be more effective if the selections are kept in order. We can list selections either in decreasing order of value, or in increasing order of weight. Since *extend* produces selections in increasing order of weight, we choose the latter.

The result is the following algorithm for *swag*:

$swag\ w = maxWith\ value \cdot foldr\ tstep\ [([],0,0)]$
   where $tstep\ i$ $= thinBy\ (\preccurlyeq) \cdot mergeBy\ cmp \cdot map\ (extend\ i)$
          $extend\ i\ sn$ $= filter\ (within\ w)\ [sn, add\ i\ sn]$
          $cmp\ sn_1\ sn_2 = weight\ sn_1 \leqslant weight\ sn_2$

This is our final algorithm for the knapsack problem. As to its running time, suppose that all weights are integers. Each thinning step brings selections with equal weights together and eliminates all but one of them, thereby maintaining a list of at most $w + 1$ selections, each with a different weight from 0 up to w. This list can be computed in $\Theta(w)$ steps in the worst case. There are n items to process, so the running time is $O(nw)$ steps. That appears to make the algorithm a linear-time one. However, if weights are arbitrary positive real numbers, then there is no guarantee that only $w + 1$ selections are maintained at each step. In fact all 2^n selections might have to be kept, each with a different total weight and value. That means the algorithm can be exponential in n for non-integral weights.

10.5 A general thinning algorithm

The last two examples seem very similar (even more so when Exercise 10.20 is answered), so let's end the chapter by solving an abstract problem that captures all of the essential ideas behind thinning when *candidates* is expressed in the following way:

$candidates :: [Data] \rightarrow [Candidate]$
$candidates = foldr\ (concatMap \cdot extend)\ [anon]$

Here *anon* is some initial candidate.
   Consider a specification of the form

$best :: [Data] \rightarrow Candidate$
$best \leftarrow MinWith\ cost \cdot filter\ good \cdot candidates$

There are four ritual steps in calculating a thinning algorithm to solve this problem. The first step is to fuse *filter good* with *candidates*. This step is possible if

$good\ (extend\ d\ x) \;\Rightarrow\; good\ x$

In other words, if a candidate is bad, then no extension of the candidate can ever be good. The candidate *anon* has to be good, otherwise there are no good candidates. We can now reason

     $filter\ good \cdot concatMap\ (extend\ d)$
$=$ $\{$ since $filter\ p \cdot concatMap = concatMap\ (filter\ p)\ \}$
     $concatMap\ (filter\ good \cdot extend\ d)$
$=$ $\{$ assumption $\}$
     $concatMap\ (filter\ good \cdot extend\ d) \cdot filter\ good$

This establishes the fusion condition and so

$$filter\ good \cdot foldr\ (concatMap \cdot extend)\ [anon] = foldr\ step\ [anon]$$

where

$$step\ d = concatMap\ (filter\ good \cdot extend\ d)$$

The second step is to introduce thinning. Suppose $\preccurlyeq$ is a comparison function for which $x \preccurlyeq y \Rightarrow cost\ x \leqslant cost\ y$ for all good candidates x and y. We can then appeal to the thin-introduction law to refine the specification of *best* to read

$$best \leftarrow MinWith\ cost \cdot ThinBy\ (\preccurlyeq) \cdot foldr\ step\ [anon]$$

The third step is to fuse $ThinBy\ (\preccurlyeq)$ and *foldr*. With

$$tstep\ d \leftarrow ThinBy\ (\preccurlyeq) \cdot step\ d$$

we have

$$foldr\ tstep\ [anon] \leftarrow ThinBy\ (\preccurlyeq) \cdot foldr\ step\ [anon]$$

provided the fusion condition

$$tstep\ d \cdot ThinBy\ (\preccurlyeq) \leftarrow ThinBy\ (\preccurlyeq) \cdot step\ d$$

holds. With the specification of *tstep* above, the proviso follows from

$$ThinBy\ (\preccurlyeq) \cdot step\ d \cdot ThinBy\ (\preccurlyeq) \leftarrow ThinBy\ (\preccurlyeq) \cdot step\ d$$

which, as we have seen in (10.1) of Section 10.3, follows from the assumption

$$x \preccurlyeq y \ \Rightarrow\ \forall v \in goodext\ d\ y : \exists u \in goodext\ d\ x : u \preccurlyeq v$$

where $goodext\ d\ x = filter\ good\ (extend\ d\ x)$. As a result we have

$$best = minWith\ cost \cdot foldr\ step\ [anon]$$
$$\mathbf{where}\ step\ d = thinBy\ (\preccurlyeq) \cdot concatMap\ (filter\ good \cdot extend\ d)$$

The fourth and final step is to make thinning more effective by keeping the candidates in order. Suppose *value* is some function on candidates such that *extend* produces new candidates in, say, increasing order of *value*. Then we have as the final algorithm

$$best = minWith\ cost \cdot foldr\ step\ [anon]$$
$$\mathbf{where}\ step\ d\ = thinBy\ (\preccurlyeq) \cdot mergeBy\ cmp \cdot map\ (filter\ good \cdot extend\ d)$$
$$cmp\ x\ y = value\ x \leqslant value\ y$$

It is possible, with more or less effort, to reformulate the three problems in this chapter as instances of this general scheme, but the reformulation does not add significantly to the understanding of the three algorithms. What is important is that the derivation of a thinning algorithm follows a more or less standard path.

10.6 Chapter notes

The theory of thinning algorithms was described in [2], and developed further by Sharon Curtis and Shin-Cheng Mu in their doctoral theses [3, 7]. The general thinning theorem, along with a number of applications, appeared in [4] and [5]. The knapsack problem has a long history, see [6], and a version of the thinning method applied to this problem appears in [1].

References

[1] Joachim H. Ahrens and Gerd Finke. Merging and sorting applied to the zero–one knapsack problem. *Operations Research*, 23(6):1099–1109, 1975.

[2] Richard S. Bird and Oege de Moor. *The Algebra of Programming*. Prentice-Hall, Hemel Hempstead, 1997.

[3] Sharon Curtis. *A Relational Approach to Optimization Problems*. DPhil thesis, Oxford University Computing Laboratory, 1996. Technical Monograph PRG-122.

[4] Oege de Moor. A generic program for sequential decision processes. In *Programming Languages: Implementations, Logics and Programs*, volume 982 of *Lecture Notes in Computer Science*, pages 1–23, Springer-Verlag, Berlin, 1995.

[5] Oege de Moor. Dynamic programming as a software component. In *Circuits, Systems, Computers and Communications*, IEEE, 1999. Invited talk.

[6] Silvano Martello and Paolo Toth. *Knapsack Problems: Algorithms and Computer Implementations*. John Wiley and Sons, Chichester, 1990.

[7] Shin-Cheng Mu. *A Calculational Approach to Program Inversion*. DPhil thesis, Oxford University Computing Laboratory, 2003. Research Report PRG-RR-04-03.

Exercises

Exercise 10.1 Is *ThinBy* $(\preccurlyeq)$ $[\,]$ well-defined?

Exercise 10.2 Give a linear-time algorithm for *thinBy* $(\preccurlyeq)$ that processes the list from left to right.

Exercise 10.3 Here is a specification of a version of *thinBy* that computes shortest thinnings:

$$thinBy\ (\preccurlyeq)\ xs \leftarrow MinWith\ length\ (candidates\ (\preccurlyeq)\ xs)$$

Give a definition of *candidates*. You can assume a function $subseqs :: [a] \rightarrow [[a]]$ that returns all the subsequences of a sequence.

Exercise 10.4 Following on from the previous exercise, give a quadratic-time algorithm for *thinBy*. No justification is required.

Exercise 10.5 Is the refinement law $id \leftarrow ThinBy\ (\preccurlyeq)$ valid for all possible definitions of $\preccurlyeq$?

Exercise 10.6 Give an implementation *thinBy* of *ThinBy* for which the equation

$$thinBy\ (\preccurlyeq) = thinBy\ (\preccurlyeq) \cdot thinBy\ (\preccurlyeq)$$

is false.

Exercise 10.7 The idempotency of *ThinBy* is captured as two refinements:

$$ThinBy\ (\preccurlyeq) \leftarrow ThinBy\ (\preccurlyeq) \cdot ThinBy\ (\preccurlyeq)$$
$$ThinBy\ (\preccurlyeq) \cdot ThinBy\ (\preccurlyeq) \leftarrow ThinBy\ (\preccurlyeq)$$

The first refinement is easy. Why? For the second we have to show for all *xs* that, if *ys* ← *ThinBy* ($\preccurlyeq$) *xs* and *zs* ← *ThinBy* ($\preccurlyeq$) *ys*, then *zs* ← *ThinBy* ($\preccurlyeq$) *xs*. Why is this assertion true?

Exercise 10.8 The thin-introduction law is also captured as two refinements:

$$MinWith\ cost \leftarrow MinWith\ cost \cdot ThinBy\ (\preccurlyeq)$$
$$MinWith\ cost \cdot ThinBy\ (\preccurlyeq) \leftarrow MinWith\ cost$$

The first refinement is easy. Why? Prove that the second refinement holds under the proviso $x \preccurlyeq y \Rightarrow cost\ x \leqslant cost\ y$.

Exercise 10.9 Prove the thin-elimination law, namely that

$$wrap \cdot MinWith\ cost \leftarrow ThinBy\ (\preccurlyeq)$$

provided $cost\ x \leqslant cost\ y \Rightarrow x \preccurlyeq y$.

Exercise 10.10 Prove the thin-filter law, namely that

$$filter\ p \cdot ThinBy\ (\preccurlyeq) = ThinBy\ (\preccurlyeq) \cdot filter\ p$$

provided $x \preccurlyeq y \wedge p\ y \Rightarrow p\ x$.

Exercise 10.11 Prove the thin-map law, namely that

$$map\ f \cdot ThinBy\ (\preccurlyeq) \leftarrow ThinBy\ (\preccurlyeq) \cdot map\ f$$

provided $x \preccurlyeq y \Rightarrow f\ x \preccurlyeq f\ y$.

Exercise 10.12 Give an example to show that the law

$$ThinBy\ (\preccurlyeq) \cdot concat = concatMap\ (ThinBy\ (\preccurlyeq))$$

does not hold.

Exercise 10.13 For the layered network problem, prove that

$$filter\ connected \cdot foldr\ op\ [[\,]] = foldr\ step\ [[\,]]$$

where

$$op\ es\ ps\ \ = [e : p \mid e \leftarrow es, p \leftarrow ps]$$
$$step\ es\ ps = [e : p \mid e \leftarrow es, p \leftarrow ps, linked\ e\ p]$$

Exercise 10.14 Suppose in the layered network problem that there exists some k such that the vertices in each layer are labelled with integers in the range 1 to k. This can always be achieved by renaming the vertices, so there is no loss of generality in the assumption. Then optimal paths from each vertex j can be stored as the jth element of an array indexed from 1 to k. That idea leads to the following version of *mcp*:

$mcp :: Nat \rightarrow Net \rightarrow Path$
$mcp\ k = snd \cdot minWith\ fst \cdot elems \cdot foldr\ step\ start$
$\quad$ **where** $start \qquad = array\ (1,k)\ [(v,(0,[]))\ |\ v \leftarrow [1..k]]$
$\qquad\qquad step\ es\ pa = accumArray\ better\ initial\ (1,k)\ (map\ insert\ es)$
$\qquad\qquad\qquad$ **where** $initial \qquad = ...$
$\qquad\qquad\qquad\qquad\ insert\ (u,v,w) = ...$
$\qquad\qquad better\ (c_1,p_1)\ (c_2,p_2) = \textbf{if}\ c_1 \leqslant c_2\ \textbf{then}\ (c_1,p_1)\ \textbf{else}\ (c_2,p_2)$

Complete the algorithm by giving the definitions of *initial* and *insert*.

Exercise 10.15 Give a definition of $mergeBy :: (a \rightarrow a \rightarrow Bool) \rightarrow [[a]] \rightarrow [a]$.

Exercise 10.16 In the coin-changing problem, suppose we had defined $\preccurlyeq$ by

$$t_1 \preccurlyeq t_2 = (residue\ t_1 \leqslant residue\ t_2) \wedge (count\ t_1 \leqslant count\ t_2)$$

Now consider the list of tuples generated when the amount is 13 and the denominations are $[1,x,5,10]$. Both $([1,0],3,1)$ and $([0,1],8,1)$ are on this list after processing the denominations $[5,10]$. Thinning with $\preccurlyeq$ eliminates the latter. Why is this wrong? (Hint: choose x.)

Exercise 10.17 The function *extend* in the coin-changing problem was defined by

$$extend\ d\ (cs,r,k) = [(cs \mathbin{+\mkern-10mu+} [c], r - c \times d, k + c)\ |\ c \leftarrow [0..r\ \text{div}\ d]]$$

How should *mkchange* be redefined if the term $cs \mathbin{+\mkern-10mu+} [c]$ is replaced by the more efficient $c : cs$?

Exercise 10.18 The final algorithm for the coin-changing problem was

$$mkchange\ n = coins \cdot minWith\ cost \cdot foldr\ tstep\ [([],n,0)]$$

What additional simplification is possible?

Exercise 10.19 In the definition of *choices* in the knapsack problem we defined the local function

$$extend\ i\ sn = filter\ (within\ w)\ [sn, add\ i\ sn]$$

What minor optimisation to this definition is possible?

Exercise 10.20 To fuse *ThinBy* $(\preccurlyeq)$ and *choices* in the knapsack problem, we have to verify the fusion condition

$$ThinBy\ (\preccurlyeq)\ (step\ i\ (ThinBy\ (\preccurlyeq)\ sns)) \leftarrow ThinBy\ (\preccurlyeq)\ (step\ i\ sns)$$

where $step\ i = concatMap \cdot extend\ i$. Prove that this condition holds.

Exercise 10.21 There is another way of defining the function *selections*, namely

$selections :: [Item] \rightarrow [Selection]$
$selections = foldr\ step\ [([],0,0)]$
$\quad\quad\quad\quad$ **where** $step\ i\ sns = sns \mathbin{+\!\!+} map\ (add\ i)\ sns$

Write down the final thinning algorithm for this version of *selections*.

Exercise 10.22 The knapsack problem was specified using *MaxWith value*. But presumably the thief would prefer a selection that not only had the maximum value, but also had minimum weight. How would you modify the specification to take this aspect into account?

Exercise 10.23 In the integer knapsack problem, selections have the type

type $Selection = ([(Nat, Name)], Value, Weight)$

Along with each item name there is a count of the number of times the item is chosen. We can specify *swag* by

$swag :: Weight \rightarrow [Item] \rightarrow Selection$
$swag\ w \leftarrow extract \cdot MaxWith\ value \cdot choices\ w$

where *extract* retains only the chosen items:

$extract :: Selection \rightarrow Selection$
$extract\ (kns, v, w) = (filter\ nonzero\ kns, v, w)$
$\quad\quad\quad\quad\quad$ **where** $nonzero\ (k, n) = k \neq 0$

Define *choices*. Hence write down a thinning algorithm for the integer knapsack problem.

Exercise 10.24 Why is it impossible to write down an executable specification for the fractional knapsack problem? It is, however, possible to show that a greedy algorithm works. The method is to consider items in decreasing order of value-to-weight ratio. At each step, the whole of the next item is chosen if the weight constraint is satisfied, otherwise the maximum possible proportion of the next item is chosen and the algorithm terminates. That way, up to the whole of the capacity of the knapsack can be used. If all weights are integers, then it is possible to express the greedy algorithm using rational arithmetic. Selections therefore have type

type $Selection = ([(Rational, Name)], Value, Weight)$
type $Value = Rational$
type $Weight = Rational$

Write down the definition of a function *gswag* that has the type

$gswag :: Weight \rightarrow [Item] \rightarrow [(Rational, Name)]$

Hint: one answer is to sort the values in increasing order of value-to-weight ratio and then to process from right to left.

Answer 10.1 Yes, we have $[] = ThinBy (\preccurlyeq) []$.

Answer 10.2 One possibility is

$thinBy (\preccurlyeq) = foldl\ bump\ [] \cdot reverse$
    where $bump\ []\ x$ $= [x]$
            $bump\ (y:ys)\ x \mid x \preccurlyeq y$ $= x:ys$
                     $\mid y \preccurlyeq x$ $= y:ys$
                     $\mid otherwise = x:y:ys$

Another method, which may not give the same answer, is to define

$thinBy (\preccurlyeq) []\ \ = []$
$thinBy (\preccurlyeq) [x] = [x]$
$thinBy (\preccurlyeq) (x:y:xs)$
   $\mid x \preccurlyeq y$ $= thinBy (\preccurlyeq) (x:xs)$
   $\mid y \preccurlyeq x$ $= thinBy (\preccurlyeq) (y:xs)$
   $\mid otherwise = x:thinBy (\preccurlyeq) (y:xs)$

Answer 10.3 The straightforward definition of *candidates* is

$candidates (\preccurlyeq) xs = [ys \mid ys \leftarrow subseqs\ xs, ok\ xs\ ys]$
    where $ok\ xs\ ys = and\ [or\ [y \preccurlyeq x \mid y \leftarrow ys] \mid x \leftarrow xs]$

The prelude functions *and* and *or* return the conjunction and disjunction of a list of Booleans.

Answer 10.4 One definition is

$thinBy (\preccurlyeq) = foldr\ gstep\ []$
    where $gstep\ x\ ys = $ **if** $any\ (\preccurlyeq x)\ ys$ **then** ys **else** $x:filter\ (not \cdot (x \preccurlyeq))\ ys$

where the prelude function *any p* is defined by $any\ p = or \cdot map\ p$. This computes a shortest thinning; but the proof that it does so is rather involved, and is omitted.

Answer 10.5 No, it holds only if $\preccurlyeq$ is reflexive.

Answer 10.6 The following definition of *thinBy* removes at most one element:

$thinBy (\preccurlyeq) []\ \ \ \ \ \ \ \ = []$
$thinBy (\preccurlyeq) [x]\ \ \ \ \ \ = [x]$
$thinBy (\preccurlyeq) (x:y:xs) = $ **if** $x \preccurlyeq y$ **then** $x:xs$ **else** $x:thinBy (\preccurlyeq) (y:xs)$

For example,

$thinBy (\leqslant) [1,2,3] = [1,3]$
$thinBy (\leqslant) [2,1,3] = [2,1]$

Thinning twice can remove two elements, so *thinBy* is not idempotent.

Answer 10.7 The first refinement follows from the identity law and the monotonicity of functional composition under refinement. The second refinement follows from the transitivity of $\preccurlyeq$ and transitivity of $\sqsubseteq$, the subsequence relation.

Answer 10.8 The first follows from the identity law. For the second we have to show that $ys \leftarrow ThinBy\ (\preccurlyeq)\ xs$ and $y \leftarrow MinWith\ cost\ ys$, then $y \leftarrow MinWith\ cost\ xs$. This fact follows easily from the proviso.

Answer 10.9 We have to show that

$$x \leftarrow MinWith\ cost\ xs \quad \Rightarrow \quad [x] \leftarrow ThinBy\ (\preccurlyeq)\ xs$$

This comes down to $cost\ x \leqslant cost\ y \Rightarrow x \preccurlyeq y$ for all $y \in xs$, which is just the proviso.

Answer 10.10 We have to show that

$$ys \leftarrow ThinBy\ (\preccurlyeq)\ xs \wedge zs = filter\ p\ ys$$
$$\Rightarrow \quad zs \leftarrow ThinBy\ (\preccurlyeq)\ (filter\ p\ xs)$$
$$zs \leftarrow ThinBy\ (\preccurlyeq)\ (filter\ p\ xs)$$
$$\Rightarrow \quad (\exists ys : ys \leftarrow ThinBy\ (\preccurlyeq)\ xs \wedge zs = filter\ p\ ys)$$

For the first implication we have $zs \sqsubseteq ys \sqsubseteq xs$, since $\sqsubseteq$ is transitive. Furthermore, it follows from $ys \leftarrow ThinBy\ (\preccurlyeq)\ xs$ and the proviso that, if $x \in xs$ and $p\ x$, then there exists a $y \in ys$ such that $y \preccurlyeq x$ and $p\ y$. Hence $y \in zs$, and so zs is a valid refinement of $ThinBy\ (\preccurlyeq)\ (filter\ p\ xs)$.

For the second implication take ys to be the subsequence of xs consisting of zs together with all the elements of xs not satisfying p. Thus $zs = filter\ p\ ys$. Suppose $x \in xs$; either $p\ x$ holds, in which case there exists a $z \in zs$ such that $z \preccurlyeq x$, or $p\ x$ does not hold, in which case $x \in ys$ and $x \preccurlyeq x$. Hence ys is a valid refinement of $ThinBy\ (\preccurlyeq)\ xs$.

Answer 10.11 Suppose $ys \leftarrow ThinBy\ (\preccurlyeq)\ xs$. We have to show that

$$map\ f\ ys \leftarrow ThinBy\ (\preccurlyeq)\ (map\ f\ xs)$$

This follows from the proviso and the fact that

$$ys \sqsubseteq xs \quad \Rightarrow \quad map\ f\ ys \sqsubseteq map\ f\ xs$$

The other thin-map law

$$ThinBy\ (\preccurlyeq) \cdot map\ f \leftarrow map\ f \cdot ThinBy\ (\preccurlyeq)$$

is also straightforward.

Answer 10.12 Let $x \preccurlyeq y = (x \leqslant y)$. Then

$$[1] \leftarrow ThinBy\ (\preccurlyeq)\ (concat\ [[1],[2]])$$

but

$$concat\ [ThinBy\ (\preccurlyeq)\ [1], ThinBy\ (\preccurlyeq)\ [2]] = [1,2]$$

Answer 10.13 We have to show

$$filter\ connected\ (op\ es\ ps) = step\ es\ (filter\ connected\ ps)$$

The proof is

$$filter\ connected\ (op\ es\ ps)$$
$$=\quad \{\ \text{definition of } op\ \}$$
$$[e:p\ |\ e \leftarrow es, p \leftarrow ps, connected\ (e:p)]$$
$$=\quad \{\ \text{definition of } connected\ \}$$
$$[e:p\ |\ e \leftarrow es, p \leftarrow filter\ connected\ ps, linked\ e\ p]$$
$$=\quad \{\ \text{definition of } step\ \}$$
$$step\ es\ (filter\ connected\ ps)$$

Answer 10.14 We can define *mcp* by

$$mcp :: Nat \rightarrow Net \rightarrow Path$$
$$mcp\ k = snd \cdot minWith\ fst \cdot elems \cdot foldr\ step\ start$$
$$\textbf{where } start \qquad = array\ (1,k)\ [(v,(0,[]))\ |\ v \leftarrow [1..k]]$$
$$step\ es\ pa = accumArray\ better\ initial\ (1,k)\ (map\ insert\ es)$$
$$\textbf{where } initial \qquad = (maxInt, [])$$
$$insert\ (u,v,w) = (u,(add\ w\ c,(u,v,w):p))$$
$$\textbf{where } (c,p) = pa\ !\ v$$
$$better\ (c_1,p_1)\ (c_2,p_2) = \textbf{if } c_1 \leqslant c_2 \textbf{ then } (c_1,p_1) \textbf{ else } (c_2,p_2)$$

The value *maxInt* and the function *add* are as defined in Dijkstra's algorithm:

$$maxInt :: Int$$
$$maxInt = maxBound$$

$$add\ w\ c = \textbf{if } c == maxInt \textbf{ then } maxInt \textbf{ else } w + c$$

Each call of *step* takes $O(k+e)$, where e is the number of edges in the current layer, so the total running time is $O(dk^2)$ as there are $O(dk^2)$ edges in total.

Answer 10.15 One definition is

$$mergeBy :: (a \rightarrow a \rightarrow Bool) \rightarrow [[a]] \rightarrow [a]$$
$$mergeBy\ cmp = foldr\ merge\ []$$
$$\textbf{where } merge\ xs\ [] \qquad = xs$$
$$merge\ []\ ys \qquad = ys$$
$$merge\ (x:xs)\ (y:ys)$$
$$|\ cmp\ x\ y \qquad = x:merge\ xs\ (y:ys)$$
$$|\ otherwise = y:merge\ (x:xs)\ ys$$

Answer 10.16 Because if $x = 4$ the tuple $([0,1,2],0,3)$ would not be produced and the minimum-cost solution would not be found.

Answer 10.17 Simply replace *coins* by *reverse · coins*.

Answer 10.18 Since *tstep* produces answers in decreasing order of residue, we can write

$$mkchange \; n = coins \cdot last \cdot foldr \; tstep \; [([],n,0)]$$

Answer 10.19 Since only selections that satisfy the capacity constraint are maintained, we could have defined

$$extend \; i \; sn = sn : filter \; (within \; w) \; [add \; i \; sn]$$

Other definitions are of course possible.

Answer 10.20 A direct attack fails because $ThinBy \; (\preccurlyeq) \cdot extend \; i = extend \; i$. Instead we have to show that (10.2) holds, namely that, if $sn_1 \preccurlyeq sn_2$, then

$$\forall en_2 \in extend \; i \; sn_2 : \exists en_1 \in extend \; i \; sn_1 : en_1 \preccurlyeq en_2$$

This comes down to the fact that $add \; i \; sn_1$ is a valid choice if $add \; i \; sn_2$ is, and that

$$sn_1 \preccurlyeq sn_2 \implies add \; i \; sn_1 \preccurlyeq add \; i \; sn_2$$

Answer 10.21 The definition is

$$swag \; w = maxWith \; value \cdot foldr \; tstep \; [([],0,0)]$$
$$\textbf{where} \; tstep \; i \; sns = thinBy \; (\preccurlyeq) \; (mergeBy \; cmp \; [sns, sns'])$$
$$\textbf{where} \; sns' = filter \; (within \; w) \; (map \; (add \; i) \; sns)$$
$$cmp \; sn_1 \; sn_2 = weight \; sn_1 \leqslant weight \; sn_2$$

Answer 10.22 One solution is to introduce a cost function

$$cost :: Selection \to (Value, Weight)$$
$$cost \; sn = (value \; sn, negate \; (weight \; sn))$$

and replace *maxWith value* by *maxWith cost*. Another solution would be to replace *maxWith value* by $maxBy \; (\preccurlyeq)$, where

$$sn_1 \preccurlyeq sn_2 = value \; sn_1 < value \; sn_2 \; \vee$$
$$(value \; sn_1 == value \; sn_2 \wedge weight \; sn_1 \geqslant weight \; sn_2)$$

That would involve a new maximisation function

$$maxBy :: (a \to a \to Bool) \to [a] \to a$$
$$maxBy \; (\preccurlyeq) = foldr1 \; higher$$
$$\textbf{where} \; higher \; x \; y = \textbf{if} \; x \preccurlyeq y \; \textbf{then} \; y \; \textbf{else} \; x$$

Answer 10.23 The definition is

$$choices :: Weight \rightarrow [Item] \rightarrow [Selection]$$
$$choices\ w = foldr\ (concatMap \cdot choose)\ [([],0,0)]$$
$$\quad\quad\quad \textbf{where } choose\ i\ sn = [add\ k\ i\ sn \mid k \leftarrow [0..max]]$$
$$\quad\quad\quad\quad\quad \textbf{where } max = (w - weight\ sn)\ \text{div } weight\ i$$

$$add :: Nat \rightarrow Item \rightarrow Selection \rightarrow Selection$$
$$add\ k\ i\ (kns,v,w) = ((k, name\ i):kns, k \times value\ i + v, k \times weight\ i + w)$$

The function *add k* selects *k* copies of the next item, where *k* is constrained so that the knapsack capacity is not exceeded. Note that values of *k* are chosen in increasing order, so the weights of selections are in increasing order. The thinning algorithm is then defined by

$$swag\ w = extract \cdot maxWith\ value \cdot foldr\ tstep\ [([],0,0)]$$
$$\textbf{where } tstep\ i \quad\quad = thinBy\ (\preceq) \cdot mergeBy\ cmp \cdot map\ (choose\ i)$$
$$\quad\quad choose\ i\ sn = [add\ k\ i\ sn \mid k \leftarrow [0..max]]$$
$$\quad\quad\quad\quad \textbf{where } max = (w - weight\ sn)\ \text{div } weight\ i$$
$$\quad cmp\ sn_1\ sn_2 = weight\ sn_1 \leqslant weight\ sn_2$$

Answer 10.24 In the fractional knapsack problem there is an infinite, in fact an uncountably infinite, number of choices for each item, one for each real number x in the range $0 \leqslant x \leqslant 1$. So no executable specification is possible. When the weights are integers, each choice is a rational number r in the range $0 \leqslant r \leqslant 1$, reducing the number of choices to a countably infinite number. The greedy algorithm is

$$gswag :: Weight \rightarrow [Item] \rightarrow [(Rational, Name)]$$
$$gswag\ w = extract \cdot foldr\ (add\ w)\ ([],0,0) \cdot sortBy\ cmp$$

$$extract :: Selection \rightarrow [(Rational, Name)]$$
$$extract\ (rns, \_, \_) = reverse\ rns$$

$$add :: Weight \rightarrow Item \rightarrow Selection \rightarrow Selection$$
$$add\ w\ i\ (rns, vn, wn) = \textbf{if } wn == w \textbf{ then } (rns, vn, wn)$$
$$\quad\quad\quad\quad \textbf{else } ((r, name\ i):rns, vn + r \times vi, wn + r \times wi)$$
$$\quad\quad\quad\quad \textbf{where } r \quad = min\ 1\ ((w - wn)/wi)$$
$$\quad\quad\quad\quad\quad\quad wi = fromIntegral\ (weight\ i)$$
$$\quad\quad\quad\quad\quad\quad vi = fromIntegral\ (value\ i)$$

$$cmp :: Item \rightarrow Item \rightarrow Ordering$$
$$cmp\ i_1\ i_2 = compare\ (value\ i_1 \times weight\ i_2)\ (value\ i_2 \times weight\ i_1)$$

For example, *gswag* 50 *items* returns the answer

$$[(1\ \%\ 1, \text{"Jewellery"}), (1\ \%\ 1, \text{"TV"}), (11\ \%\ 14, \text{"Laptop"})]$$

Quite how the thief steals eleven-fourteenths of a laptop we leave to your imagination.

Chapter 11

Segments and subsequences

By definition, a *segment* of a list is a contiguous subsequence of the list. Thus "arb" is a segment of "barbara" while "bab" is a subsequence but not a contiguous one. A segment that begins a list is called a *prefix* or an *initial* segment, and one that ends a list a *suffix* or *tail* segment. Segments are also called *factors* or *substrings* in the literature, but we will reserve the word 'segment' for the contiguous subsequences. A list can have an exponential number of subsequences but only a quadratic number of segments.

Problems involving segments and subsequences abound in computing. For example, they arise in genomics, text processing, data mining, and data compression. Whole books have been written on 'stringology' and many interesting, subtle, and useful algorithms have been discussed and analysed over the years. In this chapter we confine our attention to three simply stated problems, one involving segments and two involving subsequences. The segment problem is the most complicated of the three, so we will begin with the two problems about subsequences.

11.1 The longest upsequence

Given a sequence of elements from an ordered type, the function *lus* computes some longest subsequence whose elements are in strictly increasing order (in other words, a *longest upsequence*):

$$lus :: Ord\ a \Rightarrow [a] \rightarrow [a]$$
$$lus \leftarrow MaxWith\ length \cdot filter\ up \cdot subseqs$$

For example, "lost" is a longest upsequence of "longest". The test *up* can be defined by

$$up :: Ord\ a \Rightarrow [a] \rightarrow Bool$$
$$up\ xs = and\ (zipWith\ (<)\ xs\ (tail\ xs))$$

The function *subseqs* can be defined in a number of ways (see the exercises); here are two, both based on *foldr*. The first is to write

$$subseqs :: [a] \to [[a]]$$
$$subseqs = foldr\ step\ [[\,]]$$
$$\textbf{where}\ step\ x\ xss = xss + map\ (x\!:)\ xss$$

The second way is to write

$$subseqs :: [a] \to [[a]]$$
$$subseqs = foldr\ (concatMap \cdot extend)\ [[\,]]$$
$$\textbf{where}\ extend\ x\ xs = [xs, x\!:xs]$$

The second method is essentially the one used in the definition of *selections* in the knapsack problem of the previous chapter. For the sake of variety we will adopt the first definition. In either case, straightforward implementation of *lus* leads to an algorithm with exponential time simply because there are an exponential number of subsequences that have to be checked. Our aim is to do better; in fact there is an $O(n \log n)$ time algorithm for the problem.

The first step in the standard recipe is to fuse *filter up* and *subseqs* to arrive at

$$lus \leftarrow MaxWith\ length \cdot foldr\ step\ [[\,]]$$
$$\textbf{where}\ step\ x\ xss = xss + map\ (x\!:)\ (filter\ (ok\ x)\ xss)$$
$$ok\ x\ ys\quad = null\ ys \vee x < head\ ys$$

Only upsequences are kept at each step. An element x can be added to the front of an upsequence *ys* if either *ys* is the empty sequence or its first element is greater than x.

The next step is to see whether a greedy algorithm is possible. Can we keep a single longest upsequence at each step? No, because while "ab" is the unique longest upsequence of "xab", the longest upsequence of "uvwxab" is "uvwx", so "x" cannot disappear from view and we need to keep more than one upsequence in play. A similar argument holds if the input is processed from left to right, so the failure is not due to use of *foldr*. The same argument shows that no obvious divide-and-conquer algorithm is possible either: we can split the input into two and compute a longest upsequence for each half, but these two upsequences do not provide sufficient information to determine a longest upsequence of the whole input. That all means we need to keep more than one candidate in play. So we introduce a thinning step:

$$lus \leftarrow MaxWith\ length \cdot ThinBy\ (\preccurlyeq) \cdot foldr\ step\ [[\,]]$$

We have to ensure

$$xs \preccurlyeq ys \;\Rightarrow\; length\ xs \geq length\ ys$$

for the thin-introduction step to be valid, but what else do we need? Well, when

building upsequences from right to left, one upsequence is clearly better than another
if it is no shorter and its first element, if it exists, is bigger. For instance, "jot" is
a better upsequence to keep in play than "dot" because the former allows more
symbols to be prefixed while maintaining an upsequence ("ijot" is an upsequence
but "idot" is not). We also want to keep the empty sequence as a candidate. That
all suggests defining $\preccurlyeq$ by

$$
\begin{aligned}
[] &\preccurlyeq [] &&= \textit{True} \\
(x:xs) &\preccurlyeq [] &&= \textit{False} \\
[] &\preccurlyeq (y:ys) &&= \textit{False} \\
(x:xs) &\preccurlyeq (y:ys) &&= x \geqslant y \wedge \textit{length } xs \geqslant \textit{length } ys
\end{aligned}
$$

The first and fourth clauses ensure that $\preccurlyeq$ is reflexive and the length condition holds.

The next step is to fuse $\textit{ThinBy}\ (\preccurlyeq)$ and $\textit{foldr step}\ [[\,]]$. To this end we reason as
follows:

$$
\begin{aligned}
&\textit{ThinBy}\ (\preccurlyeq)\ (\textit{step } x\ xss) \\
=\quad &\{\ \text{definition of } \textit{step}\ \} \\
&\textit{ThinBy}\ (\preccurlyeq)\ (xss + \!\!+ \textit{map}\ (x:)\ (\textit{filter}\ (ok\ x)\ xss)) \\
=\quad &\{\ \text{distributive law of } \textit{ThinBy}\ \} \\
&\textit{ThinBy}\ (\preccurlyeq)\ (\textit{ThinBy}\ (\preccurlyeq)\ xss + \!\!+ \textit{ThinBy}\ (\preccurlyeq)\ (\textit{map}\ (x:)\ (\textit{filter}\ (ok\ x)\ xss))) \\
\rightarrow\quad &\{\ \text{thin-map law (see below)}\ \} \\
&\textit{ThinBy}\ (\preccurlyeq)\ (\textit{ThinBy}\ (\preccurlyeq)\ xss + \!\!+ \textit{map}\ (x:)\ (\textit{ThinBy}\ (\preccurlyeq)\ (\textit{filter}\ (ok\ x)\ xss))) \\
=\quad &\{\ \text{thin-filter law (see below)}\ \} \\
&\textit{ThinBy}\ (\preccurlyeq)\ (\textit{ThinBy}\ (\preccurlyeq)\ xss + \!\!+ \textit{map}\ (x:)\ (\textit{filter}\ (ok\ x)\ (\textit{ThinBy}\ (\preccurlyeq)\ xss)))
\end{aligned}
$$

The thin-map and thin-filter laws rely on the facts that

$$
\begin{aligned}
xs \preccurlyeq ys &\Rightarrow x:xs \preccurlyeq x:ys \\
xs \preccurlyeq ys \wedge ok\ x\ ys &\Rightarrow ok\ x\ xs
\end{aligned}
$$

whose proofs are left as exercises. Hence, defining $\textit{tstep}$ by

$$
\textit{tstep } x\ xss = \textit{thinBy}\ (\preccurlyeq)\ (\textit{step } x\ xss)
$$

we have

$$
\textit{foldr tstep}\ [[\,]] \leftarrow \textit{ThinBy}\ (\preccurlyeq) \cdot \textit{foldr step}\ [[\,]]
$$

and so $\textit{lus} \leftarrow \textit{MaxWith length} \cdot \textit{foldr tstep}\ [[\,]]$. Finally, the thinning process can be
made more effective by keeping subsequences in increasing order of length. That
all leads quite quickly to

$$
\begin{aligned}
\textit{lus} &= \textit{last} \cdot \textit{foldr tstep}\ [[\,]] \\
\textit{tstep } x\ xss &= \textit{thinBy}\ (\preccurlyeq)\ (\textit{mergeBy cmp}\ [xss, yss]) \\
&\quad \mathbf{where}\ yss = \textit{map}\ (x:)\ (\textit{filter}\ (ok\ x)\ xss) \\
&\qquad\quad\ \ \textit{cmp xs ys} = \textit{length } xs \leqslant \textit{length } ys
\end{aligned}
$$

Ignoring length calculations, this version of $\textit{lus}$ takes $O(nr)$ steps, where n is the length of the input and r is the length of the longest upsequence. At most $r+1$ upsequences are kept in play at each stage and these can be updated in $O(r)$ steps.

To discover the path for further optimisation we need to look more closely at the computation. Observe that at a typical stage a list of upsequences $[xs_0, xs_1, ..., xs_k]$ is maintained in which xs_j has length j, and $head\ xs_j > head\ xs_{j+1}$ for $1 \leqslant j < k$. After applying $tstep\ x$ to this list, we obtain a new list

$$[xs_0, ..., xs_j, x : xs_j, xs_{j+2}, ..., xs_k]$$

where $head\ xs_j > x \geqslant head\ xs_{j+1}$ (assuming the heads of xs_0 and xs_{k+1} are infinitely large and infinitely small, respectively). For example, since

$$foldr\ tstep\ [[]]\ \texttt{"ripper"} = [\texttt{""},\texttt{"r"},\texttt{"pr"},\texttt{"ipr"}]$$

we obtain

$$foldr\ tstep\ [[]]\ \texttt{"kripper"} = [\texttt{""},\texttt{"r"},\texttt{"pr"},\texttt{"kpr"}]$$
$$foldr\ tstep\ [[]]\ \texttt{"cripper"} = [\texttt{""},\texttt{"r"},\texttt{"pr"},\texttt{"ipr"},\texttt{"cipr"}]$$
$$foldr\ tstep\ [[]]\ \texttt{"tripper"} = [\texttt{""},\texttt{"t"},\texttt{"pr"},\texttt{"ipr"}]$$

That means $tstep$ can be redefined to read

$$tstep\ x\ ([] : xss) = [] : search\ x\ []\ xss$$
$$\textbf{where}\ search\ x\ xs\ [] \quad = [x : xs]$$
$$search\ x\ xs\ (ys : xss)$$
$$| \ head\ ys > x = ys : search\ x\ ys\ xss$$
$$| \ otherwise \quad = (x : xs) : xss$$

This version of $tstep$ finds the required insertion point by linear search from left to right: the first ys such that $head\ ys \leqslant x$ is replaced by $x : xs$, where xs is the upsequence immediately preceding ys. If there is no such ys, then $x : xs$ is added to the end of the list, as in the $\texttt{"cripper"}$ example above. Length calculations no longer appear and the running time of lus is $O(nr)$ steps. In an imperative setting, the running time can be improved to $O(n \log r)$ steps by using an array and binary search to locate the required insertion point. However, since the array also has to be updated at each step, and array updates take linear time in a purely functional setting, this solution does not improve the running time. The alternative is to use a balanced binary search tree, but we will leave the details to Exercise 11.6.

11.2 The longest common subsequence

The problem of finding the longest common subsequence of two sequences has many applications in computing, basically because such a subsequence is a useful measure of how similar the two sequences are. In this section we consider a function

$$lcs :: Eq\ a \Rightarrow [a] \rightarrow [a] \rightarrow [a]$$

so that *lcs xs ys* returns a longest common subsequence of *xs* and *ys*. The problem is interesting because of the number of different ways to solve it. We begin with a specification of the problem, in fact with two specifications. The first is to define

$$lcs \; xs \; ys \leftarrow MaxWith \; length \; (intersect \; (subseqs \; xs) \; (subseqs \; ys))$$

where *intersect* returns the common elements of two lists. The second specification, and the one we will use, is to define

$$lcs \; xs \leftarrow MaxWith \; length \cdot filter \; (sub \; xs) \cdot subseqs$$

where the test *sub xs ys* determines whether *ys* is a subsequence of *xs*:

$$
\begin{aligned}
sub \; xs \quad & [] \quad = True \\
sub \; [] \quad & (y:ys) = False \\
sub \; (x:xs) \; & (y:ys) = \textbf{if } x == y \textbf{ then } sub \; xs \; ys \textbf{ else } sub \; xs \; (y:ys)
\end{aligned}
$$

The first specification maintains symmetry between *xs* and *ys*, while the second breaks it. The advantage of the second specification is simply that it places us in familiar territory for ferreting out a thinning algorithm.

For a functional programmer happy with recursion as their basic tool there is a simple way to solve the problem, which is to write

$$
\begin{aligned}
lcs \; [] \quad & ys \quad = [] \\
lcs \; xs \quad & [] \quad = [] \\
lcs \; (x:xs) \; (y:ys) = & \textbf{if } x == y \textbf{ then } x:lcs \; xs \; ys \\
& \textbf{else } longer \; (lcs \; (x:xs) \; ys) \; (lcs \; xs \; (y:ys))
\end{aligned}
$$

The function *longer* returns the longer of two lists. This solution is an attractive one because there are no *subseqs*, *filter*, or *intersect* operations, and it can be justified by starting with the symmetric specification of *lcs* and considering the various cases that can arise. However, this solution takes exponential time, and the reason it does so is because it involves computing the solutions to the same subproblems many times over. The way to solve this problem is by dynamic programming, so we will return to this solution in the next part of the book.

For a mathematician there is another way to solve the problem. Mathematicians like to reduce problems with unknown solutions to problems with known solutions. We can do that here. After the previous section we know that the function *lus* for computing a longest upsequence can be solved reasonably efficiently and, with a little bit of cleverness, we can compute *lcs* in terms of *lus*. The solution takes the form

$$lcs \; xs \; ys = decode \; (lus \; (encode \; xs \; ys)) \; ys$$

We encode *xs* and *ys* as a single list over an ordered alphabet, solve the longest upsequence problem on this encoded list, and then decode the result. Here is how we encode the two sequences. Suppose ys is the list

0	1	2	3	4	5
'b'	'a'	'a'	'b'	'c'	'a'

The positions of the elements are recorded above the elements. Let xs be the string
"baxca". For each letter in xs we record the positions in ys at which this letter
occurs, but in reverse order. Thus

$$posns \text{ 'b'} = [3,0], \quad posns \text{ 'a'} = [5,2,1], \quad posns \text{ 'x'} = [],$$
$$posns \text{ 'c'} = [4], \quad posns \text{ 'a'} = [5,2,1]$$

The encoded string is the concatenation $[3,0,5,2,1,4,5,2,1]$ of these positions. The
longest upsequence of this list is $[0,1,4,5]$, which decodes to "baca", the longest
common subsequence of xs and ys. We leave it as an exercise to show why the trick
works, and also to supply the definitions of *encode* and *decode*. In the worst case
the encoded string can have length $\Theta(n^2)$ when both inputs have length n, so the
computation of *lus* can take $\Theta(n^2 \log n)$ steps. A thinning approach can bring this
worst case time down to $\Theta(n^2)$ steps.

The first step in the standard recipe is to fuse *filter* $(sub\ xs)$ and *subseqs*. The
success of this step relies on the fact that $sub\ xs\ (y:ys) \Rightarrow sub\ xs\ ys$. In words, if
$y:ys$ is a subsequence of xs, then so is ys. Here is the result of the fusion step:

$$lcs\ xs \leftarrow MaxWith\ length \cdot foldr\ step\ [[]]$$
where $step\ y\ yss = yss + filter\ (sub\ xs)\ (map\ (y:)\ yss)$

Instead of filtering at the end, we can filter at each step.

The next step is to check whether a greedy algorithm is possible. The longest
common subsequence of "abc" and "cab" is "ab", which cannot be extended
leftwards to the longest common subsequence of "abc" and "abcab", namely
"abc". So we cannot maintain a single subsequence at each step, and have to
introduce thinning. In order to determine which subsequences to keep we need to
know the *position* of each subsequence in xs. A subsequence can occur more than
once in a sequence; for example "ba" appears four times in "baabca", in positions
$[0,1],[0,2],[0,5],[3,5]$. When building subsequences from right to left, that is
adding elements to the front of subsequences, we want the position that is lexically
the largest, namely $[3,5]$ in the above example. Such a choice gives the greatest
freedom in adding common elements to the front of the sequence. We do not need the
full position in calculations, but only the position of the first element. So the position
of "ba" we want is 3, the rightmost position at which the last occurrence of "ba"
in "baabca" starts. The rightmost position of the empty sequence in "baabca" is
6. We will set the position of a sequence ys in a sequence xs to be -1 if ys is not
a subsequence of xs. The definition of *position* is left as an exercise.

A subsequence can be discarded if there is another subsequence whose length
and position are at least as large. Hence for fixed xs we can define

$$ys \preccurlyeq zs = length \; ys \geqslant length \; zs \wedge position \; xs \; ys \geqslant position \; xs \; zs$$

The thin-introduction law is now applicable, giving that $lcs \; xs$ is a refinement of

$$MaxWith \; length \cdot ThinBy \; (\preccurlyeq) \cdot foldr \; step \; [[\,]]$$

The next step is to fuse $ThinBy$ with $foldr$. We can keep subsequences in increasing order of position, and therefore in decreasing order of length, by merging at each step. Moreover, the term $filter \; (sub \; xs)$ can be removed from the computation if all sequences with negative positions are discarded. That leads to

$$
\begin{aligned}
&lcs \; xs = head \cdot foldr \; tstep \; [[\,]] \\
&\quad \textbf{where } tstep \; y \; yss = thinBy \; (\preccurlyeq) \; (mergeBy \; cmp \; [yss, zss]) \\
&\qquad \textbf{where } zss \qquad\quad = dropWhile \; negpos \; (map \; (y:) \; yss) \\
&\qquad\qquad negpos \; ys = position \; xs \; ys < 0 \\
&\qquad\qquad ys \preccurlyeq zs \quad = length \; ys \geqslant length \; zs \wedge \\
&\qquad\qquad\qquad\qquad\qquad position \; xs \; ys \geqslant position \; xs \; zs \\
&\qquad\qquad cmp \; ys \; zs = position \; xs \; ys \leqslant position \; xs \; zs
\end{aligned}
$$

The final optimisation is to avoid multiple computations of $position$ and $length$. To this end we represent a subsequence us of xs by a quadruple (p, k, ws, us) in which

$$
\begin{aligned}
p &= position \; xs \; us \\
k &= length \; us \\
ws &= reverse \; (take \; p \; xs)
\end{aligned}
$$

For example, the representation of "ba" as a subsequence of "baabca" is the quadruple $(3, 2, "aab", "ba")$. The function $cons \; x$ which replaces $(x:)$ is defined by

$$
\begin{aligned}
&cons \; x \; (p, k, ws, us) = (p - 1 - length \; as, k + 1, tail \; bs, x : us) \\
&\qquad\qquad\qquad\qquad \textbf{where } (as, bs) = span \; (\neq x) \; ws
\end{aligned}
$$

For example,

$$
\begin{aligned}
cons \; 'b' \; (3, 2, "aab", "ba") &= (0, 3, "", "bba") \\
cons \; 'x' \; (3, 2, "aab", "ba") &= (-1, 3, \bot, "bba")
\end{aligned}
$$

If $x : us$ is not a subsequence of xs, then the first component is negative and the third is undefined. Now we can define

$$
\begin{aligned}
&lcs \; xs = ext \cdot head \cdot foldr \; tstep \; start \\
&\quad \textbf{where } start \qquad = [(length \; xs, 0, reverse \; xs, [\,])] \\
&\qquad\quad tstep \; y \; yss = thinBy \; (\preccurlyeq) \; (mergeBy \; cmp \; [yss, zss]) \\
&\qquad\qquad \textbf{where } zss \qquad = dropWhile \; negpos \; (map \; (cons \; y) \; yss) \\
&\qquad\qquad\qquad negpos \; ys = psn \; ys < 0 \\
&\qquad\qquad\qquad q_1 \preccurlyeq q_2 \quad = psn \; q_1 \geqslant psn \; q_2 \wedge lng \; q_1 \geqslant lng \; q_2 \\
&\qquad\qquad\qquad cmp \; q_1 \; q_2 = psn \; q_1 \leqslant psn \; q_2
\end{aligned}
$$

where ext, psn, and lng are the selector functions

$$ext\ (p, k, ws, us) = us$$
$$psn\ (p, k, ws, us) = p$$
$$lng\ (p, k, ws, us) = k$$

This algorithm takes $O(mn)$ steps, where m and n are the lengths of xs and ys.

11.3 A short segment with maximum sum

Our third problem is easy to state but not so easy to solve, at least not with an efficient algorithm. Given a list of positive and negative integers, the problem is simply to return a segment of the list that has the largest possible sum subject to the segment not being too long. Thus we want to compute mss, where

$$mss :: Nat \rightarrow [Integer] \rightarrow [Integer]$$
$$mss\ b \leftarrow MaxWith\ sum \cdot filter\ (short\ b) \cdot segments$$

and *short* is defined by

$$short :: Nat \rightarrow [a] \rightarrow Bool$$
$$short\ b\ xs = (length\ xs \leqslant b)$$

For example,

$$mss\ 3\ [1, -2, 3, 0, -5, 3, -2, 3, -1] = [3, -2, 3]$$

The function *segments* is defined below. Straightforward computation of *mss* takes $O(bn)$ steps. There are $\Theta(bn)$ short segments in a list of length n, and we can generate all of them, along with their sums, in this time. Finding one with a maximum sum takes linear time, so the algorithm takes $O(bn)$ steps. However, b may be quite large, and $O(n)$ is a much better bound on the algorithm. The aim of this section is to describe an algorithm with such a bound. The algorithm is interesting because a significant change of representation is required to achieve the desired efficiency, but it is still basically a thinning algorithm.

First of all, here is one definition of *segments*:

$$segments :: [a] \rightarrow [[a]]$$
$$segments = concatMap\ inits \cdot tails$$

The segments of the list are therefore obtained by taking all the prefixes of all the suffixes. As we will see, this leads to an algorithm that processes the input from right to left. We could also have chosen to take all suffixes of all prefixes, in which case the algorithm proceeds from left to right. The functions *inits* and *tails* were discussed in Chapter 2 and are provided in the library *Data.List*. Both functions include the empty list as a prefix or suffix, so the empty list appears $n + 1$ times in the segments of a list of length n. There are easy modifications to the definitions of *inits* and *tails* that produce only nonempty segments. However, allowing the empty segment as a candidate means that a short segment with maximum sum in a list of negative numbers is the empty sequence.

We can now reason

$\quad$ *MaxWith sum · filter (short b) · segments*
$=\quad$ { definition of *segments* }
$\quad$ *MaxWith sum · filter (short b) · concatMap inits · tails*
$=\quad$ { since *filter p · concat = concat · map (filter p)* }
$\quad$ *MaxWith sum · concatMap (filter (short b) · inits) · tails*
$=\quad$ { distributive law }
$\quad$ *MaxWith sum · map (MaxWith sum · filter (short b) · inits) · tails*
$\rightarrow\quad$ { with *msp b ← MaxWith sum · filter (short b) · inits* }
$\quad$ *MaxWith sum · map (msp b) · tails*

Summarising this calculation, we have shown that

$\quad$ *mss b ← MaxWith sum · map (msp b) · tails*
$\quad$ *msp b ← MaxWith sum · filter (short b) · inits*

The new function *msp* computes a short prefix with maximum sum. For example,

$\quad$ *msp* $4\,[-2,4,4,-5,8,-2,3,1] = [-2,4,4]$
$\quad$ *msp* $6\,[-2,4,4,-5,8,-2,3,1] = [-2,4,4,-5,8]$

The new form of *mss* suggests an appeal to the *Scan Lemma*, an essential tool when dealing with problems involving segments. The Scan Lemma was mentioned in Answer 1.12, but here it is again:

$\quad$ *map (foldr op e) · tails = scanr op e*

Applied to a list of length n, the left-hand side requires $\Theta(n^2)$ applications of *op*, while the right-hand side requires only $\Theta(n)$ applications. The function *scanr* is a Haskell function in the library *Data.List*, whose definition is basically as follows:

$\quad$ *scanr* $:: (a \rightarrow b \rightarrow b) \rightarrow b \rightarrow [a] \rightarrow [b]$
$\quad$ *scanr op e* $[\,] \qquad = [e]$
$\quad$ *scanr op e* $(x:xs) = op\ x\ (head\ ys):ys$ **where** $ys = scanr\ op\ e\ xs$

For example,

$\quad$ *scanr* $(\oplus)\ e\ [x,y] = [x \oplus (y \oplus e), y \oplus e, e]$

Later on, we will need the companion function *scanl*:

$\quad$ *scanl* $:: (b \rightarrow a \rightarrow b) \rightarrow b \rightarrow [a] \rightarrow [b]$
$\quad$ *scanl op e* $[\,] \qquad = [e]$
$\quad$ *scanl op e* $(x:xs) = e:scanl\ op\ (op\ e\ x)\ xs$

For example,

$\quad$ *scanl* $(\oplus)\ e\ [x,y] = [e, e \oplus x, (e \oplus x) \oplus y]$

The Scan Lemma suggests we look for a definition of *msp* as an instance of *foldr*. Then we would obtain a definition of *mss* in terms of *scanr*. More precisely, if we can find a definition of *msp* in the form

$$msp\ b = foldr\ (op\ b)\ [\,]$$

then we can refine *mss* to read

$$mss\ b \leftarrow MaxWith\ sum \cdot scanr\ (op\ b)\ [\,]$$

As it happens there is such a definition of *msp*, but it doesn't help:

$$msp\ b = foldr\ (op\ b)\ [\,]\ \textbf{where}\ op\ b\ x\ xs = msp\ b\ (x:xs)$$

This identity cannot serve as a legitimate Haskell definition of *msp* because it is circular. In effect it states no more nor less than that $msp\ b\ (x:xs)$ is a prefix of $x:msp\ b\ xs$. Exercise 11.13 asks for a proof of this assertion.

Instead we will follow the standard thinning recipe. The first step is to fuse *filter* (*short b*) with *inits*, thereby producing only short prefixes. The function *inits* can be expressed in terms of *foldr*:

$$inits :: [a] \rightarrow [[a]]$$
$$inits = foldr\ step\ [[\,]]\ \textbf{where}\ step\ x\ xss = [\,] : map\ (x:)\ xss$$

Since the elements of *xss* are lists in increasing order of length from 0 up to k, where k is the length of *xss*, we have

$$filter\ (short\ b)\ (step\ x\ xss) = \textbf{if}\ length\ (last\ xss) == b$$
$$\textbf{then}\ [\,] : map\ (x:)\ (init\ xss)$$
$$\textbf{else}\ \ [\,] : map\ (x:)\ xss$$

In words, if adding a new element to the front of the list increases its length beyond b, then we can simply cut out the last list. An appeal to the fusion law of *foldr* then leads to

$$msp\ b \leftarrow MaxWith\ sum \cdot foldr\ (op\ b)\ [[\,]]$$

where

$$op\ b\ x\ xss = [\,] : map\ (x:)\ (cut\ b\ xss)$$
$$cut\ b\ xss = \ \textbf{if}\ length\ (last\ xss) == b\ \textbf{then}\ init\ xss\ \textbf{else}\ xss$$

Later on we will see how to make the computation of *cut* more efficient.

The next step is to introduce thinning, refining *msp* to read

$$msp\ b \leftarrow MaxWith\ sum \cdot ThinBy\ (\preccurlyeq) \cdot foldr\ (op\ b)\ [[\,]]$$

An appropriate choice of preorder $\preccurlyeq$ is

$$xs \preccurlyeq ys = (sum\ xs \geqslant sum\ ys) \wedge (length\ xs \leqslant length\ ys)$$

In words, there is no point in keeping a prefix if there is another prefix that is shorter and whose sum is at least as large. For example, optimal thinning of

$$foldr \ (op \ 7) \ [[]] \ [-2, 4, 4, -5, 8, -2, 3, 9]$$

produces the prefixes

$$[], [-2, 4], [-2, 4, 4], [-2, 4, 4, -5, 8], [-2, 4, 4, -5, 8, -2, 3]$$

of length at most 7 with sums $0, 2, 6, 9, 10$. These prefixes are in increasing order of length as well as increasing order of sum.

The next step, another appeal to fusion, is to thin at each step rather than just once at the end. Thinning can be implemented by taking advantage of the fact that the prefixes are in strictly increasing order of length and in strictly increasing order of sum. This means we only have to delete a nonempty prefix if its sum is less than or equal to zero. That gives

$$
\begin{aligned}
msp \ b \quad &= last \cdot foldr \ (op \ b) \ [[]] \\
op \ b \ x \ xss &= [] : thin \ (map \ (x:) \ (cut \ b \ xss)) \\
thin \quad &= dropWhile \ (\lambda xs. \ sum \ xs \leqslant 0)
\end{aligned}
$$

In other words, we cut from the end of the list to keep the prefixes short, and thin from the front of the list to keep sums positive. The prefix with the largest sum is the last prefix in the sequence. Now we can define

$$mss \ b = maxWith \ sum \cdot map \ last \cdot scanr \ (op \ b) \ [[]]$$

However, this definition of op will not suffice for the final algorithm. Even ignoring the cost of cutting and thinning, the map operations mean that computation of op on a list of length k takes $O(k)$ steps. In the worst case, when the input is a list of positive numbers, we have $k = b$, so the total running time of mss is $O(bn)$ steps for an input of length n. That's no better than before. The way to achieve a bound of $O(n)$ steps is by changing the representation of the list of prefixes.

The idea is simple enough: represent the list of prefixes by their differences. For example, instead of maintaining the list

$$[[], [-2, 4], [-2, 4, 4], [-2, 4, 4, -5, 8], [-2, 4, 4, -5, 8, -2, 3]]$$

we maintain the partition $[[-2, 4], [4], [-5, 8], [-2, 3]]$ of the last element. More precisely, suppose we define the abstraction function

$$
\begin{aligned}
abst &:: [[a]] \rightarrow [[a]] \\
abst &= scanl \ (+\!\!+) \ []
\end{aligned}
$$

Then

$$
\begin{aligned}
abst \ &[[-2, 4], [4], [-5, 8], [-2, 3]] \\
&= [[], [-2, 4], [-2, 4, 4], [-2, 4, 4, -5, 8], [-2, 4, 4, -5, 8, -2, 3]]
\end{aligned}
$$

In particular, $last \cdot abst = concat$. To effect the change in representation we need a function, opR say, so that

$$abst \ (opR \ b \ x \ xss) = op \ b \ x \ (abst \ xss)$$

Then, by the fusion law of *foldr*, we have

$$abst \cdot foldr \ (opR \ b) \ [\,] = foldr \ (op \ b) \ [[\,]]$$

since $abst \ [\,] = [[\,]]$. Note that we seek to apply the law in the anti-fusion or *fission* direction, splitting the fold on the right into two functions. To define *opR* we need the function

$$cutR \ b \ xss = \textbf{if} \ length \ (concat \ xss) == b \ \textbf{then} \ init \ xss \ \textbf{else} \ xss$$

as a replacement for *cut*. The function *cutR* satisfies

$$cut \ b \ (abst \ xss) = abst \ (cutR \ b \ xss)$$

We also need a replacement for *thin*, which we will call *thinR*. This function will satisfy

$$[\,] : thin \ (map \ (x:) \ (abst \ xss)) = abst \ (thinR \ x \ xss)$$

We can now define *opR* by

$$opR \ b \ x \ xss = thinR \ x \ (cutR \ b \ xss)$$

Here is the proof that this choice works:

$$
\begin{aligned}
&\quad abst \ (opR \ b \ x \ xss) \\
&= \quad \{ \text{definition of } opR \} \\
&\quad abst \ (thinR \ x \ (cutR \ b \ xss)) \\
&= \quad \{ \text{above property of } thinR \} \\
&\quad [\,] : thin \ (map \ (x:) \ (abst \ (cutR \ b \ xss))) \\
&= \quad \{ \text{above property of } cutR \} \\
&\quad [\,] : thin \ (map \ (x:) \ (cut \ b \ (abst \ xss))) \\
&= \quad \{ \text{definition of } op \} \\
&\quad op \ b \ x \ (abst \ xss)
\end{aligned}
$$

Now, putting everything together, we have

$$
\begin{aligned}
&\quad mss \ b \\
&= \quad \{ \text{definition of } mss \text{ in terms of } msp \} \\
&\quad maxWith \ sum \cdot map \ (msp \ b) \cdot tails \\
&= \quad \{ \text{definition of } msp \text{ in terms of } foldr \} \\
&\quad maxWith \ sum \cdot map \ (last \cdot foldr \ (op \ b) \ [[\,]]) \\
&= \quad \{ \text{definition of } opR \} \\
&\quad maxWith \ sum \cdot map \ (last \cdot abst \cdot foldr \ (opR \ b) \ [\,]) \cdot tails \\
&= \quad \{ \text{Scan Lemma} \} \\
&\quad maxWith \ sum \cdot map \ (last \cdot abst) \cdot scanR \ (opR \ b) \ [\,] \\
&= \quad \{ \text{since } last \cdot abst = concat \} \\
&\quad maxWith \ sum \cdot map \ concat \cdot scanR \ (opR \ b) \ [\,]
\end{aligned}
$$

Hence

$$mss\ b = maxWith\ sum \cdot map\ concat \cdot scanr\ (opR\ b)\ []$$

It remains to give the definition of *thinR*:

$$thinR\ x\ xss = add\ [x]\ xss$$
$$\textbf{where}\ add\ xs\ xss$$
$$\qquad |\ sum\ xs > 0 = xs:xss$$
$$\qquad |\ null\ xss\quad = []$$
$$\qquad |\ otherwise\ = add\ (xs +\!\!+ head\ xss)\ (tail\ xss)$$

For example,

$$add\ [-5]\ [[-2,3],[6],[-1,4]] = add\ [-5,-2,3]\ [[6],[-1,4]]$$
$$= add\ [-5,-2,3,6]\ [[-1,4]]$$
$$= [[-5,-2,3,6],[-1,4]]$$

If the current segment has positive sum, then it is added to the front of the list of segments; otherwise it is concatenated with the next segment and the process is repeated. If no segment has positive sum, then the empty list is returned. The function *add* is similar to the function *collapse* we considered in Section 1.5 and indeed was the inspiration for *collapse*.

The final step is to ensure that all the *length*, *concat*, *init*, *sum*, and $+\!\!+$ operations are implemented efficiently. Firstly, we tuple partitions and segments with their sums and lengths. Secondly, since partitions are processed at both ends, we need symmetric lists (see Chapter 3) to ensure that *init* and *cons* operations take constant time. Finally, to make segment concatenation efficient, we introduce an accumulating function. Here are the relevant definitions:

> **type** *Partition* $= (Sum, Length, SymList\ Segment)$
> **type** *Segment* $= (Sum, Length, [Integer] \rightarrow [Integer])$
> **type** *Sum*$\quad = Integer$
> **type** *Length*$\ = Nat$

We use the functions *sumP*, *lenP*, and *segsP* to extract the components of a partition, and *sumS*, *lenS*, and *segS* to extract the components of a segment. The function *opR* is replaced by *opP*, defined by

$$opP\ b\ x\ xss = thinP\ x\ (cutP\ b\ xss)$$

where *cutP* is defined by

$$cutP :: Length \rightarrow Partition \rightarrow Partition$$
$$cutP\ b\ xss = \textbf{if}\ lenP\ xss == b\ \textbf{then}\ initP\ xss\ \textbf{else}\ xss$$

$$initP :: Partition \rightarrow Partition$$
$$initP\ (s,k,xss) = (s-t,k-m,initSL\ xss)\ \textbf{where}\ (t,m,\_) = lastSL\ xss$$

and *thinP* is defined by

$$thinP :: Integer \to Partition \to Partition$$
$$thinP\ x\ xss = add\ (x, 1, ([x] +\!\!+))\ xss$$

$$add :: Segment \to Partition \to Partition$$
$$add\ xs\ xss\ |\ sumS\ xs > 0 \quad = consP\ xs\ xss$$
$$\quad\quad\quad\quad\quad |\ lenP\ xss == 0 = emptyP$$
$$\quad\quad\quad\quad\quad |\ otherwise \quad\quad = add\ (catS\ xs\ (headP\ xss))\ (tailP\ xss)$$

The subsidiary functions are defined by

$$consP :: Segment \to Partition \to Partition$$
$$consP\ xs\ (s, k, xss) = (sumS\ xs + s, lenS\ xs + k, consSL\ xs\ xss)$$

$$emptyP :: Partition$$
$$emptyP = (0, 0, nilSL)$$

$$headP :: Partition \to Segment$$
$$headP\ xss = headSL\ (segsP\ xss)$$

$$tailP :: Partition \to Partition$$
$$tailP\ (s, k, xss) = (s - t, k - m, tailSL\ xss)\ \textbf{where}\ (t, m, \_) = headSL\ xss$$

$$catS :: Segment \to Segment \to Segment$$
$$catS\ (s, k, f)\ (t, m, g) = (s + t, k + m, f \cdot g)$$

The final definition of *mss* is now given by

$$mss\ b = extract \cdot maxWith\ sumP \cdot scanr\ (opP\ b)\ emptyP$$

$$extract :: Partition \to [Integer]$$
$$extract = concatMap\ (flip\ segS\ [\,]) \cdot fromSL \cdot segsP$$

We have *flip segS* $[\,]$ *xs* = *segS xs* $[\,]$, so the accumulating function of a segment is applied to the empty list at the very end of the computation, and the results are concatenated to produce the final answer.

It remains to time the program. With the exception of *add*, all the other functions appearing in *opP* take constant time. The function *add* takes an additional number of steps proportional to the number of segments deleted. But the total number of segments deleted cannot exceed the total number added, which is at most n for an input of length n. Thus *add* takes amortised constant time. Computing *extract* can take $O(b)$ steps, so the total time for computing a short segment with maximum sum is $O(n + b) = O(n)$ steps, as we promised at the outset.

11.4 Chapter notes

There are a number of books on stringology, including [1, 2, 6]. All three of these texts discuss the longest common subsequence problem and other related problems, such as the edit-distance problem and the problem of optimal alignment. Gusfield [6] describes the reduction of the longest common subsequence problem to the longest upsequence problem used in this chapter. The upsequence problem is a favourite example in formal program design for showing the use of loop invariants, and is treated in [5, 4] as well as in a number of other places.

The maximum-sum short segment problem was discussed in [7]. Other problems about finding segments with various properties are described in [3] and [8].

References

[1] Maxime Crochemore, Christof Hancart, and Thierry Lecroq. *Algorithms on Strings*. Cambridge University Press, Cambridge, 2007.

[2] Maxime Crochemore and Wojciech Rytter. *Jewels of Stringology*. World Scientific Publishing, Singapore, 2003.

[3] Sharon Curtis and Shin-Cheng Mu. Calculating a linear-time solution to the densest-segment problem. *Journal of Functional Programming*, 25:e22, 2015.

[4] Edsger W. Dijkstra and Wim H. J. Feijen. *A Method of Programming*. Addison-Wesley, Reading, MA, 1988.

[5] David Gries. *The Science of Programming*. Springer, New York, 1981.

[6] Dan Gusfield. *Algorithms on Strings, Trees, and Sequences*. Cambridge University Press, Cambridge, 1997.

[7] Yaw-Ling Lin, Tao Jiang, and Kun-Mao Chao. Efficient algorithms for locating the length-constrained heaviest segments with applications to biomolecular sequence analysis. *Journal of Computer and System Sciences*, 65(3):570–586, 2002.

[8] Hans Zantema. Longest segment problems. *Science of Computer Programming*, 18(1):39–66, 1992.

Exercises

Exercise 11.1 Precisely how many segments and subsequences are there of a list of n distinct elements? How many segments are there of length at most b?

Exercise 11.2 Write down a definition of *subseqs* that produces subsequences in ascending order of length. No length calculations are allowed.

Exercise 11.3 With the definitions of $\preccurlyeq$ and *ok* given in the longest upsequence problem, we claimed

$$xs \preccurlyeq ys \qquad\qquad \Rightarrow \quad x:xs \preccurlyeq x:ys$$
$$xs \preccurlyeq ys \wedge ok\ x\ ys \quad \Rightarrow \quad ok\ x\ xs$$

Prove these claims.

Exercise 11.4 Can the definition of $\preccurlyeq$ in the longest upsequence problem be replaced by

$$xs \preccurlyeq ys = length\ xs \geqslant length\ ys \wedge xs \geqslant ys$$

or not?

Exercise 11.5 Suppose we defined an upsequence to be one whose elements are only weakly increasing. Thus we change *up* to read

$$up \; xs = and \; (zipWith \; (\leqslant) \; xs \; (tail \; xs))$$

Write down a definition of *tstep* for which $lwus = last \cdot foldr \; tstep \; [[\,]]$.

Exercise 11.6 As mentioned in the text, the longest upsequence problem can be solved in $O(n \log r)$ steps by using a balanced binary search tree. The aim of the following three exercises is to construct such a solution. The material depends on Section 4.3 and Section 4.4, so reread those sections first. Recall the definition

data *Tree a* = *Null* | *Node Int* (*Tree a*) *a* (*Tree a*)

from Section 4.3. A list $xss = [xs_0, xs_1, ..., xs_k]$ of upsequences is represented by a tree *t* of type *Tree* [*a*] such that *flatten t* = *xss*. The leftmost value xs_0 is the empty sequence. As a warm-up exercise, define the function *rmost* that returns the last entry xs_k.

Exercise 11.7 Following on, the new definition of *lus* takes the form

$$lus :: Ord \; a \Rightarrow [a] \rightarrow [a]$$
$$lus = rmost \cdot foldr \; update \; (Node \; 1 \; Null \; [\,] \; Null)$$
$$\textbf{where} \; update \; x \; t = modify \; x \; (split \; x \; t)$$

The value of *split x t* is a pair of trees, the first of which is a tree whose labels consist of the empty list and lists $y : xs$ for which $y > x$, and the second is a tree whose labels are lists $y : xs$ for which $y \leqslant x$. This function is defined exactly as in Section 4.4:

$$split :: Ord \; a \Rightarrow a \rightarrow Tree \; [a] \rightarrow (Tree \; [a], Tree \; [a])$$
$$split \; x \; t = sew \; (pieces \; x \; t \; [\,])$$

However, the definition of *pieces* is different. This time we have

$$pieces :: Ord \; a \Rightarrow a \rightarrow Tree \; [a] \rightarrow [Piece \; [a]] \rightarrow [Piece \; [a]]$$

where, as in Section 4.4, we have

data *Piece a* = *LP* (*Tree a*) *a* | *RP a* (*Tree a*)

Recall that a left piece *LP l x* is missing its right subtree, and a right piece *RP x r* is missing its left subtree. The definition of *pieces x t ps* is different because the labels of *t*, apart from the leftmost label [ ], are in *decreasing* rather than increasing order. Give the modified definition of *pieces*.

Exercise 11.8 The definition of *sew* is the same as in Section 4.4, so it remains to define *modify x* (t_1, t_2). If t_2 is not *Null*, then *modify* returns a tree that results from combining t_1 and a modified tree obtained from t_2 by replacing the leftmost label of t_2 with $x : xs$, where *xs* is the rightmost label of t_1. If t_2 is *Null*, then a new node with label $x : xs$ is created. As a final task, define *modify* in terms of the function *combine* from Section 4.4.

Exercise 11.9 Write down the definitions of *encode* and *decode* for which

$$lcs\ xs\ ys = decode\ (lus\ (encode\ xs\ ys))\ ys$$

Show that each upsequence of *encode xs ys* corresponds to a common subsequence of *xs* and *ys* with the same length.

Exercise 11.10 One way of defining the function *position* is by using a helper function:

$$position\ xs\ ys = help\ (length\ xs)\ (reverse\ xs)\ (reverse\ ys)$$

Define *help*, making sure that the result is negative if *ys* is not a subsequence of *xs*.

Exercise 11.11 Recall that for a given *xs* the preorder $\preccurlyeq$ for the longest common subsequence problem was defined by

$$ys \preccurlyeq zs = length\ ys \geqslant length\ zs \wedge position\ xs\ ys \geqslant position\ xs\ zs$$

Show that

$$\begin{aligned} ys \preccurlyeq zs \wedge sub\ xs\ zs &\Rightarrow sub\ xs\ ys \\ ys \preccurlyeq zs &\Rightarrow y:ys \preccurlyeq y:zs \end{aligned}$$

Hence justify the refinement

$$tstep\ y\ (ThinBy\ (\preccurlyeq)\ yss) \leftarrow ThinBy\ (\preccurlyeq)\ (step\ y\ yss)$$

where $tstep\ y\ yss \leftarrow ThinBy\ (\preccurlyeq)\ (step\ y\ yss)$.

Exercise 11.12 Express *tails* as an instance of *scanr* and *inits* as an instance of *scanl*.

Exercise 11.13 Show that $msp\ b\ (x:xs)$ is a prefix of $x:msp\ b\ xs$.

Exercise 11.14 A similar but much simpler problem about segments is to find a segment with maximum sum with no length restrictions:

$$mss \leftarrow MaxWith\ sum \cdot segments$$

Write down a definition of *msp* for which

$$mss \leftarrow MaxWith\ sum \cdot map\ msp \cdot tails$$

Find a function *step* for which $msp = foldr\ step\ [\,]$, and hence construct a simple linear-time algorithm for *mss*.

Answers

Answer 11.1 Every element can be included or excluded in a subsequence, giving 2^n subsequences in total. The number of nonempty segments of length j is $n-j+1$, so the total number of nonempty segments is

$$\sum_{j=1}^{n}(n-j+1) = \sum_{j=1}^{n}j = n(n+1)/2$$

The number of nonempty segments of length at most b is

$$\sum_{j=1}^{b}(n-j+1) = \sum_{j=0}^{b-1}(n-j) = bn - \sum_{j=0}^{b-1}j = bn - b(b-1)/2$$

Answer 11.2 Perhaps the simplest method is to maintain a list of lists of subsequences, the first list being all the subsequences of length 0, the second list all the subsequences of length 1, and so on. This list can be updated as each new element is processed, and then can be concatenated at the end of the computation. Thus we have

$$subseqs = concat \cdot foldr\ op\ [[[\ ]]]$$

where

$$op :: a \rightarrow [[[a]]] \rightarrow [[[a]]]$$
$$op\ x\ (xss : xsss) = xss : step\ x\ xss\ xsss$$

$$step\ x\ xss\ [\ ] \qquad\qquad = [map\ (x:)\ xss]$$
$$step\ x\ xss\ (yss : ysss) = (map\ (x:)\ xss \mathbin{+\!\!+} yss) : step\ x\ yss\ ysss$$

Answer 11.3 We have

$$x : xs \preccurlyeq x : ys$$
$$\Leftarrow \quad \{\ \text{definition of } \preccurlyeq \}$$
$$length\ xs \geqslant length\ ys$$
$$\Leftarrow \quad \{\ \text{definition of } \preccurlyeq \}$$
$$xs \preccurlyeq ys$$

The second claim is immediate if both xs and ys are the empty sequence. Otherwise we can argue

$$u : us \preccurlyeq v : vs \wedge ok\ x\ (v : vs)$$
$$\Rightarrow \quad \{\ \text{definition of } \preccurlyeq \text{ and } ok\ \}$$
$$u \geqslant v \wedge x < v$$
$$\Rightarrow \quad \{\ \text{definition of } ok\ \}$$
$$ok\ x\ (u : us)$$

Answer 11.4 No. We have $xs \preccurlyeq [\ ]$ for all xs, so the empty list would be removed by any thinning step.

Answer 11.5 The only change is to replace $>$ by $\geqslant$:

$$tstep\ x\ (xs : xss) = xs : search\ xs\ x\ xss$$
$$\textbf{where } search\ xs\ x\ [\ ] \qquad\quad = [x : xs]$$
$$search\ xs\ x\ (ys : xss)\ |\ head\ ys \geqslant x = ys : search\ ys\ x\ xss$$
$$\qquad\qquad\qquad\qquad\quad |\ otherwise \quad\ = (x : xs) : xss$$

Answer 11.6 The definition of *rmost* is

$rmost :: Tree\ [a] \rightarrow [a]$
$rmost\ (Node\ \_\ l\ xs\ Null) = xs$
$rmost\ (Node\ \_\ l\ xs\ r)\qquad = rmost\ r$

Answer 11.7 The definition of *pieces* is

$pieces\ x\ Null\ ps = ps$
$pieces\ x\ (Node\ \_\ l\ xs\ r)\ ps$
$\quad |\ null\ xs \vee (x < head\ xs) = pieces\ x\ r\ (LP\ l\ xs : ps)$
$\quad |\ otherwise\qquad\qquad = pieces\ x\ l\ (RP\ xs\ r : ps)$

Answer 11.8 The definition of *modify* is

$modify :: a \rightarrow (Tree\ [a], Tree\ [a]) \rightarrow Tree\ [a]$
$modify\ x\ (t_1, t_2) = combine\ t_1\ (replace\ (x : rmost\ t_1)\ t_2)$
$replace :: [a] \rightarrow Tree\ [a] \rightarrow Tree\ [a]$
$replace\ xs\ Null\qquad\qquad\quad = Node\ 1\ Null\ xs\ Null$
$replace\ xs\ (Node\ h\ Null\ ys\ r) = Node\ h\ Null\ xs\ r$
$replace\ xs\ (Node\ h\ l\ ys\ r)\qquad = Node\ h\ (replace\ xs\ l)\ ys\ r$

Answer 11.9 Here are possible definitions:

$encode\ xs\ ys = concatMap\ (posns\ ys)\ xs$
$posns\ ys\ x\quad = reverse\ [i\ |\ (i, y) \leftarrow zip\ [0..]\ ys, y == x]$
$decode\ us\ ys = pick\ us\ (zip\ [0..]\ ys)$
   where
      $pick\ [\,]\ pys\qquad\qquad\quad = [\,]$
      $pick\ (u : us)\ ((p, y) : pys) = \textbf{if}\ u == p\ \textbf{then}\ y : pick\ us\ pys$
                                       $\textbf{else}\ \ pick\ (u : us)\ pys$

Each upsequence of *encode xs ys* obviously decodes to a subsequence of *ys* of the same length since any list of increasing positions in *ys* corresponds to a subsequence of *ys*. Each upsequence also corresponds to a subsequence of *xs*, as we can see by defining

$decode_1\ us\ xs\ ys = pick\ us\ [(posns\ ys\ x, x)\ |\ x \leftarrow xs]$
   where
      $pick\ [\,]\qquad psxs\qquad\quad = [\,]$
      $pick\ (u : us)\ ((ps, x) : psxs) = \textbf{if}\ u \in ps\ \textbf{then}\ x : pick\ us\ psxs$
                                       $\textbf{else}\ \ pick\ (u : us)\ psxs$

Then $decode_1\ (lus\ (encode\ xs\ ys))\ xs\ ys$ decodes to a subsequence of *xs*.

Answer 11.10 The definition is

$$help\ p\ xs\ [\,] \quad = p$$
$$help\ p\ [\,]\ ys \quad = -1$$
$$help\ p\ (x:xs)\ (y:ys)$$
$$\quad |\ x == y \quad = help\ (p-1)\ xs\ ys$$
$$\quad |\ otherwise = help\ (p-1)\ xs\ (y:ys)$$

Answer 11.11 For the first condition it is sufficient to observe that

$$position\ xs\ ys \geqslant position\ xs\ zs$$

implies that *ys* is a subsequence of *xs* if *zs* is.

For the second condition we can prove that

$$position\ xs\ ys \geqslant position\ xs\ zs \ \Rightarrow\ position\ xs\ (y:ys) \geqslant position\ xs\ (y:zs)$$

by case analysis: either $position\ xs\ (y:zs) = -1$, in which case the result is immediate, or $position\ xs\ (y:zs) \geqslant 0$, in which case both $y:zs$ and $y:ys$ are subsequences of *xs* and the position of $y:ys$ is at least as large as the position of $y:zs$.

For the last part, we argue

$$ThinBy\ (\preccurlyeq)\ (step\ y\ yss)$$
$$=\quad \{\ \text{definition of }step\ \}$$
$$ThinBy\ (\preccurlyeq)\ (yss \mathbin{+\!\!+} filter\ (sub\ xs)\ (map\ (y:)\ yss))$$
$$=\quad \{\ \text{distributive law of }ThinBy\ \}$$
$$ThinBy\ (\preccurlyeq)\ (ThinBy\ (\preccurlyeq)\ yss \mathbin{+\!\!+}$$
$$\qquad\qquad ThinBy\ (\preccurlyeq)\ (filter\ (sub\ xs)\ (map\ (y:)\ yss)))$$
$$\rightarrow\quad \{\ \text{thin-filter law}\ \}$$
$$ThinBy\ (\preccurlyeq)\ (ThinBy\ (\preccurlyeq)\ yss \mathbin{+\!\!+}$$
$$\qquad\qquad filter\ (sub\ xs)\ (ThinBy\ (\preccurlyeq)\ (map\ (y:)\ yss)))$$
$$=\quad \{\ \text{thin-map law}\ \}$$
$$ThinBy\ (\preccurlyeq)\ (ThinBy\ (\preccurlyeq)\ yss \mathbin{+\!\!+}$$
$$\qquad\qquad filter\ (sub\ xs)\ (map\ (y:)\ (ThinBy\ (\preccurlyeq)\ yss)))$$
$$\rightarrow\quad \{\ \text{given }tstep\ y\ yss \leftarrow Thinby\ (\preccurlyeq)\ (step\ y\ yss)\ \}$$
$$tstep\ y\ (ThinBy\ (\preccurlyeq)\ yss)$$

Answer 11.12 We have

$$tails = scanr\ (\lambda x\ xs.\ [x] \mathbin{+\!\!+} xs)\ [\,]$$
$$inits = scanl\ (\lambda xs\ x.\ xs \mathbin{+\!\!+} [x])\ [\,]$$

Answer 11.13 Suppose $msp\ b\ xs = ys$ and suppose to the contrary that $x:ys$ is a proper prefix of $msp\ b\ (x:xs)$. That means

$$msp\ b\ (x:xs) = x:ys \mathbin{+\!\!+} zs$$

for some nonempty sequence *zs*. But

$$sum \; (ys + zs) = sum \; ys + sum \; zs \leqslant sum \; ys$$

by definition of $msp \; b \; xs$, and

$$x + sum \; ys < x + sum \; ys + sum \; zs$$

by definition of $msp \; b \; (x : xs)$, so $sum \; zs$ is both positive and negative, giving rise to a contradiction.

Answer 11.14 We have

$$msp \leftarrow MaxWith \; sum \cdot inits$$

We can find a greedy algorithm for msp, maintaining a prefix with maximum sum at each step. Tupling sum computations, we then have

$$msp \qquad = snd \cdot foldr \; step \; (0, [\,])$$
$$step \; x \; (s, xs) = \textbf{if } x + s > 0 \textbf{ then } (x + s, x : xs) \textbf{ else } (0, [\,])$$

And now

$$mss = snd \cdot maxWith \; fst \cdot scanr \; step \; (0, [\,])$$

Chapter 12

Partitions

By definition, a *partition* of a nonempty list is a division of the list into nonempty segments. For example, ["par", "tit", "i", "on"] is one partition of the string "partition". Partitions arise in a variety of problems. For instance, the segment problem of the previous chapter involved partitioning the prefixes of a list to achieve efficiency. In one version of Mergesort the input is partitioned into runs of non-decreasing elements before merging. In operations research, the scheduling of a sequence of activities can often be specified in terms of partitioning the activities. Partitions also arise in various data-compression and text-processing algorithms. In this chapter we will confine ourselves to just two examples. The first is a simple scheduling problem, while the second involves breaking paragraphs into lines.

12.1 Ways of generating partitions

First of all, let us look at some of the ways we can generate all the partitions of a list. A partition of a list of type $[A]$ has type $[[A]]$, so a list of partitions has type $[[[A]]]$. To improve readability, we introduce the type synonyms

type *Partition a* = [*Segment a*]
type *Segment a* = [*a*]

A list of partitions now has the more readable type [*Partition a*]. By definition, *xss* is a partition of *xs* just in the case that

$$concat\ xss = xs \ \wedge \ all\ (not \cdot null)\ xss$$

In particular, the empty list is the only partition of the empty list. The following recursive definition of *parts* can be derived from the specification above:

$$parts :: [a] \rightarrow [Partition\ a]$$
$$parts\ [] = [[]]$$
$$parts\ xs = [ys : yss \mid (ys, zs) \leftarrow splits\ xs, yss \leftarrow parts\ zs]$$

Each partition is generated by taking a nonempty prefix of the input list as the first segment, and then following it with a partition of the remaining suffix. The function *splits* splits a nonempty list *xs* into a pair of lists (ys, zs) such that *ys* is nonempty and $ys \mathbin{+\!\!+} zs = xs$:

$$splits :: [a] \rightarrow [([a], [a])]$$
$$splits\ [] \quad = []$$
$$splits\ (x:xs) = ([x], xs) : [(x:ys, zs) \mid (ys, zs) \leftarrow splits\ xs]$$

There are other ways of defining *parts*, including inductive definitions based on either *foldr* or *foldl*. One definition of *parts* in terms of *foldr* is

$$parts :: [a] \rightarrow [Partition\ a]$$
$$parts = foldr\ (concatMap \cdot extendl)\ [[]]$$

where *extendl* extends a partition on the left:

$$extendl :: a \rightarrow Partition\ a \rightarrow [Partition\ a]$$
$$extendl\ x\ [] \ = [cons\ x\ []]$$
$$extendl\ x\ p \ = [cons\ x\ p, glue\ x\ p]$$

$$cons, glue :: a \rightarrow Partition\ a \rightarrow Partition\ a$$
$$cons\ x\ p \quad = [x] : p$$
$$glue\ x\ (s:p) = (x:s) : p$$

The two ways of extending a nonempty partition with a new element on the left are to start a new segment, or to 'glue' the element onto the first segment, provided such a segment exists.

The corresponding definition of *parts* in terms of *foldl* is

$$parts :: [a] \rightarrow [Partition\ a]$$
$$parts = foldl\ (flip\ (concatMap \cdot extendr))\ [[]]$$

where, this time, *extendr* extends a partition on the right:

$$extendr :: a \rightarrow Partition\ a \rightarrow [Partition\ a]$$
$$extendr\ x\ [] = [snoc\ x\ []]$$
$$extendr\ x\ p \ = [snoc\ x\ p, bind\ x\ p]$$

$$snoc, bind :: a \rightarrow Partition\ a \rightarrow Partition\ a$$
$$snoc\ x\ p = p \mathbin{+\!\!+} [[x]]$$
$$bind\ x\ p = init\ p \mathbin{+\!\!+} [last\ p \mathbin{+\!\!+} [x]]$$

The functions *snoc* and *bind* are the dual variants of *cons* and *glue* (*bind* has the merit of being pronounceable, while *eulg* is not). Of course, *snoc* and *bind* do not take constant time, but we can deal with that problem as and when the need arises.

It seems like a free choice as to whether to use a definition of *parts* in terms of *foldr* or *foldl*, but for some problems the right choice is important. Many problems about partitions ask for a partition in which all of its component segments satisfy some property, *ok* say. Consider the task of proving that

$$filter\ (all\ ok) \cdot parts = foldr\ (concatMap \cdot okextendl)\ [[\ ]]$$

where the definition of *okextendl* – the *ok* left-extensions – is

$$okextendl\ x = filter\ (ok \cdot head) \cdot extendl\ x$$

The context-sensitive fusion condition is that

$$filter\ (all\ ok)\ (concatMap\ (extendl\ x)\ ps) =$$
$$concatMap\ (okextendl\ x)\ (filter\ (all\ ok)\ ps)$$

for all partitions *ps* of the same list. To prove it, one needs the assumption that *ok* is *suffix-closed*, meaning that, if *ok* $(xs + ys)$ holds, then so does *ok ys*. Details are left as an exercise. Dually, if we start out with the definition of *parts* in terms of *foldl*, then the required assumption is that *ok* is *prefix-closed*, meaning that *ok xs* holds if *ok* $(xs + ys)$ does. Many predicates, including those used in the following sections, are both prefix-closed and suffix-closed, so there is a free choice of which definition of *parts* to adopt. But sometimes only one of these properties holds, and that dictates the choice of definition for *parts*.

12.2 Managing two bank accounts

Our first problem is a simple example of a scheduling problem. It can be introduced in the following way. A certain individual, whom we will call Zakia, has two online bank accounts, a current account and a savings account. Zakia uses the current account only for a fixed and known sequence of transactions (deposits and withdrawals), such as salary, standing orders, and utility bills. For security reasons, Zakia never wants more than a certain amount C in her current account, where C is some fixed amount assumed to be at least as large as any single transaction. To maintain this security condition, Zakia wants to set up an automatic sequence of transfers between her current and deposit accounts so that at the beginning of each group of transactions money can be transferred into or out of the current account to cope with the next group of transactions. To minimise traffic, Zakia wants the number of such transfers to be as small as possible.

Abstractly stated, the problem is to find a shortest partition of a list of positive and negative integers into a list of *safe* segments. A segment $[x_1, x_2, ..., x_k]$ is safe if there is an amount r, the residue in the current account at the beginning of such a sequence, such that all of the sums

$$r,\ r + x_1,\ r + x_1 + x_2,\ ...,\ r + x_1 + x_2 + \cdots + x_k$$

lie between 0 and the given bound C. For example, if $C = 100$, the sequence $[-20, 40, 60, -30]$ is safe because we can take $r = 20$. But $[40, -50, 10, 80, 20]$

is not safe because r has to be at least 10 to cope with the first withdrawal and $10 + 40 - 50 + 10 + 80 + 20 = 110$, which is greater than C. It is left as an exercise to show that, if a segment is safe, then so is every prefix and suffix of the segment.

To simplify the safety condition, let m and n be the maximum and minimum of the sums $0, x_1, x_1 + x_2, ..., x_1 + x_2 + \cdots + x_k$, so $n \leqslant 0 \leqslant m$. Then it is required that there exists an r such that $0 \leqslant r + n \leqslant C$ and $0 \leqslant r + m \leqslant C$. These two conditions are equivalent to $m \leqslant C + n$ (see the exercises). Hence, supposing C is provided as a global value c, we can define

$$safe :: Segment\ Int \to Bool$$
$$safe\ xs = maximum\ sums \leqslant c + minimum\ sums$$
$$\textbf{where}\ sums = scanl\ (+)\ 0\ xs$$

The function msp (a minimum safe partition) can now be specified by

$$msp :: [Int] \to Partition\ Int$$
$$msp \leftarrow MinWith\ length \cdot filter\ (all\ safe) \cdot parts$$

The function msp returns a partition, not the sequence of transfers that have to be made between the two accounts. We will leave it as an exercise to show how the transfers can be computed from the final partition.

The first step in the standard recipe is to fuse the filter operation with the generation of partitions. Since $safe$ is both prefix-closed and suffix-closed, we can use either definition of $parts$. Choosing the definition of $parts$ in terms of $foldr$, we obtain

$$msp \leftarrow MinWith\ length \cdot safeParts$$

where $safeParts$ is defined by

$$safeParts\ \ \ \ = foldr\ (concatMap \cdot safeExtendl)\ [[]]$$
$$safeExtendl\ x = filter\ (safe \cdot head) \cdot extendl\ x$$

At each step only safe partitions are computed. It is assumed that every singleton transaction is safe, so a new transaction can always start a new segment. But it can only be glued to a segment if the result is safe, which means that the segment itself is also safe.

The next step in the recipe is to introduce thinning. Before doing so, we should first check whether or not a greedy algorithm is possible. Consider, for example, the transactions $[4, 4, 3, -3, 5]$. Taking $C = 10$, there are two safe partitions of shortest length, namely $[[4], [4, 3, -3, 5]]$ and $[[4, 4], [3, -3, 5]]$. While the former can be extended to a safe partition $[[5, 4], [4, 3, -3, 5]]$ of length 2 by gluing 5, the second one cannot, because $[5, 4, 4]$ is not a safe segment. It follows that we cannot get away with maintaining an arbitrary shortest safe partition. But that leaves open the possibility of a greedy algorithm with a modified cost function

$$cost\ p = (length\ p, length\ (head\ p))$$

In words, we may be able to maintain a shortest partition whose first segment is also as short as possible. Such a definition would be perfectly acceptable because minimising *cost* also minimises *length*. Recalling the standard calculation for a greedy algorithm, we can reason

$$
\begin{aligned}
& MinWith\ cost \cdot concatMap\ (safeExtendl\ x) \\
=\ & \{\ \text{distributing } MinWith\ cost\ \} \\
& MinWith\ cost \cdot map\ (MinWith\ cost \cdot safeExtendl\ x) \\
\rightarrow\ & \{\ \text{with } add\ x \leftarrow MinWith\ cost \cdot safeExtendl\ x\ \} \\
& MinWith\ cost \cdot map\ (add\ x) \\
\rightarrow\ & \{\ \text{greedy condition (see below)}\ \} \\
& add\ x \cdot MinWith\ cost
\end{aligned}
$$

The definition of *add* can be simplified to read

$$
\begin{aligned}
add\ x\ [] \quad &= [[x]] \\
add\ x\ (s:p) &= \textbf{if } safe\ (x:s) \textbf{ then } (x:s):p \textbf{ else } [x]:s:p
\end{aligned}
$$

In words, a partition with a cheaper cost is obtained by gluing rather than starting a new segment. The context-sensitive greedy condition holds if

$$
cost\ p_1 \leqslant cost\ p_2 \;\Rightarrow\; cost\ (add\ x\ p_1) \leqslant cost\ (add\ x\ p_2)
$$

for any two partitions p_1 and p_2 of the same list, all of whose segments are safe.

To see whether or not the greedy condition holds, consider the four possible values of $q_1 = add\ x\ p_1$ and $q_2 = add\ x\ p_2$, namely

$$
\begin{array}{lll}
q_1 = cons\ x\ p_1 & q_2 = cons\ x\ p_2 & \text{(12.1)} \\
q_1 = cons\ x\ p_1 & q_2 = glue\ x\ p_2 & \text{(12.2)} \\
q_1 = glue\ x\ p_1 & q_2 = cons\ x\ p_2 & \text{(12.3)} \\
q_1 = glue\ x\ p_1 & q_2 = glue\ x\ p_2 & \text{(12.4)}
\end{array}
$$

Firstly, suppose $|p_1| < |p_2|$, where, for brevity, $|p|$ abbreviates *length p*. Then $|q_1| < |q_2|$ except for case (12.2). But in this case we have $|q_1| \leqslant |q_2|$ and $|head\ q_1| < |head\ q_2|$, and therefore $cost\ q_1 \leqslant cost\ q_2$ for all values of q_1 and q_2.

Secondly, suppose $|p_1| = |p_2|$ and $|s_1| \leqslant |s_2|$, where $s_1 = head\ p_1$ and $s_2 = head\ p_2$. By the assumption that p_1 and p_2 are partitions into safe segments of the same list, it follows that s_1 is a prefix of s_2. Here case (12.2) cannot arise. In the remaining three cases it is easy to check that $cost\ q_1 \leqslant cost\ q_2$. So the greedy condition does indeed hold.

That means the following greedy algorithm solves the bank accounts problem:

$$
\begin{aligned}
& msp :: [Int] \rightarrow Partition\ Int \\
& msp = foldr\ add\ [] \\
& \qquad \textbf{where } add\ x\ [] \quad = [[x]] \\
& \qquad\qquad\quad add\ x\ (s:p) = \textbf{if } safe\ (x:s) \textbf{ then } (x:s):p \textbf{ else } [x]:s:p
\end{aligned}
$$

Ignoring the cost of computing *safe*, this is a linear-time algorithm. Computation of *safe* can be made to take constant time by tupling and is left as an exercise.

The lesson to be learned from the bank accounts problem is that it is as well to check whether a greedy algorithm is possible for a problem before embarking on an attack by thinning. But, out of interest, suppose we had gone ahead with a thinning strategy anyway. Then we would have

$$msp \leftarrow MinWith\ length \cdot ThinBy\ (\preccurlyeq) \cdot safeParts$$

where $\preccurlyeq$ has to be chosen so that

$$p_1 \preccurlyeq p_2 \ \Rightarrow\ length\ p_1 \leqslant length\ p_2$$

A sensible choice of $\preccurlyeq$ is the partial preorder

$$p_1 \preccurlyeq p_2 = length\ p_1 \leqslant length\ p_2 \ \wedge\ length\ (head\ p_1) \leqslant length\ (head\ p_2)$$

With this choice one can establish the fusion condition

$$ThinBy\ (\preccurlyeq) \cdot step\ x \rightarrow ThinBy\ (\preccurlyeq) \cdot step\ x \cdot ThinBy\ (\preccurlyeq)$$

where $step\ x = concatMap\ (safeExtendl\ x)$. Hence

$$msp = minWith\ length \cdot foldr\ tstep\ [[\,]]$$
$$\textbf{where}\ tstep\ x = thinBy\ (\preccurlyeq) \cdot concatMap\ (safeExtendl\ x)$$

This algorithm thins at each step. Moreover, one can prove by induction that, with the definition of *thinBy* given in Chapter 8, at most *two* partitions are kept at each stage. Therefore a thinning algorithm based on $\preccurlyeq$ will be almost as efficient as the greedy one.

There is another point of interest. Both the greedy algorithm and the thinning algorithm may return a schedule in which transfers occur before they seem necessary. For example, with $C = 100$ we obtain

$$msp\ [50, 20, 30, -10, 40, -90, -20, 60, 70, -40, 80]$$
$$= [[50], [20, 30, -10, 40, -90], [-20, 60], [70], [-40, 80]]$$

whereas the alternative solution

$$[[50, 20, 30, -10], [40, -90], [-20, 60], [70, -40], [80]]$$

also has length five and might seem less suspicious to any tracking software employed by Zakia's bank that might reasonably expect transfers to occur only when necessary. Exercise 12.12 asks for a solution to this problem.

12.3 The paragraph problem

The paragraph problem is the problem of splitting a text into lines in the best possible way. To begin with, we introduce the following type synonyms:

type *Text* = [*Word*]
type *Word* = [*Char*]
type *Para* = [*Line*]
type *Line* = [*Word*]

It is assumed that a text consists of a nonempty sequence of words, each word being a nonempty sequence of non-space characters. A paragraph therefore consists of at least one line.

The major constraint on paragraphs is that all lines have to fit into a specified width. For simplicity, we assume a single globally defined value *maxWidth* that gives the maximum width a line can possess. A reasonable generalisation, which we will not pursue, is to allow different lines to have different maximum widths. For example, paragraphs in newspapers often are arranged with varying widths to fit alongside pictures with varying contours. Instead we specify

$$para :: Text \rightarrow Para$$
$$para \leftarrow MinWith\ cost \cdot filter\ (all\ fits) \cdot parts$$

The function *fits* determines whether a line will fit into the required width:

$$fits :: Line \rightarrow Bool$$
$$fits\ line = width\ line \leqslant maxWidth$$

$$width :: Line \rightarrow Nat$$
$$width = foldrn\ add\ length\ \textbf{where}\ add\ w\ n = length\ w + 1 + n$$

The function *foldrn*, a general fold over nonempty lists, was defined in Chapter 8. The width of a line consisting of a single word is the length of the word, while the width of a line consisting of at least two words is the sum of the lengths of the words plus the number of inter-word spaces. This definition is appropriate when every character, including the space character, has the same width, but it can be adapted to fonts in which characters have different widths. It is assumed that no single word exceeds the maximum line width, so *para* is well-defined for every input.

It remains to define *cost* and to choose a definition of *parts* either in terms of *foldr* or in terms of *foldl*. The predicate *fits* is both prefix-closed and suffix-closed, so it seems like a free choice. However, if we use *foldr*, then we can arrive at solutions that, like Zakia's bank accounts problem, allow short first lines in order to ensure longer subsequent lines. The appearance of such a paragraph might appear strange, so we will use *foldl* instead.

That means we can fuse the filtering with the generation of partitions to arrive at

$$para \leftarrow MinWith\ cost \cdot fitParts$$

where

$$fitParts = foldl\ (flip\ (concatMap \cdot fitExtend))\ [[[]]]$$
$$\textbf{where}\ fitExtend\ x = filter\ (fits \cdot last) \cdot extendr\ x$$

Only those partitions whose lines fit into the maximum width are generated at each step.

Finally, how should we define the cost of a paragraph? There are at least five reasonable answers. Firstly, we could define

$$cost_1 = length$$

Here a best possible paragraph is one with the fewest lines. We could also define

$$cost_2 = sum \cdot map\ waste \cdot init$$
$$\textbf{where}\ waste\ line = maxWidth - width\ line$$

Here the cost of a paragraph is the sum of the waste of each line, taken over all lines except the very last (where wasted space does not detract from the appearance). A third definition sums the squares of the wasted space:

$$cost_3 = sum \cdot map\ waste \cdot init$$
$$\textbf{where}\ waste\ line = (optWidth - width\ line)^2$$

The definition depends on another globally defined constant $optWidth$, whose value is at most $maxWidth$ and which specifies the optimum width of each line of a paragraph. With this version, which is similar to the one used in TEX, lines that deviate only a little from the optimum width are penalised less heavily than with $cost_2$. Finally, two more definitions of $cost$ are

$$cost_4 = foldr\ max\ 0 \cdot map\ waste \cdot init$$
$$\textbf{where}\ waste\ line = maxWidth - width\ line$$

$$cost_5 = foldr\ max\ 0 \cdot map\ waste \cdot init$$
$$\textbf{where}\ waste\ line = (optWidth - width\ line)^2$$

Here it is the maximum waste that is minimised. Use of $foldr\ max\ 0$ rather than $maximum$ is needed to ensure that the cost of a paragraph consisting of a single line is zero. The last four definitions of cost assume that a paragraph is a nonempty sequence of lines ($init$ is undefined on an empty list), but we can also set the cost of an empty paragraph to zero.

There is an obvious greedy algorithm for the paragraph problem:

$$greedy = foldl\ add\ [\ ]$$
$$\textbf{where}\ add\ [\ ]\ w = snoc\ w\ [\ ]$$
$$add\ p\ w\ = head\ (filter\ (fits \cdot last)\ [bind\ w\ p, snoc\ w\ p])$$

The algorithm works by adding each word to the end of the last line of the current paragraph until no more words will fit, in which case a new line is started. A more efficient version is discussed in the exercises. This algorithm is essentially the one used by Microsoft Word and many other word processors.

So, for which definition of $cost$ does the greedy algorithm work? The answer is that *cost* has to satisfy two properties. Firstly, provided the result fits, adding a new word to the end of a line is never worse than starting a new line:

$$\textit{fits} \; (\textit{last} \; (\textit{bind} \; w \; p)) \;\;\Rightarrow\;\; \textit{cost} \; (\textit{bind} \; w \; p) \leqslant \textit{cost} \; (\textit{snoc} \; w \; p)$$

Secondly, as should be familiar by now, the greedy condition

$$\textit{cost} \; p_1 \leqslant \textit{cost} \; p_2 \;\;\Rightarrow\;\; \textit{cost} \; (\textit{add} \; p_1 \; w) \leqslant \textit{cost} \; (\textit{add} \; p_2 \; w)$$

should hold. The greedy condition does not hold when the cost of a paragraph is simply the number of lines (see the exercises), but it does if we strengthen this measure by redefining $cost_1$ to read

$$cost_1 \; p = (\textit{length} \; p, \textit{width} \; (\textit{last} \; p))$$

That is to say, a best paragraph is one that minimises the number of lines and, among such paragraphs, one that has a shortest last line. The proof is similar to the one in the bank accounts problem. As in the previous proof, let $q_1 = \textit{add} \; p_1 \; w$ and $q_2 = \textit{add} \; p_2 \; w$. There are four possible cases:

$$q_1 = \textit{bind} \; w \; p_1 \qquad q_2 = \textit{bind} \; w \; p_2 \tag{12.5}$$

$$q_1 = \textit{bind} \; w \; p_1 \qquad q_2 = \textit{snoc} \; w \; p_2 \tag{12.6}$$

$$q_1 = \textit{snoc} \; w \; p_1 \qquad q_2 = \textit{bind} \; w \; p_2 \tag{12.7}$$

$$q_1 = \textit{snoc} \; w \; p_1 \qquad q_2 = \textit{snoc} \; w \; p_2 \tag{12.8}$$

Suppose $cost_1 \; p_1 \leqslant cost_1 \; p_2$. Firstly, if $|p_1| < |p_2|$, where again $|p|$ abbreviates *length* p, then $|q_1| < |q_2|$ except in case (12.7). But in case (12.7) we have

$$|q_1| \leqslant |q_2| \;\wedge\; \textit{width} \; (\textit{last} \; q_1) < \textit{width} \; (\textit{last} \; q_2)$$

which implies $cost_1 \; q_1 < cost_1 \; q_2$. Secondly, suppose

$$|p_1| = |p_2| \;\wedge\; \textit{width} \; (\textit{last} \; p_1) \leqslant \textit{width} \; (\textit{last} \; p_2)$$

Here, case (12.7) cannot arise. In cases (12.5) and (12.8) we have

$$|q_1| = |q_2| \;\wedge\; \textit{width} \; (\textit{last} \; q_1) = \textit{width} \; (\textit{last} \; q_2)$$

while in case (12.6) we have $|q_1| < |q_2|$. So $cost_1 \; q_1 \leqslant cost_1 \; q_2$ in all cases. The greedy algorithm therefore minimises the number of lines in a paragraph.

The greedy algorithm also works for $cost_2$, the cost function that sums the waste of each line except the last. We claim that

$$cost_1 \; p_1 \leqslant cost_1 \; p_2 \;\;\Rightarrow\;\; cost_2 \; p_1 \leqslant cost_2 \; p_2$$

For the proof, suppose p_1 consists of the lines $[l_{1,1}, l_{1,2}, ..., l_{1,k}]$, with $w_{1,j}$ as the width of $l_{1,j}$. Then, abbreviating *maxWidth* to M, we have

$$cost_2 \; p_1 = (M - w_{1,1}) + (M - w_{1,2}) + \cdots + (M - w_{1,k-1})$$
$$= (k-1) \, M - (T - (w_{1,k} + k - 1))$$

where T is the total width of the text. Thus $(T - (w_{1,k} + k - 1))$ is the sum of the widths of all lines except the last because $k-1$ inter-word spaces are replaced by newlines. Similarly, if p_2 consists of the lines $[l_{2,1}, l_{2,2}, ..., l_{2,m}]$, then

$$cost_2\ p_2 = (m-1)\ M - (T - (w_{2,m} + m - 1))$$

Suppose $cost_1\ p_1 \leqslant cost_1\ p_2$, so $(k, w_{1,k}) \leqslant (m, w_{2,m})$. If $k < m$, then

$$cost_2\ p_2 \geqslant cost_2\ p_1 + M + w_{2,m} - w_{1,k} > cost_2\ p_1$$

because $w_{1,k} < M$. If, on the other hand, $k = m$ and $w_{1,k} \leqslant w_{2,m}$, then

$$cost_2\ p_2 = cost_2\ p_1 + w_{2,m} - w_{1,k} \geqslant cost_2\ p_1$$

In either case we have $cost_2\ p_1 \leqslant cost_2\ p_2$.

However, the greedy algorithm does not work for the other definitions of cost described above. Take $maxWidth = 10$ and $optWidth = 8$ and consider the two partitions

$$p_1 = [[w_6, w_1], [w_5, w_3], [w_4], [w_7]]$$
$$p_2 = [[w_6], [w_1, w_5], [w_3, w_4], [w_7]]$$

in which $length\ w_i = i$ for each word w_i. The partition p_1 is the one returned by the greedy algorithm. We have

$$cost_3\ p_1 = sum\ [(8-8)^2, (8-9)^2, (8-4)^2] = 17$$
$$cost_3\ p_2 = sum\ [(8-6)^2, (8-7)^2, (8-8)^2] = 5$$

$$cost_4\ p_1 = maximum\ [10-8, 10-9, 10-4] = 6$$
$$cost_4\ p_2 = maximum\ [10-6, 10-7, 10-8] = 4$$

$$cost_5\ p_1 = maximum\ [8-8, 8-9, 8-4]\quad = 4$$
$$cost_5\ p_2 = maximum\ [8-6, 8-7, 8-8]\quad = 2$$

With all these measures of cost, p_2 is a better partition than p_1, so the greedy algorithm does not lead to the best solution. That means we need a thinning algorithm for these particular cost functions.

More generally, we will describe a thinning algorithm for any *admissible* cost function, meaning that if

$$cost\ p_1 \leqslant cost\ p_2\ \wedge\ width\ (last\ p_1) = width\ (last\ p_2)$$

then

$$cost\ (bind\ w\ p_1) \leqslant cost\ (bind\ w\ p_2)\ \wedge\ cost\ (snoc\ w\ p_1) \leqslant cost\ (snoc\ w\ p_2)$$

As can easily be checked, all the cost functions introduced above are admissible cost functions.

Suppose p_1 and p_2 satisfy these two conditions. Then for any completion

$$q_2 = init\ p_2 + [last\ p_2 + [l_0]] + [l_1] + \cdots + [l_k]$$

of p_2 to a full paragraph, there is a similar completion

$$q_1 = init\ p_1 + [last\ p_1 + [l_0]] + [l_1] + \cdots + [l_k]$$

of p_1. Moreover, $cost\ q_1 \leqslant cost\ q_2$. Hence the partial paragraph p_2 can never lead to a better solution than p_1 and can be eliminated from the computation. Note carefully that this conclusion depends on the last lines of p_1 and p_2 having *equal* widths: if the last line of p_1 had width smaller than that of p_2, then every valid completion of p_2 remains a valid completion of p_1, but the cost of the latter may not be smaller than the cost of the former.

Taken together, all of this means thinning with $\preccurlyeq$ is appropriate, where

$$p_1 \preccurlyeq p_2 = cost\ p_1 \leqslant cost\ p_2 \ \wedge \ width\ (last\ p_1) == width\ (last\ p_2)$$

However, instead of using *thinWith* $(\preccurlyeq)$ we can customise the thinning step by keeping the list of partitions *ps* in increasing order of width of last line. Then the partitions in *map* (*bind w*) *ps* are also in this order. Moreover, the partitions in *map* (*snoc w*) *ps* all have the same last line, the shortest one possible. Thinning this list means retaining only the single partition

$$minWith\ cost\ (map\ (snoc\ w)\ ps)$$

when beginning a new line. Therefore thinning can be implemented by the following definition:

$$para = minWith\ cost \cdot foldl\ tstep\ [[\,]]$$
$$\textbf{where}\ tstep\ [[\,]]\ w = [[[w]]]$$
$$tstep\ ps\ w\ = minWith\ cost\ (map\ (snoc\ w)\ ps):$$
$$filter\ (fits \cdot last)\ (map\ (bind\ w)\ ps)$$

It is easy to see that at most $M = maxWidth$ partitions are kept in play at each step, since no last line can have width more than M. We will leave it to the exercises to show how to memoise *cost* and *width*, and how to implement *snoc* and *bind* efficiently, so that *tstep* takes $O(M)$ steps. Hence the paragraph problem for n words takes $O(M\,n)$ steps. It is possible with a more sophisticated algorithm to eliminate the dependence of this bound on M for certain definitions of cost, but we will not go into the details.

12.4 Chapter notes

The problem of managing two bank accounts is an updated reworking of the security van problem invented by Hans Zantema and discussed in Section 7.5 of [2]. There are many articles on the paragraph problem, including two, [1] and [3], written by ourselves. In [3] it is shown how to remove the dependence on the maximum line width in the running time for some definitions of cost. For a thorough discussion of the line-breaking algorithm used in TEX see [4].

References

[1] Richard S. Bird. Transformational programming and the paragraph problem. *Science of Computer Programming*, 6(2):159–189, 1986.

[2] Richard S. Bird and Oege de Moor. *The Algebra of Programming*. Prentice-Hall, Hemel Hempstead, 1997.

[3] Oege de Moor and Jeremy Gibbons. Bridging the algorithm gap: A linear-time functional program for paragraph formatting. *Science of Computer Programming*, 35(1):3–27, 1999.

[4] Donald E. Knuth and Michael F. Plass. Breaking paragraphs into lines. *Software: Practice and Experience*, 11(11):1119–1184, 1981.

Exercises

Exercise 12.1 How many partitions of a list of length $n > 0$ are there?

Exercise 12.2 Why is the clause *parts* $[] = [[]]$ necessary in the first definition of *parts*?

Exercise 12.3 Give another definition of *parts* in terms of *foldr*, one that at each step does all the *cons* operations before the *glue* operations.

Exercise 12.4 Give the details of the proof that

$$\textit{filter } (\textit{all ok}) \cdot \textit{parts} = \textit{foldr } (\textit{concatMap} \cdot \textit{okextendl}) \, [[\,]]$$

provided *ok* is suffix-closed. (Hint: it is probably best to express the fusion condition in terms of list comprehensions.)

Exercise 12.5 Which of the following predicates on nonempty sequences of positive numbers are prefix-closed and which are suffix-closed?

$$\begin{aligned}
\textit{leftmin xs} \ \ &= \textit{all } (\textit{head xs} \leqslant) \, \textit{xs} \\
\textit{rightmax xs} &= \textit{all } (\leqslant \textit{last xs}) \, \textit{xs} \\
\textit{ordered xs} \ \ &= \textit{and } (\textit{zipWith } (\leqslant) \, \textit{xs } (\textit{tail xs})) \\
\textit{nomatch xs} \ &= \textit{and } (\textit{zipWith } (\neq) \, \textit{xs } [0..])
\end{aligned}$$

Do each of these predicates hold for singleton lists?

Exercise 12.6 Suppose that $n \leqslant 0 \leqslant m$. Show that

$$(\exists r : 0 \leqslant r + n \leqslant C \wedge 0 \leqslant r + m \leqslant C) \ \Leftrightarrow \ m \leqslant C + n$$

Exercise 12.7 Show that the predicate *safe* in the bank accounts problem is both prefix-closed and suffix-closed.

Exercise 12.8 Suppose $C = 10$. What is the value of $msp\ [2,4,50,3]$ when msp is the greedy algorithm for the bank accounts problem and when msp is defined by the original specification?

Exercise 12.9 The function add in the bank accounts problem does not take constant time because the safety test can take linear time. But we can represent a partition p by a triple

$$(p, minimum\ (sums\ (head\ p)), maximum\ (sums\ (head\ p)))$$

where $sums = scanl\ (+)\ 0$. Write down a new definition of msp that does take linear time.

Exercise 12.10 The function msp returns a partition, not the transfers that have to be made to keep the current account in balance. Show how to define

$$transfers :: Partition\ Int \rightarrow [Int]$$

by computing a pair (n, r) of nonnegative numbers for each segment, where n is the minimum that has to be in the current account to ensure the segment is safe and r is the residue after the transactions in the segment.

Exercise 12.11 Consider the thinning algorithm for the bank accounts problem. Suppose that at some point in the computation there are two partitions of the form $[y]:ys:p$ and $(y:ys):p$. This could happen as early as the second step, producing the partitions $[[y],[z]]$ and $[[y,z]]$. Show that adding in a new element x and thinning the result will produce either a single partition, or two partitions of the above form.

Exercise 12.12 How can Zakia address the suspicious feature of the given solution to the bank accounts problem, namely that transfers can occur before they are absolutely necessary?

Exercise 12.13 The function $runs$ used in Mergesort is specified by

$$runs :: Ord\ a \Rightarrow [a] \rightarrow Partition\ a$$
$$runs \leftarrow MinWith\ length \cdot filter\ (all\ ordered) \cdot parts$$

Without looking back to the section on Mergesort, write down a greedy algorithm for computing $runs$. Why does the greedy algorithm work?

Exercise 12.14 Show that the greedy condition fails when the cost of a paragraph is simply the number of lines.

Exercise 12.15 The greedy algorithm for the paragraph problem can be made more efficient in two steps. This exercise deals with the first step and the following exercise with the second step. Consider the function $help$ specified by

$$p +\!\!+ help\ l\ ws = foldl\ add\ (p +\!\!+ [l])\ ws$$

Prove that

$$greedy\ (w:ws) = help\ [w]\ ws$$
$$\textbf{where}\ help\ l\ [\ ] \qquad = [l]$$
$$help\ l\ (w:ws) = \textbf{if}\ width\ l' \leqslant maxWidth$$
$$\textbf{then}\ help\ l'\ ws\ \textbf{else}\ l:help\ [w]\ ws$$
$$\textbf{where}\ l' = l +\!\!+ [w]$$

Exercise 12.16 For the second step, memoise *width* and eliminate the concatenation with the help of an accumulating function parameter.

Exercise 12.17 In the thinning version of the paragraph problem, can we replace *filter* by *takeWhile*?

Exercise 12.18 Show that the cost functions described in the text for the paragraph problem are all admissible.

Exercise 12.19 With some admissible cost functions, the thinning algorithm may select a paragraph with minimum cost but whose length is not as short as possible. How can this deficiency be overcome?

Exercise 12.20 The refinement

$$snoc\ w \cdot MinWith\ cost \leftarrow MinWith\ cost \cdot map\ (snoc\ w)$$

follows from the condition

$$cost\ p_1 \leqslant cost\ p_2 \quad \Rightarrow \quad cost\ (snoc\ w\ p_1) \leqslant cost\ (snoc\ w\ p_2)$$

Does this condition hold for $cost_3$?

Exercise 12.21 Suppose we had gone for a right-to-left thinning algorithm for the paragraph problem, using a definition of *parts* based on *foldr*. This time a cost function is admissible if

$$cost\ (glue\ w\ p_1) \leqslant cost\ (glue\ w\ p_2) \quad \wedge \quad cost\ (cons\ w\ p_1) \leqslant cost\ (cons\ w\ p_2)$$

provided that

$$cost\ p_1 \leqslant cost\ p_2 \quad \wedge \quad width\ (head\ p_1) = width\ (head\ p_2)$$

As can be checked, all five cost functions introduced in the text are admissible in this sense. Write down the associated thinning algorithm. Give an example to show that the two different thinning algorithms produce different results for $cost_3$.

Exercise 12.22 The final exercise is to make the thinning algorithm for the paragraph problem more efficient. Setting $rmr = reverse \cdot map\ reverse$, we can represent a paragraph p by a triple

$$(rmr\ p, cost\ p, width\ (last\ p))$$

The last two components memoise $cost$ and $width$, while the first component means that $snoc$ and $bind$ can be implemented in terms of $cons$ and $glue$. More precisely, we have

$$snoc\ w \cdot rmr = rmr \cdot cons\ w$$
$$bind\ w \cdot rmr = rmr \cdot glue\ w$$

Write down the resulting algorithm, assuming the cost function is $cost_3$.

Answers

Answer 12.1 There are 2^{n-1} partitions.

Answer 12.2 Because with the single clause

$$parts\ xs = [ys:yss \mid (ys,zs) \leftarrow splits\ xs, yss \leftarrow parts\ zs]$$

we would have $parts\ [] = []$, from which it follows that $parts\ xs = []$ for all xs.

Answer 12.3 The definition is

$$parts = foldr\ step\ [[]]$$
$$\mathbf{where}\ step\ x\ [[]] = [[[x]]]$$
$$step\ x\ ps\ = map\ (cons\ x)\ ps \mathbin{+\!\!+} map\ (glue\ x)\ ps$$

Answer 12.4 In terms of list comprehensions, the fusion condition takes the form

$$[p' \mid p \leftarrow ps, p' \leftarrow extendl\ x\ p, all\ ok\ p']$$
$$= [p' \mid p \leftarrow ps, all\ ok\ p, p' \leftarrow extendl\ x\ p, ok\ (head\ p')]$$

for all partitions ps of the same list. With the given definition of $extendl$, the fusion condition follows if we can show that

$$[cons\ x\ p \mid p \leftarrow ps, all\ ok\ (cons\ x\ p)]$$
$$= [cons\ x\ p \mid p \leftarrow ps, all\ ok\ p \wedge ok\ (head\ (cons\ x\ p))]$$
$$[glue\ x\ (s:p) \mid s:p \leftarrow ps, all\ ok\ (glue\ x\ (s:p))]$$
$$= [glue\ x\ (s:p) \mid s:p \leftarrow ps, all\ ok\ (s:p) \wedge ok\ (head\ (glue\ x\ (s:p)))]$$

Since $cons\ x\ p = [x]:p$ and

$$all\ ok\ ([x]:p) = all\ ok\ p \wedge ok\ [x]$$

the first condition holds. Since $glue\ x\ (s:p) = (x:s):p$ and, provided ok is suffix-closed, we have

$$all \; ok \; ((x:s):p) = all \; ok \; p \wedge ok \; (x:s)$$
$$= all \; ok \; p \wedge ok \; s \wedge ok \; (x:s)$$
$$= all \; ok \; (s:p) \wedge ok \; (x:s)$$

the second condition holds.

Answer 12.5 The predicates *leftmin* and *nomatch* are prefix-closed but not suffix-closed, while *rightmax* is suffix-closed but not prefix-closed. Finally, *ordered* is both prefix-closed and suffix-closed. All predicates hold for singletons (in the case of *nomatch* no positive integer is 0).

Answer 12.6 We can reason

$$(\exists r : 0 \leqslant r+n \leqslant C \wedge 0 \leqslant r+m \leqslant C)$$
$$\Leftrightarrow \quad \{ \text{ arithmetic } \}$$
$$(\exists r : -n \leqslant r \leqslant C-n \wedge -m \leqslant r \leqslant C-m)$$
$$\Leftrightarrow \quad \{ \text{ arithmetic } \}$$
$$(\exists r : max \; (-n) \; (-m) \leqslant r \leqslant min \; (C-n) \; (C-m))$$
$$\Leftrightarrow \quad \{ \text{ assuming } n \leqslant 0 \leqslant m \}$$
$$(\exists r : -n \leqslant r \leqslant C-m)$$
$$\Leftrightarrow \quad \{ \text{ logic } \}$$
$$m \leqslant C+n$$

Answer 12.7 If all the sums $r, r+x_1, r+x_1+x_2, ..., r+x_1+x_2+\cdots+x_k$ lie between 0 and C, then certainly every prefix of these sums does too. Taking $r' = r+x_1$, we have that all the sums $r', r'+x_2, ..., r'+x_2+\cdots+x_k$ also lie between 0 and C, so *safe* is suffix-closed as well as prefix-closed.

Answer 12.8 For the greedy algorithm we have

$$msp \; [2,4,50,3] = [[2,4],[50],[3]]$$

but for the original specification the answer is the undefined value. Since the segment [50] is not safe, there is no partition into safe segments.

Answer 12.9 We have

$$msp = part \cdot foldr \; add \; ([],0,0)$$
where
$$part \; (p,n,m) = p$$
$$add \; x \; pnm \; | \; null \; (part \; pnm) \quad = cons \; x \; pnm$$
$$\qquad\qquad\quad | \; safe \; (glue \; x \; pnm) = glue \; x \; pnm$$
$$\qquad\qquad\quad | \; otherwise \qquad\qquad = cons \; x \; pnm$$
$$cons \; x \; (p,n,m) \quad = ([x]:p, min \; 0 \; x, max \; 0 \; x)$$
$$glue \; x \; (s:p,n,m) = ((x:s):p, min \; 0 \; (x+n), max \; 0 \; (x+m))$$
$$safe \; (p,n,m) \qquad = max \; 0 \; (-n) \leqslant min \; c \; (c-m)$$

Answer 12.10 The values (n,r) for the segments in a partition can be computed by the function *endpoints*, where

$$endpoints :: [Int] \rightarrow (Int, Int)$$
$$endpoints\ xs = \textbf{if}\ n < 0\ \textbf{then}\ (-n, x - n)\ \textbf{else}\ (0, x)$$
$$\textbf{where}\ n\quad = minimum\ sums$$
$$x\quad = last\ sums$$
$$sums = scanl\ (+)\ 0\ xs$$

For example,

$$map\ endpoints\ [[40, -85, 55], [-32, 79], [80], [-21, 80]]$$
$$= [(45, 55), (32, 79), (0, 80), (21, 80)]$$

The current account has to have a balance of 45 to ensure the first segment is safe. At the end of the segment we can transfer $55 - 32$ to the savings account to ensure a credit of 32 for the next segment; and so on. Hence we can define

$$transfers = collect \cdot map\ endpoints$$
$$collect :: [(Int, Int)] \rightarrow [Int]$$
$$collect\ xys = zipWith\ (-)\ (map\ fst\ xys + [0])\ ([0] + map\ snd\ xys)$$

For example,

$$collect\ [(45, 55), (32, 79), (0, 80), (21, 80)] = [45, -23, -79, -59, -80]$$

Assuming a zero balance at the beginning, 45 has to be transferred to the current account to ensure the first segment is safe; the remaining amounts are what can be transferred to the deposit account at the end of each segment, leaving a zero balance in the current account at the end of all the transactions.

Answer 12.11 After adding x, there are three possible lists of partitions that can result:

$$[[x] : [y] : ys : p, [x, y] : ys : p, [x] : (y : ys) : p, (x : y : ys) : p]$$
$$[[x] : [y] : ys : p, [x, y] : ys : p, [x] : (y : ys) : p]$$
$$[[x] : [y] : ys : p, [x] : (y : ys) : p]$$

Furthermore,

$$[x] : (y : ys) : p \preccurlyeq [x] : [y] : ys : p$$
$$[x] : (y : ys) : p \preccurlyeq [x, y] : ys : p$$

Hence, after thinning by *thinBy* the following partitions are left in each case:

$$[[x] : (y : ys) : p, (x : y : ys) : p]$$
$$[[x] : (y : ys) : p]$$
$$[[x] : (y : ys) : p]$$

The first pair of partitions also has the same form as in the question, so at most two partitions are generated at each step.

Answer 12.12 The obvious answer is for Zakia to use a greedy algorithm that processes from left to right:

$$msp = foldl\ add\ [\ ]$$
$$\textbf{where}\ add\ [\ ]\ x = [[x]]$$
$$add\ p\ x\ = head\ (filter\ (safe \cdot last)\ [bind\ x\ p, snoc\ x\ p])$$

The answer to Exercise 12.15 shows how to make this version efficient. The validity of the left-to-right algorithm depends on the fact that *safe* is prefix-closed.

Answer 12.13 The definition is

$$runs :: Ord\ a \Rightarrow [a] \rightarrow Partition\ a$$
$$runs = foldr\ add\ [\ ]$$
$$\textbf{where}\ add\ x\ [\ ]\quad = [[x]]$$
$$add\ x\ (s:p) = \textbf{if}\ ordered\ (x:s)\ \textbf{then}\ (x:s):p\ \textbf{else}\ [x]:s:p$$

The greedy algorithm works because exactly the same reasoning as in the bank accounts problem applies, with *safe* replaced by *ordered*. Furthermore, the test in the definition of *add* can be simplified to $x \leqslant head\ s$.

Answer 12.14 Take $maxWidth = 10$ and consider the two paragraphs

$$p_1 = [[6,1],[5,3],[4]]$$
$$p_2 = [[6],[1,5],[3,4]]$$

both of which have the same length. We have

$$add\ 4\ p_1 = [[6,1],[5,3],[4,4]]$$
$$add\ 4\ p_2 = [[6],[1,5],[3,4],[4]]$$

so the greedy condition fails.

Answer 12.15 We have

$$foldl\ add\ (p + [l])\ [\ ] = p + [l]$$

so $help\ l\ [\ ] = [l]$. Next, if $add\ p\ w = bind\ w\ p$, then we have

$$foldl\ add\ (p + [l])\ (w:ws) = foldl\ add\ (p + [l + [w]])\ ws$$

which shows that $help\ l\ (w:ws) = help\ (l + [w])\ ws$. Finally, if $add\ p\ w = snoc\ w\ p$, then

$$foldl\ add\ (p + [l])\ (w:ws) = foldl\ add\ (p + [l] + [[w]])\ ws$$

which shows that $help\ l\ (w:ws) = l:help\ [w]\ ws$.

Answer 12.16 The result is

$$greedy\ (w:ws) = help\ ((w:), length\ w)\ ws$$
$$\textbf{where}$$
$$\quad help\ (f, d_1)\ [\,] \qquad = [f\ [\,]]$$
$$\quad help\ (f, d_1)\ (w:ws)$$
$$\qquad |\ d_2 \leqslant maxWidth = help\ (f \cdot (w:), d_2)\ ws$$
$$\qquad |\ otherwise \qquad = f\ [\,] : help\ ((w:), d)\ ws$$
$$\qquad \textbf{where}\ d_2 = d_1 + 1 + d; d = length\ w$$

Answer 12.17 Yes, the paragraphs are in increasing width of last line, so testing can be abandoned as soon as a last line does not fit.

Answer 12.18 The first inequality holds because $cost\ (bind\ w\ p) = cost\ p$. For the second inequality we have

$$cost\ (snoc\ w\ p) = cost\ p \oplus waste\ (last\ p)$$

where $\oplus$ is either $+$ or max. The result follows because $\oplus$ is monotonic and the waste of a line depends only on its width.

Answer 12.19 Define a new cost function $cost'\ p = (cost\ p, length\ p)$. The function $cost'$ is admissible if $cost$ is.

Answer 12.20 No. Take the two paragraphs

$$p_1 = [[6,1],[5,3],[4]]$$
$$p_2 = [[6],[1,5],[3,4]]$$

whose costs, assuming $maxWidth = 10$ and $optWidth = 8$, are 1 and 5 respectively. We have

$$cost_3\ (snoc\ 4\ p_1) = cost_3\ [[6,1],[5,3],[4],[4]] = 17$$
$$cost_3\ (snoc\ 4\ p_2) = cost_3\ [[6],[1,5],[3,4],[4]] = 5$$

Answer 12.21 The thinning algorithm is

$$para = minWith\ cost \cdot foldr\ tstep\ [[\,]]$$
$$\quad \textbf{where}\ tstep\ w\ [[\,]] = [[[w]]]$$
$$\qquad tstep\ w\ ps \qquad = cons\ w\ (minWith\ cost\ ps):$$
$$\qquad\qquad\qquad\qquad filter\ (fits \cdot head)\ (map\ (glue\ w)\ ps)$$

Take $maxWidth = optWidth = 16$. Here is just one example that shows different outputs:

```
Here is just              Here is just one
one example that          example that
shows different           shows different
outputs:                  outputs:
```

The paragraph on the left was produced by the right-to-left algorithm, while the one on the right was produced by the left-to-right one. The widths of the first layout are $[12, 16, 15, 8]$ while those of the second are $[16, 12, 15, 8]$ so the costs are the same.

Answer 12.22 The algorithm is

$para = thePara \cdot minWith\ cost \cdot thinparts$
   where

$thePara\ (p, \_, \_) = reverse\ (map\ reverse\ p)$

$cost\ (\_, c, \_)\quad = c$

$ok\ (\_, \_, k)\qquad = k \leqslant maxWidth$

$thinparts\ (w : ws) = foldl\ step\ (start\ w)\ ws$

$start\ w\qquad\qquad = [([[w]], 0, length\ w)]$

$step\ ps\ w\qquad\quad = minWith\ cost\ (map\ (snoc\ w)\ ps):$
$\qquad\qquad\qquad\quad takeWhile\ ok\ (map\ (bind\ w)\ ps)$

$snoc\ w\ (p, c, k)\ = (cons\ w\ p, c + (optWidth - k)^2, length\ w)$

$bind\ w\ (p, c, k)\ = (glue\ w\ p, c, k + 1 + length\ w)$

PART FIVE

DYNAMIC PROGRAMMING

The term *Dynamic Programming* was coined by Richard Bellman in 1950 to describe his research into multi-stage decision processes. The word *programming* was chosen as a synonym for *planning* to mean the process of determining the sequence of decisions that have to be made, while *dynamic* suggested the evolution of the system over time. These days, dynamic programming as a technique of algorithm design means something much more specific. It involves a two-stage process in which a problem, usually but not necessarily an optimisation problem, is formulated in recursive terms and then some efficient way of computing the solution is found. Unlike a divide-and-conquer problem, the subproblems generated by the recursive solution can overlap, so naive execution of the recursive algorithm will involve solving the same subproblem many times over, possibly an exponential number of times.

One way to understand the problem of overlap is to look at the *dependency graph* associated with a recursive function. This is a directed graph whose vertices represent function calls and whose directed edges show the dependency of each call on recursive calls. While the dependency graph of a divide-and-conquer algorithm is a tree of some kind with no shared vertices, the graph of a dynamic programming algorithm is an acyclic directed graph, possibly with many shared vertices. A vertex is shared if there is more than one incoming edge to the vertex.

The first job in solving an optimisation problem by dynamic programming is simply to obtain a recursive solution. As with thinning algorithms, the key step is to exploit a suitable monotonicity condition. This condition enables an optimal solution to a problem to be expressed in terms of optimal sub-solutions. When the shape of the recursion is inductive, a thinning algorithm is appropriate; when it is not, the techniques of dynamic programming come into play.

Having obtained a recursive description of the solution, there are basically two ways to ensure that sub-solutions are not computed more than once. One is called *memoisation*. Here the recursive, top-down structure of the computation is preserved but sub-solutions are remembered and stored in a table for subsequent retrieval. Thus at each recursive call one first checks to see whether the call has been made before, in which case the solution is retrieved from the table; otherwise the solution is computed recursively and the result is stored.

The second method, and the one we will focus on, is called *tabulation*. Here, the computation switches to a bottom-up scheme in which, by careful planning (or 'programming'), the simplest partial results are computed first, and then solutions to larger subproblems are computed in an appropriate order until the complete solution is obtained. For some problems, installing a tabulation can be viewed as the problem of finding a shortest path in a suitable layered network derived from the dependency graph. We considered the layered network problem in Chapter 10, and we will look at it again in the following chapter.

Each approach, the top-down and bottom-up methods, has its advantages and disadvantages. Memoisation is in principle easy to install but does require a systematic way of coding the arguments of the recursive function so that they can be used as indices in a table, usually an array of some kind. These arguments also have to be testable for equality. A top-down approach ensures that only those values actually needed for the full computation are computed. Tabulation requires a more wholesale change to the structure of the solution but, if the tabulation scheme is chosen well, each solution can be determined easily from the solutions to the associated subproblems. On the other hand, some simple tabulation schemes may involve computing the solutions to subproblems not actually required for the full solution.

The aim of the next two chapters is to look at a number of problems for which dynamic programming is a viable technique, and to examine the various kinds of tabulation scheme that can arise. In imperative programming most tabulation schemes involve arrays of various kinds, but in functional programming other representations can prove superior.

Chapter 13

Efficient recursions

In this chapter we introduce the essential ideas of dynamic programming by looking at the recursive formulation of some simple problems, examining the dependency graph associated with each recursion, and finding a suitable tabulation scheme for implementing the recursion efficiently. Most problems for which dynamic programming is appropriate are optimisation problems of one kind or another, but the first two problems, the Fibonacci function and the problem of computing binomial coefficients, are not. We will also give dynamic programming solutions for the knapsack problem of Chapter 10 and the longest common subsequence problem of Chapter 11. Two additional problems, the minimum-edit problem and the shuttle-bus problem, are also described. All these examples illustrate the range of possibilities for different tabulation schemes.

13.1 Two numeric examples

Perhaps the simplest example of a recursion that involves the same calculation being repeated many times over is the Fibonacci function:

$fib :: Nat \rightarrow Integer$
$fib\ n =$ **if** $n \leqslant 1$ **then** $fromIntegral\ n$ **else** $fib\ (n-1) + fib\ (n-2)$

We use *Integer* arithmetic for the result since values of *fib* grow large very quickly. Direct evaluation of *fib* on an argument $n > 1$ involves *fib k* evaluations of *fib* on the argument $n - k$ for $1 \leqslant k < n$, so direct evaluation takes an exponential number of steps (see Exercise 13.1).

The dependency graph of the computation of *fib* for $n = 7$ is pictured in Figure 13.1. This is a directed acyclic graph with a single root, labelled with 7, and directed edges from a node to the two recursive calls associated with the node.

One way of making the computation more efficient is to use a one-dimensional array:

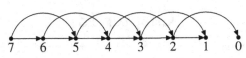

Figure 13.1 The dependency graph of *fib* 7

$fib :: Nat \rightarrow Integer$
$fib\ n = a\ !\ n$
   where $a\ = tabulate\ f\ (0,n)$
        $f\ i = \textbf{if}\ i \leqslant 1\ \textbf{then}\ fromIntegral\ i\ \textbf{else}\ a\ !\ (i-1) + a\ !\ (i-2)$

The function *tabulate* is defined by

$tabulate :: Ix\ i \Rightarrow (i \rightarrow e) \rightarrow (i,i) \rightarrow Array\ i\ e$
$tabulate\ f\ bounds = array\ bounds\ [(x,f\ x) \mid x \leftarrow range\ bounds]$

The declaration $a = tabulate\ f\ (0,n)$ in the definition of *fib* builds an array a whose ith entry for $i > 1$ is the unevaluated expression $a\ !\ (i-1) + a\ !\ (i-2)$. Thus *tabulate* takes linear time. Array entries are evaluated only when required, and then they are evaluated at most once. Therefore the above definition of *fib* takes linear time. We will use *tabulate* again when tabulating with arrays.

However, using an array for the tabulation of *fib* is overkill because at each step of the computation only the two previous values of *fib* are required. The table therefore need consist of only two entries. This observation leads to the following simple definition:

$fib :: Nat \rightarrow Integer$
$fib\ n = fst\ (apply\ n\ step\ (0,1))$
      where $step\ (a,b) = (b,a+b)$

The 'table' consists of a pair of values. It is easy to show by induction that

$apply\ n\ step\ (0,1) = (fib\ n, fib\ (n+1))$

so the above program is correct. This solution also takes linear time. In fact there is even a logarithmic-time algorithm for computing *fib*, see Exercise 13.3.

The second example concerns computing binomial coefficients. The standard definition is, of course,

$$\binom{n}{r} = \frac{n!}{r!\,(n-r)!}$$

and can be easily implemented by

$binom :: (Nat, Nat) \rightarrow Integer$
$binom\ (n,r) = fact\ n\ \text{div}\ (fact\ r \times fact\ (n-r))$
        where $fact\ n = product\ [1 .. fromIntegral\ n]$

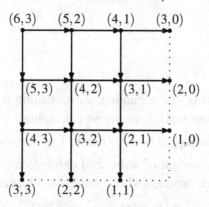

Figure 13.2 Computation of *binom* $(6,3)$

We can also define binomial coefficients recursively. If $0 < r < n$, then

$$\binom{n}{r} = \binom{n-1}{r} + \binom{n-1}{r-1}$$

Furthermore,

$$\binom{n}{0} = \binom{n}{n} = 1$$

That leads to the following recursive definition of *binom*:

> *binom* :: $(Nat, Nat) \to Integer$
> *binom* $(n, r) = $ **if** $r == 0 \vee r == n$ **then** 1
>   **else** *binom* $(n-1, r) + binom$ $(n-1, r-1)$

Like the Fibonacci function, this definition of *binom* can take exponential time if executed directly.

The dependency graph for *binom* on the argument $(6, 3)$ is pictured in Figure 13.2. It takes the form of a two-dimensional grid, so a simple tabulation scheme can be based on a two-dimensional array:

> *binom* :: $(Nat, Nat) \to Integer$
> *binom* $(n, r) = a\,!\,(n, r)$
>   **where** $a = tabulate\,f\ ((0, 0), (n, r))$
> $f\,(i, j) = $ **if** $j == 0 \vee i == j$ **then** 1 **else** $a\,!\,(i-1, j) + a\,!\,(i-1, j-1)$

The function *tabulate* was defined above. However, half of the entries, namely those for (i, j) where $i < j$, consist of the undefined value $\perp$, so the array program is wasteful of space.

A better solution can be based on a single list. Observe that the values of *binom* for the grid in Figure 13.2 are given by

20	10	4	1
10	6	3	1
4	3	2	1
1	1	1	1

and that each row consists of the running sums, reading from right to left, of the elements in the row below it. That means we can define

$$binom\ (n,r) = head\ (apply\ (n-r)\ (scanr1\ (+))\ (replicate\ (r+1)\ 1))$$

The function *scanr1*, a variant of *scanr* and defined only for nonempty lists, is another Standard Prelude function whose values are illustrated by

$$scanr1\ (\oplus)\ [x_1, x_2, x_3] = [x_1 \oplus (x_2 \oplus x_3), x_2 \oplus x_3, x_3]$$

This method takes $r(n-r)$ additions to compute $\binom{n}{r}$, but no multiplications.

13.2 Knapsack revisited

For our next example of dynamic programming, let us take a second look at the knapsack problem from Section 10.4. Recall the following declarations:

> **type** *Name* $= String$
> **type** *Value* $= Nat$
> **type** *Weight* $= Nat$
> **type** *Item* $= (Name, Value, Weight)$
> **type** *Selection* $= ([Name], Value, Weight)$
>
> *name* $(n, \_, \_)$ $= n$
> *value* $(\_, v, \_)$ $= v$
> *weight* $(\_, \_, w) = w$

In Section 10.4 we specified *swag* by

> *swag* :: *Weight* $\rightarrow$ [*Item*] $\rightarrow$ *Selection*
> *swag w* $\leftarrow$ *MaxWith value · choices w*

where *choices* was defined by a *foldr*. This time we define the choices recursively:

> *choices* :: *Weight* $\rightarrow$ [*Item*] $\rightarrow$ [*Selection*]
> *choices w* [] $\quad = [([], 0, 0)]$
> *choices w* $(i : is) = $ **if** $w < wi$ **then** *choices w is*
> $\qquad\qquad\qquad\qquad$ **else** *choices w is* $+\!\!+$ *map* (*add i*) (*choices* $(w - wi)$ *is*)
> $\qquad\qquad\qquad\qquad$ **where** $wi = weight\ i$
>
> *add* :: *Item* $\rightarrow$ *Selection* $\rightarrow$ *Selection*
> *add i* $(ns, v, w) = (name\ i : ns, value\ i + v, weight\ i + w)$

Each item is considered in turn and, weight permitting, either added to the selection or not.

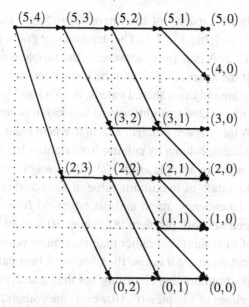

Figure 13.3 Knapsack with capacity 5, and four items with weights 3, 2, 2, 1

It is easy to show that the monotonicity condition

$$\textit{value sn}_1 \leqslant \textit{value sn}_2 \;\Rightarrow\; \textit{value (add i sn}_1) \leqslant \textit{value (add i sn}_2)$$

holds. That means

$$\textit{add i} \cdot \textit{MaxWith value} \leftarrow \textit{MaxWith value} \cdot \textit{map (add i)}$$

Using this fact and the distributive law of *MaxWith*, an easy calculation gives us the
following recursive version of *swag*:

```
swag :: Weight → [Item] → Selection
swag w []     = ([], 0, 0)
swag w (i : is) = if w < wi then swag w is
              else better (swag w is) (add i (swag (w − wi) is))
              where wi = weight i

better :: Selection → Selection → Selection
better sn₁ sn₂ = if value sn₁ ⩾ value sn₂ then sn₁ else sn₂
```

In words, if there are no items to choose from, then the result is the empty selection
with zero weight and zero value. Otherwise the choice is the better of packing the
next item, assuming the weight of the knapsack allows it, and not packing it. In
either case, the remaining selection is the best possible for the remaining items and
the remaining capacity.

Suppose the carrying capacity of the knapsack is 5 and there are four items
to choose from, with weights $3, 2, 2, 1$. The dependency graph for this instance is
pictured in Figure 13.3. A pair (w, r) represents the problem of computing *swag*
when the capacity of the knapsack is w and the last r items are left to choose from.
In this instance there are only two shared values, at $(3, 1)$ and $(0, 1)$, but in general
there will be many more. One straightforward tabulation scheme is to use a two-
dimensional array. A more space-efficient alternative is to reuse a one-dimensional
array, building the solution column by column from right to left, each column being
represented by the entries in a single array. Yet a third way is to recast the problem
as one of computing a path of maximum value in a layered network. Each layer
is a column in the dependency graph and the edges go from layer to layer. We
considered the layered network problem in Chapter 10, except that there we were
looking for a path of minimum cost rather than maximum value. If the capacity of
the knapsack is w and there are n items, then finding a best path will take $O(nw)$
steps, so the dynamic programming algorithm has the same asymptotic complexity
as the thinning algorithm of Chapter 10. However, the computational overhead in
recasting the knapsack problem as a layered network problem is quite large.

Instead, we will build the solution column by column from right to left, but
using a list rather than an array. For example, here is part of Figure 13.3 redrawn
horizontally to show the dependence of each column, now a row, on the one below
it. The row also shows the dependencies for $(4, 2)$ and $(1, 2)$, values not required in
the recursive solution:

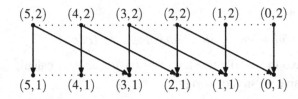

Each new entry in a row depends on the previous entry in the same row and, possibly,
an entry further to the right. All these additional entries are shifted by the same
amount, namely the weight of the current item being considered. We can therefore
define

$$swag :: Weight \rightarrow [Item] \rightarrow Selection$$
$$swag\ w = head \cdot foldr\ step\ start$$
$$\textbf{where}\ start\quad = replicate\ (w + 1)\ ([\,], 0, 0)$$
$$step\ i\ row = zipWith\ better\ row\ (map\ (add\ i)\ (drop\ wi\ row))$$
$$+\!\!\!+\ drop\ (w + 1 - wi)\ row$$
$$\textbf{where}\ wi = weight\ i$$

This solution is of comparable speed to the thinning algorithm of Section 10.4, and slightly faster than one based on a one-dimensional array, but it does depend on all weights being integers, an assumption not needed in the thinning algorithm.

13.3 Minimum-cost edit sequences

Our next example of dynamic programming concerns another way of comparing the similarity of two strings. One such measure, as we saw in Section 11.2, is the length of the longest common subsequence of the two strings. Another measure is to count the cost of transforming one string into the other by a sequence of simple edit operations. There are various possible edit operations, but we will allow just the following four:

- The operation *Replace x y* replaces the current character x in the first string xs by y and then moves on to the next character of xs. It is supposed that x and y are different characters.
- The operation *Copy x* has the same effect as *Replace x x*.
- The operation *Delete x* deletes the current character x in xs and moves on to the next character.
- The operation *Insert y* inserts a new character y before the current character of xs, and then moves on to the next character.

These edit operations are encapsulated in the data type

data *Op* = *Copy Char* | *Replace Char Char* | *Delete Char* | *Insert Char*

The character being replaced, copied, or deleted from the first string is made explicit in the edit operation. In this way, the edit sequence transforming the second string into the first can be obtained by interchanging insert and delete operations and swapping the arguments of a replace. One can also recover both the source and the target string from the edit sequence alone. More precisely, we can define

$reconstruct :: [Op] \rightarrow ([Char], [Char])$
$reconstruct = foldr\ step\ ([], [])$
$\quad$ **where** $step\ (Copy\ x)\quad (us, vs) = (x : us, x : vs)$
$\qquad\quad step\ (Replace\ x\ y)\ (us, vs) = (x : us, y : vs)$
$\qquad\quad step\ (Insert\ x)\quad (us, vs) = (us, x : vs)$
$\qquad\quad step\ (Delete\ x)\quad (us, vs) = (x : us, vs)$

Each edit operation has an associated cost. We suppose that the cost of a replace is less than the combined costs of an insert and a delete, for otherwise there would be no point in having a replace operation. Furthermore, the cost of a copy operation is assumed to be zero; then two identical strings can be transformed into one another with zero cost. Here is an example where the cost of an insert or delete is 2 units and the cost of a replace is 3 units:

```
i*nstitution*
constitue**nt
3 2 0 0 0 0 0 0 3 2 2 0 2
```

The string "institution" is transformed into "constituent" by replacing i by c, inserting an o, copying the next six characters, replacing t by e, deleting the next two characters, copying n and finally inserting t. The two strings have been aligned by using a * character to indicate insertions or deletions. The total cost of this sequence of edits is 14 units, which is the smallest possible cost when the individual edits are costed as above. The function *cost* yields the sum of the individual edit costs:

$$cost :: [Op] \rightarrow Nat$$
$$cost = sum \cdot map\ ecost$$

$$\begin{aligned} ecost\ (Copy\ x) &= 0 \\ ecost\ (Replace\ x\ y) &= 3 \\ ecost\ (Delete\ x) &= 2 \\ ecost\ (Insert\ y) &= 2 \end{aligned}$$

The problem of computing *mce* (a minimum-cost edit) is now specified by

$$mce :: [Char] \rightarrow [Char] \rightarrow [Op]$$
$$mce\ xs\ ys \leftarrow MinWith\ cost\ (edits\ xs\ ys)$$

The function *edits* returns all possible edit sequences:

$$\begin{aligned} edits &:: [Char] \rightarrow [Char] \rightarrow [[Op]] \\ edits\ xs\ [] &= [map\ Delete\ xs] \\ edits\ []\ ys &= [map\ Insert\ ys] \\ edits\ (x:xs)\ (y:ys) &= [pick\ x\ y:es \mid es \leftarrow edits\ xs\ ys] \mathbin{+\!\!+} \\ & \quad [Delete\ x:es \mid es \leftarrow edits\ xs\ (y:ys)] \mathbin{+\!\!+} \\ & \quad [Insert\ y:es \mid es \leftarrow edits\ (x:xs)\ ys] \end{aligned}$$

$$pick\ x\ y = \textbf{if}\ x == y\ \textbf{then}\ Copy\ x\ \textbf{else}\ Replace\ x\ y$$

The primary monotonicity condition for this problem is that

$$cost\ es_1 \leqslant cost\ es_2 \quad \Rightarrow \quad cost\ (op:es_1) \leqslant cost\ (op:es_2)$$

for all edit operations *op*, where es_1 and es_2 are edit sequences in *edits xs ys*. That leads to the recursive formulation

$$\begin{aligned} mce\ xs\ [] &= map\ Delete\ xs \\ mce\ []\ ys &= map\ Insert\ ys \\ mce\ (x:xs)\ (y:ys) &= minWith\ cost\ [pick\ x\ y:mce\ xs\ ys, \\ & \qquad\qquad\qquad\qquad Delete\ x:mce\ xs\ (y:ys), \\ & \qquad\qquad\qquad\qquad Insert\ y:mce\ (x:xs)\ ys] \end{aligned}$$

However, we can go one step further. Provided it is available, a *Copy* operation at

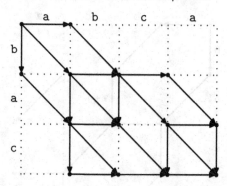

Figure 13.4 Computation of *mce* "abca" "bac"

any step is always the best possible choice. The proof of this greedy condition is left to Exercise 13.10. That means we can rewrite the third clause of *mce* to read:

$$mce\ (x:xs)\ (y:ys) = \textbf{if}\ x == y\ \textbf{then}\ Copy\ x : mce\ xs\ ys\ \textbf{else}$$
$$minWith\ cost\ [Replace\ x\ y : mce\ xs\ ys,$$
$$Delete\ x : mce\ xs\ (y:ys),$$
$$Insert\ y : mce\ (x:xs)\ ys]$$

The dependency graph for *mce* "abca" "bac" is pictured in Figure 13.4. There is a single diagonal edge when two characters match; otherwise there are three edges.

It remains to implement a suitable tabulation scheme. As with the knapsack problem, we can compute entries row by row from right to left:

$$mce\ xs\ ys = head\ (foldr\ (nextrow\ xs)\ (firstrow\ xs)\ ys)$$

The first row of edit operations is given by *firstrow = tails · map Delete*. To see how to define *nextrow*, observe that the next edit sequence to be added to the new row, say at position i, depends on one of three values: (i) the edit sequence at position $i+1$ of the new row (for a delete operation); (ii) the edit sequence at position i of the previous row (for an insert operation); and (iii) the edit sequence at position $i+1$ of the previous row (for a replace operation). These last two values can be obtained with the help of a zip, so we can define

$$nextrow :: [Char] \rightarrow Char \rightarrow [[Op]] \rightarrow [[Op]]$$
$$nextrow\ xs\ y\ row = foldr\ step\ [Insert\ y : last\ row]\ xes$$
$$\textbf{where}\ xes = zip3\ xs\ row\ (tail\ row)$$
$$step\ (x, es_1, es_2)\ row = \textbf{if}\ x == y\ \textbf{then}\ (Copy\ x : es_2) \qquad : row\ \textbf{else}$$
$$minWith\ cost\ [\ Replace\ x\ y : es_2,$$
$$Delete\ x : head\ row,$$
$$Insert\ y : es_1] \qquad : row$$

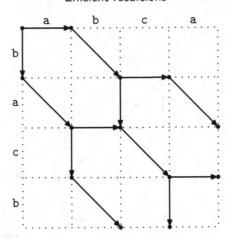

Figure 13.5 Computation of *lcs* "abca" "bacb"

Finally, *cost* computations should be memoised for efficiency, but we will leave that as an exercise. In the worst case the time required to find the edit sequence with minimum cost is then $\Theta(mn)$ steps, where m and n are the lengths of the two strings.

13.4 Longest common subsequence revisited

The above tabulation scheme for the minimum-cost edit sequence problem can be adapted to the longest common subsequence problem. Recall the recursive definition of *lcs* from Chapter 11:

$$
\begin{aligned}
&lcs :: Eq\ a \Rightarrow [a] \rightarrow [a] \rightarrow [a] \\
&lcs\ [\,]\ ys \qquad = [\,] \\
&lcs\ xs\ [\,] \qquad = [\,] \\
&lcs\ (x:xs)\ (y:ys) = \textbf{if}\ x == y\ \textbf{then}\ x:lcs\ xs\ ys \\
&\qquad\qquad\qquad\qquad\quad \textbf{else}\ longer\ (lcs\ (x:xs)\ ys)\ (lcs\ xs\ (y:ys))
\end{aligned}
$$

The dependency graph for *lcs* "abca" "bacb" is pictured in Figure 13.5. There is a single diagonal edge when two characters match; otherwise there are two edges. As with *mce*, we can compute *lcs* row by row from right to left. This time, the first row of entries is a list of empty lists and the entries of a new row each depend on one of three further entries, the same three entries as we had with *mce*. Hence we can define

$$
lcs\ xs = head \cdot foldr\ (nextrow\ xs)\ (firstrow\ xs)
$$

where

> $firstrow \; xs = replicate \; (length \; xs + 1) \; [\,]$
> $nextrow \; xs \; y \; row = foldr \; (step \; y) \; [[\,]] \; (zip3 \; xs \; row \; (tail \; row))$
> $step \; y \; (x, cs_1, cs_2) \; row = \textbf{if } x == y \textbf{ then } (x : cs_2) : row$
> $\qquad\qquad\qquad\qquad\qquad \textbf{else } longer \; cs_1 \; (head \; row) : row$

The time required to find the longest common subsequence of two lists of lengths m and n is $\Theta(mn)$ steps in the worst case, the same time as with the thinning algorithm.

13.5 The shuttle-bus problem

Our final example in this chapter is another scheduling problem. Consider a shuttle-bus that runs from an airport to a city centre. It takes on passengers only at the airport, but it can drop them off at various points along the route. We suppose that the possible stops are numbered from 0 (the airport) to n (the city centre). In the interests of getting all passengers to their destinations as quickly as possible, the bus driver is willing to make up to k intermediate stops. The problem is to program the computer on board the bus to calculate a schedule of at most k intermediate stops that minimises the total cost for a given group of passengers, where the cost to a single passenger getting off at stop m is the absolute value of the difference between the desired stop number and m.

All that is important about passengers is the number of them who wish to get off at a particular stop, so we define

> **type** $Passengers = [(Count, Stop)]$
> **type** $Count = Nat$
> **type** $Stop \quad = Nat$

For example, $[(3, 1), (10, 2), (5, 3), (15, 4), (4, 5), (10, 8), (22, 10)]$ is a possible passenger list, indicating that three people want to get off at stop 1, ten at stop 2, and so on. It is assumed that the passenger list is given in increasing order of stop number and that the stops are numbered between 1 and n inclusive.

A schedule of k intermediate stops is a subsequence of $1, 2, ..., n-1$ of length at most k. However, it turns out to be computationally simpler to describe the journey in terms not of stops but of the individual 'legs' of the journey, where a leg is a pair of stops:

> **type** $Leg = (Stop, Stop)$

For example, the subsequence $[2, 5, 7]$ of three intermediate stops is represented (assuming $n = 10$) by the sequence of legs $[(0, 2), (2, 5), (5, 7), (7, 10)]$. With this

representation, the total cost to a list of passengers for a sequence of legs is defined
by

$$cost :: Passengers \rightarrow [Leg] \rightarrow Nat$$
$$cost\ ps\ [\,] \qquad = 0$$
$$cost\ ps\ ((x,y):ls) = legcost\ qs\ (x,y) + cost\ rs\ ls$$
$$\mathbf{where}\ (qs,rs) = span\ (atmost\ y)\ ps$$

where

$$atmost\ y\ (c,s)\ = s \leqslant y$$
$$legcost\ ps\ (x,y) = sum\ [c \times min\ (s-x)\ (y-s) \mid (c,s) \leftarrow ps]$$

The leg cost of (x,y) is the cost to all passengers who wish to get off after stop x but
before or at stop y. Clearly, the closer stop is the one with smaller cost. For example,
with the above passenger list and sequence of legs, the cost is

$$legcost\ [(3,1),(10,2)] \qquad (0,2) +$$
$$legcost\ [(5,3),(15,4),(4,5)]\ (2,5) +$$
$$legcost\ [\,] \qquad\qquad\quad (5,7) +$$
$$legcost\ [(10,8),(22,10)] \qquad (7,10)$$

which is $3 \times (2-1) + (5 \times (3-2) + 15 \times (5-4)) + 0 + 10 \times (8-7) = 33$. In
particular, the five passengers who want to get off at stop 3 do best by walking there
from stop 2.

Now we can specify *schedule* by

$$schedule :: Nat \rightarrow Nat \rightarrow Passengers \rightarrow [Leg]$$
$$schedule\ n\ k\ ps \leftarrow MinWith\ (cost\ ps)\ (legs\ n\ k\ 0)$$

where *legs* returns the set of possible sequences of legs from a given position:

$$legs :: Nat \rightarrow Nat \rightarrow Stop \rightarrow [[Leg]]$$
$$legs\ n\ k\ x$$
$$\quad \mid x == n \quad = [[\,]]$$
$$\quad \mid k == 0 \quad = [[(x,n)]]$$
$$\quad \mid otherwise = [(x,y):ls \mid y \leftarrow [x+1..n], ls \leftarrow legs\ n\ (k-1)\ y]$$

When $k = 0$, the only possible leg is the one that goes straight from x to n without
making any intermediate stops; otherwise every possible leg beginning with x is
chosen.

The next step is to obtain a recursive definition of *schedule*. For the base cases
we have

$$MinWith\ (cost\ ps)\ (legs\ n\ k\ n) = MinWith\ (cost\ ps)\ [[\,]] \qquad = [\,]$$
$$MinWith\ (cost\ ps)\ (legs\ n\ 0\ x) = MinWith\ (cost\ ps)\ [[(x,n)]] = [(x,n)]$$

For the recursive case of *legs* we can reason

$$cost\ ps\ ((x,y):ls)$$
$$= \quad \{ \text{definition of } cost \text{ with } (qs,rs) = span\ (atmost\ y)\ ls \}$$
$$legcost\ qs\ (x,y) + cost\ rs\ ls$$
$$\leqslant \quad \{ \text{assuming } cost\ rs\ ls \leqslant cost\ rs\ ls' \}$$
$$legcost\ qs\ (x,y) + cost\ rs\ ls'$$
$$= \quad \{ \text{definition of } cost \}$$
$$cost\ ps\ (x,y):ls'$$

Hence

$$cost\ rs\ ls \leqslant cost\ rs\ ls' \Rightarrow cost\ ps\ ((x,y):ls) \leqslant cost\ ps\ ((x,y):ls')$$

That leads to the following recursive definition of *schedule*:

$$schedule\ n\ k\ ps = process\ ps\ k\ 0\ \textbf{where}$$
$$process\ ps\ k\ x$$
$$\quad |\ x == n \quad = []$$
$$\quad |\ k == 0 \quad = [(x,n)]$$
$$\quad |\ otherwise = minWith\ (cost\ ps)\ [\ (x,y):process\ (cut\ y\ ps)\ (k-1)\ y$$
$$\quad\quad\quad\quad\quad\quad\quad\quad\quad\quad |\ y \leftarrow [x+1..n]]$$
$$\quad cut\ y = dropWhile\ (atmost\ y)$$

The next step is tabulation. Let (k,x) represent the call *process* $(cut\ x\ ps)\ k\ x$. Then (k,x) depends on all of $(k-1,x+1), (k-1,x+2), ..., (k-1,n)$. This is a layered recursion, so we can turn the problem into one of finding a shortest path in a layered network. Alternatively, we can build a table row by row. Suppose we define

$$table\ ps\ k = [process\ (cut\ x\ ps)\ k\ x\ |\ x \leftarrow [0..n]]$$

In particular,

$$schedule\ n\ k\ ps = head\ (table\ ps\ k)$$

The bottom row of the table is given by

$$table\ ps\ 0 = [[(x,n)]\ |\ x \leftarrow [0..n-1]] ++ [[]]$$

It remains to show how *table ps k* is computed from *table ps* $(k-1)$. The idea is to define *step* so that

$$table\ ps\ k = step\ (table\ ps\ (k-1))$$

To this end, let *ptails* return the *proper* tails of a list, that is, all the tails except the list itself:

$$ptails\ [] \quad\quad = []$$
$$ptails\ (x:xs) = xs:ptails\ xs$$

Then we can define

$step\ t = zipWith\ entry\ [0..n-1]\ (ptails\ t) + [[]]$
$entry\ x\ ts = minWith\ (cost\ (cut\ x\ ps))\ (zipWith\ (:)\ [(x,y)\ |\ y \leftarrow [x+1..n]]\ ts)$

Putting these pieces together, we arrive at the final algorithm

$schedule\ n\ k\ ps = head\ (apply\ k\ step\ start)$
   where
       $start$ $= [[(x,n)]\ |\ x \leftarrow [0..n-1]] + [[]]$
       $step\ t$ $= zipWith\ entry\ [0..n-1]\ (ptails\ t) + [[]]$
       $entry\ x\ ts = minWith\ (cost\ (cut\ x\ ps))$
                    $(zipWith\ (:)\ [(x,y)\ |\ y \leftarrow [x+1..n]]\ ts)$

The algorithm can be made more efficient in various ways, including by memoising *cost*, but we will leave these optimisations as exercises.

13.6 Chapter notes

The story behind the term 'dynamic programming' is described in [4]. An early account of dynamic programming by Bellman appears in his book [1]. Various tabulation schemes for recursive programs are presented in [2]. The minimum edit distance problem has applications in computational biology and is discussed in most books on stringology, including [5]; see also [6, 8]. The shuttle-bus problem appears, in different guises, in [3] and as an elevator problem in [7]. The Wikipedia entry on dynamic programming contains a wealth of other examples.

References

[1]   Richard Bellman. *Dynamic Programming*. Princeton University Press, Princeton, NJ, 1957.
[2]   Richard S. Bird. Tabulation techniques for recursive programs. *ACM Computing Surveys*, 12(4):403–417, 1980.
[3]   Eric V. Denardo. *Dynamic Programming: Models and Applications*. Prentice-Hall, Upper Saddle River, NJ, 1982.
[4]   Stuart Dreyfus. Richard Bellman on the birth of dynamic programming. *Operations Research*, 50(1):48–51, 2002.
[5]   Dan Gusfield. *Algorithms on Strings, Trees, and Sequences*. Cambridge University Press, Cambridge, 1997.
[6]   Gonzalo Navarro. A guided tour of approximate string matching. *ACM Computing Surveys*, 33(1):31–88, 2001.
[7]   Steven S. Skiena and Miguel A. Revilla. *Programming Challenges*. Springer, New York, 2003.
[8]   Robert A. Wagner and Michael J. Fischer. The string-to-string correction problem. *Journal of the ACM*, 21(1):168–173, 1974.

Exercises

Exercise 13.1 Let $T(n)$ denote the number of additions in computing *fib* from its recursive definition. Given that *fib* $n = \Theta(\varphi^n)$, where $\varphi = (1 + \sqrt{5})/2$ is the Golden Ratio, prove that $T(n) = \Theta(\varphi^n)$.

Exercise 13.2 Give an efficient one-line definition of the function *fibs* that returns the infinite list of all the Fibonacci numbers.

Exercise 13.3 The following two identities hold for $n > 2$:

$$fib\ (2 \times n) \qquad = fib\ n \times (2 \times fib\ (n+1) - fib\ n)$$
$$fib\ (2 \times n + 1) = fib\ n \times fib\ n + fib\ (n+1) \times fib\ (n+1)$$

Using these facts, show how to compute *fib* n in $O(\log n)$ steps. As a hint, note that the linear-time algorithm for *fib* can be phrased in the form

$$fib = fst \cdot foldr\ step\ (0,1) \cdot unary$$
$$\textbf{where } step\ k\ (a,b) = (b, a+b)$$
$$unary\ n = [1..n]$$

The logarithmic version is obtained by modifying the definition of *step* and replacing *unary* by *binary*, where *binary* returns the binary expansion of a number, least significant digit first:

$$binary\ n = \textbf{if } n == 0 \textbf{ then } [] \textbf{ else } r : binary\ q$$
$$\textbf{where } (q,r) = n\ \text{divMod}\ 2$$

For example, *binary* $6 = [0,1,1]$.

Exercise 13.4 Consider the function

$$fob :: Nat \rightarrow Integer$$
$$fob\ n = \textbf{if } n \leqslant 2 \textbf{ then } fromIntegral\ n \textbf{ else } fob\ (n-1) + fob\ (n-3)$$

Show how to evaluate *fob* in linear time.

Exercise 13.5 The Stirling numbers can be defined for $0 \leqslant r \leqslant n$ by the recurrence

$$stirling :: (Nat, Nat) \rightarrow Integer$$
$$stirling\ (n,r)$$
$$\quad | \ r == n \quad = 1$$
$$\quad | \ r == 0 \quad = 0$$
$$\quad | \ otherwise = fromIntegral\ r \times stirling\ (n-1,r) + stirling\ (n-1,r-1)$$

Give a suitable tabulation scheme for computing *stirling* efficiently.

Exercise 13.6 An extreme form of dependency graph arises when every value depends on every previous value, as in the function f, where

$$f\ n = \textbf{if } n == 0 \textbf{ then } 1 \textbf{ else } sum\ (map f\ [0..n-1])$$

How would you compute this particular recursion efficiently?

Exercise 13.7 Why does the monotonicity condition

$$value\ sn_1 \leqslant value\ sn_2 \Rightarrow value\ (add\ i\ sn_1) \leqslant value\ (add\ i\ sn_2)$$

hold for the knapsack problem?

Exercise 13.8 Here is a solution to the knapsack problem based on a one-dimensional array, similar to the one in the text except that values in each row go from left to right:

$$swag\ w\ items = a\ !\ w$$
   where
       $a = foldr\ step\ start\ items$
       $start = listArray\ (0,w)\ (replicate\ (w+1)\ ([],0,0))$
       $step\ item\ a = ...$

Your task is to define *step*.

Exercise 13.9 Write down all the possible values of *mce* "abca" "bac".

Exercise 13.10 The purpose of this exercise is to establish the greedy condition for the minimum-cost edit problem by showing that, at any point in the sequence, if the two remaining strings begin with the same character, then starting with a copy operation always leads to a best possible solution. Suppose a best sequence does not begin with a copy, so it has to begin with either a delete or an insert (a replace is not possible as the first two characters are the same). The two situations are dual, so suppose it begins with k delete operations, where $k > 0$. Thereafter, there are three possibilities for the next edit operation: a copy (if available), a replace, or an insert. What alternative edit sequence beginning with a copy and with the same cost is possible in the first two cases? What alternative sequence beginning with a copy is possible in the third case? The necessary assumption is that $c \leqslant r \leqslant d+i$, where c is the cost of a copy, r the cost of a replace, d the cost of a delete, and i the cost of an insert.

Exercise 13.11 We can memoise cost computations in the final algorithm for the edit sequence problem by pairing edit sequences with their costs. In particular, let us introduce

type $Pair = (Nat, [Op])$

Now the first row is defined by

$firstrow :: [Char] \rightarrow [Pair]$
$firstrow\ xs = foldr\ nextentry\ [(0, [])]\ xs$
    where $nextentry\ x\ row = cons\ (Delete\ x)\ (head\ row) : row$

where *cons* is defined by

$cons\ op\ (k, es) = (ecost\ op + k, op : es)$

Write down the modified definition of *nextrow* (hint: it also uses *cons*) and hence construct a new definition of *mce*.

Exercise 13.12 By definition a *distance* function $d :: A \times A \rightarrow \mathbb{R}^+$, where $\mathbb{R}^+$ is the set of nonnegative real numbers, is a function with the following four properties:

1. $d(x, y) \geqslant 0$.
2. $d(x, y) = 0$ if and only if $x = y$.
3. $d(x, y) = d(y, x)$.
4. $d(x, y) \leqslant d(x, z) + d(z, y)$ for all z.

Show that *dist* is a distance function, where

$dist\ (xs, ys) = cost\ (mce\ xs\ ys)$

For this reason the minimum-cost edit sequence problem is often referred to as the *edit distance* problem.

Exercise 13.13 Let k denote the length of the longest common subsequence of xs and ys. Show that

$cost\ (mce\ xs\ ys) \leqslant length\ xs + length\ ys - 2 \times k$

given that the only edit operations allowed are copy, insert, and delete, with costs 0, 1, and 1, respectively. Show that the inequality can be strengthened to an equality.

Exercise 13.14 It may seem in the light of Exercise 13.10 that a minimum edit sequence can be obtained from a longest upsequence in the following way: partition the two sequences according to their longest upsequence, giving

$xs_0 +\!\!+ [x_0] +\!\!+ \cdots +\!\!+ xs_{n-1} +\!\!+ [x_{n-1}] +\!\!+ xs_n$
$ys_0 +\!\!+ [x_0] +\!\!+ \cdots +\!\!+ ys_{n-1} +\!\!+ [x_{n-1}] +\!\!+ ys_n$

where $[x_0, ..., x_{n-1}]$ is the longest common subsequence. For example,

"bdacb" = "b" +\!\!+ "d" +\!\!+ "" +\!\!+ "a" +\!\!+ "c" +\!\!+ "b" +\!\!+ ""
"ddacc" = "" +\!\!+ "d" +\!\!+ "d" +\!\!+ "a" +\!\!+ "c" +\!\!+ "" +\!\!+ "c"

The sequences xs_j and ys_j have no characters in common, so their minimum edit sequence can be determined by applying as many replace operations as possible, followed by either a number of deletes or a number of inserts. Does this idea work?

Exercise 13.15 To define an efficient version of the shuttle-bus function *schedule* we need to split up the passenger list by defining

$$split \ n \ ps = [cut \ 0 \ ps, cut \ 1 \ ps, ..., cut \ n \ ps]$$

Give a definition of *split*.

Now we can memoise *cost* computations by defining

$$schedule :: Nat \rightarrow Nat \rightarrow Passengers \rightarrow [Leg]$$
$$schedule \ n \ k \ ps = extract \ (apply \ k \ step \ start) \ \textbf{where}$$
$$extract = snd \cdot head$$
$$start \quad = zipWith \ entry \ pss \ [0..n-1] + [(0,[])]$$
$$\qquad\qquad \textbf{where} \ entry \ ps \ x = (legcost \ ps \ (x,n),[(x,n)])$$
$$pss \quad = split \ n \ ps$$
$$step \ t \quad = ...$$

Each sequence of legs is paired with its cost. Define the local value *step t*.

Exercise 13.16 Recall the coin-changing problem of Section 7.3:

$$mkchange :: [Denom] \rightarrow Nat \rightarrow Tuple$$
$$mkchange \ ds \leftarrow MinWith \ count \cdot mktuples \ ds$$

where *count = sum* and

$$mktuples \ [1] \ n \quad = [[n]]$$
$$mktuples \ (d:ds) \ n = concat \ [\ map \ (c:) \ (mktuples \ ds \ (n-c \times d))$$
$$\qquad\qquad\qquad\qquad\qquad | \ c \leftarrow [0..n \ div \ d]]$$

What is the monotonicity condition that yields a recursive definition of *mkchange*? Write down the recursive definition and suggest a suitable tabulation scheme.

Answers

Answer 13.1 We have $T(0) = T(1) = 0$ and $T(n) = T(n-1) + T(n-2) + 1$ for $n \geqslant 2$. By induction one can then show $T(n) = fib \ (n+1) - 1$. Since $fib \ n = \Theta(\varphi^n)$, where φ is the Golden Ratio, the result now follows.

Answer 13.2 We have

$$fibs :: [Integer]$$
$$fibs = 0:1:zipWith \ (+) \ fibs \ (tail \ fibs)$$

Answer 13.3 We have

$$fib = fst \cdot foldr \ step \ (0,1) \cdot binary$$
$$\qquad \textbf{where} \ step \ k \ (a,b) = \textbf{if} \ k == 0 \ \textbf{then} \ (c,d) \ \textbf{else} \ (d,c+d)$$
$$\qquad\qquad\qquad \textbf{where} \ c = a \times (2 \times b - a)$$
$$\qquad\qquad\qquad\qquad d = a \times a + b \times b$$

Answer 13.4 The solution is the same as the one for *fib* except that we maintain three values at each step:

$$fob\ n = fst3\ (apply\ n\ step\ (0,1,2))$$
$$\textbf{where}\ step\ (a,b,c) = (b,c,a+c)$$
$$fst3\ (a,b,c) = a$$

Answer 13.5 The simplest solution is to use a two-dimensional array:

$$stirling\ (n,r) = a\ !\ (n,r)$$
$$\textbf{where}\ a = tabulate\ f\ ((0,0),(n,r))$$
$$f\ (i,j)\ |\ i == j \quad = 1$$
$$|\ j == 0 \quad = 0$$
$$|\ otherwise = fromIntegral\ j \times a\ !\ (i-1,j) + a\ !\ (i-1,j-1)$$

As an alternative we can go for a solution with the same shape as *binom*:

$$stirling\ (n,r) = head\ (apply\ (n-r)\ step\ (replicate\ (r+1)\ 1))$$
$$\textbf{where}\ step\ row = scanr1\ (+)\ (zipWith\ (\times)\ [r',r'-1..0]\ row)$$
$$r' = fromIntegral\ r$$

This method computes row $(n,r), (n-1,r-1), ..., (n-r,0)$ from the previous row $(n-1,r), (n-2,r-1), ..., (n-r-1,0)$, starting with the row $(r,r), ..., (0,0)$, all of whose entries are 1.

Answer 13.6 A trick question, because $f\ n = 2^{n-1}$ for $n \geqslant 1$.

Answer 13.7 Because $value\ (add\ i\ sn) = value\ i + value\ sn$.

Answer 13.8 The definition is

$$step\ item\ a = a\ //\ [(j, next\ j\ item)\ |\ j \leftarrow [0..w]]$$
$$\textbf{where}\ next\ j\ i = \textbf{if}\ j < wi\ \textbf{then}\ a\ !\ j\ \textbf{else}\ better\ (a\ !\ j)\ (add\ i\ (a\ !\ (j-wi)))$$
$$\textbf{where}\ wi = weight\ i$$

The array-based solution has the same asymptotic complexity as the list-based version but is slightly slower.

Answer 13.9 There are three answers, all with cost 6:

```
abca*      *abca      ab*ca
*b*ac      ba*c*      *bac*
```

Answer 13.10 In the first two cases we can start with a copy and k deletes, to arrive at the same spot as k deletes followed by either a copy or a replace. Since $c \leqslant r \Rightarrow c + kd \leqslant kd + r$, the first sequence gives an edit sequence with smaller cost. In the third case we can start with a copy and $k-1$ deletes. This time, we have $c \leqslant d + i \Rightarrow c + (k-1)d \leqslant kd + i$, so again the first sequence has smaller cost.

Answer 13.11 The definition is basically the same as before except that (:) is replaced by *cons*:

$$nextrow :: [Char] \to Char \to [Pair] \to [Pair]$$
$$nextrow\ xs\ y\ row = foldr\ step\ [cons\ (Insert\ y)\ (last\ row)]\ xes$$
> **where**
> $xes = zip3\ xs\ row\ (tail\ row)$
> $step\ (x, es_1, es_2)\ row =$ **if** $x == y$ **then** $(cons\ (Copy\ x)\ es_2) : row$ **else**
> $minWith\ fst\ [cons\ (Insert\ y)\ es_1,$
> $cons\ (Replace\ x\ y)\ es_2,$
> $cons\ (Delete\ x)\ (head\ row)] : row$

Now we have

$$mce\ xs\ ys = extract\ (foldr\ (nextrow\ xs)\ (firstrow\ xs)\ ys)$$
> **where** $extract = snd \cdot head$

Answer 13.12 The first two properties are immediate. Changing deletes into inserts and vice versa, and swapping the arguments of a replace, we get an edit sequence of the same cost for changing the second list into the first, so the third property is satisfied. For the fourth and final property we have

$$cost\ (mce\ xs\ ys) \leqslant cost\ (mce\ xs\ zs) + cost\ (mce\ zs\ ys)$$

because we can concatenate a minimum edit sequence turning xs into zs with a minimum edit sequence turning zs into ys to get an edit sequence turning xs into ys.

Answer 13.13 Let zs be a longest common subsequence of xs and ys. Construct an edit sequence that deletes all elements of xs not in zs, inserts all elements of ys not in zs, and copies the common elements. The cost of this edit sequence is at most

$$(length\ xs - length\ zs) + (length\ ys - length\ zs)$$

and so a minimum cost edit sequence is also bounded by this quantity. To show equality we have to prove there is no cheaper edit sequence. Given a minimum sequence es, consider the string zs of length k that results from performing all the deletes in es on xs. Since ys can be constructed from zs by applying insertions alone, it follows that zs is a common subsequence of xs and ys. Hence

$$cost\ (mce\ xs\ ys) \geqslant length\ xs + length\ ys - 2 \times k$$

Since a longest common subsequence has length at least k, equality is established.

Answer 13.14 No, not as stated. For the example strings we would obtain

```
b d * a c b
* d d a c c
2 0 2 0 0 3
```

with cost 7. But a better edit is given by

```
b d a c b
d d a c c
3 0 0 0 3
```

with cost 6.

Answer 13.15 One sensible way of defining *split* is as follows:

$$split\ n\ ps = scanl\ op\ ps\ [1 .. n]$$
$$\textbf{where}\ op\ qs\ x = dropWhile\ (atmost\ x)\ qs$$

The definition of *step* is

$$step\ t = zipWith3\ entry\ pss\ [0 .. n-1]\ (ptails\ t) + [(0,[])]$$
$$entry\ ps\ x\ ts = minWith\ fst\ (zipWith\ cons\ [x+1 .. n]\ ts)\ \textbf{where}$$
$$cons\ y\ (c,ls) = (legcost\ (takeWhile\ (atmost\ y)\ ps)\ (x,y) + c, (x,y) : ls)$$

Answer 13.16 The monotonicity condition is that

$$count\ cs_1 \leqslant count\ cs_2 \Rightarrow count\ (c:cs_1) \leqslant count\ (c:cs_2)$$

That means

$$(c:) \cdot MinWith\ count \leftarrow MinWith\ count \cdot map\ (c:)$$

Hence we can define

$$mkchange\ [1]\ n \quad = [n]$$
$$mkchange\ (d:ds)\ n = minWith\ count\ [\ c:mkchange\ ds\ (n-c \times d)$$
$$| c \leftarrow [0 .. n\ \text{div}\ d]]$$

Let (k,n) denote the call *mkchange* (*drop k ds*) n. Then (k,n) depends on all of $(k-1,n),(k-1,n-d),(k-1,n-2d),....$ The recursion is layered, so we can use the layered network algorithm for the tabulation scheme. Alternatively, one can compute the partial solutions row by row.

Chapter 14

Optimum bracketing

A surprising variety of subtly different algorithms arises from the single idea of trying to bracket an expression $X_1 \otimes X_2 \otimes \cdots \otimes X_n$ in the best possible way. We assume that $\otimes$ is an associative operation, so the manner in which the brackets are inserted does not affect the expression's value. However, different bracketings may have different costs, and the aim of the exercise is to find one whose cost is as small as possible. Depending on how the cost is defined, finding the best solution may take constant, linear, linearithmic, quadratic, or cubic time.

Here is a simple example; others will be given later on. Take $\otimes$ to be matrix multiplication, an associative operation but not in general a commutative one. The cost of multiplying a $p \times q$ matrix by a $q \times r$ matrix is $O(p \times q \times r)$ additions and multiplications, and the result is a $p \times r$ matrix. Now consider the four matrices X_1, X_2, X_3, X_4 with the following dimensions:

$$(10, 20), \quad (20, 30), \quad (30, 5), \quad (5, 50)$$

With the cost taken as exactly $p \times q \times r$, the five possible ways of bracketing the four matrices have costs 47500, 18000, 28500, 6500, and 10000, the best one being $(X_1 \otimes (X_2 \otimes X_3)) \otimes X_4$ with cost

$$20 \times 30 \times 5 + 10 \times 20 \times 5 + 10 \times 5 \times 50 = 6500$$

There is no obvious method for bracketing the matrices to achieve minimum cost. Greedy strategies, like doing the cheapest (or most expensive) multiplication first, do not work. However, as we will see later on, there is a fairly straightforward dynamic programming algorithm to compute the best bracketing, one whose running time is $\Theta(n^3)$ steps for n matrices.

The right way of phrasing the bracketing problem is simply to ask for a leaf-labelled binary tree of minimum cost with a given list as fringe. Each bracketing corresponds to a particular tree. For simplicity, the elements at the leaves of the tree are taken to be the sizes of the objects to be bracketed, not the objects themselves. We will refer to such sizes as *weights* to avoid confusion with the use of *size* to describe the number of nodes in a tree. Problems like this were considered in Chapter 8. In particular we looked at Huffman coding, which can be regarded as a version of optimal bracketing in which $\otimes$ is assumed to be commutative as well as associative, so the fringe can be any permutation of the given list. In this chapter we will also tackle the restricted version of Huffman coding without commutativity, in which the fringe has to be exactly the given list. Another example that can be solved using the techniques of this chapter is to find an optimum binary search tree, a problem we will tackle in Section 14.5.

14.1 A cubic-time algorithm

The problem is based on the following data type of binary trees:

data $\mathit{Tree}\ a = \mathit{Leaf}\ a \mid \mathit{Fork}\ (\mathit{Tree}\ a)\ (\mathit{Tree}\ a)$

We will refer to such trees as *leaf* trees to avoid confusion with other kinds of tree we will need later on. A leaf tree will be displayed using parentheses. For example, the leaf tree

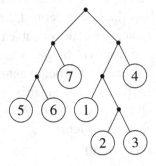

is displayed as $(((5\ 6)\ 7)\ ((1\ (2\ 3))\ 4))$.

Given *Weight* as the type of weights, the function *mct* determines a tree with minimum cost:

$$mct :: [\mathit{Weight}] \rightarrow \mathit{Tree}\ \mathit{Weight}$$
$$mct \leftarrow \mathit{MinWith}\ cost \cdot mktrees$$

The function *mktrees* returns a list of all possible trees with a given fringe. Two definitions were given in Chapter 8, but here is another way:

$$mktrees :: [a] \rightarrow [\mathit{Tree}\ a]$$
$$mktrees\ [w] = [\mathit{Leaf}\ w]$$
$$mktrees\ ws\ = [\ \mathit{Fork}\ t_1\ t_2$$
$$\qquad\qquad | \ (us, vs) \leftarrow splitsn\ ws, t_1 \leftarrow mktrees\ us, t_2 \leftarrow mktrees\ vs]$$

The function *splitsn* (see Exercise 8.7) splits a list of length at least two into two nonempty lists in all possible ways. The above recursive definition directs us towards a dynamic programming solution, while the inductive definitions of Chapter 8 suggest heading for a greedy or thinning algorithm. In any case, as mentioned in Exercise 8.8, there are

$$\binom{2n-2}{n-1}\frac{1}{n}$$

trees with a fringe of length n, so all definitions of *mktrees* take exponential time.

It remains to define *cost*. There is a range of possible definitions, but we will only consider cost functions that conform to the following general scheme:

> **type** *Cost = Nat*
>
> *cost* :: *Tree Weight* $\rightarrow$ *Cost*
> *cost* (*Leaf w*) $= 0$
> *cost* (*Fork t_1 t_2*) $=$ *cost t_1* $+$ *cost t_2* $+f$ (*weight t_1*) (*weight t_2*)
>
> *weight* :: *Tree Weight* $\rightarrow$ *Weight*
> *weight* (*Leaf w*) $= w$
> *weight* (*Fork t_1 t_2*) $= g$ (*weight t_1*) (*weight t_2*)

Thus the cost of forming a tree is the sum of the costs of forming its two component subtrees plus some function f of their weights. The weight of a leaf is the value at the leaf, while the weight of a fork is some further function g of the weights of its component trees. For the matrix multiplication problem we have the definitions

> **type** *Weight = (Nat, Nat)*
>
> f :: *Weight* $\rightarrow$ *Weight* $\rightarrow$ *Cost*
> f (p,q) (q',r) $|$ $q == q'$ $= p \times q \times r$
>
> g :: *Weight* $\rightarrow$ *Weight* $\rightarrow$ *Weight*
> g (p,q) (q',r) $|$ $q == q'$ $= (p,r)$

Other interesting instantiations of f and g will be given later on. We suppose throughout that g is an associative operation, so two trees have the same weight if they have the same fringe. This fact alone is sufficient for us to write down a recursive definition of *mct* and obtain a cubic-time solution by tabulation. Since the weights of all trees in *mktrees ws* are the same, we have

$$cost\ u_1 \leqslant cost\ u_2 \wedge cost\ v_1 \leqslant cost\ v_2 \Rightarrow cost\ (Fork\ u_1\ v_1) \leqslant cost\ (Fork\ u_2\ v_2)$$

where u_1 and u_2 are trees in *mktrees us*, and v_1 and v_2 are trees in *mktrees vs*. That means we can refine *mct* to read

> *mct* [w] $= Leaf\ w$
> *mct ws* $= minWith\ cost$ [*Fork* (*mct us*) (*mct vs*) $|$ (*us, vs*) $\leftarrow$ *splitsn ws*]

Assuming *cost* takes constant time, the running time $T(n)$ of this version of *mct* for a fringe of length n satisfies

$$T(n) = \sum_{k=1}^{n-1} (T(k) + T(n-k)) + \Theta(n)$$

with solution $T(n) = \Theta(3^n)$ (see Exercise 14.2).

The next task is to find some suitable tabulation scheme. As a first step we can make the computation more efficient by encoding a tree as a triple of values, the cost of the tree, its weight, and the tree itself:

> **type** *Triple* = (*Cost*, *Weight*, *Tree Weight*)

With *cost*, *weight*, and *tree* now returning the first, second, and third components of a triple, we have

> *mct* :: [*Weight*] → *Tree Weight*
> *mct* = *tree* · *triple*
>
> *triple* :: [*Weight*] → *Triple*
> *triple* [*w*] = (0, *w*, *Leaf w*)
> *triple ws* = *minWith cost* [*fork* (*triple us*) (*triple vs*) | (*us*, *vs*) ← *splitsn ws*]
>
> *fork* :: *Triple* → *Triple* → *Triple*
> *fork* (c_1, w_1, t_1) (c_2, w_2, t_2) = ($c_1 + c_2 + f\ w_1\ w_2, g\ w_1\ w_2, Fork\ t_1\ t_2$)

The simplest way of implementing a tabulation scheme is to use a two-dimensional array. The idea is to store the values of

> *table* :: (*Int*, *Int*) → [*Weight*] → *Triple*
> *table* (*i*, *j*) = *triple* · *drop* (*i* − 1) · *take j*

in an array. The value of *table* (*i*, *j*) is the solution when the inputs are the elements of the segment $w_i, w_{i+1}, ..., w_j$ for $1 \leqslant i \leqslant j \leqslant n$. The array-based algorithm takes the form

> *mct ws* = *tree* (*table* (1, *n*)) **where**
>   *n* = *length ws*
>   *weights* = *listArray* (1, *n*) *ws*
>   *table* (*i*, *j*)
> | *i* == *j* = (0, *weights* ! *i*, *Leaf* (*weights* ! *i*))
> | *i* < *j* = *minWith cost* [*fork* (*t* ! (*i*, *k*)) (*t* ! (*k* + 1, *j*)) | *k* ← [*i* .. *j* − 1]]
>   *t* = *tabulate table* ((1, 1), (*n*, *n*))

The function *tabulate* was defined in the previous chapter:

> *tabulate* :: *Ix i* ⇒ (*i* → *e*) → (*i*, *i*) → *Array i e*
> *tabulate f bounds* = *array bounds* [(*x*, *f x*) | *x* ← *range bounds*]

New entries to *table* are computed by looking up other entries in the array. Another array, *weights*, is used solely for quick access to the given weights.

Assuming f and g take constant time, it takes $\Theta(j-i)$ steps to compute entry (i,j) of the array for $i \leqslant j$, so the total time $T(n)$ is given by

$$T(n) = \sum_{i=1}^{n} \sum_{j=i}^{n} \Theta(j-i) = \Theta(n^3)$$

In summary, the above tabulation scheme requires cubic time and quadratic space. The only assumption we made was that the function g for combining weights was associative. We can do better if we suppose more about f and g, and that is the topic of the following section.

14.2 A quadratic-time algorithm

It is possible to shave a factor of n off the running time if we make some more assumptions about f and g. Let $r(i,j)$ denote the location of the first best split for the segment $w_i, ..., w_j$ of the input. That is, if $r = r(i,j)$, then r is the smallest integer in the range $i \leqslant r < j$ such that $(w_i \ldots w_r)\,(w_{r+1} \ldots w_j)$ is the top-level split in a best bracketing. We focus on the smallest r because our standard definition of $minWith$ happens to return the smallest best split, but the result below also holds when r is the largest position for a best split. In either case, $r(i,i)$ is undefined because a single value cannot be split. However, we can set $r(i,i) = i$ for completeness.

The result we want to prove is that, under certain conditions on f and g, the function r is monotonic; in symbols,

$$r(i,j-1) \leqslant r(i,j) \leqslant r(i+1,j) \tag{14.1}$$

for $i < j$. The proof is postponed to Section 14.4. That means we can revise the tabulation of mct to manipulate quadruples of values, the first component of which records the position of a best split. With $cost$, $weight$, and $tree$ now returning the second, third, and fourth components of a quadruple, and $root$ returning the first, we have

$mct\ ws = tree\ (table\ (1,n))$ **where**
$\quad n = length\ ws$
$\quad weights = listArray\ (1,n)\ ws$
$\quad table\ (i,j)$
$\quad\quad |\ i == j \quad\ = (i, 0, weights\,!\,i, Leaf\ (weights\,!\,i))$
$\quad\quad |\ i+1 == j = fork\ i\ (t\,!\,(i,i))\ (t\,!\,(j,j))$
$\quad\quad |\ i+1 < j \quad = minWith\ cost\ [fork\ k\ (t\,!\,(i,k))\ (t\,!\,(k+1,j))$
$\quad\quad\quad\quad\quad\quad\quad\quad\quad\quad\quad\quad |\ k \leftarrow [r(i,j-1)..r(i+1,j)]]$
$\quad r(i,j) = root\ (t\,!\,(i,j))$
$\quad t = tabulate\ table\ ((1,1),(n,n))$
$\quad fork\ k\ (\_,c_1,w_1,t_1)\ (\_,c_2,w_2,t_2) = (k, c_1+c_2+f\ w_1\ w_2, g\ w_1\ w_2, Fork\ t_1\ t_2)$

The case $i+1=j$ has to be treated separately (see Exercise 14.4). The monotonicity of r is exploited in the third clause defining *table*. It is immediate from the definition that it takes $\Theta(r(i+1,j) - r(i,j-1))$ steps to compute entry (i,j) of the table when $i+1 < j$. The total time $T(n)$ needed to compute entry $(1,n)$ can be estimated by counting the cost of computing each entry of the table along each diagonal d, where $d = j - i$:

$$T(n) = \Theta(n) + \sum_{d=2}^{n-1}\sum_{i=1}^{n-d} \Theta(r(i+1,i+d) - r(i,i+d-1))$$

The first two diagonals, $d = 0$ and $d = 1$, can be computed in $\Theta(n)$ steps. We have

$$\sum_{i=1}^{n-d} r(i+1,i+d) - r(i,i+d-1) = r(n-d+1,n) - r(1,d) = \Theta(n)$$

since $i \leqslant r(i,j) \leqslant j$. That gives $T(n) = \Theta(n^2)$.

It remains to give the conditions on f and g that ensure (14.1). In Section 14.4 we will show that (14.1) follows from the *quadrangle inequality* (QI)

$$i \leqslant i' \leqslant j \leqslant j' \;\Rightarrow\; C(i,j) + C(i',j') \leqslant C(i,j') + C(i',j) \qquad (14.2)$$

where $C(i,j)$ is the minimum cost of bracketing the segment $w_i, ..., w_j$ of the input $w_1, ..., w_n$. In words, the sum of the costs for two overlapping intervals is at most the cost of the union of the intervals plus the cost of their intersection. The conditions on f and g are those required to ensure the quadrangle inequality holds. The simplest conditions are when f and g are the same function. It is possible to formulate conditions when $f \neq g$ (see Exercise 14.9), but they are rather complicated and it is difficult to find examples to satisfy them, so we will consider only the case $f = g$.

There are two conditions. Setting $f = g = (\bullet)$ for readability, the first condition is that the quadrangle inequality should also hold for the weight function

$$W(i,j) = w_i \bullet w_{i+1} \bullet \cdots \bullet w_j$$

Thus

$$i \leqslant i' \leqslant j \leqslant j' \;\Rightarrow\; W(i,j) + W(i',j') \leqslant W(i,j') + W(i',j)$$

The second condition is that W should be monotonic in the sense that

$$i' \leqslant i \leqslant j \leqslant j' \;\Rightarrow\; W(i,j) \leqslant W(i',j')$$

The monotonicity condition can be simplified (see the exercises) to read

$$A \leqslant A \bullet B \;\wedge\; B \leqslant A \bullet B$$

for all weights A and B. Similarly, the quadrangle inequality can be simplified to read

$$(A \bullet B) + (B \bullet C) \;\leqslant\; (A \bullet B \bullet C) + B$$

for all weights A, B, and C. For example, with $(\bullet) = (+)$, the monotonicity and QI conditions are immediate, provided sizes are nonnegative. With $(\bullet) = (\times)$, the QI condition is $0 \leqslant B(A-1)(C-1)$, which holds if all weights are positive. The monotonicity condition also holds if all weights are positive. However, the QI condition fails for $(\bullet) = max$, and the monotonicity condition for $(\bullet) = min$.

We emphasise that these conditions are sufficient for an $O(n^2)$ algorithm, but not necessary conditions. Proof of (14.1) is a little complicated; for now we just accept the result and move on to examples.

14.3 Examples

So far, we have a cubic-time algorithm if g is associative, and a quadratic-time one if $f = g$ and the monotonicity and QI conditions are satisfied. But it is also possible to have a linear-time, or even constant-time, algorithm, depending on the values of these two functions. To appreciate the range of possibilities, we will now look at a number of instructive examples.

Concatenation. The first example, an old friend, concerns the best way to concatenate a list of lists. It takes m steps to concatenate a list of length m with a list of length n and the result is a list with length $m+n$, so we can take $f = (\ll)$, where $m \ll n = m$, and $g = (+)$. That means there is a cubic-time algorithm to determine the best way of concatenating lists of lists.

However, there is a much simpler method. Suppose the lists are xs_j for $1 \leqslant j \leqslant n$. The minimum possible cost of carrying out the concatenation is given by $\sum_{j=1}^{n-1} x_j$, where x_j is the length of xs_j. To see this, observe that each element of xs_j for $1 \leqslant j < n$ has to be concatenated with some list to its right, contributing at least x_j to the cost. The minimum cost can be achieved by bracketing from the right. In other words, the standard definition $concat = foldr \, (\mathbin{+\!\!+}) \, []$ is, as expected, the best possible way to concatenate a list of lists. One can regard this solution as taking constant time since no work has to be done in finding the best bracketing. Of course, it takes linear time actually to build the tree. Essentially the same result, namely that bracketing from the right is optimal, holds for $f = (\ll)$ and $g = (\times)$. The dual result, namely that folding from the left is optimum, holds if $f = (\gg)$, where $m \gg n = n$.

Adding numbers. Next, what is the best way of adding a list of decimal integers together? Integer addition is commutative as well as associative, but we will ignore this fact in what follows. Here the problem is to compute $\sum_{k=1}^{n} x_k$, where x_k is an integer with d_k digits. We will suppose that adding an m-digit integer to an n-digit integer takes $(m \min n)$ steps and yields an integer of size $(m \max n)$. Thus $f = min$ and $g = max$. These estimates are not quite accurate for integer addition, owing to possible carries, so the claim below holds only when no carries are involved in any addition. Since g is associative, there is a cubic-time solution. However, there is a simple constant-time solution: any way of bracketing the additions is as good as any other. We claim that the cost of any bracketing is the sum of the lengths of the integers minus a maximum length. More precisely, let $S(i,j) = \sum_{k=i}^{j} d_k$ and $M(i,j) = \text{Max}_{k=i}^{j} d_k$. Then we claim that the cost $C(1,n)$ of adding n numbers is $C(1,n) = S(1,n) - M(1,n)$, irrespective of the bracketing. The proof is by induction. For the base case we have

$$C(1,1) = 0 = S(1,1) - M(1,1)$$

since the cost of performing no additions is zero. For the induction step, we have

$$
\begin{aligned}
& C(1,n) \\
= \quad & \{ \text{ assuming an initial split at position } j \,\} \\
& C(1,j) + C(j+1,n) + (M(1,j) \text{ min } M(j+1,n)) \\
= \quad & \{ \text{ induction } \} \\
& S(1,j) - M(1,j) + S(j+1,n) - M(j+1,n) + (M(1,j) \text{ min } M(j+1,n)) \\
= \quad & \{ \text{ definition of } S \,\} \\
& S(1,n) - M(1,j) - M(j+1,n) + (M(1,j) \text{ min } M(j+1,n)) \\
= \quad & \{ \text{ arithmetic: } x + y = x \text{ min } y + x \text{ max } y \,\} \\
& S(1,n) - (M(1,j) \text{ max } M(j+1,n)) \\
= \quad & \{ \text{ definition of } M \,\} \\
& S(1,n) - M(1,n)
\end{aligned}
$$

All ways of summing the numbers therefore have the same cost, so the way the brackets are inserted is immaterial. It therefore takes no work to find the solution, though of course again it takes linear time to build the tree.

Multiplying numbers. Next, consider the cost of multiplying a list of decimal numbers together, assuming that multiplying an m-digit number by an n-digit number takes exactly $m \times n$ multiplications and gives an answer of length $m + n$. Thus $f = (\times)$ and $g = (+)$. Again, these estimates are not quite accurate for integer multiplication, owing to possible carries. As in the case of addition, we can improve on the cubic-time algorithm because any way of bracketing the multiplications has the same cost as any other. To define this cost, let $S(i,j) = \sum_{k=i}^{j} d_j$ and $Q(i,j) = \sum_{k=i}^{j} d_k^2$. Then the common cost is given by

$$C(1,n) = (S(1,n)^2 - Q(1,n))/2$$

The proof is by induction. The base case is

$$C(1,1) = 0 = (S(1,1)^2 - Q(1,1))/2$$

The induction step is

Figure 14.1 The Amoeba Fight Show

$$C(1,n)$$
$$= \quad \{ \text{ assuming an initial split at } j \}$$
$$C(1,j) + C(j+1,n) + S(1,j)\,S(j+1,n)$$
$$= \quad \{ \text{ induction } \}$$
$$(S(1,j)^2 - Q(1,j) + S(j+1,n)^2 - Q(j+1,n))/2 + S(1,j)\,S(j+1,n)$$
$$= \quad \{ \text{ arithmetic: } (x^2 + y^2)/2 + xy = (x+y)^2/2 \}$$
$$(S(1,n)^2 - Q(1,n))/2$$

Therefore the multiplications can be performed in any order. This is also a constant-time solution.

Multiplying matrices. As we have seen, the situation changes when the objects to be multiplied are matrices, not numbers. In this case the function r is not monotonic. For example, take the four matrices M_1, M_2, M_3, M_4 with dimensions 2×3, 3×2, 2×10, and 10×1, respectively. As can easily be verified, the best order to compute $M_1 M_2 M_3$ is to parenthesise it as $(M_1 M_2) M_3$ with root 2, while the best way to compute $M_1 M_2 M_3 M_4$ is to parenthesise it as $M_1 (M_2 (M_3 M_4))$ with root 1. That means that only the cubic-time dynamic programming solution applies. In fact there is an $O(n \log n)$ solution for the matrix multiplication problem (see the chapter notes) but it is too complicated to be described here.

Amoeba fight show. This example owes its setting to [13]. Imagine a line of cannibalistic amoebae, each separated from its neighbour by a sliding door, as shown in Figure 14.1. Removing a door enables two neighbouring amoebae to fight. The winner of the fight is always the heavier amoeba, which absorbs its lighter companion, increasing its weight in the process. The duration of the fight is proportional to the weight of the lighter amoeba. At the end of all the fights is a single fat amoeba whose weight has been increased by the sum of all the losers. The compère wants the show to be over as quickly as possible, for fast audience turnover. What is the best way of arranging the fights, that is, the best order for removing the sliding doors?

More prosaically, we seek an optimum bracketing where the relevant definitions are $f = min$ and $g = (+)$. There is therefore a cubic-time algorithm for the problem. However, we can put a lower bound to the cost of a show: each amoeba except one has to lose its life. That means the minimum cost is at least the sum of the weights of all the amoebae except a largest one. This bound can be achieved by the simple expedient of letting a heaviest amoeba fight at each step. The solution is not unique, for the two fights $((((3\ 6)\ 2)\ 1)\ 5)$ and $(3\ (((6\ 2)\ 1)\ 5))$ both have minimum cost 11. One method for constructing a best bracketing is given by

$$mct\ xs = foldr\ Fork\ e\ (map\ Leaf\ ys)$$
$$\textbf{where}\ e = foldl\ Fork\ (Leaf\ z)\ (map\ Leaf\ zs)$$
$$(ys, z : zs) = span\ (\neq maximum\ xs)\ xs$$

We split a sequence into those elements before a (first) maximum value and those afterwards. For example, $[3, 6, 2, 1, 5]$ is split into the two component lists $[3]$ and $[6, 2, 1, 5]$. Note that the first element of the second list is a maximum element. The two lists are combined by folding from the left the elements in the second list, and then folding the result from the right with the first list. This algorithm takes linear time. But it is not an example of a greedy algorithm, at least not one built on the inductive definition of *mktrees* in Chapter 8. For example, there are three trees over $[2, 1, 7, 3]$ with minimum cost, namely $(2\ (1\ (7\ 3)))$, $(2\ ((1\ 7)\ 3))$, and $((2\ (1\ 7))\ 3)$, but none of them can be extended to the unique solution $((((9\ 2)\ 1)\ 7)\ 3)$ for the fringe $[9, 2, 1, 7, 3]$.

Restricted Huffman coding. The cost function for Huffman coding is given by $\sum_{j=1}^{n} x_j d_j$, where d_j is the depth of the leaf containing x_j. As we saw in Section 8.2, the same cost function is given by taking $f = g = (+)$ in the optimum bracketing version of the problem. In the restricted version of Huffman coding the fringe of the final tree has to be exactly the list of elements in the input. In Huffman's algorithm the pair whose joint weight is the smallest is combined at each step, but that idea does not work for the restricted version. For example, the best tree for the fringe $[10, 13, 9, 14]$ is $((10\ 13)\ (9\ 14))$, whose cost is 92, but combining the smallest pair at each step would lead to the tree $((10\ (13\ 9))\ 14)$ with cost 100. Other ideas, like choosing a split that best equalises the sum of weights in each half, also do not work. However, the monotonicity and quadrangle inequality conditions hold, so there is a quadratic-time algorithm for the problem. There is also another, quite different algorithm for this particular instance, the Garsia–Wachs algorithm, which we will discuss in Section 14.6. The Garsia–Wachs algorithm can be implemented to take $O(n \log n)$ steps for an input of length n.

Cartesian sums. Consider the associative operation $\oplus$ defined by

$$xs \oplus ys = [x + y \mid x \leftarrow xs, y \leftarrow ys]$$

This function arose in Section 5.5 in connection with sorting. The cost of computing $\oplus$ on two lists of lengths m and n is $m \times n$ additions, and the result is a list of length $m \times n$, so we have $f = g = (\times)$. The problem is to combine a list of nonempty lists of numbers with $\oplus$. As we have seen, the monotonicity and quadrangle inequality conditions are satisfied for this problem, provided each list has a positive length, so a best bracketing can certainly be found in quadratic time.

Boustrophedon product. Finally, consider an operation known as the *boustrophedon product* of two lists. Some combinatorial generation algorithms involve running up and down one list in between generating successive elements of another list, rather like the shuttle on a loom or an ox ploughing a field. The word *boustrophedon* means 'ox-turning' in ancient Greek. The boustrophedon product $\langle\!+\!\!+\!\rangle$ of two lists can be defined by

$$(\langle\!+\!\!+\!\rangle) :: [a] \rightarrow [a] \rightarrow [a]$$
$$[] \quad \langle\!+\!\!+\!\rangle \; ys = ys$$
$$(x:xs) \; \langle\!+\!\!+\!\rangle \; ys = ys + x : (xs \; \langle\!+\!\!+\!\rangle \; reverse \; ys)$$

For example

$$[3,4] \; \langle\!+\!\!+\!\rangle \; [0,1,2] = [0,1,2,3,2,1,0,4,0,1,2]$$
$$\texttt{"abc"} \; \langle\!+\!\!+\!\rangle \; \texttt{"xyz"} = \texttt{"xyzazyxbxyzczyx"}$$

The function $\langle\!+\!\!+\!\rangle$ is associative, though this fact is not obvious. So, what is the best way of computing the boustrophedon product of a list of lists? The cost of computing $\langle\!+\!\!+\!\rangle$ for two lists of lengths m and n is proportional to the length of the result, namely $m + m \times n + n$. Thus $f = g = (\bullet)$, where $m \bullet n = m + m \times n + n$. The monotonicity and quadrangle inequality conditions hold for this problem, so there is a quadratic-time algorithm for computing the best way of bracketing the boustrophedon product of a list of lists.

14.4 Proof of monotonicity

This section is devoted solely to the proof of (14.1). The result can be restated in the form

$$r(i,j) \leqslant r(i,j+1) \quad \text{and} \quad r(i,j) \leqslant r(i+1,j) \tag{14.3}$$

where $r(i,j)$ is the smallest integer in the range $i \leqslant r < j$ for which the best bracketing for $w_i, \ldots, w_j$ begins with the split $(w_i \ldots w_r)(w_{r+1} \ldots w_j)$.

Let $C(i,j)$ denote the minimum cost of bracketing $w_i, \ldots, w_j$, and $W(i,j)$ the weight of the resulting expression. Thus $W(i,j) = w_i \bullet w_{i+1} \cdots w_{j-1} \bullet w_j$, where $f = g = (\bullet)$. Define $C_k(i,j)$ for $i \leqslant k < j$ by

$$C_k(i,j) = C(i,k) + C(k+1,j) + W(i,j)$$

Thus $C_k(i,j)$ is the cost of the bracketing $(w_i, \ldots, w_k)(w_{k+1}, \ldots, w_j)$. Now (14.3) follows from the assertion that, if r is the smallest value in the range $i \leqslant r < j$ such that $C(i,j) = C_r(i,j)$, then

$$i \leqslant q < r \;\Rightarrow\; C_r(i,j+1) < C_q(i,j+1)$$
$$i < q < r \;\Rightarrow\; C_r(i+1,j) < C_q(i+1,j)$$

In turn, these assertions follow from

$$i \leqslant q < r \;\Rightarrow\; C_q(i,j) + C_r(i,j+1) \leqslant C_q(i,j+1) + C_r(i,j) \tag{14.4}$$

$$i < q < r \;\Rightarrow\; C_q(i,j) + C_r(i+1,j) \leqslant C_q(i+1,j) + C_r(i,j) \tag{14.5}$$

By definition of r we have $C_r(i,j) < C_q(i,j)$ for $i \leqslant q < r$, so (14.4) and (14.5) give

$$0 < C_q(i,j) - C_r(i,j) \;\leqslant\; C_q(i,j+1) - C_r(i,j+1)$$
$$0 < C_q(i,j) - C_r(i,j) \;\leqslant\; C_q(i+1,j) - C_r(i+1,j)$$

In turn, (14.4) and (14.5) follow from the quadrangle inequality (14.2), namely

$$i \leqslant i' \leqslant j \leqslant j' \;\Rightarrow\; C(i,j) + C(i',j') \leqslant C(i,j') + C(i',j)$$

Assuming (14.2), we can prove (14.4) by arguing

$$
\begin{aligned}
& C_q(i,j) + C_r(i,j+1) \\
={} & \quad \{\text{ definition of } C_k \} \\
& C(i,q) + C(q+1,j) + W(i,j) + C(i,r) + C(r+1,j+1) + W(i,j+1) \\
\leqslant{} & \quad \{\, (14.2), \text{ as } q+1 \leqslant r+1 < j < j+1 \,\} \\
& C(i,q) + C(q+1,j+1) + W(i,j+1) + C(i,r) + C(r+1,j) + W(i,j) \\
={} & \quad \{\text{ definition of } C_q \text{ and } C_k \} \\
& C_q(i,j+1) + C_r(i,j)
\end{aligned}
$$

The proof of (14.5) is similar.

It remains to prove (14.2). The proof is by induction on $j' - i$. The claim is trivially true when $i = i'$ or $j = j'$, so (14.2) holds when $j' - i \leqslant 1$. For the induction step we need to consider the cases $i' = j$ and $i' < j$ separately.

Case A: $i < i' = j < j'$. In this case (14.2) reduces to

$$C(i,j) + C(j,j') \leqslant C(i,j') \tag{14.6}$$

if $i < j < j'$. Suppose $C(i,j') = C_r(i,j')$, where $i \leqslant r < j'$. There are two subcases, depending on whether $r < j$ or $j \leqslant r$. If $r < j$, then we reason

$$
\begin{aligned}
& C(i,j) + C(j,j') \\
\leqslant{} & \quad \{\text{ since } C(i,j) \leqslant C_r(i,j) \text{ for } i \leqslant r < j \} \\
& C(i,r) + C(r+1,j) + W(i,j) + C(j,j') \\
\leqslant{} & \quad \{\text{ induction } (14.6), \text{ since } j' - r - 1 < j' - i \text{ as } i < r+1 \} \\
& C(i,r) + C(r+1,j') + W(i,j) \\
\leqslant{} & \quad \{\text{ assumption; see below }\} \\
& C(i,r) + C(r+1,j') + W(i,j') \\
={} & \quad \{\text{ definition of } r \} \\
& C(i,j')
\end{aligned}
$$

The assumption on W is the case $i = i'$ of the monotonicity condition

$$i' \leqslant i \leqslant j \leqslant j' \;\Rightarrow\; W(i,j) \leqslant W(i',j')$$

The case $j \leqslant r$ is handled in the same way and requires case $j = j'$ of the monotonicity condition on W.

Case B: $i < i' < j < j'$. In this case suppose the two terms on the right-hand side of (14.2) are minimised at r and s, so

$$C(i',j) = C_r(i',j) \quad\text{and}\quad C(i,j') = C_s(i,j')$$

where $i' \leqslant r < j$ and $i \leqslant s < j'$. Again there are two symmetric subcases. If $s \leqslant r$, then we reason

$$
\begin{aligned}
&C(i,j) + C(i',j') \\
\leqslant\; &\{\text{ definitions of } r \text{ and } s\ \} \\
&C_s(i,j) + C_r(i',j') \\
=\; &\{\text{ definition of } C_k\ \} \\
&C(i,s) + C(s+1,j) + W(i,j) + C(i',r) + C(r+1,j') + W(i',j') \\
=\; &\{\text{ induction }\} \\
&C(i,s) + C(s+1,j') + W(i,j) + C(i',r) + C(r+1,j) + W(i',j') \\
\leqslant\; &\{\text{ assumption; see below }\} \\
&C(i,s) + C(s+1,j') + W(i,j') + C(i',r) + C(r+1,j) + W(i',j) \\
=\; &\{\text{ definition of } C_k\ \} \\
&C_s(i,j') + C_r(i',j) \\
=\; &\{\text{ definition of } r \text{ and } s\ \} \\
&C(i,j') + C(i',j)
\end{aligned}
$$

The assumption is just the quadrangle inequality condition on W. The case $r \leqslant s$ is handled similarly and also requires the quadrangle inequality. This completes the proof of (14.1).

14.5 Optimum binary search trees

We turn next to a close cousin of optimum bracketing, namely the problem of building an *optimum* binary search tree. One way to build a binary search tree was described in Section 4.3, where we showed how to balance a tree so that no search takes more than logarithmic time. In practice, however, different keys have different probabilities of occurring as the argument of a search. A better organisation would be to have keys with a high frequency of occurring closer to the root. For example, suppose we wanted to search for all occurrences of the nine-letter words in this book, say for the purpose of preparing an index. It turns out that the word 'algorithm' appears much more frequently than 'condition' or 'operation', so that key should be closer to the root of the tree.

Suppose we are given probabilities $p_1, p_2, ..., p_n$, expressed as integer frequency counts, so that p_j is the probability that the argument of a successful search is the value x_j in a list $x_1, x_2, ..., x_n$ of increasing values. Suppose $q_0, q_1, ..., q_n$ is another list so that q_j is the probability that the argument of an unsuccessful search falls between the two values x_j and x_{j+1}. By convention, q_0 represents the probability that the search argument is less than x_1 and q_n the probability that it is greater than x_n. We can install these values in a modified binary search tree in which *Null* nodes are replaced by leaf nodes containing q-values, and internal nodes are augmented with p-values.

Thus we define a binary search tree to be

$$\textbf{data } BST \; a = Leaf \; Nat \mid Node \; Nat \; (BST \; a) \; a \; (BST \; a)$$

For example, ignoring x-values, a simple example is

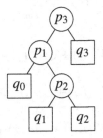

The cost of this tree is $2q_0 + 2p_1 + 3q_1 + 3p_2 + 3q_2 + p_3 + q_3$, which is the scalar product of the result of flattening the tree and the depths of the nodes, where the depths of non-leaf nodes are counted from 1 rather than 0. In general,

$$cost :: BST \; a \rightarrow Nat$$
$$cost \; t = sum \; (zipWith \; (\times) \; (flatten \; t) \; (depths \; t))$$

where

$$flatten :: BST \; a \rightarrow [Nat]$$
$$flatten \; (Leaf \; q) \qquad = [q]$$
$$flatten \; (Node \; p \; l \; x \; r) = flatten \; l \mathbin{+\!\!+} [p] \mathbin{+\!\!+} flatten \; r$$

$$depths :: BST \; a \rightarrow [Nat]$$
$$depths = from \; 0$$
$$\textbf{where } from \; d \; (Leaf \; \_) \qquad = [d]$$
$$from \; d \; (Node \; \_ \; l \; \_ \; r) = from \; (d+1) \; l \mathbin{+\!\!+} [d+1] \mathbin{+\!\!+} from \; (d+1) \; r$$

We saw a similar definition of cost in Huffman coding. Moreover, as with the cost function in Huffman coding, we can express *cost* recursively:

$$cost \; (Leaf \; q) \qquad = 0$$
$$cost \; (Node \; p \; l \; x \; r) = cost \; l + cost \; r + weight \; (Node \; p \; l \; x \; r)$$

$$weight \; (Leaf \; q) \qquad = q$$
$$weight \; (Node \; p \; l \; x \; r) = p + weight \; l + weight \; r$$

It follows that the cost $C(i,j)$ of building a binary search tree with frequency counts

$p_{i+1}, ..., p_j$ and $q_i, ..., q_j$ is given by

$$C(i,j) = \text{Min}_{k=i}^{j-1} (C(i,k) + C(k+1,j)) + w(i,j)$$

where $w(i,j) = q_i + p_{i+1} + \cdots + q_{j-1} + p_j + q_j$. The function w is monotonic and satisfies the quadrangle inequality, so (14.1) holds and there is a quadratic-time dynamic programming algorithm for constructing a binary search tree with minimum cost.

14.6 The Garsia–Wachs algorithm

When the frequency counts p_j are all zero, so only the costs of unsuccessful searches matter, the problem of finding an optimum search tree is essentially the same as that of the restricted version of Huffman coding in which the fringe has to be exactly the given list. In turn, this is exactly the instance of optimum bracketing in which $f = g = (+)$. For these particular values of f and g there is another, quite different algorithm for computing a tree with minimum cost. The algorithm is known as the *Garsia–Wachs* algorithm and is fairly easy to describe – at least in an unoptimised form – but even the best current proof of its correctness has some tricky details, so we will omit it. References to published proofs are given in the chapter notes.

The Garsia–Wachs algorithm is a two-stage process (see Exercise 14.14 as to why two stages appear to be necessary). In the first stage we build a tree from the given list of weights, and in the second stage we rebuild it. With *Weight* as a synonym for *Int*, we have

> *gwa* :: [*Weight*] → *Tree Weight*
> *gwa ws* = *rebuild ws* (*build ws*)

With *Label* as another synonym for *Int*, the types of *build* and *rebuild* are

> *build* :: [*Weight*] → *Tree Label*
> *rebuild* :: [*Weight*] → *Tree Label* → *Tree Weight*

The result of *build ws* is a tree whose fringe is not *ws* but some permutation of the labels [1..n], where n is the length of *ws*. The critical property of this tree concerns the depths of its leaves. Suppose the depths are $d_1, d_2, ..., d_n$, where d_j is the depth of *Leaf j*. Then there is a tree with minimum cost and fringe *ws* in which the depth of the leaf labelled with w_j is d_j. As an example, suppose *build* applied to [27, 16, 11, 70, 21, 31, 65] produces the tree

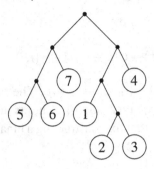

The list of depths in numerical order of leaf value is $[3,4,4,2,3,3,2]$. The claim, which we will not prove, is that there is a minimum-cost tree for the given input whose depths in fringe order constitute exactly this list, and that tree is

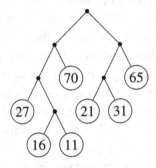

This tree can be obtained from the one above by a simple bottom-up algorithm. The starting point is a list of pairs, the first component of each pair being a leaf containing the required label w_j, and the second component being the depth d_j. For our example this is the list

$$(27,3) \ (16,4) \ (11,4) \ (70,2) \ (21,3) \ (31,3) \ (65,2)$$

in which a pair (w,d) represents ($Leaf \ w, d$). This list of pairs is reduced to a single pair by repeatedly combining the first two adjacent pairs in the list with the same depth until only a single pair remains. When two pairs with a common depth are combined, the depth is reduced by one. Thus for our example we get the sequence of steps pictured in Figure 14.2, ending with a single tree and a final depth of 0. This process is not guaranteed to work for all lists of depths, but it does work for those that result from the first stage of the Garsia–Wachs algorithm. For example, the tree $((1 \ 3) \ 2)$ has depths $[2,1,2]$ in numerical order of leaf label, but no adjacent pair has the same depth, so no pair can be combined, and the reduction process fails to make progress.

The obvious way to implement this reduction process is by a function *reduce*:

$$
\begin{array}{lllllll}
(27,3) & (16,4) & (11,4) & (70,2) & (21,3) & (31,3) & (65,2) \\
(27,3) & ((16\ 11),3) & & (70,2) & (21,3) & (31,3) & (65,2) \\
((27\ (16\ 11)),2) & & & (70,2) & (21,3) & (31,3) & (65,2) \\
(((27\ (16\ 11))\ 70),1) & & & & (21,3) & (31,3) & (65,2) \\
(((27\ (16\ 11))\ 70),1) & & & & (21,3) & (31,3) & (65,2) \\
(((27\ (16\ 11))\ 70),1) & & & & ((21\ 31),2) & & (65,2) \\
(((27\ (16\ 11))\ 70),1) & & & & (((21\ 31)\ 65),1) & & \\
(((((27\ (16\ 11))\ 70)\ ((21\ 31)\ 65))),0)
\end{array}
$$

Figure 14.2 Combining trees

---

reduce :: $[(Tree\ Label, Depth)] \rightarrow Tree\ Label$
reduce = *extract · until single step* **where**
  extract $[(t,\_)] = t$
  step $(x:y:xs) = $ **if** *depth* $x == $ *depth* y **then** *join* $x\ y:xs$ **else** $x:step\ (y:xs)$
  join $(t_1,d)\ (t_2,\_) = (Fork\ t_1\ t_2, d-1)$

where *Depth* is a synonym for *Int* and *depth* = *snd*. The function *step* is applied
repeatedly until it produces a singleton list. However, this definition of *reduce*
can take quadratic time because *step* can take linear time. The inefficiency arises
because, if *step* finds the first pair to be joined at positions k and $k+1$, then the next
call of *step* will repeat the unsuccessful search on the first $k-2$ elements when it
could begin a new search at position $k-1$, the earliest position at which two depths
could be the same. One way to avoid the inefficiency is to use a *foldl* and a recursive
definition of *step*, redefining *reduce* to read

reduce :: $[(Tree\ Label, Depth)] \rightarrow Tree\ Label$
reduce = *extract · foldl step* $[]$ **where**
  extract $[(t,\_)] = t$
  step $[]\ y\quad = [y]$
  step $(x:xs)\ y = $ **if** *depth* $x == $ *depth* y **then** *step xs* $(join\ x\ y)$ **else** $y:x:xs$
  join $(t_1,d)\ (t_2,\_) = (Fork\ t_1\ t_2, d-1)$

The first argument to *step* maintains the invariant that no two adjacent pairs on the
list have the same depth; this list is kept in reverse order for efficiency. To maintain
the invariant, *step* is called recursively whenever two pairs are joined. Each call of
step takes time proportional to the number of *join* operations, and there are exactly
$n-1$ of these operations in total, so *reduce* now takes linear time.

Having dealt with *reduce*, we can now define *rebuild*:

rebuild :: $[Weight] \rightarrow Tree\ Label \rightarrow Tree\ Weight$
rebuild ws = *reduce · zip* $(map\ Leaf\ ws) \cdot sortDepths$

The function *sortDepths* sorts the depths of a tree into increasing order of label value. Since labels take the form $[1, 2, ..., n]$, where n is the number of nodes in the tree, sorting can be accomplished in linear time by using an array:

$sortDepths :: Tree\ Label \rightarrow [Depth]$
$sortDepths\ t = elems\ (array\ (1, size\ t)\ (zip\ (fringe\ t)\ (depths\ t)))$

The functions *size*, which counts the number of nodes in a tree, *fringe* and *depths* can be computed in linear time, so *sortDepths* and *rebuild* each take linear time.

It remains to deal with the first stage of the Garsia–Wachs algorithm, the function *build*. This is where the intricacy of the algorithm resides. The plan of attack is to develop a quadratic-time solution first, and then improve it to a linearithmic one by a suitable choice of data structure.

For input $[w_1, w_2, ..., w_n]$, the starting point is a list

$$(0, w_0), \quad (1, w_1), \quad (2, w_2), \quad ..., \quad (n, w_n)$$

of pairs of leaves and weights, so (j, w) abbreviates $(Leaf\ j, w)$. The first pair $(0, w_0)$ is a sentinel pair in which $w_0 = \infty$. Use of a sentinel simplifies the description of the algorithm but is not essential (see the exercises). The following two steps are now repeated until just two pairs remain, the sentinel pair and one other:

1. Given the current list $[(0, w_0), ..., (t_p, w_p)]$, where $p > 1$, find the largest j in the range $1 \leqslant j < p$ such that $w_{j-1} + w_j \geqslant w_j + w_{j+1}$, equivalently, $w_{j-1} \geqslant w_{j+1}$. Such a j is guaranteed to exist since $w_0 = \infty$. Replace the two pairs (t_j, w_j) and (t_{j+1}, w_{j+1}) by a single pair $(t_*, w_*) = (Fork\ t_j\ t_{j+1}, w_j + w_{j+1})$, giving a new list

$$(0, w_0), \quad (t_1, w_1), \quad ..., \quad (t_{j-1}, w_{j-1}), \quad (t_*, w_*), \quad (t_{j+2}, w_{j+2}), \quad ..., \quad (t_p, w_p)$$

2. Now move (t_*, w_*) to the right over all pairs (t, w) for which $w < w_*$.

At the end of this process there are just two pairs left, the sentinel and a second pair whose first component is the required tree.

Here is an example. Suppose we begin with the list

$$(0, \infty), \quad (1, 10), \quad (2, 25), \quad (3, 31), \quad (4, 22), \quad (5, 13), \quad (6, 18), \quad (7, 45)$$

The first pair to be combined is $(5, 13)$ and $(6, 18)$ (because $22 \geqslant 18$). The result is shifted zero places to the right, giving

$$(0, \infty), \quad (1, 10), \quad (2, 25), \quad (3, 31), \quad (4, 22), \quad ((5\ 6), 31), \quad (7, 45)$$

The next pair to be combined is $(4, 22)$ and $((5\ 6), 31)$ (because $31 \geqslant 31$). The result is shifted one place to the right, giving

$$(0, \infty), \quad (1, 10), \quad (2, 25), \quad (3, 31), \quad (7, 45), \quad ((4\ (5\ 6)), 53)$$

The next pair to be combined is $(1, 10)$ and $(2, 25)$, giving

$$(0,\infty),\quad (3,31),\quad ((1\ 2),35),\quad (7,45),\quad ((4\ (5\ 6)),53)$$

The remaining three steps are similar in that they all involve combining the second two pairs:

$$(0,\infty),\quad (7,45),\quad ((4\ (5\ 6)),53),\quad ((3\ (1\ 2)),66)$$
$$(0,\infty),\quad ((3\ (1\ 2)),66),\quad ((7\ (4\ (5\ 6))),98)$$
$$(0,\infty),\quad (((3\ (1\ 2))\ (7\ (4\ (5\ 6)))),164)$$

The first component of the second pair is the final tree. Note that the sentinel plays a passive role and is never combined with another pair.

The obvious way to implement this algorithm is repeatedly to scan the whole list from right to left at each step, looking for the largest j such that $w_{j-1} \geqslant w_{j+1}$. However, a better way of organising the search stems from the following observation. Say that a sequence $w_1, w_2, \ldots$ is *two-sorted* if $w_1 < w_3 < w_5 < \cdots$ and $w_2 < w_4 < w_6 < \cdots$. It follows from the definition of j in step 1 that the sequence $w_j, \ldots, w_p$ is two-sorted. Suppose that the following sequence of weights is produced by step 2:

$$w_0,\quad w_1,\quad w_2,\quad \ldots,\quad w_{j-1},\quad w_{j+2},\quad \ldots,\quad w_{k-1},\quad w_*,\quad w_k,\quad \ldots,\quad w_p$$

Again, both $w_k, \ldots, w_p$ and $w_{j+2}, \ldots, w_{k-1}, w_*$ are two-sorted because $w_{k-2} < w_*$. Furthermore, we know that $w_{j+r} < w_* \leqslant w_k$ for $2 \leqslant r < k - j$. That means the next pair to be combined is the first one in the following list of three possibilities:

1. w_k and w_{k+1}, provided $w_* \geqslant w_{k+1}$;
2. w_{j+2} and w_{j+3}, provided $w_{j-1} \geqslant w_{j+3}$;
3. w_i and w_{i+1}, provided $1 \leqslant i < j - 1$ and $w_{i-1} \geqslant w_{i+1}$.

These cases can be captured by expressing *build* in terms of *foldr* and a new function *step*:

$$build :: [Weight] \rightarrow Tree\ Label$$
$$build\ ws = extract\ (foldr\ step\ [\,]\ (zip\ (map\ Leaf\ [0\,..])\ (infinity : ws)))$$
$$\textbf{where}\ extract\ [\_,(t,\_)] = t$$
$$infinity = sum\ ws$$

No weight arising during the algorithm can be greater than the sum of the input weights, so this definition of *infinity* is adequate. The function *foldr step* [] scans the input from right to left, looking for the next pair to be combined. To define *step*, we first introduce

$$\textbf{type}\ Pair = (Tree\ Label, Weight)$$
$$weight :: Pair \rightarrow Weight$$
$$weight\ (t,w) = w$$

Then *step* is defined by

$$step :: Pair \rightarrow [Pair] \rightarrow [Pair]$$
$$step\ x\ (y:z:xs)\ |\ weight\ x < weight\ z = x:y:z:xs$$
$$\qquad\qquad\qquad\qquad |\ otherwise \qquad\qquad = step\ x\ (insert\ (join\ y\ z)\ xs)$$
$$step\ x\ xs \qquad\quad = x:xs$$

$$join :: Pair \rightarrow Pair \rightarrow Pair$$
$$join\ (t_1, w_1)\ (t_2, w_2) = (Fork\ t_1\ t_2, w_1 + w_2)$$

$$insert :: Pair \rightarrow [Pair] \rightarrow [Pair]$$
$$insert\ x\ xs = ys \mathbin{+\mkern-10mu+} step\ x\ zs$$
$$\qquad \textbf{where}\ (ys, zs) = splitList\ x\ xs$$
$$\qquad\qquad splitList\ x\ xs = span\ (\lambda y.\ weight\ y < weight\ x)\ xs$$

The function *insert* makes use of an instance *splitList* of the general utility function *span* to find the right place for a combined pair to be inserted, and calls *step* again to deal with Case 1. The recursive call to *step* in the definition of *step* deals with Case 2, and Case 3 is handled by the right-to-left search in *foldr step* [ ]. Note that the second argument of both *step* and *insert* is always a two-sorted list, a fact we will exploit later on.

In the worst case (see Exercise 14.13), the running time of *build* is quadratic in the length of the input. That means that the algorithm is no better than the dynamic programming algorithm seen earlier. The main culprit is the function *insert*, which can take linear time in the worst case. If we could arrange that *insert* took logarithmic time, then the total running time of the Garsia–Wachs algorithm would be reduced to $O(n \log n)$ steps. Such an implementation is indeed possible, because the second argument to *insert* is not an arbitrary list of pairs but one that is two-sorted on second components.

The revised implementation is carried out in two stages. The first stage is to rewrite *build* in terms of a new data type *List Pair*, designed for representing lists of pairs that are two-sorted on second components. The following six operations are to be provided:

$$emptyL\ :: List\ a$$
$$nullL\ \ :: List\ a \rightarrow Bool$$
$$consL\ \ :: a \rightarrow List\ a \rightarrow List\ a$$
$$deconsL :: List\ a \rightarrow (a, List\ a)$$
$$concatL :: List\ a \rightarrow List\ a \rightarrow List\ a$$
$$splitL\ \ :: Pair \rightarrow List\ Pair \rightarrow (List\ Pair, List\ Pair)$$

Most of these operations are self-explanatory. The first five functions work for lists

of any type, but the function *splitL* is specific to *List Pair*. This function is the
analogue of *splitList* used in the definition of *insert*.

The function *build* is replaced by a new version *buildL*, basically the same as
before except that certain list operations are replaced with *List* operations:

$buildL :: [Weight] \rightarrow Tree\ Label$
$buildL\ ws = extractL\ (foldr\ stepL\ emptyL\ (start\ ws))$
$\quad\quad\textbf{where}\ start\ ws = zip\ (map\ Leaf\ [0..])\ (infinity:ws)$
$\quad\quad\quad\quad\quad infinity = sum\ ws$

$extractL :: List\ Pair \rightarrow Tree\ Label$
$extractL\ xs = t$
$\quad\textbf{where}\ (\_,ys)\quad\ = deconsL\ xs$
$\quad\quad\quad\ ((t,\_),\_) = deconsL\ ys$

$stepL :: Pair \rightarrow List\ Pair \rightarrow List\ Pair$
$stepL\ x\ xs = \textbf{if}\ nullL\ xs \vee nullL\ ys \vee weight\ x < weight\ z$
$\quad\quad\quad\quad\ \textbf{then}\quad consL\ x\ xs$
$\quad\quad\quad\quad\ \textbf{else}\quad stepL\ x\ (insertL\ (join\ y\ z)\ zs)$
$\quad\quad\quad\quad\ \ \textbf{where}\ (y,ys) = deconsL\ xs$
$\quad\quad\quad\quad\quad\quad\quad\ (z,zs) = deconsL\ ys$

$insertL :: Pair \rightarrow List\ Pair \rightarrow List\ Pair$
$insertL\ x\ xs = concatL\ ys\ (stepL\ x\ zs)$
$\quad\quad\quad\quad\ \textbf{where}\ (ys,zs) = splitL\ x\ xs$

The second stage is to implement *List* so that the six operations above take at most
logarithmic time. Then *buildL* will take linearithmic time. There are various options,
and we choose an implementation based on a modification of the balanced binary
search trees of Section 4.3, henceforth called *search* trees to distinguish them from
the leaf trees constructed by the algorithm. To motivate the modification, consider
the search tree

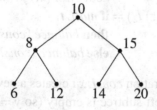

whose nodes are labelled with pairs of leaf trees and their weights, although only the
weights are shown. Flattening this tree produces a list of weights which is two-sorted
but not sorted. Now suppose we want to insert a new pair with weight w into this
search tree. We cannot use straightforward binary search because the labels of the
search tree are not in increasing order of weight. Instead, as well as comparing w

with the weight of the leaf tree at the root, we must also compare it with the weight of the preceding leaf tree in the list. Only if w is greater than both these weights can we continue by searching the right subtree; otherwise we have to search the left subtree. In order to avoid repeatedly having to discover the weight of the preceding leaf tree, we can install this tree at the root of a search tree. If there is no preceding leaf tree, then we can artificially install a copy of the leaf tree. That leads to the tree

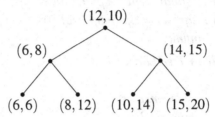

$$(12, 10)$$

$$(6, 8) \qquad\qquad (14, 15)$$

$$(6, 6) \quad (8, 12) \quad (10, 14) \quad (15, 20)$$

The data type *List Pair* is now introduced as an instance of

data *List a = Null | Node Int (List a) (a, a) (List a)*

in which nodes are labelled with pairs of values. As in Section 4.3, the first label of a *Node* records the height of the tree, which is needed in order to maintain balance. The implementations of *emptyL* and *nullL* are immediate:

emptyL :: List a
emptyL = Null

nullL :: List a → Bool
nullL Null = True
nullL _   = False

The operation *consL* adds a new pair as a leftmost element of a binary tree:

consL :: a → List a → List a
consL x Null   = node Null (x, x) Null
consL x (Node _ t₁ (y, z) t₂) = **if** *nullL t₁*
                                 then *balance (consL x t₁) (x, z) t₂*
                                 else *balance (consL x t₁) (y, z) t₂*

For an empty tree t, the operation *consL x t* creates a new node with label (x, x). For a nonempty tree t whose left subtree is empty (so $y = z$), *consL x t* creates a new node with label (x, x) and, since x is now the preceding value of z, assigns (x, z) as the new value at the root. Otherwise *consL x* is applied to the left subtree of t. The definition makes use of the two smart constructors, *node* and *balance*, described in Section 4.3. Recall that *node* is invoked only when the two trees have heights that differ by at most one, and *balance* only when the two heights differ by at most two.

Next, the function *deconsL* is defined by

> *deconsL* :: *List a* → (*a*, *List a*)
> *deconsL* (*Node* _ t_1 (*x*, *y*) t_2) = **if** *nullL* t_1 **then** (*y*, t_2)
> > **else** (*z*, *balance* t_3 (*x*, *y*) t_2)
> > **where** (*z*, t_3) = *deconsL* t_1

This searches along the left spine of a tree to find the first element.

The next function is *concatL*, which is essentially the second version of the function *combine* defined in Section 4.3:

> *concatL* :: *List a* → *List a* → *List a*
> *concatL* t_1 *Null* = t_1
> *concatL* *Null* t_2 = t_2
> *concatL* t_1 t_2 = *gbalance* t_1 (*x*, *y*) t_3
> > **where** *x* = *lastL* t_1
> > (*y*, t_3) = *deconsL* t_2

The subsidiary function *lastL* returns the last value in a nonempty tree:

> *lastL* :: *List a* → *a*
> *lastL* (*Node* _ t_1 (*x*, *y*) t_2) = **if** *nullL* t_2 **then** *y* **else** *lastL* t_2

In the third clause of *concatL* the last value in t_1 and the first value in t_2 are combined as a new root. The definition of *concatL* makes use of the general rebalancing function *gbalance* defined in Section 4.3.

The final function *splitL* is similar to the function *split* defined in Section 4.4. The difference is that *splitL x t* has to split the tree *t* into a pair of trees (t_1, t_2) in which t_1 consists of the initial segment of *t* whose weight components are all less than *weight x*, and t_2 is the remaining final segment of *t*. To carry out this process, we split a tree into pieces and then sew the pieces together again to make the final pair of trees. Thus

> *splitL* :: *Pair* → *List Pair* → (*List Pair*, *List Pair*)
> *splitL x t* = *sew* (*pieces x t*)

The only difference between this definition of *splitL* and the definition of *split* in Section 4.4 is in the definition of *pieces*:

> **data** *Piece a* = *LP* (*List a*) (*a*, *a*) | *RP* (*a*, *a*) (*List a*)
>
> *pieces* :: *Pair* → *List Pair* → [*Piece Pair*]
> *pieces x t* = *addPiece t* [ ] **where**
> > *addPiece Null ps* = *ps*
> > *addPiece* (*Node* _ t_1 (*y*, *z*) t_2) *ps* = **if** *weight x* > *max* (*weight y*) (*weight z*)
> > > **then** *addPiece* t_2 (*LP* t_1 (*y*, *z*) : *ps*)
> > > **else** *addPiece* t_1 (*RP* (*y*, *z*) t_2 : *ps*)

As we saw in Section 4.4, *splitL* takes logarithmic time in the size of the tree. This completes the definition of the Garsia–Wachs algorithm.

14.7 Chapter notes

The standard example of optimum bracketing, presented in most texts on algorithm design, is matrix multiplication. In fact, there is an $O(n \log n)$ algorithm for the multiplication of n matrices due to Hu and Shing, see [6, 7], though the details are quite complicated. For an alternative method of tabulation that uses trees with shared subtrees rather than arrays to record partial results, see [1, Chapter 21]. The quadratic-time algorithm was first described for the particular case of optimum binary search trees in [11]. Our proof of the conditions under which r is monotonic is an extension of the proof given by Yao in [14]. Yao's paper also considers other examples for which the monotonicity and QI conditions hold.

The amoeba fight show example was first described in [13]. For combinatorial applications of the boustrophedon product, see [1, Chapter 28].

The Garsia–Wachs algorithm has an interesting history. It was first discussed in terms of restricted Huffman coding in [4], where a cubic-time algorithm was proposed. As a special case of optimum binary search trees, this was reduced to a quadratic-time algorithm in [11]. A different method was described by Hu and Tucker in [8]; it is also presented in [5] and in the first edition of [12]. According to Knuth, "no simple proof [of the Hu–Tucker algorithm] is known, and it is quite possible that no simple proof will ever be found." Then along came a modification of the Hu–Tucker algorithm, the Garsia–Wachs algorithm [3], which was adopted in the second edition of [12]. The best proof of its correctness, while still not exactly simple, is discussed in [10]; see also [9]. A functional description of the Garsia–Wachs algorithm in ML, though one that uses some non-pure functional techniques, was given in [2]. All of these articles describe only the quadratic-time version of the algorithm. There is a fairly short appendix to [3], written by Robert E. Tarjan, that outlines how to implement the $O(n \log n)$ version. Knuth also mentions the sub-quadratic algorithm in an exercise [12, Section 6.2.2, Exercise 45], which is answered fairly cryptically on page 713. As far as we know, our description of an optimal, purely functional implementation of the Garsia–Wachs algorithm is new.

References

[1]   Richard Bird. *Pearls of Functional Algorithm Design*. Cambridge University Press, Cambridge, 2010.

[2]   Jean-Christophe Filliâtre. A functional implementation of the Garsia-Wachs algorithm. In *ACM SIGPLAN Workshop on ML*, pages 91–96, 2008.

[3]   Adriano M. Garsia and Michelle L. Wachs. A new algorithm for minimum cost
      binary trees. *SIAM Journal on Computing*, 6(4):622–642, 1977.
[4]   Edgar N. Gilbert and Edward F. Moore. Variable-length binary encodings. *Bell
      Systems Technical Journal*, 38(4):933–967, 1959.
[5]   Te Chiang Hu. *Combinatorial Algorithms*. Addison-Wesley, Reading, MA, 1982.
[6]   Te Chiang Hu and Man-Tak Shing. Computation of matrix chain products, part I.
      SIAM Journal on Computing, 11(2):362–373, 1982.
[7]   Te Chiang Hu and Man-Tak Shing. Computation of matrix chain products, part II.
      SIAM Journal on Computing, 13(2):228–251, 1984.
[8]   Te Chiang Hu and Alan C. Tucker. Optimal computer search trees and variable-length
      alphabetic codes. *SIAM Journal on Applied Mathematics*, 21(4):514–532, 1971.
[9]   Marek Karpinski, Lawrence L. Larmore, and Wojciech Rytter. Correctness of
      constructing optimal alphabetic tree revisited. *Theoretical Computer Science*,
      180(1–2):309–324, 1997.
[10] Jeffrey H. Kingston. A new proof of the Garsia-Wachs algorithm. *Journal of
      Algorithms*, 9(1):129–136, 1988.
[11] Donald E. Knuth. Optimum binary search trees. *Acta Informatica*, 1(1):14–25, 1971.
[12] Donald E. Knuth. *The Art of Computer Programming*, volume 3: Sorting and
      Searching. Addison-Wesley, Reading, MA, second edition, 1998.
[13] Lambert Meertens. Algorithmics: Towards programming as a mathematical activity.
      In J. W. de Bakker, M. Hazewinkel, and J. K. Lenstra, editors, *Mathematics and
      Computer Science*, volume 1 of *CWI Monographs*, pages 289—334. North-Holland
      Publishing Company, Amsterdam, 1986.
[14] Frances F. Yao. Efficient dynamic programming using quadrangle inequalities. In
      ACM Symposium on the Theory of Computing, pages 429–435, 1980.

Exercises

Exercise 14.1 Write down the five ways of bracketing $X_1 \otimes X_2 \otimes X_3 \otimes X_4$. How
many ways of bracketing five Xs are there?

Exercise 14.2 Show that if $T(1) = 1$ and

$$T(n) = n + \sum_{k=1}^{n-1} (T(k) + T(n-k))$$

then $T(n) = (3^n - 1)/2$.

Exercise 14.3 Suppose that the function *cost* associated with optimum bracketing
is generalised to read

$$cost\,(Leaf\ w) \quad = 0$$
$$cost\,(Fork\ t_1\ t_2) = h\,(cost\ t_1)\,(cost\ t_2) + f\,(size\ t_1)\,(size\ t_2)$$

Under what conditions on h would the cubic-time algorithm in the text still work?
What might be an appropriate value of h if both subtrees could be computed in
parallel?

Exercise 14.4 Suppose we replace the definition of *table* (i,j) in the quadratic algorithm for *mct* by

$$table\ (i,j)$$
$$|\ i == j\quad = (i, 0, weights\ !\ i, Leaf\ (weights\ !\ i))$$
$$|\ otherwise = minWith\ cost\ [fork\ k\ (t\ !\ (i,k))\ (t\ !\ (k+1,j))$$
$$|\ k \leftarrow [r(i,j-1)..r(i+1,j)]]]$$

What goes wrong?

Exercise 14.5 Show that the monotonicity condition

$$i' \leqslant i \leqslant j \leqslant j' \;\Rightarrow\; S(i,j) \leqslant S(i',j')$$

follows from $A \leqslant A \bullet B$ and $B \leqslant A \bullet B$ for all sizes A and B.

Exercise 14.6 Similarly, show that the quadrangle inequality

$$i \leqslant i' \leqslant j \leqslant j' \;\Rightarrow\; S(i,j) + S(i',j') \leqslant S(i,j') + S(i',j)$$

follows from $(A \bullet B) + (B \bullet C) \leqslant (A \bullet B \bullet C) + B$.

Exercise 14.7 Show that the quadrangle inequality fails for $(\bullet) = max$.

Exercise 14.8 Verify the monotonicity and quadrangle inequality conditions when $m \bullet n = m + m \times n + n$, where m and n are nonnegative.

Exercise 14.9 When $f \neq g$ the conditions that ensure (14.1) are as follows. With $f = (\circ)$ and $g = (\bullet)$ the first condition is that

$$A \circ B \leqslant A \circ (B \bullet X) \;\wedge\; A \circ B \leqslant (X \bullet A) \circ B$$

This generalises the monotonicity condition. The generalisation of the QI condition is more complicated. First of all, say that X is a *right-factor* of Y if $Y = X$ or $Y = Z \bullet X$ for some Z. Dually, X is a *left-factor* of Y if $Y = X$ or $Y = X \bullet Z$ for some Z. The two conditions are firstly that, if $C \bullet D$ is a right-factor of $A \bullet B$, then

$$A \circ B + C \circ (D \bullet X) \;\leqslant\; A \circ (B \bullet X) + C \circ D$$

and secondly that, if $C \bullet D$ is a left-factor of $A \bullet B$, then

$$A \circ B + (X \bullet C) \circ D \;\leqslant\; (X \bullet A) \circ B + C \circ D$$

As we said in the text, it is difficult to find useful examples in which these conditions are satisfied. Do they hold when $m \circ n = m$ and $(\bullet) = (+)$? How about $m \circ n = m$ and $(\bullet) = (\times)$?

Exercise 14.10 Given that the boustrophedon product $\langle +\!\!+ \rangle$ satisfies the two equations

$$(xs +\!\!+ [x] +\!\!+ ys)\ \langle +\!\!+ \rangle\ zs = (xs\ \langle +\!\!+ \rangle\ zs) +\!\!+ [x] +\!\!+ (ys\ \langle +\!\!+ \rangle\ rev\ xs\ zs)$$
$$reverse\ (ys\ \langle +\!\!+ \rangle\ zs)\quad = reverse\ ys\ \langle +\!\!+ \rangle\ rev\ xs\ zs$$

where the function *rev* is defined by

$$rev \ xs \ zs = \textbf{if } even \ (length \ xs) \textbf{ then } reverse \ zs \textbf{ else } zs$$

prove that $\langle \# \rangle$ is associative.

Exercise 14.11 Suppose in Section 14.4 that $r(i,j)$ is defined to be the *largest* best split rather than the smallest. Then (14.3) is proved by showing that $C_q(i,j+1) \geqslant C_r(i,j+1)$ for $i \leqslant q < r$, and $C_q(i+1,j) \geqslant C_r(i+1,j)$ for $i+1 \leqslant q < r$. Prove that these two facts follow from (14.4) and (14.5).

Exercise 14.12 Use of a special sentinel in the building phase of the Garsia–Wachs algorithm is not essential, provided we change the definition of *build* to read

$$build = endstep \cdot foldr \ step \ [\,] \cdot zip \ (map \ Leaf \ [1 ..])$$

Give the definition of *endstep*.

Exercise 14.13 Consider the following input to *build*:

$$[k, k, k+1, k+1, ..., 2k-1, 2k-1]$$

How long does *build* take?

Exercise 14.14 One may wonder whether the two stages of the Garsia–Wachs algorithm are necessary. To show that they are, we can consider two obvious simplifications, neither of which contains a labelling stage. One is to follow the algorithm for Huffman coding by combining at each step two adjacent trees with minimum combined weight. Ties can be broken arbitrarily by choosing the first such pair. However, unlike Huffman coding, the combined tree is not moved over other trees in order to maintain the same fringe. Here are the steps for input $[4,2,4,4,7]$:

```
(4,4)    (2,2)    (4,4)    (4,4)    (7,7)
((4 2),6)          (4,4)    (4,4)    (7,7)
((4 2),6)         ((4 4),8)          (7,7)
(((4 2) (4 4)),14)                   (7,7)
((((4 2) (4 4)) 7),21)
```

The second simplification is to start off with the same input as above, and to follow step 1 of the function *build*, but again not to move the result. Here is the computation for the same input as above:

```
(4,4)    (2,2)    (4,4)    (4,4)    (7,7)
(4,4)   ((2 4),6)          (4,4)    (7,7)
((4 (2 4)),10)             (4,4)    (7,7)
((4 (2 4)),10)            ((4 7),11)
(((4 (2 4)) (4 7)),21)
```

What are the costs of these two trees? Compute $gwa \ [4,2,4,4,7]$ and show that it has a lower cost.

Exercise 14.15 Show that the Garsia–Wachs algorithm does not work when $\circ$ and $\bullet$ are both $\times$.

Answers

Answer 14.1 The five ways are

$$X_1 \otimes (X_2 \otimes (X_3 \otimes X_4))$$
$$X_1 \otimes ((X_2 \otimes X_3) \otimes X_4)$$
$$(X_1 \otimes X_2) \otimes (X_3 \otimes X_4)$$
$$(X_1 \otimes (X_2 \otimes X_3)) \otimes X_4$$
$$((X_1 \otimes X_2) \otimes X_3) \otimes X_4$$

There are 14 ways to bracket five terms.

Answer 14.2 Rewriting the right-hand side gives us

$$T(n) = n + 2 \sum_{k=1}^{n-1} T(k)$$

Setting $T(n) = (f(n) - 1)/2$ to get rid of the n on the right, we have

$$\frac{f(n) - 1}{2} = 1 + \sum_{k=1}^{n-1} f(k)$$

which is solved by taking $f(n) = 3^n$.

Answer 14.3 The condition $x \leqslant u \wedge y \leqslant v \Rightarrow h\,x\,y \leqslant h\,u\,v$ suffices to ensure the monotonicity condition

$$cost\ u_1 \leqslant cost\ u_2 \wedge cost\ v_1 \leqslant cost\ v_2 \ \Rightarrow\ cost\ (Node\ u_1\ v_1) \leqslant cost\ (Node\ u_2\ v_2)$$

and therefore a recursive definition of *mct*. In a parallel setting we could take h to return the maximum of two numbers.

Answer 14.4 In the case $i + 1 = j$ the result would be

$$minWith\ cost\ [fork\ i\ (t!\,(i,i))\ (t!\,(i+1,i+1)),$$
$$fork\ (i+1)\ (t!\,(i+1,i+1))\ (t!\,(i+2,i+1))]$$

But $t!\,(i+2, i+1)$ is not defined.

Answer 14.5 If $i' = i$ and $j = j'$ there is nothing to prove. If $i' = i$ and $j < j'$, then monotonicity follows from $A \leqslant A \bullet B$, where $A = S(i,j)$ and $B = S(j+1,j')$. Dually, if $i' < i$ and $j = j'$, then monotonicity follows from $B \leqslant A \bullet B$, where $A = S(i',i)$ and $B = S(i+1,j)$. Finally, if $i' < i$ and $j < j'$, then monotonicity follows from $B \leqslant A \bullet B \bullet C$, where $A = S(i',i)$, $B = S(i+1,j)$, and $C = S(j+1,j')$. But this last condition follows from the first two.

Answer 14.6 If $i' = i$ or $j = j'$, then the result is immediate. Otherwise, we set $A = S(i,i')$, $B = S(i'+1,j)$, and $C = S(j+1,j')$. Then the result follows from

$$(A \bullet B) + (B \bullet C) \leqslant (A \bullet B \bullet C) + B$$

Answer 14.7 The quadrangle inequality reads

$$A \max B + B \max C \leqslant A \max B \max C + B$$

But if $B < C < A$ this simplifies to $A + C \leqslant A + B$, which is false.

Answer 14.8 Monotonicity holds because $m \leqslant m + mn + n$ and the quadrangle inequality

$$a + ab + b + b + bc + c \ \leqslant \ a + a(b + bc + c) + b + bc + c + b$$

simplifies to $0 \leqslant a(b+1)c$, which also holds.

Answer 14.9 In the case $(\bullet) = (+)$, monotonicity simplifies to $A \leqslant X + A$, and the remaining conditions simplify to $A + X + C \leqslant X + A + C$. Both conditions hold for nonnegative numbers. In the case $(\bullet) = (\times)$, monotonicity simplifies to $A \leqslant XA$, which holds, but the remaining conditions simplify to $A + XC \leqslant XA + C$, which does not hold for all A, X, and C.

Answer 14.10 The proof of

$$(xs \ \langle\!+\!\!+\rangle \ ys) \ \langle\!+\!\!+\rangle \ zs = xs \ \langle\!+\!\!+\rangle \ (ys \ \langle\!+\!\!+\rangle \ zs)$$

is by induction on xs. The base case is easy, and for the induction step we can argue

$$\begin{aligned}
& ((x\!:\!xs) \ \langle\!+\!\!+\rangle \ ys) \ \langle\!+\!\!+\rangle \ zs \\
= \quad & \{ \text{ definition } \} \\
& (ys +\!\!+ [x] +\!\!+ (xs \ \langle\!+\!\!+\rangle \ reverse \ ys)) \ \langle\!+\!\!+\rangle \ zs \\
= \quad & \{ \text{ first equation, with } rs = rev \ xs \ zs \ \} \\
& (ys \ \langle\!+\!\!+\rangle \ zs) +\!\!+ [x] +\!\!+ ((xs \ \langle\!+\!\!+\rangle \ reverse \ ys) \ \langle\!+\!\!+\rangle \ rs) \\
= \quad & \{ \text{ induction } \} \\
& (ys \ \langle\!+\!\!+\rangle \ zs) +\!\!+ [x] +\!\!+ (xs \ \langle\!+\!\!+\rangle \ (reverse \ ys \ \langle\!+\!\!+\rangle \ rs)) \\
= \quad & \{ \text{ second equation } \} \\
& (ys \ \langle\!+\!\!+\rangle \ zs) +\!\!+ [x] +\!\!+ (xs \ \langle\!+\!\!+\rangle \ (reverse \ (ys \ \langle\!+\!\!+\rangle \ zs))) \\
= \quad & \{ \text{ definition } \} \\
& (x\!:\!xs) \ \langle\!+\!\!+\rangle \ (ys \ \langle\!+\!\!+\rangle \ zs)
\end{aligned}$$

Answer 14.11 By definition of r, we have $C_q(i,j) \geqslant C_r(i,j)$ for $i \leqslant q < r$, so (14.4) gives

$$0 \leqslant C_q(i,j) - C_r(i,j) \ \leqslant \ C_q(i,j+1) - C_r(i,j+1)$$

and (14.5) gives

$$0 \leqslant C_q(i,j) - C_r(i,j) \ \leqslant \ C_q(i+1,j) - C_r(i+1,j)$$

Answer 14.12 The definition is

> $endstep :: [Pair] \rightarrow Tree\ Label$
> $endstep\ [(t, \_)]\ \ \ = t$
> $endstep\ (x : y : xs) = endstep\ (insert\ (join\ x\ y)\ xs)$

Answer 14.13 The input is a two-sorted list, so the first pair is combined at the first step, giving the list

> $[k+1, k+1, ..., 2k-1, 2k-1, 2k]$

Again this list is two-sorted. It follows that *build* takes $\Theta(k^2)$ steps in the worst case.

Answer 14.14 The cost of the first tree is 49, and the cost of the second is 51. We have

> $gwa\ [4, 2, 4, 4, 7] = ((4\ (2\ 4))\ (4\ 7))$

with cost 48.

Answer 14.15 For example, with input $[5, 10, 6, 8, 7]$ the Garsia–Wachs algorithm produces the tree $((5\ 10)\ (7\ (6\ 8)))$ with cost 17234, while an optimum tree is $(((5\ 10)\ 6)\ (8\ 7))$ with cost 17206.

PART SIX

EXHAUSTIVE SEARCH

Sometimes there seems to be no better approach than to examine every possible candidate in order to find one with a particular property or to show that none exists. That, in essence, is exhaustive search. Many of the algorithms we have met so far started life as exhaustive search algorithms. By exploiting various monotonicity conditions they were then transformed into more efficient alternatives – greedy, thinning, or dynamic-programming algorithms, algorithms whose running times were typically a low-order polynomial in the size of the input.

However, for many problems, even quite simply stated ones, no algorithm with a guaranteed polynomial running time is known. For example, there is no known algorithm for determining the factors of a positive integer that takes polynomial time in the number of its digits. There *is* such an algorithm for determining whether an integer is prime or not, but the method is non-constructive and gives no hint of what the potential divisors might be. The problems tackled in the remainder of this book fall into a similar category of ignorance, and the algorithms we will describe all take greater than polynomial time in the worst case. In fact most will take exponential time.

The main problem with an exponential-time algorithm is that it severely limits the sizes of problem instances that can be solved. Take, say, an algorithm whose running time is $\Theta(2^n)$ in the worst case. If we can improve the algorithm to one with a thousand-fold increase in speed, then the size of problem that can be tackled in the same allotted time increases from n to $n + 10$, while a quadratic-time algorithm allows an increase in problem size from n to about $30n$. That is a big difference.

Even when faced with a potentially exhaustive search, there are still a number of ways in which to squeeze as much efficiency as possible out of the process. One avenue of attack is to arrange the generation of candidates in such a way that the transition from one candidate to the next is as fast as possible. It may be possible to postpone exploration of less likely paths in favour of those paths that some heuristic deems to be more likely to lead to a solution. The choice of representation of the candidates can be tuned to minimise the total amount of space required by an exhaustive search. Finally, low-level implementations of the basic steps can sometimes be found to make them as fast as possible. Functional languages are at a disadvantage as far as the last two aspects are concerned because the use of space is difficult to control in a purely functional setting, and implementations that depend on low-level memory operations often cannot be described without introducing procedural features such as mutable arrays into the language.

Most of the problems we will discuss in the following two chapters deal with games and puzzles of various kinds. Apart from being intriguing and fun to study, puzzles provide a fertile ground for looking at exhaustive search, if only for the reason that a good puzzle should be one in which there is no obvious route to a solution.

Chapter 15

Ways of searching

As every good detective knows, an exhaustive search can be organised in different ways. The present chapter introduces the two main variations, *depth-first* search and *breadth-first* search. These different ways of searching are illustrated with the help of games and puzzles of various kinds. Good detectives also know how to prioritise certain lines of enquiry, in the hope that they will prove to be more fruitful than others. One general way of doing so is embodied in *heuristic search*, a topic we will consider in the following chapter. Another way is to formulate possible plans for achieving a given goal and then to try each plan in turn until one is successful. One example of a planning algorithm is considered in the final section of this chapter. We begin, however, with two examples in which the nature of the search is not made explicit.

15.1 Implicit search and the *n*-queens problem

Sometimes the set of candidates can be described directly, so let us start out with the simple idea of an exhaustive search based on the pattern

$\quad$ *solutions = filter good · candidates*

The function *candidates* generates a list of possible candidates from some given data, and the filter operation extracts those that are 'good'. No particular search method is explicit in this formulation because it depends on the precise way in which the list of possible candidates is generated.

$\quad$ The pattern above returns all the good candidates, but to find just one – assuming of course that one exists – we can use the idiom

$\quad$ *solution = head · solutions*

There is no loss of efficiency in extracting a single solution by this device because, under lazy evaluation, only the first element of *solutions* will ever be computed. This simple idea, known as the *list of successes* technique, was recognised early on as a useful aspect of a lazy functional programming language such as Haskell. However, as we will see below, it does not follow that the work for finding any one of n possible solutions takes $1/n$ of the total time; depending on the precise definition of *candidates*, it may take nearly as much time to find the first solution as to find all of them.

As a first example we will look at a well-known puzzle whose history goes back over 150 years. The puzzle is to arrange n queens on an $n \times n$ chessboard so that no queen attacks any other. Each queen therefore has to be placed on the board in a different row, column, and diagonal from any other queen. (Chess players refer to *ranks* and *files* rather than rows and columns, but we will stick with the standard matrix nomenclature with rows labelled from top to bottom and columns from left to right.) The first two constraints imply that any solution is necessarily a permutation of the numbers 1 to n in which the jth element is the number of the column in which the queen in row j is placed. For example, for the 8-queens problem there are 92 solutions, of which one is 15863724. The queen in the first row is in column 1, the queen in the second row is in column 5, and so on. Each solution is therefore a permutation of 1 to n in which no queen attacks any other along a diagonal. Thus, for each queen at position (r, q) there can be no other queen at any position (r', q') for which $r + q = r' + q'$ or $r - q = r' - q'$. Each *left* diagonal (top left to bottom right) is identified by coordinates with a common difference and each *right* diagonal (top right to bottom left) by coordinates with a common sum. The diagonal safety condition can be implemented by

$$safe :: [Nat] \to Bool$$
$$safe\ qs = check\ (zip\ [1\,..]\ qs)$$

$$check\ [] \qquad\qquad = True$$
$$check\ ((r, q):rqs) = and\ [abs\ (q - q') \neq r' - r \mid (r', q') \leftarrow rqs] \wedge check\ rqs$$

Now we can simply write

$$queens :: Nat \to [[Nat]]$$
$$queens = filter\ safe \cdot perms$$

where *perms n* generates all permutations of 1 to n. One efficient definition of this function was given in the very first chapter:

$$perms\ n = foldr\ (concatMap \cdot inserts)\ [[\,]]\ [1\,..\,n]$$
$$\textbf{where}\ inserts\ x\ [] \qquad = [[x]]$$
$$inserts\ x\ (y:ys) = (x:y:ys):map\ (y:)\ (inserts\ x\ ys)$$

With very little effort it seems we have arrived at a reasonable program for solving the puzzle. However, this is a very bad way of solving the problem. Generating the permutations of 1 to n takes $\Theta(n \times n!)$ steps, and each safety test takes $\Theta(n^2)$ steps, so the full algorithm takes $\Theta(n^2 \times n!)$ steps because the safety test has to be applied to $n!$ permutations.

A better idea is to generate only those permutations that can be extended to safe permutations. The idea is to exploit the following property of *safe*:

$$safe\,(qs + [q]) = safe\,qs \wedge newDiag\,q\,qs$$

where

$$newDiag\,q\,qs = and\,[abs\,(q - q') \neq r - r' \mid (r', q') \leftarrow zip\,[1\,..]\,qs]$$
$$\textbf{where } r = length\,qs + 1$$

The test *newDiag* ensures that the next queen is placed on a fresh diagonal. However, it is difficult to make use of this property with the above definition of *perms* because new elements are inserted into the middle of previously generated partial permutations. Instead we can use another definition of *perms*:

$$perms\,n = help\,n\ \textbf{where}$$
$$help\,0 = [[]]$$
$$help\,r = [xs + [x] \mid xs \leftarrow help\,(r-1), x \leftarrow [1\,..n], notElem\,x\,xs]$$

The difference between this definition and the previous one is that each new element is added to the end of a previous permutation, not somewhere in the middle. That means we can fuse part of *filter safe* into the generation of permutations to arrive at

$$queens_1\,n = help\,n\ \textbf{where}$$
$$help\,0 = [[]]$$
$$help\,r = [qs + [q] \mid qs \leftarrow help\,(r-1), q \leftarrow [1\,..n],$$
$$notElem\,q\,qs, newDiag_1\,(r, q)\,qs]$$
$$newDiag_1\,(r, q)\,qs = and\,[abs\,(q - q') \neq r - r' \mid (r', q') \leftarrow zip\,[1\,..]\,qs]$$

The safety of previously placed queens is guaranteed by construction. The test *newDiag*₁ takes only $\Theta(n)$ steps and the resulting search is faster by a factor of n.

There is a dual solution in which the order of the generators is swapped and new elements are added to the front of a previous permutation rather than to the rear:

$$queens_2\,n = help\,n\ \textbf{where}$$
$$help\,0 = [[]]$$
$$help\,r = [q : qs \mid q \leftarrow [1\,..n], qs \leftarrow qss, notElem\,q\,qs, newDiag_2\,q\,qs]$$
$$\textbf{where } qss = help\,(r-1)$$
$$newDiag_2\,q\,qs = and\,[abs\,(q - q') \neq r' - 1 \mid (r', q') \leftarrow zip\,[2\,..]\,qs]$$

The computation of *help* $(r-1)$ is brought out in a **where** clause, for otherwise it would be recomputed for each possible placement. A revised version of *newDiag* is needed because queens are now added to the front of a list.

The two functions *queens*₁ and *queens*₂ generate exactly the same solutions in exactly the same order, so which is better? It might be thought that *queens*₂ should be faster than $queens_1$, if only because the operation of adding a queen to the front of a list is a constant-time operation, while adding a queen to the rear takes linear time. Indeed, the second version *is* faster when all the solutions are computed. But the situation changes dramatically when we want just the first solution. For example, computing the first element of $queens_2$ 9 is much slower than computing the first element of $queens_1$ 9. To see why, consider the first solution 136824975 (out of 352 possible solutions). This solution is computed from left to right by $queens_1$, and the first elements of the partial permutations are generated as follows:

$$1, \ 13, \ 135, \ 1352, \ 13524, \ 135249, \ 1357246, \ 13682497, \ 136824975$$

Most of the work takes place in generating the seventh and eighth partial permutation, since 135249 cannot be extended on the right to a solution and neither can 1357246. In each case that means more partial permutations have to be generated before finding one that can be extended. The remaining partial permutations can be easily extended and so require far less work.

Contrast this effort with that required by $queens_2$, which computes from right to left and generates exactly the same list of partial permutations. This time much more work is done at each step in order to find the next partial permutation that begins with a 1. For example, the partial permutation 13524 has to be replaced by 35249 in order to allow a 1 to be added to the front, and this involves generating about 400 intermediate permutations. The same phenomenon is exhibited at each step of the process, causing $queens_2$ to perform a lot more work than $queens_1$ before it returns the first solution. Of course, it performs correspondingly less work in computing the remaining solutions. The lesson of the story is that the order in which the choices for the next move are made can significantly influence the running time for finding the first solution.

Here is another solution to the n-queens problem, one in which the search strategy *is* made explicit. The general idea, which we will revisit later when we discuss depth-first and breadth-first search, is to reformulate the search in terms of two finite sets, a set of *states* and a set of *moves*, and three functions

$moves :: State \rightarrow [Move]$
$move \ \ :: State \rightarrow Move \rightarrow State$
$solved :: State \rightarrow Bool$

The function *moves* determines the legal moves that can be made in a given state, and *move* returns the state that results when a given move is made. The function *solved* determines which states are a solution to the puzzle. Phrased in this way, the problem is essentially one of searching a directed graph in which the vertices represent states and the edges represent moves.

The following algorithm for listing the set of solved states works only under certain assumptions, given below:

$$solutions :: State \rightarrow [State]$$
$$solutions\ t = search\ [t]$$

$$search :: [State] \rightarrow [State]$$
$$search\ [] \quad = []$$
$$search\ (t:ts) = \textbf{if}\ solved\ t\ \textbf{then}\ t:search\ ts\ \textbf{else}\ search\ (succs\ t \mathbin{+\!\!+} ts)$$

$$succs :: State \rightarrow [State]$$
$$succs\ t = [move\ t\ m \mid m \leftarrow moves\ t]$$

In words, if the current state is not a solved state, then its successors are added to the front of the states waiting to be explored. This way of dealing with successor states is typical of *depth-first search*. Regarding the assumptions, the major one is that the underlying graph is acyclic, for otherwise *search* would loop indefinitely if any state is repeated. The second assumption is that no further moves are possible in any solved state, for otherwise some solved states would be missed, and the third is that no state can be reached by more than one path, for otherwise some solved states would be listed more than once.

These three assumptions are all satisfied in the *n*-queens problem, and we can immediately install the definitions

$$\textbf{type}\ State = [Nat]$$
$$\textbf{type}\ Move = Nat$$

$$moves :: State \rightarrow [Move]$$
$$moves\ qs \quad = [q \mid q \leftarrow [1..n], notElem\ q\ qs, newDiag_2\ q\ qs]$$

$$move :: State \rightarrow Move \rightarrow State$$
$$move\ qs\ q = q:qs$$

$$solved :: State \rightarrow Bool$$
$$solved\ qs \quad = (length\ qs == n)$$

The function $newDiag_2$ was defined above. A state is solved if it is a full permutation of $1..n$, and the set of moves consists of the legal positions at which the next queen can be placed. The resulting algorithm is as fast as $queens_1$ in finding the first solution.

The definition of *search* can be modified to count only the number of solutions. Counting the number of solutions to the *n*-queens problem is a time-consuming operation. For example, in an experiment in 2006 it took 26613 days of CPU time to count the number of solutions to the 25-queens problem, which turns out to be 2207893435808352. No-one currently knows how many solutions there are when $n = 28$. Nevertheless, we can try to put on speed with the algorithm above by using a more compact representation of states. We will describe a representation that uses three *bit vectors*. The three vectors determine which left diagonals, columns, and right diagonals cannot be used for the next queen. For example, consider the

5-queens problem, and suppose the last two rows have been filled in as follows, with row 3 waiting to be filled:

The three vectors for this state are 11000, 01010, and 00100. The first, 11000, determines which left-to-right diagonals are attacked by a queen. We cannot place a queen in either column 1 or column 2 because it would be under attack by an existing queen along a left-to-right diagonal. The middle vector, 01010, determines which columns are attacked, and the third, 00100 determines which right-to-left diagonals are under attack. The columns that can be used for the next row are calculated by taking the complement of the bitwise union of these three sequences:

$$complement\ (11000\ .|.\ 01010\ .|.\ 00100) = 00001$$

The bitwise union operator .|. and the *complement* function are taken from the Haskell library *Data.Bits*, as are some further operations described below. The result 00001 means we can place a queen only in column 5.

As another example, consider the possibilities for placing a queen in row 4 when row 5 has a queen in column 4. Here the three relevant vectors are 00100, 00010, and 00001. We have

$$complement\ (00100\ .|.\ 00010\ .|.\ 00001) = 11000$$

so a queen in row 4 can be placed only in columns 1 and 2. Suppose we choose column 2 (as in the first example), a choice which is represented by the bit vector 01000. We can then update the diagonal and column information by

$$shiftL\ (00100\ .|.\ 01000)\ 1 = 11000$$
$$00010\ .|.\ 01000\qquad\quad\ = 01010$$
$$shiftR\ (00001\ .|.\ 01000)\ 1 = 00100$$

These three vectors appeared in the first example. The operation *shiftL* shifts a bit vector a designated number of places to the left, introducing trailing 0s. Similarly, *shiftR* shifts a bit vector a designated number of places to the right, introducing leading 0s. In each of the computations above the shift is by just one place. A state is solved when all the bits in the column vector are 1.

Haskell provides a number of sizes for bit vectors in the *Data.Word* library, including *Word8*, *Word16*, *Word32*, and *Word64*, each of which is a n-bit unsigned integer type for $n = 8, 16$, and so on. We will choose *Word16*, which will allow us to solve the n-queens problem for $n \leqslant 16$. For $n < 16$ we can use a *mask* to mask out bits. For example, for $n = 5$ the mask would be a 16-bit vector all of whose bits are 0 except for the last five bits, which are all 1. Numerically, the mask is a bit representation of $2^n - 1$ for $0 \leqslant n \leqslant 16$, so we can define

$mask :: Word16$
$mask = 2^n - 1$

Recomputing *mask* at every point would affect the efficiency of the search, so we make it local to the complete counting algorithm:

type $State = (Word16, Word16, Word16)$
type $Move = Word16$

$cqueens :: Nat \rightarrow Integer$
$cqueens \; n = search \; [(0,0,0)]$ **where**
   $search :: [State] \rightarrow Integer$
   $search \; [] \quad = 0$
   $search \; (t:ts) = $ **if** $solved \; t$ **then** $1 + search \; ts$ **else** $search \; (succs \; t \mathbin{+\!\!+} ts)$
   $solved :: State \rightarrow Bool$
   $solved \; (\_, cls, \_) = (cls == mask)$
   $mask :: Word16$
   $mask = 2^n - 1$
   $succs :: State \rightarrow [State]$
   $succs \; t = [move \; t \; b \mid b \leftarrow moves \; t]$
   $move :: State \rightarrow Move \rightarrow State$
   $move \; (lds, cls, rds) \; m = (shiftL \; (lds \mathbin{.|.} m) \; 1, cls \mathbin{.|.} m, shiftR \; (rds \mathbin{.|.} m) \; 1)$
   $moves :: State \rightarrow [Move]$
   $moves \; (lds, cls, rds) = bits \; (complement \; (lds \mathbin{.|.} cls \mathbin{.|.} rds) \mathbin{.\&.} mask)$

The function *bits* extracts the bits from a vector as a sequence of bit vectors each containing a single set bit:

$bits :: Word16 \rightarrow [Move]$
$bits \; v = $ **if** $v == 0$ **then** $[]$ **else** $b : bits \; (v - b)$
   where $b = v \mathbin{.\&.} negate \; v$

See the exercises for an alternative, slightly less efficient definition. For example,

$bits \; 11010 = [00010, 01000, 10000]$

The expression $v \mathbin{.\&.} negate \; v$, where $.\&.$ is bitwise conjunction, returns the least significant bit; for example

$11010 \mathbin{.\&.} negate \; 11010 = 11010 \mathbin{.\&.} 00110 = 00010$

Repeatedly subtracting the least significant bit from the vector yields all the bits. When the counting algorithm was compiled and run, it delivered the fact that the 16-queens problem has 14772512 solutions in close to a minute of CPU time.

15.2 Expressions with a given sum

Here is a different kind of puzzle that can also be solved using the direct approach. The problem involves constructing arithmetic expressions that evaluate to a given sum. A simple version of the problem asks for a list of all the ways the operators $\times$ and $+$ can be inserted into a list of digits 1 to 9 so as to make a total of 100. Two such ways are

$$100 = 12 + 34 + 5 \times 6 + 7 + 8 + 9$$
$$100 = 1 + 2 \times 3 + 4 + 5 + 67 + 8 + 9$$

In this particular version of the problem, no parentheses are allowed in forming expressions and, as usual, $\times$ binds more tightly than $+$. Here we can write

$$solutions :: Nat \rightarrow [Digit] \rightarrow [Expr]$$
$$solutions\ n = filter\ (good\ n \cdot value) \cdot expressions$$

where *expressions* builds a list of all arithmetic expressions that can be formed from a given list of digits, *value* delivers the value of such an expression, and *good* tests whether the value is equal to a given target value.

Let's consider *expressions* first. Each expression is the sum of a list of terms, each term is the product of a list of factors, and each factor is a nonempty list of digits. For example, the expression

$$12 + 34 + 5 \times 6 + 7 + 8 + 9$$

can be represented by the compound list

$$[[[1,2]],\ [[3,4]],\ [[5],[6]],\ [[7]],\ [[8]],\ [[9]]]$$

That means we can define expressions, terms, and factors just with the help of suitable type synonyms:

type *Expr* $=$ [*Term*]
type *Term* $=$ [*Factor*]
type *Factor* $=$ [*Digit*]
type *Digit* $=$ *Nat*

One simple way to define *expressions* follows the earlier definition of *perms*:

$$expressions :: [Digit] \rightarrow [Expr]$$
$$expressions = foldr\ (concatMap \cdot glue)\ [[\,]]$$

$$glue :: Digit \rightarrow Expr \rightarrow [Expr]$$
$$glue\ d\ [\,] \qquad\qquad = [[[[d]]]]$$
$$glue\ d\ ((ds:fs):ts) = [((d:ds):fs):ts, ([d]:ds:fs):ts, [[d]]:(ds:fs):ts]$$

To explain *glue*, observe that only one expression can be built from a single digit d, namely $[[[d]]]$. An expression built from more than one digit can be decomposed into a leading factor, ds say, which is part of a leading term $ds:fs$, and a remaining expression, a list of terms *ts*. A new digit can be added to the front of an expression in exactly three ways: by extending the leading factor with the new digit, by starting a new factor, or by starting a new term. For example, $2 \times 3 + \cdots$ can be extended on the left with a new digit 1 in one of the following three ways:

$$12 \times 3 + \cdots$$
$$1 \times 2 \times 3 + \cdots$$
$$1 + 2 \times 3 + \cdots$$

It is immediate from this definition that there are $6561 = 3^8$ expressions one can build from nine digits, indeed 3^{n-1} expressions from a list of *n* digits.

The function *value* can be implemented as a function *valExpr*, where

$$valExpr :: Expr \rightarrow Nat$$
$$valExpr = sum \cdot map\ valTerm$$

$$valTerm :: Term \rightarrow Nat$$
$$valTerm = product \cdot map\ valFact$$

$$valFact :: Factor \rightarrow Nat$$
$$valFact = foldl\ op\ 0\ \textbf{where}\ op\ n\ d = 10n + d$$

Finally, a good expression is one whose value is equal to the target value:

$$good :: Nat \rightarrow Nat \rightarrow Bool$$
$$good\ n\ v = (v == n)$$

Evaluating *solutions* 100 [1..9], and displaying the results in a suitable fashion, yields the seven solutions

$$100 = 1 \times 2 \times 3 + 4 + 5 + 6 + 7 + 8 \times 9$$
$$100 = 1 + 2 + 3 + 4 + 5 + 6 + 7 + 8 \times 9$$
$$100 = 1 \times 2 \times 3 \times 4 + 5 + 6 + 7 \times 8 + 9$$
$$100 = 12 + 3 \times 4 + 5 + 6 + 7 \times 8 + 9$$
$$100 = 1 + 2 \times 3 + 4 + 5 + 67 + 8 + 9$$
$$100 = 1 \times 2 + 34 + 5 + 6 \times 7 + 8 + 9$$
$$100 = 12 + 34 + 5 \times 6 + 7 + 8 + 9$$

The computation does not take too long, as there are only 6561 possibilities to check. However, on another day the target value may be much larger and there may be many more digits, so let us see what we can do to optimise the search.

One obvious step is to memoise value computations to save recomputing values from scratch each time. Better still, we can exploit a monotonicity condition to achieve a partial fusion of the filter test into the generation of expressions. The situation is exactly the same as with the *n*-queens problem. The key insight is that expressions built out of positive digits, using just juxtaposition, $\times$, and $+$, have values that are as least as large as their constituent expressions. A formal statement is given as an exercise. So we can pair expressions with their values and only generate expressions whose values are *at most* the target value.

A technical difficulty is that we cannot determine the values of a new expression, obtained by gluing a new digit to the front, from the values of the digit and expression alone; we need the values of the leading factor and the leading term as well. So we will define the *component* values to be

> **type** *Values* = (*Nat, Nat, Nat, Nat*)
>
> *values* :: *Expr* → *Values*
> *values* ((*ds* : *fs*) : *ts*) = (10 ^ *length ds*, *valFact ds*, *valTerm fs*, *valExpr ts*)

The additional first component of this quadruple is included simply to make the evaluation of *valFact* more efficient. The value of an expression whose component values are (*p, f, t, e*) is $f \times t + e$.

Here is the revised definition of *solutions*:

> *solutions* :: *Nat* → [*Digit*] → [*Expr*]
> *solutions n* = *map fst* · *filter* (*good n*) · *expressions n*

The function *expressions n* generates expressions whose value is at most *n*:

> *expressions* :: *Nat* → [*Digit*] → [(*Expr, Values*)]
> *expressions n* = *foldr* (*concatMap* · *glue*) [([], ⊥)]
>   **where** *glue d* = *filter* (*ok n*) · *extend d*
>
> *extend d* ([], _) = [(([[[*d*]]]), (10, *d*, 1, 0))]
> *extend d* ((*ds* : *fs*) : *ts*, (*p, f, t, e*)) = [(((*d* : *ds*) : *fs*) : *ts*, (10 × *p*, *p* × *d* + *f*, *t*, *e*)),
>   (([*d*] : *ds* : *fs*) : *ts*, (10, *d*, *f* × *t*, *e*)),
>   ([[*d*]] : (*ds* : *fs*) : *ts*, (10, *d*, 1, *f* × *t* + *e*))]

Finally, the tests *good* and *ok* are defined by

> *good n* (*ex*, (*p, f, t, e*)) = (*f* × *t* + *e* == *n*)
> *ok n*   (*ex*, (*p, f, t, e*)) = (*f* × *t* + *e* ⩽ *n*)

The result is a program for *solutions* that is many times faster than the first version.

15.3 Depth-first and breadth-first search

In Section 15.1 we implemented a simple version of depth-first search that used three functions:

> *moves* :: *State* → [*Move*]
> *move* :: *State* → *Move* → *State*
> *solved* :: *State* → *Bool*

The search, which produced a list of all the solved states, was valid provided three assumptions were satisfied, the main one being that the underlying digraph was acyclic. However, in many applications this assumption does not hold. It is perfectly possible that some sequence of moves can lead to a state being repeated, so the associated digraph will contain cycles. We will assume, though, that $move\ t\ m \neq t$ for all states t and moves m, so the graph does not contain loops. The second assumption, namely that final states cannot be arrived at by more than one sequence of moves, is not needed if we want to enumerate all the sequences of moves that lead to solved states rather than the solved states themselves. The third assumption was that no further moves are possible in a solved state, a reasonable restriction we will continue to assume.

Let us therefore consider how to implement a function

$$solutions :: State \rightarrow [[Move]]$$

for computing all *simple* sequences of moves that lead to a solved state. A sequence of moves is simple if no intermediate state is repeated during the moves. Without this restriction the set of solutions could be infinite. To maintain the restriction, we need to remember both the sequence of moves in a path and the list of intermediate states, including the initial state, that arises as a result of making the moves. Hence we define

type $Path = ([Move], [State])$

where the second component of a path is a nonempty list of states. The simple successors of a path are defined by

$$succs :: Path \rightarrow [Path]$$
$$succs\ (ms, t : ts) = [\ (ms \mathbin{+\!\!+} [m], t' : t : ts)$$
$$\qquad\qquad\qquad\quad |\ m \leftarrow moves\ t, \textbf{let}\ t' = move\ t\ m, notElem\ t'\ ts]$$

The intermediate states in a path are recorded from right to left. That means a path leads to a final state defined by

$$final :: Path \rightarrow State$$
$$final = head \cdot snd$$

Next, the function *paths* takes a list of simple paths and produces all the possible completions. Here are two ways to define *paths*:

$$paths_1 :: [Path] \rightarrow [Path]$$
$$paths_1 = concat \cdot takeWhile\ (not \cdot null) \cdot iterate\ (concatMap\ succs)$$
$$paths_2 :: [Path] \rightarrow [Path]$$
$$paths_2\ ps = concat\ [p : paths_2\ (succs\ p)\ |\ p \leftarrow ps]$$

In $paths_1$ the list of paths is repeatedly extended by applying *succs* until no more extensions are possible. Under this definition, the simple paths are generated in ascending order of length. In $paths_2$ each path is followed immediately by its successors, so paths are not necessarily produced in ascending order of length. We will rewrite these two definitions in a moment. Now we can define $solutions_1$ by

$$solutions_1 :: State \rightarrow [[Move]]$$
$$solutions_1 = map\, fst \cdot filter\, (solved \cdot final) \cdot paths_1 \cdot start$$

The initial state is converted into a singleton containing the empty path:

$$start :: State \rightarrow [Path]$$
$$start\, t = [([], [t])]$$

The function $paths_1$ enumerates all simple paths, and the result is filtered for those paths that lead to a solved state, which are then processed to produce the moves. The definition of $solutions_2$ is the same but with $paths_1$ replaced by $paths_2$.

The two definitions of $paths$ can be rewritten with the help of a little calculation. First consider the expression

$$exp = foldr\, f\, e \cdot takeWhile\, p \cdot iterate\, g$$

An easy calculation, left as an exercise, leads to the equivalent recursive definition

$$exp\, x = \textbf{if } p\, x \textbf{ then } f\, x\, (exp\, (g\, x)) \textbf{ else } e$$

Hence $paths_1$ can be put in the form

$$paths_1\, ps = \textbf{if } null\, ps \textbf{ then } [] \textbf{ else } ps + paths_1\, (concatMap\, succs\, ps)$$

We can now show that

$$paths_1\, (ps + qs) = ps + paths_1\, (qs + concatMap\, succs\, ps)$$

for all ps and qs. The proof is by induction on ps. The base case is immediate, and for the induction step we argue

$$
\begin{aligned}
& paths_1\, (p:ps + qs) \\
=\ & \{ \text{definition of } paths_1 \} \\
& p:ps + qs + paths_1\, (concatMap\, succs\, (p:ps + qs)) \\
=\ & \{ \text{definition of } concatMap \} \\
& p:ps + qs + paths_1\, (succs\, p + concatMap\, succs\, (ps + qs)) \\
=\ & \{ \text{introducing } ps' = ps + qs \text{ and } qs' = succs\, p \} \\
& p:ps' + paths_1\, (qs' + concatMap\, succs\, ps') \\
=\ & \{ \text{induction, expanding the abbreviation} \} \\
& p:paths_1\, (ps + qs + succs\, p) \\
=\ & \{ \text{introducing } qs'' = qs + succs\, p \} \\
& p:paths_1\, (ps + qs'') \\
=\ & \{ \text{induction again, expanding the abbreviation} \} \\
& p:ps + paths_1\, (qs + succs\, p + concatMap\, succs\, ps) \\
=\ & \{ \text{definition of } concatMap \} \\
& p:ps + paths_1\, (qs + concatMap\, succs\, (p:ps))
\end{aligned}
$$

This completes the proof. In particular, setting $(ps, qs) = ([], ps)$ we obtain

$$paths_1 \ (p:ps) = p:paths_1 \ (ps +\!\!+ succs \ p)$$

That means $solutions_1$ can be rewritten in the form

$$
\begin{aligned}
&solutions_1 = search \cdot start \ \textbf{where} \\
&\quad search \ [] \qquad = [] \\
&\quad search \ ((ms, t:ts):ps) \\
&\quad\quad | \ solved \ t \ \ = ms:search \ ps \\
&\quad\quad | \ otherwise = search \ (ps +\!\!+ succs \ (ms, t:ts))
\end{aligned}
$$

The only assumption is that no moves are possible in solved states. This method is known as *breadth-first search* (BFS). In BFS, the frontier – the list of paths waiting to be explored further – is maintained as a *queue*, with new entries added to the rear of the queue. What the above calculation demonstrates is that BFS does indeed produce solutions in ascending order of length of path.

Turning to $paths_2$, we can reason

$$
\begin{aligned}
&paths_2 \ (p:ps) \\
&= \quad \{ \ \text{definition of } paths_2 \ \} \\
&\quad concat \ [p':paths_2 \ (succs \ p') \mid p' \leqslant p:ps] \\
&= \quad \{ \ \text{definition of } concat \text{ and } paths_2 \ \} \\
&\quad p:paths_2 \ (succs \ p) +\!\!+ paths_2 \ ps \\
&= \quad \{ \ \text{since } concat \ (xss +\!\!+ yss) = concat \ xss +\!\!+ concat \ yss \ \} \\
&\quad p:paths_2 \ (succs \ p +\!\!+ ps)
\end{aligned}
$$

Hence we obtain the following alternative definition of $solutions_2$:

$$
\begin{aligned}
&solutions_2 = search \cdot start \ \textbf{where} \\
&\quad search \ [] \qquad = [] \\
&\quad search \ ((ms, t:ts):ps) \\
&\quad\quad | \ solved \ t \ \ = ms:search \ ps \\
&\quad\quad | \ otherwise = search \ (succs \ (ms, t:ts) +\!\!+ ps)
\end{aligned}
$$

This method is known as *depth-first search* (DFS). This time, the frontier is managed as a *stack*, with new entries added to the front of the stack. With DFS, the solutions are not produced in ascending order of length, though all solutions will still be produced. These two definitions of *solutions* are not quite the usual ways in which DFS and BFS are described (see below), but it is instructive that both can be derived from clear specifications.

The point about BFS producing solutions in order of length would seem to tip the scales in favour of $solutions_1$. But there is a downside: under BFS, the frontier can be exponentially longer than under DFS. Suppose each state has K successors, and the first solved state occurs at level n, meaning there is a sequence of n moves that leads to a solved state. Under DFS the frontier will increase in size by K at each step, so the final frontier will have length $K n$. Under BFS, all the successors of all the states at a distance of at most n away from the solved state will be queued up in the frontier, so the frontier has a length of K^n. Consequently, BFS can use exponentially more space than DFS. Worse, as defined above it can also take exponentially longer time, because computing $(ps +\!\!+ succs\ p)$ takes time proportional to the length of ps.

One way to make the algorithm faster, though it will not reduce the space complexity, is to use a dedicated *Queue* data type to ensure that adding elements to the rear is a constant-time operation. Another alternative is to introduce an accumulating parameter, defining $search_1$ by

$$search_1\ pss\ ps = search\ (ps +\!\!+ concat\ (reverse\ pss))$$

Then, after some simple calculation which we will again leave as an exercise, we arrive at

$$solutions_1 = search\ [\,]\cdot start\ \textbf{where}$$
$$search\ [\,]\ \ [\,]\ \ = [\,]$$
$$search\ pss\ [\,]\ \ = search\ [\,]\ (concat\ (reverse\ pss))$$
$$search\ pss\ ((ms,t:ts):ps)$$
$$\quad|\ solved\ t\ \ \ = ms:search\ pss\ ps$$
$$\quad|\ otherwise = search\ (succs\ (ms,t:ts):pss)\ ps$$

In fact, there is another version of *search* in which the accumulating parameter is a list of paths rather than a list of lists of paths:

$$search\ qs\ [\,]\ \ \ = \textbf{if}\ null\ qs\ \textbf{then}\ [\,]\ \textbf{else}\ search\ [\,]\ qs$$
$$search\ qs\ ((ms,t:ts):ps)$$
$$\quad|\ solved\ t\ \ \ = ms:search\ qs\ ps$$
$$\quad|\ otherwise = search\ (succs\ (ms,t:ts) +\!\!+ qs)\ ps$$

This version has a different behaviour from the previous one, in that successive frontiers are traversed alternately from left to right and from right to left, but the solutions will still be produced in ascending order of length.

Each of the search functions considered above produces all the solutions. If just one solution is required, then there is a further space-saving idea. The problem with each of the previous searches is that a list of the intermediate states has to be kept as part of each path in order to ensure that each path is a simple one, and this adds significantly to the total space required. By moving the membership test to the top level, we can guarantee not only that each path is simple, but also that only one path to a given state is maintained.

Here are the details. A path now consists of a sequence of moves and the final state that results, so the definition of *succs* has to be changed to read

$$succs\ (ms,t) = \lfloor (ms +\!\!+ [m], move\ t\ m) \mid m \leftarrow moves\ i\rfloor$$

Now we can define

$$solution_1 :: State \rightarrow Maybe \, [Move]$$
$$solution_1 \, t = search \, [] \, [([],t)]$$
$$\textbf{where} \, search \, ts \, [] \quad = Nothing$$
$$search \, ts \, ((ms,t):ps)$$
$$| \, solved \, t \quad = Just \, ms$$
$$| \, elem \, t \, ts \, = search \, ts \, ps$$
$$| \, otherwise = search \, (t:ts) \, (ps + succs \, (ms,t))$$

The first argument to *search* is a list of visited states, states whose successors have already been added to the frontier. Using a list means that the membership test can take linear time. As an alternative we can make use of the efficient set operations of Section 4.4. The Haskell library *Data.Set* also provides the necessary operations, so we can import it

import *Data.Set* (*empty, insert, member*)

and define

$$solution_1 :: State \rightarrow Maybe \, [Move]$$
$$solution_1 \, t = search \, empty \, [([],t)]$$
$$\textbf{where} \, search \, ts \, [] \quad = Nothing$$
$$search \, ts \, ((ms,t):ps)$$
$$| \, solved \, t \quad = Just \, ms$$
$$| \, member \, t \, ts = search \, ts \, ps$$
$$| \, otherwise \quad = search \, (insert \, t \, ts) \, (ps + succs \, (ms,t))$$

This version of *solution_1* guarantees that *member* and *insert* operations both take logarithmic time. This method of searching is what is usually given as the definition of BFS. The companion function

$$solution_2 :: State \rightarrow Maybe \, [Move]$$
$$solution_2 \, t = search \, empty \, [([],t)]$$
$$\textbf{where} \, search \, ts \, [] \quad = Nothing$$
$$search \, ts \, ((ms,t):ps)$$
$$| \, solved \, t \quad = Just \, ms$$
$$| \, member \, t \, ts = search \, ts \, ps$$
$$| \, otherwise \quad = search \, (insert \, t \, ts) \, (succs \, (ms,t) + ps)$$

is what is usually given as the definition of DFS. Neither function is suitable for producing all solutions, but they will certainly produce one solution if one exists.

15.4 Lunar Landing

Let us now see how DFS and BFS can be put to work in solving another puzzle. This one is called *Lunar Landing* (it is also known as *Lunar Lockout*) and is an addictive solitaire game invented by Hiroshi Yamamoto and publicised by Nob Yoshigahara, the famous Japanese inventor of *Rush Hour*, a puzzle we will consider later on. Although it can be played on boards of different shapes and sizes, the standard is a 5×5 square of cells, of which the centre cell is designated as an escape hatch. On the board is a human astronaut and a number of bots, each occupying a single cell. The aim of the game is to get the astronaut safely into the escape hatch. Both the astronaut and the bots can move only horizontally or vertically. The catch is that beyond the boundary of the board lies infinite space, and no bot or human ever wants to go there. Consequently, each move involves moving a piece as far as possible in a straight line until it comes to rest next to another piece which is blocking the path into infinite space. The aim is to find a sequence of moves that enables the astronaut to land exactly on the escape hatch.

Here is an example board, in which the astronaut is piece number 0, there are five bots numbered from 1 to 5, and the escape hatch is marked with a $\times$:

In this position only bots 3 and 5 can move; the astronaut and the remaining bots would shoot off into infinite space if moved. Bot 3 can move downwards one cell and bot 5 upwards one cell. The longest sequence of moves involving bot 3 alone is *3D 3R 3U 3R 3D*. In words, bot 3 can move down, right, up, right, and down until it ends up just above bot 4. Bot 5, on the other hand, can engage in an infinite sequence of moves. The two sequences of moves

> *5U 5R*
> *5U 5R 5U 5R 5D 5L 5D 5R*

both result in the same final position in which bot 5 ends up to the left of bot 4. The last six moves of the second sequence can be repeated ad infinitum. Nevertheless, there is a unique nine-move solution to the puzzle. Pause for a moment to see if you can find it.

The answer is the nine moves

> *5U 5R 5U 2L 2D 2L 0U 0R 0U*

Bot 5 in three moves ends up below bot 1, then bot 2 in three moves ends up to the right of bot 3, and finally the astronaut can escape in three more moves.

There is another solution involving 12 moves but only two pieces:

5U 5R 5U 5R 5D 5L 0U 0R 0U 0R 0D 0L

Notice that in this solution the astronaut passes *over* the escape hatch during her third move, but only lands on it at the final move. There are example boards for which there are an infinite number of solutions, so the associated digraph is cyclic.

The first decision concerns how to represent the board. The obvious method is to use Cartesian coordinates, but a more compact representation is to number the cells as follows:

$$
\begin{array}{ccccc}
1 & 2 & 3 & 4 & 5 \\
7 & 8 & 9 & 10 & 11 \\
13 & 14 & 15 & 16 & 17 \\
19 & 20 & 21 & 22 & 23 \\
25 & 26 & 27 & 28 & 29 \\
\end{array}
$$

Cells that are a multiple of 6 represent the left and right borders, which will help in determining the moves. The escape hatch is cell 15. A board is a list of occupied cells with the first cell, at position 0, naming the location of the astronaut. For example, the board above is represented by the list $[26, 3, 11, 13, 22, 25]$. Hence we define

type *Cell* $= Nat$
type *Board* $= [Cell]$

solved :: *Board* $\rightarrow$ *Bool*
solved $b = (b\,!!\,0 == 15)$

The next decision is how to represent moves. Rather than take a move to be a named piece and a direction, we will represent a move by a named piece, its current position, and the finishing point of the move:

type *Name* $= Nat$
type *Move* $= (Name, Cell, Cell)$

A move can be recast in terms of directions by *showMove*, where

showMove :: *Move* $\rightarrow$ *String*
showMove $(n, s, f) = show\ n \mathbin{+\!\!+} dir\ (s, f)$

$dir\ (s, f) = $ **if** $abs\ (s - f) \geqslant 6$ **then** (**if** $s < f$ **then** "D" **else** "U")
$\qquad\qquad\qquad\qquad\qquad\qquad$ **else** (**if** $s < f$ **then** "R" **else** "L")

The function *move* is defined by

move :: *Board* $\rightarrow$ *Move* $\rightarrow$ *Board*
move $b\ (n, s, f) = b_1 \mathbin{+\!\!+} f : b_2$ **where** $(b_1, \_ : b_2) = splitAt\ n\ b$

It remains only to define *moves*, which takes the form

$$moves :: Board \rightarrow [Move]$$
$$moves\ b = [(n,s,f) \mid (n,s) \leftarrow zip\ [0..]\ b, f \leftarrow targets\ b\ s]$$

The function *targets*, which determines the destination cells of moves, is defined in terms of the four possible paths for moving a piece:

$$targets :: Board \rightarrow Cell \rightarrow [Cell]$$
$$targets\ b\ c = concatMap\ try\ [ups\ c, downs\ c, lefts\ c, rights\ c]$$

$$\textbf{where}\ try\ cs \mid null\ ys\quad = [\,]$$
$$\qquad\qquad\quad \mid null\ xs\quad = [\,]$$
$$\qquad\qquad\quad \mid otherwise = [last\ xs]$$
$$\qquad\qquad \textbf{where}\ (xs,ys) = span\ (\notin b)\ cs$$

$$ups\ c\quad = [c-6, c-12..1]$$
$$downs\ c = [c+6, c+12..29]$$
$$lefts\ c\quad = [c-1, c-2..c - c \bmod 6 + 1]$$
$$rights\ c = [c+1, c+2..c - c \bmod 6 + 5]$$

Each of the various directions is examined in turn to see if there is a blocking piece along the path. If there is, the cell adjacent to the blocker is a possible target for a move. Putting these functions together, we can compute all the simple solutions for a given board by

$$safeLandings = map\ (map\ showMove) \cdot solutions$$

where *solutions* is, say, the breadth-first version defined in the previous section. When *solutions* was run on the example board, it produced 25 simple solutions, of which the first two were those described above.

15.5 Forward planning

With both DFS and BFS we have basically the strategy of trying sequences of random moves until finding one that works. For some games and puzzles, indeed for some real-life problems, it is possible to improve on random search by suitable *forward planning*. The subject of planning algorithms is a broad one, and we will consider only one very simple situation. Suppose it is known that a certain sequence *ms* of moves is sufficient to take the starting state into a goal state. Such a sequence of moves constitutes the *game plan*. Now, it may or may not be the case that the first move *m* in *ms* is a valid move in the starting state. If it is, then move *m* is made and the algorithm carries on with the rest of the plan. If not, then it may be possible to find one or more lists of *preparatory* moves, each of which – provided they can be carried out – leads to a state in which move *m* is a legal move. After making these preparatory moves, the move *m* can then be made, in which case the rest of the plan is carried out as before. However, some of these preparatory moves may, in turn, require further preparatory moves to be made, so the planning process may have to be repeated. In the case that no preparatory moves can be found for a given move to be valid, a random move is made instead. It is because of this last possibility that a planning algorithm should be thought of as an extension of, rather than an alternative to, depth-first or breadth-first search.

Here is an example. Suppose you wanted to move a grand piano to an upstairs room. One sensible game plan is first to move the piano into the hallway, then to lift the piano up the stairs, and finally to move the piano into the required room. The first step may not be possible because (i) the pathway to the door is blocked by a chair, and (ii) the piano will not go through the door without removing its legs. In such a case the preparatory moves would consist of, in either order, moving the chair and removing the legs of the piano. The first task, say moving the chair, might be possible, but the second task would first involve obtaining a suitably large screwdriver for unscrewing the legs. Once the task of moving the piano into the hallway is accomplished, the next step, lifting the piano up the stairs, may not be possible without calling on the help of a number of friends to assist in the lifting. And so on.

Here are the details. Abstractly, a plan is a sequence of moves:

type *Plan* = [*Move*]

The game plan is provided by a function

$\quad$ *gameplan* :: *State* → *Plan*

The problem is solved in a given starting state by making the moves in *gameplan*. An empty plan means success. Otherwise, if the first move in the current plan can be carried out, then the move is made and the plan proceeds with the remaining moves. If it cannot, then we make use of a function

$\quad$ *premoves* :: *State* → *Move* → [*Plan*]

for formulating additional plans. Given a state and a move, each alternative plan in *premoves* should enable the move to be made, provided the moves in the plan are executed first. The first move in each plan returned by *premoves* may in turn require further preparatory moves to be made, so we have to form new plans by iterating *premoves*:

$\quad$ *newplans* :: *State* → *Plan* → [*Plan*]
$\quad$ *newplans* t [] $\quad$ = []
$\quad$ *newplans* t (m : ms) = **if** *elem* m (*moves* t) **then** [m : ms] **else**
$\qquad\qquad\qquad$ *concat* [*newplans* t (*pms* ++ m : ms)
$\qquad\qquad\qquad\qquad$ | *pms* ← *premoves* t m, *all* ($\notin$ ms) *pms*]

The result of *newplans* is a possibly empty list of nonempty but finite plans, the first move of which *can* be made in a given state. Plans cannot contain repeated moves.

If, in order to make a certain move, a plan requires that move to be made first, then clearly the plan is cyclic and cannot be implemented.

Using just the two new functions *newplans* and *gameplan*, we can now formulate a search based on an extended type of path and frontier:

$$\textbf{type } Path \quad = ([Move], State, Plan)$$
$$\textbf{type } Frontier = [Path]$$

This time, a path consists of the moves already made, the current state, and a plan for the remaining moves. We can define the planning algorithm to have the same structure as the time-efficient version of breadth-first search considered above:

$$psolve :: State \rightarrow Maybe\,[Move]$$
$$psolve\; t = psearch\,[]\,[]\,[(([],t,gameplan\;t)]\;\textbf{where}$$
$$\quad psearch :: [State] \rightarrow Frontier \rightarrow Frontier \rightarrow Maybe\,[Move]$$
$$\quad psearch\;ts\,[]\,[] = Nothing$$
$$\quad psearch\;ts\;qs\,[] = psearch\;ts\,[]\;qs$$
$$\quad psearch\;ts\;qs\,((ms,t,plan):ps)$$
$$\quad\;\; |\;solved\;t \quad = Just\;ms$$
$$\quad\;\; |\;elem\;t\;ts \quad = psearch\;ts\;qs\;ps$$
$$\quad\;\; |\;otherwise \; = psearch\;(t:ts)\;(bsuccs\;(ms,t,plan)\mathbin{+\!\!+} qs)$$
$$\qquad\qquad\qquad\qquad (asuccs\;(ms,t,plan)\mathbin{+\!\!+} ps)$$

In *psearch*, all plans in the main frontier are tried first in a depth-first manner until one of them succeeds or all fail. The function *asuccs* is defined by

$$asuccs :: Path \rightarrow [Path]$$
$$asuccs\;(ms,t,plan) = [(ms \mathbin{+\!\!+} [m], move\;t\;m,p)\mid m:p \leftarrow newplans\;t\;plan]$$

In particular, if *elem m (moves t)*, then

$$asuccs\;(ms,t,m:plan) = [(ms \mathbin{+\!\!+} [m], move\;t\;m, plan)]$$

If all plans fail, we can make some legal move at random and start again with a new game plan. The function *bsuccs* is defined by

$$bsuccs :: Path \rightarrow [Path]$$
$$bsuccs\;(ms,t,\_) = [\;(ms \mathbin{+\!\!+} [m], t', gameplan\;t')$$
$$\qquad\qquad\qquad \mid m \leftarrow moves\;t, \textbf{let } t' = move\;t\;m]$$

Such additional plans are necessary for completeness: plans may fail even though there is a solution. This is a consequence of the fact that plans are executed greedily and moves that can be made are made. Note that, if *newplans* returns the empty list, so does *asuccs*. In such a case, *psolve* reduces to simple breadth-first search.

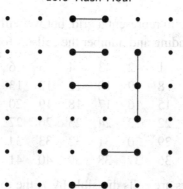

Figure 15.1 A simple Rush Hour grid

15.6 Rush Hour

Let us now see how forward planning can help with another sliding-block puzzle. This one is called *Rush Hour*, and is played on a 6×6 grid. Covering some of the cells of the grid are cars and trucks, which are placed either horizontally or vertically. Cars occupy two cells, while trucks occupy three. Horizontal vehicles can move left or right and vertical vehicles up or down, provided their path is not obstructed by another vehicle. One fixed cell, three places down along the right-hand side of the grid, is special, and is called the *exit cell*. One vehicle is also special. It is horizontal and occupies cells to the left of the exit cell. The object of the game is simply to move the special car to the exit cell.

A very simple starting grid, reminiscent of a real car-park situation, is pictured in Figure 15.1. Down the middle of the grid is a line of cars, the fourth of which has moved one place forwards. The special car, the third one, cannot exit the car park because its path is impeded by a vertical truck. To enable the special car to exit, the truck has to move two places down (which counts as two moves), which in turn requires the fourth car to move back into line (one move). The puzzle therefore has a fairly obvious five-move solution (the special car takes two moves to get to the exit). There are nine possible starting moves on the grid – the first car can move one step left or right, the second car one step left, and so on – and breadth-first search could involve examining about 9^5 moves before finding the shortest five-move solution. Simple planning, on the other hand, leads at once to the answer. Of course, most starting grids that come with the puzzle are considerably more difficult: there are starting grids that take 93 moves to solve! Furthermore, as we will see, planning is not guaranteed to find a shortest solution.

There are various ways to represent a grid, but we will take essentially the same approach as in Lunar Landing and number the cells as follows:

$$
\begin{array}{cccccc}
1 & 2 & 3 & 4 & 5 & 6 \\
8 & 9 & 10 & 11 & 12 & 13 \\
15 & 16 & 17 & 18 & 19 & 20 \\
22 & 23 & 24 & 25 & 26 & 27 \\
29 & 30 & 31 & 32 & 33 & 34 \\
36 & 37 & 38 & 39 & 40 & 41
\end{array}
$$

The left and right borders are cells divisible by 7; the top border consists of cells with negative numbers and the bottom border consists of cells with numbers greater than 42. The exit cell is cell 20. A grid state can be defined as a list of pairs of cells, with each pair (r,f) satisfying $r < f$ and representing the rear and front cells occupied by a single vehicle. The vehicles in the grid are named implicitly by their positions in the list, with the special vehicle being vehicle 0, so the first pair of numbers in the grid represents the cells occupied by vehicle 0, the second pair vehicle 1, and so on. For example, the grid of Figure 15.1 is represented by

$$[(17,18), \ (3,4), \ (10,11), \ (12,26), \ (32,33), \ (38,39)]$$

This representation is captured by introducing the type synonyms

> **type** $Cell$ $= Nat$
> **type** $Vehicle = (Cell, Cell)$
> **type** $Grid$ $= [Vehicle]$

The list of occupied cells in the grid can be constructed in increasing order by filling in the intervals associated with each vehicle and merging the results:

> $occupied :: Grid \rightarrow [Cell]$
> $occupied = foldr \ merge \ [] \cdot map \ fill$
>
> $fill :: Vehicle \rightarrow [Cell]$
> $fill \ (r,f) = \textbf{if} \ horizontal \ (r,f) \ \textbf{then} \ [r..f] \ \textbf{else} \ [r, r+7..f]$
>
> $horizontal :: Vehicle \rightarrow Bool$
> $horizontal \ (r,f) = f - r < 6$

The next decision concerns the representation of moves. A simple representation is to say that a move consists of a vehicle's name and the target cell:

> **type** $Name = Nat$
> **type** $Move = (Name, Cell)$

For example, if a car occupies the cells $(24,25)$ then the possible target cells are 23 and 26. The valid moves are defined by

> $moves :: Grid \rightarrow [Move]$
> $moves \ g = [(n,c) \mid (n,v) \leftarrow zip \ [0..] \ g, c \leftarrow steps \ v, notElem \ c \ (occupied \ g)]$

The function *steps* is defined by

$$steps\ (r,f) = \textbf{if}\ horizontal\ (r,f)$$
$$\textbf{then}\ [c \mid c \leftarrow [f+1,r-1], c \bmod 7 \neq 0]$$
$$\textbf{else}\ [c \mid c \leftarrow [f+7,r-7], 0 < c \wedge c < 42]$$

Each step involves moving a vehicle a step in one of two directions, left or right for horizontal vehicles, and up or down for vertical vehicles. In each case the target of the move has to be an unoccupied cell.

The function *move* is implemented by

$$move :: Grid \rightarrow Move \rightarrow Grid$$
$$move\ g\ (n,c) = g_1 +\!\!+ [adjust\ v\ c] +\!\!+ g_2$$
$$\textbf{where}\ (g_1, v : g_2) = splitAt\ n\ g$$

$$adjust :: Vehicle \rightarrow Cell \rightarrow Vehicle$$
$$adjust\ (r,f)\ c = \textbf{if}\ f < c\ \textbf{then}\ (c-f+r, c)\ \textbf{else}\ (c, c+f-r)$$

Finally, a puzzle is solved if the front of the special car is at the exit cell:

$$solved :: Grid \rightarrow Bool$$
$$solved\ g = snd\ (head\ g) == 20$$

Having defined *moves*, *move*, and *solved*, one can now implement a breadth-first or a depth-first search following the standard recipe.

Turning to *psolve*, it seems we need only define *gameplan* and *premoves*. However, the definition of *newplans* given in the previous section needs to be modified in order to work with Rush Hour. To see why, suppose the first move in the current plan is $(0, 19)$, moving the special car one step right from its initial position $(17, 18)$. Assume further that cell 19 is currently blocked by a vehicle, so there is a need for preparatory moves that move this vehicle out of the way. Now it is perfectly possible that one of these preparatory moves is $(0, 16)$, moving the special vehicle one step left. After executing these moves, we see that $(0, 19)$ is no longer a valid move because it requires car 0 to move two steps forward.

To solve this problem, we will allow multi-step moves in plans, but expand them to single-step moves before computing new plans. Thus we redefine *newplans* to read

$$newplans :: Grid \rightarrow Plan \rightarrow [Plan]$$
$$newplans\ g\ [] \quad\quad = []$$
$$newplans\ g\ (m : ms) = mkplans\ (expand\ g\ m +\!\!+ ms)$$
$$\textbf{where}\ mkplans\ (m : ms) = \textbf{if}\ elem\ m\ (moves\ g)\ \textbf{then}\ [m : ms]\ \textbf{else}$$
$$concat\ [\,newplans\ g\ (pms +\!\!+ m : ms)$$
$$\mid pms \leftarrow premoves\ g\ m, all\ (\notin ms)\ pms\,]$$

Each move is expanded into a sequence of legal moves before new plans are made.

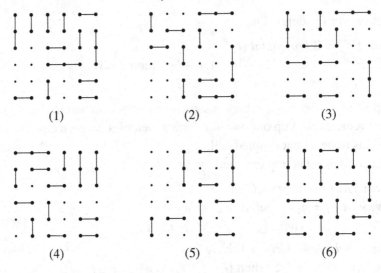

Figure 15.2 Six Rush Hour problems

Furthermore, *premoves* now returns a list of possibly multi-step moves rather than a list of sequences of moves. The function *expand* is defined by

$$expand :: Grid \to Move \to [Move]$$
$$expand\ g\ (n,c) = \textbf{if}\ horizontal\ (r,f)$$
$$\textbf{then if}\ f < c\ \textbf{then}\ [(n,d) \mid d \leftarrow [f+1..c]]$$
$$\textbf{else}\ [(n,d) \mid d \leftarrow [r-1,r-2..c]]$$
$$\textbf{else if}\ f < c\ \textbf{then}\ [(n,d) \mid d \leftarrow [f+7,f+14..c]]$$
$$\textbf{else}\ [(n,d) \mid d \leftarrow [r-7,r-17..c]]$$
$$\textbf{where}\ (r,f) = g\ !!\ n$$

Given the ability to make use of multi-step moves, we can define *gameplan* by

$$gameplan :: Grid \to Plan$$
$$gameplan\ g = [(0,20)]$$

To define *premoves*, observe that, if a move cannot be made it is because the target cell is blocked by a vehicle, which therefore has to be moved out of the way. Each additional plan therefore consists of a single, possibly multi-step move:

$$premoves :: Grid \to Move \to [Plan]$$
$$premoves\ g\ (n,c) = [[m] \mid m \leftarrow freeingmoves\ c\ (blocker\ g\ c)]$$

$$blocker :: Grid \to Cell \to (Name, Vehicle)$$
$$blocker\ g\ c = head\ [(n,v) \mid (n,v) \leftarrow zip\ [0..]\ g, elem\ c\ (fill\ v)]$$

The function *blocker* returns the name of the blocking vehicle and the cells occupied by its front and rear. To define *freeingmoves*, observe that, if a vehicle with length

Puzzle	bfsolve	moves	psolve	moves	dfsolve	moves
(1)	0.80s	34	0.08s	38	0.42s	1228
(2)	0.44s	18	0.03s	27	0.42s	2126
(3)	0.20s	55	0.12s	57	0.11s	812
(4)	16.83s	93	0.28s	121	17.27s	15542
(5)	4.14s	83	1.06s	119	3.47s	4794
(6)	0.78s	83	0.08s	89	0.27s	1323

Figure 15.3 Running times and move counts for the six Rush Hour problems

k is horizontal, then in order to free cell c we have to move the vehicle either rightwards to cell $c+k$ or leftwards to cell $c-k$. If the vehicle is vertical, then the move is downwards to cell $c+7k$ or upwards to $c-7k$. In each case the destination cell has to be on the grid. For a horizontal vehicle (r,f) we have $k=f-r+1$, while for a vertical vehicle $k=(f-r)/7+1$. Hence we can define

$freeingmoves :: Cell \rightarrow (Name, Vehicle) \rightarrow [Move]$
$freeingmoves\ c\ (n,(r,f)) =$
  if $horizontal\ (r,f)$
  then $[(n,j) \mid j \leftarrow [c-(f-r+1),c+(f-r+1)], a<j \wedge j<b]$
  else $[(n,j) \mid j \leftarrow [c-(f-r+7),c+(f-r+7)], 0<j \wedge j<42]$
  where $a = r-r \bmod 7; b = f-f \bmod 7+7$

This completes the planning algorithm for Rush Hour.

So, is *psolve* better than a BFS or a DFS solution, and if so, by how much? Pictured in Figure 15.2 are six Rush Hour grids, the bottom three of which are amongst the hardest known starting grids. Each puzzle was tackled using *bfsolve* (a BFS to find one solution), *psolve*, and also *dfsolve* (a DFS to find one solution). The computations were run using GHCi, with the results given in Figure 15.3. In each case, *psolve* is faster than *bfsolve*, varying from a factor of two to a factor of 60 in the case of puzzle (4). On the other hand, in no case did *psolve* find solutions with the minimum number of moves. As can be seen from the table, *dfsolve* found solutions with many more moves than necessary.

15.7 Chapter notes

The 8-queens puzzle was first described in 1848; many mathematicians, including Gauss, have worked on the problem. See [10], and also [4] which contains an explicit formula for computing a single solution for the n-queens problem for all $n \geqslant 4$. Using a massively parallel approach, the value of $Q(27)$, the number of solutions for the 27-queens problem, was found to be 234907967154122528 in September

2016; see [7]. Other values of $Q(n)$ appear as sequence A000170 in the On-line Encyclopedia of Integer Sequences (OEIS), see [11]. The bit-vector approach was first described by Qiu Zongyan [12] and later rediscovered by Martin Richards [9].

The problem of computing expressions with a given sum appears in [1, Chapter 6]. Knuth [6, Section 7.2.1.6, Exercise 122] also discusses the problem, and gives other variants of the problem, such as allowing parentheses and further arithmetic operations.

Lunar Landing is available at www.thinkfun.com/products, as is Rush Hour. Lunar Landing is also known as *Lunar Lockout* and the *UFO puzzle*. A computer analysis of the puzzle on boards of different shapes and sizes can be found in [8]. The planning algorithm for Rush Hour was first described in [1]. The complexity of the problem is discussed in [3] and the hardest known starting grid is taken from [2]. For more information on planning algorithms, consult [5].

References

[1]   Richard Bird. *Pearls of Functional Algorithm Design*. Cambridge University Press, Cambridge, 2010.

[2]   Sébastien Collette, Jean-François Raskin, and Frédéric Servais. On the symbolic computation of the hardest configurations of the Rush Hour game. In *Computers and Games*, volume 4630 of *Lecture Notes in Computer Science*, pages 220–233. Springer-Verlag, Berlin, 2006.

[3]   Gary W. Flake and Eric B. Baum. Rush Hour is PSPACE-complete, or "Why you should generously tip parking lot attendants". *Theoretical Computer Science*, 270(1):895–911, 2002.

[4]   Eric J. Hoffman, J. C. Loessi, and Robert C. Moore. Construction for the solutions of the *m* queens problem. *Mathematics Magazine*, 42(2):66–72, 1969.

[5]   Steven M. LaValle. *Planning Algorithms*. Cambridge University Press, Cambridge, 2006.

[6]   Donald E. Knuth. *The Art of Computer Programming*, volume 4A: Combinatorial Algorithms. Addison-Wesley, Reading, MA, 2011.

[7]   Thomas B. Preusser and Matthias R. Engelhardt. Putting queens in carry chains, N° 27. *Journal of Signal Processing Systems*, 88(2):185–201, 2017.

[8]   John Rausch. Computer analysis of the UFO puzzle. http://www.puzzleworld.org/puzzleworld/art/art02.htm, 1999.

[9]   Martin Richards. Backtracking algorithms in MCPL using bit patterns and recursion. http://www.cl.cam.ac.uk/~mr10/backtrk.pdf, University of Cambridge Computer Laboratory, 2009.

[10]   Walter William Rouse Ball. *Mathematical Recreations and Essays*. Macmillan, New York, 1960.

[11]   Neil Sloane. The on-line encyclopedia of integer sequences. https://oeis.org/, 1996.

[12]   Qiu Zongyan. Bit-vector encoding of *n*-queen problem. *ACM SIGPLAN Notices*, 37(2):68–70, 2002.

Exercises

Exercise 15.1 What simple optimisation would make $queens_1$ run faster?

Exercise 15.2 Consider the solution for the 4-queens problem based on the function *search*. Write down the successive arguments of *search* up to the point that the first solution is found.

Exercise 15.3 In the solution to the n-queens problem based on bit vectors, there is another, non-recursive definition of *bits* which uses the *Data.Bits* function *bit*. The value of *bit i* is a bit vector with bit i set to 1 and all other bits set to 0. Give the alternative definition as a list comprehension.

Exercise 15.4 In Section 15.2 the definition of *solutions* $100 [1..9]$ used limited-precision integers. Why is this justified?

Exercise 15.5 Consider again the two functions *solutions* and $solutions_1$ for computing the number of ways a list of digits can be combined to give a target value. Recall that the latter is an optimised version of the former based on the monotonicity of expressions built out of $\times$ and $+$. What would you expect the value of

$$solutions\ 100\ [0..9] == solutions_1\ 100\ [0..9]$$

to be?

Exercise 15.6 Express the condition that expressions built out of juxtaposition, $\times$, and $+$ never decrease the value of an expression more formally as a property of *glue*. Does the condition hold when the digit 0 is allowed in expressions?

Exercise 15.7 If we allowed decimal points in expressions, then there are other ways of making 100, including

$$100 = 1 \times .2 + .3 + 45 + 6.7 \times 8 + .9$$
$$100 = 1 \times 23 \times 4 + 5.6 + .7 + .8 + .9$$
$$100 = 1 \times 23 \times 4 + 5 + .6 + .7 + .8 + .9$$

In Haskell, .6 isn't a legal expression and one has to write 0.6 instead, but never mind. Are there any other ways? Write a program to find out. As a hint, there are seven ways to extend $2 \times 3 + \cdots$ on the left with a new digit 1, six ways to extend $.2 \times 3 + \cdots$, and five ways to extend $2.3 \times 4 + \cdots$. Base the program on the following type synonyms:

```
type Expr   = [Term]
type Term   = [Factor]
type Factor = ([Digit], [Digit])
```

A factor (xs, ys) contains the digits xs before the decimal point and the digits ys after the point. Either xs or ys can be the empty list but not both.

Exercise 15.8 Supposing we allowed exponentials in expressions, there is at least one other way to make 100:

$$100 = 1 + 2\,\hat{}\,3 + 4 \times 5 + 6 + 7 \times 8 + 9$$

Are there any other ways? Write a program to find out. Again, no parentheses are allowed. Base the program on the following type synonyms:

> **type** *Expr*   = [*Term*]
> **type** *Term*   = [*Expo*]
> **type** *Expo*   = [*Factor*]
> **type** *Factor* = [*Digit*]
> **type** *Digit*   = *Integer*

Here a digit is an *Integer* and the values of expressions are *Integer* values because the numbers involved can exceed the range of fixed-precision arithmetic. Each term is now a product of a nonempty list of exponentials; for example

$$12\,\hat{}\,3 \times 4\,\hat{}\,5 + 6 \times 7$$

would be represented by

$$[[[[1,2],[3]],\ [[4],[5]]],\ [[[6]],[[7]]]]$$

Assume that exponentiation associates to the left, so that, for example, $2\,\hat{}\,3\,\hat{}\,2 = 64$. (In Haskell, exponentiation associates to the right, but solving the problem with this order of association would involve such huge numbers that the program would crash.)

Exercise 15.9 Given that

$$exp = foldr\,f\,e \cdot takeWhile\,p \cdot iterate\,g$$

show that

$$exp\ x = \textbf{if}\ p\ x\ \textbf{then}\ f\ x\ (exp\ (g\ x))\ \textbf{else}\ e$$

Exercise 15.10 Recall that in order to optimise BFS we defined

$$search_1\ pss\ ps = search\ (ps + concat\ (reverse\ pss))$$

Calculate $search_1\ pss\ (p : ps)$, assuming the first state in p is not a solved state.

Exercise 15.11 Given is a permutation of $[0..n]$. The aim is to sort the permutation into increasing order using only moves that interchange 0 with any neighbour that is at most two positions away. For example, $[3, 0, 4, 1, 2]$ can produce $[0, 3, 4, 1, 2]$, $[3, 4, 0, 1, 2]$, and $[3, 1, 4, 0, 2]$ in a single step. Can the aim always be achieved? Write a breadth-first search to find the shortest sequence of moves. (*Hint*: one possible representation of states and moves is

> **type** *State* = (*Nat*, *Array Nat Nat*)
> **type** *Move* = *Nat*

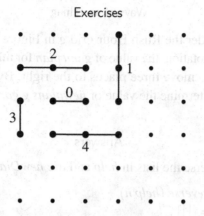

Figure 15.4 A Rush Hour grid

The first component of a state is the location of 0 in the array, and a move is an integer giving the target position for 0.)

Exercise 15.12 Imagine a row of differently sized jugs, given in ascending order of their capacity. Initially all jugs are empty except for the last, which is full to the brim with water. The object is to get to a situation in which one or more jugs contains exactly a given target amount of water. A move in the puzzle consists of filling one jug with water from another jug, or emptying one jug into another. (Water cannot simply be discarded.) Suppose *cap* is a given array that determines the capacity of each jug, and *target* is a given integer target. Decide on the representation of states and moves and give the functions *moves*, *move*, and *solved*. Hence use breadth-first search to find the unique shortest solution for the particular instance of three jugs, with capacities 3, 5, and 8, and a target amount of 4.

Exercise 15.13 There are *m* elves and *m* dwarves on a river bank. There is also a rowing boat that can take them to the other side of the river. All elves can row, but only *n* of the dwarves can. The boat can contain up to *p* passengers, one of whom has to be a rower. The problem is to transport the elves and dwarves safely to the other side in the shortest number of trips, where a trip is safe if the dwarves on either side of the river, or in the boat, never outnumber the elves. For the avoidance of doubt, the boat empties completely before new passengers get on. The exercise simply asks for a suitable way to model states and for the definitions of *moves*, *move*, and *solved*.

Exercise 15.14 Write a function *showMoves* :: [*Move*] → *String* for Lunar Landing so that, for example, the moves *5U 5R 5U 2L 2D 2L 0U 0R 0U* are recorded as *5URU 2LDL 0URU*. The Haskell *Data.List* function *groupBy* may prove useful.

Exercise 15.15 Consider the Rush Hour grid g in Figure 15.4. Using directional rather than cell-based notation, the value of *gameplan* for this grid is $0RRR$, meaning the special car 0 has to move three places to the right. By listing the appropriate values of *premoves*, determine the value of *newplans g gameplan*.

Answers

Answer 15.1 Just reverse the lists in *help* and use $newDiag_2$:

$$queens\ n = map\ reverse\ (help\ n)$$
$$\mathbf{where}\ help\ 0 = [[\,]]$$
$$help\ r = [q:qs \mid qs \leftarrow help\ (r-1), q \leftarrow [1..n],$$
$$notElem\ q\ qs, newDiag_2\ q\ qs]$$

Answer 15.2 The successive arguments of *search* are

$$[[\,]]$$
$$[[1],[2],[3],[4]]$$
$$[[3,1],[4,1],[2],[3],[4]]$$
$$[[4,1],[2],[3],[4]]$$
$$[[2,4,1],[2],[3],[4]]$$
$$[[2],[3],[4]]$$
$$[[4,2],[3],[4]]$$
$$[[1,4,2],[3],[4]]$$
$$[[3,1,4,2],[3],[4]]$$

Answer 15.3 One non-recursive definition of *bits* is

$$bits :: Word16 \rightarrow [Word16]$$
$$bits\ v = [b \mid b \leftarrow map\ bit\ [0..15], v\ .\&.\ b == b]$$

Answer 15.4 The largest value of an expression is 123456789, which is less than 2^{29}, so *Int*-arithmetic is adequate. Of course, when the input is longer than nine digits, we should use *Integer* arithmetic.

Answer 15.5 You would probably expect the answer to be *True*, but you would be wrong. The left-hand side returns 17 solutions, while the right-hand side returns only 14. One answer returned by *solutions* but not by $solutions_1$ is

$$100 = 0 \times 1 + 2 \times 3 + 4 + 5 + 6 + 7 + 8 \times 9$$

The reason for the discrepancy is that the monotonicity condition fails when the digit 0 is allowed in expressions. In particular,

$$101 = 1 + 2 \times 3 + 4 + 5 + 6 + 7 + 8 \times 9$$

but when this expression is extended by the digit 0, the result can drop in value.

Answer 15.6 The monotonicity condition can be expressed by

$$elem\ y\ (glue\ d\ x)\ \Rightarrow\ value\ x \leqslant value\ y$$

The proof follows from the fact that, if x and y are positive integers, then the larger of x and y is no greater than any of the expressions $10\,x+y$, $10\,y+x$, $x+y$, or $x \times y$. The claim does not hold when zero values are allowed, because $x \leqslant x \times 0$ is false for positive x. It also does not hold when exponentiation is allowed, because $x \leqslant y\,\hat{}\,x$ is false unless $y > 1$. It also does not hold when decimal points are allowed in expressions.

Answer 15.7 First of all, the seven ways of extending $2 \times 3 + \cdots$ are

$$.12 \times 3 + \cdots \qquad 12 \times 3 + \cdots \qquad 1.2 \times 3 + \cdots$$
$$.1 \times 2 \times 3 + \cdots \qquad 1 \times 2 \times 3 \ldots$$
$$.1 + 2 \times 3 + \cdots \qquad 1 + 2 \times 3 + \cdots$$

The monotonicity condition fails when decimal points are allowed, so only the naive program works. We will just give the modified version of *glue*, which is

$$glue :: Digit \rightarrow Expr \rightarrow [Expr]$$
$$glue\ d\ [\,] = [[[([d],[\,])]],[[([\,],[d])]]]$$
$$glue\ d\ (((xs,ys):fs):ts)$$
$$\quad |\ null\ xs \quad = (((xs,d:ys):fs):ts):rest$$
$$\quad |\ null\ ys \quad = [((([\,],d:xs):fs):ts,(([d],xs):fs):ts] + rest$$
$$\quad |\ otherwise = rest$$
$$\mathbf{where}\ rest = [((d:xs,ys):fs):ts,$$
$$\qquad\qquad\qquad (([d],[\,]):(xs,ys):fs):ts,$$
$$\qquad\qquad\qquad (([\,],[d]):(xs,ys):fs):ts,$$
$$\qquad\qquad\qquad [(([d],[\,]))]:((xs,ys):fs):ts,$$
$$\qquad\qquad\qquad [(([\,],[d]))]:((xs,ys):fs):ts]$$

It turns out that there are 198 ways to make 100 when decimal points are allowed.

Answer 15.8 The monotonicity condition fails when exponentiation is allowed, so only the naive program works. Here is a modified version of *glue*:

$$glue :: Digit \rightarrow Expr \rightarrow [Expr]$$
$$glue\ d\ [\,] \qquad\qquad = [[[[[d]]]]]$$
$$glue\ d\ (((ds:fs):es):ts) = [((((d:ds):fs):es):ts,$$
$$\qquad\qquad\qquad\qquad (([d]:(ds:fs)):es):ts,$$
$$\qquad\qquad\qquad\qquad (([[d]]:((ds:fs):es)):ts,$$
$$\qquad\qquad\qquad\qquad [[[d]]]:(((ds:fs):es):ts)]$$

An expression can be extended on the left in four ways.

It turns out that there are just three ways to make a century using exponentiation:

$$100 = 1 \,\hat{}\, 23 + 4 + 5 \times 6 + 7 \times 8 + 9$$
$$100 = 1 \,\hat{}\, 2 \,\hat{}\, 3 + 4 + 5 \times 6 + 7 \times 8 + 9$$
$$100 = 1 + 2 \,\hat{}\, 3 + 4 \times 5 + 6 + 7 \times 8 + 9$$

Answer 15.9 We have

$exp\ x$
$=$ { definition of *iterate* }
$foldr\ f\ e\ (takewhile\ p\ (x:iterate\ g\ (g\ x)))$
$=$ { definition of *takeWhile*, assuming $p\ x$ }
$foldr\ f\ e\ (x:takeWhile\ p\ (iterate\ g\ (g\ x)))$
$=$ { definition of *foldr* }
$f\ x\ (foldr\ f\ e\ (takeWhile\ p\ (iterate\ g\ (g\ x))))$
$=$ { definition of *exp* }
$f\ x\ (exp\ (g\ x))$

On the other hand, $exp\ x = e$ if $p\ x$ is false.

Answer 15.10 The calculation is as follows, assuming the first state in p is not a solved state:

$search_1\ pss\ (p:ps)$
$=$ { definition of $search_1$ }
$search\ (p:ps + concat\ (reverse\ pss))$
$=$ { definition of *search*, given assumption }
$search\ (ps + concat\ (reverse\ pss) + succs\ p)$
$=$ { definition of *concat* and *reverse* }
$search\ (ps + concat\ (reverse\ (succs\ p:pss)))$
$=$ { definition of $search_1$ }
$search_1\ (succs\ p:pss)\ ps$

Answer 15.11 Yes, the aim can always be achieved. One way is first to get the largest element into its final position and then apply the same method recursively, leaving the largest element untouched. To get the largest element into its final position, first position 0 one place to the right of the largest element. For example, counting positions from 1, the single move 2 converts $[4, 1, 3, 0, 2]$ to $[4, 0, 1, 3, 2]$, while the two moves 4 and 3 convert $[3, 0, 1, 4, 2]$ to $[3, 4, 0, 1, 2]$. Let j be the position of the largest element. Repeatedly apply the moves $j, j + 2, j + 1, j + 3$, and so on, followed by a final move $n - 1$, to shuffle the largest element to the right. Continuing the example, the moves 2, 4, 3, and 5 convert $[3, 4, 0, 1, 2]$ to $[3, 1, 2, 4, 0]$, which, followed by move 4, yields $[3, 1, 2, 0, 4]$.

The relevant definitions for a breadth-first search are

$start :: [Nat] \rightarrow State$
$start\ xs = (hole\ x, x)$
   where $x = listArray\ (1, length\ xs)\ xs$
      $hole\ x = head\ [j \mid j \leftarrow [1..], x!j == 0]$
$moves :: State \rightarrow [Move]$
$moves\ (j, x) = [k \mid k \leftarrow [j-1, j-2, j+1, j+2], a \leqslant k \wedge k \leqslant b]$
         where $(a, b) = bounds\ x$
$move :: State \rightarrow Move \rightarrow State$
$move\ (j, x)\ k = (k, x // [(j, x!k), (k, x!j)])$
$solved :: State \rightarrow Bool$
$solved\ (j, x) = sorted\ (elems\ x)$
   where $sorted\ xs = and\ (zipWith\ (\leqslant)\ xs\ (tail\ xs))$

For example,

$solution\ (start\ [4, 1, 3, 0, 2]) = Just\ [3, 1, 2, 4, 3, 5, 4, 2, 1]$

A total of nine moves sorts the numbers.

Answer 15.12 A simple representation is to use an array of naturals for states and two naturals, the source and destination jugs, for the moves:

type $State\ = Array\ Nat\ Nat$
type $Move = (Nat, Nat)$

The possible moves in a given state consist of a pair of distinct integers in which the source jug is nonempty and the target jug is not full:

$moves :: State \rightarrow [Move]$
$moves\ t = [(j, k) \mid j \leftarrow indices\ t, k \leftarrow indices\ t, j \neq k, 0 < t!j, t!k < cap!k]$

The puzzle is solved when the target value appears in the array:

$solved :: State \rightarrow Bool$
$solved\ t = elem\ target\ (elems\ t)$

Finally, to determine the result of a move, observe that the total quantity of water in the two jugs remains the same, and either the source is emptied or the target is filled to its capacity. That leads to

$move :: State \rightarrow Move \rightarrow State$
$move\ x\ (j, k) = $ **if** $t \leqslant c$ **then** $x // [(j, 0), (k, t)]$ **else** $x // [(j, t - c), (k, c)]$
      where $t = x!j + x!k; c = cap!k$

The unique solution of length six for the three-jugs problem is

$[(3, 2),\ (2, 1),\ (1, 3),\ (2, 1),\ (3, 2),\ (2, 1)]$

Answer 15.13 Data for the problem is defined by three numbers (m,n,p), where m is the total number of elves (the same as the number of dwarves), n is the number of dwarves who can row, and p is the maximum number of passengers allowed in a boat:

> **type** $Data = (Nat, Nat, Nat)$

One possible definition of a state is a quadruple

> **type** $State = (Bool, Nat, Nat, Nat)$

In a state (b,e,d,r) the boolean b is *True* if the boat is empty and at the left bank and *False* if it is empty and at the right bank. The values (e,d,r) are the numbers of elves, the number of non-rowing dwarves, and the number of dwarves who can row, on the left bank of the river, so the corresponding values on the right bank are $(m-e, m-n-d, n-r)$. Assuming everyone is initially on the left bank, the initial state is

> $start :: Data \to State$
> $start\ (m,n,p) = (True, m, m-n, n)$

The puzzle is solved if nobody is left on the left bank:

> $solved :: State \to Bool$
> $solved\ t = (t == (False, 0, 0, 0))$

A state is safe if the dwarves never outnumber the elves on either bank. If (e,d,r) are the numbers on the left bank, then we require

$$(e == 0 \lor e \geqslant d+r) \land (m-e == 0 \lor m-e \geqslant m-(d+r))$$

which simplifies to

> $safe :: Nat \to State \to Bool$
> $safe\ m\ (b,e,d,r) = (e == 0 \lor e == m \lor e == d+r)$

A move consists of the number of elves, non-rowing dwarves, and dwarves who can row, representing the passengers carried on the boat:

> **type** $Move = (Nat, Nat, Nat)$

A move is legal if it contains at most p people, at least one rower, and if the dwarves do not outnumber the elves:

> $legal :: Nat \to Move \to Bool$
> $legal\ p\ (x,y,z) = x+y+z \leqslant p \land (x \geqslant 1 \lor z \geqslant 1) \land (x == 0 \lor x \geqslant y+z)$

The function *move* is now defined by

> $move :: State \to Move \to State$
> $move\ (True, e, d, r)\ (x,y,z) = (False, e-x, d-y, r-z)$
> $move\ (False, e, d, r)\ (x,y,z) = (True, e+x, d+y, r+z)$

A move consists of the boat travelling from one side of the river to the other, and emptying all passengers onto the river bank. The function *moves* is defined by

$$moves :: Data \rightarrow State \rightarrow [Move]$$
$$moves\ (m,n,p)\ t@(b,e,d,r)$$
$$= [(x,y,z) \mid x \leftarrow [0..i], y \leftarrow [0..j], z \leftarrow [0..k],$$
$$legal\ p\ (x,y,z) \wedge safe\ m\ (move\ t\ (x,y,z))]$$
$$\textbf{where}\ (i,j,k) = \textbf{if}\ b\ \textbf{then}\ (e,d,r)\ \textbf{else}\ (m-e,m-n-d,n-r)$$

For example, the $(3,1,2)$ problem has four solutions, each involving 13 crossings in total.

Answer 15.14 One possibility:

$$showMoves :: [Move] \rightarrow [String]$$
$$showMoves = map\ showMove \cdot groupBy\ sameName$$
$$\textbf{where}\ sameName\ m_1\ m_2 = name\ m_1 == name\ m_2$$
$$name\ (n,\_,\_)\quad = n$$
$$showMove\ ms\quad = show\ (name\ (head\ ms)) \mathbin{+\!\!+}$$
$$concatMap\ dir\ [(s,f) \mid (\_,s,f) \leftarrow ms]$$

Answer 15.15 We have, again writing moves in expanded, directional form:

$$premoves\ g\ 0R = [[1DDD]]$$
$$premoves\ g\ 1D = [[4L]]$$
$$premoves\ g\ 4L = [[3U],[3DD]]$$
$$premoves\ g\ 3U = [[2R]]$$
$$premoves\ g\ 2R = [[1DD]]$$

But the move $1DD$ repeats part of $1DDD$, so this plan is rejected. We are left with a single plan, namely

$$newplans\ g\ gameplan = [3DD, 4L, 1DDD, 0RRR]$$

All moves in this plan can be carried out, leading to the solution.

Chapter 16

Heuristic search

In the search methods we have looked at so far, we have always chosen the first path on the frontier for expansion, the only difference between breadth-first and depth-first search being the order in which we added newly formed paths to the frontier. In heuristic search, we make use of a given estimate of how likely it is that each path will lead to a good result, and we choose next the one with the best expectation. The hope is that, if the estimate is reasonably accurate, then we will find an optimum path more quickly. With heuristic search the frontier is managed as a priority queue in which the priorities are estimates of how good a path is. At each step the path with the highest priority is chosen for further expansion. Heuristic search is useful only when searching for a single solution to a problem.

The primary example of heuristic search is the problem of finding a route between two towns in a network of roads. The cost of getting to the final destination from a given town can be estimated as the straight-line distance between the two towns, the distance a crow would have to fly. No real route could have a shorter distance, so this is an *optimistic* estimate. The choice of the next partial route for further exploration will be one that minimises the sum of the cost of the route so far and the estimate of how much further there is to travel. Contrast this with Dijkstra's algorithm, which always explores a partial route whose cost is the minimum so far, ignoring any estimate for completing the journey. Route-finding algorithms have many applications in artificial intelligence, including robotics, games, and puzzles. We will take a look at some examples later on.

Heuristic search is usually described using the terminology of graphs and edges rather than states and moves. We will assume throughout this chapter that graphs consist of a finite number of vertices and directed edges, and that the cost (or weight) of each edge is always a positive number. We describe two closely related algorithms for carrying out heuristic search, each of which depends on a different assumption about the estimating function. We revisit the necessary operations of priority queues,

and also describe a new structure, a *priority search queue*, that can help to improve
the running time of the search.

16.1 Searching with an optimistic heuristic

By definition, an estimating function or *heuristic* is a function h from vertices to
costs such that $h(v)$ estimates the cost of getting from vertex v to a closest goal (in
general, there may be a number of possible goals rather than one single destination).
Such a function is said to be *optimistic* if it never overestimates the actual cost. In
symbols, if $H(v)$ is the minimum cost of any path from vertex v to a closest goal,
then $h(v) \leqslant H(v)$ for all vertices v. If there is no path from v to a goal, then $h(v)$ is
unconstrained. An optimistic heuristic is also called an *admissible* heuristic. In this
section we give two algorithms that work whenever the heuristic is optimistic and
there is a path from the source to a goal.

The first algorithm is a very basic form of heuristic search, which we will call T*
search simply because the underlying algorithm is really a tree search. Here are the
types we need, with the exception of *Vertex*, which depends on the application:

> **type** *Cost* $= Nat$
> **type** *Graph* $= Vertex \rightarrow [(Vertex, Cost)]$
> **type** *Heuristic* $= Vertex \rightarrow Cost$
> **type** *Path* $= ([Vertex], Cost)$

We assume that a graph is given not as a list of vertices and edges, but as a function
from vertices to lists of adjacent vertices together with the associated edge costs.
This function corresponds to the function *moves* of the previous chapter, except that
now we assume each move from one state to another is associated with a certain
cost. A path is a list of vertices along with the cost of the path. For efficiency, paths
will be constructed in reverse order, so the endpoint of a path is the first element in
the list of vertices:

> $end :: Path \rightarrow Vertex$
> $end = head \cdot fst$
>
> $cost :: Path \rightarrow Cost$
> $cost = snd$
>
> $extract :: Path \rightarrow Path$
> $extract\ (vs, c) = (reverse\ vs, c)$

In terms of states and moves, a path would be a triple consisting of a list of moves,
an end state, and the cost of the moves. We will also make use of the following
operations on priority queues from Section 8.3:

$$insertQ \quad :: Ord \; p \Rightarrow a \to p \to PQ \; a \; p \to PQ \; a \; p$$
$$addListQ :: Ord \; p \Rightarrow [(a,p)] \to PQ \; a \; p \to PQ \; a \; p$$
$$deleteQ \quad :: Ord \; p \Rightarrow PQ \; a \; p \to ((a,p), PQ \; a \; p)$$
$$emptyQ \quad :: PQ \; a \; p$$
$$nullQ \quad :: PQ \; a \; p \to Bool$$

To recap: *insertQ* adds a new value with a given priority to the queue; *addListQ* adds a list of value–priority pairs to an existing queue; *deleteQ* deletes a value with the lowest priority from the queue, returning the value, its priority, and the remaining queue; *emptyQ* is the empty queue; and *nullQ* is a test for whether the queue is empty or not. In what follows we will not need *deleteQ* to return the priority of a value, so we introduce the variant

$$removeQ :: Ord \; p \Rightarrow PQ \; a \; p \to (a, PQ \; a \; p)$$
$$removeQ \; q_1 = (x, q_2) \; \textbf{where} \; ((x, \_), q_2) = deleteQ \; q_1$$

Here now is the definition of *tstar*:

$$tstar :: Graph \to Heuristic \to (Vertex \to Bool) \to Vertex \to Maybe \; Path$$
$$tstar \; g \; h \; goal \; source = tsearch \; start$$
$$\quad \textbf{where} \; start = insertQ \; ([source], 0) \; (h \; source) \; emptyQ$$
$$\qquad tsearch \; ps \; | \; nullQ \; ps \quad = Nothing$$
$$\qquad\qquad\qquad | \; goal \; (end \; p) = Just \; (extract \; p)$$
$$\qquad\qquad\qquad | \; otherwise \quad = tsearch \; rs$$
$$\qquad \textbf{where} \; (p, qs) = removeQ \; ps$$
$$\qquad\qquad\quad rs \quad = addListQ \; (succs \; g \; h \; p) \; qs$$

As inputs to *tstar* we have a graph, a heuristic function, a test for whether a vertex is a goal or not, and the source vertex. The frontier is maintained as a priority queue of paths and their costs, initially containing the single path [*source*] with cost 0 and priority $h(source)$. If the queue is not empty, then a path with the lowest estimate of how much it costs to complete the journey is selected. If the selected path ends at a goal node, then that path is the result; otherwise its successor paths are added to the queue. The subsidiary function *succs* returns a list of possible successor paths:

$$succs :: Graph \to Heuristic \to Path \to [(Path, Cost)]$$
$$succs \; g \; h \; (u:vs, c) = [((v:u:vs, c+d), c+d+h \; v) \; | \; (v, d) \leftarrow g \; u]$$

Note carefully that the priority of a new path is not simply the estimate of how far away the endpoint is from a goal, but the *sum* of the cost of getting to the endpoint and the estimate of the remaining cost. It is left as an exercise to show that taking the estimate alone as the priority can lead to a solution that is not the shortest.

The *tstar* algorithm is not a very satisfactory one. One fundamental flaw is that it is not guaranteed to terminate. For example, consider the graph

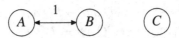

with source vertex A and an isolated goal vertex C. Instead of terminating with *Nothing*, the function *tstar* goes into an infinite loop, constructing longer and longer paths A, AB, ABA, $ABAB$, and so on, in a fruitless attempt to find the goal. A similar phenomenon occurs with the graph

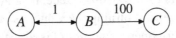

and the optimistic heuristic $h = const\ 0$. Only after 100 oscillations between A and B will *tstar* discover the path ABC with cost 101. Even worse, with the graph

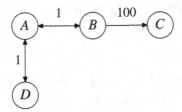

tstar will oscillate about 2^{50} times between A, B, and D before finding the final path. Hence *tstar* can be very inefficient. We will remedy both these problems below.

Nevertheless, provided there is a path from the source to a goal, *tstar* will find one with minimum cost. The only provisos are that h be optimistic and that edge costs are positive numbers. Say a path from the source vertex s is a *good* path if it can be completed to a path with minimum cost. We show that at each step of *tstar* there is a good path on the frontier and, moreover, some good path will eventually be selected for further expansion at a subsequent step. The claim is clearly true initially. For the induction step, suppose p is a good path on the frontier, with endpoint v say. Let $c(p)$ be the cost of p, so

$$c(p) + h(v) \leqslant c(p) + H(v) = H(s)$$

since h is optimistic. Recall that $H(v)$ is the minimum cost of any path from v to a goal and s is the starting vertex. Suppose some bad path q, with endpoint u say, is chosen at the next step, so

$$c(q) + h(u) \leqslant c(p) + h(v) \leqslant H(s)$$

However, u cannot be a goal state, for otherwise

$$c(q) + h(u) = c(q) + 0 > H(s)$$

since q is a bad path. The final step of the proof is to observe that bad paths cannot be added indefinitely to the frontier before a good path is selected for expansion.

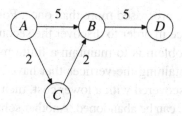

Figure 16.1 A simple graph

Let $\delta > 0$ be the minimum cost of any edge (recall that graphs are finite, so there are finitely many edges). A path of length k therefore has cost at least $k\delta$, so no bad path of length greater than $H(s)/\delta$ can be added to the frontier before a good path is selected for expansion.

Here is an example to show *tstar* at work. Consider the graph of Figure 16.1, in which A is the source vertex and D is the goal. Suppose h is the optimistic heuristic

	A	B	C	D
h	9	1	5	0

The successive queue entries in priority order are as follows (paths are written in the normal left-to-right direction):

$A\ (0+9)$
$AB\ (5+1),\quad AC\ (2+5)$
$AC\ (2+5),\quad ABD\ (10+0)$
$ACB\ (4+1),\quad ABD\ (10+0)$
$ACBD\ (9+0),\quad ABD\ (10+0)$

The algorithm starts off with the single queue entry $A\ (0+9)$, where the first component of the sum is the distance from the source vertex A and the second component is the heuristic value. Subsequent paths in the queue are as above. Although the non-optimal path ABD is inserted into the queue at the second step, it is never selected; instead the final path returned by the algorithm is $ABCD$ with cost 9. As this example demonstrates, *tstar* works best when the underlying graph is acyclic.

The obvious way to remedy the fact that *tstar* may not terminate is to maintain a second argument that records which vertices have already been visited, meaning their successors have been added to the queue. That way, no vertex is processed more than once. After all, this was exactly what was done in depth-first and breadth-first search. However, the idea does not work: it is possible that a second path to the same vertex with a smaller cost, and hence a better estimate, may be found later on, so vertices may have to be processed more than once. For example, in Figure 16.1 the vertex B is visited twice in order to discover the second, shorter path to D.

One solution to the problem is to maintain a finite map from vertices to path costs instead of a set containing the vertices that have already been visited. If a new path to a vertex is discovered with a lower cost, then the path can be explored further. Otherwise the path can be abandoned. Another solution, involving a stronger assumption about the heuristic function h, is left to the following section.

The finite map can be implemented as a simple association list of vertex–cost pairs, but a more efficient alternative is to make use of the Haskell library *Data.Map* and the three operations

> $empty$ :: $Ord\ k \Rightarrow Map\ k\ a$
> $lookup$ :: $Ord\ k \Rightarrow k \rightarrow Map\ k\ a \rightarrow Maybe\ a$
> $insert$ :: $Ord\ k \Rightarrow k \rightarrow a \rightarrow Map\ k\ a \rightarrow Map\ k\ a$

The last two operations take logarithmic rather than linear time. To avoid name clashes, we use a qualified import:

import qualified *Data.Map* **as** *M*

Here now is the definition of a revised search, the algorithm known as A* search:

> $astar$ :: $Graph \rightarrow Heuristic \rightarrow (Vertex \rightarrow Bool) \rightarrow Vertex \rightarrow Maybe\ Path$
> $astar\ g\ h\ goal\ source = asearch\ M.empty\ start$
>   **where** $start = insertQ\ ([source], 0)\ (h\ source)\ emptyQ$
> $asearch\ vcmap\ ps\ |\ nullQ\ ps\ \ \ \ \ \ \ = Nothing$
> $|\ goal\ (end\ p)\ \ \ = Just\ (extract\ p)$
> $|\ better\ p\ vcmap = asearch\ vcmap\ qs$
> $|\ otherwise\ \ \ \ \ \ = asearch\ (add\ p\ vcmap)\ rs$
>   **where** $(p, qs) = removeQ\ ps$
> $rs\ \ \ \ \ = addListQ\ (succs\ g\ h\ p)\ qs$
> $better$ :: $Path \rightarrow M.Map\ Vertex\ Cost \rightarrow Bool$
> $better\ (v : vs, c)\ vcmap = query\ (M.lookup\ v\ vcmap)$
>   **where** $query\ Nothing = False$
> $query\ (Just\ c') = c' \leqslant c$
> add :: $Path \rightarrow M.Map\ Vertex\ Cost \rightarrow M.Map\ Vertex\ Cost$
> $add\ (v : vs, c)\ vcmap = M.insert\ v\ c\ vcmap$

The additional argument *vcmap* to *asearch* is a finite map of vertex–cost pairs. The test *better* determines of a path whether or not another path to the same endpoint but with a smaller cost has already been found. If so, the path can be abandoned. The operation *M.lookup* looks up a vertex in the finite map, returning *Nothing* if there is no binding, and the associated cost if there is. The function *better* returns

True just in the case that there is such an associated cost and it is no larger than the given cost. The function *add* adds a new vertex–cost pair, or overwrites an old binding with the same vertex and the new cost.

Let us first prove that *astar* terminates for all inputs. There are a finite number of simple paths in a finite graph, paths that do not contain repeated vertices. Because the edge weights are positive numbers, no non-simple path can have a smaller cost than the corresponding simple path to the same destination. Let M denote the maximum cost taken over all simple paths, of which there are a finite number. Then any vertex can be processed at most M times during the computation because each processing step requires a path with a strictly smaller cost than before. It follows that *astar* terminates after Mn steps at the very most, where n is the number of vertices in the graph. If no path from the source to the target has been found, then no such path exists, and the algorithm correctly returns *Nothing*.

To show that *astar* terminates with a minimum-cost path from the source to a goal, assuming there is one, we can follow the proof of the correctness of *tstar*. We only have to show that at every step there is a good path on the frontier. Say that a path p with endpoint v is *open* if p is on the frontier and there is no entry (v,c) recorded by the finite map with $c \leqslant c(p)$. Otherwise, say that p is *closed*. Open paths are candidates for further expansion, while closed paths are not.

Let $P = [v_0, v_1, ..., v_n]$ be an optimal path from the source v_0 to a goal v_n and let P_j denote the initial segment $[v_0, v_1, ..., v_j]$ for $0 \leqslant j < n$. We show that at each step there is an open path p with endpoint v_j for some j and such that $c(p) = c(P_j)$. Hence p can be completed to an optimal path. The assertion holds at the very first step because P_0 is open. Otherwise, let D be the set of vertices v_i for which there is a closed path q from v_0 to v_i on the frontier with $c(q) = c(P_i)$. The set D is not empty, because it contains v_0. Let v_i be the vertex with largest index in D and set $j = i + 1$. Define p to be the path q followed by the single edge (v_i, v_j) with cost c. Then p is an open path and

$$c(p) = c(q) + c = c(P_i) + c = c(P_j)$$

That completes the proof that *astar* correctly returns an optimal solution.

16.2 Searching with a monotonic heuristic

Now we turn to a second solution to the problem with *tstar*. This time we need to assume more about the heuristic function h, namely that it is *monotonic*. A heuristic h is monotonic if $h(u) \leqslant c + h(v)$ for every edge (u, v, c) of the graph, where c is the cost of the edge. Provided $h(v) = 0$ for every goal vertex v, it is the case that a monotonic heuristic is optimistic; we leave the proof as an exercise. We do not need a finite map in the case of a monotonic heuristic because, as we will see below, no vertex is processed more than once. It is therefore sufficient to keep a set of the processed vertices. A simple list would do, but it is more efficient to use the set operations of Section 4.4. Alternatively, we can use the Haskell library *Data.Set*, which contains the operations

$$
\begin{aligned}
&empty \quad :: Ord\ a \Rightarrow Set\ a \\
&member :: Ord\ a \Rightarrow a \rightarrow Set\ a \rightarrow Bool \\
&insert \quad :: Ord\ a \Rightarrow a \rightarrow Set\ a \rightarrow Set\ a
\end{aligned}
$$

The functions *member* and *insert* take logarithmic time. To avoid name clashes, we use a qualified import:

import qualified *Data.Set* **as** *S*

Under the assumption that *h* is monotonic, the following *monotonic search* algorithm *mstar* will find an optimum path to a goal, provided one exists:

$$
\begin{aligned}
&mstar :: Graph \rightarrow Heuristic \rightarrow (Vertex \rightarrow Bool) \rightarrow Vertex \rightarrow Maybe\ Path \\
&mstar\ g\ h\ goal\ source = msearch\ S.empty\ start \\
&\quad \textbf{where}\ start = insertQ\ ([source], 0)\ (h\ source)\ emptyQ \\
&\qquad msearch\ vs\ ps\ |\ nullQ\ ps \qquad = Nothing \\
&\qquad\qquad\qquad\quad |\ goal\ (end\ p) = Just\ (extract\ p) \\
&\qquad\qquad\qquad\quad |\ seen\ (end\ p) = msearch\ vs\ qs \\
&\qquad\qquad\qquad\quad |\ otherwise \qquad = msearch\ (S.insert\ (end\ p)\ vs)\ rs \\
&\qquad\quad \textbf{where}\ seen\ v = S.member\ v\ vs \\
&\qquad\qquad\quad (p, qs) = removeQ\ ps \\
&\qquad\qquad\quad rs \qquad = addListQ\ (succs\ g\ h\ vs\ p)\ qs
\end{aligned}
$$

This variation on A* search is the one most like breadth-first or depth-first search, in that there is a simple set *vs* to record vertices that have been visited to ensure that no vertex is ever processed more than once. We show below that, once a path *p* to a vertex *v* has been found, then *p* has the minimum cost of any path from the source to *v*, so no further paths to *v* need be considered. The modified definition of *succs* reads

$$
\begin{aligned}
&succs :: Graph \rightarrow Heuristic \rightarrow S.Set\ Vertex \rightarrow Path \rightarrow [(Path, Cost)] \\
&succs\ g\ h\ vs\ p = [extend\ p\ v\ d\ |\ (v, d) \leftarrow g\ (end\ p), not\ (S.member\ v\ vs)] \\
&\qquad\qquad \textbf{where}\ extend\ (vs, c)\ v\ d = ((v : vs, c + d), c + d + h\ v)
\end{aligned}
$$

This is more efficient than the previous version because a successor path is never added to the frontier if its endpoint has already been processed.

For the proof that *mstar* works correctly, suppose path *p* to vertex *v* was found before another path p' to *v*. We have to show that $c(p) \leqslant c(p')$. Let q' be the initial segment of p' that was on the frontier when *p* was selected; let q' end at vertex *u* and let *r* be the continuation of q' that begins at *u* and constitutes p'. Then

$c(p)$

$\leqslant$ { since p was selected in favour of q' }

$c(q') + h(u) - h(v)$

$=$ { by definition of path costs }

$c(p') - c(r) + h(u) - h(v)$

$\leqslant$ { since h is monotonic and r is a path from u to v }

$c(p')$

The last step makes use of a generalisation of monotonicity, namely that, if r is a path from u to v, then $h(u) \leqslant c(r) + h(v)$. We leave the proof as an exercise. In conclusion, *mstar* returns an optimal solution if one exists.

The example of Figure 16.1 shows that *mstar* can return a non-optimal solution if h is optimistic but not monotonic. The heuristic function

	A	B	C	D
h	9	1	5	0

is not monotonic: the edge from C to B has cost 2 but $h(C) > 2 + h(B)$. As before, the algorithm starts off with the single entry A $(0+9)$. In the next step the queue has two entries AB $(5+1)$, AC $(2+5)$. The path with the lowest priority is AB, so the next queue is ABD $(10+0)$, AC $(2+5)$. The next path to be expanded is AC and, since B has already been processed, the next queue consists of the single entry ABD $(10+0)$, which is the final non-optimal result.

Here is a more elaborate example that illustrates another aspect of the *mstar* algorithm:

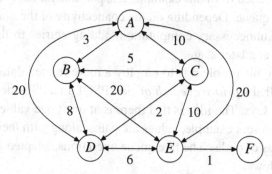

The source node is A and the single goal is F. Suppose h is the monotonic function

	A	B	C	D	E	F
h	10	10	5	5	0	0

The first queue has the single entry A $(0+10)$. Vertex A is added to the visited list, and the next queue is

AB $(3+10)$, AC $(10+5)$, AE $(20+0)$, AD $(20+5)$

Vertex B is added to the visited list, and the next queue is

$ABC\ (8+5),\quad AC\ (10+5),\quad ABD\ (11+5),\quad AE\ (20+0),\quad ABE\ (23+0),$
$AD\ (20+5)$

The queue contains redundant entries, since there are two paths to each of C, D, and E, only one of which in each case will ever be further explored. We will see how to deal with redundancy later on. Note also that the revised definition of *succs* means that the additional path ABA is not added to the queue because A has already been visited. Vertex C is added to the visited list, and the next queue is

$AC\ (10+5),\quad ABCD\ (10+5),\quad ABD\ (11+5),\quad ABCE\ (18+0),\quad AE\ (20+0),$
$ABE\ (23+0),\quad AD\ (20+5)$

There are now three paths to each of D and E on the queue, two of which are redundant. The path with the lowest priority is AC with cost 10, but this path is abandoned since C has been added to the visited list and a better path ABC with cost 8 has already been found. Instead, $ABCD$ is selected, D is added to the visited list, and the next queue is

$ABD\ (11+5),\quad ABCDE\ (16+0),\quad ABCE\ (18+0),\quad AE\ (20+0),$
$ABE\ (23+0),\quad AD\ (20+5)$

There are four remaining paths to E on the queue, three of which are redundant. The (first) path with the lowest priority is ABD, but this is rejected since D is on the visited list. Instead the path $ABCDE$ is chosen, and after one more step the final path $ABCDEF$ with cost 17 is returned.

As can be appreciated from this example, it is possible for many redundant entries to be added to the queue. Depending on the connectivity of the graph, that can lead to a good deal of unnecessary computation, adding entries to the queue only to delete them again at a later stage.

One solution to this problem is to employ a more refined data structure than a priority queue, called a *priority search queue* (PSQ). In a PSQ there are values and priorities but also *keys*. The idea is that there is at most one value in a PSQ with a given key. In the present example, values are paths, along with their costs, and keys are the end vertices of paths. The five queue operations, adapted to priority search queues, are as follows:

$insertQ\ ::(Ord\,k, Ord\,p) \Rightarrow (a \rightarrow k) \rightarrow a \rightarrow p \rightarrow PSQ\,a\,k\,p \rightarrow PSQ\,a\,k\,p$
$addListQ::(Ord\,k, Ord\,p) \Rightarrow (a \rightarrow k) \rightarrow [(a,p)] \rightarrow PSQ\,a\,k\,p \rightarrow PSQ\,a\,k\,p$
$deleteQ\ ::(Ord\,k, Ord\,p) \Rightarrow (a \rightarrow k) \rightarrow PSQ\,a\,k\,p \rightarrow ((a,p),PSQ\,a\,k\,p)$
$emptyQ\ ::PSQ\,a\,k\,p$
$nullQ\quad ::PSQ\,a\,k\,p \rightarrow Bool$

The type *PSQ* has three parameters: values, keys, and priorities. The first three functions, *insertQ*, *addListQ*, and *deleteQ*, take an extra argument, a function for

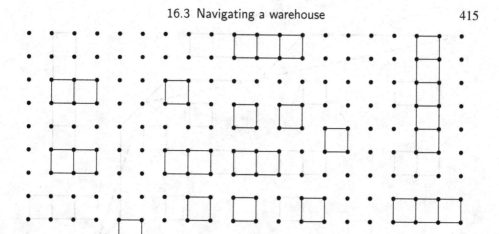

Figure 16.2 A warehouse with obstacles

extracting keys from values. For both *astar* and *mstar* the key function is *end* for extracting the endpoint of a path. The function *insertQ* works as follows: if there is no value with the given key in the queue, then the value is added to the queue along with its priority. If there is such a value, only the value with the smaller priority is kept. The function *addListQ* takes a key function and a list of value–priority pairs, and inserts them into a queue as before. The remaining functions are also as before. The three main queue operations each take logarithmic time in the size of the queue. The *astar* and *mstar* algorithms are unchanged except for an additional argument to the queue operations. It is beyond our scope to go into the details of how to implement priority search queues, but see the chapter notes for references. In fact, the Haskell libraries in the Hackage repository provide a number of implementations of PSQs, including *PSQueue* and *psqueues*, though the functions provided are slightly different in each case.

16.3 Navigating a warehouse

We will give two illustrations of A* search, the first of which concerns the problem of navigating around a warehouse filled with obstacles. This is the task that would face an autonomous vehicle which has to find a path from a given starting point in the warehouse to a given destination, taking care to avoid collisions. For example, consider the warehouse shown in Figure 16.2, which contains a haphazard collection of unit-sized boxes. What is wanted is a path from the top-left corner of the warehouse to the bottom-right corner. Sections of the path have to be straight lines starting at one grid point and ending at another, avoiding any box along the way.

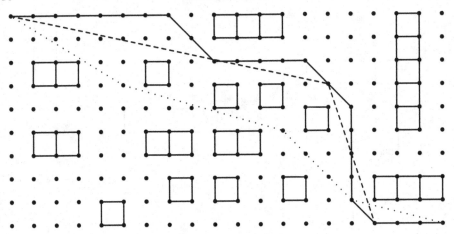

Figure 16.3 The continuous line shows an optimal fixed-angle path with cost
25.07. The dashed line is a variable-angle path with cost 23.64 and the dotted path
is an optimal variable-angle path with cost 21.48.

Different solutions are available depending on precisely how the vehicle is allowed to move between grid points. The most restrictive rule is that it can move at
each step only horizontally or vertically to an adjacent grid point. A more relaxed
rule would allow the vehicle to move diagonally at a 45 degree angle, so each grid
point has up to eight rather than four neighbours. In either of these scenarios the
target of each edge that makes up a path has to be unoccupied by a box. Finally, the
vehicle may be allowed in one step to move from any one grid point to any other,
turning through an arbitrary angle to do so. Not only has the target to be unoccupied
by a box, the step has to avoid touching any line segment that forms part of the
perimeter of a box. Figure 16.3 shows three such solutions. Firstly, the continuous
line describes a path that moves only from one grid point to a neighbouring one,
allowing diagonal moves. The cost of this path is the sum of the costs of the edges,
where an edge costs 1 for a horizontal or vertical move and $\sqrt{2}$ for a diagonal move,
so distances are Euclidean. The path consists of 18 straight moves and 5 diagonal
moves, for a total distance of $18 + 5\sqrt{2} = 25.07$. There are other paths with the
same minimum cost, but we will leave finding them as an exercise. The other two
paths are both variable-angle paths obtained by different means. The dotted line
shows a path in which every point on the grid that is visible to a starting point is
a possible neighbour. Finally, the dashed line is a path obtained by smoothing the
fixed-angle path in a manner described below.

The layout of a warehouse can be described in terms of a *grid*. The points on a grid
of size $m \times n$ are defined by coordinates (x, y), where $1 \leqslant x \leqslant m$ and $1 \leqslant y \leqslant n$, with
the four lines $x = 0$, $x = m+1$, $y = 0$, and $y = n+1$ acting as barriers. Obstacles are

made up of unit-size boxes each occupying four grid points. The vertex identifying each box is, say, its top-left corner. Hence we define

type *Coord* = *Nat*
type *Vertex* = (*Coord*, *Coord*)
type *Box* = *Vertex*
type *Grid* = (*Nat*, *Nat*, [*Box*])

boxes :: *Grid* → [*Box*]
boxes (_, _, *bs*) = *bs*

The four corners of a box are given by

corners :: *Box* → [*Vertex*]
corners (*x*, *y*) = [(*x*, *y*), (*x*+1, *y*), (*x*+1, *y*−1), (*x*, *y*−1)]

In the fixed-angle solution, the neighbours of a grid point are any of its eight adjacent grid points that are not boundary points or points occupied by a box. The function *neighbours* can be defined in a number of ways, including by using a fixed array:

type *Graph* = *Vertex* → [*Vertex*]

neighbours :: *Grid* → *Graph*
neighbours grid = *filter* (*free grid*) · *adjacents*

adjacents :: *Vertex* → [*Vertex*]
adjacents (*x*, *y*) = [(*x*−1, *y*−1), (*x*−1, *y*), (*x*−1, *y*+1),
$\qquad\qquad\qquad$ (*x*, *y*−1), (*x*, *y*+1),
$\qquad\qquad\qquad$ (*x*+1, *y*−1), (*x*+1, *y*), (*x*+1, *y*+1)]

free :: *Grid* → *Vertex* → *Bool*
free (*m*, *n*, *bs*) = (*a*!)
$\quad$ **where** *a* = *listArray* ((0, 0), (*m*+1, *n*+1)) (*repeat True*)
$\qquad\qquad$ // [((*x*, *y*), *False*) | *x* ← [0 .. *m*+1], *y* ← [0, *n*+1]]
$\qquad\qquad$ // [((*x*, *y*), *False*) | *x* ← [0, *m*+1], *y* ← [1 .. *n*]]
$\qquad\qquad$ // [((*x*, *y*), *False*) | *b* ← *bs*, (*x*, *y*) ← *corners b*]

Recall that // is the array update function. A grid point is free if it is not on a horizontal or vertical border and not occupied by a box. Use of an array means that the neighbours of a grid point can be computed in constant time.

The fixed-angle path can now be computed using the function *fpath*, a modification of *mstar* of the previous section. This time we will need the definitions

type *Dist* = *Float*
type *Path* = ([*Vertex*], *Dist*)

end :: *Path* → *Vertex*
end = *head* · *fst*

> *extract* :: *Path* → *Path*
> *extract* (*vs*, *d*) = (*reverse vs*, *d*)

We can now define *fpath* by

> *fpath* :: *Grid* → *Vertex* → *Vertex* → *Maybe Path*
> *fpath grid source target* = *mstar* (*neighbours grid*) *source target*

Since the heuristic function is fixed and there is only one goal, the type of *mstar* changes to

> *mstar* :: *Graph* → *Vertex* → *Vertex* → *Maybe Path*

The three arguments to *mstar* now consist of a graph, a source vertex, and a target vertex. We will not write out the modified definition of *mstar* because the only real difference is a new version of *succs*, which now takes the target vertex as an argument instead of the heuristic function:

> *succs* :: *Graph* → *Vertex* → *S.Set Vertex* → *Path* → [(*Path*, *Dist*)]
> *succs g target visited p* =
>   [*extend p v* | *v* ← *g* (*end p*), *not* (*S.member v visited*)]
>   **where** *extend* (*u* : *vs*, *d*) *v* = ((*v* : *u* : *vs*, *dv*), *dv* + *dist v target*)
>   **where** *dv* = *d* + *dist u v*

Definition of the Euclidean distance function *dist* is left as an exercise. The heuristic function is monotonic, so *fpath* is guaranteed to find a shortest path under the stated travel restrictions if such a path exists.

   Computing a variable-angle path involves an additional complication: not only does the endpoint of each segment of the path have to be unoccupied, but also the segment itself cannot cross any border of any box. Such a crossing may be somewhere between two grid points. For example, only the two endpoints of the path segment in

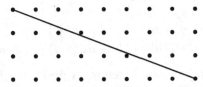

are grid points, but we have to ensure that no border edge of any box crosses the segment. A detailed implementation is postponed to the exercises, but suppose we have a function

> *visible* :: *Grid* → *Segment* → *Bool*

where

> **type** *Segment* = (*Vertex*, *Vertex*)

that determines of a grid and a segment whether or not the segment is unimpeded by a box. Then the variable-angle path of Figure 16.3 that arises by smoothing the fixed-angle path is computed by

vpath :: *Grid* → *Vertex* → *Vertex* → *Maybe Path*
vpath grid source target =
  mstar (*neighbours grid*) (*visible grid*) *source target*

where this time *mstar* has the type

mstar :: *Graph* → (*Segment* → *Bool*) → *Vertex* → *Vertex* → *Maybe Path*

and is defined in the same way as before except for a new definition of *succs*:

succs g vtest target vs p =
  [*extend p w* | *w* ← *g* (*end p*), *not* (*S.member w vs*)]
  where *extend* (*v* : *vs*, *d*) *w* = **if** *not* (*null vs*) ∧ *vtest* (*u*, *w*)
                          then ((*w* : *vs*, *du*), *du* + *dist w target*)
                          else ((*w* : *v* : *vs*, *dw*), *dw* + *dist w target*)
                          where *u* = *head vs*
                              du = *d* − *dist u v* + *dist u w*
                              dw = *d* + *dist v w*

The extra argument of *succs* is the visibility test *vtest* = *visible grid*. Each time a successor *w* of a vertex *v* is added to the list we check that the parent *u* of *v*, if it exists, is visible to *w*. If it is, then the vertex *v* is removed from the path, and the added edge proceeds directly from *u* to *w*. Such a smoothing step will never increase the cost of a path and may decrease it. The running time of this algorithm is proportional to the fixed-angle path version except for the additional time spent evaluating visibility checks.

Finally, the optimal variable-angle path of Figure 16.3 can be obtained as an instance of *fpath* that takes the neighbours of a grid point to be all points on the grid visible to it:

neighbours (*m*, *n*, *bs*) (*x*₁, *y*₁) =
  [(*x*₂, *y*₂) | *x*₂ ← [1..*m*], *y*₂ ← [1..*n*], *visible* (*m*, *n*, *bs*) ((*x*₁, *y*₁), (*x*₂, *y*₂))]

However, this method is costly and only realistic for small grids.

16.4 The 8-puzzle

The 8-puzzle is an example of a class of problems known as sliding-block puzzles. It is a smaller version of the famous 15-puzzle popularised by Sam Loyd in the 1880s. The puzzle consists of eight tiles arranged in a 3 × 3 grid with one empty space (the 15-puzzle is identical except there are 15 tiles on a 4 × 4 grid). An example is shown in Figure 16.4. Tiles are numbered from 1 to 8, and any tile adjacent to the empty space can be moved into it. The aim is to get from some given initial grid to a given

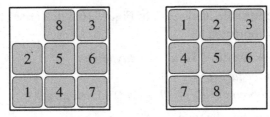

Figure 16.4 An initial grid of the 8-puzzle and the required final grid

final grid, such as the one pictured on the right of the figure. In other sliding-block puzzles the tiles can be of different sizes and may be coloured rather than numbered. The aim is to slide the pieces around to get to some pleasing final arrangement from a given starting point.

The popularity of the 15-puzzle arose partly because Loyd asked for a solution to an impossible problem: he gave an initial grid for which there was no sequence of moves that could lead to the final grid. In fact, whatever the final grid happens to be, only half the initial grids are solvable. The same holds true for the 8-puzzle. The proof turns on three ideas, the first of which is the *parity* of a permutation. The parity of a permutation is the parity of its *inversion count*, a concept introduced in Section 7.2. The inversion count is the number of pairs of elements of a permutation p that are out of place, namely when $i < j$ and $p(i) > p(j)$. If we imagine the empty space to be a 0, then the final permutation 123456780 of Figure 16.4 has an inversion count of 8, while the initial permutation 083256147 has a count of 14. So both permutations have even parity.

Next, a *transposition* of a permutation is when any two different elements are swapped. We claim that any transposition changes the parity of the permutation. To see this, consider the transposition (i,j), where without loss of generality we suppose that i occurs before j in the list $p(1), p(2), ..., p(n)$. Let s be the segment between i and j and let L_i be the number of elements of s less than i, and B_i the number of elements bigger than i; similarly for L_j and B_j. It follows that $L_i + B_i = L_j + B_j = m$, where m is the length of s. The inversion count c of the permutation p can now be expressed as

$$c = c_0 + L_i + B_j$$

where c_0 is the contribution to the inversion count of elements outside the segment s. The inversion count after the transposition is given by

$$c' = c_0 + L_j + B_i \pm 1$$

where the final term is positive if $i < j$ and negative if $i > j$. That means

$$c' = (c - L_i - B_j) + L_j + B_i \pm 1 = c - 2L_i + 2L_j \pm 1$$

so c' is odd if c is even and vice versa. This shows in particular that if the initial and final permutations are both even, then the first can lead to the second only with an even number of moves.

The third idea involves *Manhattan* distances. The Manhattan distance of a tile is the number of vertical and horizontal moves required to place the tile in its correct place in the final grid. For example, the Manhattan distance of each of the five tiles 1, 2, 4, 7, 8 in the first grid of Figure 16.4 is two, because each tile has to move two places to reach its final resting place. The three remaining tiles, tiles 3, 5, and 6, each have a Manhattan distance of zero, and the Manhattan distance of the empty space is four. Each move in the puzzle corresponds to a transposition of the empty space with a tile, and each transposition changes both the parity of the permutation and the parity of the Manhattan distance of the empty space.

It follows that starting with an *EE* permutation (even parity of permutation and even parity of the Manhattan distance of the empty space) can only lead to an *OO* or an *EE* permutation and never to an *OE* or *EO* one. Similarly an *OE* or *EO* permutation can never lead to a permutation in which the two parities are the same. The final step in the proof is to observe that the four classes, *EE*, *OE*, *EO*, and *OO*, divide the set of permutations into equal sizes. For the proof, consider the row in which the empty space occurs. Transposing the two tiles in the row changes the parity of the permutation but not the Manhattan distance of the empty space. This produces a bijection between *OE* and *EE* and a bijection between *EO* and *OO*, so they must all be of equal size.

The next task is to consider what heuristic functions might be useful in solving the 8-puzzle. At least half a dozen functions have been proposed in the literature, but we will discuss just two of the best known. The first is to take $h(g)$ simply to be the number of tiles in the grid g that are out of place. As we have seen, in Figure 16.4 there are five out-of-place tiles, so $h(g) = 5$. The function h is monotonic (see the exercises), so *mstar* is guaranteed to find a shortest path.

The second function is the sum of the Manhattan distances of the tiles from their current positions to their final resting places (but not including the Manhattan distance of the blank space). For our example we have $h(g) = 10$ because the Manhattan distance of each out-of-place tile is 2. The Manhattan heuristic is a refinement of the out-of-place heuristic in that it takes account of how out of place each tile is. The Manhattan heuristic is also monotonic.

The next decision concerns the representation of the grid. An obvious choice is a 3×3 array, but this representation can be quite wasteful of space, so we will go for a more compact one. The idea is to encode a permutation such as 083256147 as a string of digits, more specifically as an element of *Text*, a time- and space-efficient encoding of Unicode text defined in the Haskell library *Data.Text*. Since many of the functions imported by this library have names that clash with Standard Prelude functions, we import the library as a qualified module:

> **import qualified** *Data.Text* **as** *T*

We define a state of the grid by

> **type** *Position* = *Nat*
> **type** *State*   = (*T.Text*, *Position*)
>
> *perm* :: *State* → *String*
> *perm* (*xs*,*j*) = *T.unpack xs*
>
> *posn0* :: *State* → *Position*
> *posn0* (*xs*,*j*) = *j*

The position component of a state is the position of the empty space 0 in the permutation encoded by the text component, a number between 0 and 8. The function *unpack* unpacks a text into a string. The two states of our running example are therefore represented by

> *istate*,*fstate* :: *State*
> *istate* = (*T.pack* "083256147",0)
> *fstate* = (*T.pack* "123456780",8)

where *pack* :: *String* → *Text* is another library function in *Data.Text*.

Each move can shift the position of the empty space to one of its vertical or horizontal neighbours. An efficient definition of *moves* is given by

> **type** *Move* = *Nat*
>
> *moves* :: *State* → [*Move*]
> *moves st* = *moveTable* ! (*posn0 st*)
>
> *moveTable* :: *Array Nat* [*Nat*]
> *moveTable* = *listArray* (0,8) [[1,3],   [0,2,4],   [1,5],
>   [0,4,6],[1,3,5,7],[2,4,8],
>   [3,7],   [4,6,8],   [5,7]]

The array *moveTable* lists the neighbours of grid points explicitly. For example, the neighbours of grid point 0 are 1 and 3, while grid point 4 has neighbours 1, 3, 5, and 7. The function *move* can be defined by

> *move* :: *State* → *Move* → *State*
> *move* (*xs*,*i*) *j* = (*T.replace* t_y t_0 (*T.replace* t_0 t_x (*T.replace* t_x t_y *xs*)),*j*)
>   **where** t_0 = *T.singleton* '0'
> t_y = *T.singleton* '?'
> t_x = *T.singleton* (*T.index xs j*)

This is a three-step process in which the character *x* at position *j* in the text is replaced by some new character '?', the empty space by x, and finally '?' by the empty space. The functions *replace* and *index* are also library functions of the module *Data.Text*, as is *singleton*, which converts a single character into a text.

To solve a given instance we should first check whether a solution is possible. We will leave it as an exercise to define the two functions

$icparity \; :: State \rightarrow Bool$
$mhparity :: State \rightarrow State \rightarrow Bool$

where *icparity* returns *True* if the parity of the inversion count is even, and *mhparity* returns *True* if the Manhattan distance of the empty space in the initial state to its resting place in the final state is even. We can then define

$possible :: State \rightarrow State \rightarrow Bool$
$possible \; is \; fs = (mhparity \; is \; fs == (icparity \; is == icparity \; fs))$

That is, a solution is possible if either the Manhattan parity is even and the inversion parities agree, or the Manhattan parity is odd and the inversion parities disagree. This uses the fact that the Manhattan distance of the empty space in the final state is zero and therefore has even parity.

Here now is the definition of the out-of-place heuristic:

type $Heuristic = State \rightarrow State \rightarrow Nat$

$h_1 :: Heuristic$
$h_1 \; is \; fs = length \; (filter \; p \; (zip \; (perm \; is) \; (perm \; fs)))$
    where $p \; (c,d) = c \neq \; '0' \wedge c \neq d$

The two permutations are aligned and the number of out-of-place tiles is counted.

In order to define the Manhattan heuristic, we will need the coordinates of the grid points, which we can take to be

$$(0,0) \quad (0,1) \quad (0,2)$$
$$(1,0) \quad (1,1) \quad (1,2)$$
$$(2,0) \quad (2,1) \quad (2,2)$$

The coordinates of a state are given by a list of coordinates in tile order, showing which coordinate position each tile occupies. For example, with the permutation 083256147 these coordinates are

$$[(2,0), \; (1,0), \; (0,2), \; (2,1), \; (1,1), \; (1,2), \; (2,2), \; (0,1)]$$

Thus tile 1 occupies position $(2,0)$, tile 2 occupies position $(1,0)$, and so on. If we introduce the type synonym

type $Coord = (Nat, Nat)$

then the coordinates in tile order are given by

$$coords :: State \rightarrow [Coord]$$
$$coords = tail \cdot map\ snd \cdot sort \cdot addCoords$$
$$\textbf{where}\ addCoords\ st = zip\ (perm\ st)\ gridpoints$$
$$gridpoints\quad = map\ (divMod\ 3)\ [0..8]$$

Each tile is associated with its coordinate position by *addCoords*, the result is sorted into tile order, and the tiles are discarded. The leading position, the position of the empty space, is also dropped.

Now we can define the Manhattan heuristic by

$$h_2 :: Heuristic$$
$$h_2\ is\ fs = sum\ (zipWith\ d\ (coords\ is)\ (coords\ fs))$$
$$\textbf{where}\ d\ (x_0, y_0)\ (x_1, y_1) = abs\ (x_0 - x_1) + abs\ (y_0 - y_1)$$

The *mstar* algorithm maintains a queue of paths, where a path is defined by

$$\textbf{type}\ Path = ([Move], Nat, State)$$

$$key :: Path \rightarrow State$$
$$key\ (ms, k, st) = st$$

Each path records a sequence of moves, the length of the sequence, and the final state at the end of the moves. The algorithm makes use of priority search queues and the library *Data.Set* as used in Section 16.2:

$$mstar :: Heuristic \rightarrow State \rightarrow State \rightarrow Maybe\ [Move]$$
$$mstar\ h\ istate\ fstate =$$
$$\quad \textbf{if}\ possible\ istate\ fstate\ \textbf{then}\ msearch\ S.empty\ start\ \textbf{else}\ Nothing$$
$$\quad \textbf{where}\ start = insertQ\ key\ ([], 0, istate)\ (h\ istate\ fstate)\ emptyQ$$
$$\qquad msearch\ vs\ ps \mid st == fstate \quad = Just\ (reverse\ ms)$$
$$\qquad\qquad\qquad\quad \mid S.member\ st\ vs = msearch\ vs\ qs$$
$$\qquad\qquad\qquad\quad \mid otherwise \qquad = msearch\ (S.insert\ st\ vs)\ rs$$
$$\qquad\quad \textbf{where}\ ((ms, k, st), qs) = removeQ\ key\ ps$$
$$\qquad\qquad\quad rs = addListQ\ key\ (succs\ h\ fstate\ (ms, k, st)\ vs)\ qs$$

The revised definition of *succs* is

$$succs :: Heuristic \rightarrow State \rightarrow Path \rightarrow S.Set\ State \rightarrow [(Path, Nat)]$$
$$succs\ h\ fstate\ (ms, k, st)\ vs$$
$$\quad = [\ ((m : ms, k + 1, st'), k + 1 + h\ st'\ fstate)$$
$$\qquad \mid m \leftarrow moves\ st, \textbf{let}\ st' = move\ st\ m, not\ (S.member\ st'\ vs)]$$

Both the out-of-place and the Manhattan heuristics find a solution much more quickly than breadth-first search, with the Manhattan heuristic proving superior in many examples. Here for comparison purposes are typical running times with GHCi and numbers of steps, where *bfsolve* computes a solution using a simple breadth-first search, in each case returning the same solution $[3, 6, 7, 8, 5, 4, 1, 0, 3, 6, 7, 4, 5, 8]$:

	time	moves
bfsolve	0.60s	6450
mstar h_1	0.02s	138
mstar h_2	0.01s	35

From the initial state 032871456, there is an even more dramatic improvement in computing the solution $[1, 4, 3, 6, 7, 4, 1, 0, 3, 4, 5, 2, 1, 4, 5, 8, 7, 6, 3, 0, 1, 4, 7, 8]$:

	time	moves
bfsolve	920.01s	312963
mstar h_1	3.37s	15765
mstar h_2	0.41s	2032

16.5 Chapter notes

The first description of A* search was given in 1968, see [2], as part of a project for building a robot that could plan its own actions. A definitive study of the algorithm was later given in [1]. A general study of heuristics and how to choose good ones can be found in Judea Pearl's book [6]. Applications of heuristic techniques to problems in artificial intelligence can be found in [7], among many other books. Priority search queues are described in [3]. The variable-angle path planning algorithms are taken from [5]. The 15-puzzle was invented by Noyes P. Chapman, not Sam Loyd, and a proof that only a half of the initial positions were solvable was first given in 1879, see [4].

References

[1]   Rina Dechter and Judea Pearl. Generalised best-fit search strategies and the optimality of A*. *Journal of the ACM*, 32(3):505–536, 1985.

[2]   Peter E. Hart, Nils J. Nilsson, and Bertram Raphael. A formal basis for the heuristic determination of minimum cost paths. *IEEE Transactions on Systems Science and Cybernetics*, 4(2):100–107, 1968.

[3]   Ralf Hinze. A simple implementation technique for priority search queues. In B. C. Pierce and X. Leroy, editors, *ACM International Conference on Functional Programming*, pages 110–121, 2001.

[4]   William W. Johnson and William E. Story. Notes on the 15-puzzle. *American Journal of Mathematics*, 2(4):397–404, 1879.

[5]   Alex Nash and Sven Koenig. Any-angle path planning. *Artificial Intelligence Magazine*, 34(4):85–107, 2013.

[6]   Judea Pearl. *Heuristics: Intelligent Search Strategies for Computer Problem Solving*. Addison-Wesley, Reading, MA, 1984.

[7]   Stuart J. Russell and Peter Norvig. *Artificial Intelligence: A Modern Approach*. Prentice-Hall, Upper Saddle River, NJ, third edition, 2003.

Exercises

Exercise 16.1 Is the function H well-defined if edge costs are not constrained to be positive? Is H well-defined if edge costs are positive but not necessarily integers?

Exercise 16.2 Consider the graph

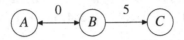

and the optimistic heuristic $h(A) = h(B) = 4$ and $h(C) = 0$. Will *tstar* find the path ABC?

Exercise 16.3 Why is Dijkstra's algorithm a special case of A* search?

Exercise 16.4 Give a simple graph to show that *tstar* does not always return a shortest path if the priority is just the heuristic estimate for completing the journey.

Exercise 16.5 The function *insert* of *Data.Map* has type

$$insert :: Ord\ k \Rightarrow k \to a \to Map\ k\ a \to Map\ k\ a$$

What assumption has been made about the use of *insert* in *astar* and *mstar*?

Exercise 16.6 Is the heuristic that returns the straight-line distance between a town and the closest goal a monotonic heuristic?

Exercise 16.7 Let the minimum edge cost be c. Is the constant function $h(v) = c$ optimistic?

Exercise 16.8 Show that, if $h(v) = 0$ for every goal vertex v, then h is optimistic if h is monotonic.

Exercise 16.9 Define $f(p) = c(p) + h(v)$, where v is the endpoint of path p. Show that, if p is a prefix of q, then $f(p) \leqslant f(q)$.

Exercise 16.10 How many other fixed-angle paths with 18 straight moves and 5 diagonal moves are there in the grid of Figure 16.3?

Exercise 16.11 Define the function *dist* used in the warehouse problem.

Exercise 16.12 Determining whether or not two arbitrary line segments intersect is a fundamental task in computational geometry. The full algorithm is a little complicated, as a number of different cases have to be considered. However, in the warehouse situation the task can be simplified somewhat, even though a number of cases still have to be distinguished. First of all, what does one have to show if the segment of the path under construction is horizontal, vertical, or a diagonal slope at an angle of 45 degrees?

Exercise 16.13 Following on from the previous question, in the remaining case we have to check that the endpoint of the segment is free from obstruction, and that no border of any box crosses the segment. The borders of the boxes in a grid can be defined by

$$borders :: Grid \rightarrow [Segment]$$
$$borders = concatMap \, (edges \cdot corners) \cdot boxes$$
$$\textbf{where } edges \, [u, v, w, x] = [(u, v), (w, v), (x, w), (x, u)]$$

However, testing all border segments for whether they cross a given segment s will involve border segments that may be far away from s. It is better to filter the borders for those that are near s in some suitable sense. What is a suitable definition of *near*?

Exercise 16.14 Following on, the definition of *visible* now takes the form

$$visible :: Grid \rightarrow Segment \rightarrow Bool$$
$$
\begin{aligned}
visible \, g \, s \mid hseg \, s \quad &= all \, (free \, g) \, (ypoints \, s) \\
\mid vseg \, s \quad &= all \, (free \, g) \, (xpoints \, s) \\
\mid dseg \, s \quad &= all \, (free \, g) \, (dpoints \, s) \\
\mid eseg \, s \quad &= all \, (free \, g) \, (epoints \, s) \\
\mid otherwise &= free \, g \, (snd \, s) \wedge all \, (not \cdot crosses \, s) \, es
\end{aligned}
$$
$$\textbf{where } es = filter \, (near \, s) \, (borders \, g)$$

A segment satisfies *hseg* if it is horizontal, *vseg* if it is vertical, *dseg* if the sum of the two coordinates of the endpoints of the segment is the same, so the diagonal is left to right, and *eseg* if the difference of the coordinates is the same. Write suitable definitions of the remaining functions, apart from *crosses*.

Exercise 16.15 It remains to define *crosses*. For this we need to determine the orientation of a triangle. The function

$$orientation :: Segment \rightarrow Vertex \rightarrow Int$$
$$orientation \, ((x_1, y_1), (x_2, y_2)) \, (x, y)$$
$$= signum \, ((x - x_1) \times (y_2 - y_1) - (x_2 - x_1) \times (y - y_1))$$

returns -1 if the orientation of the triangle ABC, where $A = (x_1, y_1)$, $B = (x_2, y_2)$, and $C = (x, y)$, is anti-clockwise, $+1$ if ABC is clockwise, and 0 if the points A, B, and C are collinear. For example, in Figure 16.5 the orientation of ABC is anti-clockwise and ABD is clockwise. Thus, if CD is a border of some box, then the segment crosses it. On the other hand, the segment does not cross EF even though ABE and ABF have opposite orientations. Why will the crossing test not be applied to EF? Hence define *crosses*.

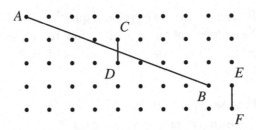

Figure 16.5 *ABC* and *ABE* are anti-clockwise, while *ABD* and *ABF* are clockwise

---

Exercise 16.16 Consider the 3-puzzle, in which there are three tiles and a blank in a 2×2 grid. Which of the 24 possible initial states are solvable if the final permutation of the tiles is 1230?

Exercise 16.17 Show that the out-of-place heuristic h for the 8-puzzle is monotonic. Show also that this would not be true if we counted whether or not the blank tile was out of place.

Exercise 16.18 Show that the Manhattan heuristic is monotonic, but only because the distance of the blank tile is not included in the sum.

Exercise 16.19 Define the functions *icparity* and *mhparity*, where *icparity* returns *True* if the parity of the inversion count is even, and *mhparity* returns *True* if the Manhattan distance of the blank tile in the initial state to its resting place in the final state is even.

Answers

Answer 16.1 Not if the graph has cycles with negative costs. As to the second part, yes, but not if the graph is infinite. Imagine an infinite graph with a single source s, a single target t, and an infinite number of other vertices v_i. There is an edge from s to v_i with cost $1/i$ and an edge from each v_i to t with cost 1. In this case $H(s)$ is not well-defined.

Answer 16.2 No. After two steps the queue contains $ABC\ (5+0), ABA\ (0+4)$. The path ABA is chosen for further expansion, and this leads to an infinite loop. The above graph is disallowed if all edge costs are positive, which is why the assumption that edge costs are positive is necessary.

Answer 16.3 Because Dijkstra's algorithm is the special case of A* search when the heuristic function is $h = const\ 0$. This function is both optimistic and monotonic (provided edge costs are positive), so Dijkstra's algorithm is also a special case of M* search.

Answer 16.4 A graph with three vertices suffices:

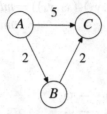

The source vertex is A and the goal vertex is C. We take $h(A) = 4$, $h(B) = 2$, and $h(C) = 0$. Tree search will select the path AC with cost 5, but the shortest path is ABC with cost 4.

Answer 16.5 That *Ord Vertex*.

Answer 16.6 Yes, in a metric space, monotonicity amounts to the triangle inequality being satisfied.

Answer 16.7 No. If v is a goal, then $h(v) = c$ while $H(v) = 0$.

Answer 16.8 Let $[v, v_1, v_2, ..., v_n]$ be a shortest path from v to a goal v_n, with edge costs $[c_1, c_2, ..., c_n]$. If h is monotonic, then

$$h(v) \leqslant c_1 + c_2 + \cdots + c_n + h(v_n) = H(v)$$

since $h(v_n) = 0$. Note the necessity of h returning 0 on any goal vertex.

Answer 16.9 It is sufficient to show that this holds when p' is p without its last vertex. Suppose u is the endpoint of p' and the edge (u, v) has cost d. Then

$$f(p') = c(p') + h(u) \leqslant c(p') + d + h(v) = f(p)$$

by monotonicity.

Answer 16.10 We counted 16 paths in total.

Answer 16.11 We have

> $dist :: Vertex \to Vertex \to Dist$
> $dist\ (x_1, y_1)\ (x_2, y_2) = sqrt\ (fromIntegral\ (sqr\ (x_2 - x_1) + sqr\ (y_2 - y_1)))$
> **where** $sqr\ x = x \times x$

Answer 16.12 In each of these three cases the segment goes only through grid points, so we have to check only that all these points are unimpeded by boxes.

Answer 16.13 We need only consider borders that lie within the rectangular area determined by s. Hence

$$near :: Segment \rightarrow Segment \rightarrow Bool$$
$$near\ ((x_1,y_1),(x_2,y_2))\ ((x_3,y_3),(x_4,y_4)) = min\ x_1\ x_2 \leqslant x_3 \wedge x_4 \leqslant max\ x_1\ x_2 \wedge$$
$$min\ y_1\ y_2 \leqslant y_3 \wedge y_4 \leqslant max\ y_1\ y_2$$

Answer 16.14 We can write

$$hseg\ ((x_1,y_1),(x_2,y_2)) = x_1 == x_2$$
$$vseg\ ((x_1,y_1),(x_2,y_2)) = y_1 == y_2$$
$$dseg\ ((x_1,y_1),(x_2,y_2)) = x_1 + y_1 == x_2 + y_2$$
$$eseg\ ((x_1,y_1),(x_2,y_2)) = x_1 - y_1 == x_2 - y_2$$

and also

$$ypoints\ ((x_1,y_1),(x_2,y_2)) = [(x_1,y) \mid y \leftarrow [min\ y_1\ y_2 .. max\ y_1\ y_2]]$$
$$xpoints\ ((x_1,y_1),(x_2,y_2)) = [(x,y_1) \mid x \leftarrow [min\ x_1\ x_2 .. max\ x_1\ x_2]]$$
$$dpoints\ ((x_1,y_1),(x_2,y_2)) = [(x,x_1 + y_1 - x) \mid x \leftarrow [min\ x_1\ x_2 .. max\ x_1\ x_2]]$$
$$epoints\ ((x_1,y_1),(x_2,y_2)) = [(x_1 - y_1 + y,y) \mid y \leftarrow [min\ y_1\ y_2 .. max\ y_1\ y_2]]$$

Answer 16.15 The segment EF lies outside the rectangle determined by AB and is therefore excluded from consideration by the *near* test. The function *crosses* is defined by

$$crosses\ s\ (v_1,v_2) = orientation\ s\ v_1 \times orientation\ s\ v_2 \leqslant 0$$

Either the two vertices v_1 and v_2 straddle the segment s, or one of them lies on the segment.

Answer 16.16 The final state is of type EO, so only initial states of type EO or OE are solvable. These are the 12 permutations:

0123 0231 0312 1023 1203 1230 2031 2301 2310 3012 3102 3120

Answer 16.17 Let u be a state of the 8-puzzle and v be the state that results when any tile t is exchanged with the blank tile. Such a move changes the value of $h(u)$ by $+1$ if t was in its correct place, by 0 if neither the starting point nor the endpoint of t is its correct place, or -1 if the endpoint of t is its correct place. In all cases we have $h(u) \leqslant 1 + h(v)$, given that the cost of a move is 1.

If we counted whether or not the empty space was out of place, then a move could reduce the value of $h(u)$ by 2 if both t and the empty space were now in their correct places. But that requires $h(u) \leqslant h(u) - 1$, which is impossible.

Answer 16.18 A similar argument to the previous question applies. Moving a tile can increase or decrease the value of the heuristic by 1 (and by -2 if the empty space is included in the sum and both tiles are in their correct places after the swap).

Answer 16.19 We have

$$icparity :: State \rightarrow Bool$$
$$icparity = even \cdot ic \cdot perm$$

$$mhparity :: State \rightarrow State \rightarrow Bool$$
$$mhparity\ is\ fs = even\ (dist\ (posn0\ is)\ (posn0\ fs))$$
$$\textbf{where}\ dist\ i\ j = abs\ (x_0 - x_1) + abs\ (y_0 - y_1)$$
$$\textbf{where}\ (x_0, y_0) = i\ \text{divMod}\ 3$$
$$(x_1, y_1) = j\ \text{divMod}\ 3$$

The function *ic* for computing the inversion count was defined in Section 7.2.

Index

Printed in the United States
By Bookmasters